Following the Fairways

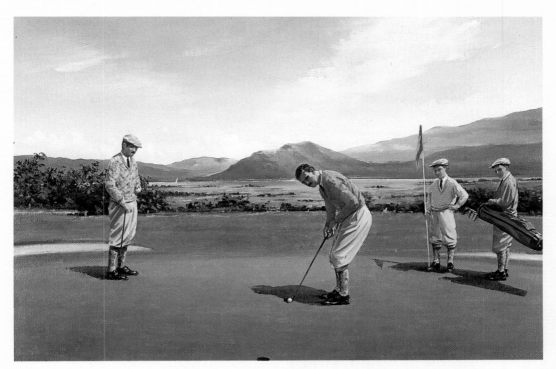

Artist: **Alec MacDonald** **PUTTING** *Courtesy of:* **Rosenstiel's**

Editor Nick Edmund

KENSINGTON WEST PRODUCTIONS

HEXHAM ENGLAND

Acknowledgements

Kensington West Productions Ltd
5 Cattle Market, Hexham,
Northumberland, NE46 1NJ
Tel (01434) 609933, Fax (01434) 600066
E mail: kensingtonwest@compuserve.com

Editor
Nick Edmund

Assitant Editors
Karen Ryan, Mark Scandle

Design
Diane Ridley

Cartography
Camilla Charnock, Craig Semple

Origination
Pre-Press Limited Hong Kong

Printing
**Liang Yu Printing Factory Limited,
Hong Kong**

Front Cover:
Royal Dublin, Dewy Morning 16th
*Artist: **John McNulty***

*Artist: **Graeme W Baxter** ROYAL BIRKDALE*
*Courtesy of: **Baxter Prints***

There have been all manner of hands that have guided the production of this, our updated, revised and expanded eleventh edition of Following the Fairways.

The company acknowledges the kind and generous advice of many golf professionals, secretaries and enthusiasts from all parts of Great Britain and Ireland. It is only by constant updating that a guide of this type maintains its value.

In our endeavour to illustrate the book, we have been kindly assisted by the Burlington Gallery, Rosenstiel's and other collectors of golfing memorabilia. A particular thank you to Bob Pringle of Old Troon Antiques. The colour work is all credited and we are most grateful to all our featured artists for giving us permission to use their works. We are especially grateful to Graeme Baxter, a renowned contemporary artist of the ancient game, for allowing us to use some of his works as illustrations.

We greatly appreciate the assistance of the many people who helped us in selecting hotels, restaurants and pubs around the country, particularly those golf secretaries who so kindly gave so much time marking our card. We are confident that you will relish savouring some of our suggestions, but do please let us know if you come across a 19th hole that you can recommend. We are also grateful to the hoteliers who have helped us produce feature pages for the book.

I would like to thank Bernhard Langer for penning our foreword. A great player and ambassador for this fine sport.

I am also extremely grateful to Jameson Irish Whiskey for their sponsorship and support. We are delighted to associate Following the Fairways with a company whose belief in quality is the same as our own. I would also like to thank Jamie Cunningham of Professional Sports Partnerships for his advice and contributions.

Finally, I would like to thank Nick Edmund, author of the golf editorial, for his tremendous efforts in providing such distinguished copy and I thank all those companies who have helped with the production for their accomplished work.

Julian West

*Artist: **Graeme W Baxter** ROYAL TROON*
*Courtesy of: **Baxter Prints***

Foreword

The fairways of Great Britain and Ireland hold many fond memories for me. Whilst I learnt golf in Germany, it could be said that I learnt about tournament golf in the home of the great game.

In Great Britain itself, I will always treasure the memory of my first European Tour victory at St Pierre in the 1980 Dunlop Masters. When the list of the other venues where I have won was shown to me recently, I counted myself incredibly fortunate to have played and won on so many prestigious courses.

The Emerald Isle has also proved kind to me. Interestingly enough, my first Irish Open victory was at the magnificent Royal Dublin (1984) whilst my second was at Portmarnock (1987). Both courses taught me a great deal about links golf.

The Links at Portmarnock was always going to be a special project. The challenge was to create a golf course which was in balance with the landscape, whilst using it to its maximum potential. I hope all golfers will enjoy the challenge which it offers.

Golf is a great game. I hope that all readers of Following the Fairways enjoy discovering both the "renowned courses" and the "hidden gems" listed in this excellent publication.

Enjoy the book and I hope that we meet Following the Fairways *soon.*

Bernhard Langer

Artist: **A Weaver WELL HOLED** Courtesy of: **Rosenstiel's**

Editor's Note:

Bernhard Langer has won European Tour events in team and individual competitions at the following courses in Great Britain and Ireland. St Pierre (twice), Moor Park, Haggs Castle, St Mellion (twice), Sunningdale, Wentworth (three times), The Belfry (twice), Portmarnock, St Andrews Old Course, Mount Juliet, The K Club and The Oxfordshire.

Introduction

You are at Portsalon in a remote, hidden corner of County Donegal. The rather bulky golfing guide had promised that the journey was worth making. You walk slightly nervously, however, towards the 1st tee: the book had warned you not to hook your opening drive into Lough Swilley, and that water threatened again at the par three 2nd and this was followed by a vertigo-inducing tee shot and tough approach to the 3rd. But, yes, it had also told you that the accompanying views were overwhelming. To your left—between the golf course and the sea—is (officially) 'the second most beautiful beach in the world'. On your right side, and semi-circling round in front of you, are the Knockinalla Mountains which tumble into heather-clad foothills. It is such a stunning backdrop, how can you possibly concentrate? Moments later, 'Crack!' Straight down the middle. You are on your way—thankfully, following the fairways.

First published in 1986, *Following the Fairways* seeks to guide the golfer (and perhaps his or her non-golfing partner) on a leisurely journey around the golf courses of Great Britain and Ireland, suggesting some of the best 18 holes—links, parkland, clifftop and heathland, and recommending superior 19th holes—places to eat, drink and sleep along the way.

Following the Fairways can properly be described as a 'Where to play—where to stay' golf guide. Our intention over the years has been to try to establish it as the most informative, entertaining and authoritative book of its kind. We have also tried to make it different from all the others and if we have achieved this goal at the expense of it fitting into your glove compartment then we make no apologies! The book's content has changed considerably in the past decade but with so much happening on and off the fairways it has needed to. Moreover, the first edition was a purely British affair whereas something like a quarter of the book is now devoted to a celebration of golf in the Emerald Isle.

Probably the most striking difference between *Following the Fairways* and other golf course guides is that we have chosen to illustrate the text with a wealth of golfing fine art, ranging from classics to contemporary. Some of these pictures have never been seen in print before.

Apart from extending the book's scope to include golf in Ireland, the biggest impact on its content has been the 'golf course boom' of the late 1980s and early 1990s. Several of the 'Championship Courses' highlighted in this book (see below) were not in existence in 1986. We believe it is precisely because it explores the best of these new developments that *Following the Fairways* can claim to be the most up to date golf course guide.

So how does the book work? Beyond the introductory pages which, in addition to the **'British Golf Venue of the Year'** and **'International Golf Venue of the Year'** awards include our **'Best of Following the Fairways'** suggestions, the journey begins in Cornwall and ends in the West of Ireland. For easy reference the book is divided into 30 chapters or 'golfing areas', each with its own attractive hand drawn map. Each golf course within the area is included within a detailed directory section which we term **'Complete Golf'**. For each club we list the telephone number, address and course yardages, together with approximate green fees and visitor policy. Some 2500 golf clubs are listed. Over 750 of the golf courses, as well as perhaps three times as many nearby hotels, inns and restaurants are recommended in the golf area text, or **'Choice Golf'**.

Many of the leading golf courses in Great Britain and Ireland are given special editorial attention. These featured courses comprise the aforementioned **'Championship Golf'** and 130 such courses are now included. Among their number are all the famous courses of Great Britain and Ireland, including every one of the Open Championship venues plus the likes of Walton Heath, Gleneagles, Ballybunion, Sunningdale and Royal Dornoch. All details relating to these entries are carefully revised with each edition.

In addition to the 'greats', many lesser known but beautifully situated courses are also featured in Championship Golf—places we believe no holidaying golfer would want to miss, for instance: Machrihanish on the Mull of Kintyre, Connemara in Co Galway, St Enodoc in Cornwall, Castletown on the Isle of Man, Bamburgh Castle in Northumberland, Nefyn in North Wales, Rosapenna and Portsalon in Co Donegal and Tenby in South Wales. The 'new' courses are also well represented by the likes of Slaley Hall, Loch Lomond, Druids Glen, Ballyliffin, Bowood, The Roxburghe, Portal and, in this edition for the first time, Skibo Castle, Celtic Manor, Carden Park, Powerscourt and The Warwickshire. Overall, we think it is a well balanced collection of the old and new, inland and seaside courses.

Before reading on, as editor I would like to thank everyone in Britain and Ireland who has assisted me over the years in my endeavours to produce the golf editorial. Special thanks are owing to Sean McCann of Golf and Travel and, of course, to my wife, Teresa and our little son George for continuing to put up with my golfing wanderlust. Finally, I would like to thank Jameson Whiskey for generously sponsoring this 11th edition, Bernhard Langer for providing the foreword, and wish you, the reader, good weather, good company and good fortune as you follow the fairways of Great Britain and Ireland.

Nick Edmund
Editor

Artist: **Alec MacDonld** **IN THE BUNKER**
Courtesy of: **Rosenstiel's**

Opening Strokes

Choice Golf

England

Wales

Scotland

Ireland

Complete Golf

England

Wales

Scotland

Ireland

Artist: Peter Munro BALLYBUNION, 11TH HOLE
Courtesy of: **Rosenstiel's**

Contents Championship Golf

Par for the Course

1. (4) OUTSTANDING GOLF AND ACCOMMODATION

The Old Course Hotel, The Duke's Course, Fife
Sunlaws House, The Roxburghe, Roxburghshire
Portmarnock Hotel & Golf Links, Co Dublin
Carden Park, Cheshire

2. (5) ENGLISH INNS AND GOLF

The Inn at Whitewell and Royal Lytham
The Whipper-In, Oakham and Luffenham Heath
The Hoste Arms, Burnham and Royal Norfolk
The Worsley Arms, Worsley and Ganton
The Nobody Inn, Doddiscombleigh and Manor
House Hotel, Moretonhampstead

3. (4) GOLF AND BEACHES

Portsalon and Ballymastocker Bay, Co Donegal
Saunton and Saunton Sands, Devon
Royal Dornoch and Embo/Dornoch Bay, Highland
Tralee and 'Ryans Daughter' Beach, Co Kerry

4. (4) GOOD HOTELS NEAR GOOD GOLF - SCOTLAND

The Old Course Hotel and St Andrews (Fife)
Greywalls and Muirfield (Lothian)
Balbirnie House and Balbirnie (Fife)
Letham Grange, Colliston (Tayside)
Sunlaws House, The Roxburghe (Kelso)

5. (4) GOLF AND HISTORIC HOUSES (ACCOMMODATION)

Woburn and Woburn Abbey (Flitwick Manor)
Bamburgh Castle and Lindisfarne (Linden Hall)
Bowood and Bowood House (Queenwood Golf Lodge)
Murrayshall and Scone Palace (Murrayshall)

6. (3) GOLF AND SHOPPING (ACCOMMODATION)

York and Fulford (Mount Royale)
Bath and Castle Combe (The Manor House)
Edinburgh and Muirfield (Johnstounburn House)

7. (5) GOOD HOTELS NEAR GOOD GOLF - ENGLAND

Slaley Hall and Slaley Hall (Northumberland)
South Lodge and Mannings Heath (Sussex)
Horsted Place and East Sussex National (Sussex))
Forest of Arden (Warwickshire)
Hawkstone Park and Hawkstone Park (Shropshire)

8. (4) HOME FROM HOMES

Glin Castle, Co Limerick, Ireland (Ballybunion)
Dupplin Castle, Perthshire, Scotland (Blairgowrie)
Bardrochat, Ayrshire, Scotland (Turnberry)
Waterville House, Co Kerry, Ireland (Waterville)

9. (4) DORMY HOUSES

Burnham & Berrow, Somerset, England
Royal Porthcawl, Mid Glamorgan, Wales
Royal Lytham, Lancashire, England
Co Louth, Baltray, Ireland

10. (4) GOLF AND PUBS

Nefyn and The Ty Coch Inn, Gwynedd
Thurlestone and The Village Inn, Devon
Waterville and The Smugglers Inn, Co Kerry
Elie and The Ship Inn, Fife

11. (4) GOLF AND SEAFOOD

Old Head and Ahernes, Youghal
St Enodoc and The Seafood Restaurant, Padstow
Royal Portrush and Ramore, Portrush
Machrinanish and Lock 16 Restaurant, Crinan

12. (3) GOLF & CASTLES

Windsor Castle and Sunningdale
Harlech Castle and Royal St David's
Culzean Castle and Turnberry

13. (4) GOOD HOTELS NEAR GOOD GOLF - WALES

Marriott St Pierre Hotel and St Pierre (Gwent)
Penally Abbey and Tenby (Dyfed)
Celtic Manor and Celtic Manor (Gwent)
St Davids Hotel and Northop Country Park (Clwyd)

14. (5) FAMOUS HOTELS WITH GOLF COURSES

Turnberry, Ayrshire, Scotland
Gleneagles, Perthshire, Scotland
Kildare Hotel Golf & Country Club, Kildare,
Ireland
Mount Juliet, Kilkenny, Ireland
The Belfry, Warwickshire, England

15. (4) OLD AND NEW

Royal St Georges and Chart Hills (Kent)
Portmarnock Golf Club and Portmarnock Hotel
& Golf Links (Co. Dublin)
Dornoch and The Carnegie Golf Links (Highland)
Rolls of Monmouth and Celtic Manor (Wales)

16. (5) FISHING AND GOLF

The K Club, The River Liffey and The K Club
Gliffaes, The River Usk and Rolls of Monmouth
Kinnaird, The River Tay and Blairgowrie
Mount Falcon, The River Moy and Enniscrone
Sunlaws House, The River Teviot and The Roxburghe

17. (4) GOOD HOTELS NEAR GOOD GOLF - IRELAND

Adare Manor (Co Clare)
The Kildare Hotel & Country Club (Co Kildare)
Luttrellstown Castle (Co Dublin)
Mount Juliet (Co Kilkenny)

18. (4) GOLF COURSES AND RESTAURANTS

Royal Dublin and The Unicorn
St Andrews and The Peat Inn, Peat Inn
Gullane and La Potiniere, Gullane
Stoke Poges and the Fredricks, Maidenhead

**It has to be the most self indulgent but satisfying round of all: eighteen of the best 19th holes.
Presumably one wakes up at The Old Course Hotel, St Andrews and dines at Fredericks at
Maidenhead—five star pampering all the way.**

Jameson 'Spirit of Ireland'

JAMESON

Established — Since 1780

SINE METU

Triple Distilled

IRISH WHISKEY

A word of welcome from the distillers of Jameson Irish Whiskey. Jameson, the world's most popular Irish whiskey is part of the renowned welcome and hospitality to be found in Ireland, not only on the 1000's of golf courses, but also in our famous bars and restaurants. Over the years Jameson has been associated with many golf events including our own internationally renowned amateur golfing tournament — The Jameson International Golf Challenge and the Smurfit European Open. Therefore, Jameson is pleased to be associated with this book.

Irish whiskey is an intrinsic part of Irish life and whether you are relaxing after an exhilarating round of golf or enjoying the warmth of an Irish pub, there is always an occasion to savour a glass of Jameson Irish Whiskey.

We hope you will enjoy using this year's 'Following the Fairways'

John Jameson & Son

Whiskey was invented in Ireland in the sixth century and predates Scotch Whisky by over seven hundred years. Irish Monks, in the sixth century discovered perfume distillation when on missionary work in the Middle East. They quickly discovered a somewhat different use for the process: they found that if a mash of barley and water was fermented with yeast and then heated in a potstill, the alcohol could be separated and retained. This resulting spirit, which had wondrous powers, was named Uisce Beatha or "The Water of Life".

What Makes Jameson Irish Whiskey Different?

TRIPLE DISTILLATION — SMOOTHER TASTE

Triple Distillation is the hallmark of the great Irish Whiskeys. Jameson is distilled three times in traditional copper pot stills, guaranteeing its smooth taste and absolute purity.

Most Scotch whiskies, by contrast, are distilled just twice, (Bourbon is usually distilled only once).

NO SMOKY TASTE

The malt for Jameson is deliberately dried in a closed kiln so that the grain is dried by clean hot air. This allows the subtleties of the malt to come through.

In Scotland, open peat fires are used, and this imparts a smoky flavour to the barley.

MELLOW FLAVOUR

Irish Whiskey is produced from barley (both malted and unmalted) and pure, clean water. It is aged in used oak casks, which ensures a mellow flavour and a golden hue. The main ingredient in Bourbon, by contrast, is corn. Bourbon is aged in new casks, giving it a heavy, sweetish flavour. Irish Whiskey is drier and more subtle.

THE DIFFERENT ARTS

In Ireland, distilling is considered the important art, while in Scotland, blending is paramount. Every brand of Irish Distillers whiskey is created in one of our own distilleries, where the quality of each drop can be controlled from start to finish.

In Scotland, a blender may buy 'fillings' from as many as thirty or forty different distilleries. This produces the typical Scotch 'blended' whiskey.

THE SPELLING

Perhaps one of the most obvious differences is in the spelling of the product. In Ireland and America, whiskey is spelt with an 'e', whereas in Scotland and Canada it is 'whisky', without the 'e'.

Whisky
Whiskey

JAMESON '98 INTERNATIONAL GOLF CHALLENGE

EVENT HISTORY

Jameson, the world's leading Irish whiskey, hosts the 6th annual Jameson International Golf Challenge this October in Ireland. Since its inauguration in 1993, the Challenge has grown in stature to involve over 22,000 participants in national qualifiers from all over the world.

THE TOURNAMENT — THE JAMESON TRIPLE

This year's Jameson International Golf Challenge is located in Portmarnock, Co. Dublin, the ancestral home of John Jameson who founded his whiskey distillery in Dublin in 1780. Combining the uniqueness which places Jameson triple distilled whiskey at the forefront of spirits brands worldwide, the 1998 Jameson International Golf Challenge stands apart from the rest as a perfect opportunity to play a three day handicap event on three of the most outstanding links courses in the world. The competition is based on teams of four golfers, with the three best scores to count each day. Each team will play in pairs, on the three courses, with two golfers from another team.

WINNER'S 1997

Richard Burrows, Chairman Irish Distillers Group (top left) presents the 1997 winners.

PLAY FOR YOUR COUNTRY

An important and exciting dimension to the Jameson International Golf Challenge is the Inter-Country Competition. The five best net individual scores from each country, each day, will be recorded and the country earning the most points over the three day period will be deemed the Champion Country. A permanent shield will be created and put on display with the winning country inscribed on it.

THE TROPHY

The Jameson Global Trophy (handcrafted Irish crystal) will be awarded to each member of the team with the best net score over the three days. A fine array of prizes will also be awarded to the best gross and net individual scores and to the best team on each course, each day.

THE 1997 WINNERS

The 1997 Jameson International Golf Challenge was won by: Fred Losel, Germany and Dick Burke, Pat Dooley and John Power from Ireland, while individual prizes went to John Power, Ireland and Teemu Tyry, Finland.

UK FINAL QUALIFYING VENUE
CARDEN PARK HOTEL, GOLF RESORT AND SPA

Carden Park Hotel, Golf Resort and Spa, situated in the heart of Cheshire but only 20 minutes drive from Junction 16 of the M6, has been chosen by Jameson Irish whiskey as the venue for the UK final of their 1998 International Golf Challenge.

A true golf resort, Carden Park ranks alongside the best in the world with its two 18 hole championship courses, 9 hole par 3 course and superb Jack Nicklaus Residential Golf School, not to mention the array of other leisure activities on the 750 acre estate and the magnificent hotel with its 192 bedrooms and suites.

The Jameson event will be held on the new Nicklaus Course, a co-design by Jack and his son Steve, which is certain to test the skills of the very best. Built to the highest standards and described by Jack as a "thinking man's golf course", it incorporates several double option holes such as the 7th and 15th where golfers have to choose which fairway to attack the green from due to the positioning of the hazards.

JAMESON IRISH WHISKEY

ROYAL DUBLIN GOLF CLUB

*" By any standards, this is as traditional a
links as you will get"*
Christy O' Connor Snr.

THE ROYAL DUBLIN GOLF CLUB

- Royal Dublin is Ireland's second oldest golf club. Founded in 1885, it moved to its present home in Bull Island in 1889.
- Redesigned by H.S. Colt, the world famous Golf Course Architect from Sunningdale, in 1920.
- Royal Dublin has staged numerous championship events including the Irish Open, the Irish Open Amateurs, and the Carrolls Irish Open (won by Seve Ballesteros in 1983 and 1985 and by Bernhard Langer in 1984).
- Royal Dublin hosted the Toyota Challenge of Champions in 1986 between Jack Nicklaus and Seve Ballesteros.
- In 1959, Christy O'Connor Sr. (ten times Ryder Cup golfer) was appointed Club Professional.

PORTMARNOCK HOTEL & GOLF LINKS

Portmarnock Golf Links was designed by Masters Champion, Bernhard Langer and was officially opened in June 1995.

It is generally acknowledged as a strong contender in the bid to host the Ryder Cup when it comes to Ireland in 2005.

The 18th hole — renowned as a magnificent finishing hole, fit to embroider any golfing masterpiece with fairway bunkers, strategically located on the left and right.

"Portmarnock Hotel & Golf Links manages an uncanny blend of the traditional perspective with all that's best in modern architecture." John Redmond (Great Golf Courses of Ireland)

Portmarnock Hotel is the ancestral home of Jameson.

PORTMARNOCK HOTEL & GOLF LINKS

*"There are very few locations in Europe
that could have allowed me the opportunity
and landscape to design such a classic
championship links. I hope all those who
play it discover its magic and its
challenging beauty"*
Bernhard Langer

PORTMARNOCK GOLF CLUB

*Ben Cranshaw considered the 185 yard par 3
15th hole as one of the 'Best in the World'.*

PORTMARNOCK GOLF COURSE

- The Portmarnock Golf Course (founded 1894) has hosted the Irish Open (1976-1982 & 1986-1990) and the Walker Cup (1991).
- When Ben Cranshaw played here in 1976 he said he wanted to take the famous 15th hole home to America.
- More recently Greg Norman and Nick Faldo endorsed his opinion when they named the 185-yard par three 15th hole in their 'Best in the World' category.
- Set on Dublin's North Coast overlooking Ireland's Eye, the land was originally donated to the club by the Jameson family.

It has been described as 'nothing less than a golfing *tour de force*. Of all the outstanding new courses that have opened in Great Britain since the first edition of *Following the Fairways* was published in 1986, Chart Hills may be the best of the bunch. Certainly, it rivals the ultra-private, ultra-exclusive Loch Lomond for that title.

Chart Hills is not devastatingly beautiful in the way Loch Lomond is (although its setting in the heart of the Kent countryside is hardly unattractive) but the design and layout of the course— specifically the quality and variety of its challenges—is quite extraordinary. Within two years of its opening in 1993, *Golf World* magazine rated Chart Hills as the 'Best New Course in England', and , ever since, it has been showered with accolades. It was designed by six-time Major winner Nick Faldo, and is his first design in Europe. Interestingly, his second European design, Sporting Club Berlin, has recently been ranked by the same magazine as 'Best New Course in Continental Europe' and 'Best Course in Germany'. At Chart Hills, Faldo teamed up with leading American architect, Steve Smyers, and their combined efforts have produced a modern classic.

The course dazzles from the instant you stand on the first tee and peer down one of the most exhilarating opening holes in golf—a par five measuring 599 yards which, from a spectacularly elevated tee, plunges dramatically downhill then sweeps to the right as it twists and tumbles towards a vast and heavily contoured green. And even before you are dazzled, you are likely to be overwhelmed with hospitality, for Chart Hills' clubhouse is one of the most luxurious yet at the same time one of the most friendly and relaxing in the country. It is a place where 'service' is not confused with 'servility', and where, thank goodness, high standards are not accompanied by stuffiness.

The visitor to Chart Hills is doubly blessed before he reaches the heroic first tee, since in addition to an excellent 19th hole, Chart Hills has superb practice facilities: "The best I've ever seen in Britain", according to swing guru David Leadbetter, who chose Chart Hills as the site for the European headquarters of his celebrated Golf Academy.

Chart Hills is located at Biddenden near Headcorn. The golf course is situated on the edge of the Kent Weald, approximately an hour to an hour and a half's drive south of London, and occupies historic turf. The club's name derives from a series of Royal Charters, the first being issued in 762 AD. It was once the site of the ancient Saxon forest of Andredsweald, and the landscape is liberally sprinkled with two hundred year old oak trees. Natural streams (or what Steve Smyers would call 'creeks') wind their way across gently undulating ground, which is ideal, in fact, for golf. And of course there is another dominating feature—sand. Faldo and Smyers love bunkers and at Chart Hills they seem to be everywhere. Most are actually very strategically placed but some have been created for purely aesthetic reasons. Many of the greens are defended by old fashioned revetted pot bunkers while clusters of Alister MacKenzie-like fairway traps shape holes and pose innumerable questions for a player when he walks on to a tee. The fairways themselves have exceptional definition, particularly in high summer when the roughs turn from pale green to gold—and grow tall and wild!

Wind is a constant factor at Chart Hills. Typically, the course plays 'firm and fast' and, on occasions, it can resemble a links course. It invariably rewards the player who can shape his shots and manoeuvre the ball in the wind. Around the greens, pitch and run shots are encouraged, allowing (and again rewarding) players to use the contours of the terrain to their advantage. In short, it is a course for the intelligent and the brave—a thrilling, puzzling and, above all, immensely charming test of golf.

Notwithstanding the aforementioned showering of accolades, the powers-that-be at Chart Hills are not content to rest on their laurels. Enhancement of the course's (already good) irrigation system and extensions to the clubhouse locker room facilities have recently been carried out. The announcement that Chart Hills is to become a European Tour Final Qualifying Venue comes as no surprise and, having already successfully staged an important Women's European Tour Event, it will surely not be long before the top men players are contesting a major tournament over this magnificent, inspiring layout.

Chart Hills is indeed a golfing *tour de force*, and, most deservedly, is *Following the Fairways* British Golf Venue of the Year.

Decisions, decisions. For the past twenty years or so the holidaying British golfer has had to make some difficult choices. Should I go and play some links golf, and if so do I go to Scotland or Ireland? Or what about Wales or the West Country? Or perhaps I should head for the sun, in which case do I fly to Spain or Portugal? Then again, South Carolina sounds exotic—or maybe Florida—take the family and kill two birds with one stone? Well, we have no hesitation in recommending another option altogether. In a sense it is middle ground between Britain and Spain and, yes, it is sunny, exotic and family friendly. We suggest you follow the fairways to France. In particular, we would direct you to the south west corner of the country, to the beautiful region of Aquitaine where you can sample the contrasting delights of Bordeaux and Biarritz and, most importantly, play some sensational golf.

Of course France hasn't been totally overlooked by British golfers—the Le Touquet-Hardelot area has long been a favourite destination. But in truth it has been viewed more as a weekend jaunt than a holiday—a quick (if very pleasant) flip across the Channel. Moreover, the golfer who visits Le Touquet and Hardelot and thinks he's 'done France' is the same golfer who journeys to Chepstow, plays at St Pierre and reckons he's 'seen Wales'.

There is a wealth of outstanding golf courses in France. Many are relatively new layouts, created in the last 15 years. But whereas most of the courses constructed in Britain during this period seem to have been built over rather plain, redundant farmland, the majority of the new French courses have been created amid magnificent countryside.

The company best equipped to point you in the right direction, to enable you to discover these French golfing gems is Blue Green, the largest owner and operator of golf courses in Europe. Blue Green is a French group but has offices in Birmingham: **Blue Green UK Ltd, Grosvenor House, 11 St Paul's Square, Birmingham B3 1RB**; telephone **0121 212 0066** or fax 0121 248 4843.

Blue Green owns 29 golf clubs throughout France. Their golf courses are all of a high standard—one or two are world class—and they place a special emphasis on 'après golf', a phrase which in golf speak translates best as 'the 19th hole'. In France, traditional 19th hole comfort, ie food, drink and accommodation tend to be taken rather more seriously than in Britain. Some French clubhouses are chateaux, others are award-winning restaurants in disguise. Several of the Blue Green clubs have hotels on site, and if not on site then (without exception) there will be a nearby 'partner hotel' at which special rates and discounts are available. Après golf also encompasses alternative recreational activities and Blue Green manage several 'golf resorts'. They also run a series of highly original golf schools and operate a Privilege Card Scheme (full details of which can be obtained by contacting the above address).

Blue Green is strongly represented in and around Paris but also in areas as diverse as Brittany, the French Alps, Burgundy and Aquitaine. This latter region is fast becoming renowned for its golf. Believe it or not, classy, chic Biarritz is twinned with Augusta! It is in Aquitaine that you will find Seignosse, a quite exceptional golf course—arguably the jewel in the Blue Green crown—and *Following the Fairways'* International Golf Venue of the Year.

Seignosse is located 45 minutes drive north of Biarritz and an hour and a half south of Bordeaux. Both towns have airports, Bordeaux being regularly served by flights from the UK. A decent map of the area will alert you to two things—firstly, the region is bordered by mile upon mile of sandy beach, in fact one of the longest strands in Europe; and secondly, the landscape is dominated by a huge pine forest, Les Landes. Seignosse is very close to the sea (it is visible from the higher parts of the course) and its fairways wind their way in and out of the forest. It is dramatic terrain and perfect for golf, for it is not only sandy underfoot and heavily wooded but it is spectacularly undulating.

The course is not quite 10 years old, although you would think it is much older. It was designed by leading American architect Robert von Hagge, who also designed Les Bordes and Le Golf National, two courses that rival Seignosse for the title 'Best New Course in France'. Seignosse is invariably ranked among the top six courses in the country (the other three were all built before the last war) and has recently been considered by the US publication *Golf Magazine* for inclusion in its listing of 'The World's Top 100 Courses'. Seignosse is that good.

Water features quite prominently in the layout, yet it is certainly not overdone. The greens are quick and often two-tiered, or otherways significantly contoured. Great use has been made of the site's natural changes in elevation and there is plenty of flowing—sometimes rippling—movement in the fairways. There is no 'signature hole' as such, there are too many outstanding holes for that, but among the best are the four short holes, which range from the tricky downhill 5th to the big stage-like 16th; the pick of the two-shot holes are, on the front nine, the 3rd and the 7th, both sweeping dog-legs, and, on the back nine, the long 13th, the pretty drive-and-pitch 14th and the 17th with its searching approach to a green perched on the edge of a lake. But the most exhilarating hole is surely the 580 yards, par five 11th, which, from a tee sited 150 feet above the fairway, plunges dramatically downhill and then weaves its way along a majestic tree-lined valley.

As for the 19th hole—or the après golf—Seignosse has few peers. The clubhouse has a commanding location overlooking the 18th green and out across the course towards the Atlantic. A short walk from the 1st tee, situated on even higher ground, is the Golf-Hotel Blue Green Seignosse. Extremely comfortable and built in a kind of New Orleans style, it blends neatly with its striking surroundings. It has 45 bedrooms, an excellent restaurant and, to illustrate its family-friendly orientation, it has a fine outdoor swimming pool. Come to think of it, where better to celebrate that closing birdie! For gourmet golfers and true connoisseurs of the game, Seignosse is simply superb.

The Best of Following the Fairways

Advanced warning: do not take these lists to heart! After travelling the length and breadth of the British Isles the editor felt he should put down a few personal thoughts highlighting what he thought to be 'the best of Following the Fairways'. The selections are restricted to the courses which are featured in the Championship Golf section of Following the Fairways - some 130 courses. A handful of our classic courses are not featured (typically because they are very private) and this explains the absence of a few personal favourites such as The Addington, Rye, Swinley Forest and Royal Worlington. This said, the following have been carefully considered and if you feel there are some glaring omissions, the editor would be delighted to hear from you! *Please see our Jameson Irish Whiskey Competition on page 351.*

Links Courses

Most Scenic Holes:
Par 3's: Royal Co Down (4th)
                Old Head (16th)

Par 4's: Turnberry (9th)
                Royal Portrush (5th)

Par 5's: Nefyn (12th)
                Co Sligo (3rd)

Most Scenic Courses: Royal Co Down
                             Cruden Bay
                             Waterville

Undiscovered Gems: Portsalon
                             Pennard
                             The Island

**Most diffiucult/
Intimidating Holes:**
Par 3's   Carnoustie (16th)
                Royal Portrush (14th)
                Waterville (17th)

Par 4's   St Andrews (17th)
                Royal St George's (4th)
                Royal Dublin (18th)

Par 5's: Royal Liverpool (16th)
                Ballyliffin (13th)
                Portmarnock (6th)

Most Characterful Holes:
Par 3's   Hunstanton (7th)
                Lahinch (6th)

Par 4's   North Berwick (13th)
                Portsalon (3rd)

Par 5's   Prestwick (3rd)
                Royal West Norfolk (8th)

Most Characterful Courses: Prestwick
                                 North Berwick
                                 Royal West Norfolk

Most Interesting Fairways: Machrihanish
                                 Ballyliffin Old
                                 Royal St George's

Most Interesting Greens: Prestwick
                                 St Andrews
                                 Royal Dornoch

Hazards:
Most Impressive Dunes   Ballybunion
                                 Cruden Bay
                                 Hillside

Most Severe Bunkers: Royal St George's (4th)
                                 St Andrews (17th)
                                 Portmarnock Hotel (17th)

Most Threatened By Ocean: Machrihanish (1st)
                                 Old Head (4th)
                                 Ballybunion(11th)

Inland Courses

Most Scenic Holes:
Par 3's: Killarney (18th)
                Loch Lomond (5th)

Par 4's: Loch Lomond (18th)
                Isle of Purbeck (5th)

Par 5's: Roxburghe (14th)
                St Mellion (12th)

Most Scenic Courses: Loch Lomond
                             Killarney
                             Boat of Garten

Undiscovered Gems: East Devon
                             Bamburgh Castle
                             Glasson

**Most diffiucult/
Intimidating Holes:**
Par 3's   West Sussex (6th)
                Notts (13th)
                St Pierre (18th)

Par 4's   The K Club (16th)
                Royal Ashdown (17th)
                Hanbury Manor (8th)

Par 5's   Wentworth (17th)
                Loch Lomond (6th)
                Collingtree Park (18th)

Most Characterful Holes:
Par 3's   Killarney (18th)
                St Mellion (11th)

Par 4's   Liphook (9th)
                Gleneagles (3rd)

Par 5's   Slieve Russell (13th)
                Lindrick (4th)

Most Characterful Courses: Gleneagles
                                 Royal Ashdown Forest
                                 Sunningdale

Best Conditioned Fairways: Loch Lomond
                                 Sunningdale
                                 Gleneagles

Best Conditioned Greens: Walton Heath
                                 Loch Lomond
                                 Lindrick

Hazards
Most Impressive Heather: Walton Heath
                                 West Sussex
                                 Sunningdale

Most Severe Bunkers: Ganton (14th)
                                 Walton Heath (16th)
                                 Woodhall Spa (12th)

Most Threatened By Water: The K Club (16th)
                                 The Belfry (18th)
                                 Druids Glen (17th)

The Best of Following the Fairways

Links Courses

Inland Courses

Greatest Holes		**Greatest Holes:**	
Short Par 3's	Royal Troon (8th) Lahinch (11th) Ballybunion (8th)	*Short Par 3's*	Gleneagles (5th) RoyalAshdown (6th) Carlow (17th)
Medium Par 3's	Cruden Bay (4th) Royal Birkdale (12th) Western Gailes (7th)	*Medium Par 3's*	Moortown (10th) Druids Glen (12th) Stoke Poges (7th)
Long Par 3's	Royal County Down (4th) Ballybunion (15th) The Island (13th)	*Long Par 3's*	Killarney (18th) Notts (13th) The Berkshire (1st)
Short Par 4's	Portmarnock (14th) Machrihanish (8th) Royal Porthcawl (9th)	*Short Par 4's*	West Sussex (4th) Ganton (14th) The Belfry (10th)
Medium Par 4's	Prestwick (17th) Royal Lytham (18th) Southerness (12th)	*Medium Par 4's*	Woodhall Spa (11th) Chart Hills (4th) Sunningdale (6th)
Long Par 4's	St Andrews (17th) Ballybunion (11th) Turnberry (10th)	*Long Par 4's*	Gleneagles (13th) Slaley Hall (9th) Druids Glen (13th)
Short Par 5's	Royal Cinque Ports (16th) Carnoustie (6th) Silloth (13th)	*Short Par 5's*	Walton Heath (16th) East Devon (6th) East Sussex (10th)
Long Par 5's	St Andrews (14th) Muirfield (17th) Portmarnock (6th)	*Long Par 5's*	Chart Hills (1st) The K Club (7th) Alwoodley (8th)
Greatest Front 9	Royal Co Down Royal St Georges	**Greatest Front 9**	Sunningdale (Old) Ganton
Greatest Back 9	St Andrews Ballybunion	**Greatest Back 9**	Walton Heath Woodhall Spa
Greatest Links Courses	St Andrews Royal Co Down Carnoustie	**Greatest Inland Courses**	Woodhall Spa Walton Heath Ganton
Best New Courses	Ballyliffin (Glashedy) Portmarnock Hotel Links	**Best New Courses**	Chart Hills Loch Lomond
Best Links Under 6400 yards	Cruden Bay Machrihanish	**Best Courses Under 6400 yards**	West Sussex The Berkshire

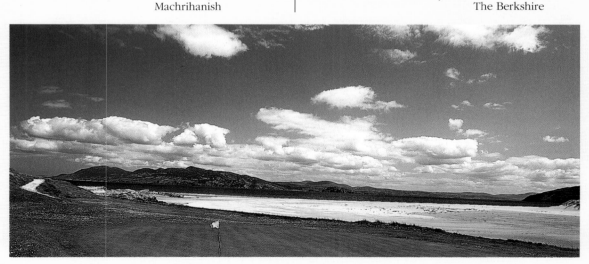

PORTSALON GOLF CLUB, CO DONEGAL, IRELAND *Courtesy of:* **David Cannon**

Have you ever tried Jameson Irish Whiskey? If not then I suggest you do. If you have then you will need no further encouragement from me. I've recently learnt that this delightfully smooth whiskey is a particularly good companion when compiling one's perfect round of golf courses. Lest you should consider in some ghastly mood of cynicism that these are the cheap words of a publisher grovelling to his major sponsor let me chide you now . . . nothing is further from the truth.

You see it happened like this . . . imagine if you will a fading light, a warmish Aga, an empty table, except for a bottle, a tumbler and a rather garish purple pen. Then allow some moments of deep reflection, as a humble golfer describes his perfect round—18 golf courses and 18 spectacular 19th holes. A journey that would bypass over 2250 other courses to be found in the British Isles—a tricky trek indeed . . . time for an inspirational drink I fancy.

Suitably refreshed I propose to start this tour of delight and discovery on the joyous fairways of Waterville, a true jewel amidst the overweighted crown of County Kerry's golf courses. Here the golf is truly tasty but delightfully remote and my first port of call is the handy Waterville House. More a country home than a hotel, it is an edifice to savour. Indeed it is fair to say that in Ireland the international golfer is heaven blessed. Let us not forget, some 30% of the world's links courses cling dramatically to the shores of this enchanting Isle. So many outstanding golf courses and some truly spectacular hotels to match. Adare Manor, Dromoland Castle, Mount Juliet, Rathsallagh, the list goes on but I digress. My second night will be spent at the Kildare Hotel and Country Club—surely one of the finest, friendliest hotels in Europe and in the K Club an outstanding golf course to match.

The temptations of Dublin are many—the delightful Royal Dublin and St Margarets spring to mind. However, for my second and third golfing treats I choose to embrace the delights of Portmarnock Golf Club where the 14th and 15th holes particularly delight one and all. Similarly gratifying is the Bernhard Langer Portmarnock

Hotel and Golf Links. Dinner at the thoroughly charming Unicorn Restaurant in Dublin followed by a night at this distinguished hotel will surely provide entertainment to compete with any.

The trickiest part of an exercise such as this is not so much what to include but what to leave out. The delightful Ballybunion, Ballyliffin, Lahinch and the 19th hole at Ashford Castle are all sadly forsaken for a trip to the North of Ireland, and a true classic—Royal County Down. One of the world's finest links, this is a course crafted more by nature than by man and its challenge is a joy to behold. A hard day following the fairways and a night at the handy Slieve Donard hotel—very satisfying indeed.

Leaving Ireland alarmingly prematurely we cross the Irish Sea to Wales, that land of dragons, sheep and many, many golf courses of excellence including that veritable classic of its type the thoroughly charming and welcoming Rolls of Monmouth, where an idyllic 18 holes of golf can be found. While there are a number of good restaurants, small hotels and pubs in the borderlands of England and Wales, my choice for its all round unspoiled nature is Gliffaes, thoroughly unpretentious, family run and some first class fishing as well.

While golfing in South Wales or anywhere in Britain you will soon surely hear tales of a relative newcomer and a hotel and resort which will match any in Europe— the incomparable Celtic Manor—36 holes here and you will surely need good rest and fare and you won't be let down. They are also building a new hotel, new golf course and a new just about everything else. Mark my words, Celtic Manor is set to be a star of the not too distant future.

Another relative youngster when compared to the Old Men of the west coast of Fife and other shores of Scotland is that Cornish outpost at St Mellion. Two excellent courses here and the Nicklaus course will challenge many a fine golfer. There is fine accommodation here as well but rather than stay I decide to visit The Manor House, Castle Combe, good golf here, and a really first

The Roxburghe, 14th Hole

class hotel as well and it is here that I rest my shoulders.

The counties of southern England offer much. Some courses are fairly private but there are some nuggets to try—East Sussex is delightful, Purbeck and the Kent coast with Princes, Deal and St Georges not to mention Rye and others is one of God's chosen kingdoms. However, I ignore their various offerings and instead embark upon another babe in arms—the tremendous, Nick Faldo-designed Chart Hills. From the opening hole this is a wonderful challenge. While the fame of this inland treat is spreading fast a better kept secret is the South Lodge Hotel in Sussex (good golf here as well)—excellent food and service and a charming place to try.

There are many remarkable attributes of the sea. Its rage, its calm, its power, its ever changing colour. Playing golf beside the sea has always been a pleasure and the Norfolk coast has a range of really excellent offerings. The finest is without question Royal West Norfolk (Brancaster), wooden sleepered bunkers and the tidal marshes of Norfolk, glorious scenery and a demanding golf course. Nearby one finds the delightful Hoste Arms, not a big hotel this but real ales and scrumptious cooking make this a real _Following the Fairways_ favourite.

So to Midland England—an extremely unglamorous description which covers numerous counties of real beauty and also a region which reveals some fine golf—as do the Home Counties, Wentworth and Sunningdale, two world class fairways. Or what of the Forest of Arden, The Belfry or the excellent Warwickshire? Well give a man a chance—my tour is tight on time and on this occasion there are beauties omitted from this area. I raise my glass and drink their health as a guilty apology for such an oversight but my spirits are lifted when I consider the delights of my forthcoming challenge—Ganton. A historic and perfectly scenic course in Yorkshire's moorland. With the bunkers successfully negotiated I set sail for another Yorkshire joy—The Worsley Arms—a hotel with real charm and service.

The Carnegie Club

As I reflect on my journey so far it is fair to consider that several of my chosen courses have been youngish in age and my next selection is also a relative junior—but what a beauty. . . . Carden Park. Here the golfer is punished for poor play on the excellent Nicklaus course and pampered at the outstanding adjoining hotel—a perfect 19th hole, and this is just as well because as the clouds begin to puff their cheeks with a troublesome breeze we set out for one of Britain's truly great courses—Royal Birkdale. The 12th is my favourite hole a difficult choice from the majestic 18.

Given that time is of no great importance in this particular crusade, I decide my next shelter should be some distance away in Cumbria—a county which offers some legendary hotels and inns. One such historic hostelry is the outstanding Farlam Hall. A mix of smiles and charm with some formal touches make this a delightful place at which to stay.

Crossing the border into Northumberland—that most charming English county—I allow myself a very personal treat, not the excellent 18 holes and hotel to be found set in the forest at Slaley Hall, but the far more lowly but equally entertaining course at Dunstanburgh Castle. A small links with a friendly 19th hole for a beer, soup and sandwich along with wonderful views to boot. There are hundreds of other courses around the coast that are similarly enchanting—some more remote than others—this just happens to be my favourite. I spend the night in the edifice which has been described as a shack and villa in the same weekend. It is neither but on a fine morning with the blue skies and fresh kippers for breakfast (Craster's of course), you are clearly close to heaven.

As another glass of Jameson Irish Whiskey warms the veins, the light fades and I cross the border into Scotland (but not that far into the home of golf) to find Hieton near Kelso. People seeking to try the celebrated courses of Scotland should add this course to their list. . . .The Roxburghe. It's outstanding. After a fine day with fine play you will smile for a month. . . . particularly if you should stay at my chosen venue, Sunlaws House, one of the finest small country house hotels in Britain.

From a relatively little known course to the most renowned in golf, St Andrews. Here we select our 19th hole from a range of first class hotels. The Old Course Hotel is the most renowned and it is here where I decide to rest my weary limbs. Today visitors can enjoy golf on the Old Course and the first class links, the Duke's Course. We choose to play the most revered course after which the hotel is named, The Old Course. It is a revered sporting venue and a privilege to play.

There are many other excellent Championship courses in Scotland. Muirfield and Carnoustie are both exceptional and there are two Meccas (if that is possible) that people speak of in the same breath of excellence—Turnberry and Gleneagles. On this occasion the coin lands on heads and I stay at Turnberry, a golf course and an hotel of excellence.

My final hostelry would arguably provide my most perfect stay—for in Skibo Castle and its revered Carnegie Club, the Highlands have an establishment of magical qualities—a visit completes my tour with heavenly proportions.

There's more light than shade in my bottle now and as I tread the stairs to bed I think of the days to come. In the mind or in practice any of the above courses and famous 19th holes and many more besides will surely satisfy the coldest heart, let alone one warmed by a smooth glass or two of Jameson Irish Whiskey.

Julian West, Publisher, Following the Fairways.

Golf In Britain

Artist: **Alec MacDonald** **DRIVING OFF** Courtesy of: **Rosenstiel's**

Following the Fairways

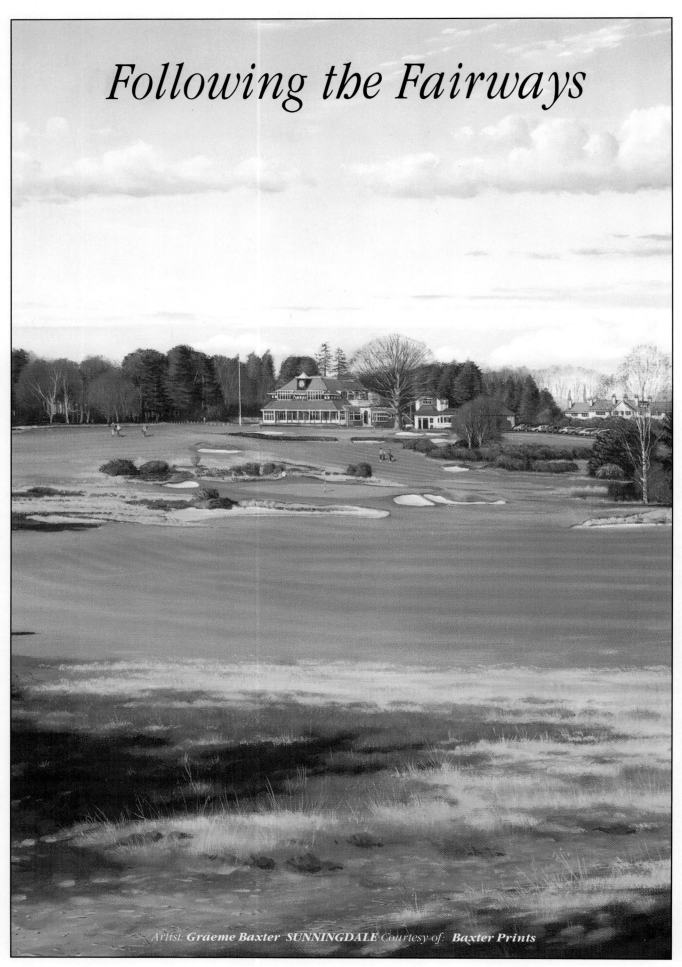

Artist: **Graeme Baxter** *SUNNINGDALE* *Courtesy of:* **Baxter Prints**

Artist: **G.Wallace** **LINKS GOLF** _Courtesy of:_ **Burlington Gallery**

Brandy for the Parson, Baccy for the Clerk'—Cornwall is the land of the smuggler's cove. It is also the land of King Arthur and the Knights of the Round Table—a land of legends. To cross the Tamar is to enter foreign soil: for centuries the Cornish Celts had more in common with the Welsh and the French Bretons than the ever-invading Anglo Saxons. Well, the Anglo-Saxons still invade but nowadays in a more peaceful manner. 'Grockles' they are called in Cornwall and they come in search of sun, sand and sea (not to mention a holiday home!) But there is also a fairly recent addition, a sub-species known as the 'golfing-grockle' who comes to Cornwall to seek out some of the finest golfing country in the Kingdom and when better than in 1999 when the century reaches its close.

The South Coast

If one commences an imaginary tour by crossing the Tamar at Plymouth, **St Mellion** Golf and Country Club (01579) 351351 has surely to be the first port of call. It is one of the few places in Britain where one might bump into Jack Nicklaus. St Mellion has an onsite hotel and two fine courses, one of which was designed by the great man and is featured later in this chapter. Not far away in Saltash, a new course has recently opened called **China Fleet**, apparently the Navy (British—not Oriental) is the guiding force behind it.

Heading westwards **Looe** Golf Club is situated on high ground to the north of Looe, near Widegates. An 18 hole moorland course, it lies somewhat at the mercy of the elements and can get exceptionally windy. Not too far away at Portwinkle the **Whitsand Bay Hotel** (01503) 30276 is an ideal place to break a journey with its own gentle 18 hole golf course stretching out along the cliffs and looking down over Whitsand Bay.

The area around Looe abounds with good hotels and restaurants with seafood not surprisingly a speciality. Hannofoe Point (01503) 263273 and Fieldhead (01503) 262689 are friendly and serve fine food. In Fowey, a restaurant to consider is Food For Thought (01726) 832221, a converted coastguard's cottage on the quayside, and the Fowey (01726) 832551 is a hotel worthy of note. Another hotel where the visitor can enjoy a little extra walking—on the cliffs as well as on the fairways is at Talland-by-Looe, the Talland Bay Hotel (01503) 272667. The Kitchen (01503) 272780 is an excellent restaurant in Polperro and in Golant, the Cormorant Hotel (01726) 833426 enjoys a glorious setting. Further inland the Old Rectory House (01579) 342617 at St Keyne offers good value.

We'll now, if you'll pardon the expression, leave the Looe area and, still heading in a clockwise direction, set sail for St Austell where we find a twin attraction for golfers: the redoubtable **Carlyon Bay** and the **St Austell** Golf Club. The St Austell course is situated on the western edge of the town off the A390. Rather shorter than Carlyon Bay but with an ample spread of gorse and numerous bunkers, it possesses plenty of challenges and attractions of its own.

Carlyon Bay is surely one of Britain's best loved hotel courses. Not a Turnberry or a Gleneagles perhaps, but very pleasing with several challenging holes and views over a number of beaches—one of which I'm told is frequented by naturists! There are numerous facilities at the hotel and it is ideal for families.

St Austell is a pleasant place to spend a day or two and golfers of course may decide to stay at Carlyon Bay Hotel itself (01726) 812304: obviously very convenient but four star comfort as well. As a first rate alternative

though, Boscundle Manor (01726) 813557 at Tregrehan is also highly recommended—the food alone is worth a trip. Heading northwards will bring one to the **Lostwithiel** Golf and Country Club (01208) 873550, where fine golf and agreeable accommodation are the order of the day. Note also the 13th century Globe Inn (01208) 872501 while in Lostwithiel.

Falmouth—a glorious harbour and seagulls aplenty. More good golf awaits. Like St Austell, there are two sets of fairways on which to exercise the swing and burn off the extra holiday calories. They are to be found at the **Falmouth** Golf Club, south west of the town (fine clifftop views over Falmouth Bay) and at the **Budock Vean** Hotel. This latter course has only nine holes but plenty of variety and is well kept.

For hotels, Budock Vean (01326) 250288 takes pride of place but others to note include the Royal Duchy (01326) 313042 and the Hotel St Michael's (01326) 312707. The opening words of The Wind in the Willows were written at the Greenbank (01326) 312440, clearly an inspiring place, while the Penmere Manor (01326) 211411 also has much to commend it. Two final thoughts for places to stay in this area are the Idle Rocks (01326) 270771 at St Mawes on the Roseland peninsula and the Meudon Hotel (01326) 250541 at Mawnan Smith.

Still heading along the south coast, the course at **Mullion** is one of the short but sweet brigade. Situated seven miles south of Helston, it can lay claim to being the most southerly on the British mainland. Nestling around the cliff edges overlooking some particularly inviting sands and with distant views towards St Michael's Mount, Mullion typifies the charm of Cornish holiday golf. With the spectacular scenery of the Lizard area, it's another good spot to spend a few days. In Mullion, or perhaps more precisely, Mullion Cove, Henscath House (01326) 240537 is perfect for the golf course and a strong mention also for the Riverside (01326) 231443 at Helford where there is some good accommodation and first rate cuisine. Penzance is another place where golfers may wish to base themselves—especially with the 18 hole **Cape Cornwall** Golf and Country Club at nearby St Just.

North Cornwall

The **West Cornwall** Golf Club lies just beyond St Ives at Lelant. A beautiful and very natural old-fashioned type of links, it was laid out a hundred years ago by the then vicar of Lelant. Like St Enodoc, it is a genuine links course—sand dunes and plenty of sea breezes—and quite short. Jim Barnes, who won both the Open and US Open was born in Lelant village.

In St Ives, two hotels to note are the Treganna Castle (01736) 795254 and the Garrack (01736) 796199—ideal for the nearby cliffs and beaches as well as the 18 hole par 59 **Treganna Castle** golf course. Slightly further afield at Carbis Bay, the aptly named Carbis Bay Hotel (01736) 795311 is particularly friendly and well recommended.

Passing numerous derelict tin and copper mines the inland course at **Tehidy Park** is soon reached. Located midway between Camborne and Portreath it presents a considerable contrast to the golf at Lelant. Here we are amidst pine trees, rhododendrons and bluebells. Getting back to the northern coast, **Perranporth** and **Newquay** look closer on the map than they are by road. Both are links type courses with outstanding sea views. Not far away at St Mawgan there is a 9 hole course, **Treloy**, and **Merlin**, an 18 hole course, has recently opened at Mawgan Porth.

In Newquay, where the crash of the Atlantic waves offers a surfers' paradise, there are several welcoming establishments. The Hotel Bristol (01637) 875181 is an ideal holiday base. A less expensive but worthy option is the Priory Lodge Hotel (01637) 874111. Connoisseurs of the public house might care to visit the Falcon at St Mawgan. Golfers at Tehidy may wish to note the Tregarthan Hotel (01209) 890399 at Mount Hawke—quite small but friendly and good value, and the Beach Dunes Hotel (01872) 572263 at Perranporth is clearly very convenient for the Perranporth links.

Further along the coast lie two marvellous golfing challenges—**St Enodoc** at Rock and **Trevose** at Constantine Bay. Trevose is the longer course but much more open and it doesn't possess the massive sandhills that are the feature of St Enodoc's links. Both courses are featured ahead.

The most convenient places for the golfing gourmet to stay are, at Trevose, the splendid Treglos Hotel (01841) 520727 and for St Enodoc, try the Molesworth Arms (01208) 812055, a pleasant 16th century coaching inn near Wadebridge. An early start can also be made from Padstow, where Rick Stein's Seafood Restaurant (01841) 532485 has a great reputation and a few fine rooms—an ideal choice for gourmet golfers who may have overindulged the night before! The Castle Rock Hotel (01208) 880300 at Port Isaac can also be recommended. This delightful fishing village also houses the 17th century Port Gaverne Hotel and Green Door Cottages (01208) 880244—where tremendous food and a charming atmosphere await. Another gem is located in Polzeath—The Cornish Cottage Hotel (01208) 862213—a delightful establishment.

Our coastal tour ends appropriately at Bude—a pleasant and unassuming seaside resort with a very good golf links, **Bude and North Cornwall,** situated almost in the town centre and renowned for its rolling fairways and excellent greens. The town has an impressive array of hotels: the Burn Court Hotel (01288) 352872 is as comfortable as any and has the advantage of overlooking the golf course. One other popular spot for golfers in town is the Camelot (01288) 352361. In Morwenstow, a fine old pub the Bush is well worth visiting. The clifftop views are breathtaking.

Inland Golf

The golf course at Tehidy was mentioned on our coastal tour, but four other inland courses definitely merit attention: the first is **Truro,** a shortish parkland course close to the charming cathedral; the second is at **Launceston,** one of the best parkland courses in the county; thirdly there is a highly rated new course near Camelford, called **Bowood**; and last but not least there is **Lanhydrock** near Bodmin which we explore in some detail ahead.

For stylish accommodation Truro golfers might wish to base themselves at the picturesque Trevispian-Vean Farm House (01872) 279514, and visitors to Bowood (which isn't far from Trevose) may opt for the comforts of the aforementioned Treglos, or the even closer Lanteglos Hotel (01840) 213551. The White Hart coaching inn is an ideal base for exploring the countryside around Launceston, as is Penhallow Manor (01566) 86206.

Lovers of angling as well as the fairways, should sample The Arundell Arms at Lifton (01566) 784666 a first class establishment in every way. However, the golf course itself is where some of the best views can be enjoyed. Located on high ground, to the west stretches Bodmin Moor—bogs and mystery—and to the east, Dartmoor—more bogs and even more mystery.

Artist: **Alec MacDonald OVER THE STREAM** *Courtesy of:* **Rosenstiel's**

St Mellion

I wonder what the golfing cynics would have said if a few years ago someone had suggested that Jack Nicklaus would one day be designing a championship course in Cornwall? 'Go tell it to the pixies', I should imagine. Well, in Cornwall myths, legends and fairy tales have a habit of turning out to be true.

St Mellion is the brainchild of farming brothers Martin and Hermon Bond. What made these charming people turn from profitable pig breeding and potato farming to golf course building remains something of a mystery. What is certain, however, is that their success has been nothing short of phenomenal.

The St Mellion story really has two parts to it. Act One commenced in the mid 1970s when the Bonds first decided to create a golf course. In short, their idea met with resounding success and a first class championship course was constructed. Within a few years, tournament golf came to Cornwall (TV cameras and all) for the first time. Ambition swelled and Act Two was conceived: 'Let's build the best course in Europe' (well, why not!) An additional two hundred acres of adjoining woodland was purchased from the Duchy of Cornwall and an approach was made to the great man himself, Jack Nicklaus. Negotiations followed and Nicklaus came over to inspect the new land. His initial thought was that the land was far too hilly and narrow—an impossible task. But of course, like the Bond brothers, Jack could never resist a challenge . . .

Plans were drawn up and at least on paper the object was a simple one, namely to build, in Jack's words, 'Potentially the world's greatest galleried golf course'. Let us just say that the construction team put in a few good hours! The end result is now ready for all the world to see. Some have described it as an 'Augusta in Cornwall'; others reckon it to be the toughest course in Britain. Perhaps the best idea is to go and judge for yourself—you'll be made most welcome.

While there is an understandable wish to play the **Nicklaus Course**, we shouldn't forget that there are two fine courses at St Mellion. When the Nicklaus course was being built, certain changes to the old championship course (now known as the **'Old Course'**) were necessary. However, it remains a worthy test of golf and is certain-ly a long way from your average 'holiday course'. Visitors are welcome to play either course, subject to making a booking with the **Advance Golf Reservations on (01579) 352002.**, fax (01579) 350537. The club's full address is the **St Mellion Golf & Country Club, St. Mellion, Saltash, Cornwall, PL12 6SD**. The green fees in 1998 are £35 per person per round on the Nicklaus Course, and £25 on the Old Course.

Although it nestles deep in the Cornish countryside, St Mellion is easily accessible from all directions. Travelling from afar most will come via Plymouth which is situated eight miles to the south east. Plymouth is linked to Exeter by the A38 and Exeter in turn to Bristol by the M5. On reaching Plymouth the A38 should be followed towards Liskeard and the turning for St Mellion is clearly signposted.

It is difficult to say which are the best holes on the Nicklaus Course. A few, however, do stand out and they exude the Nicklaus approach. The 3rd is an excellent hole—miss the fairway to the right and you can be facing a desperate uphill shot over a huge ravine to a heavi-ly protected green. On the 5th, the drive is across a lake and thereafter the fairway sweeps around to the left towards the green which has a stream running in front of it. And so it goes on, but note especially the par three 11th and par five 12th which have been likened to Augusta's 12th and 13th.

However, for all the comparisons with Augusta and Jack's best courses in America, the golfer only has to lift his eyes and look around to be reminded where he is. The surrounding scenery is unmistakably Cornish: the rolling green fields, the babbling brook with its kingfish-er and the gnarled trees that huddle around many of the greens and look as if they've endured a million English winters.

In May 1990, Benson and Hedges brought their presti-gious International Open tournament to the Nicklaus Course and victory fittingly went to one of the world's leading players, Jose-Maria Olazabal. The Spaniard was succeeded as champion by Bernhard Langer and in 1994 the trophy was claimed by Seve Ballesteros—underlining the old adage that the greatest courses produce the great-est champions.

Nicklaus Course					
Hole	Yards	Par	Hole	Yards	Par
1	400	4	10	410	4
2	518	5	11	181	3
3	356	4	12	525	5
4	175	3	13	361	4
5	315	4	14	158	3
6	420	4	15	411	4
7	480	5	16	520	5
8	135	3	17	426	4
9	375	4	18	460	4
Out	3,174	36	In	3,452	36
			Out	3,174	36
			Totals	6,626	72

St Enodoc

'It lay content
Two paces from the pin;
A steady putt and then it went
Oh, most securely in.
The very turf rejoiced to see
That quite unprecedented three.'

I suppose only Cornwall, and probably only St Enodoc come to that, could have inspired someone to write a poem about a birdie. Actually, it wasn't just 'someone', it was the Poet Laureate, Sir John Betjeman, who loved, and in later years lived beside this glorious West Country links. Everyone who visits St Enodoc, it seems, falls under a spell of some sorts. So why is it such a favourite and what are these charms?

Imagine a really classic links course:—huge sandhills, meandering, tumbling fairways, plenty of humps and hillocks, the odd awkward stance and blind shot perhaps but firm, fast greens and plenty of invigorating sea air. This is St Enodoc to a tee. Exhilarating, dramatic scenery? St Enodoc most definitely—situated on the northern coast of Cornwall and not too far from Padstow and Trevose, the views could hardly be mundane. The chance of a good score? Again yes—providing you stay on the fairways! St Enodoc, unlike all too many of today's courses won't put your length of drive on trial. It will, however, more than likely test every golf club in your bag. The holes are all very individual and bristle with old fashioned character. And then the accompanying atmosphere? Well, according to Sir John Betjeman even the turf finds time to rejoice in this splendidly relaxed environment. In short, St Enodoc is a sheer delight.

Doing his best to ensure that St Enodoc stays lost in this wonderful golfing time warp is the club's **Secretary, Mr L Guy**. He can be contacted by writing to the **St Enodoc Golf Club, Rock, Wadebridge, Cornwall, PL27 6LD**. Individual visitors are welcome throughout the week and, although it is likely to be difficult to arrange a tee time for the weekend, visitors are welcome after 2.30 pm on Saturdays. Bookings (at least four days in advance) should be made through the club's **Professional, Nick Williams, (01208) 862402**. Golfing societies, or parties of ten or more will need to make arrangements with the Secretary,s office on **(01208) 862200** or by fax on (01208) 862976. The clubhouse number is **(01208) 863216**.

Since 1982 there have been two 18 hole courses at St Enodoc. The main course is now named the **Church Course** and the newer (and considerably less testing)

one is called the **Holywell Course**. To play on the Church Course visitors must possess a maximum handicaps of 24 (28 for ladies). Green fees in 1998 for the Church Course are set at £35 a round midweek, £50 a day, with £40 per round, £55 per day payable at weekends. Fees for the Holywell Course are £15 per round, £21 per day. A round on both courses can be obtained for £40 during the week and £50 at weekends. Junior golfers (under 18) pay half rates and there are also various reductions available for those wishing to purchase weekly or fortnightly temporary memberships.

St Enodoc is much less remote and more easily reached than many people imagine. Coming by road the two towns to look for on the map are Bodmin and Wadebridge. The former is linked to Exeter by the A30 and to Plymouth by the A38. Wadebridge is 7 miles north of Bodmin. At Wadebridge the B3314 should be taken to St Minver and then a left turn should be taken at this village to Rock.

The Church Course takes its name from the tiny, half-sunken church which is situated near the far end of the links. Many years ago the church was barely visible after a violent storm practically covered it in sand. It is well worth inspecting and Sir John Betjeman is buried in the graveyard. The church almost comes into play on the celebrated 10th hole, the toughest par four on the 6243 yards, par 69 layout (the Holywell Course measures 4165 yards, par 62). As well as being the most difficult two shot hole on the course it is also one of the most memorable. The drive is downhill, but it must carry almost 200 yards to find a narrow, heavily contoured fairway;. Off to the left is a marshy area and a stream and to the right are steep sand dunes and uncompromising rough. The second shot to the green is almost as daunting as the tee shot!

Betjeman's birdie came at the 13th but the other hole that everyone talks about is the 6th. Here the golfer must confront the 'Himalayas', 'the highest sandhill, to the best of my belief, I have ever seen on a golf course' remarked the famous golf writer Bernard Darwin (another who was thoroughly enchanted by St Enodoc). With holes like the 6th it isn't difficult to see why St Enodoc is so often likened to Prestwick.

The area around Padstow is most fortunate in having both St Enodoc and Trevose so close at hand. Together they make a marvellous pair and offer two very different challenges. It is difficult to imagine anyone playing St Enodoc and not relishing a return visit . . . and who knows what an unexpected birdie might inspire!

			Church Course		
Hole	Yards	Par	Hole	Yards	Par
1	518	5	10	457	4
2	438	4	11	205	3
3	436	4	12	386	4
4	292	4	13	360	4
5	161	3	14	355	4
6	378	4	15	168	3
7	394	4	16	482	5
8	155	3	17	206	3
9	393	4	18	446	4
Out	**3,165**	**35**	**In**	**3,078**	**34**
			Out	3,165	35
			Totals	**6,243**	**69**

This delightful hotel is situated in a spectacular small cove only half a mile away from the 1000 year old fishing village of Port Isaac on the North Cornish Heritage Coast. Rich in history, much of the surrounding area consists of cliffs, headlands, beaches and old buildings which are preserved by the National Trust.

The hotel is an early seventeenth century Cornish Coastal Inn that has been carefully restored by resident proprietor Midge Ross whilst still retaining its original character, ambience and charm.

The seventeen bedrooms are all en suite with colour television, radio and direct dial telephone. The hotel is extremely comfortable with a relaxed and friendly atmosphere.

Dining at the Port Gaverne is a memorable experience with good food prepared from the best ingredients available. Chef Ian Brodey and his staff use fresh garden produce, local lamb and beef, locally landed fish, lobster and crab when in season, to create an excellent à la carte menu.

Only a few steps away from this internationally known hotel are the Green Door Cottages. These are six splendidly restored eighteenth century self contained Cornish fishermen's cottages built around an enclosed and sheltered courtyard. All are attractively and comfortably furnished with their own central heating, colour television and direct dial telephone. Overlooking the cove there are two large flats which sleep eight people.

Whether staying at the hotel, cottages or flats this is truly an ideal centre from which to explore this very special area. Swimming within the sheltered cove is always a popular choice as are diving, sailing and surfing. The more adventurous may choose inshore or shark fishing and the less energetic may choose to wander along one of the particularly spectacular coastal paths.

For golf enthusiasts Cornwall is fast becoming one of the most popular golfing holiday venues in the country. At the Port Gaverne Hotel rounds can be arranged at any of the twenty-six courses within the Royal Duchy including St Mellion, St Enodoc, Lanhydrock, Bowood Park, St Kew, Trevose, Looe and Roserrow.

Port Gaverne Hotel and Green Door Cottages
Nr Port Isaac
North Cornwall PL29 3SQ
Tel: (01208) 880244
Fax: (01208) 880151
Freephone: (0500) 657867

Trevose

To some, mention of the north coast of Cornwall will invoke thoughts of golden sandy beaches and cool, inviting seas. For others, it may conjure up images of romantic coves, wild spectacular cliffs and incessant crashing waves. Either way, the place has a certain magic and after all it was here that King Arthur is said to have met Merlin. Such is the setting of the Trevose Golf and Country Club.

Located near the quaint little fishing port of Padstow, Trevose is an ideal spot for a golfing holiday—or any kind of holiday come to that, but those who haven't made space in the boot for the golf clubs are missing out on something rather special. The club has long boasted a splendid 18 hole championship course plus an adjacent nine hole short course. Now Trevose can entice the visiting golfer with a new 'full length' par 35 nine hole course which opened in 1993, thus making 36 holes in total.

From the championship tees (handicap certificate required) the 18 hole course measures 6608 yards (par 71, SSS 72). The forward tees reduce the length by about 170 yards, while the ladies play over 5713 yards, par 73. The course can properly be described as a golf links although the visitor need have no fears of having to carry Himalayan-like sandhills. The course is fairly flat and as a rule the rough is kept short. This should ensure that the golfer spends more time admiring the scenery than searching for his golf ball. A word about the views—they are indeed tremendous, particularly those across Booby's Bay which provide a dramatic backdrop to the 4th green.

The wind at Trevose can often play a decisive role and prevent low scoring. There are a great number of well-positioned bunkers and a stream meanders through much of the course. Among the best holes one might single out

the par three 3rd, the above-mentioned 4th (a curving right to left dog-leg) the 7th and the 12th.

The clubhouse with its prime situation overlooking the course offers a whole range of first class facilities There is a large, comfortable bar and a dining room which can cater for over 100 people. For children, a separate games room is provided. Swimming, snooker and tennis are also all very much a part of the country club scene—and there is even a trendy boutique!

There is an unmistakably relaxed, holiday flavour about Trevose. The atmosphere is perhaps best epitomised by the story of four lady members involved in a foursomes game: apparently, when playing the short 16th they arrived at the green only to discover that they had been so busy chattering not one of them had remembered to tee off. . .so much for women drivers!

Trevose Golf & Country Club, Constantine Bay Padstow, Cornwall PL25 8JB	
Secretary	Patrick O'Shea (01841) 520208
Professional	Gary Alliss (01841) 520261
Green Fees	Championship £22-£33
	New Nine £15-£20
	Par Three £8-£10
Restrictions	Proof of handicap for Championship
Directions	
Four miles west of Padstow off the B3276.	

Lanhydrock

Stand on the clubhouse verandah and drink in the view. Rolling hills and patchwork fields fill the horizon. Stretching out below, amidst a beautifully wooded valley is the golf course: lush undulating fairways, splashes of dazzling white sand and slick, subtly contoured greens—framed sometimes by water hazards and nearly always by a splendid mix of trees. It is wonderful countryside and classic golfing terrain.

This is Lanhydrock and if the vision from the verandah has most golfers drooling in anticipation, so the opening hole encapsulates the spirit of the challenge ahead. The 1st is a short par four and with the tee shot being downhill to a generous landing area few should have trouble finding the fairway. The difficulty, however, comes with the approach which must be hit over a small lake to an attractively sited green which, like several at Lanhydrock, slopes from back to front—towards the water's edge.

Four strong holes are followed by a relatively modest 5th but then comes the glorious 6th. Pity the golfer who does not relish a par three where the tee shot must be struck downhill across a lake to a target green. There may be many similarly styled holes in golf but few can have been as beautifully conceived. The hole occupies its own, almost hidden, corner of Lanhydrock. The backdrop to the green comprises a steep overgrown bank, a gently cascading stream and an impressive collection of tall trees. You reach the green via an understated wooden bridge, then putt out on golf's equivalent of an open-air stage.

The best sequence at Lanhydrock begins with the 10th. The very shape of this hole encourages a swashbuckling 'bite off as much as you dare' approach. From an elevated tee the fairway plunges across a valley and regains its height just as the hole dog-legs sharply away to the right.

An ancient woodland known as Tregullan Moor envelops the 12th hole—for its entire length it is surrounded by a mass of gnarled, wizened old trees and prickly gorse. The 13th takes the golfer to the highest point on the course where the views are naturally the most spectacular . . . how often do you get the opportunity to contrast a strikingly modern clubhouse with an 18th century Cornish tin mine? !

The par five 18th can offer the chance of a closing birdie but only if the largest inland bunker in Cornwall is successfully avoided. This giant stretch of sand (Lanhydrock's version of 'Hell's Half Acre') occupies most of the land in between the 9th and 18th greens. Any hope of impressing those 'bewitched' folk on the verandah with a sneaky 'up and down' from the back of this monster? Certainly . . . in our dreams!

Lanhydrock Golf Club, Lostwithiel Road, Bodmin, Cornwall PL30 5AQ	
Manager	Graham Bond (01208) 73600
	Fax: (01208) 77325
Green Fees	WD/WE £26/round; £34/day
Restrictions	Advance booking recommended
Directions	
One mile south of Bodmin off the B3268 via the A30/A38.	

Key

*To avoid disappointment
it is advisable to telephone
in advance*

***Visitors welcome at most times*
***Visitors usually allowed on
weekdays only*
**Visitors not normally permitted
(Mon, Wed) No visitors
on specified days*

Approximate Green Fees
A	£40 plus
B	£25 to £40
C	£20 to £30
D	£15 to £25
E	under £15
F	Green fees on application

Restrictions
G *Guests only*
H—*Handicap certificate required*
H—(24) *Handicap of 24 or less*
L —*Letter of introduction required*
M—*Visitor must be a member of
another recognised club*

Bowood G.C.
(01840) 213017
Lanteglos, Camelford
(18) 6692 yards/***/B/H

Bude and North Cornwall G.C.
(01288) 352006
Burn View, Bude
(18) 6202 yards/**/B/H

Budock Vean Hotel & G.C.
(01326) 250288
Mawnan Smith, Falmouth
(9) 5153 yards/***/D/L/H

Cape Cornwall G.& C.C.
(01736) 788611
St Just, Penzance
(18) 5650 yards/**/D

Carlyon Bay Hotel G.C.
(01726) 814250
Carlyon Bay, St Austell
(18) 6463 yards/***/C

China Fleet C.C.
(01752) 848668
Saltash
(18) 6551 yards/***/F/H

Culdrose G.C.
(01326) 574121
Royal Naval Air Station, Culdrose
(18) 6432 yards/*/E/G

Falmouth G.C.
(01326) 314296
Swanpool Road, Falmouth
(18) 5680 yards/***/B/H

Holywell Bay G.C.
(01637) 830531
Holywell Bay, Newquay
(18) 2784/***/E

Isle of Scilly G.C.
(01720) 422692
St Mary's, Isles of Scilly
(9) 6001 yards/***/D

Killiow Park G.C.
(01872) 70246
Kea, Truro,
(18) 3500 yards/**/D

Lanhydrock G.C.
(01208) 73600
Lostwithiel Road, Bodmin
(18) 6185 yards/***/F

Launceston G.C.
(01566) 773442
St. Stephens, Launceston
(18) 6407 yards/**/D/H/L

Looe G.C.
(01503) 240239
Widegates, Looe
(18) 5940 yards/***/F

Lostwithiel G.& C.C.
(01208) 873550
Lower Polscoe, Lostwithiel
(18) 6098 yards/**/D/H

Merlin G.C.
(01841) 540222
Mawgan Porth, Hewquay
(18) 5227 yards/***/E

Mullion G.C.
(01326) 241176
Cury, Helston
(18) 6022 yards/**/C/H

Newquay G.C.
(01637) 874354
Tower Road, Newquay
(18) 6140 yards/***/D/H

Perranporth G.C.
(01872) 572454
Budnick Hill, Perranporth
(18) 6286 yards/***/C/H

Porthpean G.C.
(01726) 64613
Porthpean, St Austell
(9) 3266 yards/***/E

Praa Sands G.C.
(01736) 763445
Germoe Crossroads, Penzance
(9) 4104 yards/***/D/H

Radnor G.C.
((01209) 211059
Treleigh, Redruth
(9/***/E

Roserrow G. & C.C.
St Minver, Wadebridge
(01208) 863000
(18)/***/C

St Austell G.C.
(01726) 74756
Tregongeeves Lane, St Austell
(18) 6000 yards/***/F/M/H

St Enodoc G.C.
(01208) 862402
Rock, Wadebridge
(18) 6243 yards/***/B/H(24)
(18) 4165 yards/***/D

St Kew G.C.
(01208) 841500
St Kew Highway, Bodmin
(9) 2204 yards/***/E

St Mellion G.& C.C.
(01579) 352002
St Mellion, Saltash
(18) 6626 yards/**/A/H
(18) 5782 yards/**/B

Tehidy Park G.C.
(01209) 842208
Cambourne
(18) 6241 yards/***/B/H

Tregenna Castle Hotel G.C.
(01736) 797381
St Ives
(18) 3549 yards/***/F

Treloy G.C.
(01637) 878554
Treloy, Newquay
(9) 2143 yards/***/E

Trethorne G.C.
(01566) 86324
Kennards House, Launceston
(9) 3169 yards/***/E

Trevose G.& C.C.
(01841) 520208
Constantine Bay, Padstow
(18)6608 yards/***/F/H
(9) 3031 yards/***/F
(9) 1360 yards/***/F

Truro G.C.
(01872) 272640
Treliske, Truro
(18) 5347 yards/***/C/H

West Cornwall G.C.
(01736) 753401
Lelant, St Ives
(18) 5884 yards/***/B/H

Whitsand Bay Hotel G.C.
(01503) 230470
Portwrinkle, Torpoint
(18) 5800 yards/***/D/H/L

Artist: **F P Hopkins IN THE EDEN**
Courtesy of: **Burlington Gallery**

Artist: **F P Hopkins A PAINSTAKING PUTTER**
Courtesy of: **Burlington Gallery**

Artist: **Robert Guy** **WESTWARD HO!** *Courtesy of:* **Burlington Gallery**

This charming 18th century country house is situated in the historic town of Ottery St Mary and set in one of the greenest and most attractive valleys in East Devon. Formerly the home of the Coleridge family, the hotel is set in five acres of lovely grounds overlooking the Otter Valley.

Guests are offered every comfort in the 27 light and airy bedrooms, all modernised to the highest standards, to suit all tastes and requirements. In the Otterview restaurant the finest cuisine is prepared using only the freshest ingredients.

For the energetic, the hotel boasts a large indoor swimming pool, sauna, two squash courts and putting green.

There is also a host of local attractions. The hotel is ideally situated only six miles from Sidmouth and twelve miles from the centre of Exeter. Guests can visit the cathedral city, take a stroll along the South Devon coastal path among some of the most beautiful beaches

in the country, or ramble through the hills and valleys of Exmoor and Dartmoor. With many tourist attractions and National Trust properties in the area, there is something for everyone.

For those guests who wish to indulge in country pursuits, the hotel can arrange horse riding, fishing, sailing and clay pigeon shooting.

Special golf breaks are available with professional tuition packages at Woodbury Park, Axe Vale, Honiton, Sidmouth and East Devon golf clubs.

Wedding receptions, dinner dances and residential and non-residential conferences for up to 100 delegates can be accommodated. Special interest holidays and breaks are available throughout the year including painting, guided walks, antiques and literary weekends.

Salston Manor invites you to experience a special way of life—a place to relax and enjoy some of life's better things. Phone or fax for details.

Salston Manor Hotel
Ottery St Mary
Nr Exeter
Devon EX11 1RQ
Tel: (01404) 815581
Fax: (01404) 815581

Glorious Devon they call it—beaches to the north, beaches to the south and Dartmoor in the middle. Amidst all the glory are over forty golf courses, the majority of which lie either directly on the coast or within a mile or so of it. The two most widely known are both in the north of the county: Royal North Devon (Westward Ho! as it is commonly known) and Saunton. The greater number of courses, however, are on the southern coast, or to put it another way, while North Devon may have the cream, most of the tees are to be found in the south.

Firstly though, what about golf in the middle? The beautiful setting of the **Manor House** Hotel & Golf Course at Moretonhampstead is known to many. However, it is not the sole course within Dartmoor. **Okehampton** is another moorland type course and whilst not overly long, has a number of interesting holes and there is a good new course at Christow called **Teign Valley**. Away from Dartmoor, but still fairly centrally located is the parkland course at **Tiverton**, easily reached from the M5 (junction 27), and a little closer to Exeter and adjacent to Woodbury Common is the highly acclaimed **Woodbury Park**. Owned by Nigel Mansell, Woodbury has a very challenging 18 hole championship course designed by Hamilton Stutt plus a shorter 9 hole course and driving range. Note the spectacular par three 18th hole here—arguably the most dramatic closing hole in the south west.

The Manor House Hotel & Golf Course
Moretonhampstead,
Devon TQ13 8RE
Tel: (01647) 440355 Fax: (01647) 440961

West country golf is a particular delight and nowhere is it better or more appealing than at Moretonhampstead, where the gracious Manor House Hotel sits in regal splendour overlooking a golf course that is a sight for sore eyes at any time of the year. Set on the edge of Dartmoor National Park, the course provides a stunning combination of natural beauty and ideal golf terrain, perhaps without peer. A bonus is the elegant former country home that is now the Manor House, a hotel in the grand tradition.

With its many Tudor buildings, historic guildhall and impressive cathedral, Exeter makes an attractive county town. Golfwise, the city has an 18 hole course at Countess Wear, namely the **Exeter** Golf and Country Club, which has a very grand clubhouse and the course is renowned for its beautifully maintained greens, undoubtedly among the best in Devon. There are many outstanding places in which to spend a night or two when visiting this part of the world. Exeter is a likely base and here the Royal Clarence Hotel (01392) 58464 is extremely comfortable and enjoys a splendid position overlooking Cathedral Square.

Also in the city, the St Olaves Court (01392) 217736 on South Street is a delightfully secluded inn with good accommodation. One of the oldest and best known pubs in Exeter is the Ship on St Martins Lane—ideal unless you're over six feet tall!

On Dartmoor, the striking Manor House Hotel (01647) 440355 at Moretonhampstead is where many golfers will choose to hang up their spikes, but a number of splendid alternatives are at hand. Chagford offers the exceptional Gidleigh Park (01647) 432367 and the Mill End Hotel (01647) 432282. The former is lavish, the latter less so but thoroughly recommended. The White Hart in Moretonhampstead (01647) 440406 is a pleasant inn to note. In Lydford, Lydford House (01822) 820347 is comfortable, as is the Castle Inn (01822) 820242, while the Lodge Hill Farmhouse (01884) 252907 at Ashley is convenient for Tiverton. Whilst in the area, a visit to Huntsham may also be in order: Huntsham Court (01398) 361365 is a delight to those who enjoy the atmosphere of a relaxed country house. Lovers of classical music and fine food will feel particularly spoiled. After a game at Manor House, two popular pubs to note are the Nobody Inn (01392) 52394 at Doddiscombsleigh (excellent food and accommodation here as well) and the Ring of Bells in nearby historic North Bovey.

South Devon
On the east side of the River Exe and only half an hour's drive from Exeter are the courses at Sidmouth and Budleigh Salterton (**East Devon**). Both are on fairly high ground providing panoramic views out to sea. **Sidmouth** is perhaps more of a typical clifftop course with well wooded fairways and 'springy' turf, while East Devon is a cross between downland and heathland with much heather and gorse. Convenient for both courses at Ottery St Mary is the charming 18th century country house hotel, Salston Manor Hotel (01404) 815581 which also offers inclusive golf packages for Woodbury Park. East Devon's delights are detailed ahead.

To the west of the Exe estuary, the friendly **Warren** Golf Club at Dawlish offers the only true links golf in South Devon. Laid out on a narrow hook-shaped peninsula and covered in gorse with numerous natural bunkers this is Devon's answer to St Andrews—and if this sounds a little far-fetched just inspect the aerial photographs at the 19th! It is a much improved course with an interesting finishing hole that will have the wayward hitter threatening both the members in the clubhouse and/or quite possibly the passengers on a passing London to Penzance 125. A fairly near neighbour of the Warren is **Teignmouth** Golf Club. It may be near, but Teignmouth offers a totally different challenge, being situated some 900 feet above sea level on Haldon Moor. Teignmouth can become shrouded in fog during the winter, but when all is clear, it's a very pleasant course and most attractive too.

Those seeking a memorable 19th hole on their way to the south coast may have sped past Gittisham—a mistake, for Combe House (01404) 42756 provides great elegance and style. In Sidmouth, the Riviera (01395) 515201 is grand, and concessionary green fees can be arranged locally, while for a family holiday the Westcliff (01395) 513252 may be the best choice. Just east of Sidmouth, the charming Masons Arms (01297) 680300 at Branscombe is perfect for a relaxing dinner and a stopover if required. In Dawlish Warren, most convenient for the golf links is the Langstone Cliff Hotel (01626) 865155 (just roll down the hill and you're almost there). Not too far from the many courses of east Devon at Hawkchurch, near Axminster, the comfortable Fairwater Head Hotel (01297) 678349 is recommended. Just to the north west of Newton Abbot in Haytor lies the Bel Alp House Country Hotel (01364) 661217, an elegant country house offering genuine tranquillity. Another local favourite, worthy of its popularity, is the Rock Inn (01364) 661305. Just outside Teignmouth, Ness House (01626) 873480 is a small hotel offering good value breaks for golfers and also recommended is the Coombe Bank Hotel (01626) 772369 . Finally, Thomas Luny House (01626) 772976 a small Georgian town house of delightful character is ideal for a group of gourmet golfers.

The three handiest courses for those holidaying in the Torbay area are probably **Churston, Torquay** and **Newton Abbot**. The first two mentioned offer typical downland/clifftop type golf and a very different game from Newton Abbot's course at Stover where abundant heather, woods and a meandering brook are likely to pose the most challenges. A word too, on the course at **Hele Park** which has greens reputedly second to none. Speaking of challenges, mention must be made of the **Dartmouth** Golf and Country Club at Blackawton, Totnes.

One of the most pleasant and convenient places to stay in this area is the Orestone Manor House (01803) 328098 in Maidencombe. In Torquay itself, there are numerous fine hotels. The most famous hotel is the Imperial (01803) 294301, which offers all manner of splendid facilities but charges for it! The Palace Hotel (01803) 200200 is less costly, but courtesy still prevails. Perhaps the best value to be found is at Homers Hotel (01803) 213456 with its first class restaurant. Another to note is The Osborne (01803) 213311—an excellent establishment.

If you are still seeking an ideal 19th hole, the Quayside Hotel (01803) 855751 in the popular resort of Brixham is charming and the town retains a much quieter atmosphere

than its neighbour across the bay. In Dartmouth, one restaurant merits special comment: the Carved Angel (01803) 832465—a must for lovers of truly outstanding cuisine. Just outside Dartmouth, in Dittisham, Fingals at Old Coombe Manor (01803) 722398 is well worth the short trip and finally the Holne Chase Hotel (01364) 631471 in Ashburton—a glorious setting with a restaurant to match.

Heading further down the coast, the picturesque village of **Thurlestone** has one of the most popular courses in Devon. It is a superb clifftop course with several far-reaching views along the coast, on a fine day there are few better places to be. **Bigbury** lies a short distance from Thurlestone and although perhaps a little less testing it is also attractive and looks across to Burgh Island, a favourite (or hopefully an ex-favourite) haunt of smugglers. Both Thurlestone and Bigbury can be reached from Plymouth via the A379, or from the Torbay region via the A381. The Thurlestone Hotel (01548) 560382 is a perfect base not only for playing the two nearby courses, but also for exploring what is a delightful part of Devon. It also has its own very pleasant short 9 hole course. The Village Inn is a spendid pub for a post-round beverage or two. Buckland-Tout-Saints (01548) 853055 at Kingsbridge is also worthy of inclusion on any itinerary. For lovers of a good pub the Pilchard on Burgh Island is one of the best—but beware the tide! For a less pricey resting hole, the Hope and Anchor in Hope Cove is most welcoming. Salcombe with its essentially sailing fraternity offers a worthy distraction for non golfers.

Golfers in Plymouth are never far from **St Mellion**, just over the border in Cornwall. Also close to the great seafaring city, the **Elfordleigh Hotel's** (01752) 336428 9 hole golf course at Plympton is very pleasant—and not as demanding as the Nicklaus course! Towards Dartmoor, **Yelverton** is certainly one not to be missed. Designed by Herbert Fowler, the architect of Walton Heath, Yelverton lies midway between Plymouth and Tavistock on the A386. It is a classic moorland course and very attractive, with much gorse and heather.

Tavistock is also not far from Plymouth. **Tavistock** Golf Club is perhaps not as attractive as Yelverton, but worth a visit all the same. For good places to stay, the Prince Hall Hotel is a small friendly hotel in country house style while the Moorland Links Hotel (01822) 852245 at Yelverton needs little explanation and for a place to celebrate one's birdie at the 18th the Who'd of Thought It at Milton Combe sounds highly appropriate—an excellent pub which serves good value lunches.

North Devon

From Plymouth, the north coast of Devon is about an hour and a quarter's drive—from Exeter, a little less. Unless there is some urgency, a leisurely drive is recommended for the scenery is truly spectacular. A few suggestions for breaking the journey include Milton Damerel, where the Woodford Bridge (01409) 261481 is a pleasant hotel with good facilities for the sporty. Hatherleigh offers the handsome George Hotel (01837) 810454 and Clawton near Holdsworthy the delightful Court Barn (01409) 271219. Then there is Winkleigh, where the Kings Arms is a popular pub. Just beyond Winkleigh, towards Barnstaple, there is a fine 18 hole course at **Libbaton** near Umberleigh—again definitely worth breaking the journey for.

North Devon can boast one of the oldest golf clubs in England, the **Royal North Devon** Club at Westward Ho! It can also claim to have seen the lowest known score for eighteen holes of golf. In 1936 the Woolacombe Bay professional recorded a 55 on his home course—29 out and 26 back, including a hole in one at the last! As this took place on the 1st January, one cannot help wondering quite what he did the night before! Unfortunately, this course closed long ago although there are 9 holes at **Morthoe & Woolacombe** and a very popular 18 hole test at nearby **Ilfracombe**. Situated several hundred feet above sea level, this latter course offers many outstanding views of the North Devon coastline. The best hole is the par four 13th and there is an interesting selection of par three holes, one of which, the 4th, is played across a plunging ravine but measures a mere 80 yards. Whilst in the area, two notable hotels for golfing breaks in Ilfracombe are St Brannochs House Hotel (01271) 863873 and the Elmfield (01271) 863377 while yet another very recent addition to the county's golfing scene is the **Hartland Forest** Country Club near the famous 'sleepy village' of Clovelly.

Both Saunton and Westward Ho! deserve more than a fleeting visit and are featured ahead. Westward Ho! is a place for pilgrimage, but **Saunton** provides the more modern championship challenge. There are two fine courses at Saunton, the East (the championship course) and the greatly improved West. Large sandhills dominate both courses, and when the wind blows . . . .

Sleeping in the dunes is out of bounds so here are a few ideas for the 19th. Visitors to North Devon should consider Foxdown Manor (01237) 451325 at Horns Cross and the Anchorage Hotel (01271) 860655. Yeolden House (01237) 474400 in Bideford comes highly recommended, while in Saunton Sands, the hotel of the same name is first class and popular with golfers (01271) 890212. A noted nearby eating place is Otters Restaurant (01271) 813633 in Braunton. The Preston House Hotel (01271) 890472 is also close to Saunton's links and is again very highly regarded by golfers. At Fairy Cross, near Bideford, the Portledge Hotel (01237) 451262 is for the lover of peace and quiet, as is

Whitechapel Manor (01769) 573377 at South Molton (a gracious Elizabethan manor house with first class restaurant). In Northam the Durrant House Hotel (01237) 472361 is great for recuperating after an excursion to Westward Ho!

More thoughts? Recommendations are many and various: in Westward Ho! Culloden House (01237) 479421 is small but friendly and there is also the popular Buckleigh Lodge guesthouse (01237) 475988. The small town of Umberleigh provides yet more worthy country house establishments in the shape of Northcote Manor (01769) 60501 and the Highbullen Hotel (01769) 540561. A marvellous golf course and other leisure pursuits make this particularly appealing. Woolacombe offers the superb Woolacombe Bay Hotel (01271) 870388 (more first rate activities here) and the award-winning Watersmeet Hotel (01271) 870333. Then there is Penhaven Country House (01237) 451388, a lovely old rectory transformed into a hotel at Parkham near Bideford and the elegant Halmpstone Manor (01271) 830321 at Bishop's Tawton near Barnstaple.

Among a number of good eating places in the area are Gray's Country Restaurant (01271) 812809 in Knowle and the Knoll House Hotel (01271) 882548 in Kentishbury. For those who prefer to cater for themselves in one of the many pretty cottages that abound in Devon, Country Holidays (01282) 445566 and Devon and Dorset Cottages (01626) 333678 are both worth contacting.

A final thought as we leave North Devon—should it actually happen and for some peculiar reason you do get stranded in the dunes at Saunton, the chances are you will wake up to a glorious sunrise. If this is the case, let's just hope the morning's golf is equally spectacular.

Artist: **Donald McGill ISN'T IT A PITY**
Courtesy of: **Burlington Gallery**

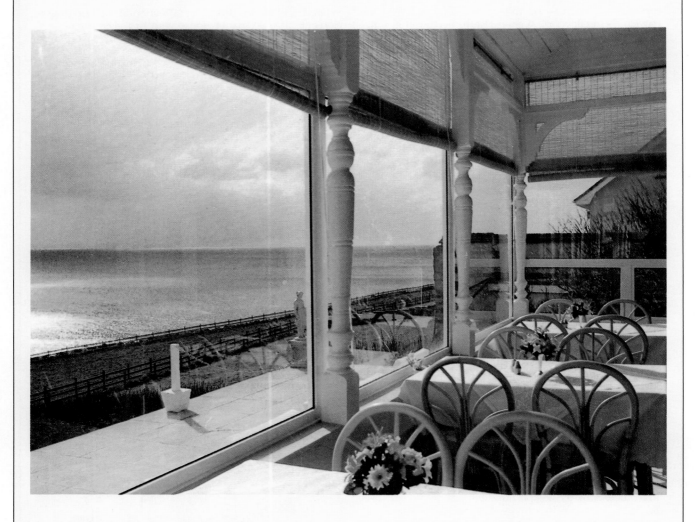

The Preston House is a gracious Victorian country house hotel standing in its own grounds and overlooking the ten mile sweep of Barnstaple's magnificent bay. The area is a veritable paradise for golfers who will find the Preston House ideally situated for two of the finest championship courses, Saunton and Royal North Devon. Guests of the hotel may take advantage of concessionary green fees and pre-booked tee times at both courses, and the management pride themselves on being able to cater for all golfers including beginners.

While Saunton lies less than half a mile from the hotel, and Royal North Devon is no more than a short drive away, there are many courses to be enjoyed in this part of Devon and a variety of other diversion on the doorstep. There is direct access to the beach where yachting, surfing and canoeing equipment can be hired and lessons are available if required. Riding and fishing can also be arranged close by and a leisurely stroll along the marvellous coastal walks is always a rewarding experience.

The hotel itself is immaculate and resplendent with antique furniture and crystal chandeliers, while the modern facilities are no less than one would expect from a hotel of this calibre.

All 15 bedrooms are individually designed to a very high standard, most with sea views. Guests can enjoy the spa bath, sauna, and solarium or relax around the heated outdoor swimming pool and admire the scenery. The conservatory is another favourite spot for guests to sit and take in the wonderful views out to sea over breakfast or lunch. In the luxurious dining room overlooking the bay guests can savour the highly commended cuisine prepared from country-fresh food, and the hotel is renowned for its home-baked ham and succulent roast sirloin of beef as well as excellent service.

The Preston House with its old world charm and grand yet informal setting assures golfers of a warm welcome, tremendous hospitality and a memorable golfing break.

Preston House Hotel
Saunton
Braunton
North Devon
Tel: (01271) 890472
Fax: (01271) 890555

Royal North Devon (Westward Ho!)

This is a club truly steeped in the history of the game. Westward Ho!, as it is commonly known, was the first English links course and being founded in 1864 the Royal North Devon Golf Club lays claim to being the oldest English club still playing over its original land. Furthermore it boasts the oldest Ladies Golf Club in the world, the Westward Ho! Ladies Golf Club, which was established in 1868. Originally designed by Tom Morris, and reconstructed by Herbert Fowler, the 18 holes are situated on Northam Burrows. The Burrows is a vast, exposed and relatively flat area of common land which stretches along the coast a couple of miles north of Bideford between Westward Ho! and Appledore.

Several of Britain's historic courses, particularly those in Scotland, have fascinating ties with common land and associated local rights which have existed since 'time immemorial', but whilst the inhabitants of St Andrews no longer use their hallowed turf for practising archery nor put their washing out to dry on the banks of the Swilcan Burn, the locals of Northam village still graze their sheep and horses on the Burrows. There can surely be no other championship course in the world where you can have teed up on the first, taken a few steps backward to survey the drive ahead only to see a sheep wander up and peer inquisitively at your ball! One shouldn't get too alarmed though, the animals are well-versed in the etiquette of the game—they generally keep a respectful distance from the fairways and greens, they take care not to bleat when you putt and what's more they certainly won't contemplate stealing your golf ball as I'm told the crows do at Royal Aberdeen.

Seriously, golf at Westward Ho! is a rich experience and given the warm welcome visitors receive, definitely to be recommended. The Secretary, **Mr Bob Fowler**, can be contacted via **The Royal North Devon Golf Club, Golf Links Road, Westward Ho! Bideford, Devon EX39 1HD**, tel: **(01237) 473817**.

If you are considering a trip to the club you may find it advisable to telephone first in order to check if any tee reservations have been made. Fine weather can make the course particularly popular during the holiday season but it is now possible to pre-book a starting time. Societies are also welcomed and bookings can be arranged with the Secretary. In 1998, a green fee of £28 midweek (£30 at weekends) entitles the visitor to a single round with £34 midweek (£36 at weekends) payable for a full day's golf. The green fee for juniors is halved. The club's **Professional** is **Iain Higgins**, who can be reached by telephone on **(01237) 477598**.

The course can be approached from both East and West via the A39, although travellers from the West may be able to avoid the busy town of Bideford by joining the B3236 near Abbotsham. Visitors travelling from the Dartmoor region should take the A386 road which runs from Okehampton to Bideford, whilst those coming from Exeter should follow the A377 to Barnstaple, thereafter joining the A39 as above.

From the championship tees the course measures 6653 yards, par 71 and is divided into two fairly equal halves. Westward Ho! has a traditional 'out and back' layout and there are some panoramic views across Bideford Bay, especially from the 6th tee where, on a clear day, the Isle of Lundy can be seen. In theory, the links receives a degree of protection from the elements from a large bank of shingle which separates the Burrows from the beach. I say 'in theory' for this is surely one of Britain's most windswept courses. However, the wind is not the only factor that can make scoring extremely difficult. There are numerous ditches and hidden pot bunkers, there is also the famous Cape bunker at the 4th (at least 100 yards wide) and then of course, there are the Great Sea Rushes. To the uninitiated a word of caution—these giant marshland reeds, unique to Westward Ho!, can literally impale golf balls, so do as the sheep do—stay clear!

Westward Ho! is not only known for its golf course, it has literary fame as well. The village was founded a year before the golf club and was named after Charles Kingsley's adventure novel about Elizabethan seafarers. A decade or so later Rudyard Kipling attended the local college and remembered his days there in Stalky and Co. Alas, there is no record to suggest that Mr Kipling was an exceedingly good golfer but while he was studying, a young boy from Northam was out on the course caddying for sixpence a round.

The boy was destined to become Open Champion on five occasions. John H Taylor learnt his game at Westward Ho! and his great affection for the club remained throughout his long life. In 1957 the club elected him their President.

In addition to a friendly and unpretentious atmosphere, the clubhouse offers some excellent catering. It also houses the club's museum. It is most interesting and contains a great variety of golfing memorabilia.

For the golfer who has confined himself to playing on gentle parkland fairways, sheltered from any wind by tall trees, a visit to Westward Ho! would probably create quite a shock to the system. But clearly, for those with even a moderate interest in the history of the game and, of course, who are not afraid of a stiff challenge, Westward Ho! is a golfing must.

Hole	Yards	Par	Hole	Yards	Par
1	478	5	10	373	4
2	416	4	11	371	4
3	421	4	12	423	4
4	349	4	13	442	4
5	136	3	14	201	3
6	406	4	15	439	4
7	397	4	16	143	3
8	192	3	17	555	5
9	497	5	18	4164	4
Out	**3,292**	**36**	**In**	**3,361**	**35**
			Out	**3,292**	**36**
			Totals	**6,653**	**71**

Set beside the River Torridge, with lawns sloping down towards the river, you will find a warm welcome at the Yeoldon House Hotel where yesterday's charms blend perfectly with today's comforts. Real hospitality and a refreshingly casual atmosphere await you here in this unique and unspoilt part of Devon.

Within an hour's drive of Yeoldon House Hotel there is an exceptional range of places to see and things to do.. Almost on the doorstep you can take a trip to Lundy Island, which offers some majestic scenery and outstanding sea bird and marine life. Visit Exmoor, the Lorna Doone country and the picturesque village of Clovelly. Rivel in miles of Coastal Footpath, and enjoy bathing and watersports on some of the finest sandy beaches in the country.

Keen golfers are surrounded by opportunities. The oldest course in England Royal North Devon (better known as 'Westward Ho'), is a mere half mile from the hotel and there are another twelve superb courses, all within an hour's drive. Salmon and trout fishing is close by, as is clay pigeon shooting, sauna, and swimming at the nearby pool.

Looking out over the lawns to the river, are the elegant 'Charters' restaurant and comfortable lounge where you can relax and watch the world go by, or enjoy a complimentary sherry before dinner. 'Charters' has an air of casual elegance where you will feel comfortable in any attire. The à la carte dinner menu changes weekly using local fresh fish, meat and vegetables. Fresh baked bread and a garden salad complement every meal, but save room for the home-made desserts! Vegetarian, diabetic and special diets are catered for, by early request.

There can surely be no better way to end such a day than in the comfort of one of the tastefully designed en suite bedrooms, each with colour TV, tea and coffee making facilities and direct dial telephone. Each bedroom holds its own charm—the cosy country style single rooms, the grand four posters room, or the split level room with its own balcony and lounge area.

Resident proprietors Kevin and Sue Jelley look forward to welcoming you to Yeoldon House and through their years of experience hope to make your stay happy and comfortable.

Yeoldon House Hotel
Durrant Lane Northam
nr Bideford Devon
EX39 2RL
Tel: (01237) 474400
Fax: (01237) 476618

Saunton

At a time when John H Taylor and Horace Hutchinson were striding the windswept fairways on Northam Burrows, across the Taw Estuary on the Braunton Burrows, other men were busy trapping rabbits. It took more than thirty years for matters to be put right.

Saunton Golf Club was founded in 1897, some three decades after Westward Ho! Like many great clubs, Saunton's beginnings were rather modest. At first there were only nine holes and the original clubhouse was a room next to the Post Office. The course was extended to 18 holes before the First World War (and a new clubhouse acquired) but it wasn't until after the war that Saunton's reputation gained momentum. Chiefly responsible was golf architect Herbert Fowler, who having reshaped Westward Ho! performed a similar task at Saunton.

In 1932 the course was selected to stage the British Ladies Championship and this was followed by the English Amateur Championship of 1937. Unfortunately the links didn't fare too well during the Second World War as it was considered the perfect place for a battle school and concrete and barbed wire covered the fairways. Reconstruction didn't begin until 1951, C K Cotton this time directing matters. Once restored the course quickly re-established itself as one of Britain's leading championship links. In the early seventies a second 18 holes were added and today the two are known as the **East** (the former 'Old Course') and the **West** Course.

At 6729 yards, par 71 (SSS 73) from the championship tees, the East Course is some 300 yards longer than the West (6403 yards par 71) and it could hardly be described as one of those that breaks you in gently—the first four holes all measure over 400 yards. There are several notable par fours early in the round, but perhaps the best

are the 12th, the 14th with its ever-narrowing fairway, and the 16th which demands a tee shot over a vast sandhill with the second needing to be carried over a deep bunker in front of the green.

On more than one occasion I have read that if Saunton had a different geography it would be an Open Championship venue. Maybe I'm missing the point, but I've never fully appreciated the 'geography' argument. Surely North Devon is no more remote than certain parts of the east and west coasts of Scotland—especially now that a motorway runs as far as Exeter (one hour's drive away). Attendance figures? Such is the popularity of golf in modern times it seems most unlikely that the crowds wouldn't flock to the area, and as for accommodation North Devon abounds with places to stay. Come to think of it, what better place for a week's holiday in July?

Saunton Golf Club, Saunton, Braunton, Devon EX33 1LG

Sec/Manager	Trevor Reynolds (01271) 812436 Fax (01271) 814241
Professional	Albert Mackenzie (01271) 812013
Green Fees	WD £30/round; £45/day WE £40/round; £55/day
Restrictions	Proof of handicap required

Directions
Follow the A361 from Barnstaple and pick up the B3231 at Braunton. The club is south of Saunton village on the B3231.

East Devon

Most clifftop courses are essentially downland or parkland in nature. Very often they are beautifully situated but the quality of the golf offered isn't quite out of the top drawer. East Devon at Budleigh Salterton is quite a rarity, for this is where heathland golf meets the sea. Laid out on cliffs some 250 to 400 feet above sea level, there are breathtaking views out to sea and along the South Devon coast in both directions. The views inland, mind you, are just as expansive, with the rolling Devon countryside presenting itself in all its glory.

But what is really special about East Devon is that the golf course takes full advantage of the location and the natural splendour of the terrain. East Devon is not as testing as somewhere like Walton Heath—it is not as long for a start—although at 6239 yards (par 70) it is not exactly short either, and the heather and gorse do not encroach to the point where they intimidate the golfer as on several of the south east's championship courses. However, variety and challenge present themselves at every hole. The layout is such that the course continually rises and falls, twists and turns. There are a couple of uphill drives and many dramatic downhill tee shots and there are some fine left and right dog-leg holes. Finally, there is the all year round quality of the putting surfaces—the best in Devon many players reckon—and for this the club must thank its excellent green keeper, who in turn must thank Mother Nature.

Probably the most outstanding sequence of holes at East Devon comes between the 6th and the 9th. What makes the par five 6th so spectacular is the choice facing the golfer after a good drive. The fairway narrows all the way to the green, out of bounds lurks to the right, thick woodland menaces to the left and if that isn't

sufficiently fear-inducing, then twenty yards short of the green is a natural gulley full of humps and hillocks. The sensible shot is to lay up but the devil-may-care golfer will not be able to resist the challenge.

After a short walk through the woods, the magnificent back tee for the 7th is reached. The tree-lined fairway dog-legs sharply to the left 50 feet below and you can't see the green as you drive. The approach is slightly uphill and the amphitheatre-like green is protected by a mischievously placed deep bunker. The next hole is a tough par three measuring over 200 yards—miss the green to the right here and a par will be a major achievement. The 9th tumbles 450 yards downhill all the way and is perhaps the best of many exhilarating downhill holes at Budleigh. In 1934, a player actually drove to the edge of the green.

East Devon Golf Club, North View Road Budleigh Salterton, Devon EX9 6DR

Secretary	Mr R Burley (01395) 443370 Fax (01395) 445547
Professional	Trevor Underwood (01395) 445195
Green Fees	WD £27/round; £35/day WE £35/round; £42/day
Restrictions	Proof of handicap required

Directions
The course is on the Exmouth side of Budleigh Salterton on the A376. Avoid driving through Exmouth by picking up the B3179 at Clyst St George. From the north use the A3025 Lyme Regis-Exeter road, exiting just north of Sidmouth.

Key

*To avoid disappointment
it is advisable to telephone
in advance*

***Visitors welcome at most times*
**Visitors usually allowed on
weekdays only*
*Visitors not normally permitted
(Mon, Wed) No visitors
on specified days*

Approximate Green Fees
A   £40 plus
B   £25 to £40
C   £20 to £30
D   £15 to £25
E   under £15
F   Green fees on application

Restrictions
G Guests only
H—Handicap certificate required
H—(24) Handicap of 24 or less
L —Letter of introduction required
M—Visitor must be a member of
another recognised club

Ashbury G.C.
(01837) 55453
Fowley Cross, Okehampton
(18) 5839 yards/***/D

Axe Cliff G.C.
(01297) 24371
Squires Lane, Axmouth,
(18) 5057 yards/***/C/H

Bigbury G.C.
(01548) 810207
Bigbury-on-Sea, Kingsbridge
(18) 6076 yards/***/C/H

Chulmleigh G.C.
(01769) 580519
Leigh Road, Chulmleigh
(18) 1450 yards/***/E

Churston G.C.
(01803) 842751
Churston, nr Brixham
(18) 6201 yards/***/B/H/M

Clovelly G.& C.C.
(01237) 431442
East Yagland, Wolsery, Bideford
(9) 5641 yards/***/D

Dainton Park G.C.
(01803) 813812
Totnes Road, Newton Abbot
(18) 6210 yards/***/D

Dartmouth G.& C.C.
(01803) 712650
Blackawton, Totnes
(18)7191 yards/***/B/H
(9) 2583 yards/***/D/H

Dinnaton G.C.
(01752) 892512
Ivybridge
(9) 4100 yards/***/D/H

Downes Crediton G.C.
(01363) 774464
Hookway, Crediton
(18) 5958 yards/***/C/H/M

Easewell Farm Holiday Park
(01271) 870225
Woolacombe
(9) 2426 yards/***/E

East Devon G.C.
(01395) 443370
North View Road, Budleigh
Salterton
(18) 6239 yards/***/B/H

Elfordleigh Hotel G.& C.C.
(01752) 336428
Colebrook, Plympton, Plymouth
(9) 5664 yards/**/C

Exeter G. & C.C.
(01392) 874139
Countess Wear, Exeter
(18) 6000 yards/**/C

Fingle Glen G. & C.C.
(01647) 61817
Tedburn St Mary, Exeter
(9) 2466 yards/***/D

Hele Park Golf Centre.
(01626) 336060
Ashburton Road, Newton Abbot
(9) 2469 yards/***/E

Highbullen Hotel
(01769) 540561
Chittlehamolt
(9) 2210 yards/***/F

Holsworthy G.C.
(01409) 253177
Kilatree, Holsworthy
(18) 6062 yards/***/D

Honiton G.C.
(01404) 44422
Middlehills, Honiton
(18) 5940 yards/***/C/H/M

Hurdwick G.C.
(01822) 612746
Tavistock Hamlets, Tavistock
(18) 4861 yards/***/C

Ilfracombe G.C.
(01271) 862176
Hele Bay, Ilfracombe
(18) 5893yards/***/D/H

Libbaton G.C.
(01769) 560269
High Bickington, Umberleigh
(18) 5812 yards/***/D

Manor House Hotel.
(01647) 440998
Moretonhampstead
(18) 6016 yards/***/B/H

Morthoe & Woolacombe
(01271) 870225
Morthoe, Ilfracombe
(9) 4852 yards/***/E

Newton Abbot (Stover) G.C.
(01626) 352460
Bovey Road, Newton Abbot
(18) 5899 yards/***/C/H

Okehampton G.C.
(01837) 52113
off Tors Road, Okehampton
(18) 5300 yards/***/F/H

Padbrook Park G.C.
(01884) 38286
Cullompton
(9) 6108 yards/***/E

Royal North Devon G.C.
(01237) 473817
Golf Links Road, Westward Ho!
(18) 6653 yards/***/B/H

Saunton G.C.
(01271) 812436
Saunton, nr Braunton
(18) 6729 yards/***/A/H
(18) 6403 yards/***/A/H

Sidmouth G.C.
(01395) 516407
Peak Hill, Cotmaton Road,
(18) 5109 yards/***/D

Sparkwell G.C.
(01752) 837219
Blacklands, Sparkwell, Plymouth
(9) 5772 yards/***/E

Staddon Heights G.C.
(01752) 402475
Staddon Heights, Plymstock
(18) 5681 yards/***/D/H

Tavistock G.C.
(01822) 612344
Down Road, Tavistock
(18) 6250 yards/***/C

Teignmouth G.C.
(01626) 772894
Exeter Road, Teignmouth
(18) 6227 yards/***/C/H/M

Teign Valley Golf Club
(01647) 253026
Christow, nr Exeter
(18) 5900 yards/***/D

Thurlestone G.C.
(01548) 560405
Thurlestone, nr Kingsbridge
(18) 6340 yards/***/C/H/M

Tiverton G.C.
(01884) 252187
Post Hill, Tiverton
(18) 6236 yards/***/B/H/M

Torquay G.C.
(01803) 314591
Petitor Road, St Mary Church
(18) 6198 yards/***/C/H

Torrington G.C.
(01805) 622229
Weare Trees, Torrington
(9) 4419 yards/***/D

Warren G.C.
(01626) 862255
Dawlish Warren, Dawlish
(18) 5968 yards/***/C/H

Woodbury Park G.C.
(01395) 233382
Woodbury Castle, Woodbury,
(18) 6707 yards/***/C

Wrangaton G.C.
(01364) 73229
Golf Links Road, Wrangaton
(18) 6040 yards/***/C/H

Yelverton G.C.
(01822) 852824
Golf Links Road, Yelverton
(18) 6363 yards/***/F/H/M

Artist: **Major Hopkins LADIES GOLF** *Courtesy of:* **Burlington Gallery**

Artist: **Robert Wade** **THE CADDIE** *Courtesy of:* **Rosenstiel's**

From the wild beauty of Exmoor to the mystery of Stonehenge; the Quantocks and the Mendips; Lyme Regis and Bath; Avebury, Chesil Beach and Lulworth Cove. The West Country offers so much, no wonder those of us who do not live there are more than a little envious. The golf too can be equally spectacular. There may not be a Wentworth or a St George's here but the region offers a considerable variety and there is certainly no shortage of challenge. There is a true championship links at Burnham and Berrow and a magnificent heathland-cum-clifftop course at the Isle of Purbeck. Excellent downland golf can be enjoyed at Long Ashton and Bath while Bournemouth offers some majestic heathland and parkland type courses. We shall tee off in Somerset.

Somerset

Burnham and Berrow (featured ahead) is without doubt the finest course in the county and the place where John H Taylor wielded his famous mashie to great effect. The two holiday towns of **Minehead** and **Weston-Super-Mare** house the region's other two links courses. The Minehead and West Somerset Golf Club has more than a hundred years of history—it therefore remembers the quieter days in the years 'Before Butlins'. A fairly flat and windy course, it is situated on the eastern side of the town. Visitors are welcome, though during the peak season a quick telephone call to the club is advisable. The same can be said of Weston—a slightly longer, well maintained course, located just off the main A370 Bristol road. Perhaps a nearby course on which it may be easier to arrange a game is the attractive new 18 hole parkland layout at the **Isle of Wedmore** Golf Club. After an arduous day's golf at Burnham, visitors can find more than adequate accommodation in the club's Dormy House. Some quite incredible steaks are served in the clubhouse: 'worth killing for!' according to one of my mashie wielding friends. Two recommended guesthouses to try in Burnham-on-Sea are the Warren Guest House (01278) 786726 and the Lulworth Guesthouse (01278) 784015, while further up the scale, between Burnham and Weston the Batch Farm Country Hotel (01934) 750371 comes highly recommended. Weston has a number of hotels with the Grand Atlantic situated on the seafront (01934) 626543 the town's most vaunted hostelry. The Gascony (01643) 705939 and the Alcombe House Hotel (01643) 705130 are also suitable resting places, whilst slightly farther afield, try the Luttrell Arms (01643) 821555 in Dunster—a creeper-clad hotel of some historical note. Exmoor House (01643) 821268 is also an excellent port of call.

Taunton's golf course is at Corfe, the **Taunton and Pickeridge** Golf Club. It is located close to the town's racetrack and is fairly undulating. In Taunton, the Castle (01823) 272671 is an outstanding place to stay and nearby The Mount Somerset in Lower Henlade (01823) 442500 is also a worthy suggestion. For the more energetically minded, the Cedar Falls Health Farm (01823) 433233 at Bishops Lydeard makes it all the easier to indulge elsewhere. In Yeovil, the Manor Hotel (01935) 231161 is very handy for Sherborne Golf Club over the border in Dorset.

Further north in the county is the magnificently titled **Windwhistle** Golf and Squash Club at Chard. The golf course is another laid out on high ground and offering extensive views. It's also close to the famous Cricket St Thomas Wildlife Park, where birdies and eagles abound. We would also recommend the first class par 72 layout at **Orchardleigh** near Frome.

More golf is found near Bridgwater. **Enmore Park,** located to the south of the town is a very pleasant medium length affair. The course enjoys a delightful setting and nestles around the foothills of the Quantocks. The White House Hotel (01984) 632306 at Williton is convenient for the golf club. Moving from the Quantocks to the Mendips, the **Mendip** Golf Club at Gurney Slade offers possibly the most spectacular vistas of any course in the south west. From its 4th fairway, almost 1000 feet above sea level, on a clear day it is possible to sight the Cotswolds and the Quantocks, the Welsh Mountains and the Purbeck Hills, Glastonbury Tor and Westbury's White Horse—need I go on? Mendip is an enjoyable course and very visitor-friendly. An agreeable pub to note in Gurney Slade is the George Inn.

The city of Wells is always worth inspecting. The cathedral is splendid and after a round on the **Wells** golf course a pleasant lunch can be enjoyed at Ritcher's (01749) 679085.

Everybody, they say, falls in love with Bath—the Romans did, the Georgians did and the Americans think it's cute. For visiting golfers, if the other half should come under the spell, the City has two attractive propositions: **Bath** Golf Club and **Lansdown** Golf Club. The former, commonly known as Sham Castle because of its situation adjacent to Bath's greatest fraud (there is a beautiful castle frontage but nothing else!) is laid out high above the city and provides tremendous views over the surrounding countryside. Lansdown occupies flatter ground adjacent to Bath racecourse.

Staying in Bath can be a sheer delight. The hotels in the city are among some of the finest in the country. Bath Spa (01225) 444424 and the Royal Crescent (01225) 739955 take pride of place but the Apsley House (01225) 336966, the Paradise House Hotel (01225) 317723 and the Priory (01225) 331922 can also be recommended with total confidence. The hotels themselves house excellent restaurants but other popular eating places in Bath include the Clos du Roy (01225) 444450, New Moon (01225) 444407 and the Hole in the Wall (01225) 424424. There is no shortage of guesthouses in and around Bath (the city does become incredibly busy in the summer—be warned!) while deeper in the countryside are a number of other outstanding establishments. Ston Easton Park (01761) 241631 boasts a considerable reputation as does Hunstrete House (01761) 490490. Another gem is the Homewood Park Hotel (01225) 723731 in Hinton Charterhouse. North of Bath the marvellously named Old Sodbury offers the charming Sodbury House Hotel (01454) 312847 and the Cross Hands Hotel (01454) 313000, and Dunkirk provides the Petty France Hotel (01454) 238361. Just outside Bath at Colerne is Lucknam Park (01225) 742777 a delightful early 18th century mansion converted into an hotel. Close by, near Corsham, is the stylish Rudloe Park Hotel (01225) 810555.

Dorset

The better golf courses in Dorset lie within a ten mile radius of the centre of Bournemouth. Having said that, **Sherborne** in the far north of the county is undoubtedly one of the prettiest inland courses to be found anywhere in Britain. In nearby Gillingham, you can stay at the Stock Hill House Hotel (01747) 823626 which comes with our highest recommendation and boasts an excellent restaurant to boot. Also, in Evershot, the Summer Lodge (01935) 83424 is a fine restaurant within a delightful country house hotel, and in Sturminster Newton stands Plumber Manor (01258) 472507 a gorgeous country house with most outstanding fare.

Lyme Regis, famed for its fossils and more recently its French Lieutenant's Woman, has a fairly hilly 18 hole course which lies to the east of the town. The road between Lyme Regis and Weymouth provides dramatic views over Chesil Beach and passes through some of the most beautiful villages in England. The area north of Weymouth is Thomas Hardy country. Dorchester stands in the middle of it all and **Came Down** Golf Club is well worth noting when in these parts, as is the **Dorset Heights** Golf Club at Blandford Forum. Yalbury Cottage (01305) 262382 in Lower Bockhampton offers good accommodation and the countryside has remained gloriously unspoilt. In Lyme Regis, the Alexandra (01297) 442010 is a good bet.

The **Isle of Purbeck** and **Ferndown** are featured ahead but **Parkstone** and **Broadstone** also fall in the 'must be visited' category. They are beautiful heathland courses with much heather, gorse and pine trees and each is kept in immaculate condition. In addition to a game on one or more of these great courses, there are a handful of other easier to play courses around Bournemouth and Poole, including the **Bulbury Woods** Golf Club at Lytchett Matravers west of Poole and the newer **Crane Valley** course at Verwood, north of Ferndown. Bournemouth's public courses shouldn't be overlooked either: **Meyrick Park** is very good while **Queens Park** is often described as the finest public course in England.

The Bournemouth—Poole—Swanage area abounds with hotels and restaurants. Here are just a few suggestions: in Bournemouth, the Langtry Manor (01202) 553887, the Swallow Highcliff (01202) 557702, Royal Bath (01202) 555555 and the Hotel Collingwood (01202) 557575 are all good. In Poole, the Mansion House (01202) 685666 and its first class restaurant are recommended as is the outstanding Haven Hotel (01202) 707333. Swanage offers the Pines (01929) 425211 and Christchurch, Splinters Brasserie (01202) 483454. Ferndown golfers can look to the comfortable Dormy Hotel (01202) 872121 and Parkstone players can enjoy superb food at both Isabels (01202) 747885 and the Warehouse Brasserie on the quay (01202) 677238. People wishing to get away from the sea and sand, or the water hazards and bunkers should visit Tarrant Monkton and the popular Langton Arms (01258) 830225, where a converted stables makes for a really splendid little restaurant with some good value accommodation.

Wiltshire

A decade ago there were only a dozen or so golf courses in Wiltshire, now there are over two dozen. Perhaps the two developments that have attracted most attention are the Dave Thomas designed championship course at **Bowood,** just off the A4 between Calne and Chippenham, and the dramatic layout at Castle Combe (now named the **Manor House** Golf Club) located to the north west of Chippenham, the handiwork of Peter Alliss and Clive Clark. Two very different courses, Bowood and the Manor House are both explored ahead. Recommended places to stay naturally include the Manor House (01249) 782206, situated within the 'prettiest village in England', while for Bowood any of the establishments mentioned for Bath should prove convenient. There is also the outstanding Queenwood Golf Lodge (01249) 822228 which is located within the confines of the Bowood course.

In **Wooton Bassett**, just west of Swindon, Alliss and Clark have constructed another course, thus giving Swindon's golfers three courses close to the town. The two others are **Broome Manor** and the **Swindon** Golf Club, both situated south of the town. The latter at Ogbourne St George, despite its name, is in fact closer to Marlborough than Swindon. It is an undulating, downland type course—very typical of the county's more established courses. Broome Manor is a public course and thus probably more accommodating to the visiting golfer.

Swindon is one of the fastest growing towns in the British Isles. In Blunsdon the charming Blunsdon House (01793) 721701 offers extensive leisure facilities. The Robin Hood Inn at Ogbourne St George is very handy after a game at Swindon. **Marlborough** Golf Club is a near neighbour of Swindon Golf Club, being situated to the north west of the town on the Marlborough Downs. It offers similarly wide ranging views (and is similarly breezy!). The Castle and Ball (01672) 512201 in Marlborough is an ideal 19th—it offers good food in addition to reasonably priced accommodation. Also worth a visit is the Ivy House (01672) 515333. A pleasant drive westwards will take you to Lacock near Chippenham where the Sign of the Angel (01249) 730230 is a tremendous 15th century inn and, still further west, there is a reasonable golf course at **Kingsdown.**

Dropping down the county, the **West Wilts** Golf Club at Warminster, is very well established, the new 'pay and play' **Erlestoke Sands** course, south west of Devizes is popular and t'other side of Stonehenge, **Tidworth Garrison** is certainly one of Wiltshire's top courses. It lies on Salisbury Plain and is owned by the Army. (Note the excellent Antrobus Arms (01980) 623163 in nearby Amesbury). Salisbury offers two fine challenges, to the north, **High Post** and to the south west **Salisbury and South Wilts**. In the days before Bowood and the Manor House appeared on the county's ever-changing golf map High Post was generally considered to be the leading course in the county. It's another classic downland type. Salisbury and South Wilts golf course offers some splendid views of Salisbury's cathedral. One's best base near Salisbury is probably either the Rose and Crown Hotel (01722) 327908 at Harnham or Milford Hall (01722) 417411 in Castle Street.

Artist: **Charles Lees THE GRAND MATCH**
Courtesy of: **Rosenstiels**

Burnham and Berrow

I wonder how many people have travelled along the M5 between Bristol and Exeter and wondered what lay beyond the great Iron Age fort midway between Weston-super-Mare and Bridgwater that rises out of level ground, like something from out of 'Close Encounters'. Well, many golfers will know that a short distance behind the great hill lies one of England's finest links courses.

Burnham and Berrow appeared on the golfing map in 1891 and the first professional the club engaged was no lesser a man than John H Taylor. The great man was then in fact a lad of 19 although within three years he was to win the Open Championship at Sandwich—the first of his five victories. John Henry thought very highly of what, until quite recently, had been a 'wild rabbit infested waste of sandhills' for he said it was here, at Burnham, that he was 'given the splendid opportunity of developing my mashie play' (as the course) 'necessitated very accurate approach play.'

The present day visitor to the North Somerset club is most unlikely to confront a gathering of wild rabbits (at least of the animal variety) nor, one assumes, will he possess a mashie amongst his armoury. However, despite a number of alterations made over the years, the towering sandhills remain by far the course's most dominant feature.

Not surprisingly, Burnham and Berrow is a popular course and whatever the time of year visitors would be wise to telephone the club before setting off. **Mrs E L Sloman** is the **Secretary** and she can be contacted on **(01278) 785760**, fax: **(01278) 795440**. The club's **Professional, Mark Crowther-Smith**, can be reached on **(01278) 784545**. Those interested in organising a society meeting are advised to write to the Secretary, the club's full address being, **Burnham and Berrow Golf Club, St Christopher's Way, Burnham-on-Sea, Somerset TA8 2PE.**

Green fees for 1998 are set at £36 for weekdays and £50 at weekends, fees being payable in the clubhouse. For juniors the fees are half the above rates. Persons holidaying in the vicinity (Weston-super-Mare is less than 10 miles away) might well consider the merits of a weekly ticket (£225 in 1998) or a fortnightly ticket (£410 in 1998). Furthermore, in addition to the 18 hole championship course there is also an adjacent 9 hole course situated alongside the sea. Whilst not quite up to the standard of the full championship course, at 3275 yards, par 36, it certainly represents a fine challenge and the green fee of £10 represents excellent value.

Approaching by car from both north and south the M5 is the most direct route, leaving at exit 22. Thereafter one should follow the B3140. The course is situated about a mile north of Burnham-on-Sea.

Right from the 1st hole the premium on accuracy becomes apparent. Anything short of a straight tee shot will leave a blind, not to mention very awkward second. At one time the layout of the course demanded the playing of several blind shots. However, today, accurate driving will largely eliminate such difficulties although on a number of holes the base of the flagstick will not be visible when playing the approach shot. As he or she stands on the 1st green, two features, in addition to the omnipresent sandhills, will strike the first time visitor. One is the condition of the greens which are quite superb; the other is the surrounding tangling rough—buckthorn it's called—avoid it like the plague! Burnham's 2nd is a good straight hole played from an elevated tee, whereas the 3rd, at least from the back, is one of those 'bite-off-as-much-as-you-dare' holes with the fairway dog-legging sharply to the left towards a sunken punchbowl green. From the 4th tee there is the first of several panoramic views of the Bristol Channel and distant Wales as the course moves nearer the sea. There are two strong par threes on the front nine, the 5th and the excellent 9th, which is one of the finest short holes to be found anywhere.

On reaching the turn anyone claiming to have mastered the large sandhills may well have to eat his words after playing the 10th, where a minor mountain must be carried from the tee and there is a severe drop away to the right—be warned! If the front nine is perhaps the more interesting of the halves, the second nine is probably the more testing. The 11th is a long par four and the 12th and 13th require very precise second shots. Both the short holes are exceptionally tricky and the 18th needs a couple of mighty big hits if it is to be reached in two.

Visitors should find the clubhouse atmosphere pleasantly informal. The catering is of a high standard and is offered daily between the hours of 11 am and 6 pm. With prior notice both breakfast and dinner can be arranged. Visitors might also wish to note the club's dormy house which can sleep eight.

Burnham and Berrow is a friendly club and well worth a visit. Clearly the message to all golfers who pass down the M5 oblivious to what goes on beyond the great hump is, quite simply, come on over!

Hole	Yards	Par	Hole	Yards	Par
1	380	4	10	375	4
2	421	4	11	438	4
3	376	4	12	401	4
4	511	5	13	530	5
5	158	3	14	192	3
6	434	4	15	440	4
7	450	4	16	344	4
8	494	5	17	200	3
9	170	3	18	445	4
Out	**3,394**	**36**	**In**	**3,365**	**35**
			Out	**3,394**	**36**
			Totals	**6,759**	**71**

Ferndown

Ask a group of golfers to give an example of a beautifully conditioned golf course and the chances are they'll cite the likes of Augusta National and Muirfield Village. There is little doubt that when it comes to perfectly manicured fairways and quick, ultra-true greens the American courses tend to be superior to their British counterparts. Ferndown, however, is a definite exception. Indeed the fairways and greens are often among the best kept in the whole of Britain. Someone clearly deserves a mighty large pat on the back!

There are in fact two courses at Ferndown, the **Old** and the **Presidents**. The Old Course was originally designed in 1912 by Harold Hilton, who was twice Open Champion before the turn of the century. The shorter Presidents Course, which has nine holes but eighteen tees, has a much more recent history being designed in 1969 by J Hamilton-Stutt and opened two years later.

The Old Course at Ferndown measures 6452 yards from the back tees, par and standard scratch both being 71. From the forward tees the length is reduced by a little over 200 yards. The layout is essentially one of two loops, an inner loop comprising holes one to eight and the outer containing the ninth to the eighteenth.

Ferndown's fairways are of the sandy, heathland type and are gently undulating throughout. The rough consists mainly of heather which together with the many pines and fir trees gives the course a most attractive appearance. There are a considerable number of dog-leg holes necessitating much thought from the tee. The toughest holes on the course are possibly the uphill 6th, which is normally played into the wind, the dog-leg 9th and the 11th—all fairly lengthy par fours from the back tees. One should also mention the 5th, an excellent par three where the rhododendrons provide a splash of colour in season, and the 16th, named 'Hilton's Hole'

after its illustrious architect. At 5604 yards (par 70) the Presidents Course is less demanding in terms of length but it too has its challenges and is set in equally beautiful surroundings.

Ferndown's clubhouse has a prime location, grandly surveying the course from its elevated position. On a clear day there are views across the course to the Isle of Wight.

In recent years the club has played host to many competitions and tournaments, such as the Women's English Amateur Championship in 1985 and the Hennessy Cognac Cup, a four man team competition, played over the Old Course in 1982 and 1984. The Ladies European Open visited the course in 1987, while in 1989 large crowds flocked to Ferndown to watch a most exciting Ladies British Open, won by leading American player Jane Geddes with an impressive four round total of 274.

Ferndown Golf Club, 119 Links Road, Ferndown, Wimborne, Dorset, BH22 8BU	
Sec/Manager	Eddie Robertson (01202) 874602
Professional	Iain Parker (01202) 873825
Green Fees	WD £42/round £47/day WE £50/round/day Presidents WD £15, WE £20
Restrictions	Prior arrangement; handicap certificate or letter
Directions	
The club is 6 miles north of Bournemouth on the A31 exit at Trickett's Cross.	

Isle of Purbeck

Most people are a little surprised when they learn that the Isle of Purbeck Golf Club was founded as long ago as 1892—a decade before Sunningdale and Walton Heath. They are probably even more surprised when they hear that Enid Blyton and her husband were once owners of the club. Originally only a 9 hole course, there are now 27 holes comprising the 18 hole **Purbeck** Course and an adjacent, shorter 9 hole course, the **Dene**. In 1966 a superb new clubhouse was built using the local Purbeck stone and it was around this time that more and more people began to consider seriously the quality of the golf here as well as the sheer beauty of the club's setting. Today the club is owned and managed by the Robinson family.

Swanage has become a very popular holiday centre and keen golfers might consider the merits of a temporary membership of the club. There are reductions for joint membership and for those wishing to limit their golf to the Dene course. Visitors may also wish to note that the club stages a limited number of open competitions during the summer. Information concerning these can be obtained from the club's Managing Director, Mrs Robinson. Golfing societies are encouraged to come to the Isle of Purbeck and those organising should find the club very accommodating.

The south coast possesses a number of scenic courses, but one would be very pushed to find an equal to the magnificent views provided by the Isle of Purbeck. The view from the 5th on the Purbeck Course, 'Agglestone' is particularly outstanding as you tee off from the top of an ancient Saxon burial mound. The par three 11th, 'Island', with its backdrop of pines and two-tier green is also an exceptional hole.

For those who find the modern day monster courses somewhat tedious with the great emphasis they place on

brute force (and ignorance?) the Purbeck Course should prove rather refreshing. From the back tees it measures 6248 yards (par 71) whilst from the forward tees the course is reduced to 5823 yards (par 69). From the ladies' tees the course measures 5648 yards (par 73).

When in South Dorset many visitors like to take in a spot of fossil hunting. Lyme Regis and Charmouth are within easy reach, however golfers need not look beyond the four walls of the clubhouse—it is full of old fossils. Lest I be accused of insulting the members, I should quickly explain: when the clubhouse was built several fossilised dinosaur footprints and some massive ammonites were incorporated into the interior walls. It therefore follows—and golf historians please note—that to a limited extent the Isle of Purbeck could be said to possess the oldest clubhouse in the world!

The Isle of Purbeck Golf Club, Swanage, Dorset, BH19 3AB	
Managing Director	Mrs Joan Robinson (01929) 450361
Professional	Ian Brake (01929) 450354
Green Fees	Purbeck WD £26, WE £32 per round Dene WD/WE £12 per day
Restrictions	Handicap certificates for Purbeck course
Directions	
Take A351 to Corfe Castle, then B3351 towards Studland.	

Bowood

The Golden Gate Bridge may lead you to San Francisco but the Golden Gates will lead you to Bowood. And Bowood is everything that California is not. Of all the great English country estates that in recent years have found the charms of the Royal and Ancient game impossible to resist, the development at Bowood seems destined to emerge as one of the best—best in terms of the quality and range of facilities and best in terms of the quality and condition of its 18 hole championship layout.

Notwithstanding the magnificently grand entrance to the Golf and Country Club—the above mentioned Golden Gates—there is nothing exclusive, or certainly no air of exclusivity, about Bowood. The atmosphere is extremely relaxed and informal and while there are golf club members at Bowood, visitors are actively encouraged seven days a week, with the exception of Saturday and Sunday mornings. The 19th hole facilities (the clubhouse is a beautifully restored 18th century farmhouse) include an extensive golf academy, incorporating three practice holes and a driving range.

Bowood is something of a rarity these days—a modern championship length golf course with a refreshingly unpretentious design. Architect Dave Thomas has not attempted to trade Wiltshire for Palm Springs, as one suspects many of his fellow designers might have tried to do. Lancelot 'Capability' Brown was the original architect of Bowood and surely he would have turned in his grave at any suggestion of deference to the American way! Water is a feature of the design but it doesn't lead the design, indeed it tends to frame rather than shape those holes where it is present. Each of the 18 holes certainly has an individual flavour and there is plenty of variety to accompany the subtlety of the challenge. Moreover there

is a great feeling of space at Bowood—none of the holes encroaches on another and with the gentle mounding and graded rough there is considerable definition to each hole. There are some nice touches too, such as the additional putting green beside the 1st tee, and the huge double green shared by the 5th and 14th holes.

Subtlety aside for a moment, if there are two holes at Bowood that could be said to 'take your breath away' then they are the par four 8th and the par four 11th where on each a downhill tee shot must be perfectly positioned to open up a sharply dog-legging fairway. For my money, however, the real strength of Bowood is to be found in its outstanding quartet of par five holes, namely the 3rd, 4th, 10th and 15th, and in its superb closing hole, where a deft approach is required to find a well protected and well-contoured putting surface.

Bowood Golf & Country Club, Calne, Wiltshire SN11 9PQ

Director of Golf	Nigel Blenkarne (01249) 822228 Fax (01249) 822218
Green Fees	£32/18 holes; £37/27 holes; £42/36 holes
Restrictions	No visitors before midday at weekends

Directions
The course is 10 miles south of M4 junction 17 where the A4 meets the A432. From London leave the M4 at junction 14 and follow the A4 west.

The Manor House (Castle Combe)

'Invest in land' Mark Twain advised, 'they're not building any more of it'. What value then, an area of dramatically rolling countryside bordering the beautiful Wiltshire village of Castle Combe? We are certainly talking about a very special place; it is the kind that if, some years ago, you were a golfer idly wandering across the land (daydreaming about your favourite pastime!) you would doubtless have sighed to yourself, 'my, what a marvellous setting this would make for a golf course!' Some daydreams can come true.

The Manor House Golf Club at Castle Combe opened in 1992, the 18 hole golf course that now winds its way through this spectacular piece of property was designed by Peter Alliss and Clive Clark. Not only does it make the most of the terrain (more of which later) but it genuinely 'accommodates' it. I choose this word because the golf course was never allowed to impose itself on the land and enormous care was taken at all stages of the development to preserve, and indeed encourage the natural flora and fauna and the abundant wildlife that inhabits the surrounding countryside.

At 6340 yards, par 73 from the back tees, Castle Combe is not a long course by the standards of many new 'high profile' layouts, but then added length is probably the last thing that this course needs. It opens with a relatively straightforward hole but the tempo immediately changes with the first of five really good par threes. Precision is vital at each of these short holes for the bad stroke is seriously punished. The 3rd is a classic par five, a genuine three shot hole where the terrain tumbles away from the tee in tiers to a far off island fairway; the second shot must somehow avoid a large tree, a stream and a small lake and then the approach is uphill to a green surrounded by sand. If the 3rd

is the most memorable hole on the front nine, then the 7th, a beautifully curving, tree-lined par five is technically its equal.

The second nine at Castle Combe contains an even greater selection of hazards and outstanding holes. The sequence between the 11th (a stunning short hole where the tee shot must carry a little brook to find an angled green) and the par four 14th where there are two distinct options from the tee, is superb. Then comes the extraordinary finish with the vertigo-inducing par three 17th and intimidating par four 18th with its beautifully landscaped greenside lake. The inhabitants of Castle Combe can not only claim that they reside in 'the prettiest village in England' but its golf club members can justifiably boast that they preside over 'the prettiest finish in England'.

The Manor House Golf Club, Castle Combe, Wiltshire SN14 7JW

Gen Manager	Susan Auld (01249) 783101 Fax (01249) 782992
Green Fees	WD £37.50/round; £60/day WE £50/round; £80/day
Restrictions	Proof of handicap required

Directions
The club is directly off the B4039 between Chippenham and Bath, just beyond the village of Castle Combe.

Time stands still in the Bybrook valley at the southern tip of the Cotswolds. Renowned as one of the prettiest villages in England, picturesque Castle Combe nestles in this delightful wooded valley where nothing has changed for the past 200 years. Rough-hewn limestone cottages, an ancient market cross and a packbridge over the Bybrook, —described in 1458 as 'the great town bridge'—are the epitome of a peaceful English village.

Certainly there can be no lovelier approach to any village than the narrow lane winding its way down to Castle Combe through a green tunnel of interlocking branches.

To the enchantment of this hidden village, the Manor House lends an extra fairytale dimension. Steeped in history, with parts of the house dating back to the 14th century and added to by the Jacobeans in 1664, it is the quintessential English manor. A symphony of chimneys, mullioned windows and creeper covered walls and inside welcoming log fires and inviting sofas.

There is rich wood panelling, and gleaming glass and silver in the candlelit Bybrook restaurant. There are bedrooms tucked away in romantic attics, or boasting an Elizabethan fireplace and triple aspect views. All are luxurious, some with four poster beds, others with Victorian style bathrooms. All the rooms in the main house have been restored and refurbished during the past two years to an exceptional degree, revealing hidden beams, stonework and a grain drying kiln.

Croquet, tennis and a heated outside swimming pool are all available for guests, with trout fishing on the one mile stretch of the Bybrook flowing through the 26 acres of gardens and parkland.

The Manor House is surrounded by countryside designated as an area of outstanding natural beauty. There are suggested walks through neighbouring woodland, or for the more energetic there are cycles available for visits to the many delightful nearby Cotswold villages.

Set in 200 acres of wooded valley and downland, the exceptional championship Manor House golf course, dominated by ancient oak and beech woods, was designed by Peter Allis and Clive Clark and provides interesting and challenging golf for the average golfer and good player alike.

Guests staying at the Manor House are able to enjoy one of the most spectacular and challenging 6340 yard, par 73 golf courses in the south of England.

Although lost in the heart of the Cotswold countryside, access is not difficult. The M4 motorway is only 15 minutes away and the journey from London by road takes but an hour and 40 minutes. The intersection with the M5 is only 20 minutes away, linking the Midlands, the North and South West for ease of access.

The Manor House
Castle Combe
Chippenham
Wiltshire SN14 7HR
Tel: (01249) 782206 Fax: (01249) 782159
E mail: enquiries@manor-house.co.uk
website: www.manor-house.co.uk

Key

To avoid disappointment
it is advisable to telephone
in advance

***Visitors welcome at most times
**Visitors usually allowed on
weekdays only
*Visitors not normally permitted
(Mon, Wed) No visitors
on specified days

Approximate Green Fees
A   £40 plus
B   £25 to £40
C   £20 to £30
D   £15 to £25
E   under £15
F   Green fees on application

Restrictions
G —Guests only
H—Handicap certificate required
H—(24) Handicap of 24 or less
L —Letter of introduction required
M—Visitor must be a member of
another recognised club

SOMERSET

Bath G.C.
(01225) 463834
North Road, Bath.
(18) 6369 yards/***/B/H

Brean G.C.
(01278) 751570
Coast Road, Brean
(18) 5714 yards/**/F/H

Burnham and Berrow G.C.
(01278) 785760
St Christophers Way,
Burnham-on-Sea
(18) 6668 yards/***/A/M
(9) 6332 yards/***/E

Cannington G.C.
(01278) 655050
Cannington, Bridgwater
(9) 2929 yards/***/D

Enmore Park G.C.
(01278) 671481
Enmore, Bridgwater
(18) 6406 yards/***/C

Entry Hill G.C.
(01225) 834248
Entry Hill, Bath
(9) 4206 yards/***/E

Fosseway C.C.
(01761) 412214
Charlton Lane, Midsomer Norton
(9) 4608 yards/***/D

Frome G.C.
(01373) 453410
Critchill Manor, Frome
(18) 4914 yards/***/E

Halstock G.C.
(01935) 891689
Common Lane, Halstock
(18) 4000 yards/***/E

Isle of Wedmore G.C.
(01934) 713649
Lineage, Wedmore
(18) 5850 yards/***/D

Kingweston G.C.
(01458) 43921
Compton Dundon, Somerton
(9) 4516 yards/*/F

Lansdown G.C.
(01225) 420242
Lansdown, Bath
(18) 6316 yards/***/B/H

Long Sutton G.C.
(01458) 241017
Long Load, Langport
(18) 6367 yards/***/D

Mendip G.C.
(01749) 840570
Gurney Slade, Bath
(18) 6033 yards/***/B/H

Mendip Spring G.C.
(01934) 852322
Honeyhall Lane, Congresbury
(18) 6328 yards/***/D
(9) 2287 yards/***/E

Minehead and West Somerset G.C.
(01643) 702057
Warren Road, Minehead
(18) 6228 yards/***/B

Oake Manor G.C.
(01823) 461993
Oake, Taunton
(18) 6109 yards/***/D

Orchardleigh G.C.
(01373) 454200
Frome
(18) 6810 yards/***/D

Puxton Park G.C.
(01934) 876942
Puxton, Weston-super-Mare
(18) 6600 yards/***/E

Saltford G.C.
(01225) 873513
Golf Club Lane, Saltford
(18) 6081 yards/***/B

Tall Pines G.C.
(01275) 472076
Downside, Backwell
(18) 5827 yards/***/D

Taunton and Pickeridge G.C.
(01823) 421537
Corfe, Taunton
(18) 5927 yards/***/F/H

Taunton Vale G.C.
(01823) 412220
Creech Heathfield, Taunton
(18) 6072 yards/***/D
(9) 2004 yards/***/E

Vivary Park G.C.
(01823) 333875
Taunton
(18) 4620 yards/***/E

Wells G.C.
(01749) 675005
East Horrington Road, Wells
(18) 6015 yards/***/D/H

Weston-super-Mare G.C.
(01934) 621360
Uphill Road North,
Weston-super-Mare
(18) 6251 yards/***/B/H

Wheathill G.C.
(01963) 240667
Wheathill, Somerset
(18) 5362 yards/***/E

Wincanton G.C.
(01963) 34606
Wincanton Racecourse
(9) 3333 yards/***/E

Windwhistle G. & C.C.
(01460) 30231
Cricket St Thomas, Chard
(18) 6500 yards/***/F

Worlebury G.C.
(01934) 625789
Worlebury, Weston-super-Mare
(18) 5963 yards/***/B

Yeovil G.C.
(01935) 22965
Sherborne Road. Yeovil
(18) 6144 yards/***/B/H
(9) 4876 yards/***/D/H

DORSET

Ashley Wood G.C.
(01258) 452253
Wimborne Rd, Blandford Forum
(18) 6231 yards/***/C

Bournemouth and Meyrick Park G.C.
(01202) 290862
Central Drive, Meyrick Park
(18) 5637 yards/***/D

Bridport & West Dorset G.C.
(01308) 421095
East Cliff, West Bay, Bridport
(18) 5246 yards/***/D

Broadstone G.C.
(01202) 692595
Wentworth Drive, Broadstone
(18) 6300 yards/**/A/H

Bulbury Woods G.C.
(01929) 459574
Lytchett Matravers, nr Poole
(18) 6020 yards/***/C

Came Down G.C.
(01305) 813494
Came Down, Dorchester
(18) 6244 yards/***/B/H

Canford School G.C.
(01202) 841254
Canford School, Wimborne
(9) 5918 yards/***/E/G

Chedington Court G.C.
(01935) 891413
Nr Beaminster, Dorset
(18) 6000 yards/***/D

Christchurch G.C.
(01202) 473817
Iford, Christchurch
(9) 4270 yards/***/E

Crane Valley G.C.
(01202) 814088
The Clubhouse, Verwood
(18) 6420 yards/***/C/H
(9) 2030 yards/***/E

Dorset Heights G.C.
(01258) 861386
Belchalwell, Blandford Forum
(18) 6500 yards/***/C

Dudmoor Farm
(01202) 483980
Dudmoor Lane, Christchurch
(9) 1562 yards/***/E

Dudsbury G.C.
(01202) 593499
Christchurch Road, Ferndown
(18) 6208 yards/***/F

East Dorset G.C.
(01929) 472244
Hyde, Wareham
(18) 6640 yards/***/C/H
(9) 2440 yards/***/D/H

Ferndown G.C.
(01202) 874602
Golf Links Road, Ferndown
(18) 6452 yards/***/A/H/L
(9) 5604 yards/***/C/H/L

Ferndown Forest G.C.
(01202) 876096
Forest Links Road, Ferndown
(9) 2810 yards/***/D

Halstock G.C.
(01935) 891689
Common Lane, Halstock
(18) 4351 yards/***/D

Highcliffe Castle G.C.
(01425) 272210
Lymington Road, Highcliffe-on-Sea
(18) 4686 yards/***/B/H/M

Iford Bridge G.C.
(01202) 888016
Barrack Road, Christchurch
(9) 2377 yards/***/F

Isle of Purbeck G.C.
(01929) 450354
Studland, Swanage
(18) 6295 yards/***/B/H
(9) 2022 yards/***/D

Knighton Heath G.C.
(01202) 572633
Francis Avenue, West Howe
(18) 5987 yards/**/F/H

Lyme Regis G.C.
(01297) 442963
Timber Hill, Lyme Regis
(18) 6220 yards/***/B/H

Lyons Gate G.C.
(01300) 345239
Lyons Gate, Dorchester
(9) 4200 yards/***/E

Moors Valley G.C.
(01425) 479776
Horton Road, Ringwood
(18) 6270 yards/***/E

Parkstone G.C.
(01202) 707138
Links Road, Parkstone
(18) 6250 yards/**/A/H/M

Queen's Park G.C.
(01202) 396198
Queen's Park, Bournemouth
(18) 6072 yards/***/D

Sherbourne G.C.
(01935) 812274
Higher Clatcombe, Sherbourne
(18) 5949 yards/***/B/H

Solent Meads Par Three G.C.
(01202) 420795
Hengisbury Head, Bournemouth
(18) 2325 yards/***/F

Sturminster Marshall G.C.
(01258) 858444
Moor Lane, Sturminster Marshall
(9) 4650 yards/***/E

Wareham G.C.
(01929) 554147
Sandford Road, Wareham
(18) 5603 yards/**/C/H

Weymouth G.C.
(01305) 773981
Links Road, Westham, Weymouth
(18) 6035 yards/***/B/H

WILTSHIRE

Bowood G. & C.C.
(01249) 822228
Derry Hill, Calne
(18) 7317 yards/***/B-A

Bradford-on-Avon G.C.
(01225) 868268
Trowbridge Road, Bradford-on-Avon
(9) 2297 yards/**/E

Brinkworth G.C.
(01666) 510277
Longman's Farm, Brinkworth
(18) 5900 yards/***/F

Bremhill Park G.C.
(01793) 782946
Shrivenham, Swindon
(18) 5880 yards/***/E

Broome Manor G.C.
(01793) 532403
Pipers Way, Swindon
(18) 6283 yards/***/E
(9) 2690 yards/***/E

Chippenham G.C..
(01249) 652040
Malmesbury Road, Chippenham
(18) 5540 yards/***/B/H/M

Cricklade Hotel G.C.
(01793) 750751
Common Hill, Cricklade
(9) 1830 yards/***/C

Cumberwell Park G.C.
(01225) 863322
Bradford-on-Avon
(18) 6807 yards/***/C

Erlestoke Sands G.C.
(01380) 831069
Erlestoke, Devizes
(18) 6649 yards/***/D

Hamptworth G. & C.C.
(01794) 390155
Hamptworth Road, Landford
(18) 6512 yards/**/C/H

High Post G.C.
(01722) 782219
Great Durnford, Salisbury
(18) 6297 yards/**/B/H

Highworth G.C.
(01793) 766014
Swindon Road, Highworth
(9) 3220 yards/***/E

Kingsdown G.C.
(01225) 743472
Kingsdown, Corsham
(18) 6445 yards/**/B

Manor House (Castle Combe) G. & C.C.
(01249) 782982
Castle Combe
(18) 6340 yards/***/A/H

Marlborough G.C.
(01672) 512147
The Common, Marlborough
(18) 6526 yards/***/B-A/H

North Wiltshire G.C.
(01380) 860627
Bishops Cannings, Devizes
(18) 6322 yards/**/C-A

Oaksey Park G.C.
(01666) 577995
Oaksey, Malmesbury
(9) 2900 yards/***/D

Ogbourne Downs G.C.
(01672) 841327
Ogbourne St George, Malborough
(18) 6226 yards/**/B/H

Salisbury and South Wilts. G.C.
(01722) 742645
Netherhampton, Salisbury
(18) 6528 yards/***/B-A

RCMS Shrivenham
(01793) 785725
Shrivenham, Swindon
(12) 5547 yards/*/E/G

Shrivenham Park G.C.
(01793) 783853
Penny Hooks, Shrivenham
(18) 5989 yards/***/D

Thoulstone Park G.C.
(01373) 832825
Chapmanslade, Wesbury
(18) 6300 yards/***/D

Tidworth Garrison G.C.
(01980) 842301
Bulford Road, Tidworth
(18) 6101 yards/**/D

Upavon G.C.
(01980) 630787
Douglas Avenue, Swindon
(9) 5589 yards/**/D

West Wiltshire G.C.
(01985) 213133
Elm Hill, Warminster
(18) 5709 yards/**/B-A/H

Wiltshire G.C.
(01793) 849999
Wootton Bassett, Swindon
(18) 6496 yards/**/B - A/H

Wrag Barn G.C.
(01793) 861327
Shrivenham Road, Highworth
(18) 6548 yards/**/C

Artist: **Major Hopkins A FOURSOME AT WESTWARD HO!**
Courtesy of: **Burlington Gallery**

Artist: **W.E.B. THE GREEN**
Courtesy of: **Burlington Gallery**

Artist: **F.P. Hopkins PUTTING**
Courtesy of: **Burlington Gallery**

Artist: **C.E. Brock THE PUTT** *Courtesy of:* **Sothebys**

Even if the Isle of Wight and the Channel Islands were taken away from this region it would still score top marks, both for the quality of the golf and the quality of the accompanying scenery. With the New Forest to the south, the Downs to the north and Winchester Cathedral standing proudly in the middle, Hampshire is arguably the fairest of all English counties. And amongst all this finery stand the likes of Liphook, Old Thorns, North Hants, Blackmoor and Brokenhurst Manor—five of the country's leading inland courses.

From Heathland to Links

Hampshire's traditional 'big three' of **Liphook, North Hants** and **Blackmoor** lie towards the east of the county close to the boundary with Surrey. Not surprisingly, they are staunch members of the heathland club—silver birch and pine, fir, heather and a dash of gorse. Liphook is possibly the pick of the three, though it's a close thing. Each measures between 6200 and 6300 yards and is maintained in superb condition. The **Army** Golf Club, just north of Aldershot is another fine and quite lengthy heathland type course with a reputation for separating the men from the boys, although it is perhaps not quite in the same league as the illustrious trio above. The final mention in this area goes to one of the county's newest recruits, the **Old Thorns** situated just south of Liphook. Both Liphook and Old Thorns are featured on a later page.

There's no shortage of comfortable hotels in the north of Hampshire and often quite hidden in the countryside are some delightful pubs and restaurants. Inns to ease the golfer's slumber include the Crown and Cushion in Minley and the Chequers in Well. Fleet bisects these two villages and the Lismoyne Hotel (01252) 628555 is ideally located. In Passfield, the Passfield Oak does good food and some popular real ales. In Liphook, as well as Old Thorns (01428) 724555, the Links Hotel (01428) 723773 is very handy for the 9th and 10th tees on the Liphook course. Basingstoke isn't Hampshire's most attractive town—too much London overspill—but a very good course nearby is the **Sandford Springs** Golf Club at Wolverton, built on the site of a former Roman shrine.

Winchester golfers, like those at Liphook, are doubly fortunate having two first class courses at hand: **Royal Winchester** and **Hockley**. Both are well kept downland type courses. The attractive additions to the Winchester/South Hampshire area are the **Botley Park** Hotel and Country Club (01489) 780888 and the **South Winchester** Golf Club.

In Ampfield, south of Winchester, and Romsey, also south of the cathedral town, two ideal 19th hole establishments catch the eye. In the former, Potters Heron (01703) 266611 is comfortable and convenient for the A31 and the White Horse (01794) 512431 is a welcoming inn located in Romsey's marketplace. The Old Manor House (01794) 517357 is a restaurant to make a special diversion for. In Winchester there are numerous restaurants, perhaps the best being the Old Chesil Rectory (01962) 851555. Also in Winchester, the Hotel du Vin and Bistro (01962) 841414 is not cheap but is particularly comfortable. North west of the city is Sparsholt, where one finds one of those exquisite English country house hotels, Lainston House (01962) 863588. People coming from, or returning to the west should note Middle Wallop—more specifically—Fifehead Manor (01264) 781565, a converted 16th century manor house with a good restaurant. Finally, I must point pub lovers in mid-Hampshire in the direction of Ovington where the Bush is tremendous fun.

Returning to the fairways, and switching nearer to the south coast, the **Rowlands Castle** parkland course occupies a peaceful setting. The course can play fairly long, especially from the back markers. While we're on the subject of length, a hundred years ago the links at **Hayling Island** is said to have measured 7480 yards—so much for the modern-day monster courses! Today the course is less frightening but still quite a challenge in the wind and visitors are warmly received.

If another drink is needed then two fine pubs are at hand—the Old House at Home (superb name) in Havant and the Royal Oak in Langstone: both are ideally situated for Rowlands Castle. Another establishment to sample in this area is the notable Old House Hotel (01329) 833049 in Wickham and in Botley, Cobbett's (01489) 782068 is a fine French restaurant. Finally, back on Hayling Island, we recommend the Newtown House Hotel (01705) 466131 as ideal for all visitors to the area—with a new 9 hole course at **Tournerbury** nearby it provides a choice of golf.

Southampton and the New Forest

Stoneham, without doubt the pick of the courses in the Southampton area, is located just two miles north of the town. The venue of the first Dunlop British Masters tournament back in 1946, it is quite undulating with an ample sprinkling of gorse and heather and in spring some wonderful flowers. Just outside of Portsmouth a fine 18 hole course to note is **Waterlooville**, although there are in fact a number of courses (including some very reasonable public courses, such as **Fleming Park** at Eastleigh) in and around Southampton and Portsmouth. Midway between Portsmouth and Southampton (M27 junction 7) is the **Meon Valley** Golf and Country Club. A parkland course, designed by J Hamilton Stutt, it too has an attractive setting which is not a million miles from the New Forest. For a night's rest the Meon Valley Hotel (01329) 833455 is the obvious selection, being both comfortable and highly convenient.

I'm afraid I know very little about William the Conqueror but I understand there are at least two things we should thank him for—one is the Domesday Book and the other is the New Forest—without doubt one of the most beautiful areas in Britain. There are two real golfing treats in the New Forest, one is **Bramshaw** Golf Club which is owned and run by the owners of the charming Bell Inn (01703) 812214—two 18 hole courses here, the Manor and the Forest courses—and the second is **Brokenhurst Manor,** a superb heathland course. Both venues are decidedly worth inspecting. A short distance from the New Forest, **Barton-on-Sea**'s exposed clifftop course is also worth a visit if in the area—it's not long, but with enough challenges and some spectacular views across to the Isle of Wight and Christchurch Bay.

A few ideas for the 19th hole, and we make a start at Lyndhurst and the Parkhill House Hotel (01703) 282944—a pleasant spot with a good restaurant as well. Near Bramshaw at No Man's Land is Les Mirabelles (01794) 390205, offering good French food and views of forest ponies outside. Two B's now, Beaulieu and Brockenhurst. In the former, the Montagu Arms (01590) 612324 and its fine restaurant is ideal to hang up one's clubs and in the latter a number of places should be considered; three definitely to include are Carey's Manor (01590) 623551, a great all rounder, Rhinefield House (01590) 622922, and Le Poussin (01590) 623063—a real beauty of a restaurant. Further south on the A337 we arrive at Lymington. In another good hotel setting stands the Passford House (01590) 682398 and for a stylish guesthouse, try Wheatsheaf House (01590) 679208. Among other things, the nearby South Lawn Hotel (01590) 643911 is convenient for ferries leaving for the Isle of Wight, while Limpets (01590) 675595, also in Lymington, has a tasty restaurant. Gordleton Mill (01590) 682219 is a real delight—aptly described as a restaurant with rooms, it is a classic of its type. In New Milton, we find the county's (quite probably the country's) finest country house hotel, Chewton Glen (01425) 275341.

Isle of Wight

There are no fewer than seven golf courses on the Isle of Wight. Of the two 18 hole courses, **Shanklin and Sandown** is the better (beautifully wooded with heather and gorse) and the other is **Freshwater Bay** (more of a downland/clifftop course.) Of the 9 holers, **Osborne** is the most scenic but a visit to any is appealing. All courses welcome visitors and green fees tend to compare favourably with those on the mainland. Note that in summer with the onset of holiday makers, the courses can be very busy and so a pre-match telephone call is strongly advised.

In Shanklin, the Cliff Tops (01983) 863262 stands out, though there are many good hotels on the island. Two pubs to visit in Shanklin include the Fisherman's Cottage—good food and a fine setting—and the Crab which provides more seafood in a high street position.

Elsewhere on the island, Cowes of course is busy and fun, especially during Cowes Week itself, but for our purposes Bonchurch beckons, where the Royal (01983) 852186 is a delightful restaurant with some rooms. There is also a tremendous selection of moderately priced establishments on the island. Suggestions include the Farringford Hotel (01983) 752500, The Albion (01983) 753631 at Freshwater, the Culver Lodge Hotel (01983) 403819 and the excellent St Catherine's Hotel (01983) 402392, both at Sandown.

The Channel Islands

If the Isle of Wight is good for golf, the Channel Islands are even better. **La Moye, Royal Jersey** and **Royal Guernsey** are the three outstanding 18 hole courses, although it seems the German troops didn't share this opinion during the island's four year occupation—they demolished La Moye's clubhouse and dug up the fairways at Royal Guernsey. Both have long since recovered though and all three provide tremendous holiday golf. La Moye is featured ahead.

When it comes to hotels one is quite simply spoilt for choice. In Guernsey, St Peter's Port offers a whole handful of excellent establishments. The St Pierre Park (01481) 728282 is the most luxurious hotel, and for real character La Frégate Hotel (01481) 724624 is an 18th century manor house overlooking the harbour. The Old Government House (01481) 724921 is again beautifully stylish. For a good seafood restaurant try the Absolute End (01481) 723822 and for a cosy guest house, La Girouette (01481) 63269 near Perrelle Bay.

In Jersey, St Brelade's Bay offers the Atlantic Hotel (01534) 44101 (ideal for La Moye links). Other recommended hotels here are the Hotel L'Horizon (01534) 43101, and La Place Hotel (01534) 44261. St Helier boasts the aptly named Grand Hotel (01534) 22301—note especially the restaurant which is excellent—the less expensive Almorah Hotel (01534) 21648 and in St Peter, the Mermaid (01534) 41255. Perhaps the best restaurant on the island is to be found at St Saviour—Longueville Manor (01534) 25501 is an outstanding hotel as well. In Bouley Bay is the delightfully secluded Water's Edge Hotel (01534) 862777. However, the intrepid guesthouse brigade will find more than enough to please them at Millbrook House (01534) 33036 in St Helier and Bryn-y-Mor (01534) 20295 in St Aubin. Finally in Grouville Bay near the Royal Jersey Golf Club is La Hougue Grange, a charming country house and one of those treats where the words 'fore' and 'fare' can be combined so happily!

Artist: **H Rountree** *IT'S A ONE* *Courtesy of:* **Burlington Gallery**

La Moye

England is part of the Channel Islands. Yes, England is part of the Channel Islands—at least this is what an islander will tell you. Apparently, the islands belonged to William, Duke of Normandy some time before he came over and added England to his territories.

So what of the golf in the 'mother country', the land where the great Harry Vardon was born? In short, there are three very fine courses: Royal Guernsey, Royal Jersey and La Moye. The first two certainly offer a marvellous day's golf but the general consensus is that La Moye sneaks it as the pick of an excellent trio. Its setting alone makes the course stand out, laid out as it is two hundred and fifty feet above St Ouen's Bay, Jersey's finest beach, on the south west tip of the island. From such a vantage point there are some tremendous views to be enjoyed from the course, particularly perhaps from the 13th where the four sister islands of Guernsey, Sark, Herm and Jetou can all be seen. Add to this a warm climate and of course, the quality of the championship links itself and you can see why people want to play golf here!

La Moye Golf Club was founded in 1902 by the then headmaster of the local school, one George Boomer. A course was mapped out but it didn't really take shape until James Braid added his skilful craftsmanship. Thereafter the course was left more or less untouched, so to speak, until 1977 when major alterations were made resulting in an improved and, when played from the back tees, much longer course.

The **Secretary** at La Moye is **Chris Greetham,** who can be contacted by telephone on **(01534) 43401** or by writing to: **La Moye Golf Club, La Moye, Jersey, Channel Islands**. The club **Professional, Mike Deeley** can be reached on **(01534) 43130.**

In addition to being a superb championship course, La Moye doubles as a very popular holiday course in the best sense of the word. Visitors are always made most welcome. The only specific requirement is that they must be members of a recognised golf club. It isn't essential to book a tee time but during the summer months the course can become extremely busy. Making an early start is always a good idea.

The green fees for 1998 were set at £40 per round

during the week and £45 at the weekend when only afternoon play is permitted.

As for finding the course, there really should be no problem. La Moye is only a mile or so from St Brelade and just five minutes by road from Jersey's airport. The island is such a size that it shouldn't take much more than half an hour to travel between La Moye and Royal Jersey in Grouville, though of course it depends on the traffic and on how much of Jersey you want to take in along the way.

From the championship tees, the course can be stretched to almost 6700 yards. The medal tees, however, are less exacting and the total yardage is 6416 yards, par 72—no pushover certainly, and there is often a very stiff wind. From the ladies tees the course measures 5903 yards, par 74. La Moye is a typical links type course—large sandhills, pot bunkers, the odd blind shot, gorse bushes and punishing rough (though it's not as punishing as at some). It really is full of variety with a number of dog-legs and plateau greens. Apart from the 13th and its enchanting views, many will probably remember the 17th hole best of all—a lengthy par four with the green dramatically set on the edge of the cliffs, rather like the famous 5th hole at Portrush.

The Jersey Seniors Open has established itself as a very popular event on the European Seniors Tour and the pros, inspired by the surroundings, have produced some very good scores—although La Moye has never been torn apart. Some well known names also won the Jersey Open when it used to be held here, including the Ryder Cup players Sandy Lyle, Tony Jacklin, Bernard Gallacher, Howard Clark, Ian Woosnam and Sam Torrance. So some of the best golfers in the world have played at La Moye and they have been joined by the best golfer to have played on the moon! Alan Sheppard, now Admiral Sheppard, is an honorary member. One suspects he is a rather good bunker player!

All golfers, terrestrial and non-terrestrial are sure to enjoy the club's excellent 19th. A spacious new clubhouse, it is one of a series for the club. The original burned down while the second was destroyed by German soldiers during the island's war-time occupation. Let's just wish the new one the best of British luck!

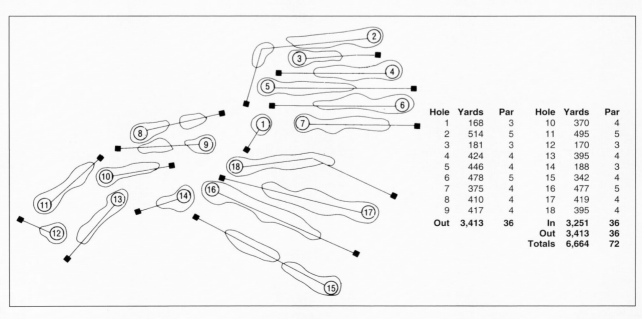

Hole	Yards	Par		Hole	Yards	Par
1	168	3		10	370	4
2	514	5		11	495	5
3	181	3		12	170	3
4	424	4		13	395	4
5	446	4		14	188	3
6	478	5		15	342	4
7	375	4		16	477	5
8	410	4		17	419	4
9	417	4		18	395	4
Out	**3,413**	**36**		**In**	**3,251**	**36**
				Out	**3,413**	**36**
				Totals	**6,664**	**72**

Liphook

Although it may sound more like a golfing nightmare than a golfing haven, Liphook is one of the most delightful inland courses in Southern England. The 18 holes straddle the Hampshire-Sussex boundary yet in character it 'belongs' to Berkshire or Surrey. Liphook is a classic heathland layout, indeed, there are many who regard it as one of *the* classic heathland courses.

Liphook was designed in 1922, principally by Arthur Croome. Blessed with a wealth of magnificent pines and silver birches, the terrain is very sandy in nature—dazzling white in parts—and in September the heather turns a beautiful shade of purple-pink. The beauty of Croome's creation is the way the course subtly blends into the landscape. There is enormous variety yet nothing appears contrived. Notwithstanding the A3 road which bisects the course, there is a very tranquil atmosphere—Liphook exudes an air of 'Merry Old England'

At 6167 yards, par 69, Liphook is not overly long, but with relatively small greens and fairways bordered by thick heather, the wayward big hitter will be punished. The nature of the challenge is evident from the outset. The course begins, rather unusually, with a long par three. It is a fairly formidable opening hole with trees all along the left, heather in front of the green and a steep fallaway to the right.

The 2nd hole features a sloping fairway and an approach over a sandy track to an attractively sited green encircled by pines. Plenty of sand and heather frame the uphill par three 3rd and then comes a big two-shotter with a fairway running parallel with the 2nd.

Bold bunkering characterises the 5th and 6th. The short 7th and down and up 8th are threatened by a railway line to the right and the front nine concludes with an intriguing (some say infuriating) par four. The second shot to the ninth is played blind over a crest to a green protected by humps and hillocks, a thoroughly old fashioned, almost links style hole.

You are encouraged to open your shoulders at the 10th and then asked to thread your tee shot between bunkers at the short 11th where a wonderful stand of pines provides a striking backcloth.

The 12th, 13th and 14th form a splendid sequence amid the most picturesque part of the course. A wide fairway at the long, steadily uphill 12th is deceptive in as much as the green is very small. The 13th 'Two Counties' has you teeing off in Sussex and holing out in Hampshire, a glorious approach across a valley to plateau green. The 14th is a teasingly short par four that dog-legs right into another handsome greensite. The uphill 15th and downhill 16th are very much a pair, and finally, a bunkerless but heather strewn par three, and a marvellous rollercoasting par five guide you back to the clubhouse.

Liphook Golf Club, Wheatsheaf Enclosure Liphook, Hants GU30 7EH	
Secretary	Major J B Morgan (01428) 723785
Professional	Ian Large (01428) 723271
Green Fees	WD £30/round, £40/day
	WE £40/round, £50/day
Restrictions	No visitors Sun am or competition Sats
	Handicap certificates required
	Booking strongly recommended
Directions	
One mile south west of Liphook off the A3 Petersfield Road.	

Old Thorns

There are two reasons why we have selected Old Thorns as one of our featured courses in this edition of *Following the Fairways*. Firstly, it is because a visit to Old Thorns can fairly be described as a unique experience and the purpose of this book, after all, is to illustrate the wealth and variety of golfing challenges that these islands have to offer. The second, just as important, is that Old Thorns is both exceptionally attractive and visitor-friendly. Nature, with a little help from course designers Peter Alliss and Dave Thomas, is chiefly responsible for the beauty of the situation. The visitor-friendly aspect is a direct result of the fact that Old Thorns isn't a golf club as such. Like The Belfry, there are no members for whom tee times must be reserved.

What about the unique experience? Old Thorns is where East meets West, not just on the golf course but at the 19th hole. Old Thorns is owned by a large Japanese publishing company, Kosaido who acquired the course and accompanying hotel only two years after its official opening in 1982. The Japanese inherited a very English set up. The centre piece of the clubhouse and hotel is a converted 150 year old tithe barn; a delightful building. The new owners have maintained, even enhanced, its traditional 'log fires in winter' ambience, but they have also added a Japanese Centre which includes a charming Japanese garden. The buildings have been extended generally to an extent that Old Thorns now boasts a splendid range of luxury facilities. The hotel has 27 well appointed rooms and guests can enjoy a genuine Japanese Shiatsu massage!

Just an hour's drive from London perhaps, but the capital can seem a world away when you arrive at the course. The surrounding countryside is some of Britain's finest; a great spread of oaks, beech trees, chestnuts and pines adorn the landscape and the golf course winds its way through the woods, gently rising and falling. Natural springs abound and much use has been made of them! Water hazards are numerous at Old Thorns; there are many streams and several times the golfer is asked to play over or across the edge of a small lake.

After holing out successfully on the tricky 18th green a stiff drink at the 19th may be in order—a glass of saki perhaps? A good meal may also be sought and some people reckon that this is where Old Thorns really comes into its own. There is a superb selection of European and Japanese cuisine in its very characterful restaurants. If you have never tried Japanese food before then the renowned Nippon Kan Restaurant and the Teppan Yaki Bar are the perfect places for an introduction. Old Thorns is guaranteed to charm you from the moment you arrive to the time you leave.

Old Thorns, Longmoor Road, Liphook, Hampshire, GU30 7PE	
Gen Manager	G M Jones
Professional	Philip Loxley (01428) 724555
	Fax (01428) 725036
Green Fees	WD £25 (£35 per day)
	WE £35
Restrictions	Book tee times with professional.
Directions	
Exit A3 at Griggs Green, just south of Liphook.	

Key

*To avoid disappointment
it is advisable to telephone
in advance*

****Visitors welcome at most times
**Visitors usually allowed on
weekdays only
*Visitors not normally permitted
(Mon, Wed) No visitors
on specified days*

Approximate Green Fees
A *£40 plus*
B *£25 to £40*
C *£20 to £30*
D *£15 to £25*
E *under £15*
F *Green fees on application*

Restrictions
*G Guests only
H—Handicap certificate required
H—(24) Handicap of 24 or less
L —Letter of introduction required
M—Visitor must be a member of
another recognised club*

HAMPSHIRE

Alresford G.C.
(01962) 733746
Cheriton Road, Alresford
(18) 5905 yards/**/C/H

Alton G.C.
(01420) 82042
Old Odiham Road, Alton
(9) 5744 yards/***/D/H

Andover G.C.
(01264) 323980
Winchester Road, Andover
(9) 6096 yards/**/C

Army G.C.
(01252) 541104
Laffans Road, Aldershot
(18) 6579 yards/**/F/H

Barton-on-Sea G.C.
(01425) 615308
Marine Drive, Barton-on-Sea,
(18) 5737 yards/***/B/H

Basingstoke G.C.
(01256) 465990
Kempshott Park, Basingstoke
(18) 6350 yards/**/B/H/G

Bishopswood G.C.
(01734) 812200
Bishopswood Lane, Tadley
(9) 6474 yards/**(Mon,Wed)/D/M

Blackmoor G.C.
(01420) 472775
Golf Lane, Whitehill, Bordon
(18) 6232 yards/**/B/H

Blacknest G.C.
(01420) 22888
Frith End, Binstead
(9) 6726 yards/***/D

Botley Park Hotel & C.C.
(01489) 780888
Winchester Road, Boorley Green
(18) 6026 yards/***/C/H

Bramshaw G.C.
(01703) 813433
Brook, Lyndhurst
(18) 6257 yards/**/B/H
(18) 5774 yards/**/B/H

Brokenhurst Manor G.C.
(01590) 623332
Sway Road, Brockenhurst
(18) 6222 yards/***/B/H(24)

Burley G.C.
(01425) 402431
Cott Lane, Burley
(9) 3135 yards/***/D/H

Cams Hall G.C.
(01329) 827222
Cams Hill, Fareham
(18) 5890 yards/**/B/H
(9) 3059 yards/**/E/H

Chilworth G.C.
(01703) 740544
Main Road, Chilworth
(9) 2347 yards/***/E

Corhampton G.C.
(01489) 877279
Sheeps Pond Lane, Droxford
(18) 6088 yards/**/B/H

Dean Farm G.C.
(01420) 489478
Kingsley
(9) 1350 yards/***/F

Dibden G.C.
(01703) 845596
Dibden, Southampton
(18) 6206 yards/***/E
(9) 1520 yards/***/E

Dummer G.C.
(01256) 397888
Dummer, Basingstoke
(18) 6556 yards/**/C

Dunwood Manor G.C.
(01794) 340549
Shootash Hill, Romsey
(18) 5885 yards/**/B/H

Fleetlands G.C.
(01705) 544492
Fareham Road, Gosport
(9) 4852 yards/***/F/G

Fleming Park G.C.
(01703) 612797
Magpie Lane, Eastleigh
(18) 4436 yards/***/E

Furzeley G.C.
(01705) 231180
Furzeley, Denmead
(9) 1858 yards/***/E

Gosport and Stokes Bay G.C.
(01705) 581625
Off Fort Road, Haslar, Gosport
(9) 5966 yards/**/D

Great Salterns G.C.
(01705) 664549
Eastern Road, Portsmouth
(18) 5970 yards/***/E

The Hampshire G.C.
(01264) 357555
Winchester Road, Goodworth
(18) 6318 yards/***/D
(9) 1050 yards/***/E

Hartley Wintney G.C.
(01252) 844211
London Road, Hartley Wintney
(9) 6096 yards/**/D

Hayling G.C.
(01705) 464446
Links Lane, Hayling Island
(18) 6489 yards/***/A/H/M/L

Hockley G.C.
(01962) 713165
Twyford, Winchester
(18) 6279 yards/**/F/G

Leckford and Longstock G.C.
(01264) 810320
Leckford, Stockbridge
(9) 3251 yards/*/F/G

Lee-on-the-Solent G.C.
(01705) 551170
Brune Lane, Lee-on-the-Solent
(18) 5959/**/B/H

Liphook G.C.
(01428) 723271
Wheatsheaf Enclosure, Liphook
(18) 6167 yards/**/A/H/L

Meon Valley G.& C.C.
(01329) 833455
Sandy Lane, Shedfield,
(18) 6519 yards/***/A
(9) 2885 yards/***/D

New Forest G.C.
(01703) 282752
Southampton Road, Lyndhurst
(18) 5742 yards/***/D

North Hants G.C.
(01252) 616443
Minley Road, Fleet
(18) 6257 yards/**/B/H/L

Old Thorns G.C.
(01428) 724555
Longmoor Road, Liphook
(18) 6533 yards/***/A

Otterbourne
(01962) 775225
Pales Lane, Otterbourne
(9) 1939 yards/***/E

Paultons G.C.
(01703) 813992
Ower, Romsey
(18) 6238 yards/***/D

Petersfield G.C.
(01730) 262725
Heath Road, Petersfield
(18) 5603 yards/**/C

Portsmouth G.C.
(01705) 201827
Crookhorn Road, Portsmouth
(18) 6139 yards/***/E

Romsey G.C.
(01703) 734637
Nursling , Southampton
(18) 5851 yards/**/B/H

Rowlands Castle G.C.
(01705) 412784
Links Lane, Rowlands Castle
(18)6627 yards/**/B/H

Royal Winchester G.C.
(01962) 852462
Sarum Road, Winchester
(18) 6218 yards/**/B/H/M

Sandford Springs G.C.
(01635) 297881
Wolverton, Basingstoke
(27) 6222 yards/**/B

Southampton Municipal G.C.
(01703) 767942
Golf Course Road, Bassett,
(18) 6218 yards/***/F
(9) 2391 yards/***/F

Southsea G.C.
(01705) 660945
The Mansion, Great Salterns
(18) 5900 yards/***/F

Southwick Park G.C.
(01705) 380131
Pinsley Drive, Southwick, Fareham
(18) 5972 yards/**/F

South Winchester G.C.
(01962) 877800
Pitt, Winchester
(18) 6697 yards/**/B/H/L

Southwood G.C.
(01252) 548700
Ively Road, Cove, Farnborough
(18) 5738 yards/***/D

Stoneham G.C.
(01703) 768151
Bassett Green Road, Bassett
(18) 6310 yards/**/B/H

Test Valley G.C.
(01256) 771737
Micheldever Road, Overton
(18) 6811 yards/***/C

Tournerbury G.C.
(01705) 462266
Tournerbury Road, Hayling Island
(9) 2956 yards/***/E

Tylney Park G.C.
(01256) 762079
Rotherwick, Basingstoke
(18) 6109 yards/**/B/H

Waterlooville G.C.
(01705) 263388
Cherry Tree Avenue, Cowplain,
Portsmouth
(18) 6647 yards/**/B/H

Weybrook Park G.C.
(01256) 320347
Aldermaston Road, Basingstoke
(18) 6100 yards/***/D

Worldham Park G.C.
(01420) 543151
Cahers Lane, Alton
(18) 5836 yards/***/D

ISLE OF WIGHT

Cowes G.C.
(01983) 292303
Crossfield Avenue, Cowes
(9) 5934 yards/***/D/H

Freshwater Bay G.C.
(01983) 752955
Afton Down, Freshwater Bay
(18) 5662 yards/***/C/H

Newport G.C.
(01983) 525076
St Georges Down, Newport
(9) 5704 yards/***/D/H

Osborne G.C.
(01983) 295421
Osborne House Estates, East Cowes
(9) 6276 yards/**/D/H

Ryde Park House G.C.
(01983) 614809
Binstead Road, Ryde
(9) 5287 yards/**(Sun, Wed)/D/H

Ryde Westridge Golf Centre
(01983) 613131
Brading Road, Ryde
(9)/***/E

Shanklin & Sandown G.C.
(01983) 403217
The Fairway, Lake, Sandown
(18) 6000 yards/**/B/H/M

Ventnor G.C.
(01983) 853326
Steep Hill Down Road
(9) 5752 yards/***/F

CHANNEL ISLANDS

Alderney G.C.
(01481) 822835
Route des Carrieres, Alderney
(9) 2528 yards/***/D

La Grande Mare
(01481) 55313
Vason Bay, Guernsey
(18) 5026 yards/***/D

La Moye G.C.
(01534) 43401
La Moye, St Brelade, Jersey
(18) 6664 yards/***/A/H/L

Les Mielles G & C.C.
(01534) 482787
Val de la Mare, St Ouens
(18) 5610 yards/***/E/H

Royal Guernsey G.C.
(01481) 47022
L'Ancresse Vale, Guernsey
(18) 6206 yards/**/B/H

Royal Jersey G.C.
(01534) 854416
Grouville, Jersey
(18) 6059 yards/***(W/E pm)/A/H

St Clements G.C.
(01524) 821938
St Clements, Jersey
(9) 3972 yards/***(Sun pm)/D

St Pierre Park G.C.
(01481) 727039
Rohais, St Peter Port, Guernsey
(9) 2511 yards/***/D

Artist: **Henry Sandham** **THE CLUB'S THE THING** *Courtesy of:* **Rosenstiel's**

Marriott Goodwood Park Hotel & Country Club

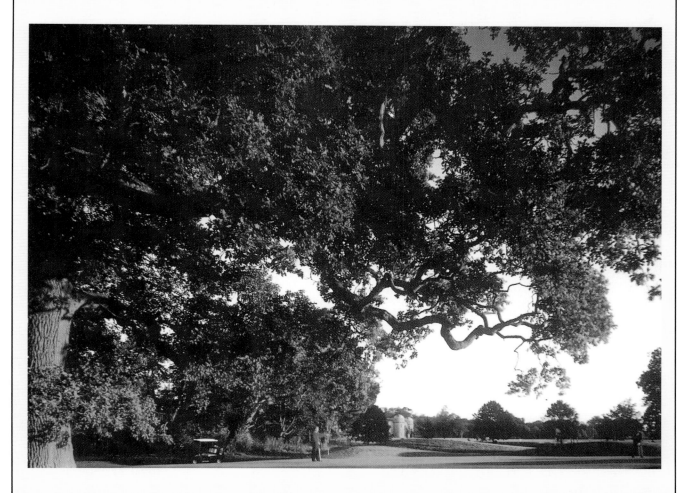

Situated within the grounds of historical Goodwood House, ancestral home to the Dukes of Richmond, the Marriott Goodwood Park Hotel & Country Club is surrounded by 12,000 acres of Goodwood Park Estate.

Sympathetically developed, the first class accommodation that distinguishes Marriott hotels provides 94 bedrooms including an elegant four poster and executive rooms.

The award-winning restaurant serves the best of modern English cuisine, and the Goodwood Sports Café Bar is available for more informal meals. The conference facilities can entertain from 10 to 150 delegates and for a uniquely sumptuous setting for a banquet or reception, the State Rooms of Goodwood House itself can be booked for functions linked to your conference.

The leisure facilities offered by the hotel include an indoor, ozone treated swimming pool, spa bath, sauna, steam room, aerobic studio, tennis courts and a fully equipped fitness gym. There is also a health and beauty salon and a solarium.

The 18 hole golf course has for its backdrop beautiful Goodwood House. Clubs and buggies are available for hire and with a golf shop, practice ground and professional tuition the player's every need, both practical and aesthetic, is catered for.

Goodwood Racing Breaks are another popular feature of the hotel with the famous racecourse only one mile away and are offered on meetings in May, June, August, and September. The elegant Glorious Goodwood meeting is held each July.

Guests wishing a more peaceful holiday will enjoy exploring the rolling Sussex Downs and a visit to Chichester is not to be missed with its harbour, cathedral and theatre. Arundel Castle is well worth a visit as is the town of Brighton.

Whether you are wanting to improve your golf handicap, visit the races, explore the sights of the South of England or simply unwind from the stress of everyday life, the thoughtful and helpful staff at Marriott Goodwood Park Hotel are waiting to welcome you.

Marriott Goodwood Park Hotel & Country Club
Goodwood
Chichester
West Sussex PO18 0QB
Tel: (01243) 775537
Fax: (01243) 520120

Sussex, where the South Downs tumble gently towards spectacular chalk cliffs or as Tennyson wrote, 'green Sussex fading into blue'. Here is the county of downland and weald, of dramatic rollercoasting cliffs, the Seven Sisters and Beachy Head.

The situation in Sussex is superb. The golf is glorious as is the countryside all around, yet at no time can you claim to be isolated—except perhaps when you visit the gorse at Ashdown Forest. West Sussex is as charming an area as one could find—the golf course of the same name is delightful and reflects the quality of some splendid nearby country house hotels—while in Rye, the golfer must visit with a packed wallet in order to seduce a member in a local drinking haunt and thus secure that elusive thing—a round of golf at Rye. A more spectacular day could not be wished for.

Tempting as it is to think of Sussex as one region, there are of course two counties, East and West, and between them they possess over sixty courses, many of which are outstandingly good. Golfers in these parts can count themselves pretty fortunate!

Close to the Coast

On a selective tour of some of the better courses on or near the Sussex coast, there seems no more logical a place to commence than in the region's south west corner and **Goodwood**—glorious Goodwood to racegoers, though the golf course is in a similarly idyllic spot, nestling in the southern foothills of the South Downs. Some four miles north of Chichester on the A286 it is in fact located just below the racecourse and has a magnificent 18th century clubhouse.

In Goodwood itself, the Marriott Goodwood Park Hotel (01243) 775537 is an excellent place to stay and very convenient for the course, but the delights of Chichester are also close at hand. Here there are a variety of attractions including numerous antique shops and the excellent Festival Theatre (01243) 781312. The Dolphin and Anchor (01243) 785121 opposite the cathedral is most welcoming and a fine place for dinner is the Droveway (01243) 528832. A theatre of the open air variety can be found at Bosham, as can the pleasant Millstream Hotel (01243) 573234.

Staying in the south west of the region, **Bognor Regis** is worth a visit—a flattish but attractive parkland course with several testing par fours. Note the Royal Norfolk (01243) 826222 in town as well as the many hotels in and around Chichester. The course at **Littlehampton** lies about seven miles east of Bognor Regis off the A259. It is the nearest one gets to a true links course in West Sussex and is always kept in first class condition. Further along the A259 at Angmering is the friendly club of **Ham Manor**. Like Bognor, it is a parkland course with an interesting layout of two distinct loops. It also boasts a beautiful clubhouse.

This corner of West Sussex is renowned for its tremendous hotels and after a day's golf there can be no better place to visit than Arundel where the Norfolk Arms (01903) 882101, a Georgian coaching inn has welcomed travellers for over two hundred years. Also to be found in Arundel are many pleasant guesthouses and inns, among them the Arden Hotel (01903) 882544, Bridge House and the Swan Hotel (01903) 882314. South of Arundel, lies Climping and the magnificent Bailiffscourt (01903) 723511, a 13th century replica offering superb comforts and an excellent restaurant. To the north of Arundel, Amberley Castle at Amberley (01798) 831992 is expensive but very good value, with a first class restaurant. Also the Boat House Restaurant (01798)

831059 has an excellent menu and is well worth a visit.

As a town Worthing is somewhat overshadowed by neighbouring Brighton (though apparently it inspired Oscar Wilde). Overshadowed or not, it has one of the leading clubs in Sussex. **Worthing** has two 18 hole courses, the Lower and the Upper. Both are exceptionally fine tests of golf. There is a reasonable public course too at Worthing, **Hill Barn**, while just north of Brighton are the new courses at **Hassocks** and **Mid Sussex**, picturesque courses at the foot of the South Downs. For a convenient 19th hole our recommendation in town is the Chatsworth Hotel (01903) 236103.

Moving into East Sussex and the town of Brighton, probably the best course in the area, and there are a number to choose from, is the **Dyke** Golf Club, located five miles north of the town centre. One of the more difficult courses in Sussex, it is on fairly high ground and provides some splendid views.

As arguably the most famous resort in Britain, it isn't surprising to find literally hundreds of hotels. Among the best are the Grand Hotel (01273) 321188 and Topps Hotel (01273) 729334. Brighton naturally has accommodation to suit everyone's taste and pockets and slightly less expensive are the Allendale Hotel (01273) 675436, the Croft Hotel and the Trouville Hotel (01273) 697384. A restaurant well worth a visit is Langans Bistro (01273) 606933.

A short distance along the A259 is Seaford. One of the older clubs in Sussex, the **Seaford** Golf Club at East Bletchington celebrated its centenary in 1987. A fair sprinkling of gorse and hawthorn is the feature of this outstanding downland course. The views too are quite spectacular being perched high above the town and overlooking the Channel. Also worth noting is the dormy house adjacent to the course.

As we continue to trek in an easterly direction, passing near to Beachy Head we arrive at Eastbourne where there are two fine courses—**Royal Eastbourne** and **Willingdon**. The former is situated very close to the town centre with the enviable address of Paradise Drive. Willingdon, north of the town off the A22, is quite a hilly course and very tough. Its interesting design has been likened to an oyster shell with the clubhouse as the pearl. In the area around Bexhill, both **Cooden Beach** and **Highwoods** are well established courses. Hotels in the area are less plentiful than in Brighton but Eastbourne does offer the exceptionally fine Grand Hotel (01323) 412345, while in Battle, Netherfield Place (01424) 774455 is extremely elegant.

Before heading inland a quick word on **Rye**. It is unquestionably one of the greatest and most natural links courses in Britain—in many people's opinion the equal of Deal and Sandwich. However, visitors are normally permitted to play only if accompanied by a Member—hence the rather flippant remark in the second paragraph! Where might such a meeting take place then? In Rye itself, the Mermaid Inn (01797) 223065 is an historic establishment standing in a steep cobbled street, while for a cosy guest house, try the Old Vicarage (01797) 222119, Little Orchard House (01797) 223831 or the listed Jeakes House (01797) 222828. A charming inn nearby is the Hayes Arms (01797) 253142 in Northiam and the Flackley Ash in Peasmarsh is a fine country house style hotel (01797) 230651.

Further Inland

If the majority of the leading courses in Sussex are located either on the coast or within a few miles of it, perhaps the most attractive courses are to be found a few more miles inland. **Piltdown**, two miles to the west of Uckfield, is a good example. Piltdown is a natural heathland course with a beautiful setting and somewhat unusually, although it shares the curiosity with Royal Ashdown, it has no bunkers—though there are certainly enough natural hazards to set the golfer thinking.

Leaving the Piltdown Men and crossing the boundary from East to West, moving from Uckfield to Cuckfield, **Haywards Heath** stands right in the middle of Sussex. A very good heathland course this, but the pride of West Sussex is undoubtedly Pulborough—the **West Sussex Golf Club**. Along with **Royal Ashdown**, **Mannings Heath** and **East Sussex National** it is featured on a later page. Not too far from Pulborough, Brian Barnes has been the driving force behind the fine new development at **West Chiltington** and where the possibility for visitors of a weekend game is a definite bonus! Still in the West three more to note are in the north of the county, and very convenient for Gatwick, the **Ifield** Golf and Country Club, **Copthorne** and the **Cottesmore** (01293) 528256, which is also a luxurious country club in very attractive surroundings. Another popular course is found at **Cowdray Park**—very pleasant and ideal should you happen to play polo as well!

Places to stay? For Cowdray, the Spread Eagle (01730) 816911 at Midhurst—the hotel and restaurant are both excellent. Similar praise can be given to the Angel (01730) 812421—a decidedly fine hotel overlooking Cowdray Park. In Bepton, the Park House Hotel (01730) 812880 is also delightful. For Pulborough, Little Thakeham (01903) 744416 at Storrington is outstanding, as is Horsted Place (01825) 750581, now linked with East Sussex National and offering excellent accommodation. The beautiful South Lodge Hotel (01403) 891711 at Lower Beeding is centrally situated for the above courses and is especially convenient for Mannings Heath.

Towards the north of East Sussex, **Dale Hill** is a much improved course with a stylish new hotel (01580) 200112 attached. Considerable investment here has resulted in both a course of challenging quality and a hotel of the highest calibre. Next comes a classic pair: **Royal Ashdown Forest** (see ahead) and **Crowborough Beacon**—two wonderfully scenic courses where the heather and gorse simply run riot. Crowborough's course is situated some 800 feet above sea level and on clear days the sea can be glimpsed from the clubhouse. Sir Arthur Conan Doyle would have taken in this view on many occasions for he lived adjacent to the course and was captain of the golf club in 1910. It really is the most beautiful of courses and has in the par three 6th one of the best short holes in Britain.

Although there may be closer places, the 16th century Middle House Hotel (01435) 872146 at Mayfield is recommended for a stay near Crowborough. As for Royal Ashdown, several ideas here. For convenience the Ashdown Forest Hotel (01342) 824866 has its own fine course in addition to being adjacent to the royal club. In Forest Row the Chequers Hotel (01342) 824394 is popular,and the Brambletye Hotel (01342) 824144 and Roebuck Hotel (01342) 823811 both come highly recommended. Nearer East Grinstead is glorious Gravetye Manor (01342) 810567 a restaurant of excellence. In Wych Cross, the Ashdown Park Hotel (01342) 824988 is well worth a visit—9 holes of golf and concessions at two good nearby courses, other leisure facilities are also good. East Grinstead also boasts an excellent guesthouse in the shape of the Cranfield Lodge (01342) 321251, very close to the new **Sweetwoods Park** 18 hole course at Cowden and another newcomer, **Chartham Park**, at Felcourt.

In the course of our brief trip no doubt several splendid 19th hole hotels have been omitted, but such is life! In order to fit in more restaurants, please forgive this somewhat hasty appraisal of some of the best in both counties. In Rusper, Ghyll Manor (01293) 871571 is first class and also provides a comfortable resting place. Returning to Alfriston, there is Moonrakers (01323) 870472—try a Hot Sussex Smokie! In Herstmonceux, the Sundial (01323) 832217 is French, whilst Jevington's Hungry Monk (01323) 482178 is outstanding. In Midhurst try Mida, in Pulborough plump for Stane Street Hollow (01798) 872819 and for a special occasion try either the Old Forge (01903) 43402 or Manley's (01903) 742331 in Storrington.

No trip to the heart of Sussex would be complete either without a visit to one of the many country houses, castles, pubs or inns. Here are a few more random thoughts for life beyond the 18th green: the White Horse Inn (01243) 535219 in Chilgrove has an excellent restaurant and the wine list is almost beyond compare, while the Shepherd and Dog in Fulking and the Lickfold Inn at Lickfold are also good. Aside from the antiques of Chichester, Arundel (an excellent castle to see here) and Petworth, which offers the superb Petworth House, there is a summer of unsurpassed opera at Glyndebourne. In contrast, a totally flamboyant place to spend time is Brighton. The streets in the old town offer several bargains while the Grand Pavilion is as striking as ever. Returning to the subject of castles, Bodiam in East Sussex is not too widely known, but nonetheless quite majestic. Any thoughts for the player who had trouble in the groping gorse at Ashdown? Well, Blackboys, the pub in the village of the same name is welcoming and resuscitating as is the Roebuck in Wych Cross (01342) 823811. Sussex, in short, is a true delight, both on and off the fairways.

*Artist: **Gwyn Hughes GOLF***
*Courtesy of: **Rosenstiel's***

West Sussex (Pulborough)

*'Concentrate your mind on the match until
you are dormy. Then look at the surrounding
scenery and expatiate on its beauties.'*
(AJ Robertson)

In the opinion of many, West Sussex, or Pulborough as it is commonly known, is quite simply the most beautiful course in England. The setting is the South Downs and seclusion is total. Commander George Hillyard founded the club in 1930 having conceived the idea, so the story goes, as he looked out of his bathroom window one day while taking his morning shave! (His house, it should be explained, overlooked the present layout). The course was designed by Sir Guy Campbell and Major CK Hutchinson and opened for play in October 1930.

In a similar vein to Woodhall Spa in Lincolnshire, Pulborough has often been described as something of an oasis, the surrounding countryside being predominantly meadow and marshland with the course lying on sandy soil and heather running throughout. Heather naturally adds charm to any golf course but it is perhaps the magnificent spread of pines, oaks and silver birch trees that are most striking at Pulborough.

Colin Simpson is the present **Club Secretary**; he may be contacted via the **West Sussex Golf Club, Wiggonholt, Pulborough, West Sussex RH20 2EN (01798) 872563** or by fax on (01798) 872033 Visitors are welcome, but strictly by appointment only; the same applies to golfing societies. It should also be noted that three ball and four ball matches are not generally permitted—singles and foursomes being preferred. The only specific restrictions on times visitors can play are before 9.30am (throughout the week), on Fridays and at weekends. The green fees for 1998 are set at £40 for a single round or £50 for a day ticket. One final introduction: **Tim Packham** is the club's **Professional**, and he may be reached by telephone on **(01798) 872426.**

While Pulborough may enjoy a gloriously peaceful setting situated right in the heart of the Sussex countryside, it could hardly be described as remote and is easily accessible from all directions. The club's precise location is about two miles east of Pulborough just off the A283 road to Storrington. The A283 links Pulborough to the outskirts of Brighton on the south coast and to Milford (near Guildford) to the north. For those approaching from westerly directions the A272 from Winchester is likely to help—it joins the A283 at Petworth approximately five miles from Pulborough. Motoring from the London area the quickest route is probably to take the M23 towards Gatwick joining the A264 at Crawley and travelling through Horsham. The A264 merges into the A29 near Billingshurst which in turn joins with Pulborough.

One of the features of Pulborough is its conspicuous absence of a par five beyond the first hole—a hole which in any event becomes a four when played from the tees of the day. At 6221 yards, (SSS 70) the par of 68 is a difficult one to match. With none of the par fours being overly short there aren't any really obvious birdie opportunities. Perhaps the best known hole on the course is the par three 6th; measuring 224 yards it requires an exceptionally accurate tee shot across water to a small green that has an out-of-bounds and tall trees directly behind it. Henry Longhurst, a great admirer of Pulborough, very aptly said of the 6th, 'If ever there was an all or nothing hole, this is it.' Immediately after the potential disaster of the 6th, the 7th requires a long uphill drive to carry over some thick heather and scrub not to mention an enormous sand bunker. With holes of such a nature and quality as the 6th and 7th it isn't unrealistic to draw a comparison between this corner of Pulborough and Pine Valley in New Jersey. It is a brave comparison (and an enormous compliment) because the North American course is generally considered to be the finest and perhaps most naturally beautiful inland course in the world.

The 6th and 7th are not the only outstanding holes, mind you: the 4th, 5th and 8th are equally memorable while on the back nine perhaps the 10th, 13th, 16th and 17th are worthy of special praise (even expatiation!) As for its 19th, West Sussex has a very comfortable clubhouse offering full catering facilities including two bars. A jacket and tie should be worn in all public rooms.

Henry Longhurst is only one of a number of celebrated admirers of Pulborough and the late Bobby Locke, four times Open Champion, considered it his favourite English course. While no major professional tournament has been played over the course (again there is a parallel to be drawn with Pine Valley) the club has hosted several national amateur championships—both men's and ladies'.

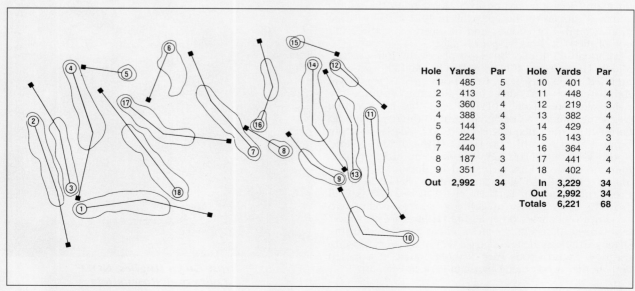

Hole	Yards	Par		Hole	Yards	Par
1	485	5		10	401	4
2	413	4		11	448	4
3	360	4		12	219	3
4	388	4		13	382	4
5	144	3		14	429	4
6	224	3		15	143	3
7	440	4		16	364	4
8	187	3		17	441	4
9	351	4		18	402	4
Out	**2,992**	**34**		**In**	**3,229**	**34**
				Out	**2,992**	**34**
				Totals	**6,221**	**68**

Royal Ashdown Forest

Although it is now less than an hour's drive from the frantic chaos of Greater London, Ashdown Forest is a place of great beauty, charm and tranquillity. And so it should be, for it was here, somewhere deep in this secluded forest of pine and silver birch, that the most famous of all 'Golden Bears', Winnie The Pooh pursued his never ending quest for honey. Such is the setting for one of Britain's most fortunate golf clubs.

In 1988 Royal Ashdown Forest celebrated its centenary. It was on Christmas Eve over a hundred years ago that the Reverend A T Scott teed up his ball and struck the very first shot. The course has changed little over the years, a fact which clearly speaks volumes for the original layout. The club acquired the title 'Royal' during Queen Victoria's reign and long before the turn of the century had established itself as one of the finest tests of golf in southern England.

Many great players have been associated with Royal Ashdown Forest over the years. The Cantelupe Club, the associate club connected to Royal Ashdown, included Abe Mitchell and Alf Padgham among its ranks and several noted amateurs have improved their technique on this most challenging course.

Casual visitors are welcomed at Royal Ashdown—rather more so, it must be said, than at some of the south east's leading courses. A recognised club handicap is, however, a requirement and it is normally advisable to telephone the club before finalising any plans. Not surprisingly the course is very popular in the summer months.

The club **Secretary, David Scrivens,** can be contacted via the **Royal Ashdown Forest Golf Club, Forest Row, East Sussex RH18 5LR tel: (01342) 822018.** Those wishing to organise a society meeting should write to Mr. Scrivens at the above address. Societies can normally be accommodated during the week, Tuesday being an exception. The green fees for 1998 were set at £35 per round (£40 per day) for weekdays with £40 per round (£45 per day) payable at weekends and on bank holidays. Visitors should note that singles and foursomes are preferred. The club **Professional** is **Martyn Landsborough** who took over in 1990 from Alf Padgham's cousin, Hector, who had been the professional for over 40 years. Martyn can be reached on **(01342) 822247.**

The club is located within Ashdown Forest, approximately 4 miles south of East Grinstead. Motoring from London and the north the A22 is by far the most direct route. This can be joined from the M25 at Junction 6. The A22 should be followed for some 4 miles beyond East Grinstead as far as Forest Row. There one should take the B2110 Hartfield road turning right after a quarter of a mile on to Chapel Lane where the club can be found. Approaching from the South the A22 can be joined from a number of roads north of Eastbourne.

The generally held view is that Royal Ashdown Forest is a particularly difficult course. On several holes a lengthy tee shot will be required in order to find the safety of the fairway. The ever-present stream and the considerable scattering of gorse and heather create a multitude of problems for the wayward golfer—and as if they were not enough, on several of the holes the fairway is exceptionally narrow and that beautiful forest will gratefully accept the result of a slice or a hook. The most celebrated hole at Royal Ashdown is probably the short 6th, the 'Island Hole' while the best of the par fours is probably the 17th with its exhilarating downhill approach.

Despite the variety of hazards, of all the country's leading courses Royal Ashdown Forest must surely be unique in not possessing a single bunker. Bernard Darwin is doubtless not the only golfer who failed to discover this fact until the conclusion of his game; as he put it, 'It is only at the end of a round that we realise with a pleasurable shock that there is not a single hideous rampart or so much as a pot bunker.' The club was prevented long ago by the Forestry Commission, or the then equivalent, from creating bunkers and their absence now forms part of the character and charm of the course. Furthermore, the undulating nature of the landscape produces some truly magnificent views over the forest and beyond.

The attractive clubhouse offers a very high standard of catering. A light lunch, such as a ploughman's, can be obtained whilst a full four course meal can also be arranged. During the months of November and December a full English breakfast is available—a welcome facility which many clubs would do well to copy. Golfers, like the forest's most famous inhabitant are hungry animals and some are more than quick to claim that the missed three footer is a result of a missed breakfast!

Hole	Yards	Par	Hole	Yards	Par
1	332	4	10	485	5
2	384	4	11	249	3
3	334	4	12	568	5
4	356	4	13	367	4
5	512	5	14	202	3
6	128	3	15	312	4
7	372	4	16	407	4
8	501	5	17	473	4
9	143	3	18	352	4
Out	**3,062**	**36**	**In**	**3,415**	**36**
			Out	**3,062**	**36**
			Totals	**6,477**	**72**

Mannings Heath

Mannings Heath is an extraordinary place. You stand on the terrace of what is possibly the finest 19th hole in England and you watch golfers descend into 'Sodom' and 'Gomorrah'. It is not quite what it seems. It is just that whoever named the opening holes on the **Waterfall Course** at Mannings Heath had a rather wry sense of humour (that or a wretched golf game). The perilous journey does not end at the 2nd as the next hole is called 'Gateway' and it leads immediately to 'Hell's Corner'. Presumably the gates of hell lie somewhere in between.

The visiting golfer shouldn't be alarmed. Mannings Heath is actually one of the most welcoming, as well as one of the most scenic courses in southern England. Nestling amidst beautiful countryside on the edge of the South Downs, the club was founded in 1905. For the best part of a century it has enjoyed a reputation as the 'hidden jewel of Sussex'! But Mannings Heath is unlikely to remain quite so hidden in the future. Two recent developments have ensured that.

The reference above to the 19th hole was not exaggerated. Mannings Heath may indeed possess the finest clubhouse in the country, and surely none is better appointed. The building in question is a beautifully restored manor house known as Fullers. Prior to the purchase of the golf club by its present owners in 1989 it was a private family residence. Today it has been tastefully converted into a clubhouse and is sumptuously furnished. Great comfort and great character combine to create a wonderfully relaxed golfing environment. . . the perfect 19th hole.

The other major development was the opening in 1996 of a second 18 holes. Sunningdale has an Old and a New, East Sussex National has an East and a West—now Mannings Heath has the **Kingfisher Course** designed by David Williams. Measuring 6217 yards, par 70, from the back markers and with full USGA greens and tees, the new course complements the old perfectly. The club cannot remain a 'hidden' jewel when it has so much to offer.

Visitors (individuals and groups) wishing to play either course can make arrangements by contacting **Jackie Brew** at the golf club on tel **(01403) 210228** and fax (01403) 270974. Mannings Heath is located two miles south of Horsham off the A28 Brighton Road. The club's full address is **Mannings Heath Golf Club, Fullers, Hammerpond Road, Horsham, West Sussex RH13 6PG.** The 1998 green fees for both courses are set at £32 per round, £42 per day midweek, and £40 per round, £55 per day at weekends.

A further two miles beyond the golf club at Lower Beeding is South Lodge—a sister property and one of the finest country house hotels in southern England. Special golfing breaks in conjunction with the club are available throughout the week.

Measuring 6378 yards, par 73 from the back markers (5405 yards, par 73 from the ladies' tees) the Waterfall Course comprises an interesting mix of woodland, parkland and heathland holes. The terrain is naturally undulating throughout—as the opening drive and the final approach underline. Mature trees line the majority of the fairways and water, invariably in the form of a winding stream, affects no fewer than eleven holes.

The most memorable holes on the Waterfall course include all three of the short holes: the 5th, 'Punchbowl', the 10th, 'Waterfall' (both these holes have a superbly elevated tee and a tantalisingly small green) and the 14th, 'Blaster', which was no doubt christened by our friend from the opening paragraph. The most celebrated two-shotter is undoubtedly the 11th, 'Valley'. It is a superb natural golf hole and features a sunken fairway bordered for its entire length by a seemingly magnetic stream and a stage-like green surrounded by trees.

Waterfall Course

Hole	Yards	Par	Hole	Yards	Par
1	325	4	10	141	3
2	289	4	11	368	4
3	399	4	12	368	4
4	372	4	13	486	5
5	184	3	14	153	3
6	377	4	15	247	4
7	425	4	16	466	5
8	499	5	17	487	5
9	376	4	18	416	4
Out	3,246	36	In	3,132	37
			Out	3,246	36
			Totals	6,378	73

One of the best kept secrets in West Sussex, South Lodge Hotel captures the essence of Victorian style and elegance, with an atmosphere of warmth and hospitality, hidden amongst 90 acres of beautiful gardens and parkland, with views over the rolling South Downs.

Built in 1883, this grey stone mansion, strewn with wisteria, was once the home of the Godman family; Frederick Ducane Godman, a keen botanist and explorer, collected hundreds of rare shrubs and trees and an outstanding variety of rhododendra and camellias, which today make the gardens at the hotel such a delight.

Dining at South Lodge is always a special occasion. In the elegant wood panelled Camellia Restaurant guests enjoy innovative menus created by top chef Lewis Hamblet, featuring local meat, game and fish, with herbs and soft fruit grown in the hotel's own wall garden.

Each of the 39 bedrooms and suites is perfectly appointed. All are individually decorated in the true country house style, sympathetically incorporating all the modern amenities one expects to find in a first class hotel.

South Lodge is an excellent base for golfers, with Royal Ashdown, East Sussex National and Pulborough all within 45 minutes drive—not to mention the two excellent championship parkland courses at nearby Mannings Heath. Racegoers too are well catered for, with Goodwood, Lingfield, Brighton, Fontwell Park and Plumpton all within easy reach—a pleasant drive through picturesque countryside.

Guests staying at the hotel may enjoy a variety of activities ranging from coarse fishing to tennis, croquet or petanque. It is also an ideal location for exploring the wealth of National Trust houses and gardens that Sussex has to offer; Petworth and Arundel are within easy reach, along with the charming coastal town of Brighton, with its famous Lanes.

South Lodge Hotel
Lower Beeding nr Horsham
West Sussex
Tel: (01403) 891711
Fax: (01403) 891766

East Sussex National

Move over Sunningdale, Wentworth and Walton Heath! These three great championship venues, all situated in the magnificent heathland belt of Surrey and Berkshire, have had to make room for a newcomer from the heart of rural Sussex.

East Sussex National has two great golf courses, the East and West, which were officially opened for play as recently as April 1990. Both were designed by the American, Robert E Cupp, formerly Jack Nicklaus' senior designer. For the first time in Great Britain, bent grasses were used throughout from tee to green and the instant result was golf course conditioning of a type never witnessed before in this country.

Both courses measure in excess of 7000 yards from their championship tees and are similarly challenging but quite different in appearance. The East Course is the 'stadium' course and was specifically designed with a view to staging big events (the European Open has already been played over the course twice) hence the gentle 'gallery mounding' very evident around the 15th and 18th greens. The West Course is more intimate than the East. The landscape rises and falls quite sharply in parts. The surrounding woodland is more dense but because of the climbs there are many spectacular views over the South Downs.

East Sussex National was first conceived in the mid 1980s when a Canadian entrepreneur purchased Horsted Place, an elegant Victorian manor house which he immediately converted into one of Britain's leading country house hotels. Various parcels of adjoining land were also acquired which, when pieced together, totalled a massive 1100 acres of prime Sussex countryside. Construction began in May 1988 on the two 18 hole championship courses and, only 23 months later, both opened for play.

Aside from the golf courses, and of course Horsted Place, East Sussex National boasts superb golf practice facilities, including three full length academy holes, one of the best golf shops in the country and a striking 27,000 sq ft clubhouse.

Individuals, groups and corporate societies are welcome at East Sussex. Visitors will invariably play the East Course as the West is reserved for members. Bookings can be made by telephoning **Reservations** on **(01825) 880232/880231** or by fax on (01825) 880012. The

visitors' green fees in summer 1998 are £55 for 18 holes, £60 for 18 holes and a three course lunch and £80 for 36 holes and a three course lunch. Seasonal discounted rates including lunch/brunch are also available. The **Director of Golf** is **Phil Lewin** and all membership and corporate enquiries can be dealt with through the Sales Office on the above number. The address for written correspondence is **East Sussex National Golf Club, Little Horsted, Uckfield, East Sussex TN22 5ES.**

There are many outstanding holes on the **East** Course but perhaps the par fives are especially memorable. Three of the four, the 7th, 10th and 14th are as good a trio as one is likely to find on any inland course, anywhere. Of these, only the 10th is realistically reachable in two shots and then only after a brave downhill second is successfully hit over water—a hole not too dissimilar to the 15th at Augusta. There is also a great finish to the East Course, with the par four 17th being perhaps the best hole on either course.

Although the challenge isn't any greater on the **West** Course, in most people's minds it has the greater number of 'pretty' holes. In fact, 'provocatively spectacular' might be the description of some. Anyone wishing to put together a 'dream nine holes' could do worse than select the 1st, 2nd, 3rd, 9th, 10th, 12th, 13th, 14th and 18th on the East Sussex National West Course. This collection would provide two outstanding short holes, on both of which the tee shot must flirt with water; a pair of genuine par fives and five two-shot holes ranging from a drive and a short iron (the dog-leg 1st) to a truly intimidating stroke one hole (the monstrous 14th). And what a dramatic finale the 18th provides! In his course notes, architect Robert Cupp gives an interesting commentary on the closing holes of the West Course. Having metaphorically walked on to the back tee at the 18th he holds his breath and surveys the view ahead:

'The player has been restricted at fourteen, tempted at fifteen, devilled at sixteen and exhausted at seventeen. Now, he stands on the elevated tee, looking across a deep chasm to a fairway lined right and left by giant oaks, and a green guarded by huge bunkers and the clubhouse beyond. The word here is "test". The reaction in tournament conditions is clammy hands'.

West Course					
Hole	Yards	Par	Hole	Yards	Par
1	363	4	10	404	4
2	517	5	11	423	4
3	136	3	12	520	5
4	354	4	13	184	3
5	504	5	14	450	4
6	396	4	15	365	4
7	192	3	16	117	3
8	408	4	17	566	5
9	392	4	18	365	4
Out	3,262	36	In	3,394	36
			Out	3,262	36
			Totals	6,565	72

Sussex Complete Golf

WEST SUSSEX

Avisford Park Hotel & G.C.
(01243) 554611
Walberton, Arundel
(9) 3009 yards/***/D

Bognor Regis G.C.
(01243) 821929
Downview Road, Felpham,
(18) 6238 yards/**/B - A/H

Burgess Hill
(01444) 870615
Cuckfield Road, Burgess Hill
(9) 4433 yards/***/F

Chartham Park G.C.
(01342) 870340
Felcourt, East Grinstead
(18) 6688 yards/***/C

Chichester Golf Centre
(01243) 533833
Hoe Farm, Hunston
(18) 6174 yards/***/C
(18) 6461 yards/***/B

Copthorne G.C.
(01342) 712508
Borers Arms Road, Copthorne
(18) 6505 yards/**/B

Cottesmore G. & C.C.
(01293) 528256
Buchan Hill, Pease Pottage, Crawley
(18) 6280 yards/***/A
(18) 5489 yards/***/B

Cowdray Park G.C.
(01730) 813599
Petworth Road, Midhurst
(18) 6212 yards/**/B/H

Effingham Park G.C.
(01342) 716528
West Park Road, Copthorne
(9) 1749 yards/***/D

Foxbridge G.C
(01403) 753303
Foxbridge Lane, Plaistow
(9) 3015 yards/***/F/G

Gatwick Manor G.C.
(01293) 538587
Lowfield Heath, Crawley Heath
(9) 1246 yards/***/E

Goodwood G.C.
(01243) 774968
Goodwood, Chichester
(18) 6401 yards/***/B - A/H

Goodwood Park G.& C.C.
(01243) 775987
(18) 6530 yards/**/D/H

Ham Manor G.C.
(01903) 783732
Angmering, Littlehampton
(18) 6216 yards/***/F/H

Hassocks G.C.
(01273) 846990
London Road, Hassocks
(18) 5754 yards/***/D

Haywards Heath G.C.
(01444) 414457
High Beech Lane, Haywards Heath
(18) 6206 yards/***/B/H

Hill Barn G.C.
(01903) 237301
Hill Barn Lane, Worthing
(18) 6224 yards/***/D

Horsham Golf Park
(01403) 271525
Worthing Road, Horsham
(9) 2061 yards/***/E

Ifield G.& C.C.
(01293) 520222
Rusper Road, Ifield, Crawley
(18) 6314 yards/**/B/H

Littlehampton G.C.
(01903) 717170
Rope Walk, Littlehampton
(18) 6244 yards/**/B

Mannings Heath G.C.
(01403) 210228
Hammerpond Road, Mannings Heath
(18) 6378 yards/**/A/H
(18) 6217 yards/**/A/H

Osiers Farm G.C.
(01798) 344097
Osiers Farm, Petworth
(18) 6191 yards/***/E

Paxhill Park G.C.
(01444) 484467
Lindfield, Haywards Heath
(18) 6196 yards/***/D

Pease Pottage G.C.
(01293) 521706
Horsham Road, Pease Pottage,
(9) 3511 yards/***/E

Pyecombe G.C.
(01273) 845372
Pyecombe, Brighton
(18) 6234 yards/**/C

Selsey G.C.
(01243) 602203
Golf Links Lane, Selsey, Chichester
(9) 5834 yards/***/D

Shillingtree G.C.
(01428) 653237
Chiddingfield, Godalming
(9) 2500 yards/***/D

Singing Hills G.C.
(01273) 835353
Albourne, Brighton
(9) 2826 yards/***/B/H
(9) 3253 yards/***/B/H
(9) 3348 yards/***/B/H

Slinfold Park G. & C.C.
(01403) 791154
Stane Street, Slinford, Horsham
(18) 6450 yards/***/B

Tilgate Forest G.C.
(01293) 530103
Titmus Drive, Crawley
(18) 6359 yards/***/D

West Chiltington G.C.
(01798) 813574
Broadford Bridge Road,
(18) 5969 yards/***/D

West Sussex G.C.
(01798) 872563
Hurston Lane, Pulborough
(18) 6221 yards/**/F/H/L

Worthing G.C.
(01903) 260801
Links Road, Worthing
(18) 6530 yards/***/F/H
(18) 5243 yards/***/F/H

EAST SUSSEX

Ashdown Forest Hotel G.C.
(01342) 824866
Chapel Lane, Forest Row
(18) 5510 yards/***/F

Beauport Park G.C.
(01424) 852977
St Leonards-on-Sea
(18) 6033 yards/***/F

Brighton and Hove G.C.
(01273) 556482
Dyke Road, Brighton
(9) 5722 yards/***/C

Cooden Beach G.C.
(01424) 842040
Cooden Sea Road, Cooden
(18) 6470 yards/***/B - A/H

Crowborough Beacon G.C.
(01892) 661511
Beacon Road, Crowborough
(18) 6279 yards/**/B/H/L

Dale Hill G.C.
(01580) 200112
Ticehurst, Wadhurst
(18) 6150 yards/***/B - A/H

Dewlands Manor G.C.
(01892) 852266
Cottage Hill, Rotherfield
(9) 3186 yards/***/B

Dyke G.C.
(01273) 857296
Dyke Road, Brighton
(18) 6611 yards/***(Sun)/B - A

Eastbourne Downs G.C.
(01323) 720827
East Dean Road, Eastbourne
(18) 6635 yards/***/D

Eastbourne Golfing Park
(01323) 520400
Lottbridge Drove, Eastbourne
(9) 5046 yards/***/D

East Brighton G.C.
(01273) 604838
Roedean Road, Brighton
(18) 6436 yards/***/H

East Sussex National G.C.
(01825) 880232
Little Horsted, Uckfield
(18) 7154 yards/*/A
(18) 7138 yards/***/A

Hastings G.C.
(01424) 852977
Battle Road, St Leonards-on-Sea
(18) 6248 yards/***/F

Highwoods G.C.
(01424) 212625
Ellerslie Lane, Bexhill-on-Sea
(18)6218 yards/***/B/H

Hollingbury G.C.
(01273) 500086
Ditchling Road, Brighton
(18) 6415 yards/***/D

Holtye G.C.
(01342) 850635
Holtye, Edenbridge
(9) 5325 yards/***/C

Horam Park G.C.
(014353) 813477
Chiddingly Road, Horam,
(9) 5864 yards/***/D

Lewes G.C.
(01273) 473245
Chapel Hill, Lewes
(18) 6218 yards/**/C

Mid Sussex G.C.
(01273) 846547
Spatham Lane, Ditchling
(18) 6227 yards/**/C

Nevill G.C.
(01892) 525818
Benhall Mill Road, Tunbridge Wells
(18) 6336 yards/**/A/H

Peacehaven G.C.
(01273) 512571
Brighton Road, Newhaven
(9) 5235 yards/***/D

Piltdown G.C.
(01825) 722033
Piltdown, Uckfield
(18) 6070 yards/**/B/H/L

Royal Ashdown Forest G.C.
(01342) 822018
Chapel Lane, Forest Row
(18) 6477 yards/**/B - A/H
(18) 5586 yards/**/B - A/H

Royal Eastbourne G.C.
(01323) 729738
Paradise Drive, Eastbourne
(18) 6109 yards/***/B
(9) 2147 yards/***/E

Rye G.C.
(01797) 225241
Camber, Rye
(18) 6301 yards/***/G
(9) 6625 yards/***/G

Seaford G.C.
(01323) 892442
East Blatchington, Seaford
(18) 6233 yards/**/F

Seaford Head G.C.
(01323) 894843
Southdown Road, Seaford
(18) 5812 yards/***/D

Sedlescombe G.C.
(01424) 870898
Kent Street, Sedlescombe
(18) 6218 yards/**/F/H

Sweetwoods Park G.C.
(01342) 850729
Cowden, Edenbridge
(18) 6400 yards/***/D

Waterhall G.C.
(01273) 508658
Devil's Dyke Road, Brighton
(18) 5775 yards/***/D

Wellshurst G.& C.C
(01435) 813636
North Street, Hellingly
(18) 5717 yards/***/C - B

West Hove G.C.
(01273) 419738
Church Farm, Hangleton, Hove
(18) 6201 yards/***/F

Willingdon G.C.
(01323) 410981
Southdown Road, Eastbourne
(18) 6049 yards/**/H

Artist: **Julian Barrow ROYAL ST GEORGE'S** *Courtesy of:* **Burlington Gallery**

From the mysterious and desolate lands of Romney Marsh to the famous White Cliffs of Dover; from the rich orchards of the Garden of England to the outskirts of Greater London; from the windswept links of Sandwich and Deal to the secluded parks of Belmont and Knole—a county of great contrasts.

Kent's reputation as one of the country's greatest golfing counties has been built around a three mile stretch of links land lying midway between St Margaret's Bay and Pegwell Bay. Within this short distance lie three Open Championship courses: **Prince's** (1932), **Royal Cinque Ports** (1909 and 1920) and **Royal St George's**. Kent has a few other fine links courses but the golfer who sticks hard to the coast will be missing out on some of the most enjoyable inland golf southern England has to offer.

Golfing Inland

In common with each of the counties that border Greater London, many of Kent's courses are gradually finding themselves more in London than in Kent. When the Blackheath golfers left their famous Common and set up base at Eltham they were doubtless surrounded by the green fields of Kent. Even Charles Darwin's village of Orpington is now feeling the pinch but the new course **Chelsfield Lakes** at Orpington is worth exploring, and happily the **West Kent** Golf Club near Bromley and nearby **Lullingstone Park** provide pleasant retreats.

Enough grousing! The ancient town of Sevenoaks is categorically in Kent and a very fortunate place too with **Wildernesse** Golf Club to the north and **Knole Park** to the south. The former is rated one of the finest inland courses in the county. With narrow fairways and quite thickly wooded, it is also one of the toughest. Knole Park is especially scenic and is one of several Kentish courses that enjoy stately surroundings, being laid out in the handsome deer park of Lord Sackville. Both Wildernesse and Knole suffered during the great hurricane of October '87 but then so did many courses in southern England.

In the south west of the county, Tunbridge Wells is a very pretty, if congested, old town. **Nevill** Golf Club is just over the border in Sussex and there are 36 holes at the **Edenbridge** Golf and Country Club, but the most exciting developments in this area are the **Hever** Golf Club which is located adjacent to the famous castle and the Anglo-Japanese creation at **Moatlands** at Brenchley. The visitor to Kent should also note **Nizels** Golf Club - a fine course and a rustic clubhouse to delight the most disillusioned golfer.

For a stopover in Sevenoaks, the Royal Oak Hotel (01732) 451109 is comfortable, as is the Bull Hotel (01732) 885522 in nearby Wrotham Heath. A number of fine restaurants are also close at hand. They include Cheevers (01892) 545524—a well regarded establishment—and the outstanding Thackeray's House (01892) 511921, both in Tunbridge Wells. If you require a place to stay in Tunbridge Wells, the Royal Wells Inn (01892) 511188 is particularly good value with a fine restaurant, and for a second place try the Spa Hotel (01892) 520331. Finally in the south western corner of the county there is an outstanding pub—great for lunches—at Speldhurst, namely the 13th century George and Dragon.

To the north of the county, both **Mid Kent's** downland course at Gravesend and **Rochester and Cobham** Park are handy for those travelling along the A2 although Rochester and Cobham is currently under alteration due to the Channel rail link. Further along this road is the attractive town of Faversham and south of the town off the A251 is Belmont Park, the estate of Lord Harris and the home of **Faversham** Golf Club. Here golf is played in the most tranquil of settings and can be particularly delightful

in autumn when the fairways abound with countless strolling pheasants.

Beyond the 18th green a few ideas emerge for a 19th hole. In Shorne, the Inn On The Lake (01474) 823333 is a fairly modern place to stay. An alternative for pub lovers is the Dickensian Leather Bottle (01474) 814327 in Cobham which also has some comfortable bedrooms. More expensive accommodation is located near Ash Green in the alarmingly named village of Fawkham where the Brands Hatch Place (01474) 872239 offers tremendous comfort and a good restaurant. Two pubs to note in the area are the Golden Eagle in Burham and the particularly pleasant and aptly named Little Gem in Aylesford. Close to Ash Green and Brands Hatch, golfers might wish to note the new **London** Golf Club, a 36 hole multi-million pound venture including a Jack Nicklaus- designed championship course. It should be emphasised, however, that this is a very private club and visitors can only play the Nicklaus (Heritage Course) as guests of a member. Back towards Faversham, a fine place to rest the spikes is the Tanyard Hotel (01622) 744705 at Boughton Monchelsea, an excellent restaurant as well as charming bedrooms are to be found. If it's just quality fare that is required, then Faversham itself houses the extremely popular Reads (01795) 535344.

Leaving Faversham, famous pheasants and all, we must make a pilgrimage. The **Canterbury** Golf Club, situated to the east of the beautiful cathedral city along the A27 is well worth a visit. Surprisingly undulating, it is a first class parkland course—one of the best in the county. South of Canterbury (via A2 and A260) at Barham is the **Broome Park** Golf and Country Club, set in the grounds of yet another famous country house—this time a beautiful 300 year old mansion, the former home of Lord Kitchener. It too is a very pleasant parkland course and quite lengthy. Whether it's the proliferation of nearby golf courses (Sandwich and Deal are just 15 miles away) or the cathedral, or even the glorious Kent countryside that attracts most, Canterbury deserves more than a short visit. Perhaps the leading hotel which also houses a commendable restaurant is the County (01227) 766266. The House of Agnes Hotel (01227) 472185 can also be recommended, and just outside the city, Howfield Manor (01227) 738294 at Chartham Hatch is a charming small country house hotel with a good restaurant. Ersham Lodge (01227) 463174 and Magnolia House (01227) 765121 also receive many favourable reports. The aforementioned glorious countryside is riddled with village pubs: two of note are the Duck Inn at Petts Bottom and the White Horse at Chilham Castle.

Maidstone may not have the appeal of Canterbury but to the south east of this busy commuter town is one of England's most attractive 'pay and play' golf courses, **Leeds Castle**. The castle itself was described by Lord Conway as the most beautiful in the world and the setting really is quite idyllic. There are nine very individual holes and as it's a public course (like Lullingstone Park, mentioned above, and **Cobtree Manor Park** on the Chatham Road) there are no general restrictions on times of play (although it can naturally get very busy). Another fairly recent golfing addition to the area is **Tudor Park** near Bearsted. Like Broome Park it is part of a country club. The golf course was designed by Donald Steel and is especially popular with golfing societies. The Tudor Park Hotel (01622) 734334 is predictably convenient.

The golf course at **Ashford** is pretty much in the middle of the county, and is strongly worth inspecting. Ashford is a heathland type course, which in itself is fairly unique to Kent and where visitors are always made to feel welcome. We're now in the heart of the Kent Downs and a variety

Artist: **William Pimm PUTTING** *Courtesy of:* **Rosenstiels**

of fine establishments beckon. Eastwell Manor (01233) 635751 takes pride of place; elegant and relaxing with a splendid restaurant—in fact outstanding in every way. In Wye, the Wife of Bath (01233) 812540 is a tremendous restaurant. An ideal tavern is the Compasses at Side Street and for an inn with good value accommodation the Chequers Inn (01233) 770217 at Smarden is recommended.

Back to the fairways and a word for **Cranbrook,** a very pleasant and greatly improved parkland course. This was the scene of Bing Crosby's last round in England. Apparently he was close to purchasing the course before his untimely death in Spain. Also in Cranbrook is one of Kent's most popular hotels, the Kennel Holt Hotel (01580) 712032—excellent for dinner and equally convenient for **Lamberhurst** Golf Club.

The final inland course demanding inspection is to be found at Biddenden, the outstanding Nick Faldo-Steve Smyers designed **Chart Hills** which opened for play in late 1993. We view the course on a later page.

Around the Coast

Switching from the rich countryside of Kent we now visit the coast. **Littlestone** is the first port of call, and the contrast is a stark one. Situated on the edge of the flatlands of Romney Marsh, it enjoys a very remote setting. Littlestone is a splendid links and an Open Championship qualifying course, which doesn't deserve to be overshadowed by Kent's more illustrious trio further along the coast. Littlestone's best holes are saved for near the end of the round—the par four 16th and par three 17th typify all that's best (and frightening!) about links golf.

Not too far from Littlestone is the town of Hythe where the Hythe Imperial (01303) 267441 is a fine base, as there are 9 holes in the 'back garden'. There is also a good course at **Sene Valley** with terrific views over Romney Bay.

North of Sandwich is the **North Foreland** Club at Broadstairs which, like Littlestone, is also an Open qualify-

ing course, although its 27 holes are more strictly clifftop than links in nature. The Castlemere (01843) 861566 in Broadstairs is another fine place to stay, as is the intimate Rothsay Hotel. To the south of Deal is **Walmer and Kingsdown**, a course providing far reaching views.

Perhaps not surprisingly, where there is one great golf links there is often another nearby: Troon, Turnberry and Prestwick in Ayrshire; Birkdale, Hillside and Formby in Lancashire. Kent's famous three, **Royal St George's, Royal Cinque Ports** and **Prince's** are all featured ahead.

Despite the great quality of golf on offer there aren't too many places along the famous three mile stretch where one can put the feet up (or the golf clubs for that matter). Anyway, in Sandwich the Bell Hotel (01304) 613388 is very comfortable and convenient: its quayside setting is also handy for the Fisherman's Wharf Restaurant (01304) 613636. St Crispin's Inn (01304) 612081 is a charming alternative. Two pubs to note in Sandwich are the King's Arms (01304) 617330 and the Fleur-de-Lis (01304) 611131. In Deal, the Black Horse Hotel (01304) 374074 and Sutherland House (01304) 362853 are popular golfing haunts. Others to note include the Royal Hotel (01304) 375555, the Kings Head (01304) 368194 and the popular Dunkerleys (01304) 375016 which comes highly recommended. St Margaret's Bay, located on National Trust land is worth a look and the Cliffe Tavern (01304) 852749 nearby is a good place to wet one's whistle and stay if you wish. The Guildford House Hotel (01304) 375015 located on Beach Street in Deal, where there is a wider choice of accommodation is another ideal 19th hole if you're playing the famous courses nearby. As a final tip it might be a good idea to take the car on a short drive to Westcliffe, where Wallett's Court (01304) 852424 is supremely welcoming (despite its name!) As we conclude our trip another thought emerges. . . . Hardelot, Le Touquet . . . Why, we could nip down to Lydd where an aeroplane can whisk us off to Le Touquet quicker than we can drive back to London. Vive le golf!

Royal St George's

Royal St George's was founded in 1887, rather ironically by two Scottish gentlemen, Dr Laidlaw Purves and Henry Lamb, after what can only be described as a rather eccentric venture. Like all good Scotsmen they had been bitten by the bug; however, both were presently living in Victorian London which meant that their golf was more or less confined to the various commons, where the game was played alongside every conceivable activity imaginable. To them golf was meant to be played on a links by the sea. Hence the pair found themselves at Bournemouth setting off in an easterly direction looking for a suitable site. Having reached the eastern shore of Kent, so the story goes, they had drawn the proverbial blank (one presumes that they experienced one of those infamous Victorian pea-soupers the day they passed through Rye). With patience no doubt wearing thin, suddenly 'land ahoy!' Doctor Purves sights a vast stretch of duneland at Sandwich. The theory is that he 'spied the land with a golfer's eye' from the tower of St Clement's Church. Quite what he was doing at the top of the tower is irrelevant—St George's had been located. Within seven short years the Open Championship had 'come south' and St George's was the first English venue.

More than one hundred years on **Gerald Watts** is the **Secretary** at St George's and he can be contacted by telephone on **(01304) 613090** or by fax on (01304) 611245. All written communication should be directed to him at **The Royal St George's Golf Club, Sandwich, Kent CT13 9PB**. As a general guide visitors are welcome between Mondays and Fridays. Gentlemen must possess a handicap of no more than 18 and ladies no more than 15 and introductions are required. There are no ladies tees and other points to note are that the 1st tee is reserved daily for members until 9.45am and between 1.00pm and 2.15pm; however, the 10th tee is usually free in the early mornings. St George's is essentially a singles and foursomes club and three ball and four ball matches are only permissible with the agreement of the Secretary.

The green fees for 1998 were set at £60 per round, £85 per day. During the months of December, January and February the £60 fee is applicable for a full day's golf. Should there be a wish to hire golf clubs, a limited supply are for hire through the **Professional, Andrew Brooks**, **(01304) 615236**. Finally, the services of a caddie can be booked via the **Caddiemaster** on **(01304) 617380**.

Please excuse the awful pun but finding Sandwich should be a 'piece of cake.' The town is linked with Canterbury to the west by the A257, a distance of approximately 15 miles, and with Deal, 6 miles south east of Sandwich, by the A258. Motoring from London, the most direct route is to head for Canterbury using a combination of the A2 and M2 and thereafter following the A257 as above. For those coming from the south coast Ashford is the place to head for: Ashford is joined to Canterbury by the A28. Sandwich can also be reached by train.

Since its first Open in 1894, won by John H Taylor, the Championship has been held at Sandwich on eleven further occasions, most recently in 1993 when Australian Greg Norman won his second Championship after an epic final day's play. The visitor will not have to tackle the course from the Open Championship tees (6860 yards) but he'll still have to confront the many dunes, the great undulations and the awkward stances that St George's is so renowned for.

It is difficult to say which is the best or most famous hole at Sandwich. The chief candidates are probably the 4th, which features the 'tallest and deepest bunker in the United Kingdom', and the short 6th, the fabled 'Maiden'. The par five 14th, 'Suez', has also witnessed much drama over the years while the 17th and 18th provide an exacting finish.

Having done battle with the elements the golfer will find the clubhouse welcoming. Excellent lunches are served daily and both breakfasts and dinners can be obtained with prior arrangement. A jacket and tie must be worn in all public rooms.

Although the 1993 Championship seems destined to be remembered as St George's greatest Open, when Nick Faldo and Payne Stewart set the course record at 63, there have been many other famous happenings: Walter Hagen won the Championship in 1922 and promptly handed his winnings straight to his caddie; Henry Cotton's opening 67-65 in the 1934 Championship (a record that stood until Nick Faldo scored 66-64 at Muirfield in 1992) and then the Harry Bradshaw broken bottle episode of 1949. After 32 years the Open returned to St George's in 1981, when American Bill Rogers won, and again four years later when Sandy Lyle became the first British winner for sixteen years. The Amateur Championship was played here for the twelfth time in 1997.

Hole	Yards	Par	Hole	Yards	Par
1	413	4	10	378	4
2	339	4	11	216	3
3	198	3	12	347	4
4	417	4	13	438	4
5	421	4	14	497	5
6	155	3	15	437	4
7	487	5	16	163	3
8	410	4	17	413	4
9	376	4	18	455	4
Out	**3,219**	**35**	**In**	**3,344**	**35**
			Out	**3,219**	**35**
			Totals	**6,560**	**70**

Chart Hills

Yⁿou and I might visit Ballybunion or Royal Dornoch on a golfing pilgrimage. Our mouths water at the prospect of tackling the great sandbelt courses of Melbourne. And we would do anything to play golf at Pine Valley in New Jersey, widely acknowledged as the finest inland course in the world. For us, the stuff of dreams—for Nick Faldo, a day at the office.

It is not that Faldo is a killjoy—quite the contrary, he has as much fun playing the great courses as anyone—it's just that nowadays whenever he makes a special visit to famous golfing shrine he is thinking 'design'. Beyond the 18th green, and after his family, golf course design has become his major interest. Moreover, when his extraordinary resolve and desire to be recognised as one of the all-time greats has been satisfied (when he is confident people will tell their grandchildren 'I saw Faldo play') golf course design will take over full time. The comparison with Jack Nicklaus is striking, and since it was a vision of Nicklaus playing at Augusta back in 1971 that ignited the golfing flame, it is also rather neat.

For some years now, Faldo has been formulating his theories on course design. In the main, these ideas have been stored in the memory bank—that is until now, or rather since he met Steve Smyers. Smyers is one of America's most talented and imaginative course architects and in many ways is a kindred soul: he thinks along the same lines as Faldo. Above all, Smyers believes that you 'feel' a great golf course and that as far as possible its design should exude, even cultivate, the natural character of the landscape. Faldo and Smyers recently joined forces to create Chart Hills.

Imagine a setting in the heart of the Kent countryside, where ancient oak trees stand proud. Imagine a golf course that has clusters of fairway bunkers reminiscent of those at Royal Melbourne; where the fairways comprise a variety of sweeping tree-lined dog-legs and island sanctuaries; where holes twist and tumble downhill in an almost links-like fashion towards huge contoured greens, and where entry to the putting surfaces is protected by winding creeks and steep revetted pot bunkers similar to Carnoustie and Muirfield. This is Chart Hills.

But one shouldn't gain the impression that Chart Hills is merely a melting pot for design theories. There has been no crude imitation, rather it is the flavour of these great courses that has been incorporated and it has been done very subtly. Indeed, the golf course doesn't so much occupy the land as seemingly melt into it. A very natural look

has been achieved and, young though it is, Chart Hills is developing its own special character and charm. It is a unique course; it has the hallmarks of a great course and, importantly (at least for the purposes of *Following the Fairways*!) it is a great course that visitors can play.

The club recommends that all those seeking to play should telephone in advance of arrival. The **Head Professional, Danny French** and his staff can be contacted on **(01580) 292148** fax (01580) 292233. Handicap certificates are required. The summer green fees in 1998 are £60 per round midweek and £70 at weekends, although a number of special packages are also available.

The 19th hole at Chart Hills has something of an American country club atmosphere, being luxurious but not overly formal. This North American ambience starts to recede the instant you stand on the 1st tee. Not only are you staring across at the green fields of Kent but below is an extraordinary opening hole, a par five of almost 600 yards that includes elements of nearly all the design influences described earlier: a Mackenzie-like spread of fairway bunkers must be confronted with the drive; to the left of the fairway the rough is savage and there is a creek off to the right but the tee shot is perhaps not quite so intimidating as it appears for the landing area is quite generous. The hole then dog-legs sharply to the right, sweeping down towards the green as the fairway narrows and becomes heavily contoured—a genuine links feel has been created. Just short of the green there is another nest of traps and guarding the front right entrance are two fairly cavernous pot bunkers. The green itself is very large and full of wicked borrows—a five at this hole is a good start !

And so the challenge continues, with dramatic holes being followed by more subtle ones and constant changes in direction and elevation. Among other outstanding holes at Chart Hills are the short 3rd (with its 'Redan' fortress-style green), the 4th (a hole that would grace Royal Melbourne), the 8th (shades of Augusta's 14th?), the 9th (a hint of Pine Valley?) and on the back nine, perhaps the finest sequence of all, the 12th, 13th and 14th.

According to Smyers, a great golf course should excite, thrill and sometimes frighten. Applying this test literally, the golfer walking off the 18th green at Chart Hills is likely to be emotionally disturbed. As for Faldo, he is on record as saying that his twin ambitions in course design are to create the best inland course in Great Britain and the best links course—Nick never was one to set himself modest goals ! Play Chart Hills, though, and you may reckon him halfway there already.

Hole	Yards	Par		Hole	Yards	Par
1	599	5		10	453	4
2	459	4		11	215	3
3	183	3		12	536	5
4	424	4		13	426	4
5	511	5		14	402	4
6	309	4		15	481	4
7	206	3		16	482	5
8	439	4		17	147	3
9	365	4		18	449	4
Out	**3,495**	**36**		**In**	**3,591**	**36**
				Totals	**7,086**	**72**

Royal Cinque Ports

In the year 55 BC Julius Caesar landed on the coast near Deal. In 1920, an American invader by the name of Walter Hagen came to Deal to play in his first Open Championship. Both came, both saw, but neither conquered. In fact, both returned whence they came, tails firmly between legs—small wonder Deal is often considered the toughest of England's championship links!

The Royal Cinque Ports golf club was founded in February 1892 by Major General J M Graham whilst at lunch in Deal's Black Horse Hotel. The 18 hole course was opened in 1895 and has required very few alterations during its distinguished history.

Very often it is Mother Nature who provides the greatest challenge at Deal. Strong winds billowing in from the sea, capable of changing direction several times during a round, can turn what appear to be modest holes into monsters. The course measures 6407 yards from the medal tees (par 70) with the championship tees extending the course to some 6787 yards (par 72). From the ladies' tees the course measures 5686 yards, (par 74).

The outward nine is generally considered the easier half—Michael Bonallack turned in 31 during his record amateur score of 65 (a record which has stood for a third of a century). Certainly the back nine is longer and Deal is renowned for its tough finish, the classic par five 16th perhaps being the most difficult (and best) hole on the course. The fairways are humpy and hillocky and well bunkered, and many of the greens stand on natural plateaux. On a clear day there are some magnificent views across the course towards the English Channel and to the distant white cliffs beyond Pegwell Bay.

Two Open Championships have been held at Deal, in 1909 and in 1920. The 1909 championship was won by the Englishman John H Taylor, his fourth victory in the event. The 1920 Open has already been referred to—the luckless Hagen in fact finished fifty third in a field of fifty four. Also entitled to feel somewhat peeved that year was Abe Mitchell who allowed George Duncan to come from thirteen strokes behind to snatch victory. Plans to stage a third championship at Deal in 1949 had to be abandoned when extensive flooding led to a temporary closure of the course.

It would not be fair, either to the Romans or Mr Hagen, to leave Deal without recording that both did eventually achieve their ambitions. The Romans returned a century later and conquered the Brits, and as for 'Sir Walter', he didn't have to wait quite so long, for in 1922 he won the first of four Open Championships, none of which though, alas, was at Deal.

Royal Cinque Ports Golf Club, Golf Road, Deal, Kent CT14 6RE	
Secretary	Colin Hammond (01304) 347007
Professional	Andrew Reynolds (01304) 374170
Green Fees	£50/day; £10 reduction after 1 pm Twilight green fee £20 Mon, Tues, Thurs after 5 pm
Restrictions	Handicap required (max 20)
Directions	

Directions
Take the M20 from London to Dover. There pick up the A258 to Deal. The course is a mile north of the town.

Prince's

One of the highlights of the magnificent 1993 Open Championship at Royal St George's was the delightful speech made at the prize presentation by the legendary American golfer, Gene Sarazen. For many years Sarazen, now in his nineties, has performed the traditional honour of hitting the first tee shot at the US Masters tournament and it is always a moving occasion. Sarazen is one of golf's greatest characters and certainly one of the finest players ever to have graced the sport. He is one of only four golfers in history (Nicklaus, Hogan and Player are the others) to have won all four of golf's grand slam events. And Sarazen's link with Prince's? It was the scene of his one British Open victory in 1932 which, no thanks to Adolf Hitler, was Prince's one and only Open Championship.

Sarazen's total score of 283 was then a record for the Open Championship but today's golfer cannot properly walk in Sarazen's footsteps for the 18 hole links was dismembered during the last War.

For a time it looked as if the military might retain the land, but in 1950 Sir Guy Campbell and John Morrison were invited to restore the links. Remarkably, given the heavily scarred landscape, seventeen of the pre-war greens could still be used. Campbell and Morrison decided, however, that they could best utilise the available land by creating three loops of nine and this is what greets the present day visitor to Prince's.

I'm not sure that 'greets' is actually the right terminology. Prince's may have lost its Open Championship status, but it has not lost its teeth. The three nines, the Dunes, Himalayas and Shore are each tremendously testing and, being a relatively exposed links, the golfer is at the mercy of the elements.

Golfers playing 36 holes will play two eighteens from the following three combinations: **Dunes/Himalayas** 6506 yards, par 71; **Himalayas/Shore** 6510 yards, par 72 and **Shore/Dunes** 6690 yards, par 72. Each course is of a similarly high standard with a plethora of plateaued greens, ridges, humps and hollows but not too many bunkers. The paucity of sandtraps is a feature of golf at Prince's and, unlike neighbouring St George's where there are many potential blind shots, the fairways tend to run parallel with the dunes as opposed to clambering over the top of them. There are few, if any, weak holes at Prince's, but if one were to single out a balanced 'nine of the best' from the 27 then I might venture a combination of the 2nd, 7th and 8th from the Himalayas; the 3rd, 6th and 9th from the Shore and the 3rd, 4th and 6th from the Dunes.

Prince's Golf Club, Sandwich Bay, Sandwich, Kent CT13 9QB	
Gen Manager	Bill Howie
Bookings	Mike Stone (01304) 611118
Professional	Chris Evans (01304) 613797
Green Fees	WD £40/round; £45/day WE £42/round; £51/Sat; £52/Sun Full day packages from £25 in winter
Restrictions	Handicap required
Directions	

Directions
Sandwich is linked to Canterbury by the A257 and to Deal by the A258. The course is four and a half miles from Sandwich railway station.

Aquarius G.C.
(0181) 693 1626
Marmora Road, Honor Oak
(9) 5246 yards/**/F/M

Ashford G.C.
(01233) 622655
Sandyhurst Lane, Ashford
(18) 6246 yards/***/B/H

Austin Lodge G.C.
(01322) 863000
nr Eynsford Station
(18) 6600 yards/***/C

Barnehurst G.C.
(01322) 523746
Mayplace Road, East Barnehurst
(9) 5448 yards/*/E

Bearsted G.C.
(01622) 738198
Ware Street, Bearsted,Maidstone
(18) 6278 yards/**/B/L/M

Birchwood Park G.C.
(01322) 662554
Birchwood Road, Wilmington
(18) 6364 yards/***/C

Boughton G.C.
(01227) 752277
Brickfield Lane, Boughton
(18) 6452 yards/***/C

Broke Hill G.C.
(01959) 533810
Sevenoaks Road, Halstead
(18) 6454 yards/***/C

Bromley G.C.
(0181) 462 7014
Magpie Hall Lane, Bromley
(9) 5538 yards/***/F

Broome Park G.& C.C.
(01227) 831701
Barham, Canterbury
(18) 6610 yards/**/B/H

Canterbury G.C.
(01227) 453532
Scotland Hills, Canterbury
(18) 6249 yards/**/B/H

Chart Hills G.C.
(01580) 292222
Weeks Lane, Biddenden
(18) 7086 yards/***/A/H

Chelsfield Lakes G.C.
(01689) 896266
Court Road, Orpington
(18) 6077 yards/***/D

Cherry Lodge G.C.
(01959) 572250
Jail Lane, Biggin Hill
(18) 6652 yards/**/B

Chestfield G.C.
(01227) 794411
103 Chestfield Road, Whitstable
(18) 6181 yards/**/B/H

Chigwell G.C.
(0181) 500 2059
High Road, Chigwell
(18) 6279 yards/**/A/H

Chislehurst G.C.
(0181) 467 3055
Camden Place, Chislehurst
(18) 5128 yards/***/B/H

Cobtree Manor G.C.
(01622) 753276
Maidstone
(18) 5716 yards/***/E

Corinthian G.C.
(01474) 707559
Gay Dawn Farm, Fawkham
(9) 6045 yards/**/D

Cranbrook G.C.
(01580) 712833
Benenden Road, Cranbook
(18) 6351 yards/**/C

Cray Valley G.C.
(01689) 831927
Sandy Lane, St Pauls Cray
(18) 5624 yards/***/D

Darenth Valley G.C.
(01959) 522944
Station Road, Shoreham
(18) 6356 yards/***/D

Dartford G.C.
(01322) 223616
Dartford Heath
(18) 5914 yards/**/B/L/M

Deangate Ridge G.C.
(01634) 251180
Hoo, Rochester
(18) 6300 yards/***/B

Edenbridge G.& C.C.
(01732) 867381
Crouch House Road, Edenbridge
(18) 6646 yards/**/C
(18) 5671 yards/**/C

Eltham Warren G.C.
(0181) 850 1166
Bexley Road, Eltham
(9) 5840 yards/***/B

Etchinghill G.C
(01303) 862280
Canterbury Road, Etchinghill.
(18) 6147 ysrds/***/D

Faversham G.C.
(01795) 890251
Belmont Park, Faversham
(18) 6030 yards/**/C

Gillingham G.C.
(01634) 853017
Woodlands Road, Gillingham
(18) 5911 yards/**/D

Hawkhurst G.C.
(01580) 752396
High Street, Hawkhurst, Cranbrook
(9) 5774 yards/**/D

Herne Bay G.C.
(01227) 373964
Eddington, Herne Bay
(18) 5466 yards/***/D/H

Hever G.C.
(01732) 700771
Hever
(18) 7002 yards/***/A/H

Hewitts G.C.
(01689) 896266
Court Road, Orpington
(18) 6077 yards/***/D

High Elms G.C.
(01689) 858175
High Elms Road, Downe
(18) 6210 yards/***/F

Holtye G.C.
(01342) 850635
Holtye Common, Cowden,
(9) 5289 yards/**/F

Hythe Imperial G.C.
(01303) 267441
Princes Parade, Hythe
(9) 5560 yards/**/B

Knole Park G.C.
(01732) 452150
Seal Hollow Road, Sevenoaks
(18) 6249 yards/**/B/H

Lamberhurst G.C.
(01892) 890241
Church Road, Lamberhurst
(18) 6232 yards/**/B

Leeds Castle
(01622) 880467
Maidstone
(9) 2880 yards/***/F

Littlestone G.C.
(01797) 363355
St Andrews Road, Littlestone
(18) 6460 yards/**/B/H

London G.C.
(01474) 879899
Stansted Lane, Ash Green
(18) 7208 yards/*/F/M
(18) 7005 yards/*/F/M

Lullingstone Park G.C.
(01959) 533793
Park Gate, Chelsfield, Orpington
(18) 6779 yards/***/F
(9) 2445 yards/***/E

Lydd G.C.
(01797) 320808
Romney Road, Lydd
(18) 6517 yards/**/D

Mid Kent G.C.
(01474) 568035
Singlewell Road, Gravesend
(18) 6206 yards/**/F/H

Moatlands G.C.
(01892) 724400
Watermans Lane, Brenchley
(18) 6460 yards/***/A/H

Nizels G.C.
(01732) 833138
Nizels Lane, Hildenborough
(18) 6279 yards/***/A

North Foreland G.C.
(01843) 862140
Convent Road, Broadstairs
(18) 6382 yards/**/B/H

Oastpark G.C.
(01634) 242818
Malling Road, Snodland
(18) 6200 yards/***/E

Parkwood G.C.
(01959) 577744
Chestnut Avenue, Westerham
(18) 6835 yards/**/C

Poult Wood G.C.
(01732) 364039
Higham Lane, Tonbridge
(18) 5569 yards/***/E

Princes G.C.
(01304) 611118
Sandwich Bay, Sandwich
(9) 3321 yards***/A/H
(9) 3492 yards***/A/H
(9) 3455 yards***/A/H

The Ridge G.C.
(01622) 844382
Chartway Street, East Sutton
(18) 6254 yards/***/B/H

Rochester & Cobham Park G.C.
(01474) 823411
Park Dale, by Rochester
(18) 6467 yards/**/B/H

Romney Warren G.C.
(01797) 362231
St Andrews Road, Littlestone
(18) 5126 yards/***/E

Royal Cinque Ports G.C.
(01304) 374007
Sandwich
(18) 6744 yards/**/F/H

Royal St Georges G.C.
(01304) 613090
Sandwich Bay Road, Sandwich
(18) 6857 yards/**/A/H

Ruxley Park G.C.
(01689) 871490
Sandy Lane, St Pauls Cray,
(18) 6027 yards/***/D

St Augustines G.C.
(01843) 590333
Cottingham Road, Cliffsend,
Ramsgate
(18) 5197 yards/***/C/H

Sene Valley G.C.
(01303) 268513
Sene, Folkestone
(18) 6320 yards/**/B/H

Sheerness G.C.
(01795) 662585
Power Station Road, Sheerness
(18) 6460 yards/**/D/H

Shortlands G.C.
(0181) 460 2471
Shortlands, Bromley
(9) 5261 yards/F/G

Sittingbourne & Milton Regis G.C.
(01795) 842261
Wormdale, Newington,
(18) 6272 yards/**/D/H/L

Sundridge Park G.C.
(0181) 460 1822
Garden Road, Bromley
(18) 6490 yards/**/A/H
(18) 6007 yards/**/A/H

Sweetwoods Park G.C.
(01342) 850729
Cowden, Edenbridge
(18) 6400 yards/***/C

Tenterden G.C.
(01580) 763987
Woodchurch Road, Tenterden
(18) 6030 yards/**/D

Tudor Park G.& C.C.
(01622) 734334
Ashford Road, Bearsted
(18) 6000 yards/***/B/H

Upchurch River Valley G.C.
(01634) 360626
Upchurch, Sittingbourne
(18) 6160 yards/***/E

Walmer & Kingsdown G.C.
(01304) 373256
The Leas, Kingsdown, Deal
(18) 6160 yards/***/C/H

Weald of Kent G.C.
(01622) 890866
Maidstone Road, Headcorn
(18) 6169 yards/***/D

Westgate & Birchington G.C.
(01843) 831115
Canterbury Road, Westgate-on-Sea
(18) 4926 yards/**/D/H/L

West Kent G.C.
(01689) 851323
West Hill, Downe, Orpington
(18) 6392 yards/**/F/H/L

West Malling G.C.
(01732) 844785
London Road, Addington, Maidstone
(18) 6142 yards/**/B
(18) 6240 yards/**/B

Whitstable & Seasalter G.C.
(01227) 272020
Collingwood Road, Whitstable
(9) 5276 yards/**/C

Wildernesse G.C.
(01732) 761199
Seal, Sevenoaks, Maidstone
(18) 6478 yards/**/B/H/L

Woodlands Manor G.C.
(01959) 523805
Tinkerpot Lane, Sevenoaks
(18) 5858 yards/**/F/H

Wrotham Heath
(01732) 884800
Seven Mile Lane, Comp, Sevenoaks
(9) 5959 yards/**/C/H

Artist: *H M Bateman* **THE IRATE GOLFER** *Courtesy of:* **Burlington Gallery**

Artist: *J Hassall* **FORE**
Courtesy of: **Burlington Gallery**

Artist: *J Hassall* **AFTER**
Courtesy of: **Burlington Gallery**

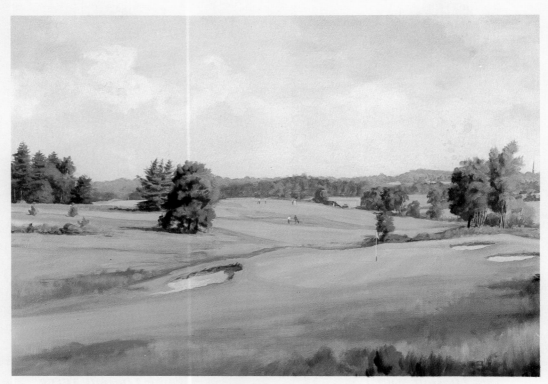

Artist: **Julian Barrow** **WALTON HEATH** Courtesy of: **Burlington Gallery**

Capital Golf

Records suggest that golf was first played in England in 1608: the venue was Blackheath in London but the participants were Scottish not English. James I (James VI of Scotland) and his courtiers are generally credited with bringing the game south of the border. The exact date that the English caught the bug is unclear. Certainly in the 18th century it was still pretty much an alien pastime—in his first English dictionary compiled in 1755 Dr Samuel Johnson described golf as 'a game played with a ball and a club or bat'.

During its formative years golf in London was largely confined to the public commons such as those at Blackheath, Clapham, Chingford and Tooting Bec, the golfers having to share their rather crudely laid out courses with 'nurse-maids, dogs, horses and stubborn old ladies and gentlemen'.

Not surprisingly when the first golf clubs started to form the tendency was to retreat from the public stage. The **Royal Blackheath** Golf Club, fittingly enough the first English club to be founded (it dates from 1787) eventually moved from the Heath and now plays on a private course at Eltham. Golf is no longer played (or at least shouldn't be!) on the commons at Clapham and Tooting Bec. However, golf does survive on those at **Wimbledon** and Chingford, the latter being the home of **Royal Epping Forest** and where golfers are still required to wear red clothing in order that they can be distinguished from other users of the common.

The majority of London clubs are for obvious reasons set in deepest suburbia and with many it is often far from clear as to whether they fall within Greater London or not. In anyone's book **Muswell Hill** is in London, which for present purposes is just as well because it's an excellent course. Measuring close to 6500 yards and quite undulating, it represents a fairly stiff test from the back tees. Other good 18 hole courses to the north of London include **Finchley** (with its elegant Victorian clubhouse), **Mill Hill** (which has something of a heathland feel to it) and **Highgate** (which is particularly pretty), while **Hampstead** has an enjoyable nine holes.

A cluster of fine courses lie a little further to the north west of the capital. Near neighbours of one another are **Northwood** and **Sandy Lodge**. The latter could be said to be sandy by name, sandy by nature—a heathland course but it can play more like a golf links at times. Anyway, it's certainly an exceptionally fine course and hosts many top class events. Northwood is in parts parkland, in parts heathland with a very good back nine. A mention also for **West Middlesex**, one of West London's better parkland courses.

On the other side of the M1 one finds **South Herts** and **Hadley Wood**. South Herts is somewhat tucked away in Totteridge but well worth finding. The club can boast having both Harry Vardon and Dai Rees among its past professionals. Hadley Wood, near Barnet is a very beautiful course designed by Alister Mackenzie with lovely tree-lined fairways. The clubhouse is very elegant too. Over towards Essex, Royal Epping Forest has been mentioned. Also within Epping Forest itself, **West Essex** is a very fine parkland course and there are two first rate public courses at **Hainault Forest**.

A 19th Hole

Before looking at a golf in the south of the metropolis a word on some of London's better hotels. Finding real value in the capital isn't easy—local knowledge helps and it may be a case of rub of the green. The following appraisal is dedicated to the American and Japanese visitor—and to any of us who have a generous expense account!

In Park Lane, the Inn on the Park (0171) 499 0888 is quite excellent and its restaurant, the Four Seasons is outstanding. Luxury of the highest order is also offered in the Dorchester (0171) 629 8888 as it proudly overlooks Hyde Park (alas no golf). The Grill Room and the Terrace are both restaurants of distinction. The international class of the Ritz (0171) 493 8181 is obvious—one can quite simply sniff the style. Nearby, Browns (0171) 493 6020 is contrastingly English and justifiably proud of it. A few more? Well, how about the Savoy (0171) 836 4343. Note the delightful settings of its restaurants the Grill Room and the River Restaurant. Guests here have temporary membership of Wentworth—a major plus for lovers of first class fairways. Another member of the Savoy group is Claridges (0171) 629 8860 —traditional to a tee but still extremely popular.

For people not wishing to stay in Central London these hotels may be of some help: in Hadley Wood the West Lodge Park (0181) 440 8311 is a superb 19th century mansion—very convenient for the many courses of South Hertfordshire. A galleried hall is one of the features of the Grym's Dyke Hotel (0181) 954 4227. The former home of W S Gilbert, this hotel is located in Harrow Weald—ideal for playing (or spectating) at **Moor Park**. Slightly further north of town, but still only twenty miles from Central London, the five star comforts of Hanbury Manor near Ware (01920) 487722 take some beating (18 great holes of golf too) while south of the capital golfers in Croydon will also find Selsdon Park Hotel (0181) 657 8811 very comfortable and convenient.

If some of the above are slightly out of the price range of the majority of ordinary mortals then it goes without saying that London provides a veritable feast of accommodation at vastly varying rates. Two recommended establishments combining comfort and value are Aston Court (0171) 602 9954 in West Kensington and in NW4 the Peacehaven Hotel (0181) 202 9758.

The South and West

Those looking for a game in south west London might consider looking in the Wimbledon area where there are several courses. **Royal Wimbledon** is just about the best in London but golfers may find it easier to arrange a game (during the week at any rate) on the nearby course at **Wimbledon Common**. **Coombe Hill** is another of the capital's most prestigious clubs—its well manicured fairways are just about visible from Royal Wimbledon. A little further out at Richmond, games can be enjoyed at **Royal Mid Surrey** (two courses here, an Outer and an Inner and a superb clubhouse which doubles as a museum to some of the great names of golf—a must for lovers of the game's history or a good lunch!) and at **Richmond** Golf Club with its superb Georgian clubhouse. There is also a public course at Richmond. A quick mention must be made here of Cannizaro House (0181) 879 1464, a truly delightful hotel on Wimbledon Common. It is perfect for the London and Surrey golfer, and also an ideal spot for the many shops to be found in Wimbledon Village. In Richmond, the Petersham 0181 940 7471 is an excellent hotel with a good restaurant (good restaurants abound in Richmond). Due west of London, **Ealing** offers a reasonable test and there are again a number of public courses in the vicinity.

South of London the Croydon area is yet another that is thick with clubs. Although it may be difficult to arrange a game on, **Addington** is generally considered the best; it is a lovely heathland course covered in heather, pines and silver birch and has in the par three 13th one of golf's toughest and most beautiful short holes. **Addington Palace** is also well thought of, as indeed is **Croham Hurst**. To make up a four, especially if one requires a base, **Selsdon Park** must be the selection— a pleasant parkland course set around the Selsdon escarpment. Seldson Park is very popular with societies. Not far from Croydon, the course at **Coulsdon Court** has a welcoming reputation and an extraordinary selection of trees. Two of the better courses towards the south east of London are **Langley Park** (at Beckenham)— heavily wooded with a particularly good series of holes towards the end of the round including an attractive par three finishing hole—and **Sundridge Park,** where indeed there are two good courses, an East and a West.

Elsewhere in the south east there is a popular public course at **Beckenham Place Park** and there are interesting layouts at **Shooters Hill** and **Dulwich and Sydenham**, but the final mention goes to **Royal Blackheath**. The club has a great sense of history and the course is full of character. Early in the round one may confront the famous 'Hamlet Cigar bunker' while its 18th isn't so much difficult as unusual, requiring a pitch over a hedge to the green. In some ways it's unfortunate that the club ever had to leave its famous common—Blackheath village is charming—but then the author of this tome may just be a little biased!

Surrey

When Providence distributed land best suited for building golf courses it wasn't done in the most democratic of spirits. Take for instance the quite ridiculous amount of majestic links land to be found along the coast of Lancashire—it's enough to make every good Yorkshireman weep. And then there's Surrey, blessed with acre upon acre of perfect inland golfing terrain—what a contrast to poor Essex!

It is probably safe to suggest that **Walton Heath, Sunningdale** and **Wentworth** are the county's three leading clubs, and each is detailed separately in this chapter. Walton and Wentworth are only two of Surrey's famous 'W Club'—there's also **Worplesdon** and **Woking, West Hill, West Surrey, West Byfleet** and to this list we can now add **Wisley** and **Wildwood**—two of the country's newest and (in the case of Wisley) most exclusive developments.

Located close to the A32 to the west of Woking, Worplesdon, West Hill and Woking Golf Clubs lie practically next door to one another. Indeed it might be possible to devise a few dramatic cross-course holes— though in view of the value of some of the adjacent properties that would have to be driven over it's perhaps not such a good idea! West Hill is generally considered to be the most difficult of the three, the fairways at times being frighteningly narrow; Worplesdon is probably the most widely known (largely due to its famous annual foursomes event), while Woking, founded a century ago, possesses the most distinctive architecture and perhaps the greatest charm. Whatever their particular merits, all three are magnificent examples of natural heathland and heather courses.

Marginally closer to the capital and still very much in the heart of the stockbroker-belt is a second outstanding trio of courses centred around Weybridge: **St George's**

Hill, New Zealand** and **West Byfleet**. Once again, these are heathland type courses where golf is played amidst heavily wooded surroundings, the combination of pines, silver birch, purple heather and, at St George's Hill and New Zealand especially, a magnificent spread of rhododendrons, making for particularly attractive settings. St George's Hill is one of the more undulating courses in Surrey and calls for several spectacular shots—indeed, many people rate it on a par with Wentworth and Walton Heath.

Golf in Surrey isn't of course all heathland and heather. **Tandridge** is one of the best downland courses in Southern England while just a short drive from Weybridge is the delightful parkland course at **Burhill**, situated some two miles south of Walton-on-Thames. Burhill's clubhouse is a particularly grand affair—at one time it was the home of the Dowager Duchess of Wellington. Much less grand, but to some of equal interest, is the Dick Turpin cottage sited on the course and reputed to have been used by the infamous highwayman (not a golfer so far as we know). Also worth noting is a nearby public course, **Silvermere**, located midway between Byfleet and Cobham where it may be easier to arrange a game—at least in theory, as it does get very busy—and where green fees are naturally lower.

Some thoughts for the 19th hole are required. Surrey is a rich county—in more ways than one. Quality golf comes in abundance, so too do first class country houses, pubs, hotels and restaurants. Here are a few suggestions. The Burford Bridge (01306) 884561 and the Thatched House (0181) 642 3131 are good choices for those visiting Walton Heath. The nearby Partners Brasserie (0181) 644 7743 is a worthy suggestion for a winning foursome. Chez Max (0181) 399 2365 in Surbiton is another for a celebratory feast of note. Another convenient hotel for Walton Heath is the Heathside Hotel (01737) 353355 in Burgh Heath. After a day's golf on any of the courses in the Woking area the Wheatsheaf Hotel (01483) 773047 is a good spot to collect one's thoughts. Another relaxing hotel is the Oatlands Park Hotel (01932) 847242—centrally located and extremely pleasant. An attractive guesthouse in Woking is Glencourt (01483) 764154. The Cricketers (01932) 862105 on Downside Common, Cobham is a sporting little pub. Two fine restaurants are Casa Romana (01932) 843470) in Weybridge, and in Reigate, La Barbe (01737) 241966. Finally, two of the county's (and the country's) finest country house hotels are in this area, again convenient for Wentworth—Pennyhill Park (01276) 471774 near Bagshot and Great Fosters (01784) 433822 near Egham—and also in Egham one can stay at the Jacobean style Anugraha Hotel (01784) 434355 which is ideal for trips to Wentworth and Sunningdale.

Generally speaking, golf in the Home Counties and golf in America have precious little in common. However, the **Foxhills** Club at Ottershaw (off the A320) can make a genuine claim to have married the two successfully. A Jacobean style manor house run on American country club lines including an outstanding range of leisure facilities, it has two championship length heathland type courses and 16 rooms to accommodate golfers in some style (01932) 872050. Not surprisingly, Foxhills is a very popular haunt for golfing societies. Another fairly newish set up in this area is the **Fernfell** Golf and Country Club at Cranleigh just south of Guildford—a worthy thought for the itinerant golfer. A hotel of considerable charm is the historic Angel (01483) 564555—well worth considering.

The country club scene may not of course appeal to all types and excellent golf in an extremely sedate atmosphere can be enjoyed at **Gatton Manor** situated in Ockley near Dorking. The course has a very scenic layout running through woods and alongside lakes. One doesn't have to look too far for a good night's rest—the manor house is now a very relaxing hotel (01306) 627555 with golf obviously very much on the menu. Note also the Punch Bowl in nearby Oakwood Hill—an excellent country pub.

Heading towards Walton Heath, if a game cannot be arranged over one of its famous courses then there is golf of a similar (if less challenging) nature at **Reigate Heath** and not too far away at **Kingswood** there is a fine parkland course. **Duke's Dene** is also well worth a trip - located in the delightful Halliloo Valley its a pleasure to play.

The rich heathland seam runs the breadth of the county and over to the west, practically straddling the three counties of Surrey, Berkshire and Hampshire, lies the superb **Camberley Heath**. There is also a first rate public course in Camberley, **Pine Ridge**, which opened in 1992. Down in the south-west corner of Surrey there is yet another outstanding trio of clubs: **Hindhead**, **West Surrey** and **Hankley Common**. Hankley Common was for many years a favourite of the late South African Bobby Locke, who once owned a house adjacent to the course. Hankley Common is widely known for its spectacular 18th hole—one of the greatest closing holes in golf. A vast gulley which seems to possess magnetic powers looms in front of the green—nine out of ten first timers fail to reach the putting surface.

The south-west corner of Surrey is particularly scenic. The hustle and bustle of London seems a world away— and of course in a way it is. In Bramley, the Bramley Grange Hotel (01483) 893434 is an ideal base from which to explore the countryside. Close to the Sussex borders lies Haslemere and another fine hotel, a timbered farmhouse on this occasion, the Lythe Hill Hotel (01428) 651251 where bedrooms in the original house have great character. People who have still not found a restaurant to visit must surely do so here for Fleur de Sel (01428) 651462 offers some simply splendid dishes and a most delightful atmosphere.

Artist: **Graeme W Baxter WENTWORTH** *Courtesy of:* **Baxter Prints**

Just 50 minutes from central London in the full splendour of the English countryside lies the little village of Bagshot and Pennyhill Park.

At the end of the winding driveway the stone-fronted, creeper-clad house stands surrounded by 112 acres of parkland and lake. This is Pennyhill Park, built in 1849 by the pioneering Canadian bridge-builder, James Hodge.

The total commitment to service at Pennyhill complements the traditions of its historic past. On entering the main hallway and with the stately sweep of the period staircase a warm welcome awaits you from attentive staff. Trained to Edwardian standards of courtesy they provide impeccable and discreet service.

Peace and tranquillity surround this house which, though old, provides every modern amenity.

You can watch polo at Smiths' Lawn Windsor, and Sunningdale and Wentworth are just two of the nearby prestigious golf courses. Pennyhill Park also has its own

9 hole golf course and other sporting facilities including tennis courts, a Roman styled swimming pool and clay pigeon shooting. The three acre lake is annually stocked with brown and rainbow trout for those in search of more tranquil pursuits.

The award-winning Latymer restaurant provides all the elegance expected of its surroundings combined with a welcoming atmosphere. The food, of mainly British produce, is served in the traditional way, and the service, known to many, is complemented by an outstanding selection of fine wines.

There are 107 bedrooms and apartments in this fine example of the English country house, all individually designed and beautifully furnished. Each room is named after a shrub or flower, save for the most luxurious Heywood suite, the namesake of the last permanent occupant of this English country manor house. Every room at Pennyhill Park is furnished and decorated using soft, elegant fabrics and comforting themes such as oak and walnut.

Pennyhill Park Hotel and Country Club
London Road Bagshot
Surrey GU19 5EU
Tel. (01276) 471774
Fax. (01276) 473217

Wentworth

*I*t is autumn. A reddish gold leaf scurries across the 18th green. The huge gallery is silent. Fully 50 yards away to the right of the fairway, close to the trees and in the rough is the young Severiano Ballesteros. He is one hole down to the legendary Arnold Palmer and he needs a miracle. The blade flashes and the ball flies towards the green. It pitches, it rolls and it drops... the eagle has landed.

A stunningly beautiful place, Wentworth is set in the heart of the famous Surrey Heath. The name first appeared on the golfing map in the mid 1920s when Harry Colt, perhaps the greatest of all British golf architects, was commissioned to design two 18 hole courses. The East Course was the first to open in 1924, with the West Course following two years later. A third 18 hole championship course, the Edinburgh, designed by John Jacobs in collaboration with Gary Player and the club's former professional, Bernard Gallacher was officially opened in 1990.

Before the War, it was the **East** Course that captured the limelight by staging the club's first important events, in 1926 an unofficial match between British and American teams and in 1932 the inaugural Curtis Cup. In the period since 1945, the longer **West** Course has taken most of the glory with the Ryder Cup in 1953, the Canada Cup—a forerunner of the World Cup—three years later, and each year since 1964 the World Matchplay Championship. Through the televising of the latter and the annual Volvo PGA Championship, the West has become arguably England's best known golf course. Every 'armchair golfer' is very familiar with the first two holes and the final six or seven on what is known affectionately (and respectfully!) as the 'Burma Road' course. The West certainly has a formidable opening and an exciting finish but arguably the two most picturesque holes on the course are rarely captured on camera—the sweeping downhill par five 4th and the 8th, a classic two-shotter where the approach is played across an attractive pond.

The owners of the club, Wentworth Group Holdings, have invested substantially in the courses and the facilities during the past decade and under Chairman, Elliott Bernerd, and Chief Executive, Willy Bauer, standards now match the best golf and country clubs in the world.

Following the completion of the **Edinburgh**, a computerised irrigation system was installed on the West, a new Halfway House built serving the East and West, another on the Edinburgh, and the outdoor heated swimming pool has been refurbished. A new tennis and health club will be opened in 1998, providing exceptional sporting facilities and superior service to encourage members to combine fitness with relaxation.

In October 1993 a major redevelopment of the clubhouse was completed. The golfing facilities are now all under one roof including the pro shop, the caddymaster, bagstore and visitors' locker rooms. The new club lounge plus dining room combining brasserie style and formal dining, Burma Bar, private meeting rooms and gabled ballroom offer plenty of flexibility for social and business entertainment.

The summer green fees for 1998 are set, per round, at £145 for the West Course with the East and Edinburgh courses at £90 and £95 respectively. Club, buggy and trolley hire and caddies may be booked in advance while special packages are available for groups of 20 or more.

Wentworth is located directly off the A30 between Bagshot and Egham, and may be approached via the M25 junction 13 or M4 through Bracknell or Windsor and Ascot. Heathrow Airport is only 15 minutes away.

Managing Director and General Manager, Julian Small and his staff ensure that all visitors feel welcome. It is advisable to pre-book a starting time and, unless accompanied by a Wentworth member, visitors are restricted to weekdays. A handicap certificate is required and the club's handicap limits are 24 (ladies 32) for the West Course and 28 (ladies 36) for the East and Edinburgh courses.

Enquiries should be addressed to: **Wentworth Club, Wentworth Drive, Virginia Water, Surrey GU25 4LS. Telephone (01344) 842201,** fax (01344) 842804.

It is spring. The PGA Championship is reaching a nailbiting climax as the two players walk down the first fairway in the sudden death play off. A decade has passed and the now legendary Ballesteros hasn't won for some time. He desperately needs a victory. The blade flashes and a 5 iron is struck 220 yards towards the green. It lands, skips, rolls and finishes two feet from the pin... El Gran Senor is back!

West Course

Hole	Yards	Par	Hole	Yards	Par
1	471	5	10	186	3
2	155	3	11	398	4
3	452	4	12	510	5
4	501	5	13	441	4
5	191	3	14	179	3
6	356	4	15	466	4
7	399	4	16	380	4
8	398	4	17	571	5
9	450	4	18	502	5
Out	**3,373**	**36**	**In**	**3,633**	**37**
			Out	**3,373**	**36**
			Totals	**7,006**	**72**

Gatton Manor Hotel, Golf & Country Club is set in 250 acres of parkland in the heart of the beautiful Surrey countryside and boasts a well established 18 hole, par 72 championship length golf course of 6653 yards. The whole course has immense character incorporating the natural waters of the River Arun. It has the advantage of three starting points at the first, fourth and tenth and veers over undulating ground through the peace and tranquillity of woods, with fourteen scenic water holes.

The enjoyable and interesting course is designed to challenge every golfer and has arguably the best finishing hole in the south. Firstly you are faced with a tee shot over water to the sloping fairway. Your second shot has to carry a stream some 50 yards from the middle of the green. The green itself is bunkered from left to right and is enclosed round the back with an interesting selection of fir trees.

Golf is certainly not all that Gatton Manor has to offer. The golfer, in his leisure moments, or indeed the non-golfer, can enjoy the benefits of the purpose-built gymnasium and health club which houses all the latest equipment, saunas, jacuzzi and solarium. Take a leisurely walk around the estate, and see many of the specimen trees and shrubs from the magnificent hybrid rhododendrons to the exotic magnolias and vast tulip tree. The estate also teems with wildlife and the keen observer can see such birds as kingfisher, greenfinch and yellowhammer, whilst animals such as otter, and roe deer are to be seen in their natural habitat. Other outdoor activities available include tennis, bowls, trout and coarse fishing. Alternatively guests can relax in the oak-beamed Golf Bar.

The attractive manor was built in 1728 and has been tastefully decorated to a high standard providing sixteen hotel rooms, all of which have en suite facilities. Adjoining the manor house is the delightful two-tiered dining room, residents' lounge, and private conference suites.

Whatever your reason for visiting Gatton Manor, you will not be disappointed. Ideally situated between London and the south coast, and within 15 miles of Gatwick airport and the M25 (exit 9), you will find Gatton Manor nestling off a quiet country lane to the west of the picturesque village of Ockley on the A29.

Gatton Manor Hotel, Golf & Country Club
Standon Lane
Ockley, nr Dorking
Surrey, RH5 5PQ
Tel: (01306) 627555
Fax: (01306) 627713
Pro Shop: (01306) 627557
E mail: gattonmanor@enterprise.net

Sunningdale

On seeing the spectacularly beautiful 18th hole at Killarney during one of his visits to Ireland, the late Henry Longhurst declared, 'What a lovely place to die'. Now whilst one rarely wishes to dwell on the subject of meeting our maker, golfers have been known to indulge in a considerable amount of speculation as to the type of course they might find on the arrival of such an occasion. There is a story of one heated discussion which involved, quite by chance, an Englishman, a Scotsman and an American. The latter argued with great conviction that a large number of the holes would, 'as sure as hell,' resemble Augusta, whilst the Scotsman vehemently insisted that even the most minute deviation from the Old Course at St Andrews would constitute an act of heresy; as for the Englishman, he naturally had no doubts whatsoever that he could stroll through the Pearly Gates and meet a second Sunningdale.

Well, perhaps the heavenly blend is a mixture of all three, but in any event, the gentleman in charge of the terrestrial Sunningdale is the **Secretary, Stewart Zuill**. Mr. Zuill may be contacted on **(01344) 621681. Keith Maxwell** is the club's resident **Professional** and he can be reached on **(01344) 620128.** In common with neighbouring The Berkshire, Sunningdale has two eighteen hole courses, the **Old,** designed in 1901 by Willie Park, and the **New** which was constructed by Harry Colt in 1922. Both are splendid, and many would say the leading examples of the famous Berkshire/Surrey heathland type course. The holes wind their way through glorious forests of conifer and pine with heather and bracken bordering each fairway. All around there are splashes of silver sand.

With its great reputation and close proximity to the capital, Sunningdale is not surprisingly very popular. Unless accompanied by a member, visitors are restricted to playing between Mondays and Thursdays and must make prior arrangement with the Secretary. A letter of introduction is also required. All written communications should be addressed to Mr. Zuill at **The Sunningdale Golf Club, Ridgemount Road, Sunningdale, Berkshire SL5 9RR.** In 1998 the green fees are set at £100 for a round on the Old Course and £75 for the New Course, while a combined ticket at £125 entitles the visitor to a round over both courses. Sets of clubs can be hired from the professional shop should the need arise. Those keen to organise a society meeting are also advised to approach Mr. Zuill via the above address.

Sunningdale is situated just off the A30, about 28 miles west of London. Motoring from the south and west the M3 (leaving at junction 3) and the M4 (junction 10) may be of assistance, while from the north both the A332 and the A330 pass through nearby Ascot. The club's precise location is some 300 yards from Sunningdale railway station.

When golfers talk of Sunningdale, invariably it is the Old Course they have in mind, this despite the fact that a large number of people consider the New to be its equal. The former has acquired such pre-eminence largely as a result of the many major professional and amateur tournaments that have been staged there. However the Old Course is perhaps best known for a single round of golf played by the legendary Bobby Jones. In qualifying for the 1926 Open Championship, which he in fact went on to win, the great man put together what has often been described as the finest 18 holes of golf ever seen. Jones' record 66, a remarkable achievement in the 1920s, comprised twelve fours and six threes—33 for the front nine and 33 for the back nine. More amazingly Jones played only 33 shots from tee to green and took 33 putts—as Bernard Darwin put it, 'incredible and indecent'.

In more recent years Sunningdale has hosted the prestigious European Open. During the 1970s the finest lady golfers assembled for the Colgate sponsored European WPGA Championship, in 1987 the Walker Cup was played at Sunningdale and in August 1997 the Weetabix British Open was staged on the Old Course.

At 6609 yards (par 72) the Old Course is slightly shorter than the New (6703 yards, par 70). The respective distances from the Ladies' tees are 5825 yards and 5840 yards (both being par 74). It seems somehow wrong to single out individual holes, each course possessing its own wealth of variety and charm. The views from the 5th and 10th tees on the Old Course are, however, particularly outstanding and the 18th also provides a spectacular closing hole as it gently doglegs towards the green and the giant spreading oak tree, very much the symbol of Sunningdale.

Sunningdale's glorious setting has been described as both 'heavenly' and 'hauntingly beautiful'. Certainly the golfer privileged to stroll up the final fairway on a summer's evening as the sun begins its leisurely dip, can be forgiven if he amends the words of Henry Longhurst and declares 'What a lovely place to be alive!'

Old Course

Hole	Yards	Par	Hole	Yards	Par
1	494	5	10	478	5
2	484	5	11	325	4
3	319	4	12	451	4
4	161	3	13	185	3
5	410	4	14	509	5
6	415	4	15	226	3
7	402	4	16	438	4
8	192	3	17	421	4
9	267	4	18	432	4
Out	**3,144**	**36**	**In**	**3,465**	**36**
			Out	**3,144**	**36**
			Totals	**6,609**	**72**

Walton Heath

Gavrilo Princip may have pulled the trigger that ignited the Great War but our history books tell us that tension in Europe had sometime earlier reached boiling point. In their palaces in St Petersburg and Berlin the Czar and the Kaiser pondered the strength of their armies. Meanwhile the great statesmen of Britain were engaged in battles of a different nature. . .

All square as they reach the 18th green on the Old Course at Walton Heath, Churchill turns to Lloyd-George and says, 'Now then, I will putt you for the Premiership'.

Herbert Fowler once said, 'God builds golf links and the less man meddles the better for all concerned'. Herbert Fowler designed Walton Heath. However, before the opening of the Old Course in May 1904, at least a little meddling was called for. The glorious heathland through which the emerald fairways were cut was once covered, or nearly covered in thick heather, in parts as much as two feet thick (the members will tell you it still is!) While many of Britain's leading clubs took several years to establish their reputations, that of Walton Heath was assured months before the first stroke was even played—in January 1904 James Braid agreed to become Walton's first professional. Braid initially signed a seven year contract and his performances in the next seven Open Championships were: 2nd, 1st, 1st, 5th, 1st, 2nd and 1st, after which he became the first ever golfer to win five Opens. Hardly surprisingly his contract was extended and so indeed began an association with the club that was to last for nearly fifty years.

In the years immediately before the first world war Walton Heath members included no fewer than 24 MPs (including Winston Churchill and Lloyd-George) and 21 members of the House of Lords. Another famous Walton golfer was W G Grace (it was once cruelly suggested that he compiled as many hundreds on the Heath as he did at the Oval). After the war a more royal flavour dominated, with the Prince of Wales becoming an Honorary Member in 1921 and Captain in 1935.

Time to leap forward to the present and introduce the club's **Secretary, Nick Lomas.** He may be contacted at **The Walton Heath Golf Club, Tadworth, Surrey KT20 7TP,** tel: **(01737) 812380.** Subject to prior arrangement with the Secretary, golfers are welcome to visit Walton Heath between Mondays and Fridays. Proof of both club membership and an official handicap is required. The green fees for 1998 are set at £68 for a full day's golf, with a reduced rate of £58 available to those teeing off

after 11.30am. The hire of golf clubs can be arranged through the club's popular **Professional, Ken MacPherson, (01737) 812152.**

Located south of London, motoring to the club is assisted greatly by the M25. Those approaching on this motorway should leave at junction 8 turning north on to the A217. The A217 should be followed for approximately 2 miles after which a left turn should be taken on to the B2032. The golf club is situated a mile or so along this road. Travelling from further afield, the M25 is linked to the M23 to the South, the M20 to the East and to the North and West by the M3, M4 and M1.

There are two great courses at Walton Heath, the **Old** and the **New** (the latter first appearing as nine holes in 1907 but later extended to the full 18). Lying adjacent to one another, each possesses the same classical heathland characteristics: sandy subsoil, heather, bracken, gorse, pines and silver birch. The finishing three holes on the Old are thought by many (including no lesser a judge than Tom Weiskopf) to be the finest on any course. The classic 16th is a very mild dog-leg to a raised green which slopes from left to right, with the right side of the green guarded by an extremely cavernous bunker. The par three 17th has sand traps practically encircling the green, creating a near island effect and the 18th requires a testing second to carry an enormous cross bunker.

Over the years Walton Heath has played host to many important tournaments. The major amateur championships have included the English Amateur and both the Ladies English Amateur and the Ladies British Open Amateur Championships. Among the professional events, twenty-two of the PGA Matchplay Championships were staged at Walton Heath and in recent years The Ryder Cup of 1981 as well as five European Open Championships.

Walton Heath has a fine clubhouse with an excellent restaurant and lounge. A jacket and tie should be worn in all public rooms after 11am. Lunches are served between 12.00 pm and 2.30pm.

Understandably wherever you turn in the clubhouse you are likely to see a reminder of the long association with James Braid. One small note sent to him from the Prince of Wales conveys a message all golfers can appreciate. It relates how the Prince came to the 18th requiring a four for a 79. After explaining how his second finished just through the green he tells how, 'with the chance of breaking 80, I couldn't stand the nerve-strain and fluffed the chip and took two putts. . .' How the mighty fall!

Old Course

Hole	Yards	Par	Hole	Yards	Par
1	235	3	10	399	4
2	442	4	11	189	3
3	289	4	12	371	4
4	441	4	13	529	5
5	391	4	14	517	5
6	427	4	15	408	4
7	174	3	16	510	5
8	494	5	17	181	3
9	400	4	18	404	4
Out	3,293	35	In	3,508	37
			Out	3,293	35
			Totals	6,801	72

Set high in the rolling hills of the Surrey countryside Selsdon Park hotel combines the ancient virtues of hospitality and courtesy with the modern attributes of efficiency and friendliness.

The hotel was purchased in March 1997 by Principal Hotels, who have added this distinctive property to their expanding portfolio of traditional hotels.

Since then a £2.5 million refurbishment has transformed the extensive facilities, making the hotel one of the highest graded in the area. The hotel now has 205 bedrooms and suites and a considerable range of conference and banqueting rooms.

An outstanding asset to Selsdon Park is the 18 hole championship golf course laid out by five-times British Open golf champion, J H Taylor. Originally cut out of the thick forest which clothed this part of the Surrey Hills, the course has been extended over the years, but the layout remains substantially as it was sixty years ago. Covering 6402 yards, this course is not perhaps for the novice, although it provides a stimulating challenge to low and high handicappers alike. Ideal for society days, a package can be tailored to met your exact requirements.

A round or two on this interesting course prepares the golfer to sample the pleasures of luncheon or dinner in the restaurant, or the more informal cuisine of the Phoenix Grill. The traditional bar lounge, warmed in winter by crackling logs, provides old world comfort while the contemporary atmosphere of the Phoenix Bar makes it an ideal place to sample the wide range of cocktails available.

Golfing weekends here are a delight, and there is plenty to occupy the time of a non-golfing partner. There is a heated outdoor swimming pool (open from May to September), a jogging trail, two hard tennis courts and two grass courts (floodlit as necessary), boules pitch and croquet lawn. A large billiard room containing four full sized snooker tables remains open for the use of resident guests until 1 am. Horse riding can be organised at a stables nearby. The Leisure Club contains a well equipped gymnasium and squash courts, while the tropical swimming pool, sunbeds, steambath, sauna and jacuzzi provide less strenuous pleasures.

Selsdon Park hotel has an almost unbeatable combination of sporting and leisure facilities to offer the golfer and non-golfer alike, together with all the amenities of a deluxe 4 star hotel.

Selsdon Park Hotel & Golf Course
Addington Road
Sanderstead
South Croydon
Surrey CR2 8YA
Tel: 0181 657 8811
Fax: 0181 651 6171

Key

*To avoid disappointment
it is advisable to telephone
in advance*

***Visitors welcome at most times*
**Visitors usually allowed on
weekdays only*
*Visitors not normally permitted
(Mon, Wed) No visitors
on specified days*

Approximate Green Fees
A £40 plus
B £25 to £40
C £20 to £30
D £15 to £25
E under £15
F Green fees on application

Restrictions
G Guests only
H—Handicap certificate required
H—(24) Handicap of 24 or less
L —Letter of introduction required
M—Visitor must be a member of
another recognised club

GREATER LONDON
(including Middlesex)

Airlinks G.C.
(0181) 561 1418
Southall Lane, Hounslow
(18) 6002 yards/***/D

Arkley G.C.
(0181) 449 0394
Rowley Green Road, Barnet
(9) 6045 yards/**/C/H

Ashford Manor G.C.
(01784) 257687
Fordbridge Road, Ashford
(18) 6343 yards/***/B/H/M

Beckenham Place Park G.C.
(0181) 650 2292
Beckenham Hill Road, Beckenham
(18) 5722 yards/***/E

Bexleyheath G.C.
(0181) 303 6951
Mount Road, Bexleyheath
(9) 5239 yards/**/D

Brent Valley G.C.
(0181) 567 1287
Church Road, Hanwell
(18) 5426 yards/***/F

Bush Hill Park G.C.
(0181) 360 5738
Bush Hill, Winchmore Hill
(18) 5809 yards/**/B/L

C & L Country Club
(0181) 845 5662
West End Road, Northolt
(9) 4440 yards/***/E

Chingford G.C.
(0181) 529 2107
Station Road, Chingford
(18) 6336 yards/***/F

Chislehurst G.C.
(0181) 467 2782
Camden Park Road, Chislehurst
(18) 5128 yards/**/C/H

Crews Hill G.C.
(0181) 363 0787
Cattlegate Road, Crews Hill, Enfield
(18) 6230 yards/**/F/H/M

Dulwich and Sydenham Hill G.C.
(0181) 693 3961
Grange Lane, College Road,
(18) 6610 yards/**/B/H(22)/L

Dyrham Park C.C.
(0181) 440 3361
Galley Lane, Barnet
(18) 6369 yards/***/F/G

Ealing G.C.
(0181) 997 0937
Perivale Lane, Greenford
(18) 6216 yards/**/B/H

Elstree G.C.
(0181) 953 6115
Watling Street, Elstree
(18) 6100 yards/***/F

Eltham Warren G.C.
(0181) 850 1166
Bexley Road, Eltham
(9) 5840 yards/**/B/H/M

Enfield G.C.
(0181) 363 3970
Old Park Road South, Enfield
(18) 6137 yards/**/B/H/M

Finchley G.C.
(0181) 346 2436
Nether Court, Frith Lane, Mill Hill
(18) 6411 yards/***/A

Fulwell G.C.
(0181) 977 7732
Wellington Road, Hampton Hill
(18) 6544 yards/**/A/L

Gryms Dyke G.C.
(0181) 428 4539
Oxhey Lane, Hatch End, Pinner
(18) 5600 yards/**/B/H

Hadley Wood G.C.
(0181) 449 4486
Beech Hill, Barnet
(18) 6473 yards/**/A/H/M

Hampstead G.C.
(0181) 455 0203
Winnington Road, Hampstead
(9) 5812 yards/***/B/H

Harrow School G.C.
(0181) 869 1253
High Street, Harrow-on-the-Hill
(9) 3690 yards/*/G

Hartsbourne G.& C.C.
(0181) 950 1133
Hartsbourne Avenue, Bushey Heath
(18) 6305 yards/*/F/G/M
(9) 5432 yards/*/F/G/M

Haste Hill G.C.
(01923) 825224
The Drive, Northwood
(18) 5794 yards/***/F

Hendon G.C.
(0181) 346 6023
Devonshire Rd, Mill Hill
(18) 6266 yards/**/B/M

Highgate G.C.
(0181) 340 1906
Denewood Road, Highgate
(18) 5982 yards/**(Wed)/B/H

Hillingdon G.C.
(01895) 233956
18 Dorset Way, Hillingdon
(9) 5459 yards/**(Thu)/C/H/M

The Holiday Inn
(01895) 444232
Stockley Road, West Drayton
(9) 3800 yards/***/E

Horsenden Hill G.C.
(0181) 902 4555
Woodland Rise, Greenford
(9) 3236 yards/***/E

Hounslow Heath G.C.
(0181) 570 5271
Staines Road, Hounslow
(18) 5901 yards/***/E

Ilford G.C.
(0181) 554 2930
Wanstead Park Road, Ilford
(18) 5251 yards/**/D

Langley Park G.C.
(0181) 650 2090
Barnfield Wood Road, Beckenham
(18) 6488 yards/**/A/H

Lee Valley G.C.
(0181) 803 3611
Picketts Lock Lane, Edmonton
(18) 4902 yards/***/D

The London Golf Centre
(0181) 841 6162
Ruislip Road, Northolt
(9) 5838 yards/***/E

London Scottish G.C.
(0181) 789 0135
Windmill Enclosure, Wimbledon
Common
(18) 5436 yards/**/F/H

Magpie Hall Lane G.C.
(0181) 462 7014
Magpie Hall Lane, Bromley
(9) 2745 yards/***/F

Mill Hill G.C.
(0181) 959 2339
Barnet Way, Mill Hill
(18) 6309 yards/***/B/H

Muswell Hill G.C.
(0181) 888 2044
Rhodes Avenue, Wood Green
(18) 6474 yards/**/B/H(24)

North Middlesex G.C.
(0181) 445 1732
Friern Barnet Lane, Whetstone
(18) 5625 yards/***/B/H

Northwood G.C.
(01923) 821384
Rickmansworth Road, Northwood
(18) 6553 yards/**/B/H

Perivale Park G.C.
(0181) 575 7116
Argyle Road, Greenford
(9) 5267 yards/***/E

Pinner Hill G.C.
(0181) 866 0963
Southview Road, Pinner Hill
(18) 6293 yards/**/F/H

Roehampton G.C.
(0181) 876 1621
Roehampton Lane, London
(18) 6046 yards/**/F/L

Royal Blackheath G.C.
(0181) 850 1795
Court Road, Eltham
(18) 6214 yards/**/A/H/L

Royal Wimbledon G.C.
(0181) 946 2125
Camp Road, Wimbledon
(18) 6300 yards/**/A/H(18)/L

Ruislip G.C.
(01895) 638835
Ickenham Road, Ruislip
(18) 5703 yards/***/D

Sandy Lodge G.C.
(01923) 825429
Sandy Lodge Lane, Northwood
(18) 6340 yards/***/F/H/M

Shooters Hill G.C.
(0181) 854 6368
Eaglesfield Road, Shooters Hill
(18) 5736 yards/**/B/H/M

Shortlands G.C.
(0181) 460 2471
Meadow Road, Shortlands, Bromley
(9) 5261 yards/*/D/G

Sidcup G.C.
(0181) 300 2150
Hurst Road, Sidcup
(9) 5722 yards/**/D/H/L

South Herts G.C.
(0181) 445 2035
Links Drive, Totteridge
(18) 6470 yards/**/F/H(24)/L

Springfield Park G.C.
(0181) 871 2468
Burntwood Lane, Wandsworth
(9) 4451 yards/**/E

Stanmore G.C.
(0181) 954 2599
Gordon Avenue, Stanmore
(18) 5881 yards/**/E-C/H

Stockley Park G.C.
(0181) 813 5700
Stockley Park, Uxbridge
(18) 6548 yards/***/A

Strawberry Hill G.C.
(0181) 894 1246
Wellesley Road, Twickenham
(9) 2381 yards/**/C

Sudbury G.C.
(0181) 902 3713
Bridgewater Road, Wembley
(18) 6282 yards/**/F/H/M

Sunbury G.C.
(01932) 772898
Sunbury
(9) 3105 yards/***/D

Sundridge Park G.C.
(0181) 460 0278
Garden Road, Bromley
(18) 6467 yards/**/A/H
(18) 6007 yards/**/A/H

Trent Park G.C.
(0181) 366 7432
Bramley Road, Southgate
(18) 6008 yards/***/D

Twickenham Park G.C.
(0181) 783 1698
Staines Road, Twickenham
(9) 6014 yards/***/E

Uxbridge G.C.
(01895) 272457
The Drive, Harefield Place, Uxbridge
(18) 5753 yards/***/D

Wanstead G.C.
(0181) 989 0604
Overton Drive, Wanstead
(18) 6262 yards/**(Wed,Thu)/B/H

West Middlesex G.C.
(0181) 574 3450
Greenford Road, Southall
(18) 6242 yards/**/C

Whitewebbs G.C.
(0181) 363 2951
Beggars Hollow, Clay Hill, Enfield
(18) 5863 yards/***/D

Wimbledon Common G.C.
(0181) 946 0294
Camp Road, Wimbledon Common
(18) 5438 yards/**/C

Wimbledon Park G.C.
(0181) 946 1250
Home Park Road, Wimbledon
(18) 5465 yards/**/B/H/L/M

Wyke Green G.C.
(0181) 560 8777
Syon Lane, Isleworth
(18) 6242 yards/**/A/H

SURREY

Addington G.C.
(0181) 777 1055
Shirley Church Road, Croydon
(18) 6242 yards/**/F/H/L

Addington Court G.C.
(0181) 657 0281
Featherbed Lane, Addington
(18) 5577 yards/***/D
(18) 5513 yards/***/D
(9) 1812 yards/***/E

Addington Palace G.C.
(0181) 654 3061
Gravel Hill, Addington
(18) 6410 yards/**/B/H/G

Banstead Downs G.C.
(0181) 642 2284
Burdon Lane, Belmont
(18) 6169 yards/**/B/H

Barrow Hills G.C.
(01344) 635770
Longcross, Chertsey
(18) 3090 yards/**/F/G

Betchworth Park G.C.
(01306) 882052
Reigate Road, Dorking
(18) 6266 yards/**(Tue,Wed)/A

Bletchingley G.C.
(01883) 744666
Church Lane, Bletchingley
(18) 6504 yards/**/B

Bowenhurst G.C.
(01252) 851695
Mill Lane, Crondham, Surrey
(9) 2007 yards/***/D

Bramley G.C.
(01483) 892696
Bramley, Guildford
(18) 5990 yards/**/B

Broadwater Park G.C.
(01483) 429955
Guildford Road, Farncombe
(9) 1323 yards/***/E

Burhill G.C.
(01932) 227345
Walton-on-Thames
(18) 6224 yards/**/F/H/L

Camberley Heath G.C.
(01276) 23258
Golf Drive, Camberley
(18) 6337 yards/**/A/H

Chessington Golf Centre
(0181) 391 0948
Garrison Lane, Chessington
(9) 1400 yards/***/E

Chiddingfold G.C.
(01428) 685888
Petsworth Road, Chiddingfold
(18) 5500 yards/***/C

Chipstead G.C.
(01737) 555881
How Lane, Coulsdon
(18) 5454 yards/**/B

Chobham G.C.
(01276) 855584
Chobham Road, Chobham
(18) 6000 yards/*/F/G/H

Clandon Regis G.C.
(01483) 224888
Epsom Road, West Clandon
(18) 6412 yards/**/B/H

Coombe Hill G.C.
(0181) 942 2284
Golf Club Drive, Kingston
(18) 6303 yards/**/A/H/L

Coombe Wood G.C.
(0181) 942 0388
George Road, Kingston Hill
(18) 5210 yards/**/F/H

Coulsdon Manor G.C.
(0181) 668 0414
Coulsdon Court Road, Coulsdon
(18) 6037 yards/***/D

Croham Hurst G.C.
(0181) 657 5581
Croham Road, South Croydon
(18) 6286 yards/**/A/H/L

Cuddington G.C.
(0181) 393 0952
Banstead Road, Banstead
(18) 6394 yards/**/A/H/L

Dorking G.C.
(01306) 886917
Chart Park, Dorking
(9) 5120 yards/**/D

Drift G.C.
(01483) 284641
The Drift, East Horsley
(18) 6425 yards/**/B

Duke's Dene G.C.
(01883) 653501
Woldingham
(18) 6390 yards/***/B

Dunsfold Aerodrome G.C.
(01483) 265472
Dunsfold Aerodrome, Godalming
(9) 6090 yards/*/E/G

Effingham G.C.
(01372) 452203
Guildford Road, Effingham
(18) 6488 yards/**/A/H/G(weekends)

Epsom G.C.
(01372) 721666
Longdown Lane South, Epsom
(18) 5701 yards/**/C

Farnham G.C.
(01252) 782109
The Sands, Farnham
(18) 6325 yards/**/B/H/M

Fernfell G.& C.C.
(01483) 268855
Barhatch Lane, Cranleigh
(18) 5599 yards/**/B

Foxhills G.C.
(01932) 872050
Stonehill Road, Ottershaw
(18) 6680 yards/**/A
(18) 6547 yards/**/A
(9) 1300 yards/**/A

Gatton Manor G.& C.C.
(01306) 627555
Ockley, Dorking
(18) 6902 yards/***/C

Goal Farm Par Three.
(01483) 473205
Gole Road, Pirbright
(9) 1283 yards/***/E

Guildford G.C.
(01483) 63941
High Path Road, Merrow
(18) 6090 yards/**/B

Hankley Common G.C.
(01252) 792493
Tilford Road, Tilford, Farnham
(18) 6418 yards/**/A/H/L

Hindhead G.C.
(01428) 604614
Churt Road, Hindhead
(18) 6373 yards/***/A/H

Hoebridge G.C.
(01483) 722611
Old Woking Road, Old Woking
(18) 6536 yards/***/D
(18) 2298 yards/***/E
(9) 2294 yards/***/E

Home Park G.C.
(0181) 977 2423
Hampton Wick, Kingston
(18) 6610/***/C

Horton Park C.C.
(0181) 393 8400
Hook Road, Ewell
(18) 5208 yards/***/D

Hurtmore G.C.
(01483) 426492
Hurtmore Road, Hurtmore
(18) 5444 yards/***/D

Kingswood G.C.
(01737) 832188
Sandy Lane, Kingswood
(18) 6880 yards/***/A/H

Laleham G.C.
(01932) 564211
Laleham Reach, Chertsey
(18) 6203 yards/**/C

Leatherhead G.C.
(01372) 843966
Kingston Road, Leatherhead
(18) 6157 yards/***/A

Limpsfield Chart G.C.
(01883) 723405
Westerham Road,Limpsfield
(9) 5718 yards/**(Thu)/C/H

Lingfield Park G.C.
(01342) 834602
Racecourse Road, Lingfield
(18) 6500 yards/**/B

Malden G.C.
(0181) 942 0654
Traps Lane, New Malden
(18) 6295 yards/**/F/H

Milford G.C.
(01483) 419200
Station Lane, Milford
(18) 6224 yards/**/B/H

Mitcham G.C.
(0181) 648 1508
Carshalton Road, Mitcham Junction
(18) 5935 yards/**/D/H(18)

Moore Place G.C.
(01372) 463533
Portsmouth Road, Esher
(9) 4186 yards/***/E

New Zealand G.C.
(01932) 345049
Woodham Lane, Addlestone
(18) 6012 yards/*/A

North Downs G.C.
(01883) 653298
Northdown Road, Caterham
(18) 5843 yards/**/B/H

Oak Park G.C.
(01252) 850880
Crondall, nr Farnham
(18) 6437 yards/***/C

Oak Sports Centre
(0181) 643 8363
Woodmansterne Road, Carshalton
(18) 6033 yards/***/D
(9) 1590 yards/***/E

Pachesham Golf Centre
(01372) 843453
Oaklawn Road, Leatherhead
(9) 1752 yards/***/E

Pine Ridge G.C.
(01276) 20770
Old Bisley Road, Frimley
(18) 6458 yards/***/D

Purley Downs G.C.
(0181) 657 8347
Purley Downs Road, Purley
(18) 6212 yards/**/A/H/M/L

Puttenham G.C.
(01483) 810498
Heath Road, Puttenham, Guildford
(18) 6204/**/C/H

Pyrford G.C.
(01483) 723555
Warren Lane, Pyrford
(18) 6201 yards/**/A/H

RAC Country Club
(01372) 276311
Woodcote Park, Epsom
(18) 6709 yards/*/F
(18) 5598 yards/*/F

Redhill G.C.
(01737) 770204
Canada Avenue, Redhill
(9) 1901 yards/***/E

Redhill and Reigate G.C.
(01737) 244433
Pendleton Road, Redhill
(18) 5238 yards/***/D

Reigate Heath G.C.
(01737) 226793
Reigate Heath, Reigate
(9) 5658 yards/**/F

Reigate Hill G.C.
(01737) 645577
Gatten Bottom, Reigate
(18) 6175 yards/**/C

Richmond G.C.
(0181) 940 1463
Sudbrook Park, Richmond
(18) 5977 yards/**/A/H

Richmond Park G.C.
(0181) 876 3205
Roehampton Gate, Richmond Park
(18) 5940 yards/***/F
(18) 5969 yards/***/F

Roker Park G.C.
(01483) 236677
Holly Lane, Guildford
(9) 3037 yards/***/E

Royal Mid Surrey G.C.
(0181) 940 1894
Old Deer Park, Richmond
(18) 5544 yards/***/A/H/M
(18) 6343 yards/***/A/H/M

Rusper G.C.
(01293) 871871
Rusper Road, Newdigate
(9) 6069 yards/**/F

St Georges Hill G.C.
(01932) 847758
St. Georges Hill, Weybridge
(18) 6600 yards/**/A/H/L
(9) 3000 yards/**/A/H/L

Sandown Golf Centre
(01372) 463340
More Lane, Esher
(9) 5656 yards/***/D
(9) 1193 yards/***/E

Selsdon Park Hotel G.C.
(0181) 657 8811
Addington Road, Sanderstead
(18) 6402 yards/***/B/H

Shillinglee Park G.C.
(01428) 653237
Chiddingfold, Godalming
(9) 2500 yards/***/D

Shirley Park G.C.
(0181) 654 1143
Addiscombe Road, Croydon
(18) 6210 yards/**/B/H

Silvermere G.C.
(01932) 867275
Redhill Road, Cobham
(18) 6333 yards/***/C

Sunningdale G.C.
(01344) 21681
Ridgemount Road, Sunningdale
(18) 6586 yards/**/A/H/L
(18) 6676 yards/**/A/H/L

Sunningdale Ladies G.C.
(01344) 20507
Cross Road, Sunningdale
(18) 3622 yards/***/B

Surbiton G.C.
(0181) 398 3101
Woodstock Lane, Chessington
(18) 6211 yards/**/A/H

Sutton Green
(01483) 766898
New Lane, Sutton Green
(18) 6305 yards/***/F

Tandridge G.C.
(01883) 712273
Oxted
(18) 6250 yards/**(Tue,Fri)/A/H

Thames Ditton and Esher G.C.
(0181) 398 1551
Portsmouth Road, Esher
(9) 5190 yards/***/D

Tyrrells Wood G.C.
(01372) 376025
Tyrrells Wood, Leatherhead
(18) 6234 yards/**/A/H/L

Walton Heath G.C.
(01737) 812380
Tadworth
(18) 6801 yards/**/A/H/L
(18) 6609 yards/**/A/H/L

Wentworth G.C.
(01344) 842201
Wentworth Drive, Virginia Water
(18) 6945 yards/**/A/H
(18) 6176 yards/**/A/H
(18) 7006 yards/**/A/H

West Byfleet G.C.
(01932) 345230
Sheerwater Road, West Byfleet
(18) 6211 yards/**/B

West Hill G.C.
(01483) 474365
Bagshot Road, Brookwood
(18) 6368 yards/**/A/H

West Surrey G.C.
(01483) 421275
Enton Green, Godalming
(18) 6300 yards/**/A/H

Wildwood G.C.
(01403) 753255
Horsham Road, Afold
(18) 6650 yards/***/A/H

Windlemere G.C.
(01276) 858727
Windlesham Road, West End,
Woking
(9) 5346 yards/***/D

Windlesham G.C.
(01276) 452220
Grove End, Bagshot
(18) 6515 yards/A/H

Wisley G.C.
(01483) 211022
Ripley, Woking
(9) 3355 yards/*/A
(9) 3473 yards/*/A
(9) 3385 yards/*/A

Woking G.C.
(01483) 760053
Pond Road, Hook Heath, Woking
(18) 6322 yards/**/A/H/M/L

Woodcote Park G.C.
(0181) 668 2788
Meadow Hill, Bridle Way, Coulsdon
(18) 6669 yards/**/B/H

Worplesdon G.C.
(01483) 472277
Heath House Road, Woking
(18) 6440 yards/**/A/H/L

 Artist: **C Harris INDOOR PRACTICE** *Courtesy of:* **Burlington Gallery**

Herts, Beds & Essex Choice Golf

Unfortunately, for all too many, the first and often lasting impression of a place can be determined by the great blue ribbons that now stretch the length and breadth of the country—Britain's ever expanding motorway network. The M1 (not to mention the M25) cuts through the heart of Hertfordshire and slices off the left ear of Bedfordshire. Between London and Luton it is a fearsome animal at the best of times and passing beyond these two counties one often draws a sigh of relief. The greater expanse of Essex fares a little better, escaping with a few nasty scratches, but in all three counties the deeper realms are not as often explored as they might be, except, needless to say, by those who live there.

The golfing breed is a little more fortunate than most. In every county in Britain he, and she, can visit courses that are tucked away in the most secluded and tranquil of settings and even in the 'there's an open space—lets build on it' 90s, Hertfordshire, Bedfordshire and Essex are not exceptions to the rule.

Hertfordshire

A glance at the map tells you that **Ashridge** in Hertfordshire isn't all that great a distance from London and the M1 but it occupies a particularly peaceful spot and the approach road which runs near **Berkhamsted** Golf Club passes through some glorious countryside—the kind that once covered much of this part of the world. Both are delightful heathland/parkland courses. Berkhamsted is best known for its conspicuous absence of bunkers though, like Royal Ashdown Forest in Sussex, it has more than enough natural hazards to test the courage of any golfer. Ashridge is perhaps most famed for its long association with Henry Cotton, for many years the club's professional. There are many fine par fours at

Ashridge, the 9th and 14th being two of the best. The approach to the latter bears an uncanny resemblance to the 17th at St Andrews—the mischievously positioned bunker front left and the road behind the green—though it's not quite as frightening! Both courses are decidedly worth a visit.

There is certainly no shortage of golf courses in Hertfordshire and several new layouts have recently opened including the **The Hertfordshire** at Broxbourne and the **Stock's Country House Hotel** (01442) 85341, situated at Aldbury, near Tring—quite close to Ashridge. In the upper realms of the county, Harpenden, convenient for those motoring along the M1, has two courses, **Harpenden** and **Harpenden Common**, the former at Hammonds End being the pick of the two. A short distance away at Wheathampstead is the **Mid Herts** Golf Club, while on the other side of the country's most famous blue ribbon lies **East Herts** near Buntingford. In the heart of Hertfordshire stands the exclusive and impressive **Brocket Hall** Golf Club near Welwyn. The greater concentration of courses, however, perhaps not surprisingly, is in the area just north of London. **Moor Park**, featured a few pages on, is the most widely known, though nearby **Porters Park** (in the quiet of Radlett) and **West Herts** (on the edge of Watford, yet similarly peaceful) also strongly merit attention.

West Herts was once more commonly known as Cassiobury Park after its location. Bernard Darwin in his famous 'Golf Courses of the British Isles' sang its praises highly: 'Of all the race of park courses, it would scarcely be possible in point of sheer beauty, to beat Cassiobury Park near Watford.' One other course to note in Hertfordshire is the first class public course at Essendon, confusingly called the **Hatfield London Country Club.**

It is possible to view the county's best courses from a

London base. This isn't to say, however, that a number of excellent establishments can't be found beyond the city limits. In Thundridge, near Ware, **Hanbury Manor** (01920) 487722 is a five star country house hotel which can boast, among many things, a golf course first laid by Harry Vardon in the 1920s and recently completely redesigned by Jack Nicklaus Jr. The course is explored on a separate page in this chapter. In **Hadley Wood**, where there is a well established 18 hole course, the West Lodge Park is an elegant mansion house (0181) 440 8311, while Boreham Wood carries a restaurant to note—Signor Battis.

The best bet if you are playing Moor Park and looking for nearby quality accommodation is the Grym's Dyke hotel 0181 954 4227 in Harrow Weald. St Albans and Harpenden, where the traffic races through, are both littered with good pubs off the busy high streets. St Albans offers its superb cathedral and the delightful St Michael's Manor (01727) 864444 which lies in its shadow. Sopwell House (01727) 864477 offers excellent leisure facilities amidst its elegant Georgian frame. Harpenden's House (01582) 449955 is a little pricey but extremely well thought of. An idea for East Herts—the Redcoats Farmhouse (01438) 729500 at Little Wymondley is very cosy.

For golfers seeking genuine excellence—a true pinnacle perhaps—the Briggens House Hotel (01279) 829955 and its elegant restaurant at Ware should serve admirably. Briggens House has its own 9 hole golf course and is only 6 miles away from Hanbury Manor.

Bedfordshire

Arguably the two leading clubs in Bedfordshire are **John O'Gaunt** at Sandy and **Beadlow Manor** near Shefford; both have more than one course. The former is more established: its two courses, the championship John O'Gaunt course and the shorter Carthegena are curiously very different in character, the John O'Gaunt being a very pretty parkland type, the Carthegena, a heathland course. Visitors to both John O'Gaunt and Beadlow Manor can expect first class facilities and a friendly welcome and for the latter the Beadlow Manor Hotel (01525) 860800 is naturally very convenient.

Another of the better courses in Bedfordshire is **Dunstable Downs,** laid out on high ground, offering remarkably extensive views—both Surrey to the south and Warwickshire to the north west can be sighted. It is a classic downland type course.

In nearby Berkhamsted, La Fiorentina (01442) 863003 is an excellent restaurant offering fine Italian food and a knowledgeable golfing host (The town is actually in Herts, but as well as being convenient for Ashridge, it is ideal for the courses of South Bedfordshire). In Whipsnade, the zoo is excellent while the downs nearby are a good place to get rid of some energy. In Dunstable the Old Palace Lodge (01582) 662201 is well worth an overnight visit. Pendley Manor (01442) 891891 is also a quality establishment.

Elsewhere in the county, **Aspley Guise and Woburn Sands** (the more famous Woburn Golf and Country Club lies over the border in Buckinghamshire) is another that provides far-reaching views and a word also for the **Bedford and County** Golf Club. Just north of the county town off the A6, near St Neots in Cambridgeshire but just within Bedfordshire, **Wyboston Lakes** is a pleasant pay and play course.

In Woburn some excellent hotels and restaurants can be found in addition to the delightful stately home and game reserve. The Paris House (01525) 290692 is an outstanding restaurant while the Bedford Arms (01525) 290441 is a welcoming Georgian coaching inn. The Black

Horse is a notable pub to visit and the Bell Inn (01525) 290280 is thoroughly recommended for its atmosphere and value. Outside the town, Moore Place (01908) 282000 in Aspley Guise is extremely relaxing and in Flitwick, the 17th century Flitwick Manor (01525) 712242 and its restaurant are tremendous. En route to the county town the Rose & Crown (0152528) 245 in Ridgmont serves a good pint and bar snacks. In Bedford itself we could call upon the services of the Moat House group—the Bedford Moat House (01234) 355131 or the less expensive Clarenden House Hotel. For grander accommodation, the Woodlands Manor (01234) 363281 in Clapham offers a delightful hotel with a quality restaurant. Finally, in the corner of Bedfordshire, Turvey offers Laws Hotel (01234) 881655: some accommodation and a good restaurant here.

Essex

Not much of Essex could be described as 'natural golfing country' yet of all England's counties this is the one that witnessed perhaps the biggest explosion in golf course site applications during the late 1980s. Strange, isn't it? Two of the top courses in the county are **Thorndon Park** (two miles south of Brentwood) and **Orsett** (two miles east of Grays and in the wonderfully named area of Mucking and Fobbing). Neither is a great distance from the M25 and both can be reached via the A128. Thorndon Park, as its name suggests, is a parkland type course situated in a former deer park belonging to Thorndon Hall—a quite stunning mansion. Orsett is much more of the heathland variety with sandy subsoil.

In a similar vein to neighbouring Hertfordshire, a number of the county's better courses have been gradually swallowed up by Greater London—the fine parkland course at **Abridge** with its splendidly luxurious clubhouse being one of them, now lying the wrong side of the M25. **Romford** is one that holds its Essex identity. A well bunkered and fairly flat course, Romford was the home of James Braid before he moved to Walton Heath. Just beyond the M25 the new Martin Gillett-designed course at Billericay, **Stock Brook Manor,** has a growing reputation.

Still further afield, both **Colchester** (the oldest town in England) and **Saffron Walden** have courses set in very pretty surroundings and for lovers of seaside golf there is a pleasant (though windy!) course at **Frinton-on-Sea**. One of the county's newest attractions is the **Five Lakes** Golf and Country Club (01621) 868888 at Tolleshunt D'Arcy, not far from Maldon, where there are 36 holes. This large complex offers an abundance of leisure facilities as well as good golf. Finally, for those visiting Chelmsford, both the **Chelmsford** Golf Club, to the south of the town and the **Channels** Golf Club to the north with its superb Elizabethan clubhouse can be recommended, as can the nearby **Warren** Golf Club at Woodham Walter (a very interesting collection of short holes here) and **The Three Rivers** Golf and Country Club in Purleigh (two courses here).

Benton Hall with 27 holes or **Stapleford Abbots** with 45 holes are also well worth ear marking for a good days golf. Essex is blessed with many outstanding hotels and restaurants. Dedham presents an ideal starting point. Here we find the superb La Talbooth (01206) 323150. This is a monument to good food, an ideal place to celebrate a special round of golf. Close by, the Maison Talbooth (01206) 322367 offers stylish accommodation. This delightful village with its views of the Stour also offers the Dedham Vale Hotel (01206) 322273 and its first class restaurant. All are also convenient for the nearby Suffolk courses. Resisting the temptation to venture further up the Stour and discover the delights of Constable country we arrive at the coast and Harwich—heading directly for the Pier (01255) 241212, where, as you may suspect, the seafood is the speciality of the house—some accommodation here as well. Further up the coast in Brightlingsea, a restaurant and a pub should be pointed out—Jacobs (01206) 302113 is the restaurant, the Cherry Tree is the pub.

More thoughts and in Arkesden a thatched pub, the Axe & Compasses provides good food and a cheerful hostelry. Saffron Walden offers the Saffron Hotel (01799) 522676 and the charming Newhouse Farm. In the quiet village of Little Walden lies The Crown—good bar food. Another Essex hotel handy for a motorway, the M11 this time, is the Green Man (01279) 442521 in Old Harlow; situated opposite the village green, the hotel totally belies the proximity of the nearby autoroute. Another Green Man (01992) 522255 is also recommended on this occasion at Toot Hill—good food here in the bar and main restaurant. Not particularly close to the county's best golf courses, but well worth a trip is the Whitehall Hotel (01279) 850603 in Broxted where the restaurant is excellent.

Finally we visit Great Dunmow, close to Stansted Airport and where the legendary Flitch trials take place. The Saracens Head Hotel (01371) 873901 in town is small-ish but pleasant. If you are rushing home and cannot spend a night in the area then dinner at the Starr (01371) 874321 may still be a possibility—it's an outstanding restaurant and now has some rooms. Incidentally, for those unfamiliar with the Flitch trials, the basic idea is to test (by some rather interesting methods) the suitability of man and woman. Not apparently a necessity for selecting one's golf partner. . .but it's a thought!

Artist: **Alec MacDonald THE BUNKER**
Courtesy of: **Rosenstiel's**

Moor Park

I don't suppose many would dispute that the R&A club-house at St Andrews is the best known 'nineteenth' in the world. However, for the title of 'most magnificent' or 'most grand' it is doubtful whether Moor Park can have many serious rivals. The Moor Park Mansion dates from the 13th century. In its illustrious history it has been the home of earls, dukes, cardinals, archbishops and even a Queen—Catherine of Aragon living there in the 16th century. During the last war the mansion was requisitioned, becoming first the headquarters of the Territorial Army, then of the ATS and later of the American 2nd Airborne Corps and it was from within Moor Park that preparations were made for the ill-fated invasion of Arnhem in 1944.

Golf first came to Moor Park in 1923, Lord Ebury founding the golf club just four years after the estate had been purchased by Lord Leverhulme. Leading architect Harry Colt was called in to design three golf courses, two of which, the **High** and the **West** courses, remain with the club, the third now being a public course (Rickmansworth) although it is in fact maintained by the Moor Park club.

The major championships staged at Moor Park are all played over the High Course. Measuring 6713 yards (par 72, SSS 72) it is some 900 yards longer than the West Course, though this at 5815 yards (par 69, SSS 68) is certainly no pushover. The High Course begins with a fairly straightforward, slightly uphill 1st but the 2nd which dog-legs to the right is one of the toughest 'fours' of the round. Towards the middle of the front nine a sliced tee shot will send a ball into some particularly pleasant properties whose gardens border the fairways (attempting to retrieve your ball is not recommended!) The back nine contains three excellent short holes including the

12th where the attractive two-tiered green is surrounded by willows and is surely one of the best par threes in the country.

Within two years of the club being founded, Moor Park played host to the 1925 PGA Matchplay Championship, won by Archie Compston. Since then, several memorable professional tournaments and pro-ams have been played here. However, perhaps the best known game of golf at Moor Park took place back in 1928. A 72 hole challenge match was played between the American Walter Hagen, the leading professional of the day, and the aforementioned Archie Compston, one of Britain's finest players. With only one hole of the final round completed the match was all over, Hagen having been defeated 18 up with 17 to play—the greatest margin of victory ever recorded in a matchplay event.

Moor Park Golf Club, Rickmansworth, Herts WD3 1QN	
Secretary	John Davies (01923) 773146 Fax (01923) 777109
Professional	Lawrence Farmer
Green Fees	£60/day (one round over both courses)
Restrictions	Proof of handicap required

Directions
Leave the M25 at junction 17 or 18. The course is off the A404 Northwood to Rickmansworth Road and about three-quarters of a mile from Moor Park station.

Hanbury Manor

There can be few golfing venues in Europe where 'Old' meets and marries 'New' as successfully and interestingly as it appears to have done at Hanbury Manor in Hertfordshire.

The 'Old' is the manor itself, which since the late 19th century has been dominated by a striking Jacobean style mansion and its wonderful grounds which, since 1918, have included a 9 hole parkland golf course. The 'New' is the recent conversion of the estate into the Hanbury Manor Golf and Country Club including restoration and transformation of the mansion into an extremely elegant five star country house hotel and the complete redesign of the golf course into an 18 hole championship length American-style golf course.

The original Hanbury Manor course was designed by Englishman Harry Vardon. Vardon was the greatest of the 'Great Triumvirate' of Vardon, Braid and Taylor who dominated golf between 1894 and 1914. The architect of the new Hanbury course is American Jack Nicklaus II, eldest son (or chief cub) of the 'Golden Bear', the greatest of the big three of Nicklaus, Palmer and Player who dominated golf from the late 1950s until the mid 1970s.

So how new, how good and how American is the course at Hanbury Manor? The official opening took place in the summer of 1991. Jack Jr was naturally present and so too were Tony Jacklin and Dave Stockton who played a friendly match billed as 'The Ryder Cup Captains' Challenge' and which, like the real thing, was won by Stockton. Both Stockton and Jacklin were very complimentary of both the condition of the course and its design. Stockton was also quoted as saying that it was, 'by far the best course I've played outside of the United States'. A shade rash, you might think—especially given that it was uttered by someone who played in several Open Championships—but Hanbury Manor undoubtedly has great potential and, while the superior conditioning of the course (it may be the best maintained course in Great Britain) and the extravagant use of water hazards give the course a very American feel, the surrounding countryside is unmistakably rural England.

Hanbury Manor is located approximately 25 miles north of London, directly off the A10, just north of the Ware turn off. It is important to note that *golf is restrict-* *ed to hotel residents, club members and their guests.* The residential green fees in 1998 are £60 weekdays and weekends. The hotel offers a number of 'packaged residential golf breaks' and those interested should telephone the hotel on **(01920) 487722** for details. The **Golf & Leisure Operations Manager, Marc Newey** and the **Head Professional, Peter Blaze** can also be contacted via the above number. Written correspondence should be addressed to **Hanbury Manor Golf and Country Club, Ware, Hertfordshire SG12 0SD.**

Only the very brave (or rash?) should attempt to tackle Hanbury Manor from the championship tees—at 7016 yards it is monstrously long and many of the par fours are beyond the reach of most mortals. From the medal tees, 6622 yards (par 72) is much more realistic, while the forward tees and ladies' tees reduce the course to 6057 yards and 5285 yards (par 72) respectively. As well as the mix of an American-type course in a very English setting, Hanbury Manor offers two very different challenges within an 18 hole round. The two nines are laid out on opposite sides of the mansion; the first nine has a much newer feel as here the Nicklaus team had to shape virgin golfing terrain (essentially farmland prior to its development) whereas on the back nine they built over the existing mature parkland of the Vardon layout. The degree of challenge, however, is comparable and both nines contain a number of dramatic and beautifully sculpted holes.

The threat of water looms as early as the twisting, downhill 2nd, one of two outstanding par fives on the front nine. The green at this hole has been raised and built at such an angle with fronting traps that even the biggest hitters are unlikely to attempt the water carry with their second shot. A small lake also features on the par three 6th and the very difficult par four 8th, but many people regard the 7th and 9th as even better holes.

On the back nine both the 10th and 15th fairways are bordered by a splendid variety of mature trees and the 13th and 17th call for dramatic do-or-die shots over water. Respite comes at the 18th, for though there is yet more water to be carried from the tee, it is not a big carry—besides, the opulent comforts of Hanbury's 19th hole are now within sight.

Hole	Yards	Par		Hole	Yards	Par
1	314	4		10	383	4
2	529	5		11	181	3
3	425	4		12	532	5
4	167	3		13	379	4
5	456	4		14	371	4
6	164	3		15	396	4
7	341	4		16	177	3
8	425	4		17	486	5
9	528	5		18	368	4
Out	**3,349**	**36**		**In**	**3,273**	**36**
				Out	**3,349**	**36**
				Totals	**6,622**	**72**

The Hanbury Manor Hotel, awarded a much sought after 5 star rating by the AA, is a country house experience to be savoured. A lovingly restored mansion with 96 bedrooms and 10 conference suites, turn of the century charm blends with every modern comfort and service that is always friendly and courteous.

The beautiful 200 acre estate provides a vast array of amenities, including a championship golf course, tennis, squash, snooker and a fully equipped health club.

The perfect place to relax or to combine business with pleasure, Hanbury Manor is easily accessible, only 25 miles north of London. The elegantly appointed bedrooms spoil the most discerning traveller, whilst fine dining is available in three enticingly different restaurants including the gourmet Zodiac Restaurant and the less formal Vardon's.

One of many highlights of a stay at Hanbury Manor will undoubtedly be the magnificent 18 hole golf course, created out of rolling Hertfordshire countryside by Jack Nicklaus II, of Golden Bear Associates. The course measures a testing 7016 yards from the championship tees, with a number of strategically placed bunkers and several picturesque water hazards providing a series of challenges for all levels of players.

The contrasting nature of the Downfield nine, beautifully sculpted out of existing meadowland and an old quarry site, and the inward half - set in breathtaking parkland with mature trees provides a remarkable variety of panoramic scenery that makes for a whole series of spectacular memories. The careful design and conditioning of the course makes Hanbury Manor one of the most beautifully manicured layouts anywhere in Britain.

Whether toning up or winding down, Hanbury provides the perfect environment for relaxing after a game on the championship standard golf course. Indoors or out, the variety of freely accessible leisure activities are numerous, making Hanbury Manor a genuine resort property. The centrepiece of the magnificently equipped leisure facilities is undoubtedly the 17m x 7m swimming pool where a warm welcome is tendered to all aquaphiles under a stunning Romanesque canopy. Steam rooms, Swedish sauna, and a jacuzzi are offered as wonderful wet alternatives and vie with the Hanbury Beauty Studio and sumptuous gymnasium for guests' attention.

Hanbury Manor has set out to offer guests a level of facilities and service that redefine traditional standards. Whether as a hotel guest, or as a member of the golf and leisure sections, Hanbury Manor is quite simply an experience not to be missed.

Hanbury Manor Hotel
Ware
Hertfordshire
SG12 0SD
Tel: (01920) 487722
Fax: (01920) 487692

Set in 320 acres of Essex countryside and surrounded by two 18 hole golf courses, Five Lakes is more than an hotel, more than a golf club and more than a country club—it's an experience! Its innovative design and modern façade, together with the comprehensive sport, leisure and health activities truly launches Five Lakes into the 21st century.

Every effort has been made to provide all the facilities that will allow you time out to recharge your batteries, rejuvenate body and mind, enjoy recreational sport or simply indulge the senses.

The hotel boasts 114 luxury en suite bedrooms and the view from their windows is only a hint of a county steeped in history and rich in legend and folklore.

There are five bars, an award-winning restaurant offering local dishes and fresh produce from the area, and a brasserie for more informal dining. For the professional organiser, the conference facilities include 18 function rooms accommodating groups from 4 to 400, and an exibition hall with over 3500 square meters of space.

The hotel's leisure facilities are unparalleled—four championship indoor tennis courts and four outdoor courts, three glass-backed squash courts, an indoor swimming pool complete with Jacuzzi, steam room and sauna, a fully equipped gymnasium, an aerobics studio, a health spa, a snooker room, a games room, a jogging trail and even a football pitch.

However, the prime focus is the two magnificent 18 hole golf courses. The par 72 championship Lakes course measuring 6767 yards and designed by Neil Coles, is used annually by the PGA European tour and was host to the Nick Faldo Challenge and the First Ladies Skins match featuring Laura Davies. The Links par 71 course measuring 6250 yards is renowned for its sweeping fairways and plush greens and provides an excellent challenge for golfers of all standards. Five Lakes also offers three putting greens, a practice range, a clubhouse with an enviable sports shop and the services of a resident golf professional.

All in all it would be hard to beat Five Lakes—a complete destination and the ultimate golfing experience.

Five Lakes Hotel, Golf & Country Club
Colchester Road
Tolleshunt Knights
Maldon, Essex
Tel: (01621) 868888
Fax: (01621) 869696

Key

To avoid disappointment
it is advisable to telephone
in advance

***Visitors welcome at most times
**Visitors usually allowed on
weekdays only
*Visitors not normally permitted
(Mon, Wed) No visitors
on specified days

Approximate Green Fees
A £40 plus
B £25 to £40
C £20 to £30
D £15 to £25
E under £15
F Green fees on application

Restrictions
G Guests only
H—Handicap certificate required
H—(24) Handicap of 24 or less
L —Letter of introduction required
M—Visitor must be a member of
another recognised club

HERTFORDSHIRE

Aldenham G.& C.C.
(01923) 853929
Church Lane, Aldenham
(18) 6500 yards/***/B

Aldwickbury Park
(01582) 760112
Piggotshill, Wheathamstead
(18) 6333 yards/**/C

Arkley G.C.
(0181) 449 0394
Rowley Green Road, Barnet
(9) 6045 yards/**/D

Ashridge G.C.
(01442) 842379
Little Gaddesden, Berkhamsted
(18) 6547 yards/**/F

Barkway Park G.C.
(01763) 849070
Nuthamstead Road, Royston
(18) 6997 yards/***/D

Batchwood Hall G.C.
(01727) 844250
Batchwood Drive, St Albans
(18) 6487 yards/**/E

Berkhamsted G.C.
(01442) 865832
The Common, Berkhamsted
(18) 6605 yards/***/B - A/H

Bishops Stortford G.C.
(01279) 654027
Dunmow Road, Bishops Stortford
(18) 6440 yards/**/C

Boxmoor G.C.
(01442) 242434
Box Lane, Hemel Hempstead
(9) 4854 yards/**/D

Brickendon Grange G.C.
(01992) 511258
Brickendon, Hertford
(18) 6315 yards/**/F/H

Briggens House Hotel
(01279) 793742
Briggens Park, Stanstead Abbots
(9) 5825 yards/***/F

Brocket Hall G.C.
(01707) 390055
Welwyn
(18) 6584 yards/*/A/G/H

Brookmans Park G.C.
(01707) 652459
Golf Club Road, Hatfield
(18) 6459 yards/***/B/H

Bushey G. & C.C.
(0181) 950 2283
High Street, Bushey
(9) 3000 yards/**/E

Bushey Hall G.C.
(01923) 222253
Bushey Hall Drive, Bushey
(18) 6099 yards/**/E

Chadwell Springs G.C.
(01920) 463647
Hertford Road, Ware
(9) 3021 yards/**/C

Chesfield Downs G.C.
(01462) 482929
Jacks Hill, Graveley
(9) 6648 yards/**/D

Cheshunt G.C.
(01992) 629777
Park Lane, Cheshunt
(18) 6608 yards/***/E

Chorleywood G.C.
(01923) 282009
Common Road, Chorleywood
(9) 2838 yards/**/D

Danesbury Park G.C.
(01438) 840100
Codicote Road, Welwyn
(9) 4150 yards/***/F/G

Dyrham Park C.C.
(0181) 440 3361
Galley Lane, Barnet
(18) 6369 yards/***/F/G

East Herts G.C.
(01920) 821923
Hamels Park, Buntingford
(18) 6455 yards/**(Wed)/F/H

Elstree G.C.
(0181) 953 6115
Watling Street, Elstree
(18) 6166 yards/***/F

Great Hadham G.C.
(01279) 843558
Great Hadham Road, Much Hadham
(18) 6854 yards/**/C

Hadley Wood G.C.
(0181) 449 4328
Beech Hill, Hadley Wood
(18) 6457 yards/**/F/H

Hanbury Manor Hotel & G.C.
(01920) 487722
Thundridge, Ware
(18) 7016 yards/*/F/G/H/M

Harpenden G.C.
(01582) 712580
Hammonds End, Harpenden
(18) 6381 yards/**/B

Harpenden Common G.C.
(01582) 712856
East Common, Harpenden
(18) 5664 yards/**/B

Hartsbourne G & C.C.
(0181) 950 1133
Hartsbourne Avenue, Bushey Heath
(18) 6305 yards/*/F/G/M
(9) 5432 yards/*/F/G/M

Hatfield London C.C.
(01707) 642624
Bedwell Park, Essendon
(18) 6854/***/C

The Hertfordshire G.C.
(01992) 466666
White Stubbs Lane, Broxbourne
(18) 6400 yards/***/C/H

Kingsway Golf Centre
(01763) 262727
Cambridge Road, Melbourn, Royston
(9) 2500 yards/***/E

Knebworth G.C.
(01438) 814681
Deards End Lane, Knebworth
(18) 6492 yards/**/B/H

Letchworth G.C.
(01707) 655051
Letchworth Lane, Letchworth
(18) 6181 yards/**/B

Little Hay G.C.
(01442) 833798
Box Lane, Hemel Hempstead
(18) 6610 yards/***/E

Manor of Groves G.& C.C.
(01279) 722333
High Wych, Sawbridgeworth
(18) 6250 yards/***/D

Mid Herts G.C.
(01582) 833385
Gustard Wood, Wheathampstead
(18) 6060 yards/*/F/H

Mill Green G.C.
(01707) 276900
Mill Green, Welwyn Garden
(18) 6713 yards/*/F/H
(18) 5823 yards/**/H

Moor Park G.C.
(01923) 773146
Moor Park Mansion, Rickmansworth
(18) 6713 yards/**/A/H
(18) 5823 yards/**/A/H

Old Fold Manor G.C.
(0181) 440 9185
Hadley Green, Barnet
(18) 6471 yards/**/B/H

Oxhey Park G.C.
(01923) 248312
Prestwick Road, South Oxhey
(9) 1637 yards/***/E

Panshanger G.C.
(01707) 338507
Herns Lane, Welwyn Garden City
(18) 7178 yards/***/F

Porters Park G.C.
(01923) 854127
Shenley Hill, Radlett
(18) 6313 yards/**/A/H

Potters Bar G.C.
(01707) 652020
Darkes Lane, Potters Bar
(18) 6279 yards/**/C/H

Redbourn G.C.
(01582) 793493
Kinsbourne Green Lane, Rickmansworth
(18) 6407 yards/**/D
(9) 1361 yards/**/E

Rickmansworth G.C.
(01923) 775278
Moor Lane, Rickmansworth
(18) 4493 yards/***/E

Royston G.C.
(01763) 242696
Baldock Road, Royston
(18) 6032 yards/**/C

Sandy Lodge G.C.
(01923) 825429
Sandy Lodge Lane, Northwood
(18) 6340 yards/***/F/H/M

Shendish Manor G.C.
(01442) 232220
Aspley, Hemel Hempstead
(9) 6076 yards/**/C/H

South Herts G.C.
(0181) 445 2035
Links Drive, Totteridge
(18) 6470 yards/**/F/H/L

Stevenage G.C.
(01438) 880424
Aston Lane, Stevenage
(18) 6451 yards/***/E

Stocks Hotel & C.C.
(01442) 851341
Stocks Road, Aldbury
(18) 7016 yards/***/A/H

Verulam G.C.
(01727) 839016
London Road, St Albans
(18) 6457 yards/**/B/H

Welwyn Garden City G.C.
(01707) 325243
High Oaks Road, Welwyn
(18) 6100 yards/**/F/H

West Herts G.C.
(01923) 224264
Cassiobury Park, Watford
(18) 6488 yards/**/C/H

Whipsnade Park G.C.
(01442) 842330
Studham Lane, Dagnall
(18) 6812 yards/**/B

Whitehill G.C.
(01920) 438495
Dane End, Ware
(18) 6636 yards/***/D/H

BEDFORDSHIRE

Aspley Guise and Woburn Sands G.C.
(01908) 583596
West Hill, Aspley Guise
(18) 6135 yards/**/B/H

Aylesbury Vale G.C.
(01245) 240196
Wing, Leighton Buzzard
(18) 6622 yards/***/D/H

Beadlow Manor Hotel G. & C.C.
(01525) 860800
Beadlow, Shefford
(18) 6238 yards/***/D/H
(9) 6042 yards/***/D/H

Bedford and County G.C.
(01234) 352617
Green Lane, Clapham
(18) 6347 yards/**/B/H

Bedfordshire G.C.
(01234) 261669
Bromham Road, Biddenham
(18)6185 yards/**/F

Chalgrave Manor G.C.
(01525) 876556
Dunstable Road, Chalgrove
(18) 6382 yards/***/D

Colmworth G.C.
(01234) 378181
New Road, Colmworth
(18) 6420 yards/***/D

Colworth G.C.
(01234) 781781
Unilever Research, Sharnbrook
(9)2500 yards/***/F/G`

Dunstable Downs G.C.
(01582) 604472
Whipsnade Road, Dunstable
(18) 6255 yards/**/F/H

Griffin G.C.
(01582) 415573
Chaul End Road, Caddington
(18) 6161 yards/**/D

Henlow G.C.
(01462) 851515
Henlow Camp, Henlow
(9) 5618 yards/*/E/G

John O'Gaunt G.C.
(01767) 260360
Sutton Park, Sandy
(18) 6513 yards/***/A/H
(18) 5869 yards/***/A/H

Leighton Buzzard G.C.
(01525) 373811
Plantation Road, Leighton Buzzard
(18) 6101 yards/**/C/H

Millbrook G.C.
(01525) 840252
Millbrook, Ampthill
(18) 6530 yards/**(Thu)/B

Mount Pleasant G.C.
(01462) 850999
Station Road, Lower Stondon
(9)6172 yards/***/D

Mowsbury G.C.
(01234) 216374
Kimbolton Road, Bedford
(18) 6514 yards/***/E

Pavenham Park G.C.
(01234) 822202
Pavenham, Bedford
(18) 6353 yards/**/D

South Beds G.C.
(01582) 591500
Warden Hill Road, Luton
(18) 6332 yards/**/C
(9) 4954 yards/**/E

Stockwood Park G.C.
(01582) 413704
London Road, Luton
(18) 6049 yards/***/E

Tilsworth G.C.
(01525) 210722
Dunstable Road, Tilsworth
(18) 5303 yards/***/E

Wyboston Lakes G.C.
(01767) 260348
Wyboston Lakes, Wyboston
(18) 5721 yards/***/D

ESSEX

Abridge G.& C.C.
(01708) 688396
Epping Lane, Stapleford Tawney
(18) 6703 yards/**/A/H

Ballards Gore G.& C.C.
(01702) 258917
Gore Road, Canewdon
(18) 7062 yards/**/C

Basildon G.C.
(01268) 533297
Clay Hill Lane, Basildon
(18) 6153 yards/***/D

Belfairs Park G.C.
(01702) 520322
Eastwood Road North, Leigh-on-Sea
(18) 5802 yards/***/D

Belhus Park G.C.
(01708) 854260
Belhus Park, South Ockendon
(18) 5188 yards/***/E

Bentley G. & C.C.
(01277) 373179
Ongar Road, Brentwood
(18) 6709 yards/**/B/H

Benton Hall G.C.
(01376) 502454
Wickham Hill, Witham
(9) 6520 yards/***/D

Birch Grove G.C.
(01206) 734276
Layer Road, Colchester
(9) 4108 yards/***/D

Boyce Hill G.C.
(01268) 793625
Vicarage Hill, Benfleet
(18) 5882 yards/**/B

Braintree G.C.
(01376) 346079
Kings Lane, Braintree
(18) 6161 yards/***/B/H

Braxted Park Estate G.C.
(01376) 572372
Maldon
(9) 1980 yards/**/E

Bunsay Downs G.C.
(01245) 222369
Little Baddow Road, Woodham Walter
(9) 2913 yards/***/F

Burnham-on-Crouch G.C.
(01621) 782282
Ferry Road, Burnham-on-Crouch
(18) 6056 yards/**/C

Burstead G.C.
(01277) 631171
Tythe Common Road, Little Burstead
(18) 6150 yards/**/C/H

Canons Brook G.C.
(01279) 421482
Elizabeth Way, Harlow
(18) 6728 yards/**/B

Castle Point G.C.
(01268) 510830
Somnes Avenue, Canvey Island
(18) 5627 yards/***/E

Channels G.C.
(01245) 440005
Little Waltham, Chelmsford
(18) 6272 yards/**/B
(18) 4779 yards/**/B

Chelmsford G.C.
(01245) 256483
Widford Road, Chelmsford
(18) 5944 yards/**/A - B/G

Chigwell G.C.
(0181) 500 2059
High Road, Chigwell
(18) 6279 yards/**/A/H

Clacton-on-Sea G.C.
(01255) 421919
West Road, Clacton-on-Sea
(18) 6244 yards/***/B/H

Colchester G.C.
(01206) 853396
Braiswick, Colchester
(18) 6319 yards/**/B

Colne Valley G.C.
(01787) 224343
Station Road, Earls Colne
(18) 6272 yards/***/F

Crondon Park
(01277) 841115
Stock Road, Stock
(18) 6585 yards/**/C

Earls Colne.
(01787) 224466
Earls Colne, Colchester
(18) 6585 yards/**/D

Epping Forest G & C.C.
(0181) 500 2549
Abridge Road, Chigwell
(18) 6048 yards/*/G/F

Essex G.C.
(01702) 601701
Eastern Avenue, Southend-on-Sea
(18) 6237 yards/***/D

Fairlop Waters G.C.
(0181) 500 9911
Barkingside, Ilford
(18) 6288 yards/***/E

Five Lakes Hotel Golf & C.C.
(01621) 868888
Tolleshunt Knights, nr Maldon
(18) 6250 yards/***/A/H
(18) 6765 yards/***/A/H

Forrester Park G.C.
(01621) 891406
Beckingham Road, Great Totham
(18) 6073 yards/**/C

Frinton G.C.
(01255) 674618
Esplanade, Frinton-on-Sea
(18) 6259 yards/***/B/H
(9) 2508 yards/***/E

Gosfield Lake G.C.
(01787) 474747
Gosfield, Halstead
(18) 6707 yards/**/C/H
(9) 4180 yards/***/E

Hainault Forest G.C.
(0181) 500 0385
Chigwell Row, Hainault Forest
(18) 5754 yards/***/F
(18) 6600 yards/***/F

Hanover G.& C.C.
(01702) 232377
Hullbridge Road, Rayleigh
(18) 6669 yards/**/B/H
(18) 3700 yards/***/D

Hartswood G.C.
(01277) 218714
King George's Playing Fields,
Brentwood
(18) 6238 yards/***/F

Harwich and Dovercourt G.C.
(01255) 503616
Station Road, Parkeston
(9) 2950 yards/***/F

Havering G.C.
(01708) 741429
Lower Bedfords Road, Romford
(18) 5237 yards/***/D

Ilford G.C.
(0181) 554 2930
Wanstead Park Road, Ilford
(18) 5251 yards/***/D

Langdon Hills G.C.
(01268) 548444
Lower Dunton Road, Bulphan
(18) 6485 yards/***/D/H

Loughton G.C.
(0181) 502 2923
Clays Lane, Debden Green
(9) 4735 yards/***/E

Maldon G.C.
(01621) 853212
Beeleigh, Langford, Maldon
(9) 6197 yards/**/C/H

Maylands G.& C.C.
(01708) 373080
Harold Park, Romford
(18) 6351 yards/**/B/L

Nazeing G.C.
(01992) 893789
Middle Street, Nazeing
(18) 6598 yards/***/B/H

North Weald G.C.
(01992) 522118
North Weald Bassett, Epping
(18) 6239 yards/**/C/H

Orsett G.C.
(01375) 891352
Brentwood Road, Orsett
(18) 6614 yards/**/A/H

Pipps Hill G.C.
(01268) 523456
Cranes Farm Road, Basildon
(9) 2829 yards/***/F

Risebridge G.C.
(01708) 741429
Lower Bedfords Road, Romford
(18) 6280 yards/***/E

Rochford Hundred G.C.
(01702) 544302
Hall Road, Rochford
(18) 6255 yards/**/F/H

Romford G.C.
(01708) 740986
Heath Drive, Gidea Park, Romford
(18) 6395 yards/**/B

Royal Epping Forest G.C.
(0181) 529 5708
Station Road, Chingford
(18) 6220 yards/***/D

Saffron Walden G.C.
(01799) 522786
Windmill Hill, Saffron Walden
(18) 6608 yards/**/A/H

St Cleres G.C.
(01268) 591798
St Cleres Hall, Stanford le Hope
(18) ***/D/H

Stapleford Abbots G.C.
(01708) 381108
Tysea Hill, Stapleford Abbots
(18) 6487 yards/**/C - A/H
(18) 5965 yards/**/C - A/H
(9) 1140 yards/**/C - A/H

Stock Brook Manor G.C.
(01277) 653616
Queens Park Avenue, Billericay
(18) 6725 yards/***/B/H
(9) 2977 yards/***/B/H

Stoke-by-Nayland G.C.
(01206) 262836
Keepers Lane, Leavenheath
(18) 6516 yards/**/B/H/M
(18) 6544 yards/**/B/H/M

Theydon Bois G.C.
(01992) 812460
Theydon Road, Epping
(18) 5480 yards/**/B/H

Thorndon Park G.C.
(01277) 810736
Ingrave, Brentwood
(18) 6481 yards/**/B/L

Thorpe Hall G.C.
(01702) 582205
Thorpe Hall Avenue, Thorpe Bay
(18) 6286 yards/**/B/H

Three Rivers G.& C.C.
(01621) 828631
Stow Road, Purleigh
(18) 6609 yards/***/C/H
(9) 1071 yards/***/C/H

Toot Hill G.C.
(01277) 365747
Toot Hill, Ongar
(18) 6013 yards/**/B/H

Top Meadow G.C.
(01708) 852239
Fen Lane, North Ockendon
(18)5500 yards/**/D
(9)1633 yards/**/D

Towerlands G.C.
(01376) 326802
Panfield Road, Braintree
(9) 2703 yards/**/E

Upminster G.C.
(01708) 222788
Hall Lane, Upminster
(18) 5926 yards/***/D/M

Wanstead G.C.
(0181) 989 3938
Wanstead, London
(18) 6262 yards/**/B/H

Warley Park G.C.
(01277) 231352
Magpie Lane, Little Warley
(27)(3 x 9)/**/B/H

Warren G.C.
(01245) 223258
Woodham Walter, Maldon
(18) 6211 yards/**/B - A/H

Weald Park G.C.
(01277) 375101
South Weald, Brentwood
(18) 6308 yards/***/B/H

West Essex G.C.
(0181) 529 7558
Sewardstonebury, Chingford
(18) 6289 yards/**/B/H

Woodford G.C.
(0181) 504 3330
Sunset Avenue, Woodford Green
(9) 5806 yards/**/C

Berks, Bucks & Oxon Choice Golf

Berkshire, Buckinghamshire and Oxfordshire—three very English counties. The region extends from the edge of the Chilterns to the edge of the Cotswolds and occupies a very prosperous part of southern Britain.

Oxfordshire

We start at **Huntercombe,** a charming golf club with an interesting history. In the early years of the century three rather old Daimler motor cars were used to ferry members to and from the local station and later a thirty seater bus was acquired for the same purpose. The course itself has passed through various owners—first a property company, then an insurance company (the Norwich Union) and later Viscount Nuffield before finally becoming a members' club in 1963. On the edge of the Chilterns at some 700 feet above sea level are some marvellous views across the Oxford Plain. The course itself is fairly flat and kept in first class condition. Nearby in Henley there are two courses worth inspecting, the more established **Henley** Golf Club and **Badgemore Park**, a course that has settled down quickly.

A suitable 19th hole? The Red Lion in Henley (01491) 572161 is commendable. In Nettlebed, the White Hart (01491) 641245 is a pleasing inn with some good value bedrooms (handy for Huntercombe) and North Stoke offers the excellent **Springs Hotel** (01491) 836687 which has a first class restaurant and its own golf course .

So to the best golf in the county and, just as The Berkshire has a Red and Blue, so **Frilford Heath** has a Red, a Blue and a Green. Frilford Heath is featured later in this chapter. Good food and drink can be found in nearby Fyfield at the White Hart. A short trip to Abingdon can be recommended, where the Upper Reaches Hotel (01235) 522311 is most welcoming. Those golfers who have missed

a crucial short putt on the 18th should consider the aptly named Dog House (01865) 390830 in Frilford Heath. We also hear good news about the recently opened Merry Miller at Cothill.

If there is a club that may one day challenge Frilford as the county's best it is the new **Oxfordshire** Golf Club at Thame, close to the M40. It is a fairly private club but if the chance of a game materialises don't pass it by! There are two courses either side of the Oxford—**North Oxford** and **Southfield** and although neither is in the Frilford Heath league both are certainly worth a game. The latter is the home of Oxford University. The Randolph (01865) 247481 is the best known of the Oxford hotels, but the part 17th century Old Parsonage (01865) 310210 will delight those who enjoy the smaller hotel—its a classic—and for first class restaurants, the Cherwell Boathouse (01865) 52746 is certainly among the best. Oxford, naturally, is more than a little used to visitors of all tastes and for reasonably priced accommodation try the Courtfield Hotel (01865) 242991. Outside in Cumnor, the Bear and Ragged Staff serves good food while a little further afield in Stanton Harcourt, the Harcourt Arms (01865) 310630 has a tremendous atmosphere, a good restaurant and accommodation. Another fine restaurant and hotel near Oxford and within striking distance of Frilford is the Plough at Clanfield (0136 781) 222. A final recommendation for the true golfing/culinary connoisseur is Le Manoir Aux Quat' Saisons (01844) 278881 in Great Milton—possibly the country's finest restaurant and a splendid hotel as well.

Back on the fairways (suitably fed one hopes!) and beyond the Oxford area there is a flattish parkland course near Bicester, the **Chesterton** Golf Club and a much improved course at **Burford**. Inching up towards the

Cotswolds there are pleasant courses at **Lyneham** and **Chipping Norton** but the best in the north of the county, although it may be a little more difficult to arrange a game upon, is clearly **Tadmarton Heath**. At less than 6000 yards in length, it is fairly short by modern standards but the narrow fairways and a great spread of gorse can make it a very difficult test. It also has a wonderfully remote setting. Right beside Tadmarton is the new course at **Rye Hill**, which is worth a visit. Not far away, the village of Deddington provides an admirable place to rest the heather-clad spikes, more specifically, the Holcombe Hotel (and restaurant) (01869) 38274. Burford offers the Lamb (01993) 823155, a truly charming Cotswold inn. A final thought, the Feathers at Woodstock (01993) 812291 is an extremely fine hotel well situated for Blenheim Palace.

Buckinghamshire

Moving into Buckinghamshire, **Woburn** (featured ahead) stands rather alone in the far north of the county. For a brief thought on where to stay, stylish Flitwick Manor (01525) 712242 is a favourite with golfers and deservedly so. In Woburn Park, the Paris House (01525) 290692 is a highly recommended restaurant, Moore Place (01908) 282000 in nearby Aspley Guise and the Bedford Arms (01525) 290441 in Woburn village also come highly recommended. In Milton Keynes, overlooking the **Abbey Hill** public golf course, is the suitably named Quality Friendly Hotel (01908) 561666 while the Red Lion Country Hotel (01908) 583117 is likely to please.

Heading down the county, the **Mentmore** Golf and Country Club boasts 36 holes of wonderfully manicured golf beneath the watchful gaze of Mentmore Towers, the former residence of the Rothschild family. **Ellesborough's** golf course is yet another with rather stately surroundings, being located on part of the property of Chequers. Quite a hilly course and well worth inspecting, not least because there are some commanding views across the Buckinghamshire countryside. Elsewhere in the centre of the county, there is a fairly lengthy parkland course at **Weston Turville**, south of Aylesbury. And just north of Aylesbury lies **Aylesbury Park**, a new course in a delightful setting.

Ideas for a 19th hole in these parts include in Ivinghoe, the Kings Head (01296) 668388, which has a splendid restaurant in a 17th century inn, and two 'Bells', the Bell (01296) 89835 in Aylesbury's market place and the Bell (01296) 630252 in Aston Clinton (note the superb wine list here). A couple of good pubs to savour are the Rising Sun at Little Hampden and the Fox at Dunsmore.

It is in southern Buckinghamshire that most of the county's better courses are to be found. **Stoke Poges** has staged many leading amateur and professional events—not at all surprisingly, this being one of the finest parkland courses in England. It also now offers some very stylish accommodation, We explore Stoke Poges on a later page, but in this area note also **Farnham Park**, a nearby public course. **Denham** Golf Club is a close neighbour of Stoke Poges lying some three miles north of Uxbridge, and as an old club handbook will tell you 'half an hours drive from Marble Arch'. (Add an extra 60 minutes nowadays if you're attempting the journey during rush hour). It is worth making the escape though for Denham enjoys a beautiful setting, deeply secluded amidst some glorious countryside. It is a very good golf course and the clubhouse is a most unusual building having been built around a 16th century tithe barn.

In equally beautiful surroundings are the **Burnham Beeches** Golf Club, four miles west of Slough and the **Lambourne** course at Burnham. Others to note in southern Buckinghamshire are **Beaconsfield**. **Harewood Downs** (at Chalfont St Giles), **Gerrards Cross** and at Denham Court the **Buckinghamshire** Golf Club designed by John Jacobs. And note that we now have The Berkshire, The Oxfordshire and The Buckinghamshire !

There are a number of very comfortable hotels in the south Buckinghamshire area. They include the Bellhouse Hotel (01753) 887211 just outside Beaconsfield, the Burnham Beeches Hotel (01628) 429955, a former hunting lodge—ideal for the golf course, the Compleat Angler Hotel (01628) 484444 at Marlow Bridge and Danesfield House (01698) 891010 just outside Marlow. This impressive hotel is particularly convenient for the newly opened **Harleyford** club. Two good pubs are the Kings Arms in Amersham and the Lions at Bledlow.

Berkshire

Berkshire—or should one say 'Royal Berkshire'—is often described as being cigar-shaped. Now whilst this may not say much for the talents of cigar-makers it does serve as a rough description in as much as the county is peculiarly long and thin. When it comes to surveying the county's twenty or so golf courses it is tempting to adopt another cigar analogy in that one end could be said to glow rather more brightly than the other.

To the east of the county there is a famous heathland belt and it is here that the twin pearls of **Sunningdale** and **The Berkshire** are to be found. Both clubs possess two 18 hole courses which for sheer enjoyment can stand comparison with anything golf has to offer. Sunningdale is better known than the Berkshire but it is difficult to imagine a more delightful setting than the tranquil, tree-lined fairways of the Red and the Blue Courses at the Berkshire—and so close to London too. Sunningdale is featured in our Surrey section; the Berkshire is described in this chapter. **Swinley Forest** is the other outstanding heathland course in the area, a veritable *paradis terrestre* indeed although individual visitors are normally only permitted to play as guests of members. Still in heather and pine country is the very attractive **East Berkshire** course at Crowthorne. Also in close proximity is the highly acclaimed—but private—**Bearwood Lakes** golf club near Wokingham, and the popular **Downshire** public course where the green fees are naturally less expensive.

Windsor is where many visiting the area will choose to spend a night or two. Pride of place must go to Oakley Court (01753) 609988. Its comfortable rooms are complemented by splendid grounds and a delightful dining room, the Oak Leaf. Melrose House (01753) 865328 meanwhile, will delight those for whom money is far from no object! In the Ascot area there are a number of good establishments. The Thatched Tavern (01344) 20874 is a pleasant place to have lunch or dinner while the Berystede Hotel (01344) 23311 is an outstanding place to stay. In Sunninghill, near Ascot, the Royal Berkshire (01344) 23322 is perhaps the *crème de la crème* and admirably reflects the quality of the nearby courses. However, a night spent in Ascot does not have to be extravagantly expensive; for affordable comfort, try the Highclere Hotel (01344) 25220. A good local pub is the Winkfield in Winkfield Row—a fine atmosphere and a charming restaurant. This area of Berkshire, of course, borders Surrey and we shouldn't forget its many delights. One tip is Pennyhill Park (01276) 471774 in Bagshot—a superb hotel and very convenient (not to mention appropriate) for the likes of Sunningdale. What Sunningdale is to golf so Cliveden (01628) 668561 is to hotels—excellence of the highest order.

Time for some more golf and **Temple's** fine course can be glimpsed from the main A23 Maidenhead to Henley Road. It has an interesting layout with many fine trees and lush fairways. Designed by Willie Park early this century, it was for a number of years the home of Henry Cotton. The course is always maintained in first class condition. The golf course at **Winter Hill** is on fairly high ground—apparently its name derives from the particularly chilling winds that sweep across in winter (I have no explanation for nearby Crazies Hill!) From the course there are some spectacular views over the Thames—definitely worth a visit. So for that matter is classy **Sonning**, situated further towards Reading. There is a reasonable course in (or on the outskirts of) **Maidenhead** and just beyond the boating villages of Goring and Streatly lies the fairly tough **Goring and Streatly** course. With the delights of Windsor Castle and Legoland close at hand **Castle Royle Golf and Country Club** is an ideal spot for those with non-golfers at hand. Its beautifully turned out and a goog challenge.

In Maidenhead, Fredrick's Hotel (01628) 635934 has a considerable reputation for comfort and warm hospitality—its dining room is also highly acclaimed—while in nearby Bray the Waterside Inn (01628) 20691 is an outstanding restaurant. The Boulters Lock Hotel (01628) 21291 on Boulters Island is a delightful place to stay. North of here in Hurley one finds yet another gem, Ye Olde Bell (01628) 825881, a very popular Norman inn. Meandering further down the Thames, recommended hotels must include the Great House at Sonning (01734) 692277 with its charming Elizabethan courtyard and also in Sonning, the French Horn (01734) 692204 is a super restaurant. In Streatly, the Swan Diplomat (01491) 873737 has a splendid riverside setting. In need of a pub? A visit to the Bell at Aldworth should do the trick. Another nearby local is the Crown and Horns at East Ilsley. Two locations with good hotel and

restaurant combinations are at Pangbourne, the Copper Inn (0118) 984 2244 and Yattendon, the Royal Oak (01635) 201325. The Beetle and Wedge (01491) 651381 rejoices in a glorious Thameside setting and offers fare of the highest order— some bedrooms are also available.

On the western edge of Reading **Calcot Park** golf course poses many interesting challenges. It can boast Guinness Book of Records fame too in that one sterling fellow sprinted round the course in a motorised cart in just over 24 minutes—a more leisurely round is suggested! Recommended 19th holes around Reading include the Ramada Hotel (0118) 958 6222 and the picturesque Bridge Cottage (01734) 713138 at Woolhampton. To the north west of Reading is the increasingly popular **Mapledurham** course and visiting golfers will find suitable accommodation at the Holiday Inn (0118) 925 9988.

Newbury is of course better known for its racing than its golf, but the **Newbury and Crookham** Golf Club close to Greenham Common and is strongly recommended. The course is hilly and well-wooded, though not overly long. Meanwhile, at nearby Donnington there is excellent accommodation and cuisine to be enjoyed (not forgetting golf) at the **Donnington Valley** Hotel and Golf Course (01635) 551199.

Before leaving Berkshire it is worth noting one of the county's more recent additions, **West Berkshire**, situated just south of the village of Chaddleworth. It is a splendid downland course, but not exactly one for the weak-kneed—it stretches to around the 7000 yard mark with one par five measuring well over 600 yards; a hearty breakfast before playing here is a must!

The Berkshire

The horse racing, golf playing residents of Ascot must number among the luckiest folk in England for right on their doorsteps lie the cream of each sport. They have of course, three golfing pearls close at hand, Sunningdale, Wentworth and The Berkshire—the youngest of the illustrious trio.

The two 18 hole courses of The Berkshire, the **Red** and the **Blue**, were designed in 1928 by Herbert Fowler—a master golf architect whose other great works include Walton Heath and Saunton. They occupy some 400 acres of Crown Land over which Queen Anne's carriage used to pass en route to the hunting in Swinley Forest.

Today, both courses give the appearance of having been hewn out of a dense forest, rather in the way that the Duke and Duchess courses were created at Woburn. This, in fact, was not the case, as much clearing of the ancient forest occurred during the First World War when the land was used for military purposes, and most of the present thick woodland is of comparatively recent origin.

The Berkshire is often described as being primarily a 'members' club', this largely through the conspicuous absence of any big-time professional golf tournament. Perhaps the club does not wish to have its tranquillity stirred or its rough trampled over by hordes of excited spectators, but this does not imply that the club closes its doors to the outside world or makes visitors unwelcome. Indeed, The Berkshire is a busy and popular club with a great number of societies, most of which choose to return year after year.

The two courses are of fairly similar length—the Red slightly longer, measuring 6369 yards to the Blue's 6260 yards, although the latter's par is one fewer at 71. The

Red course is perhaps the better known of the two, to some extent due to its comprising an unusual six par threes, six par fours and six par fives. In any event, most people agree that there is little to choose between the two, both in terms of beauty and degree of difficulty.

The Berkshire is especially famed for its glorious tree-lined fairways. There is a splendid mix of mature pines, chestnuts and silver birch and both courses are kept in the most superb condition. Much of the rough consists of heather, ensuring that the wayward hitter is heavily punished.

The club may have avoided professional tournaments, but it does play host to a number of important amateur events. The Berkshire Trophy is one of the annual highlights on the amateur calendar and before turning professional Messrs Faldo and Lyle were both winners.

The Berkshire Golf Club, Swinley Road Ascot, Berkshire SL5 8AY	
Secretary	Major P D Clarke (01344) 621496
Professional	Paul Anderson (01344) 622351
Green Fees	£50/round; £65/day
Restrictions	No visitors at weekends

Directions
The club lies just off the A332 between Ascot and Bagshot. The A332 can be joined from Windsor to the north and Guildford to the south, while driving from Reading, leave the M4 at junction 10 and follow the A329 to Ascot.

Set in two and a half acres of attractive gardens, in the midst of beautiful Berkshire countryside, Fredrick's Hotel, which dates from just after the turn of the century has successfully managed to retain its charm and traditional style whilst at the same time offering the sophisticated modern facilities required to meet the needs of today's business and leisure traveller.

From the moment you enter the immaculate reception of this luxury four star hotel with its cascading waterfall, rich furnishings, antiques and abundant flower displays, a warm and friendly welcome awaits you. 'Putting people first' is the guiding philosophy behind the running of this sumptuously equipped hotel which is indicative of the style of service that guests can expect during their stay.

The hotel's thirty seven luxuriously furnished bedrooms, including five superb suites, a number of which have their own private patio or balcony, offer guests every degree of comfort and are tastefully decorated with individuality and style and provide useful features such as hairdryers, trouser presses and ironing facilities. All rooms are equipped with direct dial telephone, radio, colour TV with satellite, minibars plus ample towelling robes and slippers. On arrival, hotel guests are greeted with a choice of either champagne, white wine or sherry and a bowl of fresh fruit is placed in every room.

Through from the reception is the Wintergarden overlooking the delightful patio where guests can relax and enjoy tea or just simply sit and enjoy the view of the gardens, beyond which lie the fairways and greens of Maidenhead Golf Club. In the hotel cocktail bar, resplendent in rich dark woods and wall hung tapestries, guests can enjoy an informal drink before sampling the culinary delights offered in Fredrick's Restaurant. Widely acknowledged and recognised by all the major guides as one of the finest restaurants in the south of England, Fredrick's offers truly outstanding cuisine. Amid the elegant decor of crystal chandeliers and crisp white linen, guests are treated to the finest gourmet cooking with imaginative and delectable dishes which are prepared from the best of fresh and seasonal ingredients under the supervision of Executive Chef, Brian Cutler.

Open daily, Fredrick's offers an extensive à la carte and table d'hôte menu plus an excellent value Sunday lunch. This combination of culinary expertise, a comprehensive wine list together with thoughtful and attentive service in delightful surroundings, ensures that every meal at Fredrick's is a special occasion.

Fredrick's Hotel and Restaurant, close to Junction 8/9 on the M4 motorway and the centre of Maidenhead, provides a highly accessible location for visitors to the Thames Valley. With a reputation for offering the best of good food, comfort and hospitality, Fredrick's is an ideal base for playing Wentworth, Sunningdale, the Berkshire and Temple and is also perfect for those attending the races at Ascot and Windsor or Henley Regatta in July.

Fredrick's Hotel and Restaurant
Shoppenhangers Road
Maidenhead
Tel: (01628) 635934
Fax: (01628) 771054

Stoke Poges

How does it go? 'The first thing we do, let's kill all the lawyers.' Never utter this Shakespearean line at Stoke Poges. Not only will it insult some of the members but it will likely stir the former Lord of the Manor. Sir Edward Coke, the first Lord Chief Justice of England (and the judge who put paid to Guy Fawkes) once owned the estate on which Stoke Poges Golf Club now stands and his presence is still greatly felt, for his towering monument can be seen from many parts of the course.

While no one disputes that the best golf in the Home Counties is to be found south west of London, especially in the celebrated heathland belt of Surrey and Berkshire, to continually visit the heather and gorse can get a little frustrating at times. For this reason alone there is good cause for investigating Stoke Poges, near Slough in southern Buckinghamshire, but there are many better reasons for doing so. Stoke Poges is arguably the finest 'established' parkland course in England; it is certainly one of the loveliest and its palatial mansion clubhouse is one of the most historic and attractive that any travelling golfer is likely to come across.

Writing in 1910, just a year after golf first came to Stoke Poges, Bernard Darwin gave his opinion on the merits of the site. 'It is a beautiful spot, and there is very good golf to be played here; the club is an interesting one, moreover, as being one of the first and most ambitious attempts in England at what is called in America, a Country Club, there are plenty of things to do at Stoke besides playing golf. We may get very hot at lawn tennis or keep comparatively cool at bowls or croquet, or, coolest of all, we may sit on the terrace or in the garden and give ourselves wholly and solely to loafing'. Well, the good news is it's still a marvellously relaxing place!

Seriously, much has happened at Stoke Poges in recent years—both on and off the fairways. A decade ago there was a 'frayed at the edges' air to the club—the course was good but a little tired looking while the mansion was, quite literally starting to crumble. Since coming under new ownership in 1993, substantial investment in the facilities has transformed Stoke Poges. The mansion has been restored to its former glory, with 21 first floor en suite bedrooms, while back on the fairways the golf course has been sympathetically upgraded, with the

addition of a further nine holes re-establishing the original 27 hole layout.

The club's **Secretary, Mr RC Pickering** may be contacted by telephone on **(01753) 717171** and by fax on (01753) 717181. The club's address is **Stoke Poges Golf Club, North Drive, Park Road, Stoke Poges, Slough SL2 4PG.** Visitors are welcome between Mondays and Fridays (with the exception of Tuesday mornings) and at weekends. Societies are also very welcome and they can make weekday bookings by telephoning the above number. All players must possess a handicap. Stoke Poges' **professional, Tim Morrison** can be reached on **(01753) 717172.**

The green fees for 1998 are £60 per round, £90 per day. A reduced rate of £35 is payable after 5pm. Junior golfers under the age of 14 and accompanied by an adult pay £15 per round.

The precise location of the golf course is 2 miles from the centre of Slough via the B416. Travellers from London should head towards Stoke Poges using either the M4 (junction 6) or the A40 (leaving at Gerrards Cross). Approaching from the south and west the M3 (junction 3) and the M4 (junction 6) are likely to prove helpful. The course is 8 miles from Heathrow.

Harry Colt was the architect of Stoke Poges. Perhaps the greatest of all golf course designers, at Stoke Poges Colt made magnificent use of a very wooded landscape. Some of the short holes he created here are among the most seductive in England. The 7th is the most talked about. It is not an especially long par three but the tee shot must be measured to perfection for the narrow green has been built at an angle and is fronted by a brook, surrounded by trees and has a devilishly positioned bunker at the back of the 'safest' side of the green. There are also at least half a dozen very good two-shot holes, and here one might single out the 4th, 6th, 8th, 12th, 17th and 18th.

The 19th hole at Stoke Poges is the spectacular mansion referred to in the second paragraph 'A dazzling vision of white stone' was Darwin's description. It was built in 1795 by one of the Penn family of Pennsylvania fame and was assaulted by Odd Job after his evil master, Goldfinger, had been caught cheating by James Bond. What a pity Lord Coke didn't catch him!

Hole	Yards	Par	Hole	Yards	Par
1	502	5	10	390	4
2	411	4	11	156	3
3	198	3	12	435	4
4	425	4	13	502	5
5	496	5	14	429	4
6	412	4	15	326	4
7	150	3	16	187	3
8	354	4	17	421	4
9	454	4	18	406	4
Out	**3,402**	**36**	**In**	**3,252**	**35**
			Out	**3,402**	**36**
			Totals	**6,654**	**71**

Flitwick Manor is situated in a peaceful corner of Bedfordshire's Green Sand Ridge, and is surrounded by picturesque countryside. However, it is a mere ten minutes drive from the M1 and within easy reach of all the main golf courses in the area.

With its exquisite bedrooms this Georgian manor is set in 50 acres of rolling grounds that were once a deer park. The gardens are impeccably manicured and extend to picturesque English countryside.

Real log fires, period antiques, the Gothic grotto and twelfth century ironstone church, the kitchen garden with its castellated walls and the large ornamental lake all retain the tradition of years gone by. There is even a croquet lawn as well as a pitch and putt for finer days!

General Manager Tim Howard and Head Chef Richard Salt continue to enhance the hotel's already enviable reputation. The interior is elegantly decorated in gracious, classical style and meals are served in one of the three dining rooms overlooking the grounds.

The restaurant continues to enjoy the coveted award of three AA rosettes, making it the highest rated restaurant in the county. The fixed-price menus are simple but modern in style—chilled, pressed terrine of Mediterranean fish is served with a succulent roast pepper dressing, while the gateau of braised lamb's sweetbreads is enhanced with a rich truffle and Madeira wine essence. As a splendid finale, hot roasted almond soufflé continues to send guests into raptures.

The 'icing on the cake' comes in the shape of seductive petits fours, including a banana ice-cream lollipop on a cocktail stick coated in Belgian chocolate. A good wine list features some impressive older vintages and well represented European selection. Staff know what pampering is all about.

Whether staying the night or simply enjoying a meal, customers become guests as soon as they walk through the door at Flitwick Manor. The gracious gravelled drive, mellowed walls, green acres, period charm and superb cuisine conspire to create a very special atmosphere that once savoured will be ever remembered.

Flitwick Manor
Church Road
Flitwick
Bedfordshire
MK45 1AE
Tel: (01525) 712242
Fax (01525) 718753

Woburn

A magnificent stately home housing one of the finest art collections in the world, the largest wildlife safari park in Europe and two of the finest inland golf courses in Britain—quite a place Woburn!

The stately home is of course Woburn Abbey which since the reign of Henry VIII has been the home of the Dukes of Bedford, while the wildlife park and the golf courses lie within the grounds of the great estate.

In a game that prides itself on its antiquity the Woburn Golf and Country Club might be described as a remarkably precocious youngster. It was founded as recently as 1976 and its two courses, aptly named the Duke's and Duchess, were not opened until 1977 and 1979 respectively. In such a short period of time Woburn has acquired an enviable reputation.

In charge of all golfing matters at Woburn is **Alex Hay** whose Celtic tones are well-known to millions of television viewers. Mr. Hay is the **Managing Director** and he may be contacted on **(01908) 370756**. The **Professional** is **Luther Blacklock**, who can be reached on **(01908) 647987**. The club fax number is (01908) 378436.

Visitors, societies and company days are all welcome from Monday to Friday at Woburn, although prior booking is essential. In addition, visitors must be members of recognised golf clubs and be able to provide proof of handicap. All written enquiries should be addressed to the Managing Director, **Woburn Golf and Country Club, Bow Brickhill, Milton Keynes, MK17 9LJ**. The green fees for 1998 were set at £110 per person per day for parties of nine and above, and £81 for parties of less than nine. This fee is inclusive of golf and lunch while dinner can also be arranged if there are 24 people or more.

Having booked a game, travelling to Woburn ought not to present too many problems. The club is located approximately 45 miles from London and 73 miles from Birmingham and is well served by major roads. Both the M1 (junction 13) and the A5 pass close by. For those using British Rail, Bletchley Station, some four miles away has good connections from both London and Birmingham. Luton and Heathrow Airports are also within fairly easy reach. The town of Woburn and the Abbey are both actually within the county of Bedfordshire while the Golf and Country Club lies a short distance over the boundary in Buckinghamshire; presumably the lions amble from county to county.

Twenty five years ago if someone had suggested that a championship course (never mind two) could have been built on the Woburn Estate, the famous lions would probably not have been the only ones to roar. The present site was then a dense forest, with giant trees and bracken restricting vision beyond a few yards. Golf architect Charles Lawrie of Cotton Pennink was called in and plans were drawn up. The bulldozers soon arrived and from amidst the pines and the chestnuts great avenues were carved. The fairways flourished on the sandy subsoil and within two years of opening, the **Duke's** Course was considered fit to stage a major professional tournament. It proved a popular decision and a succession of sponsors decided to follow suit. Following its opening, the **Duchess** matured with equal rapidity and Woburn soon possessed two precious gems.

The tournaments held at Woburn have included numerous British Masters Championships, The Ford Ladies Classic and the Weetabix Women's British Open. The British Masters winners have included such great names as Trevino, McNulty, Ballesteros, Lyle and Faldo. During the 1992 event, won in such thrilling style by Christy O'Connor Jr, Bernhard Langer was quoted as saying of the Duke's Course, 'It is as good a golf course as we play all year'.

From the back markers (or tiger tees?) the Duke's Course stretches to 6940 yards (par 72), while the Duchess measures 6651 yards (par 72). The corresponding distances for the ladies are 6060 yards (par 75) and 5831 yards (par 74). The best hole at Woburn? Not easy when there are 36 fine holes to choose from, but many people single out the picturesque short 3rd on the Duke's Course. For my money, however, the 13th is one of the best par fours in the country.

As one might expect from a modern golf and country club the facilities at Woburn are excellent. The newly rebuilt and refurbished clubhouse offers a full complement of catering, though dinners must be pre-arranged. For the sporty types there is tennis and an open-air heated swimming pool. The majority of golfers, however, will probably head for one of the two bars. . . . and toast the Duke and the Duchess.

Duke's Course

Hole	Yards	Par	Hole	Yards	Par
1	514	5	10	404	4
2	385	4	11	502	5
3	134	3	12	193	3
4	395	4	13	419	4
5	510	5	14	565	5
6	207	3	15	432	4
7	464	4	16	449	4
8	409	4	17	425	4
9	177	3	18	356	4
Out	**3,195**	**35**	**In**	**3,745**	**37**
			Out	**3,195**	**35**
			Totals	**6,940**	**72**

Frilford Heath

In 1910, just two years after the golf club was founded, Bernard Darwin described Frilford Heath as, 'A wonderful oasis in a desert of mud. The sand is so near the turf,' he enthused, 'that out of pure exuberance it breaks out here and there in little eruptions'.

The sand must be the only thing that has ever erupted at Frilford Heath. Peaceable and peaceful, this is one of England's most pleasant and understated golfing retreats. It is possibly also one of England's most underrated venues. In Darwin's day there was only one 18 hole course, but today the club has 54 holes—a third course having been built and opened for play in July 1994. They are quite marvellous tests of golf but although the club has hosted a number of important championships, its reputation is still not as widespread or as great as it merits. Moreover the condition and quality of the courses seem to be continually improving. It is always pleasing to see the construction of new tees and the careful planting of indigenous trees but at Frilford additional gorse and heather have also been introduced, and a lot of thought has clearly gone into the many subtle alterations. When added to the fact that the greens at Frilford have never been better and the rough really is rough (so rare these days) there is certainly much to admire.

Further developments during 1997-98 combine to increase the club's undoubted attractions. The clubhouse has been refurbished and extended and can now seat 120 visitors in the dining room. In addition the new 10 million gallon reservoir should be adequate for all Frilford's watering needs even in the driest of summers.

Visitors wishing to inspect any or all of the courses, the **Red, Green** and **Blue** as they are known, should make arrangements with the club's **Secretary, Mr S Styles** preferably by telephoning in advance on **(01865) 390864**. Handicap certificates are required. The **Professional** at Frilford is **Derek Craik, (01865) 390887** and the club's full address is **Frilford Heath Golf Club, Abingdon, Oxford OX13 5NW**. The green fees in 1998 are set at £45 for Monday to Friday with £60 payable at weekends and on bank holidays. After 5pm fees are reduced to £29..

The golf club is located three miles west of Abingdon off the A338 Oxford to Wantage road (an old Roman Road). It is only a few minutes from the A420, the A415 and the A34, the latter linking Oxford to the M4.

The **Red Course** (6843 yards, par 73 from the back markers) opening holes have been modified to accommodate several holes of the new Blue Course. Arguably the best sequence on the Red comes between the 5th and the 9th. The 5th is a difficult par four with a fiendish cross bunker that often comes into play as the prevailing wind is against. If the wind is blowing then the par five 6th is reachable in two, although its green, like most at Frilford, is heavily contoured. The 7th is a difficult par four—the key here being a long and accurate drive, and the stroke one 8th has a hog's back shaped fairway, making it a veritable 'beast' of a hole. Beauty follows beast though in the form of the par three 9th where the tee shot is struck over a picturesque pond. On the back nine the golfer confronts a two-tiered green on the short 11th and a saucer-shaped green on the 13th. Two other notable holes are the 12th, with its backdrop of magnificent trees and the 16th, where a new back tee has turned the hole into a very good dog-leg.

The **Green Course** (6006 yards, par 69) begins more impressively than the Red with a heavily wooded, sweeping par five followed by a most attractive par three. The 2nd is in fact one of two outstanding short holes on the front nine, the other being the 6th. The dog-leg 12th is perhaps the most memorable of the two-shot holes on this course—the drive here is over a natural lake, and there is a trio of lengthy par fours starting at the 14th, but in the right conditions the 18th is just about driveable—thus affording the perfect opportunity to show off in front of the clubhouse!

As mentioned, the **Blue Course** opened in July 1994 is maturing rapidly. Like the Red, it is of championship length, stretching to 6728 yards, par 72. The Blue Course can properly be described as a 'modern design' for in amongst the more traditional natural hazards the architect has incorporated a number of water hazard. Moreover, the bunkers are invariably large, quite shallow and strategically positioned. However, unlike many 'modern designs', Frilford's Blue Course distributes challenge and charm in equal proportion. Apparently, some members already regard it as Frilford's best 18—and that is some compliment.

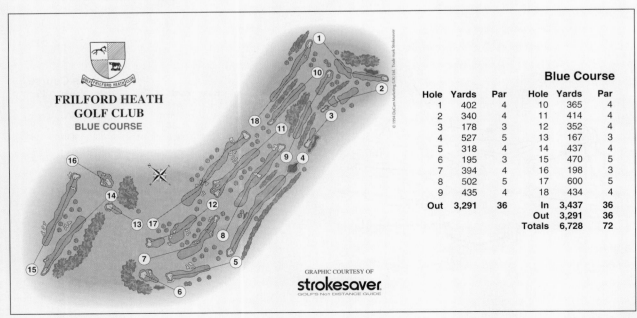

**FRILFORD HEATH
GOLF CLUB
BLUE COURSE**

GRAPHIC COURTESY OF
strokesaver
GOLF'S No1 DISTANCE GUIDE

Blue Course

Hole	Yards	Par	Hole	Yards	Par
1	402	4	10	365	4
2	340	4	11	414	4
3	178	3	12	352	4
4	527	5	13	167	3
5	318	4	14	437	4
6	195	3	15	470	5
7	394	4	16	198	3
8	502	5	17	600	5
9	435	4	18	434	4
Out	**3,291**	**36**	**In**	**3,437**	**36**
			Out	3,291	36
			Totals	6,728	72

Key

To avoid disappointment it is advisable to telephone in advance

***Visitors welcome at most times
**Visitors usually allowed on weekdays only
*Visitors not normally permitted (Mon, Wed) No visitors on specified days

Approximate Green Fees
A £40 plus
B £25 to £40
C £20 to £30
D £15 to £25
E under £15
F Green fees on application

Restrictions
G Guests only
H—Handicap certificate required
H—(24) Handicap of 24 or less
L —Letter of introduction required
M—Visitor must be a member of another recognised club

BERKSHIRE

Bearwood G.C.
(0118) 976 0060
Mole Road, Sindlesham
(9) 5624 yards/**/E/H

Bearwood Lakes G.C.
(0118) 979 7900
Wokingham
(18) 6805 yards/*/B/G

The Berkshire G.C.
(01344) 621495
Swinley Road, Ascot
(18) 6369 yards/**/A/L
(18) 6260 yards/**/A/L

Bird Hills G.C.
(01628) 7710307
Drift Road, Hawthorn Hill
(18) 6212 yards/***/D

Blue Mountain Golf Centre
(01344) 300200
Wood Lane, Binfield
(18) 6097 yards/***/D

Calcot Park G.C.
(0118) 942 7124
Bath Road, Calcot, Reading
(18) 6283 yards/**/F

Castle Royal G.C.
(01628) 829252
Knowl Hill, Reading
(18) 6700 yards/***

Datchet G.C.
(01753) 543887
Buccleuch Road, Datchet
(9) 5978 yards/**/C/E(WE)

Donnington Grove G.C.
(01635) 581000
Donnington, Newbury
(18) 7050 yards/**8/B

Donnington Valley G.C.
(01635) 32488
Old Oxford Road, Donnington
(18) 4002 yards/***/F

Downshire G.C.
(01344) 302030
Easthampstead Park, Wokingham
(18) 6382 yards/***/E

East Berkshire G.C.
(01344) 772041
Ravenswood Avenue, Crowthorne
(18) 6345 yards/***/A/H

Goring & Streatley G.C.
(01491) 873229
Rectory Road, Streatley
(18) 6255 yards/**/B

Hennerton G.C.
(01734) 401000
Crazies Hill Road, Wargrave
(9) 2730 yards/***/D

Hurst G.C.
(0118) 934 4355
Sandford Lane, Hurst, Wokingham
(9) 3013 yards/***/E

Lambourne G.C.
(01628) 666755
Dropmore Road, Burnham
(18) 6771 yards/***/A/H

Lavender Park G.C.
(01344) 890940
Swinley Road, Ascot
(9) 1104 yards/***/F

Maidenhead G.C.
(01628) 24693
Shoppenhangers Road, Maidenhead
(18) 6360 yards/**/B/H

Mapledurham G.C.
(0118) 946 3353
Chazey Heath, Mapledurham
(18) 5625 yards/***/D

Mill Ride G.C.
(01344) 886777
Mill Ride, North Ascot
(18) 6690 yards/***/A/H

Newbury & Crookham G.C.
(01635) 40035
Burys Bank Road, Greenham
(18) 5880 yards/**/B/M

Pincents Manor G.C.
(01734) 323511
Pincents Lane, Calcot
(9) 4882 yards/***/E

Reading G.C.
(0118) 947 2909
Kidmore End Road, Emmer Green
(18) 6212 yards/**(not Friday)/B

Royal Ascot G.C.
(01344) 25175
Winkfield Road, Ascot
(18) 5716 yards/**/F/G

Sand Martins G.C.
(01734) 792711
Finchampstead Road, Wokingham
(18) 6297 yards/**/B

Sonning G.C.
(0118) 969 3332
Duffield Road, Sonning
(18) 6366 yards/**/F/H

Swinley Forest G.C.
(01344) 20197
Coronation Road, South Ascot
(18)6011 yards/*/A/G/H

Temple G.C.
(01628) 824248
Henley Road, Hurley, Maidenhead
(18) 6206 yards/**/A/H

West Berkshire G.C.
(01488) 638574
Chaddleworth, Newbury
(18) 7053 yards/**/C

Winter Hill G.C.
(01628) 527613
Grange Lane, Cookham, Maidenhead
(18) 6408 yards/**/B/H

BUCKINGHAMSHIRE

Abbey Hill G.C.
(01908) 563845
Two Mile Ash, Stony Stratford
(18) 6193 yards/***/F

Aylesbury Golf Centre
(01296) 393644
Hulcott Lane, Bierton
(9) 5488 yards/***/E

Aylesbury Park G.C.
(01296) 399196
Oxford Road, Aylesbury
(18) 6146 yards/***/D

Beaconsfield G.C.
(01494) 676545
Seer Green, Beaconsfield
(18) 6487 yards/**/A/H

Buckingham G.C.
(01280) 815566
Tingewick Road, Buckingham
(18) 6082 yards/**/B/M

Buckinghamshire G.C.
(01895) 835777
Denham Court, Denham
(18) 6880 yards/**(not Friday)/A/L

Burnham Beeches G.C.
(01628) 661448
Green Lane, Burnham
(18) 6463 yards/**/A/H/L

Chalfont Park G.C.
(01494) 876293
Three Households, Chalfont St Giles
(9) 3000 yards/***/E

Chartridge Park G.C.
(01494) 791772
Chartridge, Chesham
(18) 5721 yards/***/B

Chesham and Ley Hill G.C.
(01494) 784541
Ley Hill, Chesham
(9) 5240 yards/**/F

Chiltern Forest G.C.
(01296) 630899
Aston Hill, Halton, Aylesbury
(18) 6038 yards/**/B

Denham G.C.
(01895) 832022
Tilehouse Lane, Denham
(18) 6451 yards/**(Fri)/A/H/L

Ellesborough G.C.
(01296) 622114
Butlers Cross, Aylesbury
(18) 6271 yards/**/F/H/L

Farnham Park G.C.
(01753) 647065
Park Road, Stoke Poges
(18) 6172 yards/***/E

Flackwell Heath G.C.
(01628) 520027
Treadaway Road, Flackwell Heath
(18) 6207 yards/**/B/H

Gerrards Cross G.C.
(01753) 883263
Chalfont Park, Gerrards Cross
(18) 6295 yards/**/A/H

Harewood Downs G.C.
(01494) 762184
Cokes Lane, Chalfont St Giles
(18) 5958 yards/**/B/H

Harleyford G.C.
(01628) 487878
Henley Road, Harlow
(18) 6604 yards/***/A/H

Hazelmere G.&C.C.
(01494) 714722
Penn Road, High Wycombe
(18) 6039 yards/**/B

Iver G.C.
(01753) 655615
Hollow Hill Lane, Iver
(9) 6214 yards/***/E

Ivinghoe G.C.
(01296) 668696
Wellcroft, Ivinghoe
(9) 4508 yards/***/E

Lambourne G.C.
(01628) 666755
Dropmore Road, Burnham
(18) 6746 yards/***/A/H/L

Little Chalfont G.C.
(01494) 764877
Lodge Lane, Little Chalfont
(9) 5852 yards/***/D

Mentmore G.&C.C.
(01296) 662020
Mentmore, Leighton Buzzard
(18) 6777 yards/**/B/H

Princes Risborough G.C.
(01844) 346989
Lee Road, Saunderton Lee
(9) 5017 yards/***/D

Richings Park G.C.
(01753) 655352
North Park, Iver
(18) 6200 yards/**/B

Silverstone G.C.
(01280) 850005
Silverstone Road, Stowe
(18) 6164 yards/***/D

Stoke Poges G.C.
(01753) 717171
Stoke Park, Park Road, Stoke Poges
(18) 6654 yards/**/A/H/L

Stowe G.C.
(01280) 813650
Stowe, Buckingham
(9) 4573 yards/**/F/G

Thorney Park G.C.
(01895) 422095
Thorney Mill Lane, Iver
(9) 3000 yards/**/E

Three Locks G.C.
(01525) 270470
Great Brickhill, Milton Keynes
(9) 6654 yards/***/E

Wavendon Golf Centre
(01908) 281811
Wavendon, Milton Keynes
(18) 5800 yards/***/E

Weston Turville G.C.
(01296) 24084
New Road, Weston Turville
(18) 6782 yards/***/D

Wexham Park G.C.
(01753) 663271
Wexham Street, Slough
(18) 5390 yards/***/D
(9) 2383 yards/***/E
(9) 2585 yards/***/E

Whiteleaf G.C.
(018444) 274058
Whiteleaf, Aylesbury
(9) 5391 yards/**/C/H

Windmill Hill G.C.
(01908) 378623
Tattenhoe Lane, Bletchley
(18) 6773 yards/***/E

Woburn G. and C.C.
(01908) 370756
Bow Brickhill, Milton Keynes
(18) 6940 yards/**/F/H
(18) 6641 yards/**/F/H

Wycombe Heights G.C.
(01494) 816686
Rayners Avenue, Loudwater
(18) 6300 yards/***/D

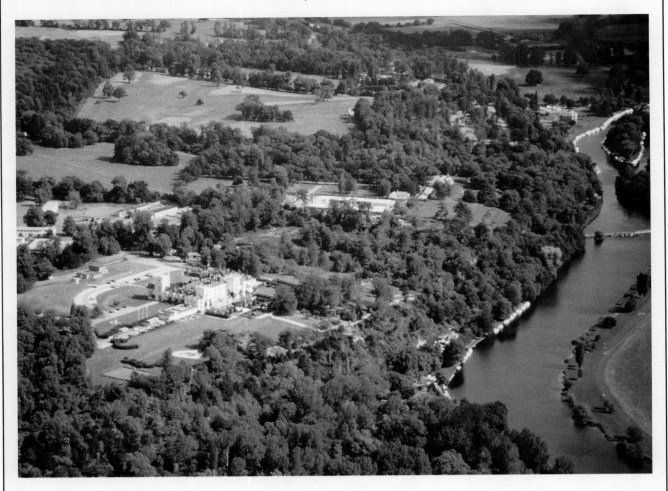

Danesfield House is set in the heart of Buckinghamshire and stands in 65 acres of beautiful English and Italian styled gardens which overlook the river Thames and Chiltern Hills. There has been a manor house on the site since 1638 but the current house, the grandest of all, was built in 1899 and opened as a luxury hotel in 1991.

In all, there are 87 individually furnished bedrooms in the main house all of which have satellite TV, minibar, 24 hour room service, two telephone lines (one to accommodate a personal fax or laptop computer), trouser press and hairdryer. Many bedrooms have the original fireplaces and balconies overlooking the Thames. There is also a range of suites, some with jacuzzis and four poster beds

The hotel offers a choice of two restaurants, the Oak Room and the less formal Orangery Mediterranean Brasserie. Both offer fine food in elegant surroundings.

Danesfield House is within easy reach of many of England's finest golf courses. The newly opened Harleyford Golf Club is right on the doorstep whilst slightly further afield we find such gems as Stoke Poges, Mentmore, Sunningdale, Woburn and Donnington Valley. For the non-golfer there is plenty at hand; Ascot and Newbury races, boating on the Thames, tennis, croquet, clay pigeon shooting, hot air ballooning and historic sites such as Windsor Castle and Blenheim Palace close by.

Danesfield House offers superb private function facilities with a range of prestigious dining suites for up to 120 guests and excellent conference facilities for up to 100 delegates.

Finding Danesfield House is no problem, situated as it is on the banks of the Thames between Marlow and Henley, approximately 45 minutes by car from central London and just half an hour from Heathrow. The hotel boasts a Thames mooring and clients can be transported to the hotel via restored steam launches. The hotel is also directly accessible via the M4 from Heathrow or even by air, by helicopter! But whatever your means of travel Danesfield House offers a luxurious retreat from the world outside.

Danesfield House
Henley Road
Marlow on Thames
Buckinghamshire SL27 2EY
Tel: (01628) 891010
Fax: (01628) 890408

Artist: **Charles Crombie RULE IV**
Courtesy of: **Rosenstiels**

Artist: **Charles Crombie RULE XIII**
Courtesy of: **Rosenstiels**

OXFORDSHIRE

Aspect Park G.C.
(01491) 578306
Remenham Hill, Henley on Thames
(18) 6369 yards/**/C/H

Badgemore Park G.C.
(01491) 573667
Badgemore Park, Henley on
Thames
(18) 6112 yards/***/B/H

Banbury G.C.
(01285) 810449
Aynho Road, Adderbury
(18) 6333 yards/***/E

Brailes G.C.
(01608) 685633
Sutton Lane, Brailes
(18) 6270 yards/**/C/M

Burford G.C.
(01993) 822149
Burford
(18) 6405 yards/**/B/H

Carswell C.C.
(01367) 870422
Carswell, Faringdon
(18) 6133 yards/***/D

Cherwell Edge G.C.
(01295) 711591
Chacombe, Banbury
(18) 5925 yards/***/E

Chesterton G.C.
(01869) 241204
Chesterton, Bicester
(18) 6224 yards/***/D/H

Chipping Norton G.C.
(01608) 642383
Southcombe, Chipping Norton
(18) 6283 yards/**/C

Drayton Park G.C.
(01235) 550607
Steventon Road, Drayton
(18) 6500 yards/***/D

Frilford Heath G.C.
(01865) 390864
Frilford Heath, Abingdon
(18) 6728 yards/***/A/H
(18) 6395yards/***/A/H
(18) 6006 yards/***/A/H

Hadden Hill G.C.
(01235) 510410
Wallingford Road, Didcot
(18) 6563 yards/***/D

Henley G.C.
(01491) 573304
Harpsden, Henley on Thames
(18) 6330 yards/**/A/H

Huntercombe G.C.
(01491) 641207
Nuffield, Henley on Thames
(18) 6301 yards/**/A/H

Lyneham G.C.
(01993) 831841
Lyneham, Chipping Norton
(18) 6669 yards/***/D

North Oxford G.C.
(01865) 554415
Banbury Road, Oxford
(18) 5805 yards/***/B/H

The Oxfordshire G.C.
(01844) 278300
Rycote Lane, Milton Common,
Thame
(18) 7187 yards/***/F/M/L

RAF Benson G.C.
(01491) 837766
Royal Air Force, Bensen
(9) 4395 yards/***/G

Rye Hill G.C.
(01295) 721818
Boon Farm, Milcombe
(18) 6569 yards/***/E

Southfield G.C.
(01865) 242158
Hill Top Road, Oxford
(18) 6230 yards/**/B/H

Tadmarton Heath G.C.
(01608) 737278
Wiggington, Banbury
(18) 5917 yards/**/B/H

Waterstock G.C.
(01844) 338093
Oxford Road, Cowley
(18) 6482 yards/***/D

Witney G.C.
(01993) 779000
Downs Road, Witney
(18) 6460 yards/***/D

Artist: **Charles Crombie XVIII**
Courtesy of: **Rosenstiels**

Artist: **Charles Crombie RULE XXXIII**
Courtesy of: **Rosenstiels**

Artist: **C.E. Brock** **THE DRIVE** Courtesy of: **Sotheby's**

A hush descends as you ponder your first swing in old Worcestershire. Apple and cherry trees are in blossom and in the distance a herd of white faced Herefords appraise your stance. You're fortunate, for several hundred years ago the air in these parts was thick with the clatter of sword against sword but now there is peace. Crack! Straight down the fairway—the echo resounds and then dies—you're on your way.

Herefordshire, Worcestershire and Gloucestershire—what a lovely trio! Bordering the principality, the region is arguably the most tranquil in England. It is an area of rich pastures and cider orchards, of small market towns and sleepy villages rather than crowded cities, and encompasses the Cotswolds and the Malverns, the beautiful Wye Valley and the splendid Vale of Evesham. Truly a green and pleasant land!

Hereford & Worcester

Herefordshire and Worcestershire have at last officially regained their separate identities—but one doubts they ever lost them. Golf courses aren't exactly plentiful, but those there are tend to be very scenic, often hidden away deep in the glorious countryside. To the north west of Hereford, **Kington** and **Herefordshire** are typical examples and both warmly welcome visitors. Kington is closer to Wales and is reputedly the highest course in either country—a place where poor golf can always be blamed on the rarified atmosphere. South of Hereford is another attractive course, **Belmont,** a newer course but one that has already gained a good reputation.

Hereford is a natural base when golfing in the area and there are a number of good hotels. The Graftonbury Hotel (01432) 356411 is a charming garden hotel with easy access to Belmont Golf Club. The Green Dragon Hotel (01432) 272506 is particularly comfortable—note the many four poster beds—and in nearby Much Birch, the Pilgrim Hotel (01981) 540742 is a splendid former rectory. The Hopbine Hotel (01432) 268722 and Castle Pool (01432) 354301 offer reasonably priced accommodation near to Hereford city centre. A short drive to Weobley reveals the Red Lion (01544) 318419, a 14th century inn in the centre of a delightful village—very handy for Herefordshire Golf Club. Ye Olde Salutation Inn (01544) 318443 is a delightful hostelry with excellent food. Near the same golf course is a good pub, the Bell at Tillington, while for Belmont, the Butchers Arms is recommended (some accommodation here too). Kington has a first class restaurant, Penrhos Court (01544) 230720—some quaint bedrooms here too. It also boasts the Oxford Arms (01544) 230322, a 16th century coaching inn near the golf course. Visitors to this pleasant area should also consider the excellent Allt-yr-Ynys Hotel (01873) 890307 in Walterstone—an ideal retreat..

Ross-on-Wye is a renowned beauty spot and the town's golf course reflects the reputation. Set in the heart of the Wye Valley and surrounded by a blaze of colour, it's hard to believe that the M50 is under a mile away (junction 4). If staying in the area, the Pengethley Manor Hotel (01989) 730211 is most charming and Peterstow Country House boasts an award-winning restaurant. Alternatively, try the New Inn (01989) 730274 in St Owens Cross where you are sure of a warm welcome.

Worcester is an attractive city with a beautiful cathedral overlooks ing the famous county cricket ground. A mile from the town centre, off the A4103, is the **Worcester** Golf and Country Club. The oldest course in the county, and possibly the finest is the appropriately

named **Worcestershire** Golf Club, two miles south of Great Malvern. Thecourse has extensive views of the Malverns, the Severn Valley and the Cotswolds. Elsewhere in the county, the **Vale** Golf and Country Club near Pershore boasts 27 testing holes and a driving range. A newer development is the **Bank House** in Bransford. The hotel here offers good leisure facilities and is ideal for a weekend away (01886) 833551. The final recommendations in Worcestershire are **Kidderminster,** the highly regarded and beautifully maintained **Blackwell** Golf Club near Bromsgrove and the relatively new **Cleobury Mortimer.**

Near Worcester, the Elms Hotel (01299) 896666 at Abberley is an outstanding country house hotel while Malvern Wells offers the delightful Cottage in the Wood hotel (01684) 575859 and an excellent restaurant, the Croque-en-Bouche (01684) 565612. Worcester itself contains the stylish Fownes Hotel (01905) 613151 and the moderately priced Giffard Hotel (01905) 726262. Browns restaurant (01905) 26263 is also well worth a visit. Great Malvern provides a charming 19th century coaching inn, the Foley Arms (01684) 573397. A highly recommended hotel in Redditch is the Old Rectory (01527) 523000,and a final suggestion is to visit Tenbury Wells where the Cadmore Lodge (01584) 810044 is an ideal setting with its own 9 hole course.

The Cottage in the Wood Hotel
Holywell Road, Malvern Wells,
Worcestershire WR14 4LG
Tel: (01684) 575859 Fax: (01684) 560662

The Cottage in the Wood Hotel and Restaurant, perched on the Malvern Hills, enjoys one of the finest views in Britain.

There are twenty bedrooms, all of different sizes and decor, some with four posters, all en suite and most with spectacular views. The hotel's restaurant is well known and highly regarded (2 AA Rosettes) with an extensive and lovingly compiled wine list.

For the sightseer, Worcester, Hereford and Gloucester are nearby and the Cotswolds and the Welsh Marches are within easy reach. Sportsmen are equally well catered for with some fine racecourses, including Cheltenham, and with special arrangements for guests at the Worcestershire golf course lying immediately beneath the hotel.

Gloucestershire

Heading into Gloucestershire, I trust that when Doctor Foster went to Gloucester he wasn't a well travelled golfer. The county has very few courses and Gloucester itself didn't possess one at all until as recently as 1976. Neighbouring Cheltenham has been a little more fortunate but, granted one or two exceptions, the quality of the golf in the county doesn't exactly match up to the undeniable quality of its scenery and hostelries.

The county's two best known courses are probably **Cotswold Hills** and **Lilley Brook**, located to the north and south of Cheltenham respectively. Both offer commanding views of the Gloucestershire countryside, especially perhaps Lilley Brook, one of southern England's most undulating courses. Each is well worth a visit and the beautiful Regency manor of the Cheltenham Park Hotel (01242) 222021 is only minutes from both.

Cleeve Hill is Cheltenham's third 18 hole course. Situated on high ground to the north of the town it can get rather cold in winter. One wag said that he enjoyed Lilley Brook in the summer as half of him was mountain goat, and Cleeve Hill in the winter because the other half of him was eskimo!

The Cheltenham area has many fine hotels, but perhaps the best known is the Queens Hotel (01242) 514724. On The Park (01242) 518898 is a popular and excellent alternative. A good hotel in the surrounding hills is the splendid Greenway (01242) 862352 in Shurdington, which offers a first class menu and beautiful grounds. Also, not far out of Cheltenham at Toddington, Woodleys (01242) 621313 is a superior guesthouse. In Cleeve Hill, the Malvern View Hotel (01242) 672017 is well thought of, a little further north in Bishops Cleeve, Cleeveway House (01242) 672585 has rooms and an outstanding restaurant.

Outside Cheltenham, **Minchinhampton** has perhaps the biggest golfing reputation. A club of great character, it celebrated its centenary in 1989. There are three very varied courses here, including the acclaimed Old course In the south of the county, **Stinchcombe Hill** is also well thought of. A first class place to stay nearby is Burleigh Court (01453) 883804, while to the north the Amberley Inn (01453) 872565 in Amberley, with its fine views over Woodchester Valley has considerable charm. For a good pub visit **Painswick** for the Royal Oak–a short golf course here too.

The 18 hole course at **Cirencester** is probably the nearest one gets to golf in the Cotswolds. Cirencester is certainly pleasant but to most of us the real Cotswolds are the many wonderfully named villages—Bourton-on-the-Water, Stow-on-the-Wold, Upper Slaughter and Lower Slaughter.

Gloucester's newish course lies within the grounds of the **Gloucester** Hotel (01452) 525653 at Robinswood Hill. A luxurious country club, there are in fact 27 holes here plus numerous leisure facilities. The 18 hole course enjoys a pleasant setting and has matured very rapidly. The same can be said of **Tewkesbury Park** Hotel's golf course (01684) 295405 which is laid out on the site of the famous Roses battle of 1471. Both hotels are comfortable and their courses are open to residents and non-residents alike. However, for a special occasion, we can recommend a stay at **Puckrup Hall** (01684) 296200, an elegant Regency house set in 40 acres of parkland with an adjacent 18 hole golf course. At Upton St Leonards, near Gloucester, Hatton Court (01452) 617412 is most relaxing.

The Forest of Dean is our next port of call—another beauty spot and some good golf too at the **Royal Forest of Dean** Golf Club in Coleford. In Coleford itself, there is the lovely 16th century Poolway House (01594) 833937.

A notable inn nearby is the Speech House (01594) 822607. Staying a few days in the area is recommended—the countryside is splendid and just eight miles away, over the border in Wales, lies Chepstow and the delights of **St Pierre**.

Then on to **Broadway** Golf Club—the course being a mile and a half or so from 'the loveliest village in England'. True to form there are some marvellous views from the golf course looking out across the Vale of Evesham. It really is a beautiful part of the world and those wishing to do some exploring will find several superb hotels, any of which will make an ideal base. The Lygon Arms (01386) 852255 in Broadway with its outstanding frontage probably takes pride of place but for excellent value the Collin House Hotel (01386) 858354 takes some beating. Both have fine restaurants. Our final recommendation in this area is Buckland Manor (01386) 852626, an hotel with an exceptional restaurant.

Across the river, the golf course at **Clevedon** stares spectacularly out across the mouth of the Severn. Clevedon is a clifftop course rather than a links and is well worth visiting. By travelling inland from Clevedon towards Bristol along the B3128, two of the city's best courses are reached before the famous suspension bridge. **Long Ashton** is immediately off the B3128, while to find **Bristol and Clifton** a left turn should be taken along the B3129. There is probably little to choose between the two, both being particularly attractive examples of downland golf. **Henbury** Golf Club is closer to the centre of Bristol, about three miles to the north in the quiet suburb of Westbury-on-Trym. Henbury is a mature parkland course with an abundance of trees, making for some very attractive and challenging holes. One final club to recommend in Bristol is **Shirehampton**—always beautifully maintained.

Perhaps one of the most stylish hotel in Bristol is the aptly named Grand Hotel (0117) 929 1645 on Broad Street. Two recommended restaurants are Harveys (0117) 927 5034 and Restaurant Lettonie (0117) 968 6456 in Stoke Bishop. An excellent base towards the north of the city at Thornbury is the Tudor-style Thornbury Castle (01454) 281182.

Anyone travelling from Bristol to Bath (or vice versa) is likely to pass within a few miles of the **Tracy Park** Golf and Country Club at Wick. If possible, a detour is recommended. Tracy Park is a newish course, built in the mid-seventies around a 400 year old mansion which acts as a rather impressive clubhouse. Although the course can get a little soggy in winter it offers a very good test of golf.

Artist: **John Horwood CHIPPING TO THE FLAG**
Courtesy of: **Burlington Gallery**

Key

To avoid disappointment
it is advisable to telephone
in advance

***Visitors welcome at most times*
**Visitors usually allowed on
weekdays only*
*Visitors not normally permitted
(Mon, Wed) No visitors
on specified days*

Approximate Green Fees
A   £40 plus
B   £25 to £40
C   £20 to £30
D   £15 to £25
E   under £15
F   Green fees on application

Restrictions
G   Guests only
H—Handicap certificate required
H—(24) Handicap of 24 or less
L —Letter of introduction required
M—Visitor must be a member of
another recognised club

GLOUCESTERSHIRE

Bristol and Clifton G.C.
(01275) 393474
Beggar Bush Lane, Failand
(18) 6294 yards/**/F/H

Broadway G.C.
(01386) 853683
Willersley Hill, Broadway
(18) 6216 yards/**/B/H

Chipping Sodbury G.C.
(01454) 319042
Chipping Sodbury, Bristol
(18) 6912 yards/***/B
(9) 6194 yards/***/E

Cirencester G.C.
(01285) 652465
Cheltenham Road, Bagendon
(18) 6021 yards/***/B/H

Cleeve Hill G.C.
(01242) 672592
Cleeve Hill, Nr Prestbury
(18) 6444 yards/**/F

Clevedon G.C.
(01275) 874057
Castle Road, Clevedon
(18) 5998 yards/**/B-A/H

Cotswold Edge G.C.
(01453) 844167
Upper Rushmire, Wotton-under-Edge
(18) 6170 yards/**/C/H

Cotswold Hills G.C.
(01242) 515264
Ullenwood, Cheltenham
(18) 6716 yards/***/B/H/L

Farrington G.C.
(01761) 241274
Farrington Gurney, Bristol
(18) 6693 yards/***/D
(9) 3022 yards/***/E

Filton G.C.
(0117) 969 4169
Golf Course Lane, Filton, Bristol
(18) 6264 yards/**/B

Forest of Dean G.C.
(01594) 832583
Lords Hill, Coleford
(18) 5682 yards/***/D

Forest Hills G.C.
(01594) 810620
Mile End Road, Coleford
(18) 5988 yards/***/D

Gloucester Hotel G.& C.C.
(01452) 411331
Matson Lane, Robinswood Hill
(18) 6135 yards/**/C/H

Henbury G.C.
(0117) 950 0044
Henbury Hill, Westbury-on-Trym
(18) 6039 yards/**/B/H

Knowle G.C.
(0117) 977 0660
Fairway, Brislington
(18) 6016 yards/**/B/H

Lilley Brook G.C.
(01204) 526785
Cirencester Road, Charlton Kings
(18) 6226 yards/**/B/H/L

Long Ashton G.C.
(01275) 392316
Long Ashton, Bristol
(18) 6077 yards/***/B/H/L

Lydney G.C.
(01594) 842614
Lakeside Avenue, Lydney
(9) 5382 yards/**/D

Mangotsfield G.C.
(0117) 956 5501
Carsons Road, Mangotsfield
(18) 5337 yards/***/E

Minchinhampton G.C.
(01453) 833860
Minchinhampton, Stroud
(18) 6295 yards/**/D/H
(18) 6244 yards/**/B/H
(18) 6270 yards/**/B/H

Naunton Downs G.C.
(01451) 850090
Naunton, Cheltenham
(18) 6174 yards/***/C

Painswick G.C.
(01452) 812180
Painswick, Stroud
(18) 4780 yards/**/D

Puckrup Hall Hotel & G.C.
(01684) 296200
Tewkesbury
(18) 6431 yards/**/B/H

Rodway G.C.
(01452) 384222
Highnam
(18) 5860 yeards/***/E

Sherdons G.C.
(01684) 274782
Manor Farm, Tredington
(9) 2654 yards/***/E

Shirehampton Park G.C.
(0117) 982 2083
Park Hill, Shirehampton
(18) 5521 yards/**/C/H

Stinchcombe Hill G.C.
(01453) 542015
Stinchcombe Hill, Dursley
(18) 5734 yards/**/C/H

Stockwood Vale G.C.
(0117) 986 6505
Keynsham, Bristol
(18) 6000 yards/***/E

Streamleaze G.C.
(01453) 843128
Bradley, Wotton-under-Edge
(18) 4582 yards/***/E

Tewkesbury Park Hotel G.C.
(01684) 295405
Lincoln Green Lane, Tewkesbury
(18) 6533 yards/**/B/H

Thornbury G.C.
(01454) 281144
Bristol Road, Thornbury
(18) 6154 yards/***/D
(18) 2195 yards/***/D

Tickenham G.C.
(01275) 856626
Clevedon Road, Tickenham
(9) 2000 yards/***/E

Tracy Park G.& C.C.
(0117) 937 2251
Bath Road, Wick, Bristol
(9) 6834 yards/***/B
(9) 6861 yards/***/B
(9) 6203 yards/***/B

West Country G.C.
(01275) 856626
Clevedon Road, Tickenham
(9) 2000 yards/***/D

Westonbirt G.C.
(01666) 880242
Westonbirt, Tetbury
(9) 4504 yards/**/F

Woodlands G. & C.C.
(01454) 619319
Woodlands Lane, Almondsbury
(18) 5550 yards/***/D

Woodspring G.C.
(01275) 394378
Yanley Lane, Long Ashton
(18) 6288 yards/***/B/H

HEREFORD & WORCESTER

Abbey Park G.& C.C.
(01527) 68006
Dagnell End Road, Redditch
(18) 6411 yards/**/D

Bank House Hotel & C.C.
(01886) 833551
Bransford, Worcester
(18) 6101 yards/**/B

Belmont Lodge G.C.
(01432) 352666
Belmont House, Belmont
(18) 6480 yards/***/F

Blackwell G.C.
(0121) 445 1944
Blackwell, Bromsgrove
(18) 6202 yards/**/A/H

Bromsgrove G.C.
(01527) 575886
Stratford Road, Bromsgrove
(9) 3159 yards/***/E

Burghill Valley G.C.
(01432) 760456
Tillington Road, Burghill
(18) 6239 yards/***/D
(9) 3075 yards/***/E

Cadmore Lodge G.C.
(01584) 810044
Berrington Green, Tenbury Wells
(9) 5130 yards/***/E

Churchill and Blakedown G.C.
(01562) 700018
Churchill Lane, Blakedown
(9) 6472 yards/**/D

Cleobury Mortimer
(01299) 271112
Wyre Common, nr. Kidderminster
(18) 6438 yards/***/C/H

Droitwich G.& C.C.
(01905) 770207
Ford Lane, Droitwich
(18) 6040 yards/**/B/H

Evesham G.C.
(01386) 860395
Cray Combe Links, Fladbury
(9) 6415 yards/**/C/H

Fulford Heath G.C.
(01564) 824758
Tanners Green Lane, Wythall
(18) 6216 yards/**/B/H

Gay Hill G.C.
0121 430 8544
Alcester Road, Hollywood
(18) 6532 yards/**/F

Habberley G.C.
(01562) 745756
Habberley, Kidderminster
(9) 5400 yards/**/D

Hereford Municipal G.C.
(01432) 344376
Holmer Road, Hereford
(9) 3060 yards/***/E

Herefordshire G.C.
(01432) 830219
Ravens Causeway, Wormsley
(18) 6100 yards/***/D

Kidderminster G.C.
(01562) 822303
Russell Road, Kidderminster
(18) 6405 yards/**/B/H

King's Norton G.C.
(01564) 826789
Brockhill Lane, Weatheroak
(27) 7060 yards/**/B

Kington G.C.
(01544) 230340
Bradnor Hill, Kington,
(18) 5840 yards/**/D

Leominster G.C.
(01568) 610055
Ford Bridge, Leominster
(9) 6100 yards/***/C/H

Little Lakes G.& C.C.
(01299) 266385
Lye Head, Bewdley
(9) 6247 yards/**/D

Ombersley G.C.
(01905) 620747
Bishops Wood Road, Ombersley
(18) 6139 yards/***/E

Perdiswell Municipal G.C.
(01905) 457189
Bilford Road, Worcester
(9) 6004 yards/***/E

Pitcheroak G.C.
(01527) 541054
Plymouth Road, Redditch
(9) 4584 yards/***/F

Redditch G.C.
(01527) 543309
Green Lane, Callow Hill
(18) 6671 yards/**/B

Ross-on-Wye G.C.
(01989) 720267
Gorsley, Ross-on-Wye
(18) 6500 yards/**/B/M

Sapey G.C.
(01886) 853567
Whitley Road, Upper Sapey
(18) 5900 yards/***/C

South Herefordshire G.C.
(01989) 780535
Hartleton, Upton Bishop
(18) 6672 yards/***/C

Tolladine G.C.
(01905) 22296
Tolladine Road, Worcester
(9) 5134 yards/**/D/H

The Vale G.& C.C.
(01386) 462781
Hill Furze Road, Bishampton
(18) 7041 yards/***/B
(9) 2960 yards/***/E

Wharton Park G.C.
(01299) 405222
Longbank, Bewdley
(18) 6600 yards/***/C

Worcester G. & C.C.
(01905) 422555
Boughton Park, Worcester
(18) 6154 yards/**/B/H

Worcestershire G.C.
(01684) 575992
Wood Farm, Malvern Wells
(18) 6449 yards/***/B/H

Wyre Forest G.C.
(01299) 822682
Zortech Avenue, Kidderminster
(18) 5790 yards/***/E

Artist: **Bill Waugh** **THE BALLESTEROS HOLE** _Courtesy of:_ **Burlington Gallery**

Birmingham

Golfers in the City of London have often been known to get frustrated at having to travel many a mile for a decent game of golf. In 1919 one obviously disgusted individual teed up at Piccadilly Circus and proceeded to play along the Strand, through Fleet Street and Ludgate Hill firing his last shot at the Royal Exchange. Such behaviour is unknown in Birmingham—as far as I'm aware, the Bull Ring and the NEC have never been peppered with golf balls. This I suspect may be because the needs of its golfing citizens have been properly attended to.

Within easy access of the town centre lie the likes of **The Belfry** and **Little Aston** to the north, **Fulford Heath, Copt Heath** and **Kings Norton** to the south, and **Sandwell Park** and **Edgbaston** somewhere in the middle. Golfers north of Birmingham are indeed particularly fortunate for, in addition to The Belfry and Little Aston, there is also **Sutton Coldfield** and **Moor Hall**. All provide extremely pleasant retreats from the noise and confusion of England's second largest city. One need hardly add that there are also a number of public courses dotted around the outskirts of Birmingham.

Despite its relative youth, The Belfry (featured ahead) has become the area's best known golfing attraction thanks largely to the thrilling Ryder Cup encounters staged there. However, Little Aston has long been regarded as one of Britain's finest inland courses and has hosted numerous major events—both amateur and professional.

Looking in and around Birmingham for places to stay a few obvious thoughts emerge. The Belfry Hotel (01675) 470301 is most luxurious and ideal for its own two courses (as well as the plethora of golf courses in the Sutton Coldfield area). It offers practically every activity under the sun. As an alternative, and very close to The Belfry is the elegant Moxhull Hall (0121) 329 2056 which provides a more intimate atmosphere. Moor Hall (0121) 3083751 also provides a most comfortable and convenient 19th hole—an attractive mansion this. Still in Sutton Coldfield, Penns Hall (0121) 351 3111 enjoys a peaceful lakeside setting, while a short distance away in Aldridge is another alternative, the Fairlawns Hotel (01922) 55122. A 9 hole par 3 course will add further to the attractions of a stay at the delightful **New Hall** (0121) 378 2442—one of the country's finest hotels—not the cheapest but thoroughly recommended. For an inexpensive hotel in the Sutton Coldfield area, we recommend the Standbridge Hotel (0121) 354 3007.

Solihull to the south of Birmingham is also surrounded by good golf. The Jarvis International (0121) 7112121 is a modernised coaching inn and a very comfortable place to stay. Another suburb, Edgbaston, provides the restaurant Sloans (0121) 4556697. Two popular pubs to visit are the Bear at Berkswell and the White Lion in Hampton-in-Arden.

More centrally in Birmingham, the Hyatt Regency (0121) 6431234 is a first rate hotel

Coventry

Like Birmingham, the city of Coventry has now been relieved of its West Midlands label and warrants its own mention. **Coventry** Golf Club enjoys a peaceful setting at Finham Park, two miles south of the city on the A444. The course is good enough to have staged the British Seniors Championship. To the north west of Coventry at Meriden, the **Forest of Arden** Golf and Country Club (featured on a later page) offers a marvellous day's golf—36 holes to savour with outstanding leisure facilities at the Country Club Hotel (01676) 522335.

The major tourist attraction in Coventry is undoubtedly the spectacular cathedral. A fine piece of modern architecture sadly not reflected in the city's hotels—but then Coventry is no different from most. De Vere Hotel (01203) 633733 near the cathedral is perhaps the best in the city. The Hearsall Lodge Hotel (01203) 674543 offers more modest accommodation but is perfectly comfortable and very convenient for **Coventry Hearsall** Golf Club, just south of the city off the A46. Another recommendation is **Nailcote Hall** (01203) 466174, west of Coventry in Berkswell, offering a 9 hole golf course, good leisure facilities and a pleasant atmosphere.

Warwickshire

Birmingham and Coventry removed, Warwickshire has been left with only a handful of courses. The county's two most popular towns are unquestionably Stratford and Warwick. Until recently Warwick had only a 9 hole course located inside its racetrack, but now, not far away from Warwick at Leek Wooton (close to junction 15 of the M40) is **The Warwickshire** where 36 holes of championship golf await (see ahead). Shakespeare-spotters who've sneaked the clubs into the boot will also be well rewarded. There are two fine 18 hole courses in Stratford, **Stratford** Golf Club and the **Welcombe Hotel** Golf Course.

The Welcombe Hotel (01789) 295252 is a beautiful mansion with comfortable rooms and a good restaurant, definitely one for lovers of good golf and fine hotels. But there are many outstanding alternatives for those spending a night or two in the Stratford area. Pride of place must go to Billesley Manor (01789) 279955 to the west of the town.

Of the countless guest houses and B&Bs in the vicinity, two that are frequently acclaimed are Moonraker House (01789) 299346 and Oxtalls Farmhouse (01789) 205277. For pubs, a short drive towards Oxhill is recommended where the Peacock and the Royal Oak (in Whatcote village) will provide excellent sustenance. Those of you choosing to play the excellent fairways of The Warwickshire and who enjoy a first class hotel, should note the elegant Ettington Park (01789) 450123—first class.

Warwick has a famous castle, and a good restaurant to note nearby is Randolphs. **Kenilworth** also has a castle (and a pretty reasonable golf course too). Here the Clarendon House (01926) 57668 is a good place to stay and a restaurant to savour is the Restaurant Bosquet (01926) 52463.

Lastly we visit Leamington Spa. It may not have the attractions of a Stratford or a Warwick but it does have a very fine golf course. **Leamington and County** is a hilly parkland course to the south of Leamington.

After an enjoyable round at Leamington, the Lansdowne (01926) 450505 is a smallish well priced hotel in town. Crandon House a comfortable farmhouse in the vicinity, but if one is looking to spoil oneself then we recommend a trip to Bishops Tachbrook and Mallory Court (01926) 330214, where superb rooms and a terrific restaurant await.

Leicestershire

The best course in Leicestershire, **Luffenham Heath,** lies over to the far east of the county, very close to the border with Lincolnshire. It is without question one of the most attractive heathland courses in England and, being in a conservation area, a haven for numerous species of wildlife. It isn't the longest of courses but then, thankfully, golf isn't always a question of how far you can belt the ball! A visit here is strongly recommended and there is no shortage of 19th holes nearby.

The splendid Rutland countryside reveals many outstanding establishments. Hambleton Hall (01572) 756991 overlooks Rutland Water and is quite tremendous and very convenient for the new course at Greetham, **Greetham Valley**. If you cannot spend the night here the restaurant is equally superb. The Whipper Inn Hotel (01572) 756971 in Oakham's market square is also most enjoyable—a fine inn with good beers, snacks and some comfortable accommodation too.

Note that this is Ruddles country and some excellent country pubs lie in wait. The King's Arms in Wing is a good example and there's a nearby maze in which to lose the children before a round of golf or a pint of County. Barnsdale Lodge (01572) 724678 is also well worth considering.

Rothley Park Golf Club, adjacent to the 13th century Rothley Court (0116) 2374141, a hotel of merit, is one of Leicestershire's most picturesque parkland courses and is within easy access of Leicester, lying some seven miles to the north west of the city, off the A6. Leicester is well served by golf courses and there are no fewer than three 18 hole municipal courses within four miles of the centre of Leicester, **Western Park** perhaps being the best of these. **Leicestershire** Golf Club, just two miles from the city centre along the A6 is one of the top courses in the county—try to avoid the ubiquitous stream that runs through it.

Leicester may not be the country's most attractive city but it does have its good points. The Haymarket theatre offers a variety of productions while the art gallery includes works by English sporting artists and, if you have business in town, the Jarvis Grand Hotel (0116)

2555599 may prove the best selection.

Looking further afield, in the north of the county the ancient town of Melton Mowbray has a fine 18 hole course sited on high ground to the north east of the town and Loughborough possesses a heathland type course, **Longcliffe**, which is heavily wooded with a wealth of bluebells, not to mention a particularly testing front nine. A game here is always a challenge.

In the south of the county, **Market Harborough's** course offers extensive views across the surrounding countryside. North west of Leicester, Charnwood Forest is one of the Midlands' most pleasant retreats, an area where heath and woodland confront rocky crags and granite outcrops.

The village of Woodhouse Eaves lies on the eastern edge of the Forest with two extremely pleasant courses at hand, **Lingdale** and **Charnwood Forest**. Though less than two miles apart they offer quite different challenges. Lingdale has a parkland setting with a trout stream flowing through it, while **Charnwood Forest** is a heathland type course—9 holes, no bunkers but several outcrops of granite around which one must navigate. The commendable Quorn Country Hotel (01509) 415050 is the 19th to shortlist.

Hinckley is linked to the centre of Leicester by the A47. Hinckley's golf course is fairly new, built over the original 9 hole Burbage Common layout. Several lakes and much gorse have to be confronted making this potentially the toughest in the county. The final mention for a round in Leicestershire goes to **Willesley Park** at Ashby-de-la-Zouch—a parkland-heathland mix with good greens and well worth a visit.

Some ideas for life beyond the 18th fairway. If a pork pie and a piece of Stilton is what you're after then

Artist: **Graeme W Baxter** **THE BELFRY** *Courtesy of:* **Baxter Prints**

Melton Mowbray is an answer to your prayers—try the George (01664) 62112—a charming inn with comfortable rooms.

In the Loughborough area the Kings Head (01509) 233222 is popular. Lovers of true style and comfort and no little love of leisure pursuits should shortlist Stapleford Park (01572) 787522—one of the best. Finally, the Crown in Old Dalby is another good pub—ideal for sampling the various local specialities.

Northamptonshire

The much admired **Northamptonshire County** course is situated five miles north of Northampton at Church Brampton, and is often referred to locally as Church Brampton. Famed for its many testing par fours, it is a splendid heather and gorse type with a fair few undulations in its 6500 yards. Rather like Liphook in Hampshire a railway line bisects the course. In the past it has staged the British Youths' Championship.

Though not as good as Church Brampton, **Northampton** Golf Club can also be recommended, as most certainly can **Collingtree Park**, Johnny Miller's spectacularly designed course (see feature page). One final mention for visitors to the county town is the **Delapre** Golf Complex where a game should be easily arranged.

For a night in Northampton, the Moat House Hotel (01604) 739988 is very modern but comfortable and handy for the town centre, while the Westone Hotel (01604) 739955 is a mansion with modern additions. For value and friendly service, Garenden Park Hotel (01509) 236557 should not disappoint.

Elsewhere in the county, there is a reasonable course at **Kettering** and not far away there is a better course at **Wellingborough**, two miles east of the town. Quite hilly and set around the former Horrowden Hall, it has several lakes and a mass of mature trees. and is certainly one of the best courses in the county.

The **Hellidon Lakes** Hotel and Country Club (01327) 262550 offers some fine golf, while good leisure facilities and accommodation make this doubly worthy of attention. Other courses to note include **Staverton Park** at Daventry, **Cold Ashby** (near the site of the famous Battle of Naseby of 1645) with its superb views across the Northamptonshire uplands and the popular **Farthingstone Hotel** Golf and Leisure Centre near Towcester.

Pleasant countryside surrounds the towns of Wellingborough and Kettering. Perhaps the best bet for accommodation near the former is the Hind (01933) 222827. In the south of the county, the Crossroads (01327) 340354 at Weedon and the Saracens Head (01327) 350414 at Towcester are both welcoming, although Farthingstone Hotel (01327) 36291 must be a good bet here.

_____ *The Warwickshire* _____

Being something of a racing man "I've gotta horse", are words that almost always fill my heart with gloom. You're trapped you see. . . . if you don't have a bet you feel dramatically foolish if the nag in question wins but more often than not the wretched beast will not deliver the goods. In golf however, my experiences are altogether different. Perched in sunny Menorca, of all places, after a decent 18 holes (lovely island, limited golf) I struck up some conversation as one does and we discussed the merits of various golf courses. "What's good and new?" I enquired of my newly found friend, who seemed to know his stuff. "The Warwickshire" he proclaimed - "It's stunning".

This little natter took place several years ago and since then the Warwickshire has been praised by many more and it is a worthy newcomer to our list of championship golf courses. Today the course is the UK flagship of the expanding Clubhaus Group and it offers golfers 36 exciting holes on four separate loops, respectively titled the **North**, **South**, **East** and **West** courses.

The courses are situated amidst 465 acres of rolling mature parkland. Avenues of trees and various water hazards provide daunting obstacles but delightful scenery. The two championship courses were designed by Karl Litten (of The Emirates course, Dubai fame), and it is fair to say that golfers of all standards will be put to the test. Despite the relative youth of these courses (The Warwickshire opened in the summer of 1993), this is definitely the type of venue that people will delight in playing. The acreage and the setting allows length and variety on all four loops. The toughest combination is the West/North—you'll certainly need a beverage or two in the excellent 19th after your round. The 7th on the North is particularly memorable. On the East the 3rd is wonderful and those who enjoy water hazards will find the West particularly appealing. The par five 7th on the South course also offers H₂O to savour.

Those who are seeking a somewhat less daunting challenge will enjoy the nine hole par three course and driving range. We mentioned the 19th previously and it is well worth mentioning again for several reasons. Firstly it is one of the best in the country, secondly you'll find good service and fare but most importantly you'll find a welcome and a half. So many golf clubhouses are so unwelcoming—for no good reason, here the opposite is the case—my friend in Menorca said so . . . But many, many more feel the same. If you're looking for a challenging round or two as well as a reason to be cheerful you should head for the middle of England and here you will find the answer to your dreams. The Warwickshire might not be winning any races but it's a real favourite in any company.

The Warwickshire, Leek Wootton, Warwick Warwickshire CV35 7QT	
Gen Manager	Martin Watson (01926) 409409
Professional	John Cook
Green Fees	WD £35 per round
	WE £45 per round
Restrictions	Handicap certificate required

Directions
Two miles off junction 15 on the M40, just off the A46 to Coventry near Kenilworth

The Belfry

To adopt lawyers' jargon, it is 'beyond any reasonable doubt' that the game of golf was invented in Scotland. A handful of golfing pioneers brought the game south and today, with the exception of a few notable areas in the north, where to live is to play golf, the sport is almost as popular south of the border.

One cannot help wondering quite what those early pioneers would have made of The Belfry project... 'American-style target gowff?...and what d'ya mean artificial burns with manmade mounds and lakes!'...'More than 7000 yards did ya say?'...'Too many whiskies m'friend, you must be oot o'your wee mind!'

The 'Belfry project' involved not only a plan to build a championship course on American lines where in due course the Ryder Cup could be staged, but also the siting of a new headquarters for the PGA. Peter Alliss and Dave Thomas were given the task of creating the showpiece, and a very great task it was, for the land they were given was flat, uninteresting and comprised one small lake, a stream and numerous acres of potato fields.

Well, the boys didn't hang about. Earth mountains were moved, the potatoes disappeared and hundreds of trees were planted. The end result in fact produced two 18 hole courses, opened in June 1977. The feature course was named the **Brabazon,** after Lord Brabazon, a former President of the PGA, and the shorter, easier course, the **Derby.**

June 1977—the month when Hubert Green survived a death threat to win the US Open and a month before Nicklaus and Watson fought out the 'Duel in the Sun' at Turnberry. So much has happened since then and to cite the history of The Belfry since its creation is almost to chart the rise of European golf—they are of course indelibly linked.

Of all Europe's successes around the world the 1985 Ryder Cup triumph at The Belfry will perhaps be remembered best of all. It was, after all, the first time the Americans had been defeated in nearly 30 years, and no other single event has been more responsible for generating the golf boom that has swept right across the continent. So successfully staged were the matches in 1989 (a tie) and 1993 (a US victory) that The Belfry has been awarded the match for a fourth time in 2001.

To prepare for the Ryder Cup, the Brabazon course is currently in the process of extensive remodelling at a cost of some £2.4 million and will not re-open for play until September 1998. However, this allows the new **PGA National** course, opened in June 1997, time to come into its own. Also designed by Dave Thomas, this is the first PGA National standard course in Europe, and at upwards of 7000 yards promises to stretch most golfers.

A key feature of The Belfry is that it is not a club—all three courses open their doors to the general public at all times, all the year round. However, golfers should note that a handicap of 24 or better (32 for ladies) is required to play the Brabazon and PGA National courses. The green fees in 1998 are £75 per round on the Brabazon, £60 per round on the PGA National and £35 per round on the Derby.

The **Golf Manager, Robert Maxfield** and his staff can be contacted on **(01675) 470301.** Special residential packages are often available and persons wishing to make reservations should contact the Sales Office on **(01675) 470033,** fax: (01675) 470256, or write to: **The Belfry, Wishaw, N Warks B76 9PR.**

In addition to being a four star hotel with a full complement of facilities, The Belfry has twenty one meeting and conference rooms, eight public bars and five restaurants open to the general public, as well as a fully equipped leisure centre and a nightclub in the hotel grounds. If after a meal and a few drinks you're still not satisfied with your golf there's a final opportunity to put things right on the impressive floodlit covered driving range.

Situated close to the country's industrial heart, there is surely no golfing complex in Britain better served by communication networks. The Belfry is one mile from the M42 (junction 9), five miles from the M6 (junction 4), nine miles from Birmingham city centre and less than ten minutes from Birmingham International Airport and the NEC railway station. The exact position of the golf club is at the apex of the A446 and A4091.

PGA National Course

Hole	Yards	Par	Hole	Yards	Par
1	353	4	10	502	4
2	538	5	11	209	3
3	196	3	12	562	5
4	405	4	13	419	4
5	448	4	14	439	4
6	541	5	15	195	3
7	464	4	16	350	4
8	224	3	17	384	4
9	443	4	18	400	4
Out	**3,612**	**36**	**In**	**3,460**	**36**
			Out	**3,612**	**36**
			Totals	**7,072**	**72**

The Belfry®

The Belfry, set in 500 acres of Warwickshire countryside, is considered to be the best located business, golf and leisure resort in the UK and a great destination for a well-earned break. The location of The Belfry is an advantage for most people. It is in the centre of the country and only ten minutes drive from Birmingham International Airport and the NEC, as well as being close to the M42.

However, it is The Belfry's famous fairways and greens that have won the hearts of people throughout the world, even if they have only seen The Brabazon on television. The Belfry is unique as the only venue to have staged the biggest golf event in the world—The Ryder Cup Matches—an unprecedented 3 times with a 4th returning in 2001. The Brabazon is regarded throughout the world as a great championship course with some of the most demanding holes in golf, but it will soon be even tougher. It is currently closed until September 1998 for a £2.4 million redevelopment which will make it even more testing; new holes are being created, streams and the lakes are being reshaped and brought more into play. But the world famous holes like the 10th (Ballesteros's hole), and the 18th, with its dangerous lakes and amphitheatre around the final green, will of course remain as they were, breathtaking and unforgettable.

In the meantime you can pit your wits against a new legend in the making, the recently opened PGA National Course, which has won the plaudits from near and far. The Dave Thomas-designed course has been used for professional competition and is already establishing itself as one of Britain's leading courses. For those who like their golf a little easier or like to get back into the swing gently, the Derby course is ideal and can be played by golfers of any standard.

The Brabazon, PGA National and Derby are open to the public. There is no membership, which means it is possible to get a taste of Ryder Cup action. There is also a putting green, plus a floodlit driving range.

The Belfry caters for golfers of every standard by running courses for beginners and residential golf schools. It is a popular venue for society golf and corporate golf continues to grow.

However, The Belfry is not just a venue for golfers, it is a Business, Golf and Leisure Resort made up of a 324 bedroom 4-star hotel, 21 conference and meeting rooms, 5 restaurants and 8 bars. The restaurants cater for every taste ranging from simple snacks to the best cuisine, which can be found in the award-winning French restaurant. There is a well-equipped Leisure Club and also the Bel Air Nightclub in the hotel grounds.

Also on site is the largest on-course golf, leisure and lifestyle shop in Europe with a wide choice of golfing and non-golfing items, such as crystal trophies and glasses, costume jewellery and corporate prizes. A mail order service is also available.

As well as The Belfry being able to cater for a wide variety of leisure interests, the surrounding area has many attractions. Cadbury World and the acclaimed Symphony Hall in Birmingham as well as the city's exciting shopping are within easy reach. However, for that little bit of extra excitement, residents receive complimentary entry to one of Britain's most popular amusement parks, Drayton Manor Family Theme Park (excluding Bank Holiday Mondays). There are plenty of other local attractions and tickets for many local places of interest can be purchased from reception.

The Belfry has a unique warm and welcoming atmosphere that will soon make you feel at home. There is so much to do and so many ways to enjoy your stay that you'll be spoilt for choice.

The Belfry
Wishaw
North Warwickshire B76 9PR
Tel: (01675) 470301
Fax: (01675) 470178

Reputedly the oldest moated manor house in England, New Hall is now a country house hotel of unrivalled style and presence. Personally run by Ian and Caroline Parkes it has been awarded 4 Red Stars by the AA, 3 AA Rosettes for food and was the AA Inspectors' Hotel of the Year for England in 1993/94. Among other accolades it also holds the highest RAC award, the Blue Ribbon for seven years.

Guests dine in the 16th century oak-panelled restaurant, where the award-winning chef creates superb cuisine which is unmistakeably English but exhibits flair and imagination. The comprehensive wine list, selected personally by Ian Parkes, contains the best of the old world but also features some superb newcomers.

Part of the restaurant lends itself to semi-private dining, while the Oak Room provides private dining for up to eight people. Boardroom facilities are also available in the Garden Room, the Sir Alfred Owen Room and the Chadwick Room, while the Great Chamber provides an inspiring setting for meetings of up to 40 people.

Set in twenty six acres of private garden and surrounded by a lily-filled moat, the hotel provides extensive leisure facilities—a croquet lawn, archery, putting, an all-weather tennis court and its own 9 hole par 3 golf course. Keen golfers will be delighted by New Hall's close proximity to The Belfry's championship course. The hotel can arrange golf here for its guests as well as at Moor Hall and Little Aston. Other championship courses in the immediate vicinity include Forest of Arden, Copt Heath and Fulford Heath. Truly a golfer's paradise.

New Hall is seven miles from the centre of Birmingham. Warwick, Coventry, Lichfield and Stratford upon Avon are all within easy reach. A veritable haven for the golfer and non-golfer alike.

New Hall
Walmley Road
Royal Sutton Coldfield
B76 1QX
Tel: 0121 378 2442
Fax: 0121 378 4637

Collingtree Park

In recent years we have grown accustomed to watching Australian Greg Norman tear golf courses apart: 62s at Doral and Glen Abbey; 63s at St Andrews, Augusta and Turnberry and 64s at Troon and St George's. A tournament isn't over, they say, whilst Greg Norman is within seven shots of the leader. In the 1970s the man with a similar reputation for shooting extraordinary, par shattering rounds was American Johnny Miller. Twice in as many weeks in 1975 he returned a score of 61. That year he won the first three tournaments he entered in America, all by very large margins and he finished one shot away from catching Jack Nicklaus in the Masters after closing rounds of 65 and 66. In 1973, he stormed through the field with a final round of 63 to win the US Open; the score still stands as the lowest ever to win a major. In 1974 he won eight tournaments on the US Tour and in 1976 charged around a dry and dusty Royal Birkdale in a course record equalling 66 on the final day of the Open to win by six strokes. He was a dashing champion whose hobby (like Norman's) was driving superfast cars. Johnny Miller is also the man who designed Collingtree Park.

Opened in May 1990, it is Miller's first course in Europe. Without question, he has produced a dramatic golf course which, in time, may be considered one of the finest of its type in England. It is certainly one of the most challenging with 11 acres of lakes to be negotiated and more than 72,000 imported trees and shrubs in a layout that can be stretched to close on 7000 yards.

Collingtree Park is much more than an exciting new golf course. In addition to Miller's creation, there is a golf academy which includes three full length practice holes, a 16 bay floodlit driving range and an indoor video teaching room and computerised custom fitting centre. All golf enquiries should be made to the **Head Professional, Geoff Pook** and his staff who may be contacted on **(01604) 700000** or by fax on **(01604) 702600** The address for written correspondence is **Collingtree Park Golf Course, Windingbrook Lane, Northampton NN4 0XN.**

For individual visitors and groups of fewer than twelve players bookings can be made up to one week in advance. Handicaps are required and green fees for 1998 are set at £20 per round during the week and £25 at the weekend. Details of corporate day packages and tuition courses can be obtained by telephoning the above number.

Travelling to Collingtree Park should be fairly straightforward. Very centrally located in the heart of England, it is just on the outskirts of Northampton, one of Britain's fastest growing towns and very close to the M1. Junction 15 is the exit to use, immediately picking up the A508 road to Northampton. This road should be followed for about half a mile and Collingtree Park's entrance is the second turning on the left. The golf course is sixty-five miles from London, thirty-five miles from Birmingham and about twenty miles from Milton Keynes.

When Johnny Miller first viewed the site in 1986 it is doubtful that he could have thought it the most natural setting for a golf course he had ever seen. Part meadowland, part wasteland, it required a massive amount of work. With the support of Jack Nicklaus' technical services team it certainly received it. Work commenced in 1987 with the movement of over 350,000 cubic metres of earth. A positive drainage system with sixteen miles of underground piping was installed and then the course was landscaped. Work still continues and minor alterations have recently been made on the 1st, 5th, 11th, 12th and 15th holes.

'I designed the course along American lines, but not without respect for the English countryside. I wanted Collingtree to combine the best of both English and American course ideas' said Miller. At 6777 yards from the medal tees and 5146 yards from the ladies' tees it is a formidable challenge. There isn't a bad hole at Collingtree Park but on the front nine the par three 5th across the edge of a lake and the 9th—one of those par fives that can be reached with two good shots but where disaster awaits the failed attempt—are especially memorable and on the much more difficult back nine there is the spectacular finishing hole, perhaps the most dramatic in Great Britain. The 18th measures 602 yards from the back tees and the third shot (you won't be going for this one in two) must be played to an island green—Florida comes to Northamptonshire! It is Miller's masterstroke and you can guarantee that almost all conversation at the 19th hole will centre around 'how did you fare at the last?' And I dare say there will be one or two tall stories.

Hole	Yards	Par	Hole	Yards	Par
1	348	4	10	350	4
2	386	4	11	387	4
3	474	4	12	192	3
4	531	5	13	423	4
5	179	3	14	543	5
6	367	4	15	170	3
7	388	4	16	422	4
8	166	3	17	401	4
9	498	5	18	602	5
Out	**3,337**	**36**	**In**	**3,440**	**36**
			Out	**3,337**	**36**
			Totals	**6,777**	**72**

Forest of Arden

If Forest of Arden has always had something of an enchanting ring to it, it is only over relatively recent times that the images conjured up would have a golfing theme. The resort, which has now firmly established itself as one of the UK's premier business, leisure and golfing destinations, has somehow managed to retain something of the countrified, unspoiled atmosphere sadly lacking from many of the modern all-purpose resorts. In actual fact, it is difficult to think of many inland venues with such a happy combination of new and old, where modern course design blends quite so harmoniously with ancient oak trees and grazing deer.

If the above sounds a little too much like the marketing blurb so favoured in glossy hotel brochures, then rest assured that this is one much-hyped golfing destination where reality will invariably meet expectation. Forget for a moment the conference delegates, aqua-aerobics or any other of Forest of Arden's manifold delights. If your poison is exhilarating golf on a course coaxed out of a classic English landscape, then look no further than the Arden course, host to the 1998 One-2-One British Masters. To the probable chagrin of its nevertheless fortunate members, Forest of Arden welcomes all authentic golfers, with starting times bookable through the **Golf Shop (01676) 526113**. Individual and group lessons can be booked through **Kim Thomas** and his team of professionals on **0958 632170**. The full address is **c/o David MacLaren, Director of Golf, Marriott Forest of Arden Hotel and Country Club, Maxstoke Lane, Meriden, Warwickshire, CV7 7HR**.

Guests are advised to contact the hotel regarding prices and any seasonal offers, although green fees for visitors are expected to be in the region of £50 during 1998. A range of residential packages are also available, with golf included on the **Arden** course and its less celebrated sister the **Aylesford**.

To find Forest of Arden, take junction 6 from the M42 and follow the A45 towards Coventry. After about a mile, turn left into Shepherds Lane by the Little Chef restaurant. You will find the hotel some one and a half miles on the left. Birmingham International Airport is only four miles away, with the world renowned National Exhibition Centre even closer.

Although it is the back nine on the Arden which is likely to have you reaching into the golf bag for camera and additional balls, the front nine does not fail to provide a stern and scenic challenge. A relatively benign opening quickly gives way to a succession of testing holes, with tortuous short holes interspersed with par fives which could leave even Tiger Woods struggling for breath. It is, however, at the 8th and 9th holes that the course really starts to bare its teeth. Both rely on water to define their challenge, with shot selection at the 8th meaning the difference between a birdie opportunity and a watery grave. The 9th is one of the favourite holes of no less celebrated a judge than Colin Montgomerie, who ranks the second shot, usually hit with a long iron at best, as one of the toughest anywhere.

The back nine derives much of its character from the ancient oaks and massive expanses of bracken which make even the most miserable scores a more bearable experience. It is, however, the herds of roaming deer that will provide perhaps the most vivid memories and the hotel's management is to be commended on its live-and-let-live approach to the estate's varied wildlife. Holes that particularly stand out from the generally scenic ambience include the 12th, 17th and 18th. The first two are both par fives, with yet more water all too ready to turn a birdie into bogey. The final hole on the Arden course also requires an airborne approach but at over two hundred yards, golfers are likely to be more confident of the culinary delights that lie beyond the green. Like its sister resort at St Pierre which also closes with a gigantic par three, the 18th is in many ways a fitting climax to a course that merits the tag of championship.

Although considerably less spectacular than the Arden, the shorter Aylesford course will nevertheless provide good golfing in a pleasant environment. If, however, your supply of golf balls has been extinguished by the Arden's water and wildlife hazards, fear not, for the resort offers a wealth of alternative attractions. With 215 bedrooms, a fully equipped leisure club, two restaurants, the celebrated Packington trout lakes and even a teaching academy for learning golf, the resort makes a great venue for golfing widows or widowers.

Hole	Yards	Par	Hole	Yards	Par
1	345	4	10	434	4
2	361	4	11	421	4
3	560	5	12	543	5
4	389	4	13	474	4
5	196	3	14	446	4
6	463	4	15	187	3
7	526	5	16	422	4
8	177	3	17	511	5
9	470	4	18	209	3
Out	**3487**	**36**	**In**	**3647**	**36**
			Out	**3487**	**36**
			Totals	**7134**	**72**

Even the name has a magical ring to it. In a classic English setting of massive oak trees and lakes teeming with trout, Marriott Forest of Arden is a world-renowned golf, leisure and conference resort.

Venue to a host of international tournaments, including the 1998 One-2-One British Masters, the centrepiece of Forest of Arden's golfing wonderland is the Arden course, one of the UK's finest inland challenges. The Arden meanders its way through ancient oak trees, crystal blue lakes and an astonishing variety of wildlife that includes a herd of roaming deer. Stretching to a formidable 7000 yards from the championship tees, the Arden provides an exhilarating challenge for golfers of all persuasions, with its 'signature hole' undoubtedly the 18th, a par three which demands a stomach-churning drive over water to a green some two hundred yards distant.

If golf is not yet your game, the less hazardous Aylesford Course and a professionally staffed Teaching Academy will provide a gentle and enjoyable introduction. For the equally energetic, the hotel also offers the very best in leisure facilities, including three state-of-the-art gymnasiums which encompass cardio vascular, resistance and free weights equipment.

After a day of arduous exercise, there are two outstanding choices for dinner. The award-winning Broadwater restaurant offers classic English and French cuisine, whilst the ever popular Long Weekend Cafe Bar, adorned with an evocative array of sporting memorabilia, serves a wide range of meals and snacks. With friendly, attentive staff, exceptional service is guaranteed in a warm, relaxed environment.

In the unlikely event that you tire of Forest of Arden's manifold charms, Warwick Castle, Kenilworth Castle and Stratford-upon-Avon provide nearby places of historic and scenic interest.

Whether for a golf break, company golf day, leisure break, wedding or conference, Marriott Forest of Arden is renowned everywhere as a truly outstanding international resort.

Marriott Forest of Arden Hotel & Country Club
Maxstoke Lane
Meriden
Warwickshire CV7 7HR
Tel: (01676) 522335
Fax: (01676) 523711

Key

To avoid disappointment
it is advisable to telephone
in advance

***Visitors welcome at most times
**Visitors usually allowed on
weekdays only
*Visitors not normally permitted
(Mon, Wed) No visitors
on specified days

Approximate Green Fees
A   £40 plus
B   £25 to £40
C   £20 to £30
D   £15 to £25
E   under £15
F   Green fees on application

Restrictions
G   Guests only
H—Handicap certificate required
H—(24) Handicap of 24 or less
L —Letter of introduction required
M—Visitor must be a member of
another recognised club

NORTHAMPTONSHIRE

Brampton Heath G.C.
(01604) 843939
Sandy Lane, Church Brampton
(18) 6054 yards/***/D

Cherwell Edge G.C.
(01295) 711591
Chacombe, Banbury
(18) 5925 yards/***/E

Cold Ashby G.C.
(01604) 740548
Stanford Road, Cold Ashby
(27) 6308 yards/**/D

Collingtree Park G.C.
(01604) 700000
Windingbrook Lane, Northampton
(18) 6821 yards/***/B/H

Corby G.C.
(01526) 260756
Stamford Road, Weldon
(18) 6677 yards/***/F

Daventry and District G.C.
(01327) 702829
Norton Road, Daventry
(9) 5812 yards/**/E

Delapre G.C.
(01604) 764036
Eagle Drive, Northampton
(18) 6356 yards/***/D
(9) 2146 yards/***/E

Elton Furze G.C.
(01832) 280189
Haden, Peterborough
(18) 6291/*/B

Embankment G.C.
(01933) 228465
The Embankment, Wellingborough
(9) 3374 yards/***/E

Farthingstone Hotel G.C.
(01327) 361291
Farthingstone, Towcester
(18) 6248 yards/***/C-B

Hellidon Lakes Hotel & C.C.
(01327) 262550
Hellidon, Daventry
(18) 6691 yards/***/C/H

Kettering G.C.
(01536) 511104
Headlands, Kettering
(18) 6036 yards/**/C/H

Kingsthorpe G.C.
(01604) 710610
Kingsley Road, Northampton
(18) 6006 yards/**/B/H

Northampton G.C.
(01604) 845102
Kettering Road, Northampton
(18) 6534 yards/**/C/H

Northamptonshire County G.C.
(01604) 843025
Sandy Lane, Church Brampton
(18) 6503 yards/***/A/H

Oundle G.C.
(01832) 273267
Benefield Road, Oundle
(18) 5900 yards/**/F

Overstone Park G.C.
(01604) 674666
Willow Lane, Little Billing
(18) 6260 yards/***/D

Priors Hall G.C.
(01536) 260756
Stamford Road, Weldon
(18) 6677 yards/***/E

Rushden G.C.
(01933) 418511
Kimbolton Road, Chelveston
(10) 6335 yards/**/C

Staverton Park G.C.
(01327) 302000
Staverton, Daventry
(18) 6634 yards/**/C/H

Wellingborough G.C.
(01933) 677234
Horrowden Hall, Great Horrowden
(18) 6620 yards/**/B/H

West Park G.& C.C.
(01327) 858092
Whittlebury, Towcester
(36) 4 x 9 7000 yards/***/B/H

LEICESTERSHIRE

Beedles Lake G.C.
(0116) 260 6759
Broome Lane, East Goscote
(18) 6412 yards/***/E

Birstall G.C.
(0116) 267 4450
Station Road, Birstall
(18) 6222 yards/***/B/H/G/L

Blaby G.C.
(0116) 278 4804
Lutterworth Road, Blaby
(9) 2600 yards/***/E

Breedon Priory G.C.
(01332) 863081
Wilson, Derby
(18) 5700 yards/**/D

Charnwood Forest G.C.
(01509) 890259
Breakback Lane, Woodhouse Eaves
(9) 5960 yards/**/C/H

Cosby G.C.
(0116) 286 4759
Chapel Lane, Cosby
(18) 6418 yards/**/B/H

Enderby G.C.
(0116) 284 9388
Mill Lane, Enderby
(9) 4356 yards/***/E

Glen Gorse G.C.
(0116) 271 4159
Glen Road, Oadby
(18) 6603 yards/**/B/H

Greetham Valley G.C.
(01780) 460444
Greetham, Oakham
(18) 6656 yards/***/C

Hinckley G.C.
(01455) 615124
Leicester Road, Hinckley
(18) 6517 yards/**(Tue)/B/H

Humberstone Heights G.C.
(0116) 276 4674
Gipsy Lane, Leicester
(18) 6444 yards/***/E

Kibworth G.C.
(0116) 279 2301
Weir Road, Kibworth Beauchamp
(18) 6282 yards/**/C

Kilworth Springs G.C.
(01858) 575974
South Kilworth Road, Lutterworth
(18) 6718 yards/***/C

Kirby Muxloe G.C.
(0116) 239 3457
Station Road, Kirby Muxloe
(18) 6303 yards/**/B/H

Langton Park G. & C.C.
(01858) 545374
Langton Hall, Leicester
(18) 6965 yards/**/B-A/H/L
(9) 3362 yards/***/D

Leicestershire G.C.
(0116) 273 6035
Evington Lane, Leicester
(18) 6330 yards/***/B/H

Leicestershire Forest G.C
(01455) 824800
Markfield Lane, Botcheston
(18) 6111 yards/***/D

Lingdale G.C.
(01509) 890703
Joe Moores Lane, Woodhouse Eaves
(18) 6545 yards/***/C

Longcliffe G.C.
(01509) 216321
Snell's Nook Lane, Nanpantan
(18) 6551 yards/**/B/H

Luffenham Heath G.C.
(01780) 720205
Ketton, Stamford
(18) 6254 yards/***/A/H

Lutterworth G.C.
(01455) 552532
Rugby Road, Lutterworth
(18) 5570 yards/**/C/H

Market Harborough G.C.
(01858) 463684
Oxendon Road, Market
Harborough
(18) 6027 yards/**/C/H

Melton Mowbray G.C.
(01664) 62118
Waltham Road, Thorpe Arnold
(18) 6222 yards/**/C/H

Oadby G.C.
(0116) 270 9052
Leicester Road, Oadby
(18) 6228 yards/***/D

Park Hill G.C.
(01509) 815454
Park Hill, Seagrave
(9) 6800 yards/***/C/H

RAF Cottesmore G.C.
(01572) 812241
Oakham, Leicester
(9) 5622 yards/*/E/G

RAF North Luffenham G.C.
(01780) 720041
North Luffenham, Oakham
(9) 6006 yards/***/F

Rothley Park G.C.
(0116) 230 2809
Westfield Lane, Rothley
(18) 6487 yards/**(Tues)/B/H/M

Rutland County G.C.
(01780) 460239
Great Casterton, Stamford
(18) 6189 yards/***/C/H

Scraptoft G.C.
(0116) 241 9138
Beeby Road, Scraptoft
(18) 6166 yards/**/B/H

Ullesthorpe Court Hotel
(01455) 209023
Frolesworth Road, Ullesthorpe
(18) 6650 yards/**/D

Western Park G.C.
(0116) 287 2339
Scudamore Road, Braunstone Frith
(18) 6532 yards/***/E

Whetstone G.C.
(0116) 286 1424
Cambridge Road, Cosby
(18) 5795 yards/**/D/H

Willesley Park G.C.
(01530) 414596
Tamworth Road, Ashby-de-la-Zouch
(18) 6304 yards/***/B/H/M

BIRMINGHAM & COVENTRY

Aston Wood G.C.
(0121) 353 0363
Blake Street, Sutton Coldfield
(18) 6480 yards/**/B/H

Blackwell G.C.
(0121) 445 1994
Blackwell, nr Bromsgrove
(18) 6202 yards/**/B/H

Bloxwich G.C.
(01922) 476593
Stafford Road, Bloxwich
(18) 6286 yards/**/F/H

Boldmere G.C.
(0121) 354 3379
Monmouth Drive, Sutton Coldfield
(18) 4463 yards/***/E

Brandhall G.C.
(0121) 552 2195
Heron Road, Oldbury, Warley
(18) 5813 yards/***/D

Bromsgrove Golf Centre
(01527) 575886
Stratford Road, Bromsgrove
(9) 3159 yards/**/E

Calderfields G.C.
(01922) 640540
Aldridge Road, Walsall
(18) 6636 yards/***/D

City of Coventry G.C.
(Brandon Wood)
(01203) 543141
Brandon Lane, Brandon, Coventry
(18) 6610 yards/***/F

Cocks Moor Woods G.C.
(0121) 444 3584
Alcester Road South, Kings Heath
(18) 5742 yards/***/F

Copt Heath G.C.
(01564) 772650
Warwick Road, Knowle, Solihull
(18) 6504 yards/**/A/H/M

Coventry G.C.
(01203) 411123
Finham Park, Coventry
(18) 6613 yards/**/A/H

Coventry Hearsall G.C.
(01203) 713470
Beechwood Avenue, Coventry
(18) 5983 yards/**/C/H

Dartmouth G.C.
(0121) 588 2131
Vale Street, West Bromwich
(9) 6060 yards/**/D

Druids Heath G.C.
(01922) 55595
Stonnal Road, Aldridge
(18) 6914 yards/**/B/H

Dudley G.C.
(01384) 233877
Turners Hill, Rowley Regis,
Warley
(18) 5715 yards/**/D

Edgbaston G.C. .
(0121) 454 1736
Church Road, Edgbaston
(18) 6118 yards/***/A/H

Enville G.C.
(01384) 872551
Highgate Common, Enville
(18) 6556 yards/**/B-A/H
(18) 6217 yards/**/B-A/H

Forest of Arden G.& C.C.
(01676) 522335
Maxstoke Road, Meriden
(18) 7100 yards/**/F/H
(18) 6525 yards/**/F/H

Gay Hill G.C.
(0121) 430 6523
Alcester Road, Hollywood,
(18) 6522 yards/**/B/H

GPT (Grange G.C.).
(01203) 451465
Copsewood, Coventry
(9) 6002 yards/**/D/H

Great Barr G.C.
(0121) 358 4376
Chapel Lane, Great Barr,
Birmingham
(18) 6546 yards/**/B/H/L

Hagley G.C.
(01562) 883701
Wassell Grove, Hagley, Stourbridge
(18) 6353 yards/**/B/H

Halesowen G.C.
(0121) 501 3606
The Leasowes, Halesowen
(18) 5754 yards/**/C

Handsworth G.C.
(0121) 554 3387
Sunningdale Close, Handsworth
(18) 6312 yards/**/C/H

Harborne G.C.
(0121) 427 3058
Tennal Road, Birmingham
(18) 6240 yards/**/A/H

Harborne Church Farm G.C.
(0121) 427 1204
Vicarage Road, Harborne
(9) 4914 yards/***/E

Hatchford Brook G.C.
(0121) 743 9821
Coventry Road, Sheldon
(18) 6164 yards/***/E

Hilltop G.C.
(0121) 554 4463
Park Lane, Handsworth
(18) 6114 yards/***/E

Himley Hall G.C.
(01902) 895207
Himley Hall Park, Dudley
(9) 3145 yards/**/E

Kings Norton G.C.
(01564) 826789
Brockhill Lane, Weatheroak
(18) 7057 yards/**/B/H
(9) 3300 yards/**/B/H

Ladbrook Park G.C.
(01564) 742264
Tanworth-in-Arden, Solihull
(18) 6427 yards/**/B-A/H

Lickey Hills G.C.
(0121) 453 3159
Rose Hill, Rednal
(18) 6010 yards/***/E

Little Aston G.C.
(0121) 353 2942
Streetly, Sutton Coldfield
(18) 6724 yards/**/F

Maxstoke Park G.C.
(01675) 466743
Castle Lane, Coleshill
(18) 6437 yards/**/A

Moor Hall G.C.
(0121) 308 6130
Four Oaks, Sutton Coldfield
(18) 6249 yards/**/B-A/H

Moseley G.C.
(0121) 444 2115
Springfield Road, Kings Heath
(18) 6285 yards/***/A/H/L

North Warwickshire G.C.
(01676) 522259
Hampton Lane, Meriden
(9) 3186 yards/**(not Thurs)/C

North Worcestershire G.C.
(0121) 475 1047
Frankley Beeches Road, Northfield
(18) 5959 yards/**/B/H

Olton G.C.
(0121) 705 1083
Mirfield Road, Solihull
(18) 6229 yards/**(Weds)/B/H

Oxley Park G.C.
(01902) 425892
Bushbury, Wolverhampton
(18) 6168 yards/***/C

Patshull Park Hotel G. & C.C.
(01902) 700100
Pattingham, Wolverhampton
(18) 6412 yards/***/B-A

Penn G.C.
(01902) 341142
Penn Common, Wolverhampton
(18) 6465 yards/**/C

Perton Park G.C.
(01902) 380103
Wrottesley Park Road, Perton
(18) 7007 yards/***/E

Pype Hayes G.C.
(0121) 351 1014
Eachelhurst Road, Walmley
(18) 5811 yards/***/E

Robin Hood G.C.
(0121) 706 0061
St Bernards Road, Solihull
(18) 6635 yards/**/B-A/H

Sandwell Park G.C.
(0121) 553 4637
Birmingham Road, West Bromwich
(18) 6470 yards/**/A/H

Sedgley Golf Centre
(01902) 880503
Sandyfields Road, Sedgley
(9) 3150 yards/**/E

Shirley G.C.
(0121) 744 6001
Stratford Road, Solihull
(18) 6510 yards/**/B-A/H

South Staffordshire G.C.
(01902) 751065
Tettenhall, Wolverhampton
(18) 6513 yards/**(Tues)/B/H

Sphinx G.C.
(01203) 451361
Sphinx Drive, Coventry
(9) 4104 yards/***/E

Stourbridge G.C.
(01384) 395566
Worcester Lane, Pedmore
(18) 6178 yards/**/C/H

Sutton Coldfield G.C.
(0121) 353 9633
Thornhill Road, Streetly
(18) 6541 yards/***/A/H

Swindon G.C.
(01902) 897031
Bridgnorth Road, Swindon
(18) 6042 yards/**/C
(9) 1135 yards/**/C

Tidbury Green G.C.
(01564) 824466
Tilehouse Lane, Shirley
(9) 2473 yards/***/E

Walmley G.C.
(0121) 377 7272
Brooks Road, Wylde Green
(18) 6537 yards/**/B

Walsall G.C.
(01922) 613512
The Broadway, Walsall
(18) 6243 yards/**/A/H

Wergs G.C.
(01902) 742225
Keepers Lane, Tettenhall
(18) 6949 yards/***/D

Widney Manor G.C.
(0121) 711 3646
Saintbury Drive, Widney Manor,
Solihull
(18) 4709 yards/***/E

Windmill Village Hotel & G.C.
(01203) 404041
Birmingham Road, Coventry
(18) 5200 yards/***/D

WARWICKSHIRE

Ansty Golf Centre
(01203) 621341
Brinklow Road, Ansty
(18) 5823 yards/***/E

Atherstone G.C.
(01827) 713110
The Outwoods, Atherstone
(18) 6239 yards/**/C/H
(18) 6006 yards/**/C/H

The Belfry G.C.
(01675) 470301
Lichfield Road, Wishaw
(18) 7177 yards/***/A/H
(18) 6186 yards/***/B/H

Bidford Grange G.C.
(01789) 490319
Bidford Grange, Bidford-on-Avon
(18) 7233 yards/***/D

Crocketts Manor G. & C.C.
(01564) 793715
Henley-in-Arden
(18) 6933 yards/***/B/H

Ingon Manor G.C.
(01789) 731857
Ingon Lane, Snitterfield
(18) 6554 yards/***/C/H

Kenilworth G.C.
(01926) 512732
Crew Lane, Kenilworth
(18) 6413 yards/***/B-A/H

Lea Marston Hotel & Leisure Complex
(01675) 470707
Haunch Lane, Lea Marston
(9) 1027 yards/***/F

Leamington & County G.C.
(01926) 425961
Whitnash, Leamington Spa
(18) 6425 yards/***/B-A/H

Newbold Comyn G.C.
(01926) 421157
Newbold Terrace, Leamington Spa
(18) 6315 yards/***/E

Nuneaton G.C.
(01203) 347810
Golf Drive, Whitestone
(18) 6412 yards/**/C/H

Purley Chase G.C.
(01203) 393118
Ridge Lane, Nuneaton
(18) 6604 yards/**/D/H

Rugby G.C.
(01788) 542306
Clifton Road, Rugby
(18) 5457 yards/**/F

Stoneleigh Deer Park G.C.
(01203) 639991
The Old Deer Park, Stoneleigh
(18)6083 yards/**/D
(9) 1251 yards/**/E

Stratford Oaks G.C.
(01789) 731982
Bearley Road, Snitterfield
(18) 6100 yards/***/D

Stratford-upon-Avon G.C.
(01789) 205677
Tiddington Road, Stratford
(18) 6309 yards/***/F/H

Warley G.C.
(0121) 429 2440
Lightswood Hill, Warley
(9) 2606 yards/***/F

Warwick G.C.
(01926) 494316
The Racecourse, Warwick
(9) 2682 yards/***(not racedays)/E

The Warwickshire G.C.
(01926) 409409
Leek Wootton, Warwick
(18) 7178 yards/***/A
(18) 7154 yards/***/A

Welcombe Hotel G.C.
(01789) 295292
Warwick Road, Stratford
(18) 6217 yards/**/A/H

Whitefields Hotel & Golf Complex
(01788) 521800
Coventry Road, Thurlaston
(18) 6433 yards/***/D/H

Artist: **Julian Barrow BRANCASTER** *Courtesy of:* **Burlington Gallery**

The counties of East Anglia, which for our purposes comprise Norfolk, Suffolk and Cambridgeshire, stretch from Constable Country in the south, through the Fens and the Broads to the tip of the Wash. For golfers this means it stretches from Felixstowe Ferry, through Thetford to Hunstanton. There are numerous other combinations capable of whetting the golfing appetite, for East Anglia is one of the game's richest regions. Certainly for quality and variety it has few equals. It is also a corner of Britain where golf has long been a popular pastime.

Norfolk

It is doubtful whether any county in England can surpass Norfolk's great range of outstanding courses. In short it offers the golfer a bit of everything. There are the magnificent links courses at **Hunstanton** and **Brancaster**, some terrifically scenic golf along the cliffs at **Sheringham** and **Cromer** and a number of superb inland courses of which **Thetford, Barnham Broom** and **Kings Lynn** are prime examples.

However, the title of 'Oldest Club' in Norfolk goes to **Great Yarmouth and Caister**, founded in 1882. A fine seaside links, it is located to the north of Great Yarmouth close to the old Roman town of Caister-on-Sea and near to the start of the A149 coastal road. Punters may wish to note that the golf course is actually situated inside part of Great Yarmouth racecourse. Anyone who does think of combining the two might look to Gorleston on Sea for a night's rest at the Cliff Hotel (01493) 662179 or in Yarmouth itself we recommend the Imperial Hotel (01493) 851113, which is a family run hotel, and the Carlton (01493) 855234.

Cromer, some twenty five miles north along the A149 is apparently famed for its crabs—the town, not the golf course I hasten to add—and also for its 150 year old lighthouse. The latter is a feature of **Royal Cromer's** attractive clifftop course. The 14th, the 'Lighthouse Hole', was played by Tony Jacklin during his '18 holes at 18 different courses helicopter round'. Several elevated tees and a generous spread of gorse make for a very interesting game.

Sheringham is only five miles further along the coast and is Norfolk's other great clifftop course. Founded some three years after Cromer in 1891 it is perhaps less exacting than its neighbour but certainly no less scenic. The view from the 5th hole is particularly stunning looking out across the rugged north Norfolk coastline.

A glorious day's golf (followed perhaps by some early evening bird watching—don't forget the binoculars) and time to relax. Well, in Sheringham, Southlands (01263) 822679 and the Beaumaris (01263) 822370 are handy, and inexpensive, whilst in nearby Weybourne the Swiss Restaurant (01263) 70220 is a splendid eating place and Maltings Hotel (01263) 70731 is a perfect base. On the road towards Brancaster (still the A149) the Blakeney area offers a glorious coastline and two beautifully situated hotels, the Manor (01263) 740376 and the Blakeney (01263) 740797.

And so on to **Brancaster** and **Hunstanton**, an outstanding pair to put it mildly. We feature both courses, or both links to be precise, later in this section. Once again, there's no shortage of places in which to relax and reflect on the day's golf. In Old Hunstanton, Le Strange Arms (01485) 534411 on Golfhouse Road, is highly thought of, as is the Fieldsend Guesthouse (01485) 532593 on Homefields Road. The village of Thornham lies between Hunstanton and Brancaster

and here one might consider the popular Lifeboat Inn (01485) 512236. To the south east of Brancaster the Old Rectory (01328) 820597 at Great Snoring is the perfect place for a particularly long rest and a little nearer at Brancaster Staithe, the Jolly Sailors (01485) 210314 is a good pub with an accompanying restaurant.

Further accommodation can be found at Titchwell, the Titchwell Manor (01485) 210221—a good value and thoroughly agreeable establishment. For two seafood restaurants we recommend the Moorings in Wells and Fishes (01328) 738588 in Burnham Market. We would also recommend the aptly named Hoste Arms (01328) 738777 a spendid 17th century inn with excellent food and accommodation. Finally, for a really homely country house in this area, the Holly Lodge (01485) 70790 at Heacham takes some beating.

Kings Lynn is our next port of call, and another very good golf course. Although the **Kings Lynn** Golf Club was founded back in 1923, it has played at Castle Rising to the north of the town since 1975. An Alliss/Thomas creation, it's very heavily wooded and quite a demanding test of golf. Returning to the town itself suggestions for an overnight stay might include the Dukes Head Hotel (01553) 774996 and Russet House (01553) 773098. Meanwhile at Knights Hill village, the Knights Hill Hotel (01553) 675566 has excellent leisure facilities and great character. A short journey to Grimston and one finds a real gem in Congham Hall (01485) 600250, an elegant and very well run Georgian manor house hotel.

The golfing visitor to Norwich, one of England's more attractive county towns, should have little difficulty in finding a game. **Sprowston Park** is a welcoming club on the edge of the city while for a fine combination of the old and the new try **Royal Norwich** and **Barnham Broom**. Both clubs have excellent parkland courses. Barnham Broom is part of an hotel and country club complex (01603) 759393 and has two courses with numerous accompanying leisure facilities.

If Norwich is to be the base though, then the Maids Head Hotel (01603) 209955 is most comfortable. Slightly less imposing, but no less comfortable, are the Grange Hotel (01603) 34734 and the Marlborough House Hotel (01603) 628005. Among many good restaurants are Adlard's (01603) 633522 (an outstanding establishment) Marcos (01603) 624044, the Brasted's (01603) 625949 and Greens Seafood (01603) 623733. Our final thought is Sprowston Manor (01603) 410871, good leisure facilities and in close proximity to the public course that lies adjacent to the hotel.

Last but not least, we must visit **Thetford**, right in the very heart of East Anglia and close to the Norfolk-Suffolk boundary. Thetford is surely one of England's most beautiful inland courses. Set amid glorious oaks, pines and silver birch trees it is also a great haven for wildlife (rather like Luffenham Heath in Leicestershire). Golden pheasant abound and one can also sight red deer and even, so I'm told, Chinese Water Deer (whatever they may be!) The green fee here is always money well spent. The second place to invest the cash is at the Bell Hotel (01842) 754455 in Thetford—a jolly good place to rest the spikes. Martine's (01842) 762000 is a restaurant to note.

Suffolk

Of the twenty or so golf clubs in Suffolk, about half were founded in the 19th century and the **Felixstowe Ferry** Golf Club which dates from 1880 is the fifth oldest club in England. Given its antiquity, and the fact that it was here that the 'father of golf writers' Bernard Darwin began to play his golf, Felixstowe Ferry is as good a place as any to begin our brief golfing tour of Suffolk.

The course lies about a mile to the north east of Felixstowe and is a classic test of traditional links golf. This part of Suffolk is fairly remote and at times it could easily be imagined that one was playing one of the better Scottish links courses. The greens are first class and the wind is often a major factor. Those looking to spend some time in this area (the courses at Ipswich and Woodbridge are only a short drive away) should note the Marlborough Hotel (01394) 285621 in Felixstowe. Lovers of fish and chips should note the splendid Felixstowe Ferry fish and chip restaurant on the beach— the finest for miles around!

The A45 links Felixstowe with Suffolk's largest town. The **Ipswich** Golf Club at Purdis Heath, three miles east of Ipswich, was designed by James Braid and is a fine heathland course. Always well maintained, the fairways wind their way between two large ponds and are bordered by heather and an attractive assortment of hardwood trees and silver birch. **Woodbridge** offers a similar type of challenge. Like the Ipswich course it's beautifully mature but is much more undulating. The golf club is located two miles east of Woodbridge along the B1084 Orford road.

The Ipswich-Woodbridge area is blessed with some outstanding places to stay and the seafood served in these parts is some of the best in Britain. In Woodbridge, Seckford Hall (01394) 385678 is superb while Melton Grange (01394) 384147 also appeals. A recent addition to the 'where to stay, where to play' map is provided by the new **Ufford Park** Hotel (01394) 383555 at Ufford, near Woodbridge. Here 18 holes of golf and numerous leisure facilities are offered in a pleasant country club setting. In Ipswich the Marlborough Hotel (01473) 257677 is both comfortable and good value and to the west of the town at Hintlesham is the 16th century **Hintlesham Hall** (01473) 652 334, where a glorious country house with an excellent restaurant and golf course await—gourmet golf itself! Other hotel suggestions in the Ipswich area would include the good value Bentley Tower Hotel (01473) 212142.

A little further up the Suffolk coast lie two delightful holiday courses: **Thorpeness** and **Aldeburgh**. Although close to the sea both are again heather and gorse types. The town of Aldeburgh is of course famed for its annual music festival and Benjamin Britten once lived next to the club's 14th fairway. Thorpeness, yet another James Braid creation, is about two miles north of Aldeburgh and is especially scenic. One hole that everyone remembers is the par three 7th, played across an attractive pond. On the 18th an unusual water tower (the 'House in the Clouds') and a restored windmill provide a unique background.

Thorpeness Golf Club has its own Golf Hotel (01728) 452176 which is naturally very convenient, and in Aldeburgh there are a number of alternatives, many of which also specialise in golfing breaks. Ideas here include the Wentworth (01728) 452312, the White Lion (01728) 452720 and the Uplands Hotel (01728) 452420. Also worth a visit is the White Horse Hotel (01728) 830694 in nearby Leiston. A final thought before moving inland is the Crown (01502) 722275 at Southwold to the north of Thorpeness—some pleasant rooms and some very good beer!

Over to the west of Suffolk the two courses that stand out are the parkland layout at **Bury St Edmunds** and the near-legendary **Royal Worlington**. Royal Worlington and Newmarket, to give its full title, is located two miles from Mildenhall, midway between Cambridge and Bury St Edmunds. A marvellous inland course with an almost links feel, it was once described as the finest 9 hole course in the world.

For a night's stopover, Bury St Edmunds offers a first rate hotel in the Angel (01284) 753926 while to the south of the town the Countrymen (01787) 312356 at Long Melford is an extremely welcoming abode. Chimneys (01787) 379806 is a first rate restaurant to look out for as is the popular Swan (01787) 247477 at Lavenham. Finally the Bedford Lodge Hotel (01638) 663175 at Newmarket is renowned for its hospitality.

Cambridgeshire

Having ventured west it is time to inspect the land of the fens and the courses of Cambridgeshire. Not exactly a county renowned for its golf, the courses tend, as one might expect, to be rather flat. One great exception though is the **Gog Magog** Golf Club situated to the south east of Cambridge which offers a tremendously enjoyable test of golf. The club takes its name from the ridge of low hills on which it lies. Apparently taking a line due east from here the next range of hills one comes across is the Ural Mountains! Among many fine holes, the par four 16th stands out and is surely one of the best (and toughest!) two-shot holes in the country.

A second good course, though not in the same league as Gog Magog, close to the famous University city belongs to the **Cambridgeshire Moat House Hotel** (01954) 249988. It is a particularly challenging course when played from the back tees with a lake and several ditches providing the challenges. Just north of Cambridge, **Girton** Golf Club is also worth inspecting.

Cambridge with its magnificent colleges is a marvellous place to spend a day or two and the Moat House is just one of many fine hotels. Of the others the Garden House Hotel (01223) 63421 perhaps takes pride of place and is particularly welcoming. It also possesses a first class restaurant. Another good eating place in town is the Marguerite (01223) 315232. Among the less expensive hotels, both Bon Accord House (01223) 411188 and the Lensfield Hotel (01223) 355017 are recommended as are Kirkwood House (01223) 313874 and Dykelands Guest House (01223) 244300. In nearby Royston, Chiswick House (01763) 60242 has great charm and Orton Hall Hotel (01733) 391111 near Peterborough is one of the finest in Cambridgeshire. Some notable hostelries in the county include the Plough and Fleece at Horningsea, the Three Horse Shoes at Madingley and the Green Man at Grantchester.

Other golf courses in Cambridgeshire which can be recommended include **Ramsey, St Ives** and **St Neots**. To the east of St Neots is the **Abbotsley** Golf Hotel (01480) 474000, and situated in the grounds is the course of the same name—one for the shortlist. In Huntingdon the Old Bridge (01480) 434700 is thoroughly recommended. A duo to note just outside of bustling Peterborough are **Peterborough Milton** and the public course, **Thorpe Wood**. Finally, in Ely there is the attractive **Ely City** course which provides some excellent views of the stunning 12th century cathedral and where, rather interestingly, the course record is held by one Lee Trevino.

Royal West Norfolk (Brancaster)

Excluding those which have staged an Open Championship, there are perhaps two courses in Britain that exude a sense of tradition, history and character above all others. One is Westward Ho! and the other is Brancaster or, to give them their correct titles, Royal North Devon and Royal West Norfolk.

Apart from their rather geographical names, they have much in common: both enjoy a wondrously remote setting yet are still fairly close to a superb championship links (Saunton and Hunstanton); both have a unique hazard (Devon's sea rushes and Norfolk's tidal marshes) and both are particularly friendly clubs, emphasising that tradition need not accompany aloofness.

Brancaster is something of a golfers' Camelot. Having reached the attractive little village there is every possibility that a high tide will have flooded the road that leads to the course. Indeed, many choose to leave their car in the village and walk the remainder of the journey. (Don't worry, it's not that far!) The golf course lies in a range of sandhills between marshland and sea. There is a story that the course was laid out on the suggestion of the Prince of Wales (later King Edward VII) having conceived the idea while out shooting on the land. Certainly it was he who bestowed patronage upon the club immediately on its foundation in 1891. The Royal flavour has continued and there have been no fewer than four Royal Captains, most recently the Duke of Kent in 1981.

The **Secretary** at Brancaster is **Major Nigel Carrington Smith** and he can be contacted on **(01485) 210087**. The club's full address is **The Royal West Norfolk Golf Club, Brancaster, Nr Kings Lynn, Norfolk, PE31 8AX.** Individual visitors and societies are both welcome at Brancaster although all visiting parties must make prior arrangements with the Secretary—an introduction is preferred. Due to increased demand, no visitors are received at any time, unless playing with a member, during the last week in July and until the end of the first week in September.

In 1998, the green fee is £43 during the week and £53 at weekends and on bank holidays. The preferred days for golfing societies are Mondays, Wednesdays and Fridays. The **Professional** at Brancaster, **Ray Kimber,** can be contacted on **(01485) 210616.**

Travelling to the course can be a lengthy journey. Brancaster is approximately eight miles from Hunstanton and twenty-five miles from Kings Lynn, to the south and south west respectively, and about thirty miles from Cromer to the east. Linking each to the other is the A149.

Like our friend Westward Ho!, Brancaster has the traditional out and back links layout. A quick glance at the scorecard tells us that one nine is considerably shorter than the other, the outward half measuring 3369 yards to the inward's 3059 yards. However, as at every good seaside course, wind direction is all important and on many occasions the back nine can play, or at least seem much longer. In total, the 6428 yards, par 71 represents a considerable test of golf. From the ladies' tees the course measures 5927 yards, par 75.

As well as the tidal marshes which come into play around the 8th and 9th, Brancaster is famed for its great wooden sleepered bunkers. Many are cross bunkers, which, as Sir Peter Allen observed, 'can be alarming to play over and frightening to play out of'. The course has received very few alterations over the years although two greens were lost to the sea in 1939 and 1940. There is no gentle beginning; the first three holes all measure over 400 yards and the great cross bunkers can come into play as early as the 3rd hole, one of the most difficult on the course. The bunker is fifty yards short of the green, which itself sits on a plateau. The 4th is a short par three but is deceptively tricky, especially into the wind. The 8th and 9th have been mentioned and the marshes must be carried twice on the 8th and from the tee on the dog-legged 9th which has a cross bunker in front of the green. The 11th and 12th are played deep amid the dunes but the 14th is perhaps the most difficult hole, with the 18th close behind—a hole with sleepered bunkers both to the front and back of the green.

The clubhouse, which is only a year younger than the course, is decidedly comfortable and is separated from the sea only by a sea wall. This famous last line of defence had to be repaired in 1991 after high seas wreaked havoc in 1990. The clubhouse also has a lovely verandah from which there are some glorious views. The setting really is something special and nobody described it better than the late Tom Scott.

'It has a quiet and restful beauty, and when you leave the clubhouse and drive across the marsh to the main road in the dusk of a summer evening, look back for a minute and perhaps you will be rewarded, as I have frequently been, with a view of the red sun setting over the sea with a golden glow. You will see too, the long shadows cast by the great sandhills, and you will hear the call of the many birds across the marshes, a sound to my mind typical of Norfolk.'

Hole	Yards	Par	Hole	Yards	Par
1	410	4	10	151	3
2	449	4	11	478	5
3	407	4	12	386	4
4	128	3	13	317	4
5	421	4	14	432	4
6	186	3	15	188	3
7	486	5	16	346	4
8	478	5	17	377	4
9	404	4	18	384	4
Out	**3,369**	**36**	**In**	**3,059**	**35**
			Out	**3,369**	**36**
			Totals	**6,428**	**71**

Hunstanton

Imagine you are standing on the tee of a particularly difficult par three hole. It is a difficult hole on a still day—188 yards long and with six deep bunkers encircling the green—but it is particularly tough on this day because the wind is dead against. You select a one iron and hit the perfect shot; so perfect that it lands a few feet from the flag and rolls into the hole. Marvellous, but what a pity this is only a practice round! A day later, in the tournament itself, you reach the 16th but this time the wind is with you. You choose a six iron and incredibly you repeat the trick—in it goes for a second hole in one. Much celebration follows at the 19th. The next day (the second of the tournament) the wind is once more at your back as you walk onto the tee of what is now your favourite hole. If a six iron was good enough yesterday, it must be good enough today you reckon. Your calculations are entirely accurate and your well struck shot never really looks like missing. Three aces in three days at the same hole! Are you a liar, a dreamer . . .or Robert Taylor?

Taylor performed this remarkable feat in the summer of 1974 on the 16th at Hunstanton. Nobody has ever matched his extraordinary achievement and probably never will.

Founded over a hundred years ago, Hunstanton Golf Club celebrated its centenary in 1991. Although it is situated on the east coast of England the course actually faces north west and looks over the Wash towards Lincolnshire. Hunstanton has the kind of geography that causes its members to lose sleep over talk of global warming. It is a very good golf course—in the opinion of many, the east coast's finest 18 hole challenge between Sandwich and Muirfield, a distance of about 400 miles. It is a boast regularly expressed by Hunstanton's members when a player from Brancaster happens to be within earshot. But theirs is a valid claim, for Hunstanton is a truly classic links course. Like Brancaster, the course runs out and back although not rigidly so, rather it meanders away from the clubhouse, reaches the 8th green and meanders its way home. The outward holes have the River Hun for company—normally it is off to the right and the inward ones are closer to the shore. At first glance, the links looks very flat, and indeed there aren't any major climbs, up or down, but the course has more than its fair share of subtle undulations and there are a number of elevated tees and plateau greens, some of which offer extensive views of both sea and country.

It isn't the views though that are likely to be best remembered after a round at Hunstanton—it is the greens and bunkers. The putting surfaces are as quick (and usually as well prepared) as any in Britain—including the Open Championship courses. As for the bunkers, they are numerous, strategically (and sometimes sadistically) placed and often quite deep. Avoid the bunkers and putt well and you'll probably score well here!

The club is very happy to receive visitors on weekdays and occasionally at weekends. All must be members of golf clubs and have current handicaps. It is worth noting that the 1st tee is reserved on weekdays before 9.30am, but in any event it is a good idea to contact the club a few days prior to any visit. The **Secretary** at Hunstanton, **Mr Malcolm Whybrow** can be approached by writing to **The Hunstanton Golf Club, Old Hunstanton, Norfolk PE36 6JQ.** Mr Whybrow can also be contacted by telephone on **(01485) 532811. Mr John Carter** is the club's **Professional** and he can be reached on **(01485) 532751.**

The green fees for 1998 are £45 per day during the week and, when available, £55 per day at weekends. Junior golfers pay half the above rates.

From the championship tees, Hunstanton measures 6735 yards, par 72 (SSS 72); while from the medal tees it is reduced by some 400 yards to 6333 yards, and for ladies the course measures 5973 yards, par 75. We have already referred to the ingenious and severe bunkering and the four par three holes emphasise this: the 4th is only 172 yards in length but has eight bunkers; the 7th is a similar length and has only one trap, but what a trap! The tee shot is an exhilarating one over a gully to a plateau green. Anything short is almost certain to plummet into a deep, yawning bunker that almost runs the entire width of the entrance—a low runner is not the desired shot here. The 14th requires a blind tee shot of 200 yards plus and again eight bunkers are waiting to greet the player who fails to find the putting surface.

The par four holes at Hunstanton offer a range of challenges. The 3rd, for instance, demands a very long approach shot if the prevailing wind is up to its tricks. By contrast, the 6th is a modest length hole but a deft touch is required to pitch onto the plateau green and the 17th and 18th provide a very strong finish. However, the best hole on the course is generally considered to be the 11th, which runs parallel to the shore. A high tee gives a spectacular view of both the hole and the surrounding countryside. At 439 yards it needs two perfectly hit shots along an ever narrowing valley-fairway to reach the green.

Numerous major amateur events have been staged at Hunstanton over the years, including the 1990 British Boys Amateur Championship, won by Michael Welch and the 1995 English Amateur Championship won by Mark Foster.

Hole	Yards	Par	Hole	Yards	Par
1	343	4	10	375	4
2	532	5	11	439	4
3	443	4	12	358	4
4	172	3	13	387	4
5	436	4	14	219	3
6	337	4	15	478	5
7	166	3	16	189	3
8	505	5	17	445	4
9	513	5	18	398	4
Out	**3,447**	**37**	**In**	**3,288**	**35**
			Out	**3,447**	**37**
			Totals	**6,735**	**72**

CAMBRIDGESHIRE

Abbotsley G.C.
(01480) 474000
Eynesbury Hardwicke, St Neots
(18) 6150 yards/***/C

Bourn G.C.
(01954) 718057
Toft Road, Bourn
(18) 6275 yards/**/C

Brampton Park G.C.
(01480) 434700
Buckden Road, Brampton
(18) 6403 yards/***/B

Cambridge G.C.
(01954) 789388
Station Road, Longstanton
(9) 3464 yards/***/D

Cambridge Meridian
(01233) 264700
Comberton Road, Toft
(18) 6277 yards/***/C

Cambridgeshire Moat House Hotel G.C.
(01954) 780555
Bar Hill
(18) 6734 yards/***/C/L/M

Elton Furze G.C.
(01733) 280189
Bullock Road, Haddon
(18) 6291 yards/*/B

Ely City G.C.
(01353) 662751
Cambridge Road, Ely
(18) 6686 yards/**/B

Girton G.C.
(01223) 276169
Dodford Lane, Girton
(18) 6085 yards/**/C

Gog Magog G.C.
(01223) 247626
Shelford Bottom
(18) 6386 yards/**/B/H/L
(9) 5833 yards/**/B/H/L

Hemingford Abbots G.C.
(01480) 495000
New Farm Lodge, Cambridge Road
(9) 5468 yards/**/F

Heydon Grange G. & C.C.
(01763) 208988
Heydon, Royston
(18) 6512/***/C
(9) 3249/***/C

Lakeside Lodge G.C.
(01487) 740540
Fen Road, Pidley
(18) 6600 yards/***/E

Malton G.C.
(01763) 262200
Meldreth, Royston
(18) 6708 yards/***/D

March G.C.
(01354) 652364
Frogs Abbey, Grange Road, March
(9) 6200 yards/**/D/H

Old Nene G.& C.C.
(01487) 813519
Muchwood Lane, Bodsey, Ramsey
(9) 5524 yards/***/E

Orton Meadows G.C.
(01733) 237478
Ham Lane, Peterborough
(18) 5800 yards/***/E

Peterborough Milton G.C.
(01733) 380489
Milton Ferry, Peterborough
(18) 6431 yards/**/A/H

Ramsey G.C.
(01487) 812600
Abbey Terrace, Ramsey,
(18) 6136 yards/**/C/H

St Ives G.C.
(01480) 468392
Westwood Road, St Ives
(9) 6052 yards/**/C/H

St Neots G.C.
(01480) 472363
Crosshall Road, St Neots
(18) 6027 yards/**/B/H

Thorney Golf Centre
(01733) 270570
English Drove, Thorney,
Peterborough
(18) 6104 yards/***/E

Thorpe Wood G.C.
(01733) 267701
Thorpe Wood, Peterborough
(18) 7076 yards/***/D

SUFFOLK

Aldeburgh G.C.
(01728) 452890
Saxmundham Road, Aldeburgh
(18)6330 yards/***/F/H
(9) 2114 yards/***/F

Brett Vale G.C.
(01473) 310718
Noakes Road, Raydon
(18) 5808 yards/***/C

Bungay and Waveney Valley G.C.
(01986) 892337
Outney Common, Bungay
(18)6063 yards/**/C/H

Bury St Edmunds G.C.
(01284) 755979
Tut Hill, Bury St Edmunds
(18) 6615 yards/**/B/H
(9) 4644 yards/**/D/H

Cretingham G.C.
(01728) 685275
Cretingham, Woodridge
(9) 2260 yards/**/E

Diss G.C.
(01379) 642847
Stutson Road, Diss
(18) 6238 yards/**/C

Felixstowe Ferry G.C.
(01394) 286834
Ferry Road, Felixstowe
(18) 6324 yards/***/C/H

Flempton G.C.
(01284) 728291
Flempton, Bury St Edmunds
(9) 6240 yards/**/C/H

Fynn Valley G.C.
(01473) 785463
Witnesham, Ipswich
(18) 5700 yards/***/D

Haverhill G.C.
(01440) 61951
Coupals Road, Haverhill
(9) 5707 yards/***/D

Hintlesham Hall G.C.
(01473) 652761
Hintlesham, Ipswich
(18) 6630 yards/***/B

Ipswich G.C.
(01473) 728941
Purdis Heath, Bucklesham Road
(18) 6405 yards/**/A/H(18)
(9) 1950 yards/***/E

Links G.C.
(01638) 663000
Cambridge Road, Newmarket
(18) 6424 yards/**/B/H

Newton Green G.C.
(01787) 377217
Newton Green, Sudbury
(18) 5488 yards/**/D/H

Rookery Park G.C.
(01502) 560380
Beccles Road, Carlton Coleville
(18) 6649 yards/**/C/H

Royal Worlington and Newmarket G.C.
(01638) 712216
Worlington, Bury St Edmunds
(9) 3105 yards/**/B/H

Rushmere G.C.
(01473) 725648
Rushmere Heath, Ipswich
(18) 6287 yards/***/C/H

Seckford G.C.
(01394) 388000
Seckford Hall Road, Woodbridge
(18) 5088 yards/***/D

Southwold G.C.
(01502) 723248
The Common, Southwold
(9) 6001 yards/***/D

St Helena G.C.
(01986) 875567
Bramfield Road, Halesworth
(18) 6580 yards/***/C/H
(9) 3059 yards/***/E/H

Stoke-by-Nayland G.C.
(01206) 262836
Keepers Lane, Colchester
(18) 6544 yards/***/B/H
(18) 6516 yards/**/B/H

Stowmarket G.C.
(01449) 736473
Lower Road, Onehouse, Stowmarket
(18) 6101 yards/***/B-A/H

Suffolk G. & C.C.
(01284) 706777
St Johns Hill, Bury St Edmunds
(18) 6212 yards/**/C

Thorpeness Golf Hotel
(01728) 452176
Thorpeness, Leiston
(18) 6241 yards/**/B

Ufford Park Hotel & G.C,
(01394) 383836
Yarmouth Road, Ufford,Woodbridge
(18) 6335 yards/***/D

Waldringfield Heath G.C.
(01473) 736768
Newbourne Road, Waldringfield
(18) 6153 yards/**/C

Woodbridge G.C.
(01394) 382038
Bromeswell Heath, Woodbridge
(18) 6314 yards/**/B/H
(9) 2243 yards/**/B/H

Wood Valley G.C.
(01502) 712244
The Common, Beccles
(9) 2781 yards/**/D

NORFOLK

Barnham Broom. Hotel.
(01603) 759393
Barnham Broom, Norwich
(18) 6603 yards/**/B/H
(18) 6470 yards/**/B/H

Bawburgh G.C.
(01603) 746390
Long Lane, Bawburgh, Norwich
(18) 6066 yards/***/D

Costessey Park G.C.
(01603) 746333
Costessey Park, Costessey
(18) 6104 yards/**/C

Dereham G.C.
(01362) 695900
Quebec Road, Dereham
(9) 6225 yards/**/C/H

Dunham G.C.
(01328) 701718
Little Dunham, Kings Lynn
(9) 2132 yards/***/D

Dunston Hall G.C.
(01508) 470444
Ipswich Road, Dunston
(9) 6408 yards/***/D

Eagles G.C.
(01553) 827147
School Road, Kings Lynn
(9) 2142 yards/***/E

Eaton G.C.
(01603) 451686
Newmarket Road, Norwich
(18) 6135 yards/***/C

Fakenham G.C.
(01328) 863534
The Racecourse, Fakenham
(9) 5879 yards/**/D

Feltwell G.C.
(01842) 827644
Thor Avenue, Feltwell, Thetford
(9) 6260 yards/**/D

Gorleston G.C.
(01493) 662103
Warren Road, Gorleston
(18) 6400 yards/***/C/H

Great Yarmouth and Caister G.C.
(01493) 728699
Beach House, Caister-on-Sea
(18) 6284 yards/**/B

Hunstanton G.C.
(01485) 532811
Golf Course Road, Old Hunstanton
(18) 6735 yards/***/A/H

Kings Lynn G.C.
(01553) 631654
Castle Rising, Kings Lynn
(18) 6646 yards/**/A/H

Links Country Park Hotel G.C.
(01263) 838383
West Runton, Cromer
(9) 4814 yards/***/C

Mattishall G.C.
(01362) 850464
South Green, Mattishall, Dereham
(9) 6218 yards/***/E

Middleton Hall G. & C.C.
(01553) 841800
Middleton, Kings Lynn
(9) 5570 yards/**/D

Mundesley G.C.
(01263) 720095
Links Road, Mundesley
(9) 5410 yards/***/C

RAF Marham G.C.
(01760) 337261
RAF Marham, Kings Lynn
(9) 5244 yards/**/E

Reymerston G.C.
(01362) 850297
Hingham Road, Reymerston
(18) 6603 yards/**/B

Richmond Park G.C.
(01953) 881803
Saham Road, Watton
(18) 6300 yards/***/C

Royal Cromer G.C.
(01263) 512884
Overstrand Road, Cromer
(18) 6508 yards/***/B/H

Royal Norwich G.C.
(01603) 429928
Drayton High Road, Hellesdon
(18) 6603 yards/**/B/H

Royal West Norfolk G.C.
(01485) 210087
Brancaster, Kings Lynn
(18) 6428 yards/**/A/G/H

Royston Park G.C.
(01366) 382133
Denver, Downham Market
(9) 6292 yards/***/B/G/H

Sheringham G.C.
(01263) 823488
Weybourne Road, Sheringham
(18) 6464 yards/**/B/H

Sprowston Park G.C.
(01603) 410657
Wroxham Road, Sprowston
(18) 5985 yards/***/D/H

Swaffham G.C.
(01760) 721611
Cley Road, Swaffham
(9) 6252 yards/**/C

Thetford G.C.
(01842) 752169
Brandon Road, Thetford
(18) 6879 yards/***/B/H

Wensum Valley G.C.
(01603) 261012
Beech Avenue, Taverham
(18) 6000 yards/**/D
(18) 4862 yards/**/D

Weston Park G.C.
(01603) 872363
Weston Longville, Norwich
(9) 3132 yards/**/C/H

Artist: **Gordon Grant Smith SELF PORTRAIT** *Courtesy of:* **Burlington Gallery**

Artist: **Michael Brown** **PREPARING TO PLAY** *Courtesy of:* **Burlington Gallery**

Derbyshire

Not wishing to be unkind, but Derby the town isn't one of Earth's more inspiring places but Derbyshire the county is a different matter altogether. The Peak District is without question one of the most scenic regions in England and commencing only a short distance north of Derby, it covers the greater part of the county. The Pennine Way of course starts in Derbyshire.

As well as being the beginning of all things beautiful, the area just north of Derby is where three of the county's leading golf courses are to be found: Kedleston Park, Breadsall Priory and Chevin. Located approximately four miles from Derby off the A111 (and well signposted) **Kedleston Park** golf course occupies a beautiful situation and is generally rated as the finest course in Derbyshire. Quite lengthy from the back tees, it has a variety of challenging holes. Eyeing the course from across a lake is the impressive Kedleston Hall, historic home of Lord Scarsdale. Lying east of Kedleston is **Morley Hayes**—a challenge to all golfers with some good par 4s.

I'm not sure what the 13th century monks would have made of **Breadsall Priory** Golf and Country Club, three miles north east of Derby at Morley, but for heathens of the 20th century it provides an ideal setting for one of the most enjoyable games in the Midlands. Golfwise, Breadsall Priory has only been on the map since 1976 but the undulating parkland course with its imported Cumberland turf greens has matured rapidly and the second 18 holes admirably complement the plush leisure centre.

Chevin lies slightly further north off the A6 at Duffield. It has an interesting layout; the first ten holes are a steady climb towards a spectacular vantage point after which holes 11 to 18 gently bring you down to earth (or at least to Duffield!) Another course to recommend in the south of the county and over towards Nottingham is the wooded layout at **Erewash Valley**, noted for its two quarry holes.

If Derby is the chosen resting place then the the Midland Hotel (01332) 345894 is a comfortable hotel and reasonably priced. La Gondola (01332) 332895 is also good. In Belper, Makeney Hall (01332) 842999 is a splendid country house hotel—a perfect place to celebrate one's closing birdie at Chevin. Breadsall Priory (01332) 832235 itself of course offers a most satisfying 19th hole and is ideal for an action packed or more leisurely weekend away. Finally, Kedleston Country House (01332) 559202 is well placed for the excellent 18 holes of Kedleston Park.

Moving up country, the picturesque town of **Matlock** has a fairly short but pleasant course situated north of the town off the Chesterfield road and **Chesterfield's** course at Walton is also well worth a visit. There are also two public courses close to the town centre. A recommendation for a memorable night is Riber Hall (01629) 582795 near Matlock—a first rate restaurant and hotel—and in Matlock itself the New Bath Hotel (01629) 583275 is well worth a visit.

The town of Buxton lies in the heart of the Peak District and is many people's idea of the perfect town. This may have something to do with the fact that some of the finest pubs in England are located round about, but it also helps that there are two excellent golf courses either side of the town—**Buxton and High Peak** and **Cavendish**. Of similar length it is difficult to say which is the better, but in any event both warmly welcome visitors at green fees that should leave a few pennies for celebrating nearby. After a day on the fairways (not to mention an evening in a Buxton pub) a suitable hotel is required. The Old Hall Hotel (01298) 22841 is a historic hotel just one mile from the Cavendish course. There is also the Lee Wood Hotel (01298) 23002 which overlooks the cricket ground. Having done my bit for the Buxton tourist board another suggestion for this delightful area can be found in Hassop. Hassop Hall (01629) 640488

is a splendid establishment whilst the nearby Riverside Country House Hotel (01629) 814275 offers good food and comfortable rooms.

Other good locals include the Old Bulls Head, Little Hucklow; in Hathersage, the George; and in Beeley, the Devonshire Arms which is near to Chatsworth, and no trip to the area would be complete without visiting this incredible stately home, perhaps England's finest. A similar comment could be made about Fischer's at Baslow Hall (01246) 583259—an excellent restaurant with rooms to match the finest 18 holes in the country.

Nottinghamshire

Moving into Nottinghamshire, the famous **Notts** Golf Club at Hollinwell is featured separately on a later page; however, in addition to this rather splendid 'Nottingham gorse affair' those visiting the county town should strongly consider the merits of **Wollaton Park**, an attractive course set amidst the deer park of a stately home and surprisingly close to the centre of Nottingham. The city's two 18 hole municipal courses are also fairly good. Slightly further afield but well worth noting are the parkland courses at **Chilwell Manor** (A6005) and **Radcliffe on Trent** (A52 east of the town).

Nottingham has no shortage of comfortable modern hotels and the Forte Crest (0115) 9470131 and the Royal (0115) 9414444 are first rate and centrally located. To the north of the city at Arnold, Bestwood Lodge (0115) 9203011 is less stylish but good value. To the south, lovers of the country house scene should delight in Langar Hall (01949) 860559 at Langar (seems to have a golfing ring to it, don't you think?) The best known pub in town is probably the Olde Trip to Jerusalem—said to be the oldest in England. Mansfield is only about 15 minutes drive from Hollinwell and here Manor Park Hotel (01623) 22644 is a highly recommended hotel while a pleasant guesthouse is Tichfield House (01623) 810356.

Two of the county's finest courses lie fairly close to one another near the centre of Nottinghamshire, **Coxmoor** and **Sherwood Forest**. The former is a moorland type course situated just south of Mansfield at Sutton in Ashfield. The Sherwood Forest course is more of a heathland type—well wooded (as one might expect given its name) with much tangling heather. Measuring over 6700 yards it is quite a test too.

Over towards the border with Lincolnshire is the attractive town of Newark with its 12th century castle and cobbled market square. **Newark** Golf Club lies four miles east of the town off the A17. Reasonably flat and quite secluded, the golf is a little less testing than at some of the county's bigger clubs. An attractive place to stay is the Old Rectory, north of Newark in Kirkton. Also in town the Old Kings Arms is a fine pub (01636) 703416.

Before inspecting Lincolnshire, a brief word on **Lindrick**. Although its postal address is in Nottinghamshire the majority of the course lies in South Yorkshire. In any event, it is featured in our Yorkshire chapter. If a night's rest is required 'this side' of the border, then Ye Olde Bell Hotel at Barnby Moor (01777) 705121 is a pleasant coaching inn and the Angel in Blyth is a friendly pub with some accommodation also.

Lincolnshire

Lincolnshire is a large county—bigger now that Humberside has disintegrated and Grimsby, Scunthorpe and Cleethorpes are all back in the fold. So now, by my reckoning there are over forty worthwhile golf courses in the county. Woodhall Spa is of course head and shoulders above the rest but although the county as a whole is unlikely to be the venue for many golfing holidays there are certainly a handful of courses well worth a visit.

Woodhall Spa is featured ahead. For those fortunate

enough to be able to spend a few days playing the course, here are some suggestions. The appropriately named Golf Hotel (01526) 353535 is a popular and convenient place in which to stay, but the Abbey Lodge (01526) 352538, Duns (01526) 352969 and Petwood House (01526) 352411 are also recommended. The Edwardian Dower House (01526) 352588 is also very pleasant. Lincoln of course may be a base and for those not minding a bit of a drive or, alternatively, The George (01780) 755171 at Stamford is quite excellent—a charming atmosphere with a very fine restaurant. Stamford in fact is a delightful town: Burghley is found here, an outstandingly attractive Elizabethan house. **Burghley Park** Golf Club is noted for its greens and its links with Mark James, while just over the county boundary in Leicestershire lies **Luffenham Heath**, a truly splendid golf course.

Lincoln was briefly mentioned and it really is an attractive city—a beautiful cathedral, a castle and a wealth of history. The White Hart (01522) 526222 is a noted hotel and there are several fine restaurants. including The Jew's House (01522) 524851, a fascinating building with first rate food. Excellent food and a great pub can be found in the Wig and Mitre (01522) 535190. The award winning D'Isney Place Hotel (01552) 538881 will lure many and disappoint none. Outside the city in Branston, the Moor Lodge Hotel (01522) 791366 is good value. The best golf to be found in **Lincoln** is at Torksey just to the north west of the city. It's a fairly sandy, heathland type course with a lovely selection of trees. **Canwick Park**, on the opposite side of Lincoln is a shorter parkland course, but challenging in its own way.

Three courses of note towards the north of the county are at **Gainsborough** (Thonock), **Market Rasen** and **Louth**. All are very welcoming. Gainsborough is owned by the Ping company and is a classic parkland layout; Market Rasen is a very good woodland type course while Louth has an attractive setting in a local beauty spot, the Hubbards Hills. A second course near Louth, **Kenwick Park**, recently opened and

already promises to be one of the region's top courses. The Limes Country House Hotel (01673) 842357 is ideal for Market Rasen, and in Louth, the Priory (01507) 602930 offers a comfortable stop-over. (There are some fine pubs in Louth too—note the Wheatsheaf). The Kenwick Park Hotel (01507) 608806 is handy for the fairways of the same name. A real beauty of a course is also to be found in Broughton, **Forest Pines**, a real gem.

Across the Humber, **Elsham** is well thought of (an old haunt of Tony Jacklin's this) and slightly nearer to Scunthorpe, **Holme Hall** at Bottesford is a championship length parkland course. Finally over to the Humberside coast, both **Grimsby** and **Cleethorpes** are also worth a game. Both towns are full of character (characters as well) and if you do play at Grimsby don't miss out on the local fish and chips—they're reckoned to be the best in Britain! In Cleethorpes, the Kingsway (01472) 601122 is a seafront hotel to note.

Skegness is a famous resort—perhaps not everyone's cup of tea, but a game here is certainly recommended for those who like their links golf. **Seacroft** is the place: flattish, windy and plenty of sand dunes—a most underrated course. Further up the coast, a less severe challenge is offered at **Sandilands** where the Grange and Links Hotel (01507) 441334 is adjacent to the course. The south of the county comprises much rich agricultural land but not too much in the way of golf. **Stoke Rochford** however is a popular parkland course and **Spalding** is worth inspecting particularly at the time of year when the famous bulbs have flourished. An 18 hole course here, and in the south west there is the very established **Belton Park** course and the much newer De Vere **Belton Woods** Hotel & Country Club (01476) 593200 which enjoys a peaceful setting outside Grantham. The hotel itself is very large but is well thought of and it has two 18 hole courses, the Lancaster and Wellington, and as there is a lot of water to be negotiated a few Barnes Wallis type shots may be called for!

"STARTING FROM SCRATCH" "DRIVEN FROM THE TEE" "HALVING A HOLE"

"A MASHIE" "ROYAL AND ANCIENT (ST ANDREWS 1798)" A HEAVY DRIVER.

"SHIES A PENNY"

Artist: **Frank Paton ROYAL AND ANCIENT** _Courtesy of:_ **Rosenstiel's**

Notts (Hollinwell)

The Notts Golf Club was founded in 1887, although the club's first home was, in fact, nearer to Nottingham itself at Bulwell Forest. Apparently the proposed move from Bulwell to Hollinwell which occurred around the turn of the century initially met with considerable opposition. Undeterred, the radicals invited Willie Park Jr to design the new course and by the time John H Taylor had added some finishing touches, not a squeak of discontent was to be heard. Messrs. Park and Taylor had presented the members with a masterpiece.

The gentleman presently looking after the interests of the Notts golfers is the **Secretary, Mr Stuart Goldie.** Visitors seeking a game are advised to contact him some time in advance of intended play. Mr Goldie can be contacted by telephone on **(01623) 753225** while the address for written correspondence is **The Notts Golf Club, Hollinwell, Derby Road, Kirkby-in-Ashfield, Nottinghamshire, NG17 7QR.**

As a general guide, visitors can play between Mondays and Fridays although it should be noted that Friday is often busy, it being Ladies' Day. The first tee is reserved for members between 12.00pm and 1.00pm on Mondays and Tuesdays, and on Wednesdays and Thursdays between 12.00pm and 2.00pm or 11.30am and 1.30pm during the winter months. Societies are welcome with Mondays and Tuesdays being the favoured days. In 1998 the green fees are £40 per round or £55 per day. Another thing visitors might wish to note is the club's popular driving range.

Since the club's move to Hollinwell in 1900 it has had, somewhat remarkably, only five professionals. Brian Waites, probably our best known 'club pro', retired recently after 29 years service. Brian made history in 1983 by becoming the oldest British player to make his debut in the Ryder Cup. Now a very successful member of the Seniors Tour, Waites has played for the Rest Of The World Seniors against the American Seniors in the United States. His successor, **Alasdair Thomas** is already well-known to local golfers having served eight years at the club as Brian's senior assistant. He and his staff may be contacted on **(01623) 753087.**

The course is located to the north west of Nottingham on the A611. Approaching from either the North or South of England, the M1 is very convenient. The motorway should be left at junction 27 at which point the A608 should be followed until it joins the A611. The club is then two miles away and is signposted off to the right.

From the championship tees, the course is something of a minor monster stretching to a shade over 7000 yards (7030 yards, par 72). Even from the forward tees, it represents a formidable test at 6619 yards. The ladies' course measures 5882 yards, par 75. If Hollinwell is a monster, then it's a pretty one (if there can be such a creature!) with a wealth of heather and gorse lining the fairways, together with some superb oaks and silver birch trees; certainly a splendid setting in which to enjoy a day's golf.

Similar to Woodhall Spa, the 1st at Hollinwell is relatively straightforward and has been described as 'ideal for the early morning top!'—something to be avoided on the lengthy 2nd, a hole famed for the huge rock which guards the back of the green known as Robin Hood's Chair. Another notable hole on the front nine is the 8th, perhaps not so intimidating from the forward tee, but from the medal tee it requires a very straight and solid drive to carry an attractive lake. Half hidden by trees to the right of the tee is the 'holy well' from which the name Hollinwell derives. Whether its waters will give you divine inspiration to tackle the back nine is debatable but it's worth a look. Actually, a prayer or two, or at least a little luck may be required when the downhill 13th is confronted. One of only three short holes, although short is hardly apt, it was once called 'an absolute terror', having 'trouble everywhere'. The 15th is another very challenging hole and the round ends with a stiff par four which, if achieved, will certainly earn you a drink at the club's comfortable 19th.

Championship golf regularly visits Hollinwell. Both Sandy Lyle and Nick Faldo have triumphed here, Lyle winning the 1975 English Open Stroke Play Championship (an event which returned to Hollinwell in 1992) as a precocious seventeen year old, and Faldo the European Tournament Players Championship of 1982. Arguably the most celebrated event was the 1970 John Player Classic when Christy O'Connor pocketed a cheque for £25,000, at the time a world record first prize—no doubt a few Irish eyes were smiling.

Hole	Yards	Par	Hole	Yards	Par
1	376	4	10	362	4
2	430	4	11	365	4
3	511	5	12	433	4
4	455	4	13	236	3
5	193	3	14	403	4
6	533	5	15	440	4
7	403	4	16	355	4
8	410	4	17	490	5
9	178	3	18	457	4
Out	**3,489**	**36**	**In**	**3,541**	**36**
			Out	**3,489**	**36**
			Totals	**7,030**	**72**

Woodhall Spa

Between them, Sunningdale and Walton Heath have seventy two holes, each with an Old and a New course. Many may disagree but if a composite eighteen were created, taking the best eighteen holes from the four courses I still don't think we would see a better (or more challenging) course than the round offered at Woodhall Spa—and I certainly don't view Sunningdale and Walton Heath as anything less than outstanding.

Woodhall Spa Golf Club was founded in 1905. The course itself was originally laid out by Harry Vardon, although substantial alterations were made firstly by Harry Colt and later by Colonel Hotchkin. A great deal has been happening of late. The club became the national golf centre of the English Golf Union in 1995. Since then they have built a second course, the Bracken Course, which comes into play in June 1998. The original course, renamed the Hotchkin Course, was recently ranked 29th best course in the world by the US publication *GOLF Magazine* and top inland course in England.

As one of the country's greatest (and most beautiful) heathland layouts, Woodhall Spa is understandably extremely popular and visitors (both individuals and societies) looking for a game must make prior arrangements with the club's **Secretary, Mr B H Fawcett,** who may be contacted via **The Woodhall Spa Golf Club, Woodhall Spa, Lincolnshire, LN10 6PU (01526) 352511** or by fax on **(01526) 352778.** The club's **Professional, Campbell Elliot** can be reached on **(01526) 353229.**

The green fees at Woodhall Spa for 1998 are £40 per round or £65 per day. Reduced rates are available to English Golf Union members (£30 per round, £50 per day) but an EGU card or a letter of introduction providing proof of such membership must be produced.

Glancing at the map, Woodhall Spa looks fairly close to Lincoln. By road the distance is, in fact, at least twenty miles. Those approaching from the cathedral city should take the B1188 towards Sleaford, taking a left fork onto the B1189 towards the village of Martin. At Martin the B1191 road should be picked up and followed to Woodhall Spa, the club being directly off this road. Those travelling from further north will probably need to use a combination of motorways before joining the A15, which links Lincoln to the M180 (junction 4). Those motoring from the south may have to do even more map-reading! The A1 is likely to be a good starting point. It should be left just north of Colsterworth and the B6403 then taken towards Ancaster and RAF Cranwell, joining the A15 just beyond the RAF base. A right fork should be taken towards the wonderful-ly named hamlet of Ashby de la Launde on the B1191 which takes us to Martin and then to Woodhall Spa.

The journey across Lincolnshire will have taken the traveller alongside many miles of flat agricultural land—hardly golfing country. Suddenly, everything changes as Woodhall Spa looms on the horizon like a glorious golfing mirage. Often described as the ultimate golfing oasis, Woodhall Spa has all the classic heathland characteristics—sandy subsoil, heather running riot and glorious tree-lined fairways.

The course measures a lengthy 6921 yards, par 73 from the championship tees, 6501 yards, par 70 from the men's tees and 5731 yards, par 73 from the ladies' tees. It is arguably most renowned for its vast cavernous bunkers and while it is almost impossible to select individual holes, perhaps those that particularly stand out are the 3rd, and a strong sequence towards the middle of the round, between the 9th and the 14th. The 11th is quite possibly the finest par four in the country and certainly one of the prettiest. A plaque beside the 12th tee records how in March 1982 two members halved the hole in one.

Another feature of Woodhall Spa is the remarkable variety of wildlife which the golfer is likely to come across (especially the more wayward hitter!) One hawkish, but obviously dedicated, individual claimed after hitting a rather poor drive to the 18th that he was 'distracted by the merry gathering of partridges and pheasants to the right of the tee and by the squirrel who was chasing a magpie across the fairway.'

Although none of the major professional tournaments has visited the course (primarily a result of its isolation) numerous major amateur events have. These have included the Youths Amateur Championship, the English Amateur Championship and the English Ladies Amateur Championship.

The members are fortunate in having a wonderfully intimate clubhouse. The atmosphere is both friendly and informal and there's an almost Colonial feel about the place—a Raffles in Lincolnshire perhaps? A full complement of catering is offered throughout the week with a variety of very reasonably priced meals.

I referred earlier to the often alarmingly deep bunkers. Apparently a competitor in the 1974 English Amateur Championship, in his endeavours to find the exit to the club, drove his car straight into a huge bunker beside the 4th green. . . .one wonders whether this might have had a little to do with the aforementioned friendly atmosphere to be found at the 19th!

Hole	Yards	Par	Hole	Yards	Par
1	361	4	10	338	4
2	411	4	11	437	4
3	415	4	12	172	3
4	414	4	13	451	4
5	148	3	14	488	5
6	510	5	15	321	4
7	437	4	16	395	4
8	192	3	17	336	4
9	555	5	18	540	5
Out	**3,443**	**36**	**In**	**3,478**	**37**
			Out	**3,443**	**36**
			Totals	**6,921**	**73**

Key

DERBYSHIRE

Alfreton G.C.
(01773) 832070
Wingfield Road, Oakerthorpe
(9) 5074 yards/**/D

Allestree Park G.C.
(01332) 550616
Allestree Hall, Derbyshire
(18) 5749 yards/***/E

Ashbourne G.C.
(01335) 342078
Clifton, Ashbourne
(9) 5359 yards/***/D

Bakewell G.C.
(01629) 812307
Station Road, Bakewell
(9) 5240 yards/**/D

Blue Circle G.C.
(01433) 620317
Cement Works, Hope
(9) 5350 yards/*/B-A/G

Bondhay G. & C.C.
(01909) 723608
Bondhay Lane, Whitwell
(18) 6785 yards/**/C

Breadsall Priory G.& C.C.
(01332) 832235
Moor Road, Morley
(18) 6201 yards/***/B/H
(18) 6028 yards/***/B/H

Burton-on-Trent G.C.
(01283) 544551
Ashby Road East, Burton-On-Trent
(18) 6555 yards/***/B/H/L

Buxton & High Peak G.C.
(01298) 23453
Town End, Buxton
(18) 5954 yards/***/B

Carsington Water
(01629) 85650
Carsington, Wirksworth
(9) 6000 yards/***/F

Cavendish G.C.
(01298) 23494
Gadley Lane, Buxton
(18) 5833 yards/***/B/H

Chapel-en-le-Frith G.C.
(01298) 812118
Manchester Road, Stockport
(18) 6119 yards/***/B

Chesterfield G.C.
(01246) 279256
Walton, Chesterfield
(18) 6326 yards/**/B/H

Chesterfield Municipal G.C.
(01246) 273887
Crow Lane, Chesterfield
(9) 6013 yards/***/E

Chevin G.C.
(01332) 841864
Golf Lane, Duffield
(18) 6057 yards/**/B

Derby G.C.
(01332) 766323
Sinfin, Derby
(18) 6153 yards/***/F

Erewash Valley G.C.
(0115) 932 4667
Stanton-by-Dale, Ilkeston
(18) 6492 yards/**/B/H

Glossop & District G.C.
(01457) 865247
Sheffield Road, Glossop
(18) 5800 yards/***/C

Grassmoor Golf Centre
(01246) 856044
North Wingfield Road, Grassmoor
(18) 5800 yards/***/E

Horsley Lodge G.C.
(01332) 780838
Smalley Mill Road, Horsley
(18) 6434 yards/***/C/H

Ilkeston G.C.
(0115) 930 4550
West End Drive, Ilkeston
(9) 4116 yards/***/E

Kedleston Park G.C.
(01332) 840035
Kedleston, Quarndon, Derby
(18) 6600 yards/***/B/H

Matlock G.C.
(01629) 582191
Chesterfield Road, Matlock
(18) 5800 yards/**/B

Maywood G.C.
(0115) 939 2306
Rushy Lane, Risely
(18) 6424 yards/**/C

Mickleover G.C.
(01332) 518662
Uttoxeter Road, Mickleover
(18) 5708 yards/***/B/H

Morley Hayes G.C.
(01332) 780480
Main Road, Morley
(18) 6800 yards/***/C

New Mills G.C.
(01663) 743485
Shaw Marsh, New Mills
(9) 5633 yards/***/F/G

Ormonde Fields G.& C.C.
(01773) 570043
Nottingham Road, Codnor, Ripley
(18) 6000 yards/***/F

Pastures G.C.
(01332) 521074
Pastures Hospital, Mickleover
(9) 5005 yards/*/F

Shirland G.& C.C.
(01773) 834935
Lower Delves, Shirland
(18) 6072 yards/**/C

Sickleholme G.C.
(01433) 651306
Saltergate Lane, Bamford
(18) 6064 yards/***(Wed am)/B

Stanedge G.C.
(01246) 566156
Walton Hay Farm, Chesterfield
(9) 4867 yards/**(pm)/C

Tapton Park G.C.
(01246) 273887
Murray House, Tapton
(18) 6010 yards/***/F

NOTTINGHAMSHIRE

Beeston Fields G.C.
(0115) 925 7062
Beeston, Nottingham
(18) 6400 yards/***/B/H

Bramcote Hills G.C.
(0115) 928 1880
Thoresby Road, Bramcote
(18) 1500 yards/***/E

Bulwell Forest G.C.
(0115) 977 0576
Hucknall Road, Bulwell
(18) 5746 yards/***/E

Chilwell Manor G.C.
(0115) 925 8958
Meadow Lane, Chilwell
(18) 6379 yards/**/C/H
(18) 5438 yards/***/C/H

College Pines G.C.
(01909) 501431
College Drive, Worksop
(18) 6663 yards/***/D

Cotgrave Place G.& C.C.
(0115) 933 3344
Stragglethorpe, Radcliffe on Trent
(27) 6560 yards/***/C

Coxmoor G.C.
(01623) 557359
Coxmoor Road, Sutton-in-Ashfield
(18) 6501 yards/**/B/H

Edwalton Municipal G.C.
(0115) 923 4775
Wellin Lane, Edwalton
(9)3360 yards/***/E

Kilton Forest G.C.
(01909) 472488
Blyth Road, Worksop
(18) 6600 yards/***(Sun)/E

Lindrick G.C.
(01909) 475282
Lindrick Common, Worksop
(18) 6606 yards/***(winter)/A/H

Mansfield Woodhouse G.C.
(01623) 23521
Leeming Lane, Mansfield Woodhouse
(9) 2446 yards/***/E

Mapperley G.C.
(0115) 926 5611
Mapperley, Nottingham
(18) 6224 yards/***/D/H

Newark G.C.
(01636) 626241
Coddington, Newark
(18) 6421 yards/***/B/H

Nottingham City G.C.
(0115) 927 6916
Bulwell, Nottingham
(18) 6218 yards/**/E

Notts G.C.
(01623) 753225
Hollinwell, Kirkby-in-Ashfield
(18) 7020 yards/**/F/H

Oakmere Park G.C.
(0115) 965 3545
Oaks Lane, Oxton
(18) 6617 yards/***/D
(9) 3495 yards/***/E

Radcliffe-on-Trent G.C.
(0115) 933 3000
Cropwell Road, Radcliffe-on-Trent
(18) 6381 yards/***/B/H

Ramsdale Golf Centre
(0115) 965 5600
Oxton Road, Calverton
(18) 6546 yards/***/D

Retford G.C.
(01777) 703733
Ordsall, Retford
(9) 6301 yards/**/C

Ruddington Grange G.C.
(0115) 921 1951
Wilford Road, Ruddington
(18) 6500 yards/**/D/H

Rufford Park G.C.
(01623) 825253
Rufford Lane, Newark
(18) 5953 yards/***/D
(9) 868 yards/***/E

Rushcliffe G.C.
(01509) 852959
Stocking Lane, East Leake
(18) 6090 yards/***/B

Serlby Park G.C.
(01777) 818268
Serlby
(9) 5325 yards/*/F/G

Sherwood Forest G.C.
(01623) 26689
Eakring Road, Mansfield
(18) 6714 yards/**/F/H

Southwell G.C.
(01636) 816501
Southwell Racecourse, Rolleston
(9) 5500 yards/***/D

Springwater G.C.
(0115) 965 4946
Moor Lane, Calverton
(9) 3203 yards/***/D

Stanton on the Wolds G.C.
(0115) 937 4885
Stanton Lane, Keyworth
(18) 6437 yards/**/B/H

Trent Lock Golf Centre
(0115) 9464398
Lock Lane, Sawley
(18)   /***/E

Wollaton Park G.C.
(0115) 978 7574
Wollaton Park, Nottingham
(18) 6494 yards/***/F

Worksop G.C.
(01909) 477731
Windmill Lane, Worksop
(18) 6651 yards/**/C

LINCOLNSHIRE

Belton Park G.C.
(01476) 567399
Belton Lane, Grantham
(9) 6412 yards/**/B/H
(9) 6109 yards/**/B/H
(9) 5857 yards/**/B/H

Belton Woods Hotel & C.C.
(01476) 593200
(18) 7021 yards/***/B/H
(18) 6875 yards/***/B/H
(9) 1184 yards/***/B/H

Blankney G.C.
(01526) 320263
Blankney, Lincoln
(18) 6402 yards/***/C/H

Boston G.C.
(01205) 350589
Horncastle Road, Boston
(18) 6483 yards/***/C/H

Burghley Park G.C.
(01780) 762100
St Martins, Stamford
(18) 6236 yards/**/C/H/L

Canwick Park G.C.
(01522) 522166
Washingborough Road, Lincoln
(18) 6257 yards/**/D

Carholme G.C.
(01522) 523725
Carholme Road, Lincoln
(18) 6114 yards/**/F

Cleethorpes G.C.
(01472) 812059
Kings Road, Cleethorpes
(18) 6015 yards/***/C

Elsham G.C.
(01652) 680291
Barton Road, Elsham
(18) 6411 yards/**/C/H

Forest Pines G.C.
(01652) 650756
Brigg, Lincs
(18) 6882 yards/***/A

Gainsborough G.C.
(01427) 613088
Thonock, Gainsborough
(18) 6620 yards/**/B/H

Gedney Hill G.C.
(01406) 330922
West Drove, Gedney Hill
(18) 5450 yards/**/E

Grimsby G.C.
(01472) 342630
Littlecoates Road, Grimsby
(18) 6058 yards/***/C/H

Holme Hall G.C.
(01724) 862078
Bottesford Road, Scunthorpe
(18) 6475 yards/**/C/H

Horncastle G.C.
(01507) 526800
West Ashby, Horncastle
(18) 5782 yards/***/D

Immingham G.C.
(01469) 575298
Immingham, Grimsby
(18) 6161 yards/**/D

Kenwick Park G.C.
(01507) 607161
Kenwick Hall, Louth
(18) 6815 yards/***/B/L

Kingsway G.C.
(01724) 840945
Kingsway, Scunthorpe
(9) 1915 yards/***/E

Kirton Holme G.C.
(01205) 290669
Holme Road, Kirton Holme
(9) 2884 yards/***/E

Lincoln G.C.
(01427) 718721
Torksey, Lincoln
(18) 6438 yards/**/C/H

Louth G.C.
(01507) 602554
Crowtree Lane, Louth
(18) 6477 yards/***/C

Manor G.C.
(01472) 873468
Laleby Manor, Grimsby
(9) 3127 yards/***/E

Market Rasen
(01673) 842319
Legsby Road, Market Rasen
(18) 6043 yards/**/C/H/L

Millfield G.C.
(01427) 718255
Laughterton, Lincoln
(18) 5583 yards/***/E
(18) 4300 yards/***/E

Normanby Hall G.C.
(01724) 720226
Normanby Park, Scunthorpe
(18) 6548 yards/***/D

North Shore G.C.
(01754) 763298
North Shore Road, Skegness
(18) 6134 yards/***/F/H

RAF Waddington G.C.
(01552) 720271
Waddington, Lincoln
(18) 5223 yards/***/F

Sandilands G.C.
(01507) 441432
Sea Lane, Sandilands
(18) 5995 yards/***/D

Scunthorpe G.C.
(01724) 866561
Burringham Road, Scunthorpe
(18) 6281 yards/**/C/H/M

Seacroft G.C.
(01754) 763020
Drummond Road, Seacroft
(18) 6501 yards/***/B/H

Sleaford G.C.
(01529) 488273
Willoughby Road, South Rauceby
(18) 6443 yards/**/B/H

South Kyme G.C.
(01526) 861113
Skinners Lane, South Kyme
(18) 6597 yards/***/D

Spalding G.C.
(01775) 680234
Surfleet, Spalding
(18) 6478 yards/***/F/H

Stoke Rochford G.C.
(01476)530275
Great North Road, Grantham
(18) 6251 yards/***/B-A/H

Sudbrook Moor G.C.
(01400) 250796
Charity Lane, Grantham
(9) 4566 yards/***/E

Sutton Bridge G.C.
(01406) 350323
New Road, Sutton Bridge, Spalding
(9) 5804 yards/**/C/H

Woodhall Spa G.C.
(01526) 352511
The Broadway, Woodhall Spa
(18) 6921 yards/***/A/H(20)
(18) 7000 yards/***/B-A

Woodthorpe Hall G.C.
(01507) 450294
Woodthorpe, Alford
(18) 5222 yards/***/E

Artist: **Charles Crombie** **WHAT SHALL I TAKE FOR THIS ?** *Courtesy of:* **Rosenstiel's**

Artist: **Charles Crombie** **THE ONLY WAY** *Courtesy of:* **Rosenstiel's**

Artist: **H. Rountree PERFECTLY PLACED** Courtesy of: **Burlington Gallery**

Staffordshire, Shropshire and Cheshire: three essential-ly rural counties. Staffordshire shares a boundary with the Midlands and Cheshire has two rather ill defined borders with the industrial areas around Manchester and Liverpool. As for Shropshire, it enjoys a splendid peace, broken only perhaps by the mooing of cows and the cries of Fore! from the county's many lush fairways.

Each of the three has a great deal to offer the visiting golfer: in Staffordshire, Beau Desert and Whittington Heath are two of the best (and prettiest) courses in the Midlands; Cheshire offers Carden Park, Tytherington, Mere, Portal and some heathland gems (we have described Hoylake and the Wirral courses in the 'Lancashire' section) while Shropshire, in addition to possessing the likes of Hawkstone Park and Patshull Park can boast at having produced two US Masters champions—both Sandy Lyle and Ian Woosnam who were bred if not born in the county.

Staffordshire
Making a start in Staffordshire, **Whittington Heath** and **Beau Desert** have already been mentioned. The former, located near Lichfield off the A51 was known until recently as Whittington Barracks. As its new name implies, it is a heathland type course with fine views towards the three spires of Lichfield Cathedral—quite possibly the county's toughest challenge. **Beau Desert** Golf Club near Hazel Slade occupies an unlikely setting in the middle of Cannock Chase. Surrounded by fir trees and spruces it also lives up to its name and is quite a haven both for golfers and for wildlife.

After a relaxing day on the golf course, some thoughts for a suitable 19th hole are in order. In Lichfield the Little Barrow Hotel (01543) 414500 is a comfortable hotel for a night's stay and Thrales (01543) 255091 is a particularly good restaurant. The George Hotel (01543) 414822, an old coaching inn, is also recommended. (Note also the new 18 hole pay-and-play course in Lichfield, the charm-ingly named **Seedy Mill.**) After a round at Beau Desert, Rugeley may be the place to head for. Here the Cedar Tree Hotel (01889) 584241 is welcoming but if a restau-rant is sought then nearby Armitage offers the Old Farmhouse (01543) 490353. On the other side of Lichfield, in Tamworth, the Castle Hotel (01827) 57181 is recom-mended.

From the heart of Cannock Chase to the heart of the Potteries, there are a number of courses in and around Stoke-on-Trent. **Trentham** and **Trentham Park**, near neighbours to the south of the city, are both well worth a visit. Each is well wooded and there are many delight-ful views. In Stoke, the North Stafford (01782) 744477, the Stakis (01782) 202361 and the Moat House (01782) 609988 are all large but comfortable hotels, while at Basford, Haydon House (01782) 711311 is more intimate but equally good and worthy of note. However, as the recommended courses are south of the town Stone may be the most convenient place to spend a night. The Stone House (01785) 815531 is particularly comfortable. East of Stoke, the Old Beams (01538) 308254 in Waterhouses is an excellent restaurant with some delightful bedrooms, while in nearby Cauldon the Yew Tree is a superb hostelry. Non golfers and golfers alike will delight in the Wedgwood Visitors Centre which is well worth a visit.

Stafford, the county town, is pretty much in the mid-dle of things. Once again a pair of 18 hole courses to note here: to the south of Stafford is **Brocton Hall** and to the north east, set in the grounds of the former home of the Earl of Shrewsbury is **Ingestre Park**. Both offer a very relaxing game. There is also an enjoyable 9 holer at **Stafford Castle**. If a bed is needed then the De Vere Tillington Hall (01785) 253531 in Stafford is pleasant and, although a bit of a drive away, Rolleston on Dove offers the engaging Brookhouse Hotel (01283) 814188, a splen-didly converted William and Mary building. Those who prefer Georgian architecture may care to consider Dovecliffe Hall (01283) 531818, a delightful restaurant with rooms.

Shropshire
Moving into Shropshire, many will wish to head straight for **Hawkstone Park** (01939) 200611 and its fine hotel. Hawkstone is featured ahead but Shropshire has a lot more than Hawkstone Park on the menu. **Patshull Park** (01902) 700100 makes a marvellous starter, especial-ly considering its closeness to the Midlands—an ideal retreat in fact. As at Hawkstone, golf is played amid very peaceful and picturesque surroundings and overnight accommodation is immediately at hand. The delightful setting of Patshull Park owes much to the fact that the land was originally landscaped by 'Capability' Brown.

Shrewsbury is a pleasant county town with many charming half-timbered buildings. **Shrewsbury** Golf Club is situated about five miles from the town centre off the A49. It is an interesting course with a railway track run-ning through the middle. The Prince Rupert Hotel (01743) 499955 in Shrewsbury is good value for an overnight stay and the oak beams and sloping floors add to the character. Fieldside Hotel (01743) 353143 has no pretensions to grandeur but is extremely comfort-able.

Travelling a little further down the A49 into southern Shropshire, **Church Stretton**, set amidst the Long Mynd Hills is well worth a visit. Not the longest course in Britain but one that offers quite outstanding views. Mynd House (01694) 722212 is an exceptionally welcom-ing establishment to head for but the Belvedere Guest House (01694) 722232 can also be recommended and those needing to quench their thirst might note the Royal Oak in Cardington (some accommodation also).

The largest town in Shropshire is Telford. It's a strange mixture of the old and the new: a modern centre yet sur-rounded by a considerable amount of history—Brunel's famous Ironbridge is here. The popular **Telford Hotel** Golf and Country Club (01952) 429977 is situated near to the Ironbridge Gorge, high above it in fact, and is easily accessi-ble from the M54 (junction 4 or 5). Full leisure facilities are offered at the hotel. Further south of Telford, towards Bridgnorth, **Lilleshall Hall** offers a very pleasant round with two nicely contrasting nines. The Hundred House Hotel (01952) 730353 is a charming Georgian inn with a first rate restaurant—an excellent choice.

To the east of Telford, **Shifnal** Golf Club is set in a glo-rious park and an old manor house serves as an impres-sive clubhouse. The Park House Hotel (01952) 460128 in Shifnal is an excellent place for a stopover and the hotel's restaurant, the Idsall Rooms is particularly good.

In the middle of Shropshire, **Bridgnorth** is one of the oldest and longest courses in the county (note the distin-guished Haywain Restaurant (01746) 780404 at Hampton Loade) and in the far south is historic **Ludlow**. It's now a fairly quiet market town but in former times was the capital of the West Marches. The golf course takes you around the town's racecourse—or is it vice versa?—Anyway, it's an interesting challenge and if a round of golf is being combined with a weekend's racing, the

Feathers (01584) 875261 in Ludlow provides an ideal place in which to relax—note the outstanding Jacobean facade. In Brimfield, near Ludlow, you might stop at the Roebuck (01584) 872230—the adjoining restaurant, Poppies (01584) 711230 is outstanding. Not too great a distance from Ludlow is Hopton Wafers where the Crown offers some first rate cooking and a fine drop of ale. A final thought, consider Dinham Hall (01584) 876464 a superb hotel.

To the north west of Shropshire three courses are recommended. **Oswestry** is one clearly to seek out—if only because this is where Ian Woosnam relaxes. Note the popular Wynnstay Hotel (01691) 655261 in town. Close to the Welsh border, **Llanymynech** (Woosie's first course) lies on high ground and is very scenic. On the 4th hole you stand on the tee in Wales and drive into England (always good for the ego). After a game here, a visit to the Bradford Arms (01691) 830582 in Llanymynech is essential as it boasts a particularly fine restaurant.

Still high in the hills another 'Llany', not Wadkins but Blodwel: Llanyblodwel is where excellent refreshment can be found—the Horseshoe, with its spectacular setting. The third recommendation, **Hill Valley** near Whitchurch, brings us down to earth. We may get wet as well with water affecting many holes on this fairly new American-style course. As well as the water there are many other challenges and it's well worth inspecting. Terrick Hall Hotel (01948) 663031 is practically adjacent to the course and in Whitchurch itself there is Dearnford Hall (01948) 662319, another fine hotel. At Weston-under Redcastle you will find **Hawkstone Park** (featured ahead) where there is also an excellent hotel (01939) 200611.

Cheshire

Cheshire could be described as the 'Surrey of the North'. In many parts it's decidedly affluent, with a great band of commuter towns lining its northern fringes. There's also a sand belt where heathland golf is found—no Sunningdale here perhaps but **Delamere Forest** and **Sandiway** would certainly be at home in either Surrey or Berkshire. Delamere is particularly good. A creation of Herbert Fowler, who also designed Walton Heath and The Berkshire, it's a marvellous heather and gorse type course—some superb trees also. The words 'temporary green' do not exist at Delamere Forest (something winter golfers might wish to bear in mind) nor apparently does the word 'par'—the old fashioned term 'bogey' being preferred as a more realistic yardstick of a hole's difficulty—at least for the non-pro.

There are a number of first class places in which to stay in the area but pride of place must go to Rookery Hall (01270) 610016 in Worleston near Nantwich. Part Georgian, part Victorian, it's a wonderful hotel with a restaurant to match. Nantwich also offers the reasonably priced Burland Farmhouse (01270) 74210. Nearer to Sandiway in Hartford, Hartford Hall (01606) 75711 is very pleasant, and in Sandiway itself Nunsmere Hall (01606) 889100 is very convenient and comfortable. In Acton Bridge the Rheingold Riverside Inn (01606) 852310 offers some really stylish food. Finally, a handy pub for Delamere is the Ring of Bells at Overton.

Mere is certainly one of the leading courses in Cheshire. Although fairly close to Sandiway and Delamere, Mere is a classic parkland course, and a beautiful one too with a testing closing stretch including the spectacular par five 18th, where a new green has been built on the edge of a small lake. After eagling the 18th at Mere the perfect place for celebration is in Lower Peeover at the Bells of Peeover (01565) 722269 (pronounced 'Peever' I'm assured). Cottons Hotel (01565) 650333 has a good local reputation and is also well placed.

The area around Wilmslow is fairly thick with clubs. **Wilmslow** itself and **Prestbury** have two of the better courses. For many years the former was the venue of the Greater Manchester Open. Both are extremely well kept. The popular Stanneylands Hotel (01625) 525225 at Wilmslow is convenient for both courses although again there are many fine hotels nearby to choose from, one strong recommendation being **Mottram Hall** (01625) 828135 at Mottram St Andrews—quite magnificent. The hotel now boasts a challenging 18 hole course, designed in fine style by Dave Thomas.

Stockport provides a dramatic contrast to rural Cheshire—not the prettiest of places perhaps but full of character. Offerton is where **Stockport** Golf Club is found. It's a good test and well worth visiting; so for that matter are the two courses at Bramhall, **Bramhall** and **Bramhall Park**. **Macclesfield's** course offers some extensive views and between Macclesfield and Prestbury is the fairly new, but highly acclaimed **Tytherington** Club. Shrigley Hall (01625) 575757 in Pott Shrigley, again near to both Prestbury and Macclesfield, has another newish golf course in a wonderful setting with views over the Cheshire Plain. Well situated for these courses is the Alderley Edge Hotel (01625) 583033 which offers some excellent food as well as first class accommodation.

Over to the far east of Cheshire, close to the Derbyshire border and the splendid Peak District is **Chapel-en-le-Frith**. A really friendly club, this and some enjoyable golf too. From the far east to the far west, Chester demands inspection—a fascinating Roman city with all manner of attractions. Two of the best places to swing a club are at Upton, namely the delightful **Upton-by-Chester** Golf Club and at **Eaton**, a parkland course to the south of the city. Just 15 minutes drive from Chester an impressive Golf and Leisure Complex opened in 1994 at **Carden Park** (01829) 73100. The hotel offers first class facilities and is thoroughly recommended.

If staying in Chester, the best hotel is the Chester Grosvenor (01244) 324024 (note the superb restaurant). Hoole Hall Hotel (01244) 350011 on the Warrington Road is less grand but is good. An interesting alternative though is the Blossoms Hotel (01244) 323186. Crabwall Manor (01244) 851666 is also outstanding in every way.

South east of Chester near Tarporley much has been happening. The **Portal** Golf and Country Club comprises 45 holes and, along with Hawkstone Park and Carden Park is explored separately in this chapter. Strongly recommended for golfers visiting Portal are the Wild Boar at Beeston (01829) 260305 a 17th century part-timbered house and the Swan Hotel in Tarporley (01829) 733838.

In the middle of the county, **Crewe** offers a pleasant 18 holes and back towards the north of the region, **Ringway** Golf Club is a good parkland challenge, but our final visit takes us to the end of a very leafy lane in Altrincham—the impressive **Dunham Forest** Golf and Country Club. Only two miles from the M56 (junction 7) and not all that far from the whirl of Manchester it nonetheless delights in an incredibly tranquil setting. The beautifully mature tree-lined fairways are a sheer delight to play on and if you cannot enjoy your golf here, well, let's just say you've got problems! The Bowdon Hotel (0161) 9287121 is a suitably relaxed establishment in which to ponder on your game.

Shaw Hill Hotel, Golf & Country Club

Standing amidst trees, lakes, streams and acres of well manicured grassland Shaw Hill is just what you want it to be. If you are seeking the tranquillity and comfort of a superbly appointed country house hotel, then that's what it is. It boasts its own demanding championship course and is the perfect venue for a sporting break. Yet is is ideally equipped for private functions and business conventions of every variety and scale. A magnificent Georgian mansion tastefully refurbished and enhanced to offer the highest level of hospitality, Shaw Hill offers everything you wish from a comfortable and welcoming hotel—only more so.

In tune with international standard of accommodation, all guest rooms are fully equipped with an en suite bath or shower, colour television and direct dial telephone.

The award-winning Vardons Restaurant enjoys an excellent reputation amongst the neighbouring community—for its delicious cuisine, extensive wine cellar and delightful setting. For drinks before and after your meal, you might venture into the Visitors Bar, a relaxed and informal lounge where light refreshments are also served.

Shaw Hill's various function rooms lend themselves admirably to private parties, wedding receptions, dinner dances, board meetings, business seminars and sales conferences. The new leisure complex provides excellent facilities for the energetic and the grounds extend the permutations still further, with scope for marqueed exhibitions and receptions, product demonstrations, golf tournaments and inspiring photographic sessions. Naturally, the hotel also accommodates every catering requirements, from canapés to banquets.

Visit Shaw Hill on a golf weekend and you are guaranteed a complimentary round each day, weather permitting, with the others at a modest additional cost. During the week these superb facilities are also available for corporate golfing days and sponsored pro-am tournaments.

Shaw Hill Hotel, Golf & Country Club
Whittle-le-Woods
Nr Chorley
Lancashire
PR6 7PP
Tel: (01257) 269221
Fax: (01257) 261223

Portal

Americans who are apt to drool at English country houses, their grounds and gardens, should head for Tarporley in Cheshire; and English golfers who believe that the only good courses being built nowadays are 'American style' designs should go with them. Portal Hall in Tarporley is the kind of dwelling that would grace the front cover of *Country Life* magazine: the house is splendid and the gardens resplendent. Adjacent to Portal Hall is the Portal Golf and Country Club and possibly the finest new golf course in the north of England.

Many of the courses constructed in Britain during the last decade tend to be either very average (due usually to the poor quality of the site or terrain) or very American—and, as somebody once remarked, there's nothing wrong with American golf courses . . . in America! The reality is that Britain doesn't have America's climate and unless there is a vast amount of money behind a project to build such a course then achieving and maintaining the standard of conditioning required is unlikely to happen. (Interestingly, how many attempts to build a Scottish style golf links in North America have succeeded?) Portal is different and very special.

Like many golf clubs, it owes its existence to the dream and ambition of one man. John Lilley was the guiding force behind the creation of Portal and while he lived to see its opening (June 1991) he is no longer with us to enjoy its success. Portal is his gift to golf. The new owners, under the enthusiastic direction of Chairman, Michael Taylor are determined to enhance this legacy. The club has recently acquired and now manages the former Oaklands Golf and Country Club which is situated just half a mile away. Thus Portal now comprises the original 18 hole Portal Course, now called the **Portal Championship** course and the former Oaklands course which has been renamed **Portal Premier**. A further nine hole course, the **Arderne**, is located close to the Portal Championship layout, so providing the complex with a total of 45 holes. A large indoor golf academy beside the Arderne course offers driving bays, chipping lanes, contoured putting greens and a unique practice bunker facility, along with the latest computerised teaching equipment. The Championship course also has an outdoor driving range and a new all-weather synthetic putting green. Plans are in hand to add a 50-bedroom facility and a leisure centre.

Individual visitors and corporate and society visitors who wish to play at the Portal Championship Course can make bookings by contacting the **Director of Golf, David Wills** on **(01829) 733933** or fax (01829) 733928. Those wishing to visit Portal Premier should telephone **Keith Brain** on **(01829) 733884**. The green fees in 1998 are £40 per round (7 days a week) for the Portal Championship course with £30 per round on weekdays and £35 at weekends on the Portal Premier course.

Portal Championship Course was designed by British architect Donald Steel. Steel considers it to be one of his best and he is justifiably very proud of his work. As you may have gathered from the preceding comments, he has not tried to fashion an American-style course amidst this very natural and very English parkland setting. There are no Nicklaus-style mounds at Portal, and Steel has no Trent Jones-like obsession with long water carries. There are, however, plenty of sweeping elevational changes—some are dramatic as at the 4th, 16th and 17th and some more subtle, as at the 2nd, 3rd, and 6ththere is also a huge variety of mature trees, as well as lakes and ponds, but they are not designed to terrify. Indeed the purpose behind their placement is as much visual as strategic.

The visual pleasure aspect is of course where Portal gains a significant advantage over most new designs. There are many strong and challenging holes—the course measures well over 7000 yards from the championship tees but it is the stunning beauty of two in particular, the par three 14th and par five 3rd that are likely to leave the most lasting impression after a visit to Portal. Stand on the stage-like green at the short 14th and you feel surrounded by cascading ponds, stately trees and rhododendron bushes—golf landscaping at its best. Stand on the tee at the long 3rd with its rockery banks of heather and shock of flowers and your mind may wander from golf to horticulture. Dangerous, as there are 600 yards of fairway and hazards to negotiate!

The 19th hole is the final treat at Portal—the clubhouse is an extraordinary circular building; its unusual design apparently reflects the turrets of nearby Beeston and Peckforton castles. In character with the whole set-up the facilities inside are first class and the atmosphere is relaxed and informal.

Portal (Championship Course)

Hole	Yards	Par	Hole	Yards	Par
1	374	4	10	501	5
2	342	4	11	433	4
3	602	5	12	520	5
4	545	5	13	395	4
5	215	3	14	135	3
6	365	4	15	422	4
7	392	4	16	189	3
8	402	4	17	437	4
9	355	4	18	413	4
Out	**3,592**	**37**	**In**	**3,445**	**36**
			Out	**3,592**	**36**
			Totals	**7,037**	**73**

The Donald Steel Championship Course, acclaimed as "Golf Course of the Year" by *Following the Fairways (1995)* is now established as one of Northern Europe's finest courses. Steel has worked on many projects, both in this country and overseas, but he regards the layout at Portal as perhaps his most accomplished work.

Portal exudes quality; a strikingly modern, yet very elegant clubhouse and a truly first rate golf course set in the scenic heartland of Cheshire with breathtaking panoramic views.

The Championship course offers 18 holes from prairie-like open fairways to elegant wooded greens. In addition there is the 9 hole Arderne Course (a test for the most skilful) the largest indoor golf academy in the UK, with golf shows, clinics and video facilities, an outdoor driving range and an extensive all-weather putting green.

The course is superbly landscaped and presented with countless flower beds, banks of heather and rockeries around trees and greens. The lakes and ponds are not merely water hazards - they are works of art with a special feature being the dramatic cascading waterfall and rock garden forming the backdrop of the 18th hole.

There are many strong and challenging holes. The course measures over 7000 yards from the Championship tees but it is the stunning beauty of two in particular—the par three

14th and par five 3rd—that are likely to leave the most lasting impression after a visit to Portal.

The 19th hole is the final treat. The clubhouse is an extraordinary circular building, its unusual design reflecting the turrets of nearby Beeston and Peckforton castles. The facilities are excellent and the atmosphere relaxed and informal. The clubhouse offers well appointed bar and dining areas with private visitors and banqueting rooms available providing first class catering and hospitality for both small and large groups.

Portal has established a reputation for having the highest standard of presentation and service in the North West of England. A team of experienced professionals and staff can organise your day from start to finish involving pre-match planning, game formats, reception, tournaments controllers, starter and the provision of unique prizes and trophies. Other features include catering before, during (via on course catering or halfway house) and after play, a large fleet of buggies, spacious wood-panelled locker rooms with private facilities and cars and golf clubs on request.

As a corporate, society or individual visitor to Portal, you will enjoy a day to remember in an ideal atmosphere in which to develop friendships, positive relationships and create business potential. In fact, Portal exudes more than quality and character - it has style. Golf in this country has waited a long time for a club and course like Portal.

Portal Golf & Country Club
Cobblers Cross Lane
Tarporley
Cheshire CW6 0DJ
Tel: (01829) 733933
Fax: (01829) 733928

Even a fairly detailed map is unlikely to show Weston-under-Redcastle, but ask a golfer for the location and it is possible he will direct you there blindfolded! The Hawkstone Park complex is set in an exquisite 400 acre north Shropshire estate and is more than just a golfer's paradise. It features two 18 hole golf courses, a six hole academy course and a range of practice facilities aimed at golfers of all standards. A purpose built golf centre has been recently opened with an excellent indoor swing analysis facility. There is also a large golf/leisure retail shop.

The 65 bedroom (en suite) hotel, classified by the English Tourist Board as 'highly recommended', is a chip shot from the course and is steeped in history. it was built as an elegant and spacious hostelry in 1790, then known as the Hawkstone Inn, to cater for visitors to one of Britain's original 18th century walking centres, now designated by English Heritage as a grade 1 landscape. The hotel today provides banqueting suite facilities for up to 200 persons and has been successful in attaining its share of the business meeting/conference market. The hotel's traditional dining room offers a table d'hote menu whilst the Terrace restaurant and bar on the top floor of the new Golf Centre offers golfers snacks and meals all day. Views of both courses can be enjoyed from the Terrace.

Also situated on the estate is the famous Historical Park and Follies. Recently restored, this unique feature allows residents and visitors the experience of breathtaking cliff walks, viewing sites of historical interest which include the famous grottos, Swiss Bridge, Monument, Gingerbread Hall and the modern day hermitage The entrance to the Historic Park and Follies provides a cafeteria, gift shop, interpretation centre and classroom facility.

Hawkstone Park Hotel & Golf Courses
Weston-under-Redcastle
Shropshire SY4 5UY
Tel: (01939) 200611
Fax: (01939) 200311 Fax Reservations: (01939) 200335

The Hawkstone Course was opened in 1920 and is built around the 12th century Red Castle, believed to be part of the King Arthur legend. The course underwent some minor alterations by James Braid in the late 1920s and has remained largely unchanged from that time. Accuracy rather than length is the key to producing a good score and is rewarding for golfers of all standards. The full length of the course from the championship tees is 6491 yards and has a par of 72. Many of the fairways are lined with oak and birch trees with breathtaking views on the 10th and 11th holes.

The Windmill Course was designed by former Ryder Cup captain and player, Brian Huggett. The grand opening of this course was on 1st May, 1995, exactly 75 years to the day that the Hawkstone Course was opened. In sharp contrast to the Hawkstone Course, the Windmill has many American style features such as round and oval tees, fairways lined with uniform mounds and large, gently undulating greens. The use of water is extensive with many challenging shots over water, if the golfer

wishes to take the risk. Like the Hawkstone Course, the Windmill has been designed with the emphasis on strategic play, rather than length. Off the championship tees the course measures 6764 yards with a par of 72.

Golf Facilities: Along with the golf courses, Hawkstone offers a variety of game improvement facilities for golfers of all standards. There are extensive practice facilities covering all aspects of the game and there is no doubt about the centrepiece attraction - an indoor swing analysis room which incorporates the latest in video/computer technology. This facility is one of the most advanced in Europe and provides a golfer with a tremendous insight into his or her swing. There is also a team of PGA qualified professionals on site who provide a comprehensive service to club members, hotel residents and visitors alike. For beginners or for those golfers who only want to play just a few holes, there is a six hole academy course, set in a beautiful silver birch wood.

Hawkstone Park

What is a man to do when his two daughters, his pride and joy, tell him that they wish to leave home? Well, such was the dilemma facing a certain Sir William Gray in 1921. His solution you might think was an admirable one—he promised to build them a golf course. For two young ladies much bitten by the bug it proved irresistible—clearly bribery of the highest calibre. In 1921 the ingenious Sir William owned Hawkstone Park, and the golf course, the subject of this tale, grew from an original nine holes to the present day Hawkstone Course.

Today probably every golfer from Land's End to John O'Groats has heard of Hawkstone Park—not because of the 'golfing Grays', but thanks to one Sandy Lyle, Open Champion of 1985 and US Masters Champion of 1988. Sandy's association with Hawkstone Park has been life-long. Whilst there is probably no truth in the rumour that he was born adjacent to the first tee he certainly grew up nearby. For many years his father Alex served as club professional and in every sense it was here that Sandy learnt his game.

Hawkstone Park is, of course, much more than the birthplace of Sandy Lyle. Today there are two 18 hole courses, the well established **Hawkstone** and the newer **Windmill** Course (built in the main over the former Weston Course which was completely redesigned and extended). Both are set in the beautiful grounds of the Hawkstone Park Hotel. A 6 hole academy course completes the picture.

The hotel itself is certainly a grand affair. In a guide book of 1824 it was described as 'more like the seat of a nobleman than an hotel' and the grounds are not only exceptionally beautiful—exotic plants and flowers abound—but are also steeped in history and legend. The hotel runs the golf courses and other than an early morning tee reservation for residents there are no general restrictions on visitors, but starting times must be pre-booked. This can be done by telephoning the **Golf Centre** on **(01939) 200611**, fax: (01939) 200311. Green fees in 1998 vary with the season. For winter months the rates are £16 midweek and £21.50 at weekends. The equivalent summer rates are £28 and £36. Those wishing to play 27 or 36 holes will be charged £42 during the week and £50 at weekends.

In summer there is a special twilight rate after 5.00 pm of £14 on weekdays and £18 at weekends. Parties of twelve or more are deemed to be golfing societies, subject again to making prior arrangements. They are equally welcome and written applications may be made in writing to **Golf Reservations** at **The Golf Centre, Hawkstone Park Hotel, Weston-under-Redcastle, Nr Shrewsbury SY4 5UY.**

It has been said that one of the reasons for Hawkstone Park enjoying such a delightfully peaceful setting is that it is 'miles from anywhere'—not strictly true: it is only seven miles south of Whitchurch, or if you prefer, twelve miles north of Shrewsbury, and is easily accessible. The A49 is the best route when approaching from either of these towns. Shrewsbury itself is linked to the West Midlands by way of the M54 and the A5, while those motoring from the north will find the M6 of assistance.

I mentioned that all 18 holes of the Windmill course were in play by April 1995—in fact, a great deal has been happening of late at Hawkstone Park. The aforementioned 'Golf Centre' is itself a new building and serves as a very modern three-tiered clubhouse, one where traditional 19th hole facilities are supplemented by a state of the art teaching academy run by the **Head Professional, Paul Wesselingh**.

Brian Huggett is the architect responsible for completely reshaping the old Weston Course and while that was a fairly modest affair, the Windmill Course measures some 6476 yards and features a series of dramatic holes where the golfer must confront do-or-die shots over and along-side water. It provides a great contrast and complement to the celebrated challenges of the Hawkstone Course. A recent visit in February when a day of beauty was stolen from May's calendar found both courses in amazing condition for the time of year.

The hotel and golf course complex provides comprehensive facilities for golf meetings at a corporate or local level. A wide range of good value golfing breaks is offered throughout the year and many golfers regularly travel great distances to sample the delights of this Shropshire golfing paradise. It's all come a long way since the days of Sir William Gray and his golf-mad daughters, but one suspects that they would approve.

Hawkstone Course

Hole	Yards	Par	Hole	Yards	Par
1	374	4	10	517	5
2	402	4	11	438	4
3	216	3	12	145	3
4	332	4	13	373	4
5	371	4	14	485	5
6	364	4	15	315	4
7	434	4	16	256	4
8	481	5	17	383	4
9	188	3	18	417	4
Out	**3,162**	**35**	**In**	**3,329**	**37**
			Out	3,162	35
			Totals	6,491	72

Carden Park

As you meander along the drive and see the deer herd grazing on the estate you will be struck by the wonderful views of the surrounding Cheshire country-side. Then as you look out across the lake on the 17th hole of the Nicklaus course you will get views of a truly outstanding 19th hole—the l;uxurious Carden Park Hotel.

Carden Park, a 750 acre estate that dates back to the 17th century is situated in the heart of Cheshire, has recently undergone a major transformation and is surely destined to become one of Europe's leading golf resorts.

With the help and guidance of Jack Nicklaus and Golden Bear International, a comprehensive range of quality golf facilities has been created to cater for the needs of all golfers—from complete beginners to scratch players.

This includes two 18 hole courses—the **Cheshire** Course and the new **Nicklaus** Course, designed by Jack and his son Steve. There is also the par 3 **Azalea** Course, a magnificent clubhouse and Europe's first Jack Nicklaus Residential Golf School.

The 6850 yards, par 72 Cheshire Course, which opened in 1993 is a stern but fair test of golf from the back tees and has played host to several championships, including the Cheshire and North Wales Open.

In 1996, in consultation with Nicklaus Design, the lay-out was revised. Now even mere mortals are assured of a thoroughly enjoyable game on this course with its wonderful mix of open parkland, feature bunkers, water, coniferous forest and a sandstone cliff. It has an interesting combination of long and short par 3s, par 4s from 360 to 470 yards, a short par 5 on which many will hope for a birdie, and three other par 5s that are real testers.

However, the jewel in the crown at Carden is the 7070 yards, par 72 Nicklaus Course, the first co-design between Jack and his son Steve, which incorporates several challenging water features and has been designed to be enjoyable for golfers of all levels of ability.

Built to the highest standards and described by Jack Nicklaus as "a thinking man's golf course", it incorporates several double option holes, such as the 7th and the 15th, where, because of the positioning of the hazards, golfers will have to choose which fairway it is best to attack the green from. As the Golden Bear said, "Players will have to really think about what they are going to do next."

In addition to this the Jack Nicklaus Residential Golf School caters for the needs of golfers at all skill levels. The philosophy, developed by Jack and his personal coach Jim Flick, is simply to help golfers play to their full potential, consistently, so that they can derive a lot more pleasure on the golf course. Courses at the school range from one to three days, and most include tuition and time for playing golf each day.

Adjacent to the first tees of the Nicklaus and Cheshire courses is the spacious two-storey clubhouse, which provides a range of excellent facilities. The ground floor supplies well appointed locker rooms with adjoining relaxation areas and an extensive golf shop. On the first floor you will find the club bar and lounge, dining room and private suites, all with verandas offering stunning views over the golf courses and the Welsh hills.

The luxurious hotel with its superb selection of 192 bedrooms and suites provides an excellent complement to the golf course's. There are a number of places to eat and the visitor can also enjoy a superbly equipped health spa and a host of other leisure activities. The estate even boasts its own vineyard!

Whatever your reason for visiting Carden Park, be it business or pleasure, you will quickly realise that you have arrived at a very special place.

Carden Park Hotel, Golf Resort & Spa, Carden, Broxton, Nr Chester CH3 9DQ

Professional	David Llewllyn (01829) 731600
Green Fees	£60 per round
Restrictions	Must have a current handicap certificate

Directions
Taking junction 20 off the M6 towards Chester, then turn off on to the A41. Follow the A41 till you reach the Broxton roundabout, head towards Wrexham and after 2 miles you will find Carden Park on your left.

Key

*To avoid disappointment
it is advisable to telephone
in advance*

***Visitors welcome at most times*
**Visitors usually allowed on*
weekdays only
*'Visitors not normally permitted
(Mon, Wed) No visitors
on specified days*

Approximate Green Fees
A   £40 plus
B   £25 to £40
C   £20 to £30
D   £15 to £25
E   under £15
F   Green fees on application

Restrictions
G   Guests only
H—Handicap certificate required
H—(24) Handicap of 24 or less
L —Letter of introduction required
M—Visitor must be a member of
another recognised club

STAFFORDSHIRE

Alsager G.& C.C.
(01270) 875700
Andley Road, Stoke-on-Trent
(18) 6206 yards/**/C/M

Barlaston G.C.
(01782) 372795
Meaford Road, Barlaston, Stone
(18) 5800 yards/**/C

Beau Desert G.C.
(01543) 422626
Hazelslade, Hednesford, Cannock
(18) 6300 yards/***/A/H

Branston G. & C.C.
(01283) 512211
Burton Road, Branston
(18) 6541 yards/**/C

Brocton Hall G.C.
(01785) 661901
Brocton
(18) 6095 yards/***/B/H/L

Burslem G.C.
(01782) 837006
Wood Farm, High Lane, Tunstall
(9) 5354 yards/**/D

Burton upon Trent G.C.
(01283) 568708
Ashby Road East, Burton-upon-Trent
(18) 6555 yards/***/B/H/L/M

Cannock Park G.C.
(01543) 578850
Stafford Road, Cannock
(18) 4559 yards/***/E

The Craythorne G.C.
(01283) 564329
Craythorne Road, Stretton
(18) 5230 yards/***/D/H

Drayton Park G.C.
(01827) 251139
Drayton Park, Tamworth
(18) 6414 yards/**/B/H

Enville G.C.
(01384) 872074
Highgate Common, Kinver
(18) 6217 yards/**/B/H

Golden Hill G.C.
(01782) 234200
Golden Hill, Stoke-on-Trent
(18) 5957 yards/***/E

Greenway Hall G.C.
(01782) 503158
Stockton Brook, Stoke-on-Trent
(18) 5676 yards/**/E

Himley Hall G.C.
(01902) 895207
School Road, Himley
(9) 3125 yards/**/F

Ingestre Park G.C.
(01889) 270845
Ingestre, Stafford
(18) 6334 yards/**/B/H

Izaak Walton G.C.
(01785) 760900
Cold Norton, Stone
(18) 6281 yards/***/D/H

Lakeside G.C.
(01889) 575667
Rugeley Power Station, Rugeley
(18) 5534 yards/*/F/G

Leek G.C.
(01538) 384779
Cheddleton Road, Leek
(18) 6240 yards/**/B/H

Manor Kingstone G.C.
(01889) 563234
Leese Hill, Kingstone, Uttoxeter
(9) 3523 yards/***/D

Meadow Vale G.C.
(01785) 760900
Cold Norton, Stone
(18) 6500 yards/***/C

Newcastle Municipal G.C.
(01782) 627596
Keele Road, Newcastle-under-Lyme
(18) 6256 yards/***/E

Newcastle-under-Lyme G.C.
(01782) 616583
Whitmore Road
(18) 6427 yards/**/B/H

Parkhall G.C.
(01782) 599584
Holme Road, Weston Coyney
(18) 2335 yards/***/E

St Thomas's Priory
(01534) 491116
Armitage, Lichfield
(18) 6637 yards/*/G

Seedy Mill G.C.
(01543) 417333
Elmshurst, Lichfield
(18) 6247 yards/***/F/H

Stafford Castle G.C.
(01785) 223521
Newport Road, Stafford
(9) 6347 yards/**/D

Stone G.C.
(01785) 813103
Filley Brooks, Stone
(9) 6299 yards/**/C

Tamworth G.C.
(01827) 53850
Eagle Drive, Tamworth
(18) 6695 yards/***/F

Trentham G.C.
(01782) 658309
Barlaston Road, Trentham
(18) 6644 yards/**/B/H

Trentham Park G.C.
(01782) 658800
Trentham Park, Trentham
(18) 6403 yards/**/B/H

Uttoxeter G.C.
(01889) 564884
Wood Lane, Uttoxeter
(18) 5468 yards/***/D

Westwood G.C.
(01538) 398385
Newcastle Road, Wallbridge, Leek
(18) 6156 yards/**/C

Whiston Hall G.C.
(01538) 266260
Whiston Cheadle
(18) 5724 yards/***/D

Whittington Heath G.C.
(01543) 432212
Tamworth Road, Lichfield
(18) 6457 yards/**/A/H

Wolstanton G.C.
(01782) 622413
Dimsdale Old Hall, Hassam Parade
(18) 5807 yards/**/C/H

SHROPSHIRE

Arscott G.C.
(01743) 860114
Arscott, Pontesbury
(18) 6035 yards/**/C

Bridgnorth G.C.
(01746) 763315
Stanley Lane, Bridgnorth
(18) 6668 yards/***/C

Chesterton Valley G.C.
(01476) 783682
Worfield, Bridgnorth
(9) 3392 yards/***/E

Church Stretton G.C.
(01694) 722281
Trevor Hill, Church Stretton
(18) 5008 yards/**/D/H

Hawkstone Park Hotel G.C.
(01939) 200611
Weston-under-Redcastle
(18) 6465 yards/***/B/H
(18) 6655 yards/***/B/H

Hill Valley G.& C.C.
(01948) 663584
Terrick Road, Whitchurch
(18) 6517 yards/***/C
(18) 5285 yards/***/C

Lilleshall Hall G.C.
(01952) 604104
Lilleshall, Newport
(18) 5906 yards/***/C/H

Llanymynech G.C.
(01691) 830542
Pant, Oswestry
(18) 6114 yards/**/D/H

Ludlow G.C.
(01584) 77285
Bromfield, Ludlow
(18) 6239 yards/***/C/H

Market Drayton G.C.
(01630) 652266
Sutton, Market Drayton
(18) 6214 yards/**/C

Meole Brace G.C.
(01743) 364050
Meole Brace, Shrewsbury
(12) 5830 yards/***/F

Mile End G.C.
(01691) 671246
Mile End, Oswestry
(9) 6136 yards/***/D

Oswestry G.C.
(01691) 610448
Aston Park, Oswestry
(18) 6046 yards/***/C/H/M

Patshull Park Hotel & G.C.
(01902) 700100
Nr Wolverhampton
(18) 6400 yards/***/B/H

Severn Meadows G.C.
(01746) 862212
Highley, Bridgnorth
(9) 2520 yards/***/E

Shifnal G.C.
(01952) 460467
Decker Hill, Shifnal
(18) 6422 yards/**/C/H/L

Shrewsbury G.C.
(01743) 872976
Condover, Shrewsbury
(18) 6212 yards/***/C/H

The Shropshire G.C.
(01952) 677866
Muxton Grange, Telford
(9) 3286 yards/***/D
(9) 3303 yards/***/D
(9) 3334 yards/***/D

Telford Moat House G.& C.C.
(01952) 429977
Great Hay, Telford
(18) 6766 yards/***/B/H

Welsh Border G.C.
(01734) 884247
Middletown, Welshpool
(9) 3250 yards/***/F

Worfield G.C.
(01746) 716541
Worfield, Bridgnorth
(18) 6801 yards/***/C

Wrekin G.C.
(01952) 244032
Ercall Woods, Wellington, Telford
(18) 5657 yards/**/C

CHESHIRE

Alder Root G.C.
(01925) 291919
Alder Root Lane, Winwick
(9) 5564 yards/***/C

Alderley Edge G.C.
(01565) 872385
Brook Lane, Alderley Edge
(9) 5839 yards/***/C/H/G

Alvaston Hall G.C.
(01270) 624341
Middlewich Road, Nantwich
(9) 1806 yards/***/E

Astbury G.C.
(01260) 272772
Peel Lane, Astbury, Congleton
(18) 6277 yards/**/B/H/G

Birchwood G.C.
(01925) 818819
Kelvin Close, Risley, Warrington
(18) 6808 yards/***/C/H

Carden Park G.C.
(01829) 731199
Carden, Tilston, Chester
(18) 6828 yards/***/B/H
(18) 7070yards/***/B/H

Chapel-en-le-Frith G.C
(01298) 812118
Manchester Road, Stockport
(18) 6119 yards/***/B

Cheadle G.C.
(0161) 4282160
Shiers Drive, Cheadle
(9) 5006 yards/(*** D/H-L

Chester G.C.
(01244) 677760
Curzon Park North, Chester
(18) 6487 yards/**/B/H

Congleton G.C.
(01260) 273540
Biddulph Road, Congleton
(18) 5103 yards/***/D

Crewe G.C.
(01270) 584099
Fields Road, Haslington, Crewe
(18) 6259 yards/**/B/H

Davenport G.C.
(01625) 876951
Middlewood Road, Higher
Poynton
(18) 6066 yards/**/B/H

Delamere Forest G.C.
(01606) 883800
Station Road, Delamere, Northwich
(18) 6305 yards/**/B

Disley G.C
(01663) 762071
Stanley Hall Lane, Stockport
(18) 6051 yards/***/B

Eaton G.C.
(01244) 335885
Guy Lane, Waverton
(18) 6446 yards/***/F/H

Ellesmere Port G.C.
(0151) 339 7689
Chester Road, Hooton
(18) 6432 yards/***/E

Frodsham G.C.
(01928) 732159
Simons Lane, Frodsham
(18) 6289 yards/**/B

Helsby G.C.
(01928) 722021
Towers Lane, Helsby, Warrington
(18) 6229 yards/**/B/H

Heyrose G.C.
(01565) 733664
Budworth Road, Knutsford
(18) 6449 yards/***/C

Knights Grange G.C.
(01606) 557406
Grange Lane, Winsford
(9) 6210 yards/***/E

Knutsford G.C.
(01565) 633355
Mereheath Lane, Knutsford
(9) 6288 yards/**/C

Leigh G.C.
(01925) 763130
Kenyon Hall, Culcheth
(18) 6861 yards/***/B/H

Lymm G.C.
(01925) 755020
Whitbarrow Road, Lymm
(18) 6304 yards/**/C/H

Macclesfield G.C.
(01625) 423227
The Hollins, Macclesfield
(18) 5625 yards/**/C/H

Malkins Bank G.C.
(01270) 583509
Betchton Road, Sandbach
(18) 6071 yards/***/E

Mere G.& C.C.
(01565) 830155
Chester Road, Mere, Knutsford
(18) 6817 yards/**(Wed,Fri)/A/H/L

Mersey Valley G.C.
(0151) 424 6060
Warrington Road, Widnes
(18) 6400 yards/**/C

Mottram Hall Hotel & G.C.
(01625) 828135
Mottram St Andrews
(18) 7006 yards/***/A/H

New Mills G.C.
(01663) 743485
Shaw Marsh, New Mills, Stockport
(9) 5707 yards/**/F

Onneley G.C.
(01782)750577
Onneley, Crewe
(9) 5584 yards/**/C

The Portal G & C.C.
(01829) 733933
Cobbler's Cross Lane, Tarporley
(18) 7037 yards/***/A/H
(9) 3250 yards/***/C

Portal Premier G.C
(01829) 733884
Forest Road, Tarporley
(18) 6508 yards/***/A

Poulton Park G.C.
(01925) 812034
Cinnamon Brow, Warrington
(9) 5512 yards/**/C

Prestbury G.C.
(01625) 829388
Macclesfield Road, Prestbury
(18) 6359 yards/**/B/H/L

Pryors Hayes G.C.
(01829) 740140
Willingdon Drove, Oscroft
(18) 5923 yards/***/C

Queens Park G.C.
(01270) 628352
Queens Park Gardens, Crewe
(9) 5370 yards/***/E

Reaseheath College G.C.
(01270) 625131
Reaseheath, Nantwich
(9) 3334 yards/***/E/G

Runcorn G.C.
(01928) 574214
Clifton Road, Runcorn
(18) 6035 yards/**/C/H

Sandbach G.C.
(01270) 762117
Middlewich Road, Sandbach
(9) 5614 yards/**/C/H

Sandiway G.C.
(01606) 883247
Chester Road, Sandiway, Northwich
(18) 6435 yards/***/A/H/L

Shrigley Hall G.C.
(01625) 575757
Shrigley Park, Pott Shrigley
(18) 6305 yards/***/B

St Michael's Jubilee G.C.
(0151) 424 6230
Dundark Road, Widnes
(18) 5612 yards/***/F/L

Tytherington G.C.
(01625) 434562
Tytherington, nr Macclesfield
(18) 6737 yards/***/B-A/H

Upton-by-Chester G.C.
(01244) 381183
Upton Lane, Upton-by-Chester
(18) 5875 yards/***/B/H

Vicars Cross G.C.
(01244) 335174
Tarvin Road, Littleton
(18) 6234 yards/**/C

Walton Hall G.C.
(01925) 266775
Warrington Road, Higher Walton
(18) 6843 yards/***/E

Warrington G.C.
(01925) 261775
Appleton, Warrington
(18) 6305 yards/***/F/H

Widnes G.C.
(0151) 424 2440
Highfield Road, Widnes
(18) 5719 yards/**/B/H

Wilmslow G.C.
(01565) 872148
Mobberley, Knutsford
(18) 6607 yards/**/A/H

Artist: **Victor Venner** **ADDRESSING THE BALL** *Courtesy of:* **Rosenstiel's**

Artist: **Bill Waugh** **ROYAL LYTHAM & ST ANNES** Courtesy of: **Burlington Gallery**

addies are not allowed on the greens when wearing 'clogs'—recorded in the minutes of a Lancashire golf club, 1894.

The Lancashire Coast

I don't suppose they appreciate it in the slightest but the many horses that race across the sands near Southport early each morning (and the donkeys that do their best to race across the same sands) are performing within a few yards of one of the greatest stretches of golfing country in the world. On the Lancashire coast between Liverpool and Blackpool lies a magnificent collection of natural golfing links. Being more specific, between Hoylake on the Wirral Peninsula and Lytham St Annes (a distance of less than 40 miles) are to be found the likes of **Royal Liverpool, Wallasey, West Lancashire, Formby, Southport and Ainsdale, Royal Birkdale, Hillside, Royal Lytham, Fairhaven and St Annes Old Links.** A truly formidable list. Hoylake, Birkdale and Lytham have, of course, each staged the Open Championship on a number of occasions, while the Amateur Championship has been played at both Hillside and Formby, and Southport and Ainsdale has twice hosted the Ryder Cup. When the wind hammers across from the Irish Sea any of the links mentioned can become treacherously difficult and the famous Lancashire sandhills rarely provide shelter from the elements. Hoylake, Birkdale, Hillside, Formby and Lytham are each featured on later pages but a visit to any of the above will certainly not meet with disappointment (though it may result in a little damaged pride!)

Having done battle with the elements, and perhaps after visiting the treacherous Gumbley's bunker at S & A or the heather and pines at Formby, a drink will be in order. A good meal and a comfy bed for the night may also be required. Here are some suggestions. The Woolton Redbourne Hotel (0151) 421 1500 is extremely comfortable and particularly convenient for Royal Birkdale. In Southport, the Scarisbrick Hotel (01704) 543000, the Prince of Wales (01704) 536688 and the Royal Clifton (01704) 533771 are probably the pick of the hotels but there are numerous others. The Metropole Hotel (01704) 536836 and the Bold Hotel (01704) 532578 are also good and amongst the less expensive options the Ambassador Hotel (01704) 543998 and the Sunningdale Hotel (01704) 538673 should not disappoint. In Formby, the Tree Tops (01704) 879651 is an ideal base.

Lytham St Annes is another golfer's paradise. It's a pleasant town and hotels to note in the area are the Chadwick (01253) 720061 on the seafront, the Clifton Arms Hotel (01253) 739898 at Lytham, the Dormy House at the course itself and the New Glendower Hotel (01253) 72324. The Dalmeny Hotel (01253) 712236 has a host of leisure facilities and a good restaurant. C'est La Vie is an ideal watering hole while Endsleigh Private Hotel (01253) 351937 and Strathmore (01253) 725478 also have good reputations. Fleetwood to the north, is a pleasant seaside links. The North Euston Hotel (01391) 876525 is an inexpensive base here.

Blackpool, famed for its 'golden mile', its great tower and impressive funfair is more of a paradise for children than golfers, but then if golf is being sneaked in on the family holiday it may be the best choice for a stay. On the North Promenade are two of the town's best hotels, the Pembroke (01253) 23434 and the Imperial (01253) 23971. Comfort here is guaranteed but there are numerous, slightly cheaper alternatives and pot luck may be the order of the day. The Sunray Private Hotel (01253) 351937, the Lynstead (01253) 351050 and the Surrey House

Hotel (01253) 51743 fall into the less glamorous category but offer pleasant accommodation and on Shaftesbury Avenue you can find the Brebyns Hotel (01253) 354263, noted for its good food. To the east, at Little Singleton there is a listed historic house and excellent hotel in the Mains Hall (01253) 885130. A restaurant in Blackpool to note is September Brasserie (01253) 23282.

It may be that some business in Liverpool has to be dealt with before one can put on one's plus fours and stride out onto the fairways. If you are staying in the Liver city the Atlantic Tower (0151) 227 4444 is a good bet. The city has a reputation for splendid Indian and Chinese food but two European establishments are our recommendations: on the one hand Ristorante Del Secolo (0151) 236 4004 and on the other La Grande Bouffe (0151) 236 3375. The nearest of the great links courses is West Lancashire, although Formby—note also the **Formby Ladies'** club here—and the Southport courses are also within easy reach. The A565 is the road to take out of Liverpool.

For the purposes of this piece Liverpool and Manchester have been included in Lancashire, a county to which they both once belonged (and still do in spirit). As the whole of what was once Merseyside has been included—it's here that Royal Birkdale and Royal Liverpool are now situated—parts of former Cheshire are also included. Confused? Let's visit the Wirral. For such a relatively small area the peninsula is fairly thick with golf clubs. In addition to the famous links at Hoylake, **Wallasey** offers another tremendous seaside test amid some impressive sand dunes while **Heswall** offers a quite outstanding parkland challenge. Situated alongside the River Dee off the A540, it's a medium length course, beautifully maintained with views towards the distant Welsh hills. A mention also for **Caldy** which is a parkland-cum-clifftop course, and for the **Wirral Ladies'** Golf Club near Birkenhead. If an hotel is sought on the Wirral then the splendidly named Bowler Hat Hotel (0151) 652 4931 at Birkenhead is most comfortable.

Inland Golf in Lancashire

Looking to play more centrally in Lancashire, the **Shaw Hill** Golf and Country Club (012572) 69221 is most definitely one to note if travelling along the M6. Located just north of Chorley at the appropriately named Whittle-le-Woods it enjoys a very peaceful setting, despite its proximity to the motorway, and is a particular favourite of golfing societies. Visitors are welcome throughout the week, and there is some high quality accommodation immediately beyond the 18th green.

On the other side of the M6, **Pleasington** Golf Club enjoys similarly secluded and picturesque surroundings. The course is situated three miles west of Blackburn along the A59 and is undoubtedly one of the best parkland courses in the north of England. You're bound to build up a good appetite here—in which case head for Northcote Manor (01254) 240555—a restaurant par excellence with some rooms as well. Still moving 'up' the country, **Preston** has a pleasantly undulating course, just north of the town. It too can easily be reached from the M6 (junction 32). The Broughton Park (01772) 864087 is a large hotel with good leisure facilities.

Another of the better inland courses in the county is **Clitheroe** Golf Club, situated on the edge of the Forest of Bowland. The course lies approximately two miles south of the town with views across to Pendle Hill.

Lancashire wouldn't be complete without mentioning its county town. There are a number of clubs at hand, perhaps the best being the **Lancaster** Golf and Country

Club located three miles south of the city on the A588 at Stodday. An attractive parkland course, it is laid out close to the River Lune estuary (and can be breezy!).

A few more ideas for the 19th hole now follow. The city of Lancaster lies west of some majestic moorland scenery. The M6 carves its way through and near to junction 34 the Posthouse Hotel (01524) 65999 is ideal for travellers. Recommended alternatives include Edenbreck House (01524) 32464 and Lancaster House (01524) 844822. A little further north in Heaton with Oxcliffe a pub with a splendid riverside setting is the Golden Ball—well worth a visit when in these parts. In Morecambe the Strathmore (01524) 421234 is welcoming and a good spot for the marvellous seaside golf to be enjoyed at Morecambe where the views will make you feel glad to be alive. Closer to the M6, **Garstang** Country Hotel & Golf Club (01995) 600950 is a newly built hotel which stands next to a fine course and is well worth a visit.

At Whitewell, amid the delightful Forest of Bowland lies the Inn at Whitewell (01200) 448222 which offers excellent bar snacks, a first rate restaurant and some charming bedrooms. If you are looking for a self-catering holiday in the region, we recommend you contact either Red Rose Cottage Holidays (01200) 27310 or Country Holidays (01282) 445533. More thoughts for celebrating after a day at Preston or Clitheroe? In Hurst Green, the Shireburn Arms Hotel (01254) 826518 is well worth a visit. Not only can you enjoy the splendid Ribblesdale countryside but also some tremendous cuisine. An alternative eating establishment, a restaurant on this occasion, is Tiffany at Great Harwood, where the fish is particularly good. In Clitheroe itself, the Swan and Royal Hotel (01200) 23130 is convenient and nearby in Slaidburn is the Parrock Head Farm Hotel (01200) 446614. In Preston, both the Gibbon Bridge (01995) 61456 and Tulketh Hotel (01772) 726250 offer excellent facilities. Finally, a recommendation for the first class **Mytton Fold** Farm Hotel (01254) 240662 which now boasts its own course at Langho, near Blackburn.

Manchester and Surrounds

And so to Manchester. The city itself is famed the world over for the liberal amount of rain that falls. Mancunians will tell you that this is pure poppycock (or something like that). Of course, the only time that rain can be guaranteed these days is during the five days of an Old Trafford test match. If you do happen to get caught in the rain, be it on the streets or the fairways, here are a few superior shelters. You ought to be able to find a room in the Britannia Hotel (0161) 228 2288 for there are 365 (one for every day of the year?) Alternatives include the Jarvis Piccadilly (0161) 236 8414, and the Portland Thistle (0161) 228 3400.

Outside the city there are many attractive options. To the north in Egerton, the Egerton House (01204) 307171 is good value as is the Last Drop Village Hotel (01204) 591131—well appointed and well run. Another thought is the Bramhall Moat House (0161) 439 8116—ideal for the many courses in northern Cheshire. Near to Manchester Airport one finds Etrop Grange (0161) 499 0500—comfortable and convenient. Altrincham has a trio to consider: the Cresta Court (0161) 927 7272 is modern but well equipped; the Bowdon (0161) 928 7121 is Victorian and comfortable; while a former coaching inn, the George and Dragon (0161) 928 9933 has most charm. Some of the very best restaurants in the Manchester area include: the Market Restaurant (0161) 834 3743 and the excellent Royal Orchid (0161) 236 5183.

It is probably a fair assessment to say that for golf courses, Manchester, rather like London, gets top marks for quantity but is a little shaky on the quality score. Certainly it compares unfavourably with Liverpool and Leeds—which is a shame because historically Manchester was the scene of some of the earliest golf outside Scotland. The **Old Manchester** Club was founded back in 1818. Its current status is 'temporarily without a course'—one can only hope that its members have found somewhere else to play—**North Manchester** perhaps? Only four miles from the city centre this is one of the best in the county. A close neighbour of North Manchester is the excellent **Manchester** Golf Club. Elsewhere around Manchester, **Stand, Whitefield** and **Worsley** (Eccles) are fine courses, while to the north **Rochdale** is well worth travelling to. There is a cluster of courses close to the River Mersey in the Didsbury/Sale area. The best is perhaps **Withington**, and there are about ten public courses in and around the city centre. Over towards Stockport, there is a very enjoyable course at **Reddish Vale** and the area around Bolton again boasts a number of courses of which **Bolton Old Links** is probably the finest. It is a tough and interesting moorland course at which visitors are always made welcome. As for the title 'Links' it may sound a bit quaint—but there again, what are we to make of Wigan Pier?

The Isle of Man

There are seven 18 hole courses on the island, with the links courses at **Castletown, Ramsey** and **Mount Murray** being particularly good. With fairly modest green fees and numerous relaxing places to stay the island would appear to be an ideal place for a golf holiday—ask Nigel Mansell who brought Greg Norman here! In Castletown, there are two restaurants to note; Silverburn Lodge (01624) 822343 and Rosa's Place (01624) 822940, whilst the Castletown Golf Links Hotel (01624) 822201 is very comfortable. Castletown golf course is featured ahead. Further up the east coast is the Mount Murray Hotel and Country Club, which opened in 1994 and provides a stern challenge to any golfer

At the other end of the island, Ramsey offers the large Grand Island Hotel (01624) 812455 and the Harbour Bistro (01624) 814182, an informal and friendly restaurant. Finally there are, of course, many places to stay in Douglas and here we can recommend the Palace Hotel (01624) 662662 and the Sefton (01624) 626011.

Artist: **Gilroy SNOW GOLF**
Courtesy of: **Burlington Gallery**

Royal Lytham & St Annes

'There goes a hundred thousand bucks . . .' the immortal words of Al Watrous after having witnessed the most magnificently outrageous stroke in golfing history. Imagine yourself in his shoes, striding down the 17th fairway, sharing the lead in the Open Championship. You have played two strokes and are safely on the edge of the green, your partner (and effectively your opponent) has driven wildly into the rough and has found a small bunker. He faces a terrifying shot over sandhills, scrub and goodness knows what else—a blind shot of fully 170 yards. Seconds later the impossible happens and his ball is lying a few yards from the hole, well inside your second. Minutes later you walk from the green having taken five to your opponent's four.

The occasion was, of course, the 1926 Open Championship at Royal Lytham and the opponent, the incomparable Bobby Jones.

In February 1986, Royal Lytham and St Annes proudly celebrated its one hundredth birthday. Few golf clubs in the world can have enjoyed such a rich and colourful history. There have been nine Open Championships, four Seniors' British Opens and many other major events.

Presently in charge of all administrative matters at Royal Lytham is the club's **Secretary, Mr L Goodwin,** who may be contacted by telephone on **(01253) 724206** and by fax on (01253) 780946. **Eddie Birchenough** is the club's **Professional** and he may be reached on **(01253) 720094.** Visitors wishing to tread the famous fairways are asked to provide a letter of introduction, but subject to this requirement they are welcome between Mondays and Fridays. Thursdays are specifically reserved as visitors' days, but restrictions apply at weekends. Advance booking is essential, preferably two to three weeks in advance,. Those wishing to write to the club should address correspondence to the Assistant Secretary, **Royal Lytham and St Annes Golf Club, Links Gate, Lytham St Annes, Lancashire FY8 3LQ.**

The green fees at Lytham in 1998 are £80 for a single round inclusive of lunch and a 'golfers welcome pack'. Dormy house facilities are available at the 19th hole (telephone the club for details) and Royal Lytham's clubhouse is a marvellous Victorian building. Golfers can enjoy the excellent catering service which is offered throughout the day.

Motoring to the course is assisted greatly by the M6 and the M61. Both northbound and southbound travellers should leave the M6 at junction 32 to pick up the M55. The M55 runs out of steam at junction 4 but a left turn will take you to Lytham St Annes. The M61 links the Greater Manchester area to the outskirts of Preston. From Preston, the A583 should be followed, joining the A584 which also runs to Lytham St Annes. The course is situated only a mile from the centre of the town close to St Annes railway station.

The railway line is, in fact, a major feature of the opening holes at Lytham, forming a continuous boundary to the right. From the medal tees the course measures 6685 yards par 71 (SSS 74) with the ladies playing over 5814 yards par 75 (SSS 75). Rather unusually, Lytham opens with a par three, which at over 200 yards is quite a testing opener, although the real threat of the railway looms on the 2nd and 3rd. The two-shot 8th is many people's favourite hole and among the short holes perhaps the 12th stands out. Normally played into a prevailing wind, it calls for a searching tee shot towards a raised and heavily guarded green. The back nine is invariably the more difficult of the two halves, although the determining factor at Lytham (as on most links courses) will nearly always be the wind. The 17th has been mentioned and a plaque marks the spot from where the Jones miracle recovery shot was played. As for the superbly bunkered 18th, it of course invokes so many Open Championship memories: Tony Jacklin's arrow straight drive en route to winning the 1969 Championship; Gary Player putting left handed from up against the clubhouse wall in 1974; Seve Ballesteros storming to victory in 1979 and again in 1988; and the most recent Championship in 1996 when Tom Lehman became the first American to win at Lytham since Jones.

The 1988 championship will always be remembered for the fantastic duel between Ballesteros and Nick Price. Price led by two shots going into the final round. He produced an almost flawless 69 yet lost by two. 'A round that happens once every 25 or 50 years' was Seve's description of his scintillating 65. Perhaps Nick Price alone can understand how Al Watrous felt.

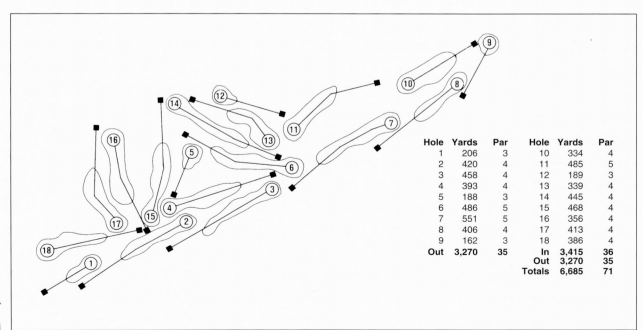

Hole	Yards	Par	Hole	Yards	Par
1	206	3	10	334	4
2	420	4	11	485	5
3	458	4	12	189	3
4	393	4	13	339	4
5	188	3	14	445	4
6	486	5	15	468	4
7	551	5	16	356	4
8	406	4	17	413	4
9	162	3	18	386	4
Out	**3,270**	**35**	**In**	**3,415**	**36**
			Out	**3,270**	**35**
			Totals	**6,685**	**71**

Ideally situated in the heart of Old Woolton village, yet only five minutes from the M62 and Liverpool International Airport, you will find the Woolton Redbourne—a Grade II listed building in the grand country house style, so typical of the late Victorian period.

Situated amidst expanses of beautiful gardens and lawns, offering superb views of the surrounding countryside, the hotel has been completely refurbished to its original splendour and offers classical Victorian ambience to the discerning traveller.

Possibly the best hotel in the north west this is a haven for the rich and famous, probably because it offers total privacy as well as luxury—a homely atmosphere together with a highly personal and friendly service.

All of the bedrooms and six suites are splendid but the Redbourne suite offers the ultimate in comfort—not only a four poster bed, but also a four poster jacuzzi.

Only two hundred yards away from the main hotel, Acrefield House, another Grade II listed building adds another dimension to the accommodation. Also set in beautifully landscaped grounds, Acrefield offers self contained two-bedroom apartments, all furnished to the very highest standard in period style. All can be reserved for one night stays but are extremely suitable for guests who stay a little longer and require that little extra space and comfort.

There is no shortage of things to do in the area. For those of a nostalgic turn of mind the hotel is in the heart of Beatles country, only two minutes away from Strawberry Fields, and Beatles tours are on offer. The surrounding scenery is quite spectacular and some interesting tours of Liverpool's architectural heritage can be arranged.

Golfers would be well advised to book one of the special Romantic Weekends. While you are savouring the delights of the nearby championship courses of Royal Liverpool, Royal Birkdale, Formby and Lytham St Annes, your partner will be pampered with breakfast in bed and then you can both enjoy champagne and a candlelit dinner to enthuse or commiserate over the day's play.

Even if you don't summon the energy to play a round of golf you could not fail to appreciate the sheer luxury of a stay at the Woolton Redbourne.

The Woolton Redbourne Hotel
Acrefield Road
Woolton, Liverpool
L25 5JN
Tel: 0151 421 1500
Fax: 0151 421 1501

Royal Birkdale

Back in 1889 your average JP was possibly not the most popular man in town. However, in a certain Mr J C Barrett, Birkdale possessed a man of rare insight and one clearly cognisant of the finer things in life. Mr Barrett was a golfer. On the 30th July 1889, he invited eight fellow addicts to his home and together they resolved to form a golf club. One can imagine their enthusiasm as they formulated their plans, perhaps over a brandy and cigars, I know not, but very quickly a clubhouse was secured—a single room in a private residence at a four shilling per week rental! Land (at £5 per year rental) was acquired and soon a nine hole course was laid out. It all sounds rather unsophisticated, but compared with today's problems of first finding a suitable site and then obtaining planning permission, I suppose it was relatively straightforward.

Although no one could question its present day status as one of the country's leading championship courses, historically Birkdale set off rather like the proverbial tortoise. Forced eviction in 1897 led to the club's rerooting in its present position where a full eighteen holes were immediately available. During the 1930s a striking art deco style clubhouse was built and John H Taylor and Fred Hawtree were commissioned to redesign the course. As one would expect, they made a splendid job of it and it was now only a question of time (and the small matter of a world war) that prevented Birkdale from staging an Open Championship. Since the war our golfing tortoise has left many of the hares behind. No fewer than seven Open Championships have now been held at Birkdale (an eighth is due in 1998) in addition to two Ryder Cups and numerous other major events.

Golfers wishing to play at Birkdale must belong to a recognised golf club and produce a current handicap certificate. Visitors should make prior arrangements with the **Secretary, Norman Crewe**. This applies to individual visitors as well as those hoping to organise a society game. Mr Crewe can be contacted at **The Royal Birkdale Golf Club, Waterloo Road, Birkdale, Southport, Merseyside PR8 2LX. Tel: (01704) 567920** and fax: **(01704) 562327**. Golf clubs may be hired from the **professional, Richard Bradbeer, (01704) 568857** and it may also be possible to obtain the services of a caddy. Individual visitors may play from Monday to Friday, green fees in 1998 being £90 per round or £110 per day, inclusive of a three course meal.

The club is situated approximately two miles from the centre of Southport close to the main A565 road. From the North this road can be reached via the A59, leaving the M6 at Preston and from the South via the M62 and M57 or alternatively, as when travelling from Manchester and the East, by taking the A580 and then following the A570 into Southport.

Whilst the course possesses many of the towering sandhills so familiar with good links golf, the holes tend to wind their way between and beneath the dunes along fairly flat valleys. From the fairways the awkward stance and blind shot are the product of poor golf, not poor fortune.

With its par fives the back nine is probably the easier half—at least to the longer hitter—although with the buckthorn and willow scrub infested rough and narrow strategically bunkered fairways the wild long hitter will be severely penalised. A journey into the rough on the 16th, however, is recommended although only to visit Arnold Palmer's plaque—placed in memory of the great man's miraculous 6 iron shot when he somehow contrived to find the green after driving deep into the undergrowth. The two finest holes at Birkdale are thought by many to be the 6th, a very demanding left to right dog-leg and the 12th, a classic par three where the green nestles in the sand dunes.

Birkdale may have a relatively short history as an Open course, but her list of champions is as impressive a list as can be found anywhere: Peter Thomson (twice), Arnold Palmer, Lee Trevino, Johnny Miller, Tom Watson—who claimed his fifth title in nine years when winning in 1983—and Ian Baker-Finch, who set alight the 1991 championship with a brilliant front nine of 29 on the final day.

The course has indeed thrown up more than its fair share of drama. Perhaps most notably in 1969 when Jack Nicklaus, ever the sportsman, conceded Tony Jacklin's very missable putt on the 18th green, so tying the Ryder Cup. In the 1961 Palmer's Open, an almighty gale threatened to blow the tented village and all inside far out into the sea. In stark contrast was the 1976 Open when fire engines were close at hand as Birkdale (and all of Britain come to that) suffered in the drought.

That 1976 championship saw the mercurial Miller at his brilliant best as he shook off first the challenge of Nicklaus and then of an inexperienced and unknown 19 year old who had a name no one at the time could pronounce. . .Severiano Ballesteros.

Hole	Yards	Par		Hole	Yards	Par
1	449	4		10	403	4
2	421	4		11	408	4
3	407	4		12	183	3
4	203	3		13	475	4
5	344	4		14	198	3
6	473	4		15	544	5
7	177	3		16	416	4
8	457	4		17	547	5
9	411	4		18	472	4
Out	**3,342**	**34**		**In**	**3,646**	**36**
				Out	**3,342**	**34**
				Totals	**6,988**	**70**

Royal Liverpool (Hoylake)

The Royal Hotel at Hoylake (alas no longer with us) played a starring role in the early history of the Royal Liverpool Golf Club. In 1869 a meeting was held there which led to the famous club's formation. Perhaps of greater significance that day, with no disrespect whatsoever to those founding members, was the presence in the hotel of a seven year old boy. John Ball, whose father was the hotel proprietor, grew to become not only Hoylake's favourite son, but also the finest amateur golfer Britain has ever produced.

In the early days, golf at Hoylake must have been at times a trifle frustrating, for the club shared the links with a racecourse and hoofprints on the fairways were a fairly common hazard. However, by 1876 the horses (doubtless equally frustrated) had found elsewhere to gallop and the golf course quickly developed into England's premier championship test. The 1869 birthdate in fact makes Hoylake England's second oldest links course—just four years younger than Westward Ho! in Devon.

Ten Open Championships and seventeen Amateur Championships later, visitors are welcome to play at Hoylake, subject to proof of handicap or letter of introduction from their home club. Special green fee rates apply in July. At all other times the rates for 1998 are £55 per round or £80 per day during the week and £70 at weekends. The tee is reserved for members until 9.30am and between 1.00pm and 2.00pm.

On weekdays, individual bookings must be made through the **Secretary, Group Captain Christopher Moore, (0151) 632 3101** or by fax on (0151) 632 6737, who will also authorise limited weekend bookings. Organisers should address written applications to: **The Secretary, Royal Liverpool Golf Club, Meols Drive, Hoylake, Wirral, Merseyside. L47 4AL.** You may also contact the club by e mail on sec@rlgc.u-net.com or at http://www.royal-liverpool.golf.com.

John Heggarty is the club's **Professional**. Through him, lessons can be booked, clubs hired, and caddies obtained. Mr Heggarty can be reached on **(0151) 632 5868.**

Hoylake is located at the tip of the Wirral peninsula, approximately ten miles west of Liverpool and fifteen miles north of Chester. The north west of England is particularly well served by motorway connections and finding the course shouldn't be a problem. Approaching from either the north or south the M6 is likely to be of assistance; it passes midway between Manchester and Liverpool and should be left at junction 19A. Thereafter the M56 can be followed towards Chester joining the M53 at junction 15. The M53 will then take you to the far end of the Wirral where the A553 Hoylake road should be picked up. (In a nutshell: M6—M56—M53—A553).

The course occupies fairly flat ground and is very exposed to the elements. It is most unusual for the wind not to blow. (You have been warned!) It was his mastery of the wind, a skill acquired playing at Hoylake that enabled John Ball to win many of his record eight Amateur Championships. His victories were achieved between 1888 and 1912. Ball's great rival during those years, both remarkably, and ironically, was a fellow Hoylake man, Harold Hilton. Hilton himself won four Amateur Championships. In addition both Hilton and Ball won the Open Championship, Ball in 1890 and Hilton twice, in 1892 and 1897. The great Bobby Jones is the only other amateur golfer to have won the Open title.

Even on those very rare occasions when all is calm, Hoylake is still an exceptionally difficult test. From the medal tees the course measures 6848 yards, par 72, and it can play every inch of its length. If the most interesting and classic links type sequence of holes occurs between the 8th and the 12th, the end of the round provides a real 'sting in the tail'. Rather like Carnoustie, Hoylake is renowned for its exacting final stretch. It contains two par fives and three par fours, any of which is capable of wrecking a potentially good score. The long 16th in particular can be cruelly punishing with its out of bounds to the right of the fairway.

The ten Opens held at Hoylake produced ten different champions and among them some of the game's greatest names: Harold Hilton, John H Taylor, Walter Hagen and Bobby Jones. The latter's victory in 1930 was the second leg of the historic grand slam.

The sole reason for the course being presently 'off the Open rota' (the last staging was in 1967 when Roberto de Vicenzo won) is that the course cannot accommodate the vast crowds that the event now attracts. Unfortunately, it is the same enthusiastic public who suffer most, for there are many who maintain that Hoylake remains the greatest of all England's championship links.

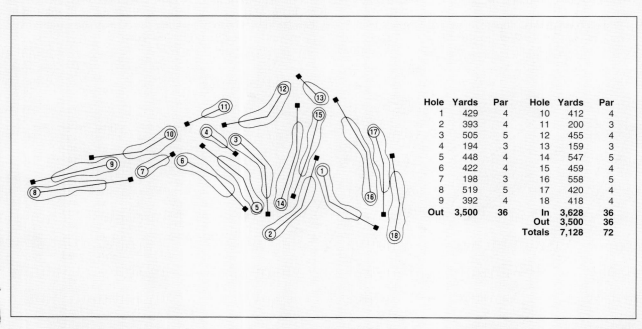

Hole	Yards	Par	Hole	Yards	Par
1	429	4	10	412	4
2	393	4	11	200	3
3	505	5	12	455	4
4	194	3	13	159	3
5	448	4	14	547	5
6	422	4	15	459	4
7	198	3	16	558	5
8	519	5	17	420	4
9	392	4	18	418	4
Out	**3,500**	**36**	**In**	**3,628**	**36**
			Out	**3,500**	**36**
			Totals	**7,128**	**72**

Hillside

If Royal Birkdale is the finest golf links in England (and most commentators seem to think it is) then Hillside must surely be number two. Why so? Well, firstly, they occupy the very same magnificent golfing country being laid out literally side by side amid a vast stretch of sandhills near Southport and, secondly, when analysing the quality of the individual golf holes people find it very difficult to separate the two courses. Perhaps it is only Birkdale's Open Championship history which accords it precedence. And why hasn't Hillside staged the 'Big One'? Presumably it's because it is only since 1967, when Hillside's back nine holes were completely reshaped, that it has deserved to be ranked alongside its more illustrious neighbour. The front nine at Hillside has long been highly regarded, but the newer second nine is really outstanding and indeed very spectacular—a bit like Ballybunion minus the Atlantic Ocean.

Since 1967 Hillside has hosted a number of important championships. In the late 1970s both the British Ladies Championship and the Amateur Championship were held here and in 1982 came the European Tour's prestigious PGA Championship. A great course and a great event produced a great winner when Tony Jacklin defeated the up-and-coming Bernhard Langer in a thrilling playoff.

From the back tees Hillside measures a daunting 6850 yards, par 72. The first two holes, however, are fairly straightforward—provided you don't hook on to the railway line! The 3rd is a really first class dog-leg hole where the approach must be played over a brook to a green that is well protected by deep traps. Stray to the right with your second shot and you'll land in a pond. Stray to the right at the next, the short 4th, and your ball will be greeted by one of three bunkers that are just as devilish as those on the 3rd. The 5th is a real teaser. It is a par five that can be reached with two

good blows, and you can see everything from the tee by virtue of a gap in the dunes fifty yards short of the green. The problem is that a seemingly magnetic sleepered bunker has been placed in the gap. Three of the next four holes are difficult dog-leg par fours. The 7th is the breather—a lovely par three played downhill towards a generous green backed by some magnificent tall pines.

The second nine commences with another outstanding short hole. The 10th measures only 147 yards but it's a much tougher green to hit than most and is ringed by a series of alarmingly cavernous bunkers—yes, Hillside is inundated with them! Of the remaining holes only the 12th and the 15th could be described as anything less than superb, with the two par fives, the 11th and 17th which both weave a path through a wonderful dune-lined valley, being possibly the best holes of the entire round.

Hillside Golf Club, Hastings Road, Hillside, Southport, Merseyside, PR8 2LU	
Sec/Manager	John Graham (01704) 567169
Professional	Brian Seddon (01704) 568360
Green Fees	WD £40/round, £50/day Sunday pm £50/round
Restrictions	No visitors on Saturdays; limited Sunday golf, handicap certificates.
Directions	
Two miles south west of Southport on A565.	

Formby

According to the traditionalist, as opposed to the pure pleasure-seeker, there is only one genuine form of golf and that is the sort played on a links. To this person golf might be just as enjoyable (and probably a darn sight easier when the wind blows!) on an inland course but it is not quite the real thing: Sunningdale, Gleneagles, Wentworth—all wonderful places but . . . By contrast, from the pure pleasure-seeker's point of view these courses may be more attractive, not because the challenge is less intimidating but because many of the best links courses tend to be fairly bleak places where the golfer is exposed. Trees are either very rare or non-existent. Often the layout of the course is a tiresome 'straight out and straight back'.

Formby is a very special place, for it is here that the traditionalist and the pure pleasure-seeker can play a round of golf together and not fall out. Formby is a links—no question about it—firm, fast seaside greens, natural sandy bunkers and some fairly prodigious sandhills. But Formby is also blessed with a plethora of pine trees which add great beauty to the scene and often considerable shelter. Many of Formby's holes weave their way a good bit below the level of the surrounding dunes, creating a feeling of privacy, or at least occasional intimacy, so rare on a links course. And Formby certainly doesn't stretch 'out and back'—in fact, the bird's eye view of the links reveals eleven distinct changes of direction.

Included among most people's favourite holes at Formby are the par five 3rd and the par three 5th; the 7th with its raised green and avenue of pines and the genuinely glorious 12th. Formby's celebrated 4-3-5-4 finish calls for some very precise shot making and at the end of the round there is every chance that the golfer will have used every club in his bag. In total the course measures 6695 yards, par 72.

Although the Open Championship has never visited

Formby the club regularly hosts important amateur events. Just a week after the Open was played at Royal Birkdale in 1991, the English Amateur was being staged 'down the road' at Formby. In the piece on Royal Birkdale, featured elsewhere in this chapter, we mentioned how in the Open of 1976 a raw and hitherto unknown 19 year old burst on to the scene finishing joint runner up to Johnny Miller. Arguably the high point of Ballesteros' career came in 1984 when he overcame Tom Watson to win his second Open title at St Andrews. Later that same summer, Formby, celebrating its centenary, hosted the Amateur Championship and another teenage Spaniard wrote his name into the history books—Jose-Maria Olazabal who produced some sensational golf to defeat a future British Ryder Cup star, Colin Montgomerie. Perhaps the Spanish Armada should have tried landing in Lancashire all those centuries ago.

Formby Golf Club, Golf Road, Formby, Liverpool, L37 1LQ	
Sec/Manager	Mr Wilcox (01704) 872164
Professional	Clive Harrison (01704) 873090 Fax (01704) 833028
Green Fees	WD £50 in Summer WD £35 in Winter
Restrictions	Limited golf is available on Sundays and Wednesdays. Handicap certificates are required.
Directions	
Formby lies 14 miles north of Liverpool and 7 miles south of Southport on the A565.	

Set on Fort Island with breathtaking views across the Irish Sea, the Castletown Golf Links Hotel's very own 18 hole championship golf course offers you a challenging course with the finest facilities and service to match.

The Castletown Golf Links Hotel occupies pride of place in the centre of a wild and beautiful course with the first tee directly opposite the hotel's entrance.

The airport is only five minutes away from the hotel. From landing on the island, you can be checked in and be on the first tee within 20 minutes.

The course offers a challenge from the beginner to the more seasoned player. Holes such as the 5th—known as 'The Road' running parallel with the main shoreline driveway leading to the hotel, and the 17th—christened 'The Gully', with a 200 yard drive across the Irish Sea, are so memorable, they will surely require a post mortem afterwards in the 19th.

The hotel itself has been refurbished and now all bedrooms and public areas offer elegance and luxuriously high standard of comfort that will undoubtedly appeal to the most discerning traveller. Golfer or not, the complete enjoyment experience awaits you—indoor pool, saunas, snooker room and solaria are here to pamper you, or walk around the course and the never ending countryside has to be given time out.

As the sun goes down over the island's mountains, enjoy the fine wines and inspirational cuisine in one of the two restaurants. Whether you choose to dine in the main restaurant or L'Orangerie, you will be sure to delve into the very best cuisine—an experience all of its own, as the islanders will recommend. Afterwards the choice is your own. Relax in one of the three bars or watch satellite TV.

The Isle of Man and Castletown Golf Links Hotel and golf course have to be seen to be believed.

The Castletown Golf Links Hotel
Derbyhaven
Isle of Man
Tel: (01624) 822201
Fax: (01624) 824633

Castletown

Was the Isle of Man ever part of the mainland? If so, which mainland? Situated almost exactly midway between Great Britain and Ireland and roughly equidistant, as the seagull flies, from England, Scotland, Northern Ireland and the Republic, it looks as if Providence deliberately positioned it in mid-ocean so that no-one could claim it as theirs.

The Irish theory, however, has much appeal. One of the Emerald Isle's greatest heroes, Finn McCool—a legend in his own lifetime if ever there was one, and the Giant who started to build the famous Causeway—was really responsible for its location. One day, Finn got out of bed on the wrong side and started to have one of those days. Finn's personality problem was his temper—the only thing about him that was short. This particular day he completely lost his rag and Finn McCool became Finn Not-so-Cool. He grabbed the largest rock he could find and hurled it 50 miles into the sea. Today, that huge rock is known as the Isle of Man.

Enough about the geography and history of the island. What of the golf? Put Castletown aside for a second and it is pretty fair, add Castletown to the equation and it is pretty excellent. What really makes Castletown is its extraordinary location on the island. Like St Andrews the course is laid out on a fairly thin strip of land but unlike St Andrews it is surrounded by water on three sides, the golf links being laid out on a very unusual, triangular peninsula. This is the Langness Peninsula, more commonly known as Fort Island, situated right on the south eastern tip of the Isle of Man only a few minutes from the island's airport at Ronaldsway.

The extraordinary location produces some amazing seascapes and, as the land 'between the sea' is more or less perfect links terrain, the architect who designed Castletown was given a mighty head start by Mother Nature. Fortunately for you and me they didn't give the task to any old architect either. The original layout was prepared by 'Old' Tom Morris—he of course was the chap who reckoned that Machrihanish was 'designed by The Almighty for playing golf'. What must he have thought of this site? (Interestingly, there is more than a hint of Machrihanish about some of the holes at Castletown). After the last war Castletown was reshaped and this time another celebrated architect was brought in to oversee the project—Mackenzie Ross, the man who converted Turnberry from a battle station into the majestic links it now is.

Unless one is fortunate enough to be a member of Castletown Golf Club, by far the easiest way of inspecting Ross's masterpiece is to stay overnight at the adjacent Castletown Golf Links Hotel. The hotel actually owns the golf course and booking a game is much easier for hotel guests. Residents have priority over visitors and pay reduced green fees. Non residents can only book tee times one month in advance. This is not to say that they are unwelcome at short notice, it is just that it may be a case of pot luck. Bookings may be made through the **Golf Secretary, Carol Kaye** on **(01624) 825435** or by fax on (01624) 824633. Visitors who do not have a tee reservation should contact the club's **Professional, Murray Crowe (01624) 822211**. The green fees for 1998 are £22.50 per day for hotel residents. Visitors pay £25 per day between Monday and Thursday and £30 at all other times.

Because of the hotel, its adjoining links and its course architect, Castletown has been called the 'Poor Man's Turnberry'. This is actually intended as a compliment.

Certainly, there is nothing poor about the hotel or its golf course—the quality of both is excellent. In fact many people believe that in its way the golf at Castletown is just as enjoyable (if a little less testing) and scenically as enchanting as the famous Ailsa Course. From its championship tees the links can be stretched to 6711 yards, par 72. The corresponding lengths from the medal and forward tees are 6534 yards and 6093 yards respectively.

Among the best holes on the course are two fine par threes, the 8th and the 13th, the sharply dog-legging 4th and a truly spectacular pair, the 5th and the 17th. The former carries a famous name, 'The Road Hole.' There are no railway sheds to drive over here but terror does lurk all the way down the right side of the fairway—a sliced drive will either end up on tarmac, the beach or the sea. Take the road away and from the back tee the 5th is almost a mirror image of the 1st at Machrihanish—it is of a similar length too at 422 yards. There are no bunkers around the green but then getting there is problematical enough.

The 17th is called 'The Gully' and again a brave long drive is needed if the direct route to the green is taken. The carry is nearly 200 yards over a deep chasm, and rocks and frothy water await the mishit shot. You stand on the 17th tee at Castletown with the knowledge that your drive could finish up in England, Scotland, Ireland or even Wales. As the great Nigel would say, only the best drivers stay on the Isle of Man.

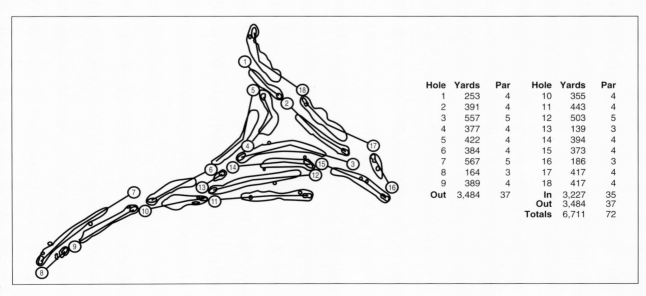

Hole	Yards	Par	Hole	Yards	Par
1	253	4	10	355	4
2	391	4	11	443	4
3	557	5	12	503	5
4	377	4	13	139	3
5	422	4	14	394	4
6	384	4	15	373	4
7	567	5	16	186	3
8	164	3	17	417	4
9	389	4	18	417	4
Out	**3,484**	**37**	**In**	**3,227**	**35**
			Out	**3,484**	**37**
			Totals	**6,711**	**72**

Key

MANCHESTER AREA

Acre Gate G.C.
(0161) 748 1226
Pennybridge Lane, Flixton
(18) 4395 yards/***/E

Altrincham G.C.
(0161) 928 0761
Stockport Road, Timperley
(18) 6162 yards/***/D

Ashton-in-Makerfield G.C.
(01942) 727267
Garswood Park, Ashton-in-
Makerfield
(18) 6250 yards/**(Wed)/C/G

Ashton-on-Mersey G.C.
(0161) 976 4390
Church Lane, Sale
(9) 3076 yards/**(Tues)/C/H

Ashton-under-Lyne G.C.
(0161) 330 1537
Gorsey Way, Ashton-under-Lyne
(18) 6209 yards/**/G

Avro G.C.
(01942) 870757
Old Hall Lane, Woodford
(9) 5735 yards/*/F/G

Blackley G.C.
(0161) 643 2980
Victoria Avenue East, Blackley
(18) 6237 yards/**(Thurs)/C

Bolton G.C.
(01204) 843067
Chorley Old Road, Bolton
(18) 6215 yards/***/B

Bolton Old Links
(01204) 840050
Links Road, Bolton
(18) 6406 yards/***/A

Bolton Open Golf
(01204) 309778
Longsight Lane, Harwood
(9)/**/E

Brackley G.C.
(0161) 790 6076
Bullows Road, Little Hulton
(9) 6006 yards/***/E

Bramhall G.C.
(0161) 439 4057
Ladythorn Road, Bramhall
(18) 6293 yards/***(Thurs)/B/M

Bramhall Park G.C.
(0161) 485 3119
Manor Road, Bramhall
(18) 6214 yards/***/B-A/L

Breightmet G.C.
(01204) 827381
Red Bridge, Ainsworth, Bolton
(9) 6416 yards/**/C

Brookdale G.C.
(0161) 681 4534
Woodhouses, Failsworth
(18) 6040 yards/***/C/H

Bury G.C.
(0161) 766 4897
Unsworth Hall, Blackford Bridge
(18) 5961 yards/**/C/H

Castle Hawk G.C.
(01706) 40841
Heywood Road, Castleton,
(18) 5398 yards/***/E
(9) 3158 yards/***/E

Cheadle G.C.
(0161) 428 2160
Shiers Drive, Cheadle
(9) 5006 yards/***(Tues/Sat)C/H/L

Chorlton-cum-Hardy G.C.
(0161) 881 5830
Barlow Hall Road, Chorlton
(18) 6003 yards/**/C/H

Crompton & Royton G.C.
(0161) 624 0986
Highbarn, Royton, Oldham
(18) 6222 yards/**(Tues/Wed)/B/H

Davyhulme Park G.C.
(0161) 748 2260
Gleneagles Road, Davyhulme
(18) 6237 yards/**(Wed)/B/H/L

Deane G.C.
(01204) 861944
Broadford Road, Deane, Bolton
(18) 5583 yards/**/C/H/M

Denton G.C.
(0161) 336 3218
Manchester Road, Denton
(18) 6290 yards/**/B/H

Didsbury G.C.
(0161) 998 9278
Ford Lane, Northenden
(18) 6273 yards/**/C/H

Disley G.C.
(01663) 762071
Stanley Hall Lane, Digby
(18) 6015 yards/***/B

Dukinfield G.C.
(0161) 338 2340
Lyne Edge, Ashton-under-Lyne
(18) 5585 yards/**/D

Dunham Forest G.& C.C.
(0161) 928 2605
Oldfield Lane, Altrincham
(18) 6636 yards/**/B/H

Dunscar G.C.
(01204) 598228
Longworth Lane, Bromley Cross
(18) 6085 yards/**/B/H

Ellesmere G.C.
(0161) 799 0554
Old Clough Lane, Worsley
(18) 5957 yards/***/C/H/M

Fairfield Golf & Sailing Club
(0161) 370 1641
Booth Road, Audenshaw
(18) 5654 yards/**/D

Flixton G.C.
(0161) 748 2116
Church Road, Flixton
(9) 6410 yards/**/D

Gathurst G.C.
(01257) 252861
Miles Lane, Shevington, Wigan
(9) 6308 yards/**(Wed)/C

Gatley G.C.
(0161) 437 2091
Styal Road, Heald Green, Gatley
(9) 5934 yards/**(Tues)/C

Great Lever & Farnworth G.C.
(01204) 656137
Lever Edge Lane, Bolton
(18) 5859 yards/**/C/H

Greenmount G.C.
(01204) 883712
Greenmount, Bury
(9) 4920 yards/**(Tues)/D/H

Haigh Hall G.C.
(01942) 833337
Haigh Country Park, Haigh, Wigan
(18) 6423 yards/***/E

Hale G.C.
(0161) 980 4225
Rappax Road, Hale
(9) 5780 yards/**(Thurs)/C

Harwood G.C.
(01204) 522878
Roading Brook Road, Bolton
(9) 5993 yards/**/D

Hazel Grove G.C.
(0161) 483 3978
Buxton Road, Stockport
(18) 6310 yards/***/B/H

Heaton Moor G.C.
(0161) 432 2134
Heaton Mersey, Stockport
(18) 5876 yards/***(Tues)/B-A

Heaton Park G.C.
(0161) 798 0295
Heaton Park, Prestwich
(18) 5849 yards/***/E

Hindley Hall G.C.
(01942) 255131
Hall Lane, Hindley, Wigan
(18) 5904 yards/**(Wed)/B/H/L

Horwich G.C.
(01204) 696980
Victoria Road, Horwich, Bolton
(9) 5404 yards/*/F/G

Houldsworth G.C.
(0161) 442 9611
Reddish, Stockport
(18) 6078 yards/**/C

Lowes Park G.C.
(0161) 764 1231
Hill Top, Bury
(9) 6043 yards/**(Wed)/C/M

Manchester G.C.
(0161) 643 2718
Rochdale Road, Middleton
(18) 6464 yards/**/B/H

Manor G.C.
(01204) 705651
Moss Lane, Kearsley
(18) 5000 yards/**/E

Marple G.C.
(0161) 427 2311
Hawk Green, Marple
(18) 5700 yards/***(Thurs)/B/H

Mellor & Townscliffe G.C.
(0161) 427 2208
Tarden, Gibb Lane, Mellor
(18) 5925 yards/**/B

North Manchester G.C.
(0161) 643 9033
Manchester Old Road, Middleton
(18) 6527 yards/***/C

Northenden G.C.
(0161) 998 4738
Palatine Road, Northenden
(18) 6469 yards/***/B/H

Oldham G.C.
(0161) 624 4986
Lees New Road, Oldham
(18) 5045 yards/***/F

Pennington G.C.
(01942) 876444
St Helens Road, Leigh
(9) 2919 yards/***/F

Pike Folds G.C.
(0161) 740 1136
Victoria Avenue, Blackley
(9) 5789 yards/**/D

Prestwich G.C.
(0161) 773 2544
Hilton Lane, Prestwich
(18) 4712 yards/**/C/H

Reddish Vale G.C.
(0161) 480 2359
Southcliffe Road, Reddish
(18)6086 yards/**/C/H

Regent Park G.C.
(01204) 844170
Chorley New Road, Bolton
(18) 6069 yards/***/E

Ringway G.C.
(0161) 904 9609
Hale Barns, Altrincham
(18) 6494 yards/***/B-A/H

Romiley G.C.
(0161) 430 2392
Goosehouse Green, Romiley
(18) 6421 yards/***/B

Saddleworth G.C.
(01457) 873653
Mountain Ash, Uppermill
(18) 5976 yards/***/B/H

Sale G.C.
(0161) 973 1638
Sale Lodge, Golf Road, Sale
(18) 6346 yards/***/B/H/M

Stamford G.C.
(01457) 832126
Huddersfield Road, Stalybridge
(18) 5701 yards/**/F

Stand G.C.
(0161) 766 3197
Ashbourne Grove, Whitefield
(18) 6425 yards/***/B/H

Stockport G.C.
(0161) 427 8369
Offerton Road, Offerton, Stockport
(18) 6326 yards/***/A/M

Swinton Park G.C.
(0161) 794 0861
East Lancashire Road, Swinton
(18) 6712 yards/**/F/H

Turton G.C.
(01204) 852235
Wood End Farm, Bromley Cross
(18) 5894 yards/**(Wed)/D

Walmersley G.C.
(0161) 764 1429
Garretts Close, Walmersley, Bury
(9) 3057 yards/**(Tues)/C

Werneth G.C.
(0161) 624 1190
Green Lane, Garden Suburb, Oldham
(18) 5363 yards/**/D

Werneth Low G.C.
(0161) 368 2503
Werneth Low Road, Hyde
(9) 5734 yards/**/C

Westhoughton G.C.
(01942) 811085
Westhoughton, Bolton
(9) 5834 yards/**/D

Whitefield G.C.
(0161) 766 2904
Higher Lane, Whitefield
(18) 6045 yards/***/B/H/L
(18) 5755 yards/***/B/H/L

Whittaker G.C.
(01706) 378310
Whittaker Lane, Littleborough
(9) 5576 yards/***(Sun)/D

William Wroe G.C.
(0161) 748 8680
Pennybridge Lane, Flixton
(18) 4395 yards/***/E

Withington G.C.
(0161) 445 9544
Palatine Road, West Didsbury
(18) 6411 yards/***(Thurs)/B/H

Worsley G.C.
(0161) 789 4202
Stableford Avenue, Monton, Eccles
(18) 6217 yards/***/B/H/L

LANCASHIRE

Accrington & District G.C.
(01254) 381614
West End, Oswaldtwistle
(18) 5954 yards/***/D

Ashton & Lea G.C.
(01772) 735282
Tudor Avenue, Lea, Preston
(18) 6289 yards/***/C

Bacup G.C.
(01706) 873170
Maden Road,Bacup
(9) 5652 yards/***(Tues)/D

Baxenden & District G.C.
(01254) 234555
Top o' th' Meadow, Baxenden
(9) 5740 yards/**/D

Beacon Park G.C.
(01695) 622700
Beacon Hill, Dalton, Up Holland, Wigan
(18) 5996 yards/***/F

Bentham G.C.
(01524) 261018
Robin Lane, Bentham
(9) 5760 yards/***/D

Blackburn G.C.
(01254) 51122
Beardwood Brow, Blackburn
(18) 6147 yards/**(Tues)/C/H

Blackpool North Shore G.C.
(01253) 351017
Devonshire Road, Blackpool
(18) 6442 yards/***(Thurs/Sat)/B/H

Blackpool Park G.C.
(01253) 397916
North Park Drive, Blackpool
(18) 6192 yards/***/E

Burnley G.C.
(01282) 421045
Glen View, Burnley
(18) 5899 yards/***/C/H

Chorley G.C.
(01257) 480263
Hall o' th' Hill, Heath Charnock, Chorley
(18) 6295 yards/**/C/H/L

Clitheroe G.C.
(01200) 422292
Whalley Road, Pendleton
(18) 6326 yards/***/B/H

Colne G.C.
(01282) 863391
Law Farm, Skipton Old Road
(9) 5961 yards/***/D

Darwen G.C.
(01254) 701287
Winter Hill, Darwen
(18) 5752 yards/***(Sat)/D

Dean Wood G.C.
(01695) 622219
Lafford Lane, Up Holland, Skelmersdale
(18) 6137 yards/**/B

Duxbury Park G.C.
(01257) 265380
Duxbury Hall Road, Chorley
(18) 6390 yards/***/E

Fairhaven G.C.
(01253) 736741
Lytham Hall Park, Ansdell, Lytham
(18) 6883 yards/***/B/H

Fishwick Hall G.C.
(01772) 798300
Glenluce Drive, Farringdon Park, Preston
(18) 6092 yards/**/B

Fleetwood G.C.
(01253) 873661
Princes Way, Fleetwood
(18) 6723 yards/***/B/H

Ghyll G.C.
(01282) 842466
Ghyll Brow, Barnoldswick
(9) 5422 yards/***(Sun)/D

Great Harwood G.C.
(01254) 884391
Whalley Road, Harwood Bar
(9) 6413 yards/***/D

Green Haworth G.C.
(01254) 237580
Green Haworth, Accrington
(9) 5556 yards/***/D

Herons Reach G.C.
(01253) 838866
East Park Drive, Blackpool
(18) 6416 yards/***/B/H

Heysham G.C.
(01524) 851011
Trumacar Park, Middleton Road, Heysham
(18) 6258 yards/***/C/H

Hurlston Hall G.C.
(01704) 840400
Hurlston Lane, Scarisbrick
(18) 6700 yards/**/C/H

Ingol Golf and Squash Club
(01772) 734556
Tanterton Hall Rd, Ingol
(18) 5868 yards/***/C

Knott End G.C.
(01253) 810576
Knott End on Sea
(18) 5789 yards/**/C/H

Lancaster G.& C.C.
(01524) 751247
Ashton Hall, Ashton-with-Stodday
(18) 6282 yards/**/B/H

Lansil G.C.
(01524) 39269
Caton Road, Lancaster
(9) 5608 yards/***/D/H

Leyland G.C.
(01772) 436457
Wigan Road, Leyland
(18) 6123 yards/**/C

Lobden G.C.
(01706) 343228
Whitworth, Rochdale
(9) 5750 yards/***/D/H

Longridge G.C.
(01772) 783291
Fell Barn, Jeffrey Hill, Longridge
(18) 5800 yards/***/C

Lytham Green Drive G.C.
(01253) 737390
Ballam Road, Lytham
(18) 6175 yards/**/B-A/H

Marland G.C.
(01706) 49801
Springfield Park, Rochdale
(18) 5237 yards/***/E

Marsden Park G.C.
(01282) 614094
Townhouse Road, Nelson
(18) 5806 yards/***/F

Morecambe G.C.
(01524) 418050
Bare, Morecambe
(18) 5766 yards/***/B/H

Mytton Fold G.C.
(01254) 240662
Langho, Blackburn
(18) 6217 yards/***/D

Nelson G.C.
(01282) 614583
Kings Causeway, Brierfield, Nelson
(18) 5967 yards/**(Thurs/Sat)/C/H

Ormskirk G.C.
(01695) 572227
Cranes Lane, Lathom, Ormskirk
(18) 6358 yards/***(Sat)/B/H/L

Penwortham G.C.
(01772) 744630
Blundell Lane, Penwortham
(18) 5915 yards/**(Tues)/B

Pleasington G.C.
(01254) 202177
Pleasington, Blackburn
(18) 6417 yards/**(Tues)/B/H

Poulton-le-Fylde G.C.
(01253) 892444
Breck Road, Poulton-le-Fylde
(9) 2979 yards/***/E

Preston G.C.
(01772) 700011
Fulwood Hall Lane, Fulwood, Preston
(18) 6233 yards/**/B/H

Rishton G.C.
(01254) 884442
Eachill Links, Blackburn
(9) 6094 yards/**/D

Rochdale G.C.
(01706) 43818
Edenfield Road, Bagslate, Rochdale
(18) 6002 yards/**/B

Rossendale G.C.
(01706) 213056
Ewood Lane, Haslingden
(18) 6267 yards/***(Sat)/B

Royal Lytham & St Annes G.C.
(01253) 724206
St Annes on Sea, Lytham
(18) 6685 yards/**/A/H/L

St Annes Old Links G.C.
(01253) 723597
Highbury Road, Lytham St Annes
(18) 6616 yards/**(Tues)/B-A/H

Shaw Hill G.& C.C.
(01257) 269221
Whittle-le-Woods, Chorley
(18) 6467 yards/***/A/H

Silverdale G.C.
(01524) 701300
Red Bridge Lane, Silverdale, Carnforth
(9) 5417 yards/***/D

Springfield Park G.C.
(01706) 56401
Springfield Park, Bolton Road, Rochdale
(18) 5209 yards/***/E

Stonyhurst Park G.C.
(01254) 826478
Hurst Green, Blackburn
(9) 5529 yards/**/D

Towneley G.C.
(01282) 451636
Todmorden Road, Burnley
(18) 5862 yards/***/E

Tunshill G.C.
(01706) 342095
Kiln Lane, Milnrow
(9) 5812 yards/**(Tues pm)/F

Whalley G.C.
(01254) 822236
Portfield Lane, Whalley, Blackburn
(9) 6258 yards/***/C

Wigan G.C.
(01257) 421360
Arley Hall, Haigh, Wigan
(9) 6058 yards/***(Tues/Sat)/B

Wilpshire G.C.
(01254) 248260
Whalley Road, Wilpshire, Blackburn
(18) 5911 yards/***/B/H

LIVERPOOL AREA

Allerton Park G.C.
(0151) 428 1048
Allerton, Liverpool
(18) 5494 yards/***/E
(9) 1845 yards/***/E

Arrowe Park G.C.
(0151) 677 1527
Arrowe Park, Woodchurch, Birkenhead
(18) 6377 yards/***/E

Bidston G.C.
(0151) 638 8685
Bidston Link Road, Wallasey
(18) 6207 yards/**/D

Blundells Hill G.C.
(01744) 24892
Blundells Lane, Rainhill
(18) 6347 yards/***/B

Bootle G.C.
(0151) 928 6196
Dunnings Bridge Road, Bootle
(18) 6362 yards/***/F

Bowring G.C.
(0151) 489 1901
Bowring Park, Roby Road, Huyton
(9) 5592 yards/***/F

Brackenwood G.C.
(0151) 608 3093
Bracken Lane, Bebington
(18) 6285 yards/***/F

Bromborough G.C.
(0151) 334 2155
Raby Hall Road, Bromborough
(18) 6650 yards/**/B

Caldy G.C.
(0151) 625 5660
Links Hey Road, Caldy, Wirral
(18) 6675 yards/**/F

Childwall G.C.
(0151) 487 0654
Naylors Road, Gateacre
(18) 6425 yards/**(Tues)/B/H

Dudley Golf Club
(0151) 428 7490
Allerton Park, Allerton
(18) 5494 yards/**/E

Eastham Lodge G.C.
(0151) 327 3003
Ferry Road, Eastham, Wirral
(15) 5813 yards/**/C/H

Formby G.C.
(01704) 872164
Golf Road, Formby
(18) 6695 yards/**(Wed/Sun))/A/H/L

Formby Ladies G.C.
(01704) 873493
Golf Road, Formby
(18) 5374 yards/***(Thurs)/B-A/H

Grand National G.C.
(0151) 523 5157
Melling Road, Aintree
(18) 6624 yards/**/E

Grange Park G.C.
(01744) 26318
Prescot Road, St Helens
(18) 6429 yards/**/B/L

Haydock Park G.C.
(01925) 228525
Golbourne Park, Newton-le-Willows
(18) 6043 yards/**(not Tues)/B/M

Hesketh G.C.
(01704) 536897
Cockle Dicks Lane, Southport
(18) 6478 yards/**/B-A/H

Heswall G.C.
(0151) 342 1237
Cottage Lane, Gayton, Heswall
(18) 6472 yards/***/A/H

Hillside G.C.
(01704) 567169
Hastings Road, Hillside, Southport
(18) 6850 yards/**/A/H/M

Hoylake Municipal G.C.
(0151) 632 2956
Carr Lane, Hoylake
(18) 6330 yards/***/E

Huyton and Prescot G.C.
(0151) 489 3948
Hurst Park, Huyton Lane, Huyton
(18) 5738 yards/**/F/L

Kirkby (Liverpool Municipal) G.C.
(0151) 546 7031
Ingoe Lane, Kirkby
(18) 6571 yards/***/F/H

Leasowe G.C.
(0151) 677 5852
Leasowe Road, Moreton, Wirral
(18) 6204 yards/***/C/H

Lee Park G.C.
(0151) 487 3882
Childwall Valley Road, Gateacre
(18) 6024 yards/***/F/L

Park G.C.
(01704) 530133
Park Road, Southport
(18) 6200 yards/**/F

Prenton G.C.
0151 608 1053
Golf Links Road, Prenton, Birkenhead
(18) 6411 yards/***/B/H

Royal Birkdale G.C.
(01704) 569903
Waterloo Road, Birkdale, Southport
(18) 6988 yards/**/A/H/L

Royal Liverpool G.C.
0151 632 3101
Meols Drive, Hoylake, Wirral
(18) 7128 yards/**/A/H/L

Sherdley Park Municipal G.C.
(01744) 813149
Sherdley Road, St Helens
(18) 5941 yards/***/E

Southport & Ainsdale G.C.
(01704) 578000
Bradshaws Lane, Ainsdale, Southport
(18) 6612 yards/**/A/H/M

Southport G.C.
(01704) 535286
Park Road West, Southport
(18) 6400 yards/***/F

Southport Old Links G.C.
(01704) 28207
Moss Lane, Southport
(9) 6486 yards/**(Wed)/C/H

Wallasey G.C.
0151 691 1024
Bayswater Road, Wallasey
(18) 6607 yards/**/B/H/M

Warren G.C.
0151 639 5730
Grove Road, Wallasey
(9) 5914/***/F

West Derby G.C.
0151 254 1034
Yew Tree Lane, Liverpool
(18) 6333 yards/**/B

West Lancashire G.C.
0151 924 1076
Hall Road West, Blundellsands, Crosby
(18) 6756 yards/***/B-A/H

Wirral Ladies G.C.
0151 652 1255
Bidston Road, Oxton, Birkenhead
(18) 4966 yards(ladies)***/F/H/L
(18) 5170 yards/(men)***F/H/L

Woolton G.C.
0151 486 2298
Doe Park, Speke Road, Woolton
(18) 5706 yards/***/B

ISLE OF MAN

Castletown G.C.
(01624) 822201
Fort Island, Derbyhaven
(18) 6711 yards/***/C

King Edward Bay G.& C.C.
(01624) 672709
Groudle Road, Onchan
(18) 5457 yards/***/D

Mount Murray G & C.C.
(01624) 661111
Santon
(18) 6709 yards/***/E-D/H

Peel G.C.
(01624) 844232
Rheast Lane, Peel
(18) 5914 yards/**/D/H

Port St Mary G.C.
(01624) 497387
Kallow Road, Port St Mary
(9) 2711 yards/***/F

Pulrose G.C.
(01624) 661558
Pulrose Road, Douglas
(18) 6080 yards/***/F

Ramsey G.C.
(01624) 812244
Brookfield, Ramsey
(18) 6019 yards/**/D/H

Rowany G.C.
(01624) 834108
Rowany Drive, Port Erin
(18) 5840 yards/***/D/H

Artist: **Linda Hartough** ROYAL BIRKDALE *Courtesy of:* **Old Troon Sporting Antiques**

Artist: **Roy Perry** **TO HALVE THE MATCH** *Courtesy of:* **Rosenstiel's**

Rudding Park Hotel is an elegant hotel set in 18th century parkland adjacent to the existing Grade II listed Rudding Park House. An inviting fire place in the foyer ensures that guests receive the warmest of Yorkshire welcomes. The luxury bedrooms are spacious, with contemporary furnishings and views over the gardens and golf course.

The Hawtree-designed par 72 course has six bunkers, wide fairways and large elevated greens, but clever use of the trees ensures variety for all levels of golfer. The undulating first seven holes snake up and down hills between mature trees and lakes. There are a few holes in an open area before returning to the parkland and the signature hole of the course. The 14th is surrounded by four bunkers, nestling among rhododendron bushes, and mature woodland.

A covered and floodlit driving range has a professionally run academy along with the latest in video technology to improve already acquired skills and also to help the beginner.

Visiting parties, be they societies or corporate clients, can enjoy the superb course, the relaxed atmosphere of the clubhouse and take full advantage of the administration service. Rudding Park takes full responsibility for the organisation of the whole day so that visitors can concentrate on enjoying their game.

The resort also offers fine conference and banqueting facilities in the Regency period Rudding Park House, with all types of functions receiving the very best of service.

Rudding Park is situated just 2 miles south of the Spa town of Harrogate and is accessible from the A1 north or south via the A661, being just off the A658.

For further information please contact **Rudding Park, Harrogate, North Yorkshire HG3 1JH Tel: (01423) 871350 Fax: (01423) 872286.**

Hole	Yards	Par	Hole	Yards	Par
1	393	4	10	499	5
2	384	4	11	211	3
3	463	4	12	393	4
4	442	4	13	341	4
5	164	3	14	176	3
6	533	5	15	398	4
7	456	4	16	488	5
8	202	3	17	389	4
9	525	5	18	414	4
Out	**3,562**	**36**	**In**	**3,309**	**36**
			Out	**3,562**	**36**
			Totals	**6,871**	**72**

While many consider the delights of Yorkshire to be exclusive to its northernmost area this is totally wrong. The small villages that nestle amid the southern Pennines or the Dales are delightful and the river Wharfe carves its way through south Yorkshire revealing extraordinary beauty along its trail. From the haunting howls of Haworth and the Bronte country to the jovial singing in a pub on Ilkley Moor, there is a rich tradition. Yorkshire folk are a proud breed—better reserve your best golf for the 18th fairway.

South Yorkshire

Perhaps the pick of the courses in the Sheffield area are the moorland course at **Hallamshire**, three miles west of the city off the A57, **Abbeydale**, a fine wooded parkland test to the south west and **Lees Hall**, a mix of parkland and meadowland, located south of the town centre and occupying a lofty situation with marvellous views over the city.

Having saved your best golf for the 18th fairway a few thoughts now emerge for the 19th. A pleasant hotel in this city of nudity is the well run Staindrop Lodge (0114) 284 6727, while the Forte Posthouse (0114) 267 0067 is particularly convenient for the Hallamshire course. Sheffield also offers the comfortable Charnwood Hotel (0114) 2589411. The city has many good Asian restaurants, one of the best being Nirmal's (0114) 2724054; whilst for French food enthusiasts we suggest the Neptune (0114) 2796677. Finally, we ought to recommend a good pub (the area is naturally riddled with them) but try the Fat Cat in downtown Sheffield—a great establishment.

Before noting some of the other courses in South Yorkshire, a brief word on **Lindrick** (featured separately). According to the postman it properly belongs in Nottinghamshire although the club's administrative ties are with Yorkshire and a great number of members live in the Sheffield area. Anyway, whichever side of the fence it's on it is quite superb! The same can be said of the Old Vicarage (0114) 2475814—a classic restaurant.

Rotherham's excellent course is located at Thrybergh Park, two miles north of the town on the A630 and is well worth inspecting. Crossing the A1 we arrive at Doncaster. The **Doncaster Town Moor** Golf Club is situated very close to the famous racetrack. Like Rotherham, it's a parkland type course though not as testing. In Doncaster, the Danum Swallow (01302) 342261 and the Grand St Leger (01302) 364111 are two recommended establishments. In the countryside surrounding the busy railway town, Cadeby provides the cosy Cadeby Inn, while in Hatfield Woodhouse the Green Tree offers a warm welcome and some good snacks. The Crown at Bawtry (01302) 710341 is a pleasant high street inn. Those seeking more creature comforts should try Hellaby Hall (01709) 702701 which is very handy for the M18 and well worth a visit.

West Yorkshire

West Yorkshire has a greater number of golf courses. Quantity is certainly matched by quality with the area just to the north of Leeds being particularly outstanding. Within a short distance of one another are **Alwoodley** and **Moortown** (both are featured ahead), **Sand Moor** and **Moor Allerton**, all of which are of championship standard.

Whilst Alwoodley, Moortown and Sand Moor are predominantly heathland and moorland in character, Moor Allerton, where there are 27 holes, is more strictly parkland. When travelling to any of the four clubs, the A61

should be taken out of Leeds itself. Moortown is probably the most widely known course in southern Yorkshire (if one excludes Lindrick), however, many consider Alwoodley to be at least its equal. Play all four if you can! An outstanding place to stay in this area — just one mile from Moortown — is Weetwood Hall (0113) 2306000; less expensive but equally welcoming is the Harewood Arms Hotel (0113) 2886566 in Harewood. Other good courses to note around Leeds are **Roundhay, Leeds, Howley Hall** and **Temple Newsham.**

Following the Wharfe into the east of West Yorkshire one finds some superb countryside. This is the land of the Brontes. In Bramhope, a far cry from the romance of the Brontes but a particularly popular hotel for businessmen visiting Leeds, is Oulton Hall (0113) 2821000. Visiting golfers will find plenty of good but inexpensive accommodation in Leeds, the Aragon Hotel (0113) 2759306 being a fine example. The gem in this area however is Pool Court at 42 The Calls (0113) 2440099—a wonderful restaurant, it is also a thoroughly engaging place to stay.

A second concentration of good golf courses is to be found to the north of Bradford, more particularly, **Northcliffe, Keighley** and **Shipley.** Northcliffe is probably the pick with some outstanding views of the nearby moors, but each is well worth a game. Yet another trio encircles Huddersfield, with **Bradley Park** to the north, **Woodsome Hall** to the south and **Huddersfield** Golf Club to the west. It was on the latter course that Sandy Herd learnt his game. The Open Champion of 1902, Herd finished in the first five in the Championship on no fewer than twelve occasions. He would have doubtless won on several of those but for a fellow called Vardon from Ganton across the way.

Two more courses in West Yorkshire demand to be visited—the first is **Ilkley** and the second is **Otley.** They are without question two of the county's most attractive courses. Our friend, the River Wharfe, winds its way through much of the Ilkley course and is a major hazard on several of the early holes. The equally charming course at Otley nestles majestically in the Wharfe valley. Beyond the fairways, the river and the rough, the gourmet golfer is well catered for in this area. Here are some suggestions. In Ilkley, the Edwardian Breakfast at Rombalds (01943) 603201 is legendary but the hotel itself and the restaurant are both thoroughly recommended too. Elsewhere in Ilkley, a town where delightful antique shops clutter the streets, one finds the Craiglands Hotel (01943) 607676 which has a setting adjoining that famous moor and is most comfortable. Another good value establishment is the Cow and Calf (01943) 607335. A restaurant renowned for its fine cuisine is the Box Tree (01943) 608484—pricey but excellent.

In Otley, Chevin Lodge (01943) 467818 built in Finnish pine is an interesting option. Bradford, Bingley, Otley—all this area is riddled with enthusiastic cricket and rugby sides as well as golfers—popular pubs for one and all include the Fox at Menston, the Malt Shovel at Harden and in Ryburn, where there would seem to be a focal point, the Old Bridge and the Over the Bridge (both provide excellent lunches—perhaps in between rounds?)

North Yorkshire

To the south and west the Yorkshire Dales, to the north and east the Yorkshire Moors. North Yorkshire is England's largest county and quite possibly England's most beautiful.

The Dales and the Moors may not sound like great golfing country and indeed by far the greater number of Yorkshire's golf courses lie in the more populated and industrial regions of South and West Yorkshire. However, golfing visitors to North Yorkshire will not be disappointed; not only does the county boast the likes of Ganton and Fulford, two of England's greatest inland courses, but there are forty or so others, the majority of which are set in glorious surroundings.

Starting from the top of the county, just south of the Tees in what was until recently Cleveland, the golf course at **Saltburn** isn't right by the sea, it's about a mile west of the town and is a well-wooded meadowland course. Around Teeside itself there are courses at Redcar (**Cleveland**), **Middlesborough** and **Billingham** but perhaps the best or most enjoyable in the area is found at **Eaglescliffe**, a hilly course where there are some marvellous views of the Cleveland Hills.

For a 19th hole, at Saltburn an excellent pub can be recommended, namely the Ship with its splendid sea views, while a little inland at Moorsholm the Jolly Sailor offers some very good food. Those playing at Eaglescliffe can enjoy midday sustenance (or evening celebration) at the Blue Bell.

York, they say, is a city everyone should visit at least once. I recommend at least twice for there are two outstanding golf courses within three miles of York Minster: **Fulford** to the south and York Golf Club at **Strensall** to the north. Fulford (see feature page) is the better known, but York is also a championship course and has many admirers. It is a fine woodland type course, laid out on the edge of Strensall Common.

Staying in York is a delight: there is a wealth of attractions—Shambles has some marvellous shops, the Minster itself is sensational, there are museums galore and some first class hotels in and around the city. The star of the show is Middlethorpe Hall (01904) 640241, a beautiful mansion house with an exquisite restaurant. The Mount Royale (01904) 628856 is another well run hotel and is less expensive, while closer to the centre of town the Judges Lodging (01904) 638733 is particularly elegant. The equally relaxing Grasmead House Hotel (01904) 629996 is excellent value.

The town centre has many tea shops and small restaurants as well as some pleasant pubs. Meltons (01904) 634341 is a particularly fine restaurant. A noted pub outside the city can be found in Wighill—the White Swan—good value bar snacks. In Fulford village two pubs very handy for the famous course are the Saddle and the Plough and convenient accommodation can be found in Hovingham at the Worsley Arms (01653) 628234, a delightfully elegant inn.

Next to York, Harrogate probably offers most to both sightseer and golfer. **Pannal** and **Harrogate** are the pick of the courses in the area, the former being a fairly lengthy championship challenge. It is moorland in nature and heavily wooded. Harrogate is possibly the more attractive with its lovely setting at Starbeck near Knaresborough. **Rudding Park**, set in 18th century parkland, is an award-winning par 72 course offering a good test of golf together with a fully equipped golf academy and driving range. Rudding Park House (01423) 871350 provides 4 star accommodation along with conference and banqueting facilities.

The town of Harrogate is renowned for its fine restaurants. They include the Drum and Monkey (01423) 502650 (superb seafood) and Cafe Fleur (01423) 503034. The restaurants in the town's hotels are generally particularly good, notably those at the Majestic (01423) 568972, the Old Swan (01423) 500055, the Studley (01423) 560425 and the Balmoral Hotel and Restaurant (01423) 508208.

The Bistro (01423) 530708 is also most attractive.

Before heading towards the dales and moors it is worth noting **Selby** in the south of the county. Laid out over fairly sandy subsoil the course could be described as part links, part parkland. An enjoyable day's golf here might be followed by a visit to Monk Fryston and its fine hotel, Monk Fryston Hall (01977) 682369.

Skipton is known as the 'Gateway to the Dales'. The ancient market town has a fine parkland course situated only a mile or so from the town centre. The views are magnificent and a mountain stream runs through the course adding to the many challenges. An appetite created, dinner is recommended at the Devonshire Arms (01756) 710441 in Bolton Abbey. If a good drink is simply all that's required then the Angel at Helton may be preferable.

Ripon is another very charming place. There are only nine holes of golf here (at **Ripon City**) though they offer great variety nonetheless. The surrounding countryside is quite stupendous. Jervaulx Abbey, founded in 1156 is well worth inspecting as is Fountains Abbey. For accommodation, Ripon has the Ripon Spa Hotel (01765) 602172 or the more modest Crescent Lodge (01765) 602331, and in nearby Boroughbridge, the Crown (01423) 322328 is a comfortable old inn. Lovers of Theakstons should make a pilgrimage to the White Bear at Masham. One other hotel of distinction in the area is the charming Feversham Arms at Helmsley (01439) 770766 noted not just for its accommodation but also for its great lunches. The village is extremely pleasant and an ideal base for touring the Yorkshire moors and dales.

Two of North Yorkshire's most beautiful courses are situated fairly close to one another in the centre of the county: **Thirsk & Northallerton** and **Bedale**. The former lies very close to Thirsk racetrack. The views here are towards the Cleveland Hills on one side and the Hambleton Hills on another. Bedale Golf Club can be found off the A684 and is known for its beautiful spread of trees.

In the north of the county, **Richmond** Golf Club enjoys glorious surroundings. The town itself has a strange mixture of medieval, Georgian and Victorian architecture and is dominated of course by the famous castle. Fine restaurants once again abound: in nearby Moulton, the Black Bull Inn (01325) 377289 is excellent, as is the Bridge Inn (01325) 350106 at Stapleton. Firmly recommended also are the Millers House (01969) 622630 at Middleham and the Burgogne Hotel (01428) 884292 in Reeth. Just south of Richmond, **Catterick Garrison's** Golf Club is well worth a visit.

Dropping back down the county, **Malton and Norton** shouldn't be overlooked. It is also particularly convenient for those heading towards Ganton on the A64. **Ganton**, thought by many to be the finest inland course in England, boasts a superb setting on the edge of the Vale of Pickering. It is explored fully on a later page. The White Swan (01751) 472288 in Pickering is welcoming place to stay and offers some excellent bar snacks.

Yorkshire's coast contrasts greatly with that of Lancashire, with spectacular cliffs rather than dunes dominating the shoreline. Not surprisingly, there are no true links courses to be found here. However, visitors to the resorts of **Filey** and **Scarborough** will be able to enjoy a game with sea and sand and near Flamborough Head there is a testing layout at **Bridlington.**

The Crown (01723) 373491 overlooking Scarborough South Bay is a busy hotel to consider. East Ayton Lodge (01723) 864227 is also handy and very pleasant too. Slightly inland at Hackness, the Hackness Grange

Country Hotel (01723) 882345 enjoys a beautiful setting and makes for a pleasant stay. There's also a pitch and putt course to sneak in some early morning practice. Meanwhile at Scalby, Wrea Head (01723) 378211 is a Victorian country house of character. Finally, situated between Scarborough and Whitby in Ravenscar, lies the **Raven Hall** Country House Hotel and Golf Course (01723) 870353, a historic house well worth a visit.

The East Riding

The East Riding, like a phoenix, has risen from the ashes of Humberside and reappears in its former glory. Unfortunately try as I may, I cannot trot off a list of wonderful golf courses. There are enough of them about but there's no Ganton here, alas. The best in the county is arguably at **Hornsea**, famed, of course for its pottery. It is a beautiful heathland course with particularly outstanding greens. One tip—try not to kill the ducks on the 11th!

Beverley is no great distance from Hornsea and the Beverley Arms (01482) 869241 is a good place for a night's rest. Tickton offers the excellent Tickton Grange (01964) 543666 and for a pleasant drink visit the White Horse in Brandesburton. The Manor House (01482) 881645 is wonderfully peaceful and offers excellent accommodation and food to complete the picture.

If one has crossed all 1542 yards of the Humber Bridge to reach the county's largest town then the **Hull** Golf Club at Kirk Ella is probably the best choice for a game, although **Hessle** has developed into a very good course too. The Waterfront (01482) 227222 is the most attractive hotel in town. The seafood in Hull ought to be sampled, Ceruttis (01482) 28501 is one of the best places to do so.

From north to south and across the breadth of the newly reunited Yorkshire the golfer can enjoy a wealth of outstanding courses and a fine array of hotels in a dramatically changing landscape. A visit is most heartily recommended.

Artist: **Victor Venner** *LUCKY DOG* *Courtesy of:* **Rosenstiel's**

The Worsley Arms Hotel is an attractive stone built Georgian inn in the heart of Hovingham, near York, with a history stretching back to Roman times. The hotel was built in 1841 by Sir William Worsley, the first Baronet. Today the hotel still belongs to the Worsley family and is privately operated by Euan and Debbi Rodger. Hovingham Hall, the family house which stands on the edge of the village was designed around 1760 by Thomas Worsley, and is now the home of Sir Marcus Worsley, the fifth Baronet. His sister, Her Royal Highness the Duchess of Kent was born there.

This country inn of renown, named Yorkshire Life's Hotel of the Year for 1997/8, has the welcoming and restful atmosphere of a pleasant country house. The spacious sitting rooms are ideal havens for morning coffee, full afternoon tea, or an aperitif.

Food is undoubtedly a highlight. The chef, Andrew Jones, with a wealth of local produce on the doorstep, aims to combine the best of traditional and modern

cooking with presentation that reflects an individual style. His food can be enjoyed in the Wyvern Restaurant or in the more informal Cricketers Bistro. In recognition of the quality of the food, the AA has, for the third year running, awarded the hotel two AA Rosettes.

The bedrooms, each with private bathroom, are individually and tastefully decorated, providing every comfort and modern facility.

The village is on the edge of a designated Area of Outstanding Natural Beauty; national parks are on the doorstep, the nearby Yorkshire Dales and the North York Moors. The area is rich in romantic and historic sites—the ruined abbeys of Rievaulx and Fountains, the castles of Helmsley and Pickering, the stately homes of Castle Howard, Duncombe Park and, of course, Hovingham Hall. Leisure pursuits abound as the hotel is ideally placed for quality racing, golfing (the championship courses of Ganton and Fulford are within half an hours drive), shooting and walking.

The Worsley Arms Hotel
Hovingham
York YO6 4LA
Tel: (01653) 628234
Fax: (01653) 628130

Ganton

They used to say at Ganton that when Harry Vardon played the course twice in the same day, in his afternoon round he'd often hit his tee shots into the very divots he'd created in the morning. The chances are that this was a little bit of Yorkshire bluff but then again the members at Ganton were fortunate to witness what were probably the very finest years of Britain's greatest ever golfer.

Vardon came to Ganton in 1896, just five years after the club's formation. Within a few weeks of his appointment he won his first Open Championship at Muirfield defeating the hat trick seeking John H Taylor in a play-off. In 1900 Vardon returned from America with the US Open trophy, by which time he'd added two more Open Championships and was half way towards his record number of six victories in that event. By the time that Vardon left the Club in 1903 the name of Ganton had been firmly put on the golfing map.

Located approximately nine miles from the sea, Ganton could hardly be called a golf links in the strict sense but it is often said that it has many of the features of links golf with crisp seaside turf and sandy subsoil. Indeed, whenever new bunkers are cut, sea-shells are often discovered lying beneath the surface—it appears that the whole of the surrounding area was once an arm of the sea.

Golfers wishing to play at Ganton must make prior arrangements with the club's **Secretary, Major R G Woolsey** who may be contacted on the **Ganton Golf Club, Ganton, Scarborough, North Yorkshire YO12 4PA. (01944) 710329** and fax (01944) 710922. The club's **Professional, Gary Brown,** can be reached on **(01944) 710260**. Subject to proof of handicap and prior arrangement, visitors are made most welcome and it is possible to pre-book starting times. The green fees for 1998 are set at £48 for a day's golf during the week with £53 payable at the weekend.

Travelling to the course is made straightforward by the A64. This road links the village directly with Scarborough to the north east (12 miles) and to both York (30 miles) and Leeds (60 miles) to the south west. If approaching from the south a combination of the A164 to Great Driffield and the B1249 will take you to within two miles of the course. Travellers from further north can avoid the City of York by heading for Thirsk and thereafter heading for Malton by way of the A170 and the B1257. Malton lies on the A64 road and, like Scarborough, is approximately twelve miles from Ganton.

Ganton enjoys a beautifully peaceful setting nestling on the edge of the Vale of Pickering and the Yorkshire Moors. While the golf course is indeed beautiful, particularly when the gorse is in full bloom, it is very rarely peaceful and when the winds sweep across it can become fearsomely difficult. There are few inland courses with such cavernous bunkers—111 of them in all! In addition to the many bunkers and the great spread of gorse, there are numerous fir trees and pines which can come into play following a wayward shot—the dog-leg 18th being a notable example, and one that provides a very testing finishing hole.

The finest hole on the course is thought by many to be the 4th, where the second has to be played across a plunging valley towards a plateau green that is heavily bunkered to the right. Another outstanding hole on the front nine is the 7th, a marvellous swinging dog-leg, and on the back nine the 15th and 16th are both highly memorable two-shotters.

The 19th at Ganton has a welcoming atmosphere and offers an extensive range of catering. (Note the famous Ganton cake—the origins of which are unknown and the recipe a secret!) Dress is informal in the men's bar until 4pm Monday to Friday, although a jacket and tie should be worn in all other public rooms.

Inevitably Ganton's name will always be linked with Vardon's. But another great player also developed his talents on the Yorkshire course—Ted Ray, the famed long hitter who won the Open in 1912 and later found fortune in America winning their Open in 1920. In winning the latter he ironically held off the challenge of the then 50 year old Vardon. The greatest event in Ganton's distinguished history was undoubtedly the great Ryder Cup match of 1949 when the home team led by three matches to one at the end of the first day only to lose eventually by seven to five. Ben Hogan, convalescing from his near fatal accident, led the American side as non-playing captain.

Three times since the last war the Amateur Championship has been held at Ganton. The most recent staging was in 1991, the centenary year for the club. The British Mid-Amateur is scheduled for 12-16th August 1998, the English Ladies' Amateur Championship for May 1999 and the Curtis Cup for June 2000.

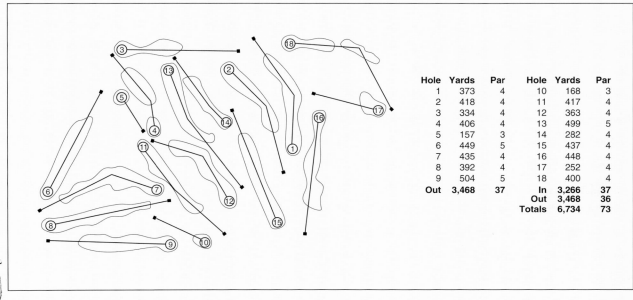

Hole	Yards	Par	Hole	Yards	Par
1	373	4	10	168	3
2	418	4	11	417	4
3	334	4	12	363	4
4	406	4	13	499	5
5	157	3	14	282	4
6	449	5	15	437	4
7	435	4	16	448	4
8	392	4	17	252	4
9	504	5	18	400	4
Out	**3,468**	**37**	**In**	**3,266**	**37**
			Out	**3,468**	**36**
			Totals	**6,734**	**73**

Moortown

Moortown enjoys an enviable situation. It lies within minutes of the town centre of Leeds, yet it also lies within minutes of the Pennines and the beauty of the Yorkshire Moors. The club was founded in the autumn of 1909 with the course being laid out by the great Alister Mackenzie. Less than twenty years after its formation Moortown was selected to host the first ever Ryder Cup to be played on British soil. It proved a momentous occasion.

The American side in 1929 was virtually identical to the one that crushed the British team 9-2 in the inaugural staging at Worcester, Massachusetts two years previously. It included Walter Hagen, the reigning British Open Champion, Gene Sarazen, Johnny Farrel the US Open Champion, Leo Diegel the US PGA Champion and Al Watrous. To cut a long story short, the British side won by six matches to four. On the final day George Duncan defeated Walter Hagen by 10 and 8 and Archie Compston defeated Gene Sarazen 6 and 4. Whatever it may have done to American pride, and I note that Wall Street collapsed later that summer, it certainly secured Moortown's place in golfing lore.

With its great spread of heather and gorse Moortown is occasionally described as heathland, although the absence of sandy sub-soil more properly makes it a moorland type course. Either way, it has the fine combination of being sufficiently testing yet not too severe.

Measuring in excess of 7000 yards from the championship tees, the generally held view is that the front nine is much the easier of the two halves; this may have something to do with the fact that it begins with what golfers usually term a 'birdiable hole', being a short par five to a fairly open green. Perhaps Moortown's finest hole is the 10th, a par three measuring 176 yards, it calls for a shot to a plateau green built on a foundation of rock; it is called 'Gibraltar'—miss it

and you're sunk. The 12th is an excellent par five, aptly titled 'The Long' for it stretches to 554 yards; the aforementioned Archie Compston once holed out here in two strokes.

The difficult, dog-leg 18th at Moortown has an alarming effect on certain people. Countless numbers, including Severiano Ballesteros, have been known to overclub and fire the ball over the green into the clubhouse area. In the 1929 Ryder Cup during one of the foursomes matches, Joe Turnesa hooked his second behind the marquee adjoining the clubhouse whereupon his partner promptly sailed it back over the marquee to within a yard of the hole. In the 1974 English Amateur Strokeplay tournament one player actually put his second into the men's bar. Opening the clubhouse windows he played his third straight out onto the green. The clubhouse certainly has a welcoming atmosphere but this would seem to be taking things a little too far!

Moortown Golf Club, Harrogate Road, Alwoodley, Leeds, LS17 7DB

Sec/Manager	Chris Moore (0113) 268 6521
Professional	Bryon Hutchinson (0113) 268 3636
Green Fees	WD £42/round, £50/day
	WE £47/round, £55/day
Restrictions	Prior arrangement with Secretary

Directions
The A61 Leeds to Harrogate road takes you directly to Moortown.

Fulford

These days golf is not only played in every foreign field but it is also played in the most unlikely of places. In 1971 astronaut Captain Alan Sheppard struck two golf shots from the surface of the moon, becoming in the process the only man able to shank a ball 200 yards. Not to be outdone, as ever, Arnold Palmer in 1977 hit three golf balls off the second stage of the Eiffel Tower, while in 1981 at Fulford, Bernhard Langer decided to take golf into further alien territory by shinning up a rather large tree and playing his chip shot to the 17th green from amidst its spreading branches.

Fulford Golf Club was founded soon after the turn of the century, but it was only as recently as 1985 that the club celebrated 50 years of playing over the present course. Televised tournament golf has undoubtedly turned the North Yorkshire club into a 'golfing household name', but in golf's more discerning circles it has for a long time possessed the reputation of having one of the country's finest inland courses.

Measuring 6775 yards from the back tees (par 72) Fulford provides quite a stern test for the club golfer, but it is no more than a medium length course for the professionals. Much of the prodigiously low scoring achieved at Fulford during those European Tour events that it has staged has, however, had precious little to do with the length of the course. As the members will quickly tell you, it simply reflects the superb condition in which the fairways and the putting surfaces are maintained. Fulford is especially renowned for its fast and very true greens. Certainly, Ian Woosnam found them much to his liking as he holed putt after putt during an extraordinary sequence of eight successive birdies during his final round in the 1985 Benson and Hedges International Tournament. Woosnam's score of 62 that day set a new course record but unfortunately it wasn't quite good enough to prevent Sandy Lyle from joining a distinguished list of

Fulford champions—a list which includes the likes of Tony Jacklin, Greg Norman and Lee Trevino.

The 'B&H' has since gone south to St Mellion and The Oxfordshire, although in the early 1990s Fulford played host to a second European Tour event, the Murphy's Cup. In keeping with the tradition of eccentricity established by Bernhard Langer in 1981, the organisers announced before the inaugural 1990 event that the first player to hole in one at the 14th would receive 'one hour's output of Murphy's Irish Stout' (estimated to be 13,750 pints)!

Most golfers probably won't be leaving Fulford with a 62 under their belt—nor one presumes will they have been shinning up the trees or downing Murphy's by the bucketload—but they are sure to be heading home contented souls having spent a day on what is unquestionably one of the country's most pleasurable golf courses.

Fulford Golf Club, Heslington Lane, Fulford, York, YO1 5DY

Sec/Manager	Ron Bramley (01904) 413579
Professional	Bryan Hessay (01904) 412882
Green Fees	WD £30/round, £40/day
	WE £40
Restrictions	Prior arrangement with secretary.

Directions
Fulford lies a mile south of York just off the A19.

The hotel is the result of the tasteful blending of two beautiful William IV detached houses. The proprietors, Richard and Christine Oxtoby, have spent a good deal of effort on restoring the former glory of these buildings and their efforts have been well rewarded.

Any traveller with an interest in English history must surely rate the fascinating city of York at least alongside London. The capital of the north and second city of the realm, it began its long and fascinating life around AD71 as a fortress to protect the Roman 9th legion. The marauding Vikings gave the city its name, derived from Jorvik or Yorvik. This period of history has been magnificently captured in the Jorvik Viking Centre, one of the most entertaining museums in the country.

The minster or cathedral is the largest medieval structure in Britain. There has been a minster on the site since the 7th century. The present one is the fourth and was started about 1220, taking 250 years to complete. The city is still protected by ancient city walls, guarded by defensive bastions, working portcullis and barbican at the Walmgate bar.

Staying in York one is surrounded by some of the most fascinating sights in the world. Wander around the Micklegate bar, where traitors' severed heads were displayed, or visit the National Rail Museum.

Relaxing afterwards in the intimate cocktail bar of the Mount Royale, or enjoying a delicious meal in the restaurant overlooking the delightful garden, enhances the whole experience. Enjoying the gracious beauty of the hotel, the style and antiquity of much of the furnishings, or slipping into the secluded heated swimming pool is the perfect way to pamper the body as well as the mind.

The hotel is ideal for the small conference or private party, and is only a short drive from the rolling Yorkshire Dales. The perfect base, offering peace and tranquillity in the heart of this wonderful city.

Mount Royale Hotel
The Mount
York, Y02 2DA
Tel: (01904) 628856
Fax: (01904) 611171

Lindrick

There are two golf courses in England whose names will be forever linked with the Ryder Cup: one is The Belfry, the other is Lindrick—and they couldn't be more different. The Belfry (perhaps one should be precise and say the Brabazon Course) is a big strapping youngster, immature in some ways though agreeable in others. Lindrick is the seasoned campaigner. It's seen a lot in its lifetime (and in fact is old enough to have received a telegram in 1991). It is no giant but it is charming, subtle and full of challenge.

Before the Ryder Cup came to Lindrick in 1957, many golfing enthusiasts knew very little of this great course, indeed some knew nothing at all. By the end of that heady, windswept week in October, none present would ever forget it. It was the last time an exclusively British and Irish team would ever beat the mighty men from across the sea.

Lindrick lies close to the boundaries of Yorkshire, Nottinghamshire and Derbyshire. Although the golf course is entirely contained within the confines of South Yorkshire, the club's postal address is Lindrick, Notts—no doubt to the considerable annoyance of every Yorkshireman! The golf course occupies the best part of 200 acres of classic English common—Lindrick Common—and is essentially heathland in nature, lying on top of limestone rock. There is a mass of gorse which, when in bloom adds great colour (though it can be a devil if you land in it!) and a wealth of oak and silver birch—a delightful setting if ever there was one.

Visitors are very welcome to test their skills in this splendid environment, although prior arrangement with the club is required. The **Secretary** is **Lieutenant Commander R J M Jack RN**, who may be contacted by telephone on **(01909) 475282** or by fax on (01909) 488685. Written correspondence should be addressed to **Lindrick Golf Club, Lindrick Common, Worksop, Notts, S81 8BH**. All bookings should be made through the Secretary's office, but as a general guide, visitors are not permitted to play on Tuesday mornings and

the first tee is normally reserved for members for an hour around lunchtime, but again it's best to check.

The green fees at Lindrick vary according to the season. In summer 1998 they were set at £45 per round on weekdays and at weekends. Reductions of fifty per cent are available to junior golfers if accompanied by an adult. The club's **Professional** is **Peter Cowen (01909) 475820**.

Although Lindrick Common may look a little isolated on the map, strangers shouldn't have too much difficulty in locating the course. Those coming from the south should find the M1 and the A1 of great assistance. The club is actually situated just off the A57 Worksop to Sheffield road, to the west of the former and is well signposted.

From the championship tees, the course measures 6606 yards, with the par a fairly tight 71. Quite refreshingly, it is not a long hitter's course—the fairway shots to the green being what Lindrick is all about—and there are some excellent par fours. The 2nd, with its slightly uphill approach, the 8th and the 17th are among the most subtle and cleverly designed holes, while the most demanding are the 7th, 12th and 13th. Perhaps the best known hole at Lindrick is the par five 4th. This requires a blind approach to a low lying green backed by trees and behind which the River Ryton flows. The green has a magnificent stage-like setting and it was here that the boundaries of Yorkshire, Derbyshire and Nottinghamshire once merged. In days of old, the stage was used for bare fist-fighting and cockfighting, contestants and spectators being able to step into a convenient county whenever unfriendly law authorities showed up.

The clubhouse at Lindrick provides golfers with a fine view of the 18th green and many a drama will have been witnessed. But I don't suppose there will ever be anything to equal the scenes of 1957 and the time when Dai Rees and his boys made the old campaigner smile.

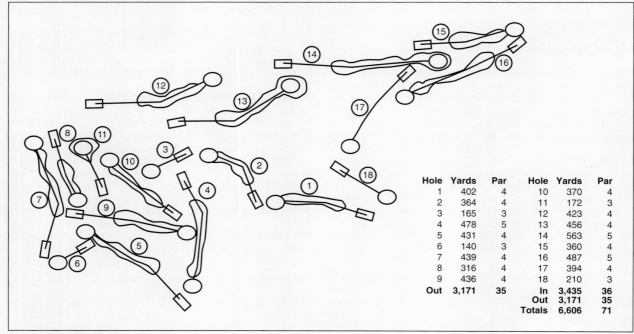

Hole	Yards	Par	Hole	Yards	Par
1	402	4	10	370	4
2	364	4	11	172	3
3	165	3	12	423	4
4	478	5	13	456	4
5	431	4	14	563	5
6	140	3	15	360	4
7	439	4	16	487	5
8	316	4	17	394	4
9	436	4	18	210	3
Out	**3,171**	**35**	**In**	**3,435**	**36**
			Out	**3,171**	**35**
			Totals	**6,606**	**71**

Alwoodley

Whereas the best links golf in the North of England is to be found on the coast of Lancashire, it is Yorkshire that has the superior collection of inland courses. By general consensus the three finest golf courses in Yorkshire are Ganton in the north, Lindrick in the south and Alwoodley, which, situated just to the north of Leeds, lies somewhere in the middle. Collectively they comprise what writer Barry Ward calls 'The Great Triumvirate of Yorkshire Golf'.

All three golf courses could be described as heathland, although parts of Ganton resemble a seaside links and both Lindrick and Alwoodley provide more than a hint of moorland golf. Alwoodley, for instance, has far more trees—predominately firs and silver birches—than a traditional heathland layout such as Walton Heath, and while the likes of Sunningdale and St Georges Hill have very little gorse to accompany the heather, the gorse at Alwoodley grows in abundance. The most distinctive feature of Alwoodley, however, owes more to the input of man than nature.

Alister Mackenzie, the creator of such golfing masterpieces as Augusta and Royal Melbourne, was the principal architect of Alwoodley. He designed several courses in Great Britain—and most of these in Yorkshire—before achieving international fame, but Alwoodley is widely acknowledged to be his premier British design. Amazingly, it was also his first. Harry Colt was originally approached (this was back in 1907) but after he had discussed the project with Mackenzie - then a medical practitioner with a keen interest in golf course architecture (and soon to be the club's first secretary) - it was Mackenzie who effectively assumed the role of course designer. The style and standard of the bunkering is the feature that particularly sets the course apart. It is very bold, almost 'flashy' in appearance, and it repeatedly turns strong holes into superb and extremely strategic ones. The other significant Mackenzie signature is the quality of the putting surfaces, which are generally quite large and always beautifully contoured.

Returning to our 'Great Yorkshire Triumvirate', despite Mackenzie's contribution Alwoodley is the least known of the trio. This is principally because, over the years, Ganton and Lindrick have regularly staged important championships—men's and women's, amateur and pro-

fessional—while Alwoodley on the other hand has preferred to maintain a much lower profile. A stubborn regard for privacy rather than any perceived 'stuffiness' has been the cause, although in recent years this resolve has eased and the club has hosted both the English and British Ladies Championships.

Provided arrangements are made in advance, visitors (who must have current handicaps) are generally welcome at Alwoodley on each day except for Tuesday's and Saturdays. For 1998 the green fee rates are £50 during the week and £60 at weekends. The club's **Secretary, Mr R C W Banks** can be contacted by telephone on **(0113) 268 1680** and by fax on (0113) 268 9458. The **Professional, John Green** can be reached on **(0113) 268 9603**. Given its close proximity to Leeds, Alwoodley enjoys a surprisingly tranquil as well as attractive setting. Its precise location is five miles north of Leeds via the A61 Harrogate road. The Club's full address is **Alwoodley Golf Club, Wigton Lane, Alwoodley, Leeds LS17 8SA**.

Measuring 6686 yards, par 72 from the back tees, Alwoodley's routing is unusual for an inland course (though similar to the West Course at Wentworth) in that it runs 'out and back' in classical links fashion. Not every hole follows this general trend, however, particularly on the outward nine, but the final six holes all confront the prevailing wind and invariably make for an exacting finish.

The outstanding holes on the front nine are the 3rd, a sweeping par five with its green set in a slight hollow, the 5th, a shortish par four but where the fairway has a pronounced left to right tilt, and the 8th, at 546 yards a big three-shotter with a chain of cross bunkers and a slightly raised green.

On the inward nine the two short holes, the tight uphill 11th and the 200 yards-plus 14th are both very challenging but arguably the two finest holes of the round must be tackled during the aforementioned tough 'finishing stretch'. The 15th has been described by Frank Penninck as 'the Pride of Alwoodley' and it features an undulating, curving fairway, some intelligent cross bunkering and an elusive plateaued green. Finally, an elevated tee at the 18th encourages the player to open his shoulders—although a legion of bunkers lie in wait, perfectly placed to thwart any hopes of a closing birdie.

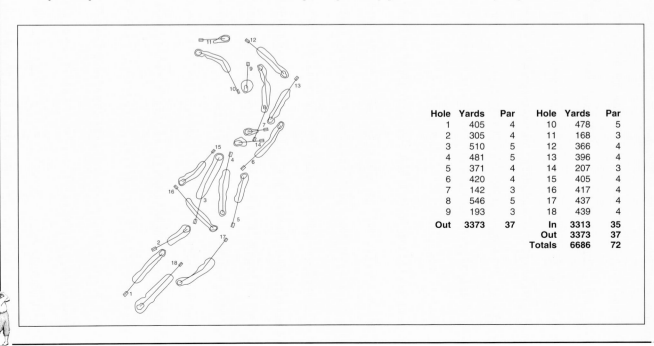

Hole	Yards	Par	Hole	Yards	Par
1	405	4	10	478	5
2	305	4	11	168	3
3	510	5	12	366	4
4	481	5	13	396	4
5	371	4	14	207	3
6	420	4	15	405	4
7	142	3	16	417	4
8	546	5	17	437	4
9	193	3	18	439	4
Out	**3373**	**37**	**In**	**3313**	**35**
			Out	**3373**	**37**
			Totals	**6686**	**72**

NORTH YORKSHIRE

Aldwark Manor G.C.
(01347) 838353
Aldwark, Alne, York
(18) 6171 yards/***/C

Ampleforth College G.C.
(01439) 770678
Helmsley, York
(10) 4018 yards/***/E

Bedale G.C.
(01677) 422451
Leyburn Road, Bedale
(18) 6565 yards/***/C

Bentham G.C.
(015242) 61018
Robin Lane, Bentham
(9) 5760 yards/***/D

Catterick G.C.
(01748) 833268
Leyburn Road, Catterick Garrison
(18) 6331 yards/***/C

Cleveland G.C.
(01642) 471798
Coatham, Redcar
(18) 6707 yards/**/C/H

Cocksford G.C.
(01937) 834253
Cocksford, Stutton
(18) 5518 yards/***/C

Crimple Valley G.C.
(01423) 883485
Hookstone Wood Road, Harrogate
(9) 2500 yards/***(pm only)/F

Drax G.C.
(01405) 860533
Drax, Selby
(9) 5510 yards/*/G

Easingwold G.C.
(01347) 821964
Stillngton Road, Easingwold
(18) 6262 yards/***/B/H

Filey G.C.
(01723) 513293
South Cliff, Filey
(18) 6104 yards/***/C/M

Forest of Galtres G.C.
(01904) 766198
Wideopen Farm, Skelton Lane
(18) 6312 yards/***/B

Forest Park G.C.
(01904) 400425
Stockton on Forest
(18) 6211 yards/***/C

Fulford G.C.
(01904) 413579
Heslington Lane, Heslington, York
(18) 6775 yards/**/A/H

Ganton G.C.
(01944) 710329
Ganton, Scarborough
(18) 6734 yards/**/A/H

Harrogate G. C.
(01423) 862999
Forest Lane Head, Starbeck
(18) 6241 yards/***/B/M

Heworth G.C.
(01904) 424618
Muncastergate, York
(11) 6141 yards/***/D

Hunley Hall G.C.
(01287) 676216
Brotton, Salrburn
(18) 6918 yards/***/C

Kilnwick Percy
(01759) 303090
Home Farm, Pocklington
(18) 6200 yards/***/D

Kirbymoorside G.C.
(01751) 431525
Manor Vale, Kirbymoorside
(18) 5958 yards/***/C

Knaresborough G.C.
(01423) 862690
Boroughbridge Road, Knaresborough
(18) 6232 yards/***/C/H

Malton and Norton G.C.
(01653) 697912
Welham Park, Malton
(18) 6456 yards/***/B/H
(18) 6267 yards/***/B/H

Masham G.C.
(01765) 689379
Swinton Road, Masham, Ripon
(9) 5244 yards/**/D

Middlesbrough G.C.
(01642) 311515
Brass Castle Lane, Marton
(18) 6106 yards/***/B

Middlesbrough Municipal G.C.
(01642) 315533
Ladgate Lane, Middlesbrough
(18) 6314 yards/***/E

Oakdale G.C.
(01423) 567162
Oakdale, Harrogate
(18) 6456 yards/***/B/M

The Oaks G.C.
(01757) 288577
(18) 6743 yards/**/B/H
Aughton, York

Pannal G.C.
(01423) 872628
Follifoot Road, Pannal, Harrogate
(18) 6659 yards/**/A/M/H

Pike Hills G.C.
(01904) 706566
Tadcaster Road, Copmanthorpe, York
(18) 6120 yards/**/D/M

Raven Hall Hotel & G.C.
(01723) 870353
Ravenscar
(9) 1938 yards/***/C

Richmond G.C.
(01748) 825319
Band Hagg, Richmond
(18) 5704 yards/***/D

Ripon City G.C.
(01765) 603640
Palace Road, Ripon
(9) 5750 yards/***/C

Romanby G.C.
(01609) 778855
Yafforth Road, Northallerton
(18) 6663 yards/***/D

Rudding Park G.C.
(01423) 844801
Rudding Park, Harrogate
(18) 6871 yards/***/C/4

Saltburn-by-the-Sea G.C.
(01287) 622812
Guisborough Road, Hobb Hill(18)
5803 yards/***/C/H

Scarborough North Cliff G.C.
(01723) 360786
Burniston Road, Scarborough
(18) 6425 yards/***/B/M

Scarborough South Cliff G.C.
(01723) 374737
Deepdale Avenue, Scarborough
(18) 6085 yards/***/B/H

Scarthingwell G.C.
(01937) 557248
Scarthingwell, Tadcaster
(18) 6759 yards/**/C

Selby G.C.
(01757) 228622
Mill Lane, Brayton Barff, Selby
(18) 6246 yards/**/B/H/M

Settle G.C.
(01729) 825288
Buckhaw Brow, Settle
(9) 4600 yards/***(Sun)/D

Skipton G.C.
(01756) 795657
NW Bypass, Skipton
(18) 6191 yards/***(Mon)/B

Swallow Hall G.C.
(01904) 448219
Crockley Mill, York
(18) 3092 yards/***/E

Teesside G.C.
(01642) 616516
Acklam Road, Thornaby
(18) 6472 yards/***(pm only)/B

Thirsk & Northallerton G.C.
(01845) 522170
Thornton-le-Street, Thirsk
(9) 6257 yards/***/C/M

Whitby G.C.
(01947) 602768
Low Straggleton, Whitby
(18) 5706 yards/***/C/H

Wilton G.C.
(01642) 465265
Wilton Castle, Redcar
(18) 6104 yards/***(not Sat)/C

York G.C.
(01904) 491840
Lords Moor Lane, Strensall, York
(18) 6285 yards/***/B

SOUTH YORKSHIRE

Abbeydale G.C.
(0114) 236 0763
Twentywell Lane, Dore, Sheffield
(18) 6419 yards/***/B

Austerfield Park G.C.
(01302) 311977
Cross Lane, N Bawtry, Doncaster
(18) 6828 yards/***/C

Barnsley G.C.
(01226) 382856
Wakefield Road, Staincross
(18) 6048 yards/***/E

Beauchief G.C.
(0114) 236 7274
Abbey Lane, Sheffield
(18) 5423 yards/***/E

Birley Wood G.C.
(0114) 264 7262
Birley Lane, Sheffield
(18) 5483 yards/***/E

Bond Hay G.C.
(01909) 723608
Bond Hay Lane, Whitwell
(18) 6700 yards/***/D

Concord Park G.C.
(0114) 257 0111
Shiregreen Lane, Sheffield
(18) 4321 yards/***/E

Crookhill Park G.C.
(01709) 862974
Conisbrough, nr Doncaster
(18) 5846 yards/***/E

Doncaster G.C.
(01302) 868316
Bawtry Road, Bessacarr, Doncaster
(18) 6220 yards/**/B/M/H

Doncaster Town Moor G.C.
(01302) 535286
Belle Vue, Doncaster
(18) 6094 yards/***(Sun am)/D

Dore and Totley G.C.
(0114) 236 0492
Bradway Road, Sheffield
(18) 6265 yards/***/B/H

Grange Park G.C.
(01709) 558884
Upper Wortley Road, Rotherham
(18) 6461 yards/***/E

Hallamshire G.C.
(0114) 230 2153
Sandygate, Sheffield
(18) 6396 yards/***/B-A

Hallowes G.C.
(01246) 413734
Hallowes Lane, Dronfield, Sheffield
(18) 6342 yards/***/B/G/H

Hickleton G.C.
(01709) 896081
Hickleton, Doncaster
(18) 6361 yards/***/C/H/M

Hillsborough G.C.
(0114) 234 9151
Worral Road, Sheffield
(18) 6035 yards/**/B/H

Lees Hall G.C.
(0114) 255 2900
Hemsworth Road, Norton, Sheffield
(18) 6137 yards/***/C

Lindrick G.C.
(01909) 475282
Lindrick Common, Worksop
(18) 6606 yards/***(Tues am)/A/H

Owston Park G.C.
(01302) 330821
Owston Hall, nr Carcroft
(9) 6148 yards/***/E

Phoenix G.C.
(01709) 363864
Pavilion Lane, Brinsworth
(18) 6145 yards/***/C/M

Ponderosa G.C
(01302) 842057
Doncaster Road, Hatfield
(18) 6002 yards/***/E

Renishaw Park G.C.
(01246) 432044
Station Road, Renishaw, Sheffield
(18) 6253 yards/**/B-A/H/M

Rotherham G.C.
(01709) 850812
Thrybergh, Rotherham
(18) 6323 yards/**/B-A

Rother Valley G.C.
(0114) 247 3000
Wales Bar, Sheffield
(18) 6602 yards/***/D

Roundwood G.C.
(01709) 523471
Rawmarsh, Rotherham
(9) 5646 yards/**/D

Sandhill G.C.
(01226) 753444
Little Houghton, Barnsley
(18) 6214 yards/***/E

Sheffield Transport G.C.
(0114) 237 3216
Meadow Head, Sheffield
(18) 3966 yards/*/F/G

Sickleholme G.C.
(01433) 651306
Saltergate Lane, Bamford, Sheffield
(18) 6064 yards/***(Wed am)/B

Silkstone G.C.
(01226) 790328
Field Head, Silkstone, Barnsley
(18) 6045 yards/**/B-A/H

Sitwell Park G.C.
(01709) 541046
Shrogswood Road, Rotherham
(18) 6203 yards/***/B/M

Stocksbridge and District G.C.
(0114) 288 2003
Townend, Deepcar, Sheffield
(18) 5200 yards/***/C/H

Tankersley Park G.C.
(0114) 246 8247
High Green, Sheffield
(18) 6212 yards/**/C

Thorne G.C.
(01405) 812084
Kirton Lane, Thorne
(18) 5366 yards/***/E

Thornhurst Park G.C
(01302) 337799
Holme Land, Owsten
(18) 6085 yards/***/E

Thorpe Marsh G.C.
(01302) 886680
Bamby Down, Doncaster
(9) 4120 yards/***/E

Tinsley Park G.C.
(0114) 256 0237
High Hazel Park, Darnall, Sheffield
(18) 6064 yards/***/E

Wath G.C.
(01709) 582000
Abdy, Blackamoor, Rotherham
(18) 5857 yards/**/C

Wheatley G.C.
(01302) 831655
Armthorpe Road, Doncaster
(18) 6345 yards/***/C/H/M

Wombwell Hillies G.C.
(01226) 754433
Wentworth View, Wombwell
(9) 2095 yards/***/E

Wortley G.C.
(0114) 288 5294
Hermit Hill Lane, Sheffield
(18) 5983 yards/**/B/H/M

WEST YORKSHIRE

Alwoodley G.C.
(0113) 268 1680
Wigton Lane, Alwoodley, Leeds
(18) 6686 yards/**/A/H/M

Baildon G.C.
(01274) 582428
Moorgate, Baildon, Shipley
(18) 6225 yards/**/D

Ben Rhydding G.C.
(01943) 608759
High Wood, Ben Rhydding, Ilkley
(9) 4711 yards/**(Wed)/D

Bingley St Ives G.C.
(01274) 562436
St Ives Estate, Bingley
(18) 6480 yards/**/B

Bracken Ghyll G.C.
(01943) 831207
Skipton Road, Addingham
(9) 6560 yards/***/D

Bradford G.C.
(01943) 875570
Hawksworth Lane, Guiseley, Leeds
(18) 6259 yards/***(Sat/Sun am)/F

Bradford Moor G.C.
(01274) 638313
Scarr Hall, Pollard Lane, Bradford
(9) 5854 yards/***/D

Bradley Park G.C.
(01484) 539988
Bradley Road, Huddersfield
(18) 6202 yards/***/D

Branshaw G.C.
(01535) 643235
Branshaw Moor, Keighley
(18) 5858 yards/**/D/H

Calverley G.C.
(0113) 256 9244
Woodhall Lane, Pudsey
(18) 5516 yards/***(Sat/Sun am)/D

Castlefields G.C.
(01484) 712108
Rastrick Common, Brighouse
(6) 2406 yards/*/F/G

City of Wakefield G.C.
(01924) 367442
Howbury Road, Wakefield
(18) 6299 yards/***/E

Clayton G.C.
(01274) 880047
Thornton View Road, Bradford
(9) 5518 yards/***(Sun)/D

Cleckheaton and District G.C.
(01274) 851266
Bradford Road, Cleckheaton
(18) 5847 yards/***/B

Crosland Heath G.C.
(01484) 653216
Felk Site Road, Huddersfield
(18) 5962 yards/***/F

Crow Nest Park G.C.
(014842) 201216
Hove Edge, Brighouse
(9) 5910 yards/***/D

Dewsbury District G.C.
(01924) 492399
The Pinnacle, Sands Lane, Mirfield
(18) 6256 yards/**/C/H

East Bierley G.C.
(01274) 681023
South View Road, Bierley, Bradford
(9) 4692 yards/***(Sun)/D

Elland G.C.
(01422) 372505
Hammerstones, Leach Lane, Elland
(9) 5526 yards/***/D

Fardew G.C.
(01274) 561229
Carr Lane, East Morton
(9) 6212 yards/***/E

Ferrybridge 'C' G.C.
(01977) 674188
Stranglands Lane, Knottingly
(9) 5138 yards/*/E/G

Fulneck G.C.
(0113) 256 5191
Fulneck, Pudsey
(9) 5564 yards/**/D

Garforth G.C.
(0113) 286 3308
Long Lane, Garforth, Leeds
(18) 6296 yards/**/B/H/M

Gott's Park G.C.
(0113) 256 2994
Armley Ridge Road, Leeds
(18) 4960 yards/***/E

Halifax G.C.
(01422) 244171
Union Lane, Ogden, Halifax
(18) 6037 yards/***/B

Halifax Bradley Hall G.C.
(01422) 374108
Stainland Road, Holywell Green
(18) 6213 yards/***/B

Halifax West End G.C.
(01422) 363293
Highroad Well, Halifax
(18) 6003 yards/***/C/H

Hanging Heaton G.C.
(01924) 461606
White Cross Road, Bennett Lane, Dewsbury
(9) 5874 yards/**/D/M

Headingley G.C.
(0113) 267 9573
Back Church Lane, Adel, Leeds
(18) 6298 yards/***/B/H

Headley G.C.
(01274) 833481
Headley Lane, Thornton,Bradford
(9) 4914 yards/***/E

Hebden Bridge G.C.
(01422) 842732
Great Mount, Wadsworth
(9) 5064 yards/***/D

Horsforth G.C.
(0113) 258 6819
Layton Road, Horsforth, Leeds
(18) 6243 yards/***/B/H

Howley Hall G.C.
(01924) 478417
Scotchman Lane, Morley, Leeds
(18) 6029 yards/***(Sat)/B/H

Huddersfield G.C.
(01484) 426203
Fixby Hall, Fixby, Huddersfield
(18) 6424 yards/***/A

Ilkley G.C.
(01943) 600214
Middleton, Ilkley
(18) 6256 yards/***/A

Keighley G.C.
(01535) 604778
Howden Park, Utley, Keighley
(18) 6149 yards/**/B/H

Leeds G.C.
(0113) 265 8775
Elmete Lane, Leeds
(18) 6097 yards/**/C/M

Leeds Golf Centre
(0113) 288 6000
Wike Ridge Lane, Shadwell
(18) 6800 yards/***/D

Lightcliffe G.C.
(01422) 202459
Knowle Top Road, Lightcliffe
(9) 5388 yards/***(Wed/Sat)/D/M

Lofthouse Hill G.C.
(01924) 823703
Leeds Road, Wakefield
(9) 3167 yards/*/E/G

Longley Park G.C.
(01484) 426932
Maple Street, Huddersfield
(9) 5269 yards/**(Thurs)/D

Low Laithes G.C.
(01924) 261844
Parkmill Flushdyke, Ossett
(18) 6468 yards/**/C

Marsden G.C.
(01484) 844253
Mount Road, Hemplow, Marsden
(9) 5702 yards/**/E

Meltham G.C.
(01484) 850227
Thick Hollins, Meltham
(18) 6145 yards/***(Wed/Sat)/B

Middleton Park G.C.
(0113) 253 3993
Middleton Park, Leeds
(18) 5233 yards/***/E

Mid Yorkshire G.C.
(01977) 704522
Havercroft Lane, Darrington
(18) 6500 yards/***/C/H

Moor Allerton G.C.
(0113) 266 1154
Coal Road, Wike, Leeds
(27) 6045 yards/**/A/H
6222 yards/**/A/H
6930 yards/**/A/H

Moortown G.C.
(0113) 268 6521
Harrogate Road, Alwoodley, Leeds
(18) 7020 yards/***/A/H

Mount Skip G.C.
(01422) 892896
Hebden Bridge
(9) 5114 yards/***/F

Normanton G.C.
(01924) 892943
Syndale Road, Normanton,
(9) 5288 yards/***(Sun)/D

Northcliffe G.C.
(01274) 584805
High Bank Lane, Shipley
(18) 6104 yards/**(Sat/Tues)/B/H

Otley G.C.
(01943) 465329
West Busk Lane, Otley
(18) 6235 yards/***(Sat)/B

Oulton Park G.C.
(0113) 282 3152
Oulton, Leeds
(18) 6241 yards/**/E

Outlane G.C.
(01422) 374762
Slack Lane, Outlane, Huddersfield
(18) 6003 yards/***/C

Painthorpe House C.C.
(01924) 255083
Painthorpe Lane, Crigglestone
(9) 4520 yards/***(Sun)/E

Phoenix Park G.C.
(01274) 667573
Dick Lane, Thornbury
(9) 4774 yards/**/F

Pontefract & District G.C.
(01977) 792241
Park Lane, Pontefract
(18) 6227 yards/**/B-A

Queensbury G.C.
(01274) 882155
Brighouse Road, Queensbury
(9) 5102 yards/***/D/M

Rawdon G.C.
(0113) 250 6040
Buckstone Drive, Rawdon, Leeds
(9) 5960 yards/**/D/H

Riddlesden G.C.
(01535) 602148
Elam Wood Road, Riddlesden
(18) 4185 yards/***/D

Roundhay G.C.
(0113) 266 2695
Park Lane, Leeds
(9) 5166 yards/***/E

Ryburn G.C.
(01422) 831355
Norland, Sowerby Bridge, Halifax
(9) 5002 yards/***/D/H

Sand Moor G.C.
(0113) 268 5180
Alwoodley Lane, Leeds
(18) 6429 yards/**/B/M

Scarcroft G.C.
(0113) 289 2311
Syke Lane, Leeds
(18) 6426 yards/***/B/H

Shipley G.C.
(01274) 563212
Beckfoot Lane, Cottingley Bridge
(18) 6218 yards/***(Tues/Sat)/B

Silsden G.C.
(01535) 652998
High Brunthwaite, Silsden
(14) 4870 yards/***/D

South Bradford G.C.
(01274) 679195
Pearson Road, Odsal, Bradford
(9) 6004 yards/**/D

South Leeds G.C.
(0113) 270 0479
Gipsy Lane, Beeston Ring Road
(18) 5890 yards/**/C/M

Temple Newsam G.C.
(0113) 264 5624
Temple Newsam Road, Leeds
(18) 6448 yards/***/E
(18) 6029 yards/***/E

Todmorden G.C.
(01706) 812986
Rive Rocks, Cross Stone
(9) 5878 yards/***/C/H

Wakefield G.C.
(01924) 258778
Woodthorpe Lane, Sandal, Wakefield
(18) 6626 yards/**/B/H

Waterton Park G.C.
(01924) 259525
The Balk, Wakefield
(18) 6274 yards/C/G

West Bowling G.C.
(01274) 724449
Newall Hall, Rooley Lane, Bradford
(18) 5770 yards/**/B/H

West Bradford G.C.
(01274) 542767
Chellow Grange, Bradford
(18) 5752 yards/***/C

Wetherby G.C.
(01937) 583375
Linton Lane, Wetherby
(18) 6235 yards/***/B/H

Whitwood G.& C.C.
(01977) 558596
Altofts Lane, Castleford
(9) 6282 yards/***/F

Willow Valley G.C.
(01274) 878624
Clifton, Brighouse
(9) ***/E

Woodhall Hills G.C.
(0113) 255 4594
Woodhall Road, Calverley, Pudsey
(18) 6102 yards/***/B

Woodsome Hall G.C.
(01484) 602971
Fenay Bridge, Huddersfield
(18) 6080 yards/***(Tues)/B/H

Woolley Park G.C.
(01226) 380144
Woolley, Wakefield
(18) 5874 yards/***/D

EAST RIDING

Beverley & East Riding G.C.
(01482) 869519
The Westwood, Beverley
(18) 6164 yards/***/D

erry G.C.
(01430) 430364
Spaldington, Howden, Goole
(18) 6651 yards/***/E

Bridlington G.C.
(01262) 606367
Belvedere Road, Bridlington
(18) 6491 yards/**(Sun pm)/D

Bridlington Links
(01262) 401584
Flanborough Road, Morton
(18) 6720 yards/***/D

Brough G.C.
(01482) 667374
Cave Road, Brough
(18) 6159 yards/**(Wed am)/B/H

Cave Castle Hotel & G.C.
(01430) 422245
South Cave, Brough
(18) 6409 yards/***/D

Cherry Burton G.C
(01964) 550924
Leconfield Road, Beverly
(9) 2278 yards/***/E

Cottingham G.C.
(01482) 842394
Spring Park Farm, Cottingham
(18) 6230 yards/**/D

Driffield G.C.
(01377) 253116
Sunderlandwick, Driffield
(18) 6199 yards/***/C

Flamborough Head G.C.
(01262) 850333
Lighthouse Road, Bridlington
(18) 5438 yards/***(Sun am)/D/M

Ganstead Park G.C.
(01482) 811280
Longdales Lane, Coniston, Hull
(18) 6801 yards/**/C/H

Grange Park G.C.
(01724) 762945
Butterwick Road,
(9) 2970 yards/***/E

Hainsworth Park G.C.
(01964) 542362
Brandesburton, Driffield
(18) 6003 yards/***/D

Hessle G.C.
(01482) 650171
Westfield Road, Cottingham, Hull
(18) 6638 yards/**(Tues am)/C/H

Hornsea G.C.
(01964) 532020
Rolston Road, Hornsea
(18) 6450 yards/***(Tues)/C

Hull G.C.
(01482) 658919
The Hall, Packman Lane, Kirk Ella
(18) 6242 yards/**/B/H

Springhead Park G.C.
(01482) 656309
Willerby Road, Hull
(18) 6439 yards/***/E

Sutton Park G.C.
(01482) 374242
Salthouse Road, Sutton, Hull
(18) 6251 yards/***/E

Withernsea G.C.
(01964) 612078
Chestnut Avenue, Withernsea
(9) 5112 yards/***/E

Artist: **Harry Eliott** **THE TEA BREAK** *Courtesy of:* **Burlington Gallery**

Artist: **Arthur Weaver** **THE GREEN** *Courtesy of:* **Burlington Gallery**

Farlam Hall was opened in 1975 by the Quinion and Stevenson families who over the years have achieved and maintained consistently high standards of food, service and comfort. These standards have been internationally recognised by all the major guides with three red stars and two rosettes from the AA, three stars and a blue ribbon from the RAC and membership of the Relais and Chateaux.

This old border house, dating in parts back to the seventeenth century was extended to its present size in Victorian times and is now set in acres of mature landscaped gardens which can be seen from the elegant lounges and dining room.

The fine silver, crystal and starched white linen, all combine to create the feeling of a more elegant era and complement the quality of the English country house style of cooking produced by Barry Quinion and his team of experienced chefs. Attentive service from the family and their local staff add the finishing touch.

There are only twelve bedrooms in this large house which allows some of the rooms to be on rather a grand scale, while the rooms designed originally for lesser family members are of a more conventional size. This variation in room size permits a wide price range in the tariff. No matter what size or shape, the same care and quality has been applied and, as with the whole house, antique and fine furniture has been used wherever possible.

This area offers a wealth of different attractions - miles of unspoilt country for walking, three golf courses within ten minutes of the hotel, and close by are Hadrian's Wall, Lanercost Priory and Carlisle with the castle, cathedral and museum. The Lake District, Scottish Borders and Yorkshire Dales provide an ideal day's touring. The hotel's proximity to the M6 also makes it an ideal overnight stop when travelling to or from Scotland.

Dogs are welcome. Closed at Christmas. Directions: Farlam Hall is two and a half miles south east of Brampton on the A689, not in Farlam Village.

Farlam Hall Hotel
Brampton
Cumbria CA8 2NG
Tel: (016977) 46234
Fax: (016977) 46683

Just as Devon is often viewed by holidaymakers as a stepping stone to Cornwall (which as a Devonian pleases me greatly!) so the far north of England is often viewed by golfers as a mere pretty pathway to the delights of Scotland—Turnberry, Gleneagles etc. Indeed, some even believe that north of Lytham there's nothing much in the way of golfing challenges until the 'Bonnie Land' is reached. To those I simply say, 'shame on you!'

Our region covers Cumbria as well as the North East. Now admittedly, Cumbria is hardly perfect golfing territory. A Sunningdale in the middle of the Lake District is hard to imagine (although some spectacular holes are clearly possible!) But there are a number of golf courses in between the fells and the lakes, and furthermore Cumbria comprises more than just the Lake District. Before the counties were rearranged and renamed in the early seventies, Cumberland was the most northerly county in the West of England and home, not only to the famous sausage, but to the **Silloth-on-Solway** Golf Club which is, dare I say it, as good a links as you'll find anywhere in England. As for the North East, **Seaton Carew** near Hartlepool offers championship golf of a very high calibre and **Slaley Hall** is full of Northumbrian promise, while even further north along the Northumberland coast lie a string of golfing pearls—**Alnmouth, Dunstanburgh, Bamburgh** and **Goswick**—good courses with breathtaking scenery.

Cumbria

Let us make a start in the Lake District with the hope that in addition to the picnic hamper and the climbing boots, we've left room in the back of the car for the golf clubs.

The Lake District is the land of poets, 'Where breezes are soft and skies are fair' (W C Bryant) and 'Where nature reveals herself in all her wildness, all her majesty' (S Roger). At Keswick the golfer meets the poet. **Keswick** Golf Club lies four miles east of the lakeland town via the A66. While the course now measures well over 6000 yards, it recently held a rather dubious claim to being the shortest course in Britain—in 1976 there was a splendid clubhouse but only five holes—no doubt some remarkable scores were returned! These days scoring is a little more difficult with several streams and some dense woodland to be avoided. As one might imagine the views are quite something and a visit will never disappoint.

Still in the Lakes we find **Kendal**, a fine parkland course, close to the town centre and only two miles from the M6 link road. Although a fair bit shorter than Keswick its first hole is often considered the toughest opener in Britain—231 yards, uphill all the way, out of bounds to the left and woods to the right! Should one make it to the 2nd the holes get much easier. However there is an infamous quarry on the right of the 15th fairway which has been known to receive more than golf balls. One frustrated chap after firing ball after ball into its murky depths decided to throw in his bag for good measure. Fortunately he didn't throw himself in as well but the word is he never played golf again. Who said it was only a game!

The Golf Club at **Windermere** should prove much more relaxing. The club recently celebrated its centenary and the course has improved considerably in the last few years. An ideal place for a game of golf while on holiday in the Lakes, we feature Windermere later page. Another first class course, still within the National Park boundary is at **Penrith,** close to the A6 but a lovely setting nonetheless with some beautiful views Ullswater and several very challenging holes. Talking of good

views, the parkland course at Ulverston enjoys commanding views of Morecambe Bay and there is also a pleasant new course at **Carus Green.**

Recommending both superior and reasonably priced establishments in the area is a difficult task, to put it mildly, simply because there are so many. But hopefully the following suggestions will be useful. Grasmere is a favourite and here Michael's Nook (015394) 35496 is an outstanding country hotel with an excellent restaurant. Antiques are dotted throughout the house and the gardens are a delight. The Wordsworth (015394) 35592 is also a grand hotel while at White Moss House (015394) 35295—the poet's former residence—another superb restaurant can be found. Another truly first class establishment in the area is the delightful Nanny Brow Hotel (015394) 32036 near Ambleside, more landscape gardens here with views to match. Nearer to Keswick, Armathwaite Hall (017687) 76551 in Bassenthwaite is charming, while for a really relaxing country inn, the Pheasant Inn (017687) 76234 in Bassenthwaite Lake can have few equals. In Keswick itself there is the Keswick Country House Hotel (01768) 772020 well suited for golf. The Brundholme (01768) 774495 is also good.

Penrith is a bustling town with numerous hotels. As an alternative to staying in town Ullswater naturally attracts and here the Sharrow Bay Hotel (017684) 86301 and its restaurant are particularly stylish. Cheaper accommodation is available nearby in one of the area's best pubs, the Queens Head at Askham, while the Old Church Hotel (017684) 86204 at Watermillock offers spectacular views and a lakeside settings. Also worth hunting out is the Brandelhow Guesthouse (01768) 64470.

Oh-so-popular Windermere offers a wealth of good hotels. Three meriting attention are the Miller Howe (015394) 42536 where breakfast is reputed to be among the best in the country, the Langdale Chase (015394) 32201 and the Lindeth Fell Country House Hotel (015394) 43286. Rogers (015394) 44954 in the High Street is another recommended restaurant. Among other first class establishments near Windermere Golf Club we can also recommend Gilpin Lodge Country House (015394) 88818 and Linthwaite House Hotel (015394) 88600, while the Burn How Garden House Hotel (015394) 46226 offers a luxurious and rather unique style of accommodation. Other ideas for a 19th hole in the Lake District must include the Old Vicarage (015395) 52381 at Witherslack, the Mortal Man (015394) 33193 at Troutbeck (wake up to a glorious setting), the Wild Boar in Crook (015394) 45225 and for a really popular pub try the Masons Arms in Cartmel Fell. Finally, consider Holbeck Ghyll (015394) 32375 a former hunting lodge and an excellent establishment.

To the south of Cumbria the highly rated **Furness** Golf Club lays claim to being the oldest in the county. A true links and being quite exposed, scoring well is often more difficult than the card suggests. An after-golf thought here is the excellent Abbey House Hotel (01229) 838282, while Eccle Riggs Manor (01229) 716398 is also recommended. Also pleasant is Bridgefield House (01229) 885239 at Spark Bridge—excellent food here—and further inland the Uplands Country House Hotel (015395) 36248 is extremely good value and the restaurant is spectacular.

Further along Cumbria's coast, **Seascale** has a somewhat underrated links. One shouldn't be put off by the thought of being close to the Seascale nuclear installations (and jokes about balls glowing in the dark are uncalled for). It's an excellent test of golf with a splendid clubhouse and good food, as well as some tremendous views towards the Wasdale Screes and the Scafell Range. North of Workington (en route to Silloth) there is a fair course at **Maryport**. There is doubtless some convenient accommodation nearby but I'll recommend a trip inland to another personal favourite, Buttermere, one of the more westerly lakes where the Bridge Hotel (017687) 70252 is very comfortable. Pickett Howe (017687) 85444 is another delightful hotel in which to stay—remote countryside and very appealing.

Silloth-on-Solway has already been referred to and is featured separately on a later page. The course certainly deserves more than a fleeting visit and two handy hotels in the town are the Queen's Hotel (016973) 31373 and the Golf Hotel (016973) 31438. Both specialise in golf packages, as for that matter does the nearby Skinburness Hotel (016973) 32332. Further east, the Kelsey Hotel (019673) 71229 comes highly recommended,

Golfers in Carlisle are well catered for with two good courses in the area, **Carlisle** and **Brampton**—or Talkin' Tarn as it is sometimes called. (We're told the Tarn End House (01697) 72340 is a magical place to eat!) Brampton, located to the east of Carlisle off the B6413, is a beautifully kept course, laid out four hundred feet above sea level with views towards the nearby hills. It is probably best described as moorland whereas Carlisle, equally well maintained, is more of a parkland type. For an overnight stop in Carlisle the Crown and Mitre (01228) 25491 is welcoming. Near Brampton, Farlam Hall (016977) 46234 is an excellent country house hotel with an outstanding restaurant and the Hare and Hounds (016977) 3456 is a comfortable inn. Fantails (01228) 560239 in Wetheral is a first class restaurant and for a pleasant waterside setting, the Crosby Lodge, an 18th century country mansion at Crosby-on-Eden (01228) 573618 is recommended.

Before leaving Cumbria, a quick mention for the somewhat isolated **Appleby** Golf Club. If you are in the vicinity it's well worth a visit. A splendid combination of moorland and heathland—very colourful. Remote, perhaps but in nearby Appleby-in-Westmorland the Appleby Manor (017683) 51571 awaits and for a nearby friendly inn note the Black Swan at Ravenstondale.

The North East

So to the North East—and what a mixture! Durham, Tyne & Wear and Northumberland. An area encompassing Tyneside, Teeside and Wearside, it also includes the Cleveland Hills, the Cheviots and the wild spectacular coast of ancient Northumbria. The area stretches from the far end of the Yorkshire Pennines and intrudes into the Scottish Borders, the greater part of Northumberland lying north of Hadrian's Wall.

The appeal of any golf course can be affected greatly by its surroundings and nowhere in Britain does the accompanying landscape seem to dictate the enjoyment of a game as much as in this part of the world. The contrast between the industrial and rural North East is dramatic. The golf courses in the former tend towards the uninspiring—Seaton Carew being one exception—whilst the likes of Bamburgh Castle and Hexham offer such magnificent scenery that the quality of the golf can often be relegated to a secondary consideration.

Durham

Beginning in the south of the region, **Seaton Carew** is far and away the best in the county. In fact, it is almost certainly the best links course on the East Coast of England, north of Norfolk. Seaton Carew is featured ahead.

The top hotel in this area for golfers is undoubtedly Hardwick Hall (01740) 620253 at Sedgefield, which is well placed for Seaton Carew and the courses in County Durham. There are a number of other good hotels in the county, although as everywhere some of them are very modern and unfortunately rather characterless. An exception to this is the Crathorne Hall Hotel (01642) 700398 at Yarm—a converted Edwardian mansion. Also handy for Seaton Carew is the Grand (01429) 266345 in Hartlepool.

Moving up to Durham itself, people often talk of Old Durham Town, but of course it's very much a city with a cathedral that has been adjudged the most beautiful building in the world. Without doubt the course to visit here is **Brancepeth Castle**, four miles south west of the city and set in very beautiful surroundings. Rather like St Pierre at Chepstow the course occupies land that was formerly a deer park, and a 13th century church and castle provide a magnificent backcloth. Perhaps the most convenient place to stay is at the Bridge Hotel (0191) 3780524 in Croxdale, a well run Toby House, but there are a number of good hotels in Durham itself including the Royal County (0191) 3866821. Just north of Durham is the historic Lumley Castle (0191) 3891111 which offers good food and accommodation overlooking the course at Chester-le-Street.

Further north, **Beamish Park** near Stanley is another laid out in a former deer park (belonging to Beamish Hall) and is worth a detour if heading along the A1. **Bishop Auckland** in the centre of the county is a pleasant parkland course. The land here belongs to the Church of England and one of the terms of the club's lease is that the course has to close on Good Friday and Christmas Day. Play then at your peril!

To the south west of Bishop Auckland, **Barnard Castle** enjoys yet another delightful setting. More of a moorland course than anything else, it has a stream that must be crossed seventeen times during a round! There are some fine establishments nearby in which to celebrate (or perhaps even dry out?) In Barnard Castle the Jersey Farm Hotel (01833) 638223 is excellent value for a night's stay while those just looking for a bar snack and a drink might visit the nearby villages of Cotherstone (The Fox and Hounds) or Romaldkirk where you find The Rose and Crown (01833) 650213, a pleasant inn with some good food A slightly longer drive to Eggleston, also possible from Bishop Auckland, and one finds the Three Tuns—famed for its pub lunches. Midway between Bishop Auckland and Darlington at Newton Aycliffe is the **Woodham** Golf and Country Club which has a growing reputation.

Darlington is the largest town in the county. It may not have the appeal of Durham but for golfers there's a twin attraction: to the north, **Haughton Grange** with its great selection of MacKenzie greens and to the south, **Blackwell Grange** with its fine variety of trees. Both courses are parkland and always well maintained. For an ideal base one doesn't really have to look further than the 17th century Blackwell Grange Moat House (01325) 380888. A good restaurant to note in the town is Sardis (01325) 461222, an Italian inspired menu here, and for a drink and some accommodation try the Kings Head (01325) 380222. Outside the town try Headlam Hall (01325) 730238 or Hall Garth (01325) 300400 where there is a nine hole course. Further north still, one should not omit **Ramside Hall** (0191) 3865282 a pleasant hotel which has just opened a first rate 18 hole course.

Tyne and Wear

Tyne and Wear is essentially a tale of two cities, Newcastle—the home of the Geordies—and Sunderland where the welcome is second to none. There are plenty of golf courses in the area but the really attractive golf lies further north along the coast. The **Northumberland** (Gosforth Park) Golf Club and **Ponteland** probably have the best two courses in Tyne & Wear. The former is situated alongside Gosforth Park Racecourse and like Seaton Carew has staged several national championships, it is renowned for its difficult finishing holes. The visitor may find it easier to arrange a game at Ponteland (at least during the week)—a particularly well-kept course this and very convenient if you happen to be flying to or from Newcastle Airport. **Whitley Bay** is another alternative. It is quite a long, windswept course with very large greens and a wide stream that can make scoring pretty difficult.

If there's one large town in England that could really do with a championship standard golf challenge it's Sunderland, a place of great character—golf architects please note! The best courses in the area are probably **Whitburn** and **Boldon**. **Wearside** also presents a number of tough holes and some pleasant views.

Staying in and around Newcastle some of the leading hotels are the Swallow Gosforth Park Hotel (0191) 236 4111, the Holiday Inn (0191) 201 9988 and the Marriott (0191) 493 2233, while Malmaison on the Quayside (0191) 245 5000 is fast developing a good name. All offer all the mod. cons. and some first class leisure facilities. Jesmond offers a multitude of less expensive hotels—Chirton House Hotel (0191) 2730407 being one example.

In Newcastle itself, the choice is tremendous. The city boasts a real 'Chinatown' along Stowell Street with a host of superb restaurants of which Ming Dynasty (0191) 261 5787 remains one of the best. For Indian (or Punjabi to be more accurate) cuisine of the highest order there can be only one selection and that is Sachins (0191) 2619035—do ring to reserve a table and get directions. An evening at 21 Queen Street (0191) 2220755 on the Quayside is always a culinary experience and there are now a number of other restaurants in the immediate vicinity to suit any palate or pocket. Finally, excellent cooking can always be found at either the Fisherman's Lodge (0191) 2813281 or the Fisherman's Wharf (0191) 2321057. Outside the city and handy for Ponteland and the airport is Horton Grange (01661) 860686 offering an elegant restaurant in pleasant surroundings.

Northumberland

Finally then, a look at Northumberland, a county with a splendid, almost mythical history. The first golf course on the way up, as it were, is **Arcot Hall**, six miles north of Newcastle and a most tranquil setting. A James Braid creation, Arcot Hall is a heathland course with a wealth of trees and a lake. The club has a sumptuous clubhouse but beware of the Grey Lady who ghosts in and out from time to time! If thoroughly frightened, many peaceful villages are at hand and some very good pubs. The Highlander at Belsay is one such place (and equally convenient incidentally after a day's golf at Ponteland).

Trekking northwards again, **Morpeth** is next on the agenda. Another pleasant course designed this time by one of James Braid's old rivals—Mr Vardon no less. One of England's finest Georgian country houses lies only a short distance away at Longhorsley—**Linden Hall** (01670) 516611. A new course opened here in 1996 and early reports are extremely positive. Also nearby is **Longhirst Hall** (01670) 791348 a 19th century stately home with its own 18 hole parkland course..

Along the rugged coast some tremendous golf lies ahead. The course at Alnmouth (**Foxton**) is very pleasing and in the village is the comfortable Marine House Hotel (01665) 830349. Just a little beyond are the magnificent castle courses of **Dunstanburgh** (at Embleton) and **Bamburgh.** The golf is fun and the scenery superb. Dunstanburgh Castle, the ruins of which were immortalised in watercolour by Turner, occupies a wondrously remote setting. The course is a genuine links, hugging close to the shore and staring out across miles of deserted beach. Bamburgh Castle is perhaps even more special and is often referred to as England's most beautiful course. Not long by any means—but the setting! Holy Island and Lindisfarne, the Cheviot Hills and a majestic castle. Furthermore, the fairways are bordered by a blaze of colour, with gorse, purple heather and numerous wild orchids. Bamburgh Castle is explored ahead. Not far from here is the fairly short but underrated course at **Seahouses**.

Having placated the golfing soul a few suggestions for the body include the Dunstanburgh Castle Hotel (as its name suggests, very handy for the golf course) and the Lord Crewe Arms (01668) 214243 in Bamburgh—good for a drink with some accommodation also. Another good resting place is to be found in Belford, the Blue Bell Hotel (01668) 213543. Warren House (01668) 214581 is another hotel just outside Bamburgh but well worth seeking out. Among several good Northumbrian pubs are the Tankerville Arms in Wooler, the Olde Ship in Seahouses, the Jolly Fisherman in Craster and the Craster Arms in Beadnell.

For centuries the town of Berwick-upon-Tweed didn't know whether it was coming or going, passing between England and Scotland like the proverbial shuttlecock. However disorientated it has a fine links course at **Goswick**, three miles south of the town. Two thoughts for what may be one's last night in England—or maybe one's first—are the Kings Arms Hotel (01289) 307454 and the excellent Marshall Meadows Country House (01289) 331133 is a thoroughly popular local spot. A little further afield try the Tillmouth Park Hotel (01890) 882255, a really pleasant place to stay.

Having sent the golfer north of Newcastle I am aware of having neglected Hexham. Just north of Hexham are the newly opened **Matfen Hall**. and the county's newest golfing gem, **Slaley Hall**, which is featured ahead. **Hexham** Golf Club is only a short drive west of Newcastle, along the A69 or A695. Slaley Hall International Resort and Spa (01434) 673350 is quite sumptuous with excellent restaurants and leisure facilities. The journey is well worth making as the course has a glorious setting and the nearby villages with their many inns. The Hadrian, at (would you believe) Wall, and the Manor House at Carterway Heads (01207) 55268 cry out for inspection. Betwixt the two, the Angel (01434) 632119 in Corbridge is good. Within similarly easy reach of Slaley Hall, is Danielle's Bistro (01434) 601122 in Hexham itself, which offers imaginative food attentively served. A golfing holiday I believe is in order—and who needs Scotland!

Slaley Hall

Despite its close proximity to Scotland, the 'royal' and 'ancient' county of Northumberland has made little impact on the history of the royal and ancient game. In the future, however, this situation is likely to change. How come? The catalyst can be found deep in the countryside at Slaley Hall near Hexham.

Slaley Hall itself is today a hotel and leisure complex of the highest order with an 18 hole golf course to match. The championship golf course was designed by Dave Thomas and opened for play in July 1989. Let us at once say that Thomas has produced a masterpiece; he himself considers it his finest work. Immediately it opened, critics were describing it as 'The Woburn of the North' and with dense forest surrounding the course it doesn't need much imagination to see why. As for the luxury hotel, following a £17 million remodelling and refurbishment programme the ultra impressive (and grandly named) Slaley Hall International Hotel Golf Resort and Spa opened its doors to the public.

Golfing visitors are welcome at Slaley Hall but they must have a handicap certificate or other valid proof of handicap. Subject to availability, they may play at any time during the week but must be resident in the hotel to book a tee time at weekends. Single tee times may be booked up to seven days in advance through the **Pro Shop (01434) 673154** while group booking enquiries should be directed to the **Golf Co-ordinator (01434) 673350** or by fax on (01434) 673152. The 1998 green fees are set at £50 per round, £70 for 27 holes and £80 for 36 holes. There is a 10% reduction for four ball groups. Golf buggies are available for hire and can be reserved in advance.

Although it genuinely is situated in deepest, rural Northumberland, visitors shouldn't have too much difficulty finding Slaley Hall. Its precise location is 6 miles south of Hexham and 2 miles west of the A68 road, between Corbridge and Consett. The quickest route from Newcastle (and its airport) is to pick up the A69 towards Hexham. Thereafter take the A68 south and follow the signs. From Hexham, the road to take for Slaley is the B6306. Approaching from further afield, the A1/M1 is likely to be of most assistance for those motoring up from the South and the Midlands, while to the north Hexham is linked to Scotland by the A68. The aforementioned Newcastle Airport is approximately 18 miles from the golf course.

In mid June 1998 the resort again plays host to the Compaq European Grand Prix which, with its £700,000 prize fund, is one of the most important events on the PGA European Tour. Won last year by Colin Montgomerie, the Grand Prix will attract many of the big names in European golf and the quality of the course should be of such a standard to test all participants.

From its championship tees Slaley Hall weighs in at a fairly formidable 7073 yards, par 72. Less daunting are the medal and 'social' tees which reduce the total length to around 6800 and 6500 yards respectively. From the ladies' tees the course measures 5862 yards, par 75.

The 1st hole offers a chance to open the shoulders, for the fairway is fairly wide, but thereafter at least a little caution may be the order of the day. The 2nd and 3rd are excellent holes—the former being a swinging dog-leg where, if you're too greedy from the tee, the conifers will swallow your ball. Fir trees are ever present at Slaley Hall, lining just about every fairway and giving the course something of an alpine feel. The golfer must do battle with streams and small lakes at the 4th, 5th, 6th and 7th. The 8th is another of Slaley's swinging dog-legs and the 9th is a truly magnificent par four played over water and through a narrow avenue of towering pines and dense rhododendrons.

On the back nine, holes 11, 12 and 13 are highly memorable; laid out close to Slaley Hall, cherry trees abound and they are a spectacular sight when in bloom. Holes 14 to 17 have a distinctly moorland feel and the 18th is a classic, though very difficult, finishing hole.

Just a year after opening, the magazine Executive Golfer International featured Slaley Hall in its June 1990 edition, and had this to say: 'We feel confident in predicting that Slaley Hall will soon become a name synonymous with major golf events—in the same league as Wentworth, Gleneagles and Turnberry. But in addition, Slaley Hall will be the total resort for all reasons and all seasons—as they say, the ultimate dream.'

In 1990 it was only a dream, but with Slaley Hall now a fully fledged European Tour venue, a fully serviced practice range with eight covered bays opening in the spring of 1998 and a second championship course, designed by Neil Coles, now complete and likely to be ready for full play by May 1999, that dream is at last being realised.

Hole	Yards	Par		Hole	Yards	Par
1	434	4		10	363	4
2	414	4		11	565	5
3	412	4		12	533	5
4	518	5		13	390	4
5	382	4		14	179	3
6	205	3		15	331	4
7	428	4		16	396	4
8	429	4		17	182	3
9	452	4		18	460	4
Out	**3,674**	**36**		**In**	**3,399**	**36**
				Out	3,674	36
				Totals	7,073	72

Slaley Hall International Hotel, Golf Resort & Spa

A unique mix of a rural location, proximity to major Northumbrian tourist attractions and possessing one of the UK's premier golf courses has rapidly turned Slaley Hall hotel into a favoured destination for golfing holidays and short breaks.

An investment of £17 million 18 months ago turned the private home into a five star standard 142 room hotel with 17 suites, two fine dining restaurants, a health and leisure club and spa, all set within a 1,000 acre estate.

Pride of place at Slaley Hall is the 18 hole championship golf course designed by Dave Thomas, which will this year host the Compaq European Tour golf event with $1,000,000 in prize money. Some of the biggest names in the sport are expected to take part.

Already, a second golf course is under construction and Slaley Hall's resident golf professional, Mark Stancer, can give expert tuition to both novice and experienced golfers round the demanding course.

In the golf clubhouse, golfers can eat all day if they wish without moving out to the two main restaurants. The pro shop next door provides the very best in golf wear for the discerning player and Slaley Hall has its own branded merchandise with gift vouchers to fill the gap when the imagination fails to come up with a special gift idea.

Guests enjoying a short golfing break can dine in the Imperial restaurant which specialises in local produce and game in addition to having a very fine wine cellar. The adjacent Fairways Brasserie caters for all day dining in a more informal atmosphere with views over the stunning 18th green.

Slaley Hall's health and leisure club has a gym equipped with state of the art fitness equipment including the latest in cardio-vascular machines. An adjoining pool area features a 23 meter deck pool, whirlpool and three waterfalls. A juice bar ensures that health enthusiasts can stick to their calorie counted meals.

The hotel's Spa facilities are not to be missed with a comprehensive range of facial and body treatments for both men and women including aromatheraphy, massage and hydrotheraphy. The golfer's recovery treatment is specially designed to look after tired muscles after a round on the course.

Slaley Hall is also a haven for walking, relaxing or as a touring base. The gardens boast a little known Japenese garden, complete with temple and watercourses. Together with the woodland walks, guests can enjoy peaceful seclusion on the estate.

Altrnatively, for golfers who prefer to keep on the move, an action packed weekend on the estate driving quad bikes, mountain biking,clay pigeon shooting or orienteering may have more appeal. Golfing conference delegates can take further advantage of the activities by putting forward competition teams to raise the temperature a little after a long day round the conference table.

Newcastle Airport is only 30 minutes away for London flights and there are mainline stations at both Newcastle and Carlisle. The hotel, hidden away in rural Northumberland, is easy to find, just 3 miles from the A68 south, off the A69 from Newcastle to Carlisle.

Slaley Hall International Hotel Golf Resort and Spa
Slaley
Hexham
Norhtumberland NE47 0BY
Tel: (01434) 673350
Fax:(01434) 673962

Silloth-on-Solway

One of the greatest ever lady golfers, Miss Cecil Leitch once said, 'If you can play Silloth you can play anywhere'. The four times British Ladies Champion and the great rival of Joyce Wethered would have been able to judge better than most for she grew up in Silloth and it was on Silloth's championship links that she and her four golfing sisters learnt to play.

Today, Silloth is perhaps one of Britain's lesser known championship links, this doubtless a result of its somewhat remote situation 23 miles west of Carlisle. Hidden away it may be but it is a journey decidedly worth making, for not only is this one of Britain's greatest tests of golf but the Silloth Club is just about the most friendly one is likely to come across.

Measuring 6614 yards, par 72 from the championship tees (6357 yards from the medal and 5780 yards, par 75 from the ladies' tees), Silloth may not sound particularly frightening, and you may just be wondering what all the fuss is about. Standing on the 1st tee with the wind hammering into your face you'll know exactly what all the fuss is about! Two shots later (hopefully!) you'll also discover why the large greens at Silloth have acquired such a marvellous reputation.

The course meanders its way through and over some classic links terrain. There are occasional spectacular vantage points—the coastal views from the 4th and 6th tees being especially memorable—and the round calls for several demanding strokes, both going out and coming home. Of the many great holes however, perhaps the par five 13th stands out. Appropriately named 'Hogs Back' it has an exceptionally narrow fairway that is heather lined on either side and a plateau green. Hit a good drive and you'll be tempted to go for the green in two—miss it and you're in deep trouble.

The club is understandably proud of the fact that it has been selected to host the British Ladies Amateur Championship on three occasions since 1976. However, it can also be proud of the courage some of its members displayed back in 1912; for this information I am greatly indebted to the club's former Secretary, John Todd. On behalf of all the clubs in the British Isles Silloth appealed against the assessment to income tax on green fees. Unfortunately for the golf clubs the learned judge found in favour of the Inland Revenue, leaving Silloth with the task of finding £433 12s. 9d. for legal expenses. 81 clubs promised contributions to help towards the debt and they eventually raised £140 11s. between them, leaving Silloth with a deficiency of almost £300. One very famous club, I am told, subscribed one shilling—and I bet you'd like to know which!

Silloth on Solway Golf Club, Silloth on Solway, Carlisle, Cumbria CA5 4BL

Secretary	John Proudlock (01697) 331304
Professional	Carl Weatherhead (01697) 332404
Green Fees	WD £25/day, WE £30/round
Restrictions	Must be a member of a recognised golf club

Directions
From the south—M6 junction 41, B5305 to Wigton, B5302 to Silloth. From the north/east—M6 junction 43, A69 to Carlisle, A595/596 to Wigton, B 5302 to Silloth.

Windermere

Whoever first coined that atrocious phrase, 'Golf is a good walk spoiled' was more than likely an idiot. One thing's for sure, he (or she) had never visited Windermere Golf Club in the Lake District. Golf not only 'takes us to such beautiful places', as Henry Longhurst used to say, but it also regularly guides us to some beautiful vantage points. Had the idiot who coined the former offering stood on the 8th tee at Windermere he would have assuredly been forced to revise his ill-informed comment. Golf, if nothing else, is a good walk with a good incentive. (Better not tell that idiot then that the 8th at Windermere is called 'Desolation!')

Founded in 1891, Windermere has always been a popular course. It never had pretensions to becoming a championship length course but has always offered an enjoyable challenge. With its outstanding views, its great swathes of heather, bracken and gorse, plus the marvellous condition in which the course is currently maintained, it is easy to understand why more and more people are calling it a 'mini Gleneagles.' Windermere is probably worthy of such flattery.

Measuring just 5122 yards and with a par of 67, there are, of course, many par three holes and, while none of the par fours is overly long, the naturally rugged landscape makes up for the lack of length. As on a links type course, awkward stances and blind shots are not uncommon at Windermere, and with the greens being fairly small a well-honed short game is often the key to a good round.

We have already singled out the 8th as Windermere's 'signature hole': from the tee the green sits roughly at eye level but in between is a deep valley of gorse. The green is table-shaped and can be extremely difficult to hit. Distraction is the last thing a golfer needs here but over the player's shoulder is a marvellous view of Morecambe Bay while stretching ahead are the magnificent mountains of the Lake District.

Among other notable holes at Windermere one might include the 2nd, a very long par three; the 4th which is the stroke index one hole with its difficult drive to an acutely angled fairway and potentially even more difficult blind approach; the 6th and 7th where you play beside an attractive little reservoir and the three closing holes, which, according to the card run 5-4-3—scores that most players will be happy to settle for!

Having introduced Windermere with a regrettable quote, it seems only appropriate to conclude with one of the more noble philosophies on life and reputedly first uttered by the legendary golfer Walter Hagen: 'You're only here for a short while; don't hurry, don't worry, but be sure to smell the flowers along the way.' Of course at Windermere, they might even be found fluttering and dancing in the breeze.

Windermere Golf Club, Cleabarrow Windermere, Cumbria LA23 3NB

Secretary	Mr K Moffat (015394) 43123
Professional	Stephen Rook (015394) 43550
Green Fees	WD £23, WE £28
Restrictions	Players must be members of golf clubs and have official handicaps

Directions
From the M6, the best exit point is junction 36. The club is a mile and a half from Bowness on the B5284.

Seaton Carew

Seaton Carew near Hartlepool is a place of extraordinary contrasts. Here is where the industrial north east collides head on with a popular seaside resort. The North Sea washes a sweep of golden sand; beyond this strand are the dunes; beyond the dunes is the lively town (where in summer sedate guesthouses jostle for prominence with noisy arcades) and beyond the town is a backdrop of towering chimneys and their modern equivalents, which at night appear lit up like giant torches. Oh, we forgot to mention one thing: on the landward side of the dunes—though occasionally wandering in amongst them—is the Seaton Carew championship golf links, the finest 18 holes on the east coast of Britain between Hunstanton in Norfolk and Muirfield in East Lothian.

A golf club was formed here in 1874. Initially, there were just 9 holes and the club was named the Durham and Yorkshire Golf Club. There were 18 holes by 1891 but the course did not properly take shape until Alister MacKenzie made major revisions to the layout in the 1920s. Fifty years later, Frank Pennink constructed four new holes and today the club maintains all 22 holes.

Championship golf regularly visits Seaton Carew and in recent years it has hosted the English Strokeplay Championship and, on two occasions, the British Boys Championship.

The challenge commences with a hole called 'The Rocket'. The name has become particularly appropriate following the recent discovery (by the club's head greenkeeper) of two unexploded war time bombs on the adjacent practice area! There is plenty of variety in the 4-5-3 start but the two outstanding sequences at Seaton Carew occur around the turn and over the closing stretch, where sand dunes, undulating terrain, traditional seaside bunkers and a mass of buckthorn conspire to provide an exacting but enjoyable finish. The 371 yards, par four 9th, 'Lagoon' is possibly the best hole on the front nine. The Lagoon—essentially marshy ground—lies to the right of the fairway yet a tee shot directed to this side sets up a much easier second to a green with a steep fall-away on the right. The 10th heads directly towards the sea and, together with the rugged 12th is the pick of Frank Pennink's 'new' holes.

The imaginative (and prophetic) soul who thought up the names 'Rocket' and 'Lagoon' was premumably not consulted with regard to the 16th—it is called 'Dog Leg'! Still, it is a fine hole and leads to a truly great hole. The 17th at Seaton Carew features a bold drive over dunes and gorse and an approach to a raised green surrounded by subtle contours—Alister MacKenzie at his best. The 18th has plenty of character too, with an out of bounds to the right and a rippling fairway.

Seaton Carew Golf Club, Tees Road, Hartlepool TS25 1DE	
Secretary	P R Wilson (01429) 261040
Professional	W Hector (01429) 890660
Green Fees	WD £29/day
	WE £40/day
Restrictions	Handicap certificates required.
Directions	
2 miles south of Hartlepool off the A178.	

Bamburgh Castle

Bamburgh Castle may be golf's ultimate 'hidden gem'. The setting is quite stunning. A number of Britain's golf courses fall within the gaze of nearby castles—Royal St. David's and Harlech Castle is perhaps the best known example, Cruden Bay and Dunstanburgh are others, but none is more dramatic than the situation at Bamburgh. Standing 150 feet high on a vast, rocky crag and covering over eight acres, Bamburgh is one of Britain's most spectacular castles. It towers over the village and is visible in all its majesty from the adjoining 18 hole links.

Apparently we have to thank the Normans for the splendid keep. It was they who built it, having acquired the original castle from Matilda, Countess of Northumberland, after threatening to take out the eyes of her captive husband—charming times!

Bamburgh has what might be described as an 'invigorating climate'. Situated on the north eastern coast of Northumberland, only Berwick-upon-Tweed lies further north in England and Bamburgh is a shade closer to the North Pole than either Prestwick, Turnberry or Troon. Despite its remoteness, the journey is a fairly straightforward one and is definitely worth making. By any standards, Bamburgh Castle is a short course, measuring 5621 yards (par 68) from the men's tees and 5098 yards from the ladies' tees (par 70). Short it may be but it isn't without its tests; there are many whin bushes and several of the fairways are flanked with tangling heather. As with every seaside course, the moods of the wind must always be considered. In any event the golfer will not have come to Bamburgh to seek golf's toughest challenge—it is the splendour of the unique setting that is to be enjoyed. The castle isn't the only sight that demands attention: there are magnificent views across to nearby Holy Island and Lindisfarne and the Cheviot Hills provide a glorious backdrop.

As for the course itself, in addition to the great spread of purple heather, a number of fairways are lined with rare wild orchids. It is hardly surprising that Bamburgh is often described as Britain's most beautiful course. Especially memorable holes at Bamburgh include the short 8th with its tee shot over a valley, the 15th—from this tee the golfer can spy no fewer than four castles—and the 17th which is guaranteed to bring the dreaming golfer down to earth.

What about the 19th? In short, exceptionally friendly (as one comes to expect in this part of England). There are no formal dress requirements and lunches and dinners are offered daily in addition to light snacks.

There is a saying used in many sports that 'a good big'un' is always better than 'a good little'un'; the golf course at Bamburgh demonstrates that the phrase has no meaning whatsoever in the world of golf.

Bamburgh Castle Golf Club, The Club House, Bamburgh, Northumberland, NE69 7DE	
Steward/Clubhouse	(01668) 214378
Secretary	Mr T C Osborne (01668) 214321
Green Fees	WD £25/day
	WE £30/round; £35/day
	5 day weekday ticket £70
Restrictions	Weekends busy
	Handicap certificates required.
Directions	
Bamburgh is linked to the A1 (6 miles away) by the B3141 and the B3142.	

Key

CUMBRIA

Alston Moor G.C.
(01434) 381675
The Hermitage, Alston
(9) 5380 yards/***/E

Appleby G.C.
(017683) 51432
Brackenber Moor, Appleby-in-Westmorland
(18) 5895 yards/***/D

Barrow G.C.
(01229) 825444
Rakesmoor Lane, Hawcoat
(18) 6209 yards/***/C

Brampton (Talkin Tarn) G.C.
(0169) 772255
Talkin Tarn,Brampton
(18) 6420 yards/***/C/H

Brayton Park G.C.
(016973) 20840
Lakeside Inn, Brayton Park
(9) 2521 yards/***/E

Carlisle G.C.
(01228) 513303
Aglionby, Carlisle
(18) 6278 yards/**/B/H

Carus Green G.C.
(01539) 721097
Burnside Road, Kendal
(18) 5642 yards/**/E

Casterton G.C.
(015242) 71592
Sedbergh Road, Casterton
(9) 3015 yards/***/E

Cockermouth G.C.
(017687) 76223
Embleton, Cockermouth
(18) 5496 yards/**/D

Dalston Hall G.C.
(01228) 710165
Dalston Hall, Dalston
(9) 2667 yards/***/E

Dunnerholme G.C.
(01229) 462675
Duddon Road, Askam-in-Furness
(10) 6181 yards/***(not Sun)/D

Eden G.C.
(01228) 573003
Crosby-on-Eden, Carlisle
(18) 6975 yards/***/D

Furness G.C.
(01229) 471232
Walney Island, Barrow-in-Furness
(18) 6363 yards/***/D

Grange Fell G.C.
(015395) 32536
Fell Road, Grange-over-Sands
(9) 4826 yards/***/D

Grange-over-Sands G.C.
(015395) 33180
Meathop Road, Grange-over-Sands
(18) 5938 yards/***/C/H

Kendal G.C.
(01539) 724079
The Heights, Kendal
(18) 5483 yards/***/C/H

Keswick G.C.
(017687) 79324
Threlkeld Hall, Keswick
(18) 6175 yards/***/C

Kirkby Lonsdale G.C.
(015242) 76365
Scaleber Lane, Barbon
(18) 6283 yards/***(Sun am)/D

Maryport G.C.
(01900) 812605
Bank End, Maryport
(18) 6272 yards/***/C

Penrith G.C.
(01768) 891919
Salkeld Road, Penrith
(18) 6026 yards/***/C/H

Seascale G.C.
(019467) 28202
The Banks, Seascale
(18) 6416 yards/***/C

Sedbergh G.C.
(015396) 21551
Catholes-Abbot Holme, Sedbergh
(9) 5504 yards/***/D

Silecroft G.C.
(01229) 774250
Silecroft, Millom
(9) 5712 yards/**/D

Silloth-on-Solway G.C.
(016973) 31304
Silloth-on-Solway
(18) 6614 yards/***/B-A/H

Silverdale G.C.
(01524) 701307
Red Bridge Lane, Silverdale
(12) 5417 yards/***/D

St Bees School G.C.
(01946) 824300
Rhoda Grove, Rheda, Frizington
(9) 5082 yards/***/E

Stonyholme Municipal G.C.
(01228) 34856
St Aidans Road, Carlisle
(18) 5783 yards/***/F

Ulverston G.C.
(01229) 582824
Bardsea Park, Ulverston
(18) 6142 yards/***/D-C/H

Windermere G.C.
(015394) 43123
Cleabarrow, Windermere
(18) 5006 yards/**/B/H

Workington G.C.
(01900) 603460
Branthwaite Road, Workington
(18) 6200 yards/***/C/M/H

CO DURHAM

Barnard Castle G.C.
(01833) 638355
Harmire Road, Barnard Castle
(18) 5838 yards/***/D

Beamish Park G.C.
(0191) 370 1382
Beamish, Stanley
(18) 6205 yards/***(not Sun)/C/H

Billingham G.C.
(01642) 533816
Sandy Lane, Billingham
(18) 6460 yards/***/B/H

Bishop Auckland G.C.
(01388) 602198
Durham Road, Bishop Auckland
(18) 6420 yards/***/B

Blackwell Grange G.C.
(01325) 464458
Briar Close, Blackwell,
(18) 5587 yards/***(Wed)/C

Brancepeth Castle G.C.
(0191) 378 0075
Brancepeth, Durham
(18) 6300 yards/**/B/H

Castle Eden & Peterlee G.C.
(01429) 836220
Castle Eden, Hartlepool
(18) 6293 yards/***/C

Chester-le-Street G.C.
(0191) 388 3218
Lumley Park, Chester-le-Street
(18) 6054 yards/**/B/H/L

Consett and District G.C.
(01207) 502186
Elmfield Road, Consett
(18) 6001 yards/**/C/H

Crook G.C.
(01388) 762429
Low Jobs Hill, Crook
(18) 6016 yards/***/D

Darlington G.C.
(01325) 355324
Haughton Grange, Darlington
(18) 6032 yards/**/B/M

Dinsdale Spa G.C.
(01325) 332297
Middleton St George, Darlington
(18) 6078 yards/**/D

Durham City G.C.
(0191) 378 0069
Littleburn Farm, Langley Moor
(18) 6326 yards/***/C

Eaglescliffe G.C.
(01642) 780098
Yarm Road, Eaglescliffe
(18) 6275 yards/***/B

Hartlepool G.& C.C.
(01429) 274398
Hart Warren, Hartlepool
(18) 6255 yards/**/C/H

Hobson Municipal G.C.
(01207) 271605
Hobson, nr Burnopfield,
(18) 6582 yards/***/E

Houghton-le-Spring G.C.
(0191) 584 1198
Copt Hill, Houghton-le-Spring
(18) 6450 yards/*/D/M

Knotty Hill G.C.
(01740) 620320
Sedgefield, Stockton-on-Tees
(18) 6668 yards/***/D

Mount Oswald G.C.
(0191) 386 7527
South Road, Durham
(18) 6101 yards/***/D

Norton G.C.
(01642) 676385
Junction Road, Norton
(18) 5870 yards/**/E

Oakleaf G.C.
(01325) 310820
School Aycliffe Lane, Newton Aycliffe
(18) 5430 yards/***/F

Roseberry Grange G.C.
(0191) 370 0670
Grange Villa, Chester-le-Street
(18) 5628 yards***/E

The Ramside
(0191) 386 9514
Ramside Hall Hotel, Carville
Prince Bishops 6851/**/H/B
Cathedral 6217/**/H/B
Bishops Cathedral 6430/**/H/B

Ryhope G.C.
(0191) 5217333
Leechmere Way, Ryhope
(9) 6000 yards/***/E

Seaham G.C.
(0191) 581 2354
Dawdon, Seaham
(18) 5972 yards/***/D

Seaton Carew G.C.
(01429) 261040
Tees Road, Hartlepool
(18) 6855 yards/***/B-A

South Moor G.C.
(01207) 232848
The Middles, Craghead, Stanley
(18) 6445 yards/**/D/H

Stressholme G.C.
(01325) 461002
Snipe Lane, Darlington
(18) 6511 yards/***/F

Woodham G. & C.C.
(01325) 320574
Burnhill Way, Newton Aycliffe
(18) 6770 yards/***/F

TYNE AND WEAR

Backworth G.C.
(0191) 268 1048
The Hall, Backworth
(9) 5930 yards/**/F

Birtley G.C.
(0191) 410 2207
Portobello Road, Birtley
(9) 5660 yards/**/D

Boldon G.C.
(0191) 536 4182
Dipe Lane, East Boldon
(18) 6348 yards/**/F

City of Newcastle G.C.
(0191) 285 1775
Three Mile Bridge, Gosforth
(18) 6508 yards/***/C

Garesfield G.C.
(01207) 561309
Chopwell, Garesfield
(18) 6603 yards/**/C

George Washington G.C.
(0191) 417 2626
Nr Washington Moat House Hotel
(18) 6604 yards/***/D

Gosforth G.C.
(0191) 285 3495
Broadway East, Gosforth
(18) 6043 yards/**/C/H

Heworth G.C.
(0191) 469 9832
Gingling Gate, Heworth
(18) 6462 yards/**/D

Newcastle United G.C.
(0191) 286 4693
Ponteland Road, Cowgate
(18) 6498 yards/**/D/M

Northumberland G.C.
(0191) 236 2009
High Gosforth Park, Newcastle upon Tyne
(18) 6640 yards/**/A/L

Parklands G.C.
(0191) 2364480
High Gosforth Park, Newcastle upon Tyne
(18) 6060 yards/***/D

Ravensworth G.C.
(0191) 487 2843
Moss Heaps, Wrekenton
(18) 5872 yards/***/C/H

Ryton G.C.
(0191) 413 3253
Stanners Drive, Ryton
(18) 6034 yards/**/D

South Shields G.C.
(0191) 456 0475
Cleadon Hills, South Shields
(18) 6264 yards/***/B/L

Tynemouth G.C.
(0191) 257 4578
Spital Dene, Tynemouth
(18) 6403 yards/**/C/M

Tyneside G.C.
(0191) 413 2742
Westfield Lane, Ryton
(18) 6055 yards/**/C/H

Wallsend G.C.
(0191) 262 1973
Bigges Main, Wallsend
(18) 6608 yards/***/D

Washington Moat House G.C.
(0191) 417 8346
Stone Cellar Road, Usworth
(18) 6604 yards/***/C

Wearside G.C.
(0191) 534 2518
Coxgreen, Sunderland
(18) 6373 yards/***/B/M/H

Westerhope G.C.
(0191) 286 9125
Whorlton Grange, Westerhope
(18) 6407 yards/**/D

Whickham G.C.
(0191) 488 7309
Hollinside Park, Whickham
(18) 6129 yards/***/C

Whitburn G.C.
(0191) 529 2144
Lizard Lane, South Shields
(18) 5773 yards/***(Tues)/D

Whitley Bay G.C.
(0191) 252 0180
Claremont Road, Whitley Bay
(18) 6617 yards/**/C

NORTHUMBERLAND

Allendale G.C.
(01434) 683926
High Studdon, Allendale
(9) 5044 yards/***/E

Alnmouth G.C.
(01665) 830231
Foxton Hall, Alnmouth
(18) 6414 yards/**/B/H

Alnmouth Village G.C.
(01665) 830370
Marine Road, Alnmouth
(9) 6078 yards/***/D/H

Alnwick G.C.
(01665) 602632
Swansfield Park, Alnwick
(18) 6250 yards/***/D

Arcot Hall G.C.
(0191) 236 2794
Dudley, Cramlington
(18) 6389 yards/**/B/H

Bamburgh Castle G.C.
(01668) 214378
The Wynding, Bamburgh
(18) 5465 yards/**/B/H

Bedlingtonshire G.C.
(01670) 822457
Acorn Bank, Bedlington
(18) 6224 yards/***/D

Belford G.C.
(01668) 212433
South Road, Belford
(9) 6304 yards/***/E

Bellingham G.C.
(01434) 220530
Boggle Hole, Bellingham
(9) 5245 yards/***/D

Berwick-upon-Tweed G.C.
(01289) 387256
Goswick, Berwick-upon-Tweed
(18) 6425 yards/**/B

Blyth G.C.
(01670) 540110
New Delaval, Blyth
(18) 6300 yards/**/D

Burgham Park G.& C.C.
(01670) 787898
Felton, Morpeth
(18) 7139 yards/***/D

Close House G.C.
(01661) 852953
Heddon-on-the-Wall
(18) 5587 yards/**/D/G

Dunstanburgh Castle G.C.
(01665) 576562
Embleton, Alnwick
(18) 6038 yards/***/D

Haltwhistle G.C.
(016977) 47367
Greenhead, Haltwhistle
(18) 5968 yards/***/E

Hexham G.C.
(01434) 603072
Spital Park, Hexham
(18) 6272 yards/***/B/H

Magdalene Fields G.C.
(01289) 306384
Berwick-upon-Tweed
(18) 6551 yards/***/D

Matfen Hall G.C.
(01434) 886500
Matfen, Hexham
(18) 6732 yards/***/C

Morpeth G.C.
(01670) 515675
The Common, Morpeth
(18) 6215 yards/***/B/H

Newbiggin-by-the-Sea G.C.
(01670) 817344
Newbiggin-by-the-Sea
(18) 6452 yards/***/B

Ponteland G.C.
(01661) 822689
Bell Villas, Ponteland
(18) 6512 yards/**/B

Prudhoe G.C.
(01661) 832466
Eastwood Park, Prudhoe
(18) 5812 yards/**/C

Rothbury G.C.
(01669) 620718
Old Racecourse, Rothbury
(9) 5146 yards/***(not Sat)/D

Seahouses G.C.
(01665) 720794
Beadnell Road, Seahouses
(18) 5462 yards/***/D

Slaley Hall G.& C.C.
(01434) 673350
Slaley, Hexham
(18) 7073 yards/***/A/H

Stocksfield G.C.
(01661) 843041
New Ridley, Stocksfield
(18) 5594 yards/***/D/H

Swarland Hall G.C.
(01670) 787010
Coast View, Swarland
(9) 6517 yards/**/D

Tynedale G.C.
(01434) 608154
Tyne Green, Hexham
(9) 5706 yards/***/D

Warkworth G.C.
(01665) 711596
The Links ,Warkworth
(9) 5856 yards/***/D

Wooler G.C.
(01668) 281137
Dodd Law, Doddington, Wooler
(9) 6353 yards/***/D

Artist: **Frank Moss Bennett** **GOLFING SCENE** *Courtesy of:* **Rosenstiels**

Golf in England

Royal Lytham & St Annes, England

The Belfry, 10th Hole, England

The Belfry, 18th Hole, England

Royal St George's, England

Wentworth, England

Sunningdale, England

*Royal St George's, England

*Royal Birkdale, England

Pictures by Graeme W Baxter courtesy of Baxter Prints, see page 352 for order details

THE FIRST, KING'S COURSE
by Robert Wade   19″ × 27″

THE CADDIE
by Robert Wade   19″ × 27″

THE LUCKY DOG by Victor Venner   12″ × 16″

ADRESSING THE BALL by Victor Venner   12″ × 16″

SEVEN IRON by Roy Perry   20″ × 30″

TO HALVE THE MATCH by Roy Perry   20″ × 30″

BALLESTEROS' HOLE, THE BELFRY
by Bill Waugh   10 ¾″ × 16″

AUGUSTA NATIONAL,16th HOLE
by Bill Waugh   16 ¼″ × 24 ¼″

see page 351 for order form.

Balls in South Wales are often large, oval-shaped and made of leather. However, those belonging to the much smaller dimpled breed—usually white, though these days sometimes shocking pink and yellow—are to be found in some particularly pleasant spots, and in a great variety of places between the Wye Valley and the Gower Peninsula. In addition to the Glamorgans and the Monmouth area our region takes in Mid Wales as well, that is the larger, less inhabited counties—'the real Wales', they'll tell you there.

Monmouth and Surrounds

For many travellers their first sample of golf in South Wales will be the impressive **St Pierre** Golf and Country Club at Chepstow (see feature page). Unfortunately, far too great a number make St Pierre their one and only stop. Further up the Wye Valley both **Monmouthshire** and the **Rolls of Monmouth** offer an outstanding game in delightful surroundings. Bounded by the River Usk, the Monmouthshire Golf Club lies half a mile west of Abergavenny at Llanfoist. In 1992 the club celebrated its centenary—quite an achievement when one considers its unusual beginnings. Laid out on ground formerly used for polo and later for horseracing, golf was started here in 1892, as the club handbook tells you, 'the result of a bet as to whether such a venture could be run successfully at Abergavenny!' Clearly the golfers backed a winner. Golf at 'The Rolls' is explored on a later page.

The Marriott St Pierre Hotel (01291) 625261 is a 14th century mansion providing a whole range of facilities. However, those not wishing to wake up next to the famous 18th green, note the Beaufort (01291) 622497, also in Chepstow and very comfortable. The Walnut Tree (01873) 852797 in Abergavenny is without doubt one of the finest restaurants in Wales and Llanwenarth Arms Hotel (01873) 810550 at Govilon to the west of Abergavenny makes an excellent base for golfing visitors. Monmouth provides the Riverside Hotel (01600) 715577 and Tallocher Farm House Hotel (01600) 740662 while the nearby Crown at Whitebrook (01600) 860254 offers award-winning cuisine and good accommodation.

Heading west of Chepstow, a very established course and one well worth a visit is **Newport** at Rogerstone. It is a very fine downland course and decidedly handy when travelling along the M4 (junction 27)—en route to Porthcawl perhaps? Undoubtedly the place to stay in Newport is the **Celtic Manor** Hotel Golf and Country Club Hotel (01633) 413000 which just happens to have two Robert Trent Jones designed golf courses right on its doorstep (see feature page).

The Glamorgans

Golfers in Cardiff (or Caerdydd) are quite fortunate having a number of well established courses close at hand. Not surprisingly they tend to be busier than the majority of Welsh courses and therefore before setting off it is especially important to contact the particular club in question. The **Cardiff** Golf Club is a superior parkland course situated some three miles from the city centre at Cyncoed. **St Mellons,** north east of the city, within easy access of the M4, is another popular parkland course—quite challenging, with several interesting holes. To the south west of Cardiff, **Wenvoe Castle**, one of the more hilly courses in South Glamorgan can be recommended as can the **Glamorganshire** course, located to the west of Penarth.

Perhaps the best hotels in Cardiff are the Marriott Hotel (01222) 399944 in the centre of the town and the Park Hotel (01222) 383471. The New House Hotel (01222) 520280 is also most appealing. Among the better restaurants, are

the ironically named Armless Dragon (01222) 382357 and the Blas-Ar Cymru (01222) 382132 which offers a delightful taste of Wales. Another good eating place is found in Penarth, the Caprice (01222) 702424, where excellent seafood accompanies fine views over the Bristol Channel. Also in Penarth, the Captain's Wife is recommended (a pub it should be added!). More pubs, and to the north and south of Cardiff are the Maenllwyd at Rudry and the beautifully thatched Bush at St Hilary. Still further south is the popular Blue Anchor at East Aberthan to the west of Penarth (superb lunches).

A short distance to the north of Cardiff, the town of Caerphilly is more famous for its castle and its cheese than for its golf; however, there is some good golf in the area, **Mountain Lakes** Golf and Country Club being particularly noteworthy and well worth a visit. Before heading off to the glorious coastal strip around Porthcawl a course certainly deserving a mention is **Aberdare**—an excellent woodland course, undoubtedly the finest in 'the Valleys'. In Coychurch, the Coed-y-Mwstwr Hotel (01656) 860621 is an extremely attractive hotel to consider.

One would have to travel many a mile to find a course the equal of **Royal Porthcawl** (also featured later this chapter) but its near neighbour to the east, **Southerndown** gets closer than most. Situated on high ground it is an outstandingly scenic downland type course measuring a little over 6600 yards (par 70). Even closer to Porthcawl is the fine links of **Pyle and Kenfig,** on more than one occasion the venue for the Welsh Amateur Stroke Play Championship. It is a very tough challenge, being open to the elements, and boasts some very large sand dunes. The **St Mary's** Golf Club offers 27 holes and numerous other attractions besides. Its close proximity to the M4 makes it very convenient. The hotel here (01656) 861100, converted from a 17th century farmhouse, is also one to note.

Additional ideas for a well earned night's rest in the area include in Porthcawl, the Atlantic Hotel (01656) 785011 and The Seabank (01656) 782261. In Nottage, the Rose and Crown (01656) 784850 is an excellent pub serving good food and with some accommodation, while another notable drinking establishment is the Prince of Wales in Kenfig. As a base for covering the whole region in style, the historic Great House at Laleston (01656) 657644 and the elegant Egerton Grey (01446) 711666 at Borth Kerry outside Barry are hard to beat.

Beyond Pyle and Kenfig the M4 heads into West Glamorgan passing through Port Talbot towards Swansea, and beyond Swansea is the beautifully secluded Gower Peninsula. If you are fortunate enough to be visiting these parts, three courses that can be strongly recommended are **Pennard** (featured ahead) **Fairwood Park**, and **Clyne.** Fairwood Park, situated close to Swansea Airport, is a second course over which racehorses once galloped. It is a much improved course and has several long par fours. Clyne offers a moorland challenge while from Pennard's clifftop course there are some splendid views out across the Bristol Channel.

A hotel for the night? Near to Swansea, the Langland Court Hotel (01792) 361545 is a comfortable clifftop inn of great character, and in nearby Mumbles, the Norton House Hotel (01792) 404891 is most relaxing. On the Gower, Fairyhill Country House (01792) 390139 is recommended, especially for its cuisine. As for a drink, there are numerous pubs. Here are two suggestions: the Joiners Arms in Bishopston and the Welcome to Town in Lanrhidian.

Mid Wales

For every person in New Zealand there are twenty sheep. Regrettably, I don't have the figures for mid Wales but I suspect they're fairly similar. The bad news is that the lack of human beings is unfortunately reflected by a low number of top class golf courses (unlike in New Zealand it should be said). However, the good news is that even during the summer months most of the courses remain relatively uncrowded, visitors are made very welcome and the green fees tend to be a lot cheaper than in most parts of Britain.

Ceredigion, Carmarthen and Pembroke

The two championship courses in this region lie on the southern coast, some 30 miles apart. Both **Tenby** (featured ahead) and **Ashburnham** were founded before the turn of the century and each has staged more than one Welsh Amateur Championship, Ashburnham in fact being a regular venue.

Located one mile west of Burry Port, Ashburnham's links is fairly close to industrial South Wales which, I suppose, extends as far as Llanelli, or at least to where the M4 from London fizzles out. The course measures 7000 yards from the championship tees and 6686 yards from the medal tees—certainly not a course for the inexperienced! Connoisseurs of the game, however, should find it an excellent challenge.

In Llanelli, the Diplomat (01554) 756156 is convenient for Ashburnham, but for a really relaxing 19th hole, golfers may prefer to stay in Tenby with its stylish Georgian harbour. Here Waterwynch House (01834) 842464 is recommended. The Tall Ships (01834) 842055 also enjoys a suitably convenient location. A local favourite is the St Brides Hotel (01834) 812304 which enjoys superb views of Carmarthen Bay and its restaurant makes the best use of locally captured lobster. Equally impressive in this respect is the excellent Penally Abbey (01834) 843033 in the quiet village of Penally and ideally situated for Tenby Golf Club. To the north, nestling in the foothills of the Black Mountains, is the town of Llandeilo and a stay at the delightful 18th century coaching inn of the Cawdor Arms Hotel (01558) 823500 is recommended. Another good hotel which also offers excellent seafood can be found in Broadhaven—the Druidstone Hotel (01437) 781221.

Moving westwards along the coast, the next 18 holes are to be found at **Milford Haven**, a medium-length parkland course to the west of the town. In days of old the former whaling town may well have been a haven but the present day 'landscape in oils' isn't everyone's cup of tea. More attractive is **St Davids** with its beautiful cathedral making it the smallest city in Britain. Unfortunately for golfing visitors there is only a modest 9 hole golf course .20 miles away at **Newport** there is a very fine golf course, and one which offers some tremendous sea views.

St Davids has many pleasing hotels, and Warpool Court (01437) 720300 is particularly good. St Non's Hotel (01437) 720239 is a good family hotel and offers special rates on St David's 9 hole course. Should one tire for some reason of the coast then the Wolfscastle Country Hotel (01437) 87225, in Wolfscastle is very welcoming (even though it may not sound like it). The 17th century Hotel Merineth (01437) 763353 in Haverford West is another comfortable hotel. The Mariners (01437) 764523 is also well worth a visit. Perhaps the most appropriate place for golfers who have played somewhat waywardly is the village of Welsh Hook—Stone Hall (01348) 840212 is the establishment recommended, an excellent restaurant with rooms. Good places for a drink include the contradictory Sailors Safety and the Ship Aground, both at Dinas, and the Golden Lion in Newport. If you are still hungry then the best tip is to visit Cardigan and the Pantry (01239) 820420. Failing the

Pantry, try the kitchen—the Castle Kitchen (01239) 615055, an informal but well run restaurant nearby.

Leaving 'Little England beyond Wales' and heading still further up the coast, the University town of **Aberystwyth** has an 18 hole course that looks out over Cardigan Bay. Try the Belle Vue Royal Hotel (01970) 617558 for a 19th hole here—a lovely hotel with seafront views over Cardigan Bay. A more impressive golf course though is **Borth and Ynyslas,** one of the oldest clubs in Wales. Borth is a superbly maintained seaside links. The B4353 road runs right alongside much of the course and is often peppered by golf balls. Taking out insurance before playing Borth is recommended.

Whether you've peppered the road or the flagsticks one of the many guesthouses in and around Borth may be the most convenient place for a good night's sleep. However, further north at Eglwysfach, 16th century Ynyshir Hall (01654) 781209 is well worth inspecting (note the nearby bird sanctuary) and in Machynlleth, the Wynnstay Arms (01654) 70294 is a cosy former coaching inn. Back in Borth, the Victoria Inn is a good pub and finally, a great example of friendly local hospitality in an elegant setting is the Conrah Country Hotel (01970) 617941 in Chancery near Aberystwyth, handy for the scenic **Penrhos** Golf and Country Club.

Inland, there is precious little golf to speak of, though there is a fairly testing hilltop course at **Carmarthen**—one which is decidedly better in summer than in winter and an attractive parkland course, **Glynhir,** near the foothills of the Black Mountain Range. The latter is a particularly friendly club situated close to the Glynhir Mansion where the first news of Wellington's victory at Waterloo is reputed to have been received by carrier pigeon. (Must have been a pretty sharp pigeon!) One doesn't have to look far for a night's stay either: in Llandybie, the Mill at Glynhir (01269) 850672 overlooks the 14th green.

Powys

The golf courses in Powys are few and far between, but those there are tend to be set amidst some splendid scenery. There is an 18 hole course at **Welshpool** up in the hills near the English border (do try to visit Powys Castle and its superb gardens if you're in the area) and two interesting 9 hole courses at Newton (**St Giles**) and at Llanidloes (**St Idloes**) in the quiet of the Cambrian Mountains (note the very fine Glansevern Arms (01686) 440240 in Pant Mawr). Two of the region's best courses are situated right in the centre of Wales, **Llandrindod Wells** and **Builth Wells**. Both are attractive courses, but Llandrindod in particular offers spectacular views. For Builth Wells there can be no finer base to play from than the Lake Country House (01591) 620202 while in the town itself is the Lion Hotel (01982) 553670, an historic inn and very pleasant too. In Llandrindod the large Metropole Hotel (01597) 823700 is very convenient, the Harp at Old Radnor is an ideal place for a drink and a snack after a round at Llandrindod, but for a real overnight treat a visit to either Llangoed Hall (01874) 754525 or to a Welsh Rarebits property (01686) 668030 is recommended.

One final course to mention, and one good enough to have held the Welsh Amateur Stroke Play Championship is **Cradoc** near Brecon. A lovely course this, and again, very scenic being within the Brecon Beacons National Park. Here's another tip: a drink at the White Swan in Llanfrynach followed by dinner and a relaxing stay at Gliffaes (01874) 730371 in Crickhowell, an ideal base from which to play many courses.

Royal Porthcawl

By common consent Royal Porthcawl is the finest course in Wales and one of the greatest championship links in the British Isles; yet like many famous clubs, Porthcawl's beginnings were rather humble. The club was founded in June 1891 and the following year a nine hole course was laid out on a patch of common land known as Lock's Common, consent having been given by the local parish vestry. Having to share the course with, amongst other things, cattle soon frustrated the members and a second nine holes were sought. These they found on the present site closer to the shore. By 1898 Lock's Common was abandoned altogether and the 'favoured' second nine holes were extended to a full eighteen. Once settled the club prospered and in 1909 patronage was bestowed. Royal Porthcawl had well and truly arrived.

The members were extremely fortunate in finding this new home for today Royal Porthcawl is not only considered to be one of Britain's finest golfing challenges but also one of the most beautifully situated. Every hole on the course provides a sight of the sea and from many points there are spectacular views across the Bristol Channel to the distant hills of Somerset and North Devon.

Presently presiding over the Royal domain is the club's helpful **Secretary, Mr Frank Prescott**. He may be contacted by telephone on **(01656) 782251** and by fax on **(01656) 771687**. The **Professional, Peter Evans**, can be reached on **(01656) 773702**. Golfers wishing to visit Royal Porthcawl can expect a warm welcome. Subject to possessing a golf club handicap there are no general restrictions; however, being an understandably popular club prior telephoning is advisable. Those wishing to organise golf society meetings should either telephone or preferably address a written application to the Secretary at **The Royal Porthcawl Golf Club, Porthcawl, Mid Glamorgan, Wales, CF36 3UW**. Tuesdays and Thursdays are the usual society days.

The green fees at Royal Porthcawl for 1998 are set at £45 per day during the week (but note that visitors are not permitted on Wednesdays) with £50 payable at weekends. A rather novel and most encouraging policy is adopted towards junior golfers. Junior members of the club can introduce an outside junior for a green fee of just £1 during weekdays.

The course is situated approximately 15 miles east of Swansea and about 20 miles west of Cardiff. The M4 makes travelling to Porthcawl fairly straightforward. Approaching from either east or west the motorway should be left at junction 37, then following the A4229 into Porthcawl. The course's precise location is towards the northern end of the town.

In the opening paragraph Porthcawl was described as a 'links'. This isn't perhaps entirely accurate for although much of the course is certainly of a links nature, some parts are more strictly downland and heathland in character and there aren't the massive sandhills that feature so prominently on the great championship links of Lancashire, and which are indeed to be found at neighbouring Pyle and Kenfig. The absence of sandhills means there is no real protection from the elements on stormy days and when the winds blow fiercely Porthcawl can be as tough a challenge as one is likely to meet.

From its championship tees the course stretches to 6685 yards (par 72, SSS 74) and from the medal tees it measures 6406 yards (par 72) with the ladies playing over 5749 yards (par 75). Good scores at Porthcawl are likely to be fashioned on the first ten holes. The 2nd, 3rd, 5th and 9th are the best of the early challenges, while from the par three 11th some very difficult holes lie ahead. The second shot from the fairway on the dog-leg 13th is one not to be hurried, as the views out across the course are quite breathtaking. The 15th and 16th are two excellent and quite lengthy par fours and the round ends with a glorious downhill finishing hole.

As for its 19th, Porthcawl has a splendid clubhouse. There is an informal men's bar where spikes may be worn, a mixed lounge (jacket and tie after 7pm) and a dining room (jacket and tie at all times). Both lunches and dinners can be arranged with prior notice, and light snacks are offered at all times except on Sundays. Since 1995 the club has also offered very good value Dormy accommodation—telephone the secretary for details.

One final thought for those wishing to explore the delights of Royal Porthcawl; I beg you to consider carefully before deciding to visit late on a November's afternoon for as the light fades and a mist starts to descend upon the links, the ghost of the Maid of Sker walks the 17th fairway—don't say you haven't been warned!

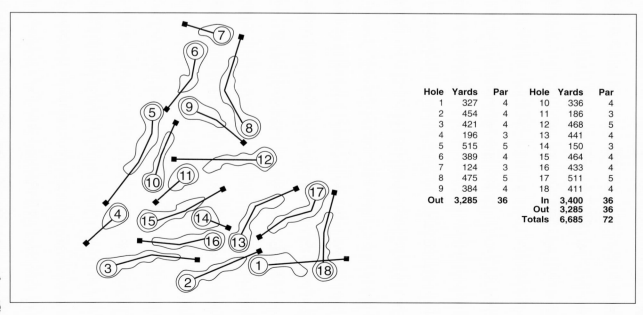

Hole	Yards	Par	Hole	Yards	Par
1	327	4	10	336	4
2	454	4	11	186	3
3	421	4	12	468	5
4	196	3	13	441	4
5	515	5	14	150	3
6	389	4	15	464	4
7	124	3	16	433	4
8	475	5	17	511	5
9	384	4	18	411	4
Out	**3,285**	**36**	**In**	**3,400**	**36**
			Out	3,285	36
			Totals	6,685	72

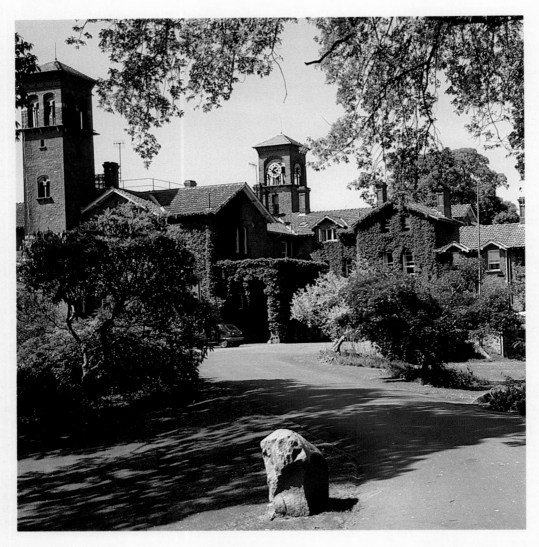

A thoroughly charming Victorian country house hotel, Gliffaes boasts fine gardens and parkland. Situated in the National Park yet only one mile off the main A40, it offers peace and tranquillity as well as being easily accessible.

Its location makes it ideal for visiting golfers. The championship course of the Rolls of Monmouth is only 30 minutes away, while top courses such as Cradoc and Abergavenny lie within ten miles. St Pierre, Builth Wells and Llandrindod Wells are also reasonably close. External facilities include fishing for salmon and trout in part of the Usk, which the hotel overlooks, tennis, bowls, putting and croquet. There are many short walks in stunning countryside with an abundance of birdlife and nearby riding or pony trekking centres.

The house, which faces due south, stands in its own 33 acres in the beautiful valley of the River Usk, midway between the Brecon Beacons and the Black Mountains. Built in 1885 as a private residence, it has been ideally adapted to provide spacious comfort in the country house tradition. There are 22 bedrooms, all individual in decor and furnishing and all with private bathrooms or showers.

The downstairs rooms include a large, panelled sitting room which leads into an elegant Regency style drawing room. From here, french windows lead to a large conservatory which opens onto the terrace. The dining room and comfortable bar also open onto the terrace, with glorious views of the surrounding hills and River Usk some 150 feet below. The billiard room has a full sized table and provides an additional sitting room with something of a club atmosphere.

Breakfast is served from a buffet table and a wide variety of light lunches are ordered in the bar. Dinner offers a good choice of freshly cooked and beautifully presented dishes. Country house standards of the old order are maintained by the resident owners, the Brabners, who have held sway here since 1948.

Gliffaes Country House
Crickhowell, Powys
Wales NP8 1RH
Tel: (01874) 730371 Fax: (01874) 730463
E mail: calls@gliffaeshotel.com

St Pierre

St Pierre was founded in 1961 and the Ken Cotton designed **Old** Course opened the following May. The first thing to strike you at St Pierre is the beautiful setting. The golf course land was originally a deer park and it has an abundance and great variety of mature trees. At the heart of the course there is also a lake covering eleven acres. Whilst the Old Course is understandably St Pierre's pride and joy, there are in fact 36 holes, as a second eighteen, the **Mathern** Course opened in 1975.

Visitors wishing to arrange a game at St Pierre must book starting times in advance. The club's **Professional, Craig Don** and his staff can be contacted by telephone on **(01291) 625261** and by fax on (01291) 629975. All written correspondence should be addressed to **Stephen Follett, Golf Operations Manager, Marriott St Pierre Hotel and Country Club, St Pierre Park, Chepstow, Gwent NP6 6YA.**.

There are no general restrictions on times of play. Officially visitors are not allowed at weekends but the rules can be bent if tee times are available. Societies are normally received only during the week unless they are resident at the hotel, in which case they may also play at weekends. Residential packages, inclusive of golf, are available on request.

The 1998 green fees are as follows: £55 for a round over the Old Course during the week and at weekends (when available), with £40 during the week and at weekends for a game on the Mathern Course. For junior golfers a single round on the Old Course is priced at £20 during the week and £25 at weekends. Junior rates for the Mathern course are £15 and £25 respectively.

The golf club is located to the south of Chepstow off the A48. The M4 links Chepstow to Cardiff and Swansea in the west and to London and Bristol in the east. Leave the M4 at junction 21, then follow the M48 as far as junction 2 taking the A4666 into Chepstow where the A48 can be joined and followed to St Pierre. The best route for those approaching from Birmingham and the north of England is probably to travel south on the M5, leaving at exit 8, thereafter picking up the M50 to Ross-on-Wye. From Ross-on-Wye a combination of the A40 and A466 provides a pleasant drive through the Wye Valley to Chepstow.

The Old and the Mathern Course differ quite considerably in length. The Old is the championship course and from the back tees measures 6762 yards (par 71). The forward tees reduce the length to 6506 yards, while for the ladies it measures 5865 yards (par 75). The respective distances for the Mathern Course are 5732 yards (par 68), 5569 yards and 5212 yards (par 70).

Despite its relative youth, the Old Course has been the venue for a remarkable number of professional events. The Dunlop Masters and Silk Cut Masters were staged regularly here—illustrious winners including Tony Jacklin, Bernhard Langer and Greg Norman. The latter on his way to a seven stroke victory in 1982 drove the 362 yards 10th with a three wood. In more recent years the Epson Grand Prix tournament was also held at St Pierre. In 1989 Seve Ballesteros produced some remarkable golf to win his first title in Wales. In 1990 the tournament changed its format from matchplay to strokeplay which resulted in a popular home victory for Ian Woosnam, and a year later Jose Maria Olazabal strolled home nine shots ahead of the field.

In September 1996 St Pierre successfully hosted the 4th Solheim Cup, the premier team event in women's golf. For two days it looked as if Europe might repeat its famous victory at Dalmahoy in 1992, but the final day's singles were won emphatically by the United States.

Perhaps the most famous hole on the Old Course is the 18th, surely one of the most dramatic finishing holes in golf. A par three of 237 yards, it requires a brave tee shot across the edge of the lake with large trees lining the left hand side of the fairway.

Standing proudly behind the green is the ivy-clad St Pierre Hotel. The hotel is in fact a former 14th century country mansion and it serves the golfer as a particularly impressive 19th. In addition to two fine restaurants, there are three bars. Celebrating at the end of a round is always to be recommended—particularly if the 18th hole has been tackled successfully.

Spare a thought though for a person by the name of Arwyn Griffiths who came to the 18th needing a three for a gross 63. A few minutes later he walked off the green having taken eleven strokes—but even he found cause for celebration, for Arwyn still won the competition!

Old Course

Hole	Yards	Par	Hole	Yards	Par
1	576	5	10	362	4
2	365	4	11	393	4
3	135	3	12	545	5
4	379	4	13	219	3
5	420	4	14	521	5
6	165	3	15	375	4
7	442	4	16	426	4
8	309	4	17	449	4
9	444	4	18	237	3
Out	**3,235**	**35**	**In**	**3,527**	**36**
			Out	**3,235**	**35**
			Totals	**6,762**	**71**

Celtic Manor

Celtic Manor is huge and it's getting bigger. It's also exciting and it's going to become more interesting still. You could say things are a happening in them there Wentwood Hills.

The Celts are passionate golfers. The Scots, Irish and Welsh delight in this most handsome game and the Welsh I have to say have struck gold with this fine development. It will in time surely become a monument to the game that so many Welshmen have served so proudly. One such star, the outstanding Ian Woosnam, refers to Celtic Manor as a golfer's dream. Beautiful, yes, challenging, yes, designed with distinction, for sure, but some may call it a nightmare! It will challenge many, tire many, frustrate others and it is already something to shout about. A visit to the splendid complex is warmly recommended.

One could describe course architect, Robert Trent-Jones Sr, as the true elder statesman of golf course design, and with his Roman Road course set amidst 1000 acres of mature woodland he has really delivered. Furthermore, late in 1998, a new championship course course, The Wentwood Hills, will provide a further 18 holes to challenge the brave. On this occasion the course is designed by Trent-Jones Jr, and is a par 72, 7200 yards in length. It is contained within the hilly landscape of the fisherman's paradise—The Usk Valley.

Celtic Manor is located in Coldra Woods, 100 minutes from Eros in Piccadilly Circus. For the clubhouse and golf courses leave the M4 at junction 24 - take the A48 towards Newport Town Centre for half a mile, and turn right at the Royal Oak. Continue up the hill, turn right at its summit drive for a half mile and the Celtic Manor Clubhouse is on your right hand side. The full address is **Celtic Manor Hotel & Country Club, Coldra Woods, Newport, Gwent, NP6 2YA**. To book a game of golf you should telephone **(01633) 410208** and the cost for the Roman Road Course is £30 per round. A current handicap certificate of 20 of below is required to play the course and you should always book your tee time well before playing. The **Professional Steve Bowen** and the **General Manager Duncan Williams** can both be contacted on the above number.

The **Roman Road** championship course offers a marvelous test. It runs along the ridge of Coldra Hill, straddling the ancient east to west Roman Road, Via Julia. The scenery offered is varied and exciting with deep ravines, steep ridges and stunning views of the neighbouring countryside. The course measures in excess of 7000 yards from the back tees with a scratch score of 74, but a par of 69. History has it that the Romans trained their gladiators over this formidable terrain—bouts of a more gentle type may be the norm today, but nevertheless the challenge remains intense throughout the course of this outstanding 18 holes.

There are numerous Trent-Jones trademarks, typically the large bunkers scattered throughout the course that would delight the giant jigsaw puzzler. There are several water carries and the greens, though often large, demand excellent approach play. The five par 3s are most significant if you are to score well—all but one measure in excess of 200 yards from the back tees.

There are a number of memorable holes and precision is vital—particularly at the 16th, a real beauty with its green protected by an ever hungry lake. This is a formidable golf course and visitors will be delighted that a huge acreage and standard of excellence has also been bestowed on the 19th hole. It's stylish and the largest in Britain. As such it's made to measure for the corporate occasion but the private party should not be deterred, this is a thoroughly welcoming establishment.

As well as the Roman Road and soon to be completed **Wentwood Hills** courses, the **Coldra Woods** course is far shorter though no less spectacularly beautiful and a delight to play. In addition there is a teaching academy with every facility which Woosnam rates as one of the best in the world.

The adjacent hotel is worthy of note and there are also numerous leisure faclilties—this really is some place, moreover in June 1999 a 400 bedroom hotel will be opened. Celtic Manor is getting bigger but we predict it is also going to get even better and that is, golfers will surely verify, the thing that counts.

Coldra Woods Course

Hole	Yards	Par	Hole	Yards	Par
1	220	3	10	403	4
2	190	3	11	182	3
3	279	4	12	130	3
4	192	3	13	162	3
5	283	4	14	191	3
6	164	3	15	243	4
7	243	4	16	196	3
8	179	3	17	186	3
9	363	4	18	288	4
Out	**2113**	**31**	**In**	**1981**	**30**
			Out	**2113**	**31**
			Totals	**4094**	**61**

Roman Road Course

Hole	Yards	Par	Hole	Yards	Par
1	455	4	10	447	4
2	529	5	11	217	3
3	423	4	12	367	4
4	205	3	13	425	4
5	586	5	14	206	3
6	335	4	15a	395	4
7	218	3	16	380	4
8	439	4	17	182	3
9	461	4	18	449	4
Out	**3651**	**36**	**In**	**3068**	**33**
			Out	**3651**	**36**
			Totals	**6719**	**69**

Tenby

Where are the loveliest beaches in Britain? Since I grew up in Devon and my ancestors came from Pembrokeshire, someone will doubtless accuse me of being biased but in my opinion the two finest places to bring out the bucket and spade are on the North Devon coast at Saunton and at Tenby in South Wales. Both have wonderful long stretches of golden sand. What makes Saunton and Tenby even more appealing—and now I will admit to bias—is that their beaches are fringed by massive sand dunes, adjacent to which are wonderful natural links courses.

Beautiful beaches aside, the courses at Saunton and Tenby are actually like 'chalk and cheese'. Saunton's design is reminiscent of Royal Birkdale with its fairways running parallel to the dunes along relatively flat valleys, whereas the layout at Tenby follows the Royal St George's approach—it careers over the top of the dunes. Tenby is an unashamedly old fashioned links—awkward stances, the occasional blind shot, hidden pot bunkers and tricky greens that sit on natural plateaux. This is what golf at Tenby is all about. It has enormous character, and for links enthusiasts it is tremendous fun.

Founded in 1888, Tenby is the oldest golf club in Wales. It is also one of the most spectacularly situated with glorious views, not only down over those golden sands but across the sea to Caldey Island.

The 1st at Tenby measures 466 yards and the opening drive must be struck straight into the sandhills. The golfer then disappears into another world. The 3rd hole is named 'Dai Rees' and was a favourite of the great Welsh golfer. It is not long but precision is everything for it features a hog's back fairway, an approach across a plunging valley to a narrow table-like green with a pot

bunker protecting the front entrance and steep banks on either side—a death or glory hole! The 4th is played from an elevated tee along a tumbling fairway bordered by huge dunes. The second shot is again downhill, this time to a blind green concealed beneath the dunes in a dell—shades of Lahinch and Prestwick! The 5th tee overlooks the beach as the course now heads off in a different direction.

Although some excellent two-shotters lie ahead, the most memorable holes from here on are the par threes—the short 6th, where the green is practically encircled by a sea of gorse, the 9th, the formidable 12th, with its crumpled fairway, and the exhilarating downhill 17th. The closing hole is the intriguingly named 'Charlie's Whiskers' and, true to form, it bristles with character. You don't need to be biased—or a lover of golden sands—to fall in love with Tenby.

Tenby Golf Club, The Burrows, Tenby, Pembroke, SA70 7NP

Secretary	J A Pearson (01834) 842978
Professional	Mark Hawkey (01834) 844447
Green Fees	WD £22 WE £26
Restrictions	Handicap certificates required.

Directions
The club is located on the west side of Tenby off the A447, near the railway station.

Pennard

Just beyond the town of Swansea, and the wonderfully named resort of Mumbles, is the Gower Peninsula and a secret, immensely scenic kingdom. It was once claimed of the Gower that smuggling was not just a profitable exercise—it was a full scale industry. Here is a land of golden beaches and hidden coves. A miniature Cornwall perhaps? Not really. The Gower is much quieter, much more 'grockle' free. And you've probably heard of St Enodoc and Trevose, but are you familiar with Pennard?

Founded around the turn of the century, Pennard Golf Club is Wales' best kept secret. It is not exactly cut off from the outside world but is genuinely tucked away. It lies just beyond the tiny village of Pennard—a church a post office and not much else—and occupies high ground that looks set to slip into the sea at any moment. The views, particularly those down across Oxwich Bay and Three Cliffs Bay are arresting, but the golf is worthy of the setting.

Pennard is not entirely undiscovered. Tom Doak, a leading American golf course architect and controversial course critic wrote of Pennard in his book *The Confidential Guide to Golf Courses*, "This is one of my all-time favourites—the site is one of the most spectacular I've ever seen."

Pennard is essentially a links course, although, as at Royal Porthcawl, there is a slight moorland-cum-downland feel to some of the holes. At 6329 yards, par 71, it is not overly long but being routinely buffeted by strong winds that roar up the Bristol Channel it can provide a very stern challenge. Much of the rough consists of thick gorse and dense, rust coloured bracken.

Like Tenby, there is a slightly eccentric, old-fashioned flavour to the links—the holes accommodate the land rather than vice versa. It is capricious wild terrain and some of the green sites border on the bizarre, but the golf is nothing if not adventurous.

The course is laid out in two distinct loops. The round starts and finishes with a strong par four but the greatest hole at Pennard is surely the 7th. Here you drive over a deep valley to find a fairway which runs alongside the ruins of a 12th century Norman castle and the site of a medieval church. Trying your best not to be distracted by the views, you must then play a deft pitch to a partially concealed, sunken green. It is a hole that personifies the character and charm of Pennard.

Pennard Golf Club, 2 Southgate Road, Swansea SA3 2BT

Secretary	Morley Howell (01792) 233131
	Fax (01792) 234797
Professional	M V Bennett (01792) 233431
Green Fees	WD £24; WE £30
Restrictions	Proof of handicap required. Avoid Tuesday mornings.

Directions
The club is eight miles west of Swansea via the A 4067 and the B 4436.

The Rolls of Monmouth

If this golf course didn't already have such a splendid name it would be necessary to invent one. 'Tranquillity Golf Club' might suffice. OK maybe that's a bit naff, but it wouldn't be in breach of the Trade Descriptions Act. The Rolls of Monmouth enjoys one of the most peaceful and secluded settings in Britain. The golf course is relatively young—it opened in 1982—but the accompanying countryside of gentle, circling hills and far off mountains cannot have altered greatly in hundreds of years.

The actual name is no mystery at all for the golf course lies within the grounds of the Rolls Estate, the former country home of Charles Stewart Rolls, who, together with Henry Royce, founded the famous Rolls Royce company. The imposing mansion that dominates the grounds and is visible from several parts of the course was largely built in the 18th century. Fortunately for we present day golfers the Rolls family were rather keen on landscaping and the grounds are blessed with a wonderful variety of trees and shrubs. Given such a setting and the fact that the Rolls course was laid out to championship specifications, incorporating several small lakes and streams, it isn't difficult to see why it has quickly established itself as one of the finest parkland tests in Britain.

The Rolls is very much a course of two halves, the two nines being laid out on opposite sides of the estate. The front nine opens fairly tamely (though prettily enough) with three gentle par fours all requiring slightly downhill approaches and the short 4th which has an attractive lake just behind the green and a semi-concealed bunker to the left. Then comes probably the most difficult series of holes in the round. The 5th has a deep ravine in front of the green and the only saving grace for the golfer is that it is a par five. The 6th is the stroke one hole and requires two very accurate shots across a severely contoured fairway and the 7th dramatically curls, tumbles and twists its way downhill for all of 500 yards until it meets a lake and a little stream. As for the green it's still another thirty yards the other side of the stream. The 8th is an outstanding par three, and the 9th, a short par four played from a spectacular high tee.

Among the more memorable holes on the back nine are the 11th, a lovely sweeping downhill par four, the sharply dog-legging 15th at the far end of the course (some splendid mountain views here) and the two par threes, the 13th and the 18th. The former has been described as 'an absolute beauty' and the latter 'an absolute horror'. Water features on both holes, but while it merely helps to shape the 13th and make it a very picturesque one-shotter, it turns the 18th into a very intimidating closing hole. 'Tranquillity'? Tell that to the match waiting on the 18th tee with all bets in the balance!

The Rolls of Monmouth Golf Club, The Hendre, Monmouth NP5 4HG

Secretary	Mrs Sandra Orton (01600) 715353 Fax: (01600) 713115
Green Fees	WD £32, WE £37 Monday Special—coffee, 18 holes of golf and lunch, £26
Restrictions	Book to make a tee reservation

Directions
The club is four miles west of Monmouth off the B4233. Monmouth is linked to Chepstow by the A466 and to Ross-on-Wye and Hereford by the A40.

One's first thoughts of North Wales are often of lakes, great castles and even greater mountains, or as a fine fellow by the name of Hywel ap Owain, 12th century Prince of Gwynedd, put it (I offer it in translation)

I love its sea-marsh and its mountains,
And its fortress by its forest and its bright lands,
And its meadows and its water and its valleys,
And its white seagulls and its lovely women.

A man who had obviously seen much of the world! Of course in the 12th century the Welsh didn't play golf, or at least if they did they kept it pretty quiet and in any case you can be pretty confident that Hywel ap Owain would have told us about it. Well, what about the golf in North Wales then? In a word, marvellous. Inland it tends to get hilly to put it mildly, and should you wish to venture up into 'them thar hills' as well as the climbing gear, don't forget to bring the waterproofs! But there again, leave room for the camera (hope you've got a large golf bag).

In the main though, it is to the coast that the travelling golfer will wish to head. Between Flint in the east and Aberdovey in southern Gwynedd are the impressive championship links of Prestatyn, Maesdu, North Wales, Conwy, Royal St Davids and of course Aberdovey itself. In addition, there are several with spectacular locations, Nefyn on the Lleyn Peninsula being an outstanding example.

Denbigh, Flint & Conwy

Before journeying around the coast though, a brief mention for some of the inland courses, with a few thoughts as to where one might stop off in order to eat, drink, be merry or simply rest the weary golf clubs. Away from the sea and sand probably the two main challenges are to be found at Wrexham and Llangollen. **Wrexham**, located just off the A53, is fairly close to the English border and indeed the views here are across the Cheshire plain. Two good holes to look out for are the 4th and 14th. Llangollen's splendid course, the **Vale of Llangollen**, is set out alongside the banks of the River Dee. There are some truly excellent holes, notably the 9th. Appropriately named the River Hole it is a really tough par four of 425 yards. The golfer who likes a spot of fishing (or perhaps even the golfing fisherman) would be in his element here and on a good day should see a few of the famous Dee salmon being landed—probably easier than netting a birdie. One name to watch in the future is the spectacular **Chirk Golf and Country Club**, south of Wrexham on the A483. Over 7000 yards of manicured fairways are complemented by a much less taxing par three course and driving range. North west of Wrexham on the road to Flint can be found the St Davids Park Hotel (01352) 840800 and **Northop Country Park** Golf Club complex. Excellent accommodation and a course now attracting PGA events make this well worth a visit.

As host to the famous International Eisteddfod Festival Llangollen has long been a popular tourist centre and there are a number of fine hotels in the town including the Hand (01978) 860303 and the Royal (01978) 860202. Also in Llangollen, Gales Wine Bar (01978) 860098 is well recommended and it also has rooms. The Bryn Howell (01978) 860331 is also good and the Cross Lanes (01978) 780555 is handy for visitors to Wrexham. Finally, visitors to Chirk should seek out the delightfully isolated Starlings Castle (01691) 718464—a charming restaurant with rooms.

In the unfortunately named town of **Mold** there is a pleasant parkland challenge, while still further north and getting nearer the coast is the **Rhuddlan** Golf Club. They say you should never rush a round at Rhuddlan. If you are heading for the tougher links courses on the coast then this is the ideal place to groove the swing. The course is laid out close to one of North Wales' famous massive fortresses in the grounds of Bodrhydden estate and overlooks the Vale of Clwyd. Just a couple of thoughts for golfers wishing to wet the whistle: the Dinorben Arms at Bodfari and the Salisbury Arms at Tremeirchion—two fine hostelries.

Exploring the countryside is a delight and there is a plentiful supply of country houses and inns to entice the traveller. A charming place to rest is the 16th century Hand Hotel (01691) 760666 at Llanarmon Dyffryn Ceiriog—all wooden beams and roaring fires—wonderful! Another thought is Soughton Hall (01352) 840811, an early 18th century mansion with good accommodation. Time to tear oneself away. The coast beckons and it's time to put that grooved swing into practice.

Prestatyn warrants first attention. Close to Pontin's holiday camp (or is it village nowadays?) it is a genuine links and when the prevailing westerly blows, can play very long (the championship tees stretch the course to 6714 yards). If a day at Pontin's isn't your cup of tea then the Traeth Ganol (01745) 853594 is worth a try. Thirsty golfers might also find the time to drive over the hill to the village of Gwaenysgor and the Eagle and Child pub—good food and good ale.

The A55 is the coastal road that should be followed to find our next port of call, the **Abergele and Pensarn** Golf Club, just west of Abergele. This course is a fairly new parkland layout lying beneath the walls of fairytale Gwyrch Castle. Games are often won or lost on the last three holes at Abergele. The round is supposed to finish five, three, five—but not many scorecards seem to!

A trio of championship courses are to be found a little further along the coast and just over the county border in Gwynedd. Golfers in Llandudno are more fortunate than most, having two fine courses to choose from: **North Wales** and **Llandudno (Maesdu)**. Both are of a high standard and each offers superb views across the Conwy estuary towards Anglesey.

The **Caernarvonshire** Golf Club lies the other side of the estuary at Conwy—yet another spectacular siting between the sea and mountains and another course where the wind can blow fiercely. A regular venue for the important Welsh Championships, it is a long course and is generally considered second only to Royal St Davids in terms of golfing challenges in North Wales. It possesses everything that makes links golf so difficult—gorse, rushes, sandhills and more gorse, rushes and sandhills—quite frightening!

The Llandudno-Conwy-Colwyn Bay area is riddled with places of interest and places to stay. Indeed it offers a veritable feast for the golfing gourmet. Here are a few thoughts. In Llandudno, famed for its Great Orme, are several excellent hotels, the Esplanade (01492) 860300 and the St Tudno Hotel (01492) 874411 (note the excellent restaurant here) are two first class examples, while slightly inland at Deganwy is the renowned 17th century Bodysgallen Hall (01492) 584466. Set amid quite idyllic grounds, the hotel offers great style as well as sumptuous cuisine. Less expensive accommodation of good quality can be found at the Bryn Cregin Garden Hotel (01492) 585266 also in Deganwy and highly recommended. Returning to Llandudno, a pair of pubs whose names you should have little difficulty in remembering are the Kings Head and the Queens Head, the latter a little to the south of the town at Llandudno Junction. Nearby in Conwy a liquid round can be enjoyed at the Liverpool Arms on the quay. There are many attractions in the area—the great castle and the town walls, Bodnant Gardens in the Conwy Valley and even the smallest house in Great Britain. Finally in Colwyn Bay among the many hotels two that merit attention are the Norfolk House (01492) 531757 and the Colwyn Bay Hotel (01492) 516555, a distinctive hotel high on a clifftop. Café Niçoise (01492) 531555 is a really good restaurant to try.

Gwynedd

Golfwise there is not a great deal more in the deeper realms of North Wales. **Ffestiniog,** famed for its mountain railway, has a short nine holes of the moorland variety but the scenery in these parts may prove a little too distracting. Ffestiniog nestles in the heart of Snowdonia and the encircling mountains are quite awe-inspiring.

Heading for the golf courses of the Lleyn Peninsular, many may wish to break their journey at Caernarfon. The castle is splendid and well worth inspecting. I suppose every golfer has at one time or another drawn up a mental listing of favourite golf courses. Anyone who has made the trip to **Nefyn** is almost certain to have the course high on such a list. A delight to play on (see feature page) Nefyn was a regular haunt of Lloyd-George, as was neighbouring **Pwllheli,** which was opened by him in 1909 when he was the Chancellor of the Exchequer. Not far from Pwllheli there is an interesting golf course at **Aberscoch.** Handy hotels for Nefyn include the Linksway (01758) 720258, Woodland Hall (01758) 720425 and the Caeau Capel Hotel (01758) 720240. The Nanhoran Arms (01758) 720203 offers special golf packages and is worthy of consideration. There are numerous pubs, including the Ty Coch Inn (almost on the course itself), and the Sportsman. Close by, situated right on the cliffs is the provocatively named Dive Inn (01758) 877246 at Tudweilog, which has an excellent restaurant. Another pleasant establishment is the lively Bryncyann Inn (01758) 720879 in Morfa Nefyn. In Pwllheli the Tower Hotel (01758) 612822, the Bel Air Restaurant (01758) 613198 and Porth Tocyn Hotel (01758) 7113303 are also recommended. A final thought is Plas Bodegroes (01758) 612363, a delightful restaurant with rooms.

A trip to the north west of Wales wouldn't be complete without a visit to Harlech, another great castle and certainly a great golf links, home of the **Royal St Davids** Golf Club (it too is explored on a later page). On the culinary side in Harlech there are two good restaurants, the Castle Cottage (01766) 780479 (some accommodation) and the Cemlyn (01766) 780425, while not far off in Talsarnau is the excellent Maes-y-Neuadd (01766) 780200 hotel and restaurant—extremely convenient for Royal St Davids, as is St Davids Hotel (01766) 780366. Finally in Harlech, Alexa House and Stable Cottages offer charming accommodation at a charming price. In Porthmadog is another good hotel, the Royal Sportsman (01766) 512015. Lastly, you cannot miss out on visiting Portmeirion, Clough Williams Ellis' attempt at creating the Italian Riviera on the coast of Wales. We recommend you stay at the Hotel Portmeirion (01766) 770228.

Heading further south and passing the splendid George III Hotel (01341) 422525 at Penmaenpool, **Aberdovey** is soon reached. The subject of favourite courses has been raised and Aberdovey was the choice of the celebrated golf writer Bernard Darwin, 'the course that my soul loves best of all the courses in the world.' It has an interesting layout, sandwiched between the sand dunes on the one side and a railway line on the other (the railway line in fact links Aberdovey to Harlech and is a pretty good service).

Golfers looking to play Aberdovey should consider the Corbett Arms (01654) 710264 and the Trefeddian Hotel (01654) 762213, which is exceptionally convenient for the course. Alternatives are the attractive Hotel Plas Penhelig (01654) 767676 which overlooks the Dovey estuary and the Penhelig Arms (01654) 767215, a delightful black and white inn with excellent food.

Isle of Anglesey

The Isle of Anglesey is linked by a road bridge to the mainland across the Menai Straits. There is a choice of six golf courses—perhaps the best two games to be found are at **Bull Bay**, near Amlwch, and at **Holyhead (Trearddur Bay)** on Holy Island. Both courses are very scenic and we have featured Holyhead separately. Bull Bay enjoys a fairly remote, and certainly spectacular setting on the island's northern coast. It is a hilly course with much gorse and several rocks to confront and when the wind blows it can be very tricky. The club handbook relates how in an exhibition match to mark the opening of the course, featuring John H Taylor and James Braid, the latter tangled with the gorse on the short third hole and finished up with an eight! There's hope for us all. Convenient resting places include the Bull Bay Hotel (01407) 830223 at Amlwch, the Lastra Farm Hotel (01407) 830906 (recommended by local golfers) and the impressive Trearddur Bay Hotel (01407) 860301 which lies adjacent to the Holyhead Golf Club. Ye Olde Bull's Head (01248) 810329 in Beaumaris is also recommended for its excellent restaurant and accommodation. In addition there are not surprisingly a vast number of reasonably priced guest houses on Anglesey—contact the Wales Tourist Board for details.

Artist: **A B Frost BEGINNER'S LUCK**
Courtesy of: **Rosenstiel's**

Royal St David's (Harlech)

With a St Andrews in Scotland and a St George's in England, it seems only right that there should be a St David's in Wales. Along with Royal Porthcawl in the South, the Royal St David's Golf Club at Harlech is one of the principality's two greatest Championship links.

The club was founded in 1894 by the Hon Harold Finch-Hatton together with Mr W H More who for twenty years acted as Hon Sec. The course itself was open for play at the end of 1894 and the opening competition was fittingly won by the greatest golfer of the day and the then reigning Amateur Champion, John Ball. St David's became Royal St David's early this century and in 1935 The Duke of Windsor (then Prince of Wales) became the club's captain.

Of its many attributes St David's is perhaps best known for its glorious setting. On the one side stretch the blue waters of Tremedog Bay, and on the other the imperious Snowdon and the other great mountains of Snowdonia National Park, while surveying all from its lofty perch is the almost forbidding presence of Harlech Castle. The massive fortress built by Edward I has known a particularly turbulent past. It played a prominent role in the War of the Roses when a great seige took place eventually ending in surrender. The seige is commemorated in the famous song 'Men of Harlech'.

The present 'Men of Harlech' to whom I should introduce you are the **Secretary, Mr D L Morkill (01766) 780361** and the club's **Professional, John Barnett** who may be contacted by telephone on **(01766) 780857** and by fax on (01766) 781110. The club's address is **Royal St David's Golf Club, Harlech, Gwynedd, LL46 2UB.**

St David's has a reputation for being one of Britain's friendliest clubs. Subject to being members of golf clubs, visitors and golfing societies are welcome at all times although those wishing to make party bookings must do so by written application to the Secretary. The cost of a day's golf in 1998 is set at £30 during the week with £35 payable at the weekend and on bank holidays.

The setting is indeed superb but the journey to get there can be a lengthy one—Harlech alas isn't like the proverbial Rome and there is just one road that travellers must join, namely the A496. From the north this road approaches from Blaenau Ffestiniog via Maentwrog (east of Porthmadog) and from the south via Dolgellau and Barmouth. Those coming from further afield may find Bala (if travelling from the north) and Welshpool (if motoring from the south) useful towns to head for. Bala links with Maentwrog by way of the A4212 and the A487, while the A458 and A470 link Welshpool to Barmouth. Finally, for those not travelling by car, the train station at Harlech may prove of assistance.

Measuring less than 6500 yards from the championship tees, St David's may not at first glance seem overly testing. However the general consensus is that the course, to adopt golfers' terminology, 'plays long'. Par is a very tight 69 and there are only two par fives on the card. Furthermore the rough can be very punishing (not to mention frustrating) and it is very rare for there not to be a stiff westerly wind.

Perhaps the most difficult holes on the course are the 10th, a long par four into the prevailing wind, and the classic 15th which requires a lengthy, angled drive followed by a precise approach. The round finishes with, to adopt another curious golfing expression, 'a nasty long short hole.'

The nineteenth at St David's matches the high standards set by the previous eighteen. There is an excellent bar for celebration or recuperation and light snacks, lunches and dinners are all offered. With prior warning a full Anglo/Welsh breakfast can also be arranged.

As one might imagine, each of the major Welsh Championships is staged regularly at St David's; in addition the British Ladies Championship, (won for the fourth time by Cecil Leitch in 1926), the British Boys Championship and both Men's and Ladies' Home International Matches have also been played at Harlech.

The conviviality of the club atmosphere has already been mentioned. Unfortunately there are still some English who consider the Welsh a little insular—a visit to Royal St David's makes one realise that Welsh golf clubs could teach many of their English counterparts a thing or two about hospitality . . .and on that controversial note, I wish you good golfing!

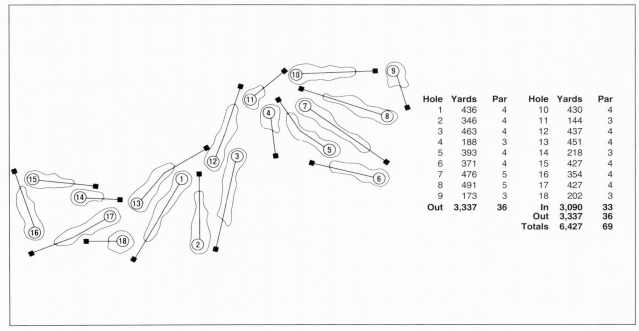

Hole	Yards	Par	Hole	Yards	Par
1	436	4	10	430	4
2	346	4	11	144	3
3	463	4	12	437	4
4	188	3	13	451	4
5	393	4	14	218	3
6	371	4	15	427	4
7	476	5	16	354	4
8	491	5	17	427	4
9	173	3	18	202	3
Out	**3,337**	**36**	**In**	**3,090**	**33**
			Out	**3,337**	**36**
			Totals	**6,427**	**69**

Holyhead (Trearddur Bay)

Which do you reckon are the best holes at Holyhead? I asked a Mancunian friend who plays the course every summer without fail. 'They're all real crackers down there', he replied. 'In fact, it's a cracking course full stop'. And he's right. Trearddur Bay, as many people call it, is one of two superb golf courses on the Isle of Anglesey, the other being Bull Bay on the island's northerly tip at Amlwch.

A glance at the scorecard tells you that the course measures only just over 6000 yards in length from the back tees, moreover, from a distance, it looks relatively tame with only one serious hill to negotiate. Look a little closer, however, and you will soon realise that not only are the fairways extremely narrow and quite undulating but the rough comprises much gorse, heather, bracken and, as my friend puts it, 'all kinds of horror stories'—the words of one who has been thrilled too often—and then there is the wind which whips across from the Irish Sea.

So you had been licking your lips contemplating a very short, straightforward par four to open proceedings but you survey the scene ahead and suddenly there is the feeling you are looking down a gun barrel. The fearless big hitter will hope to fire one up the middle and perhaps even reach the green. Most golfers however, could only feel really comfortable playing this and the next few holes wearing blinkers.

The 2nd is a very tricky par three. Clammy hands is the sensation here—go left and you must visit the local farmer—stray right and you may tumble down the edge of a cliff on to an adjacent fairway from which the pitch to the green is less than inviting. The next is a tremendous hole—a par four from the front tees but the 3rd is a genuine five from the back markers. Here the drive is hit straight into the crest of a hill. Once over the hill, there is then a gentle

climb to the green; two good straight hits—usually into the wind—will be needed to set up any chance of a birdie. Then comes the shortest hole on the course, the 4th, played directly towards the sea. Very exposed to the elements, this hole can play anything from a long iron to a sand iron.

The challenge continues throughout the round with the 9th and 10th being two especially memorable holes. It also culminates with a glorious, if fiendish, finishing hole where to the right of the fairway the gorse and bracken have been permitted to run rampant. 'Can't remember the last time I hit the 18th green in two', my friend tells me. 'In fact, I can't remember the last time I parred it—it's far too tough for me' he says. Perhaps you should give Anglesey a miss this summer, I dare to suggest. Go to Spain perhaps? 'What! Five hours for a round under a blazing hot sun instead of playing golf here . . . you must be crackers. Absolutely crackers.'

Holyhead Golf Club, Lon Garreg Fawr, Trearddur Bay, Anglesey, LL65 2YG

Sec/Manager	John Williams (01407) 763279
Professional	Stephen Elliot (01407) 762022
Green Fees	WD £17/round; £22/day
	WE £22/round; £28/day
Restrictions	Telephoning advisable

Directions
Take the A5 from Bangor to Trearddur Bay.

Nefyn

We golfers in Britain are doubly fortunate—not only do we have an infinite variety of courses to play upon (contrast, for instance, the Surrey heathland with the Scottish links), but we also possess a wealth of outstandingly scenic courses. Perhaps one of our lesser known treasures is perched on the cliffs of North Wales' western tip. Nefyn, or more precisely Nefyn and District, was founded in 1907, although the course really came into its own in 1920 when an extension was opened by James Braid and John H Taylor (where was Harry you ask!)

I suppose Nefyn could be described as a classic holiday course: to begin with there is a very pleasant drive to the club and on arrival visitors are made very welcome; the course is always well maintained with particularly pleasing fairways; whilst the golf is by no means easy, it is never too severe or unfair (indeed, unless the wind blows fiercely, good scores should definitely appear on the cards); the views as mentioned are quite stupendous and, to cap it all, there is even a pub two thirds of the way round! Well, what more could a golfer ask for?

From the back markers Nefyn stretches to 6332 yards and has a par of 72. Ian Woosnam, the 1991 US Masters Champion, holds the professional course record of 67. I am reliably informed that another model of Welsh consistency, Lloyd-George, was a frequent visitor to Nefyn and that this trend was in turn followed by Clement Attlee—who doubtless found the golf here a welcome diversion from the pressures of No 10.

After a lengthy opener which certainly invites a hearty belt from the tee (sorry, controlled power) the course moves out along by the cliff edges for a number of spectacular holes. It then turns back on itself before heading in a different direction out on to a headland where arguably

the best holes on the course, numbers 11 to 18 are found.

There is no real place on the course where you lose sight of the sea and you may just encounter the occasional sunbather who has lost his or her way. If the holiday mood really takes you, then down in a cove by the 12th green is the Ty Coch Inn. Yes, it is accessible from the course and on a really hot summer's day can doubtless be mistaken for a heavenly mirage. One cannot help wondering how many steady score cards have suddenly taken on erratic proportions from the 13th hole in!

Returning to the clubhouse you will find that full catering facilities are offered. There is a snooker room and a genuinely pleasant atmosphere in which to relax and reflect on your day. Well, if you have not enjoyed your golf at Nefyn then I must venture to suggest that you are an extremely difficult person to please!

The Nefyn & District Golf Club, Morfa Nefyn, Pwllheli, Gwynedd, LL53 6DA

Sec/Manager	J B Owens (01758) 720966
Professional	John Froom (01758) 720102
Green Fees	WD £25 (£30 per day)
	WE £30 (£35 per day)
Restrictions	Handicap certificates required.

Directions
From Colwyn Bay take the A55 towards Bangor then the A487 to Caernafon. From there the A499 and B4417 lead through Nefyn to Morfa Nefyn.

MONMOUTH & SURROUNDS

Alice Springs G.C.
(01873) 880914
Bettws Newydd, Usk
(18) 6041 yards/***/D
(18) 6400 yards/***/D

Blackwood G.C.
(01495) 223152
Cwmgelli, Blackwood
(9) 5300 yards/***/D/H/L

Caerleon G.C.
(01633) 420342
Broadway, Caerleon
(9) 3092 yards/***/E

Celtic Manor G. & C.C.
(01633) 413000
Coldra Woods, Newport
(18) 7100 yards/***/A/H
(18) 4094 yards/***/F/H

Dewstow G.C.
(01291) 430444
Caerwent, Newport
(18) 6100 yards/***/D

Greenmeadow G.C.
(01633) 862626
Treherbert Road, Croesyceiliog,
Cwmbran
(18) 5587 yards/***/F

Llanwern G.C.
(01633) 412029
Tennyson Avenue, Llanwern
(18) 6115 yards/**/B/H/L
(9) 5239 yards/**/B/H/L

Monmouth G.C.
(01600) 712212
Leasebrook Lane, Monmouth
(18) 5698 yards/***/D

Monmouthshire G.C.
(01873) 852606
Llanfoist, Abergavenny
(18) 6054 yards/***/B/H/G

Newport G.C.
(01633) 892643
Great Oak, Rogerstone, Newport
(18) 6431 yards/**/A/H/M

Oakdale G.C.
(01495) 220044
Llwynon Lane, Oakdale
(9) 1235 yards/***/E

Parc G.C.
(01633) 680933
Church Lane, Coedkernew
(18) 5136 yards/***/D

Pontnewydd G.C.
(016333) 482170
Maesgwyn Farm, West Pontnewydd
(10) 5353 yards/**/D/G

Pontypool G.C.
(01495) 763655
Lasgarn Lane, Trevethin
(18) 6046 yards/***/C/H/L

Raglan Park G.C.
(01291) 690077
Park Lodge, Raglan
(18) 6604 yards/***/D

The Rolls of Monmouth G.C.
(01600) 715353
The Hendre, Monmouth
(18) 6733 yards/***/A

St Pierre G.& C.C.
(01291) 625261
St Pierre Park, Chepstow
(18) 6762 yards/***/A/H
(18) 5732 yards/***/A/H

Shirenewton G.C.
(01291) 641642
Shirenewton, Chepstow
(18)6820/***/D

Tredegar Park G.C.
(01633) 894433
Bassaleg Road, Newport
(18) 5575 yards/***/B/H

Tredegar & Rhymney G.C.
(01685) 840743
Tredegar, Rhymney
(9) 5500 yards/***/D

Wernddu Golf Centre
(01873) 856223
Old Ross Road, Abergavenny
(18) 6600 yards/***/E

West Monmouthshire G.C.
(01495) 310233
Pond Road, Nantyglo
(18) 6118 yards/***(Sun)/D

Woodlake Park G.C.
(01291) 673933
Glascoed, Pontypool
(18) 6300 yards/***/C/H

THE GLAMORGANS

Aberdare G.C.
(01685) 872797
Abernant, Aberdare,
(18) 5874 yards/***(Sat)/D/H/L

Allt-y-Graben G.C.
(01792) 885757
Pontlliw, Swansea
(9) 2210 yards/***/E

Bargoed G.C.
(01443) 830608
Heolddu, Bargoed,
(18) 6000 yards/**/D

Bryn Meadows Golf Hotel
(01495) 225590
The Bryn, Hengoed,
(18) 6200 yards/***/C

Brynhill G.C.
(01446) 720277
Port Road, Barry,
(18) 6000 yards/***(Sun)/B/H

Caerphilly G.C.
(01222) 863441
Mountain Road, Caerphilly,
(14) 6000 yards/**/B/H

Cardiff G.C.
(01222) 753320
Sherborne Avenue, Cincoed,
(18) 6016 yards/**/B/H

Castell Heights G.C.
(01222) 886666
Blaengwynlais, Caerphilly,
(18) 7000 yards/***/E
(9) 2670 yards/***/E

Clyne G.C.
(01792) 401989
Owls Lodge Lane, Mayals,
(18) 6312 yards/***/B/H

Cottrell Park G.C.
(01446) 781781
Cottrell Park, St Nicholas, Cardiff
(18) 6176 yards/**/D/H

Creigiau G.C.
(01222) 890263
Creigiau, Cardiff,
(18) 5900 yards/**/B/G

Dinas Powis G.C.
(01222) 512727
Old Highwalls, Dinas Powis,
(18) 5377 yards/***/C/L

Earlswood G.C.
(01792) 812198
Jersey Marine, Neath
(18) 5174 yards/***/E

Fairwood Park G.C.
(01792) 297849
Upper Killay, Swansea,
(18) 6741 yards/***/B

Glamorganshire G.C.
(01222) 701185
Lavernock Road, Penarth,
(18) 6181 yards/***/B/H

Glyn Neath G.C.
(01639) 720452
Penycraig, Pontneathvaughan, t
(18) 5499 yards/**/D/H

Gower G.C.
(01792) 872480
Cefn Goleu, Three Crosses, Swansea
(18) 6400 yards/***/E

Grove G.C.
(01656) 788771
South Cornelly, Nr Porthcawl
(18) 6065 yards/***/D

I.N.C.O. G.C.
(01792) 843336
Clydach, Swansea,
(12) 6230 yards/***/F

Lakeside G.C.
(01639) 899959
Water Street, Margam, Port Talbot
(18) 4390 yards/***/E

Langland Bay G.C.
(01792) 361721
Llangland Bay, Swansea,
(18) 5830 yards/***/B

Llanishen G.C.
(01222) 755078
Cwm, Lisvane,
(18) 5296 yards/**/B/H

Llantrisant and Pontyclun G.C.
(01443) 224601
Llanelry Road, Talbot Green,
(12) 5712 yards/**/F/H/G

Maesteg G.C.
(01656) 734106
Neath Road, Maesteg,
(18) 5900 yards/***/C/H

Merthyr Tydfil G.C.
(01685) 723308
Cilsanws Mt, Cefn Coed,
(11) 5900 yards/**/F

Morlais Castle G.C.
(01685) 722822
Pant, Dowlais, Merthyr Tydfil,
(18) 6320 yards/**/D

Morriston G.C.
(01792) 796528
Clasemont Road, Morriston,
(18) 5800 yards/***/C/H

Mountain Ash G.C.
(01443) 479459
Cefnpennar, Mountain Ash,
(18) 5500 yards/***/D/H

Mountain Lakes G.C.
(01222) 861128
Blaengwynlais, Caerphilly,
(18) 5700 yards/***/C/H

Neath G.C.
(01639) 632579
Cadoxton, Neath,
(18) 6465 yards/**/C/G

Palleg G.C.
(01639) 842193
Lower Cwmtwrch, Swansea, t
(9) 3260 yards/**/D

Pennard G.C.
(01792) 233131
Southgate, Swansea,
(18) 6266 yards/***/C/H

Peterstone G.C.
(01633) 680009
Peterstone, Wentloog
(18) 6600 yards/***/C/H/M

Pontardawe G.C.
(01792) 863118
Cefn Llan, Pontardawe,
(18) 6061 yards/**/C/H

Pontypridd G.C.
(01443) 409904
Ty Gwyn Road, Pontypridd,
(18) 5650 yards/***/C/H/L

Pyle and Kenfig G.C.
(01656) 783093
Waun-y-Mer, Kenfig,
(18) 6640 yards/**/A/H

RAF St Athan G.C.
(01446) 751043
Barry, Cardiff,
(9) 5957 yards/***(Sun am)/D

Whether it's a relaxing get-away-from-it-all break or a round of golf in the Welsh countryside, the St David's Park Hotel and Northop Country Park Golf Club are a winning combination.

The four star hotel on the outskirts of Chester is now in its sixth year and is 'partnered' by the 18-hole Northop Country Park Golf Club, just minutes away.

The 145-bedroom Georgian-style hotel, designed around an inner courtyard, boasts first-class facilities, including luxury bedrooms, and private function rooms. A comprehensive choice of golfing breaks can be arranged through the hotel, including a 'three-course menu' which includes play at Royal Liverpool and Royal St David''s Golf Clubs as well as Northop.

Gourmets can indulge themselves in the Fountains Restaurant or for those with fitness in mind, the hotel has a superb leisure club which includes an indoor swimming pool, snooker room, beautician, sauna and gymnasium.

Free transfer from the hotel to the golf club can be provided where golfers can pit their wits against the challenging course designed by former Ryder Cup captain John Jacobs.

The clubhouse includes a golf shop and has all a player needs, including a sauna, gymnasium, private function suite and the Far Pavilions Restaurant providing first-class catering for individual golfers or corporate groups.

Northop's professional, David 'Lulu' Llewellyn, who partenered Ian Woosnam to World Cup victory, is also on hand to provide guidance and expertise to help even the most discerning golfer get into the swing of things.

St Davids Park Hotel
St Davids Park
Ewloe
Nr Chester CH5 3YB
Tel: (01244) 520800
Fax: (01244) 520930

Set in 247 acres of panoramic Welsh countryside the Northop Country Park Golf Club throws up many challenges for golfer of every standard.

The 18 hole, 6735 yard course has seen players return time and time again and has been host to the Welsh PGA Championship and the Cheshire and North Wales Open.

This year the crème de la crème of golfers will stride out onto the fairway to tackle the course when Northop plays host to the prestigious Glenmuir Club Professionals Championship and also the Welsh Ladies Closed Championships.

No doubt social golfers will find the course as challenging as the competitors as the Northop venture is made up of four par 3s, four par 5s, and ten par 4s with 12 changes of par in the round.

The par 3s range from the demanding 203 yard 5th hole to the picturesque 17th of 156 yards.

But the challenges don't end there—the par 4s include the tricky dog-leg 354 yard 10th and the water-bound 378 yard and 16th.

Golfers who keep their nerve at the par 4s can open their shoulders at the par 5s especially the 8th and 15th which can be reached in two. But watch out for the 11th, aptly named the 'Wooden Heartache' at 559 yards which can wreck the card.

Golfers be warned—don't relax and let your concentration slip because disaster can also strike at the 440 yard 18th which features a right-to-left dog-leg and a slightly raised green. Players need to keep their nerve as they tackle the final hole.

Former Ryder Cup Captain John Jacobs clearly used his ample experience when designing the picturesque course, however he has taken in the needs of players of every standard and the course, its fairways and clubhouse are ideal for occasional, society and corporate golfers.

For more information on the Northop Country Park Golf Club contact 01244 840440.

Northop Country Park,
Northop,
Chester,
Flintshire CH7 6WA
Tel: (01352) 840440,
Fax: (01352)840445.

Radyr G.C.
(01222) 842408
Radyr, Cardiff,
(18) 6031 yards/**/B/H/L

Rhondda G.C.
(01443) 441384
Penrhys, Rhondda,
(18)6428 yards/**/C/H

Royal Porthcawl G.C.
(01656) 782251
Porthcawl,
(18) 6600 yards/**/A/H/G

St Andrews Major G.C.
(01446) 722227
Cadoxton, Barry,
(9) 2931 yards/***/D

St Marys G. & C.C.
(01656) 860280
St Marys Hill, Pencoed,
(18) 5236 yards/***/D/H
(9) 2426 yards/***/E/H

St Mellons G.C.
(01633) 680408
St Mellons, Cardiff
(18) 6275 yards/**/C/H

Southerndown G.C.
(01656) 880476
Ewenny, Bridgend,
(18) 6613 yards/**/C-A/H

Swansea Bay G.C.
(01792) 816159
Jersey Marine, Neath,
(18) 6302 yards/***/C

Vale of Glamorgan G.C.
(01443) 222221
Hensol Park,near Bridgend
(18) 6507 yards/***/C

Virginia Park G.C.
(01222) 863919
Virginia Park, Caerphilly,
(9) 2566 yards/***/D

Wenvoe Castle G.C.
(01222) 593649
Wenvoe, Cardiff,
(18) 6411 yards/**/B/H/G

Whitchurch G.C.
(01222) 620985
Whitchurch, Cardiff,
(18) 6319 yards/**/B/H

Whitehall G.C.
(01443) 740245
Nelson, Treharris,
(9) 5750 yards/**/G

MID WALES

Aberdovey G.C.
(01654) 767602
Aberdovey
(18) 6445 yards/**/C

Aberystwyth G.C.
(01970) 615104
Bryn-y-Mor, Aberystwyth
(18) 6100 yards/***/F

Ashburnham G.C.
(01554) 832269
Cliffe Terrace, Burry Port
(18) 6916 yards/***/B-A/H

Bala G.C.
(01678) 520359
Penlan, Bala
(10) 4962 yards/**/D

Bala Lake Hotel G.C.
(01678) 520344
Bala
(9) 4280 yards/***/F

Borth and Ynyslas G.C.
(01970) 871202
Borth, Aberystwyth
(18) 6000 yards/***/C/H

Brecon G.C.
(01874) 622004
Newton Park, Llanfaes, Brecon
(9) 5218 yards/***/D

Builth Wells G.C.
(01982) 553296
Golf Club Road, Builth Wells
(18) 5376 yards/***/D/H

Cardigan G.C.
(01293) 612035
Gwbert-on-Sea, Cardigan
(18) 6600 yards/***/C/H

Carmarthen G.C.
(01267) 281493
Blaen-y-Coed Road, Carmarthen
(18) 6212 yards/***/C

Chirk G. & C.C
(01691) 774407
Chirk, nr Wrexham
(18) 6800 yards/***/C

Cilgwyn G.C.
(01570) 45286
Llangybi, Lampeter
(9) 5318 yards/***/D

Cradoc G.C.
(01874) 623658
Penoyre Park, Cradoc, Brecon
(18) 6301 yards/***/(Sun)/C

Dolgellau G.C.
(01341) 422603
Pencefn Road, Dolgellau
(9) 4512 yards/***/D

Ffestiniog G.C.
(01766) 831829
Y Cefn, Ffestiniog
(9) 5032 yards/***/F

Glyn Abbey G.C.
(01554) 810278
Pontnewydd, Trimsaren
(18) 6173 yards/***/E

Glynhir G.C.
(01269) 850472
Glynhir Road, Llandybie,
(18) 5900 yards/***(Sun)/D

Haverfordwest G.C.
(01437) 764523
Narberth Road, Haverfordwest
(18) 6005 yards/***/C

Knighton G.C.
(01547) 528646
Little Ffrydd Wood, Knighton
(9) 5320 yards/***/E

Llandrindod Wells G.C.
(01597) 823873
Llandrindod Wells
(18) 5749 yards/***/D

Llanstephan G.C.
(01267) 241526
Llanstephan
(9) 2165 yards/***/E

Llanymynech G.C.
(01691) 830983
Pant, Nr Oswestry
(18) 6114 yards/***/D

Machynlleth G.C.
(01597) 823873
Fford Drenewydd, Machynlleth
(9) 5726 yards/***/D

Maesmawr G.C.
(01686) 688303
Caersws, Newtown
(9) 2554 yards/***/E

Milford Haven G.C.
(01646) 692368
Hubberston, Milford Haven
(18) 6071 yards/***/D

Newport (Pembs) G.C.
(01239) 820244
Newport
(9) 5815 yards/***/D

Penrhos G.& C.C.
(01974) 202999
Llanrhystud, Aberystwyth
(18) 6641 yards/***/D

Old Rectory G.C.
(01873) 810373
Llangattock, Crickhowell
(9) 2878 yards/***/F

Rhosgoch G.C.
(01497) 851251
Rhosgoch, Builth Wells
(9) 4842 yards/***/E

St Giles Newtown G.C.
(01686) 625844
Pool Road, Newtown
(9) 5936 yards/**/D/H/L

St Idloes G.C.
(01686) 412559
Penrhallt, Llanidloes
(9) 5428 yards/**/D/H

St Davids City G.C.
(01437) 720312
Whitesands Bay, St Davids
(9) 5693 yards/***/D

South Pembrokeshire G.C.
(01646) 621453
Military Road, Pembroke Dock
(9) 5804 yards/***(evenings)/D

Tenby G.C.
(01834) 842978
The Burrows, Tenby
(18) 6232 yards/***/C/H

Trefloyne G.C.
(01834) 842165
Penally, Nr Tenby
(18) 6635 yards/***/D

Welsh Border Golf Complex
(01743) 884247
Bulthy, Middletown
(9) 3250 yards/***/E

Welshpool G.C.
(01938) 83249
Golfa Hill, Welshpool
(18) 5708 yards/***/D/H

NORTH WALES

Abergele & Pensarn G.C.
(01745) 824034
Tan-y-Goppa Road, Abergele
(18) 6520 yards/***/B

Abersoch G.C.
(01758) 712622
Abersoch
(18) 5910 yards/***/D/H

Betws-y-Coed G.C.
(01690) 710556
Betws-y-coed
(18) 4996 yards/***/D

Bryn Morfydd Hotel & G.C.
(01745) 890280
Llanrhaeadr, Denbigh
(18) 5601 yards/***/F
(9) 1190 yards/***/F

Caernarfon G.C.
(01286) 673783
Llanfaglan, Caernarfon
(9) 5860 yards/***/C

Caerwys G.C.
(01352) 720692
Caerwys, Mold
(9) 3080 yards/***/E

Clays Farm Golf Centre
(01978) 661406
Bryn Estyn Road, Wrexham
(18) 5600 yards/***/E

Conwy G.C.
(01492) 592423
Morfa, Conwy
(18) 6901 yards/**/B/H

Criccieth G.C.
(01766) 522154
Ednyfed Hill, Criccieth
(18) 5787 yards/***/D

Denbigh G.C.
(01745) 816669
Henllan Road, Denbigh
(18) 5650 yards/***/C

Flint G.C.
(01352) 732327
Cornist Park, Flint
(9) 5953 yards/**/D

Hawarden G.C.
(01244) 531447
Groomsdale Lane, Hawarden
(9) 5620 yards/**/C/G/H

Holywell G.C.
(01352) 713937
Brynford, Holywell
(9) 6484 yards/***/D

Kinmell Park G.C.
(01745) 833548
Bodelwyddan
(9) 1550 yards/***/E

Llandudno (Maesdu) G.C.
(01492) 876450
Hospital Road, Llandudno
(18) 6513 yards/***/B/H/M

Llandudno (North Wales) G.C.
(01492) 875325
Bryniau Road, West Shore
(18) 6247 yards/***/B/H

Llanfairfechan G.C.
(01248) 680144
Llannerch Road, Llanfairfechan
(9) 3119 yards/***/D

Mold G.C.
(01352) 741513
Clicain Road, Pant-y-Mwyn, Mold
(18) 5545 yards/***/C

Nefyn and District G.C.
(01758) 720966
Morfa Nefyn, Pwllheli
(18) 6332 yards/***/B/H

Northop Country Park
(01352) 840440
Northop, Chester
(18) 6735 yards/***/B-A

Old Colwyn G.C.
(01492) 515581
Woodland Avenue, Old Colwyn
(9) 5800 yards/**/D

Old Padeswood G.C.
(01244) 547401
Station Road, Padeswood, Mold
(18) 6639 yards/***/C

Padeswood and Buckley G.C.
(01244) 550537
Station Lane, Padeswood, Mold
(18) 5775 yards/***(Sun)/B

Penmaenmawr G.C.
(01492) 623330
Conwy Old Road, Penmaenmawr
(9) 5031 yards/***/C

Artist: **Harry Eliott ON THE FAIRWAY** *Courtesy of:* **Burlington Gallery**

Porthmadog G.C.
(01766) 514124
Morfa Bychan, Porthmadog
(18) 5838 yards/***/C/H

Prestatyn G.C.
(01745) 854320
Marine Road East, Prestatyn
(18) 6764 yards/***/C/H

Pwllheli G.C.
(01758) 612520
Golf Road, Pwllheli
(18) 6110 yards/***/C

Rhos-on-Sea G.C.
(01492) 549100
Penrhyn Bay, Llandudno
(18)

Rhuddlan G.C.
(01745) 590217
Meliden Road, Rhuddlan
(18) 6045 yards/***(Sun)/B/H

Rhyl G.C.
(01745) 353171
Coast Road, Rhyl
(9) 6185 yards/***/D

Royal St David's G.C.
(01766) 780857
Harlech
(18) 6427 yards/***/B/H

Ruthin-Pwllglas G.C.
(01824) 702296
Pwllglas, Ruthin
(10) 5418 yards/***/D

St Deniol G.C.
(01248) 353098
Penybryn, Bangor
(18) 5048 yards/***/D

St Melyd G.C.
(01745) 854405
Meliden Road, Prestatyn
(9) 5857 yards/***/C

Vale of Llangollen G.C.
(01978) 860906
Holyhead Road, Llangollen
(18) 6461 yards/***/C

Wrexham G.C.
(01978) 364268
Holt Road, Wrexham
(18) 6078 yards/***/F/H
(18) 5838 yards/***/C/H
6064 yards/***/F

ISLE OF ANGLESEY

Anglesey G.C.
(01407) 811202
Station Road, Rhosneigr
(18) 5713 yards/***/D

Baron Hill G.C.
(01248) 810231
Beaumaris
(9) 5564 yards/***/D

Bull Bay G.C.
(01407) 830960
Bull Bay Road, Amlwch
(18) 6160 yards/***/C/H

Holyhead G.C.
(01407) 763279
Trearddur Bay, Holyhead
(18) 6058 yards/***/D/H

Llangefni G.C.
(01248) 722193
Llangefni
(9) 1467 yards/***/F

Storwys Wen G.C.
(01248) 852673
Brynleg, Anglesey
(9) 2630 yards/**/D

Artist: **Harry Eliott THE CHIP SHOT** *Courtesy of:* **Burlington Gallery**

W. Linton G.C.
EDDLESTON
Innerleithen G.C.
Peebles G.C.
PEEBLES
LAUDER
Lauder G.C.
GREENLAW
Galashiels G.C.
GATTONSIDE
MELROSE
Kelso G.C.
Melrose G.C.
KELSO
TWEEDSMUIR
SELKIRK
ST. MARY'S LOCH
ETTRICKBRIDGE
Selkirk G.C.
HAWICK
Minto G.C.
Moffat
MOFFAT G.C.
BEATTOCK
Hawick G.C.
Dumfries & County G.C.
Lochmaben G.C.
Thornhill G.C.
DUMFRIES
LOCKERBIE
CANONBIE
Newton Stewart G.C.
NEWTON STEWART
NEW ABBEY
Powfoot G.C.
Stranraer G.C.
DALBEATTIE
KIPPFORD
COLVEND
POWFOOT
STRANRAER
Southerness G.C.
Portpatrick G.C.
Wigtown & Bladnoch G.C.
ROCKLIFFE
PORTPATRICK
PORT WILLIAM

Artist: **Sam Garratt PEEBLES** *Courtesy of:* **Burlington Gallery**

The two modern counties of Dumfries & Galloway and Borders encompass most of the Scottish Lowlands. A beautiful area of Britain—as of course is most of Scotland—but surely not one terribly renowned for its golf? It may not be renowned but there is still certainly no shortage of exciting and challenging courses in the area. Indeed, the very fact that the great hordes head for the more famous venues further north means that Scotland's southerly golfing gems remain by and large marvellously uncrowded.

Dumfries & Galloway

The one true championship test in this region is found at **Southerness.** Of all Scotland's great links courses this is perhaps the least widely known. We have featured MacKenzie Ross's masterpiece on a separate page.

Powfoot is a fairly close neighbour of Southerness (at least as the crow flies) the course lying five miles west of Annan off the B724. A semi-links with plenty of heather and gorse, it offers a tremendous test of golf and is an admirable companion to Southerness. Adding to the enjoyment of a round at Powfoot is the setting—the course provides extensive views towards the Cumberland Hills to the south and the Galloway Hills to the west. The Isle of Man is also visible on a clear day.

Two convenient resting places after a game at Southerness are in Rockliffe, the Baron's Craig Hotel (01556) 630225 and a little closer in Colvend, the Clonyard House (01556) 630372. Good eating places include the Criffel Inn (01387) 850244 in New Abbey, and the Pheasant in Dalbeattie (01556) 610345. Powfoot has the Golf Hotel (01461) 700254 whilst a little further away is Canonbie and an exceptional restaurant at the Riverside Inn (01387) 371512. The rooms here are also very pleasant.

Nearby there are two good 18 hole courses at Dumfries, **Dumfries and County**, to the north of the town being the pick of the two, but golfers travelling north would do well to pay **Lochmaben** a visit as well. It is a very friendly club with an interesting course designed by James Braid. The setting around the Kirk Loch is most picturesque and the course is famed for its many beautiful old trees.

When inspecting any of the above courses, Dumfries, the county's largest town is a likely base and here the Cairndale Hotel (01387) 54111 is most pleasant. Other recommended establishments in the area include the Dryfesdale (01576) 202427 in Lockerbie, the Lockerbie Manor (01576) 202610, 14th century Comlongon Castle (01387) 870283 and Allanton House (01387) 274509 with its resident farm.

Towards the western corner of Dumfries and Galloway there is more fine golf. Two 9 hole courses well worth playing are at Wigtown, **Wigtown and Bladnoch** and **Newton Stewart**. Still further west, **Stranraer,** the ferry terminal for Larne, has a fine parkland course north of the town overlooking Loch Ryan. But the clifftop course at **Portpatrick** is surely the major golfing attraction in this area, indeed it is rated by many to be one of the most beautiful courses in Britain. Apparently for many years in the last century the town was Ireland's Gretna Green—couples sailing across the Irish Sea to get hitched in Portpatrick's tiny church. The golf course provides some breathtaking scenery—particularly outstanding is the view from the 13th fairway. It can often get quite breezy and although only 5644 yards in length, the course is certainly no pushover.

Superb golf is accompanied by an exceptionally high number of first rate hotels in the area. In Castle Douglas, Milton Park (01644) 430286 is a recurring favourite while in Newton Stewart, the Kirroughtree Hotel (01671) 402141 is excellent. We would also recommend Creebridge House (01671) 402121—an extremely pleasant place to stay. Port William offers the very fine Corsemalzie House Hotel (01988) 600254. Cally Palace (01559) 814341 in Gatehouse of Fleet—a beautiful 18th century mansion—has its own golf course while a number of alternatives are found at Portpatrick. Pick of the bunch is the Knockinaam Lodge (01776) 810471 which has a glorious setting and a tremendous restaurant. Others to note are the Fernhill (01776) 810220, and the North West Castle (01776) 704413 in Portrodie.

Having sampled the delights of the coast of Southern Scotland one may head inland to the Border towns. En route one could slip 18 holes in at **Thornhill** or perhaps visit **Moffat.** The town has a very enjoyable moorland course with a marvellous setting in the valley of Annandale. The Black Bull is a welcoming hostelry after a round at Moffat and recommended places to spend an evening include the Beechwood Country House Hotel (01683) 220210 and Moffat House (01683) 220039.

Borders

The Border towns offer castles aplenty, some superb woollens and some excellent rugby. Golfwise, prior to the opening of The Roxburghe (see below) no course here could claim to be of championship proportions. However, the majority can boast spectacular settings, visitors are always encouraged and the green fees in these parts are just about the cheapest in Britain.

A cluster of courses are to be found in the centre of the county. The town of **Melrose** is famed for its ruined Abbey where the heart of Robert the Bruce is said to have been buried (gruesome stuff!) It has a fine 9 hole course and there are other equally pleasant courses at **Selkirk, Hawick, Lauder, St Boswells, Innerliethen** and **West Linton.** Kelso has an interesting layout being inside Kelso racecourse. Finally, well worth noting are **Peebles** and **Galashiels**—both are public courses, very well maintained and set amidst magnificent countryside.

Walter Scott's land really does deserve a lengthy inspection. Whether one is golfing in the Borders or simply breaking a journey, here are some ideas for places to stay. In Melrose, Burts Hotel (01896) 822285 lies in the very heart of Border country. It is a fine centre from which to explore the area and the hotel is comfortable and offers excellent food. In Peebles, there are two choice hotels: Cringletie House Hotel (01721) 730233 and the Peebles Hotel Hydro (01721) 720602. Good guesthouses are also plentiful, with Lindores (01721) 720441 and Whitestone House (01721) 720337 among the best.

Golfers who like a spot of fishing should also note the Tweed Valley Hotel (01896) 870636 in nearby Walkerburn. St Mary's Loch offers the Tibbie Shiels Inn (01750) 42231, Selkirk, Philipburn House (01750) 20747 and Tweedsmuir the cosy Crook Inn (01899) 880272. Ettrickshaws Hotel (01750) 52229 in Ettrickbridge is pleasant as is the Cross Keys Hotel (01573) 223303 in Kelso.

We end our trip, but we could equally well begin it, at Sunlaws House Hotel (01573) 450331—one of the most delightfully relaxed country house hotels you will find anywhere. Here the new **Roxburghe** course opened in 1997 and is a real treat. It is explored later in this chapter.

The Roxburghe

If I were a salmon I might well fancy other rivers than the Tweed or any of its noble tributaries to drop my anchor. I appreciate that instinctively I have little choice in this but the fishermen frequenting Sunlaws House are something of a rum team and catches are often excellent.

However if I were a salmon that enjoyed a spot of golf, well I would have to reconsider my raison d'être for things have happened of late on the Sunlaws Estate where a golf course of real excellence has been crafted in unbelievably quick time. It is the first championship course for the Borders and in time will become a place of pilgrimage for those travelling north to sample the more historic links of Fife or Ayrshire.

You will find the course by travelling north on the A68 and following signs to Kelso. Sunlaws House is just three miles south west of the border town and is clearly signposted. Rail stations are thin on the ground with Berwick upon Tweed, some 18 miles away, being the nearest station for Intercity trains.

The course is set in 200 acres and makes exceptional use of the naturally contoured parkland. It also incorporates some stunning views of the River Teviot and the Borders countryside. The course was commissioned by the Duke of Roxburghe, an extremely keen golfer himself, and designed by Dave Thomas. It was created to appeal to all standards of golfer but make no mistake it is a tough course.

Gordon Niven is the course **Professional** and **Cameron Lunn** the **Clubhouse Manager**. They can be contacted by telephone on **(01573) 450333** or by fax on (01573) 450611. Green fees start at £30 for a midweek round (£45 per day) and £40 and £60 respectively at the weekend. In addition, there are opportunities for a range of memberships including country and overseas membership.

The clubhouse has been newly constructed to offer golfers every amenity, including a relaxing Spike Bar and restaurant, and enjoys views over the 1st and across the 12th and 13th. The hotel itself is magnificent, offering

luxurious accommodation and first class food in a very special, intimate atmosphere. Hotel guests will have tee times arranged and can enjoy a host of other leisure facilities

In Scotland, The 'McNab' where one must shoot a stag, bag a brace of grouse and catch a trout in the space of 24 hours is a noted challenge for sporting enthusiasts. For those who are partial to clay pigeon shooting or wish to fish on the hotel's private beats or prefer riding, tennis, falconry or game shooting, the sportman is in paradise.

Back on the golf course, one would be hard pressed to find a more delightful hole than the par five 14th 'Viaduct' hole. Flanked by the river Teviot the hole is dominated by the Roxburghe Viaduct behind the green and is destined to become one of the most photographed holes in Scotland. As we played this hole we were distracted by the sight of a lone fisherman landing an 11lb salmon—a memorable sight indeed. A good tee shot will open up birdie opportunities for those who play a sensible shot to the front of the generous green.

Another water hole demanding nerve and commitment is the par four, 10th where careful club selection is crucial to avoid hitting the river behind the green whilst the long par four, 18th provides a testing finish to your round. Here, three deep bunkers guard the approach to the green. The course measures a giant total of 7111 yards from the championship tees and the last three holes seem extremely long (460, 398 and 437 yards respectively) and provide quite a challenge. It is at this point some may be glad of a buggy to carry them those extra final yards. Buggies and caddies can be hired from the clubhouse.

The greens are immaculate and Dave Thomas has made full use of the contours of the countryside to create rolling greens of generous proportions.

The course record, set by Nick Faldo, is 67 and I can guarantee that anyone trying to better this will thoroughly enjoy the challenge.

Hole	Yards	Par	Hole	Yards	Par
1	421	4	10	469	4
2	396	4	11	526	5
3	364	4	12	399	4
4	188	3	13	216	3
5	581	5	14	571	5
6	382	4	15	177	3
7	520	5	16	460	4
8	203	3	17	398	4
9	403	4	18	437	4
Out	**3458**	**36**	**In**	**3653**	**36**
			Out	**3458**	**36**
			Totals	**7111**	**72**

Sunlaws House Hotel & Golf Course

Sunlaws House stands in the heart of Scotland's beautiful Border Country, in 200 acres of gardens and mature parkland along the banks of the Teviot three miles from the historic town of Kelso. There has been a house on the same site as Sunlaws for nearly 500 years and from its beginnings it has always been a Scottish family house—and that, to all intents and purposes, is how it will stay.

Sunlaws has a place in history, from the faint echoes of ancient strife when English armies of the 15th and 16th centuries came marauding through Roxburghshire and the Borders, to the Jacobite rebellion of 1745. Indeed Prince Charles Edward Stuart is reputed to have stayed on November 5th 1745 and to have planted a white rose bush in the grounds.

There are 22 bedrooms, which include the splendid Bowmont Suite and six delightful rooms in the stable courtyard, all furnished with care to His Graces' own taste and all with private bathroom or shower, colour television, radio and direct dial television. Disabled guests too are provided with the amenities they need.

The restaurant, which makes use of local produce, is amongst the very finest in Scotland. The Duke's own wine list also enjoys a magnificent reputation.

The spacious public rooms are furnished with the same care and elegance, which adds to the overall atmosphere of warmth and welcome with log fires burning in the main and inner hall, drawing room, library bar and dining room throughout the winter and on cold summer evenings. A health and beauty salon provides another welcome attraction for guests wishing to further treat themselves.

Flowers and plants, from the gardens and the conservatory, will be found all over the house. Herbs too are grown for the kitchen and will be found in many of the traditional dishes that are prepared for the dining room.

Sunlaws is also the perfect centre for a host of holiday activities. Sporting and cultural interests are well served, too. Salmon and trout fishing, and a complete range of shooting are available at the hotel, with golf, horse riding, racing and fox hunting all nearby. A Dave Thomas championship golf course, the Roxburghe, is currently under construction and looks set to be an outstanding test.

Sunlaws is the perfect location for touring the Borders, with great country houses including Abbottsford, the home of Sir Walter Scott, and a number of abbeys and museums all within easy reach.

Sunlaws House
Heiton Kelso
Roxburghshire
Tel: (01573) 450 331
Fax: (01573) 450 611

Southerness

Two of Britain's greatest (and least explored) links courses stare at one another across the Solway Firth—one is on the English side at Silloth and the other lies north of the border at Southerness. As close as they appear on the map, the only way of travelling from one to the other is by a fairly lengthy drive around the coast via Gretna Green. Before the war a bridge crossed the Solway, but before the war Southerness didn't have a golf course.

Situated 16 miles south of Dumfries, in an almost forgotten corner of southern Scotland, Southerness is the only true championship links in Great Britain to have been built since 1945. (Quite a contrast to Ireland where the likes of Tralee, The European, Connemara and the new links at Ballybunion and Ballyliffin have all been constructed within the last 20 years.)

So golf came to Southerness about 500 years after it came to St Andrews but one cannot help wondering why it took so long—after all, the much more remote golfing outposts of Dornoch and Machrihanish took root in the dim and distant past and a more natural and pleasanter site for the links it is hard to imagine. Sandy terrain, rampant heather, dense bracken and prickly golden gorse all present themselves in abundance here; as for that matter do firm, fast fairways and subtly contoured greens. If Mother Nature created the wonder of the setting then Mackenzie Ross (the architect of modern Turnberry) must be credited with the production of a genuine classic.

From the championship tees the links can be stretched to 7000 yards. Most mortal golfers will still find the 6566 yards, par 69 from the white tees (or 6105 yards from the yellow tees) an awesome challenge. The course's Standard Scratch is as high as 73; several of the par fours measure in excess of 400 yards (with prodigious carries to match) and two of the par threes are well over 200 yards long. A visit to Southerness is certainly recommended but pray that your long game is in fine fettle!

Before you set off, prior communication with the club's **Secretary, Mr W D Ramage** is advisable. Visitors can book tee times beween 10.00—12.00 and 2.00—5.00 midweek and between 10.00—11.30 and 2.30—5.00 at weekends. Mr Ramage can be contacted by telephone on

(01387) 880677 and by fax on (01387) 880644. Written correspondence should be directed to **The Secretary, Southerness Golf Club, Southerness, Dumfries DG2 8AZ.** Golfing societies are equally welcome but organisers must contact the Secretary in advance. Southerness does not have a golf professional.

The green fees at Southerness compare favourably with those at many of Scotland's more celebrated championship courses. A full day's golf in 1998 costs £28 per day during the week and £40 at weekends. Junior visitors can play midweek for a green fee of just £8.

Southerness's situation is quiet rather than remote. Golfers from England, heading to or from Turnberry, Troon and Prestwick will likely drive through the town of Dumfries on the A75/A76 and Southerness is just half an hour's detour from Dumfries along the A710; a pretty drive via New Abbey. From the west the A710 approaches via Dalbeattie while Dumfries is linked to Glasgow by the A710 and the A74/M74, and to Edinburgh by the A702 and the A74.

Southerness opens with three dog-legged holes, the best of these being the 3rd, where there is a wonderfully natural green site in a wooded corner. After the short 4th with its impressively plateaued green the course doubles back on itself, then turns towards the sea. The views become more distracting but the challenge in no way diminishes. The 7th is the first of two long par threes and you aim your tee shot directly at the Solway but the best run of holes comes between the 10th, a par three surrounded by a sea of heather and the 13th, the longest par four on the card. The 12th is undoubtedly the best hole of all; here a well positioned drive (avoiding the deviously positioned fairway bunkers) is essential as the second shot must be fired towards a narrow green which sits on a plateau and looks down over a beautiful beach; deep bunkers guard the green front right and a pond will gleefully swallow any shot that strays left of centre.

The 15th is yet another outstanding par 3—expertly bunkered—while the toughest hole on the closing stretch is probably the 16th which is normally played into the teeth of the wind A four here may prove more elusive than at the par five 18th, where with the wind finally at our backs we have the chance of finding the green with two good blows.

Hole	Yards	Par	Hole	Yards	Par
1	393	4	10	168	3
2	450	4	11	390	4
3	408	4	12	421	4
4	169	3	13	467	4
5	496	5	14	458	4
6	405	4	15	217	3
7	215	3	16	433	4
8	371	4	17	175	3
9	435	4	18	495	5
Out	**3,342**	**35**	**In**	**3,224**	**34**
			Out	**3,342**	**35**
			Totals	**6,566**	**69**

Key

_To avoid disappointment
it is advisable to telephone
in advance_

***_Visitors welcome at most times_
**_Visitors usually allowed on
weekdays only_
*_Visitors not normally permitted
(Mon, Wed) No visitors
on specified days_

Approximate Green Fees
A   £40 plus
B   £25 to £40
C   £20 to £30
D   £15 to £25
E   under £15
F   Green fees on application

Restrictions
G   Guests only
H—Handicap certificate required
H—(24) Handicap of 24 or less
L —Letter of introduction required
M—Visitor must be a member of
another recognised club

BORDERS

Duns G.C.
(01361) 882194
Hardens Road, Duns
(9) 5864 yards/***/D

Eyemouth G.C.
(018907) 50551
Gunsgreen House, Eyemouth
(9) 4608 yards/***/E

Galashiels G.C.
(01896) 753724
Ladhope Recreation Ground,
Galashiels
(18) 5785 yards/***/D

Hawick G.C.
(01450) 372293
Vertish Hill, Hawick
(18) 5929 yards/**/E

Hirsel G.C.
(01890) 882678
Kelso Road, Coldstream
(18) 6092 yards/***/C

Innerleithen G.C.
(01896) 830951
Leithen Road, Innerleithen
(9) 5984 yards/***/D
Jedburgh G.C.
(01835) 863587
Dunion Road, Jedburgh
(9) 5522 yards/***/D

Kelso G.C.
(01573) 223009
Racecourse Road, Kelso
(18) 6066 yards/***/C

Lauder G.C.
(01578) 722526
Galashiels Road, Lauder
(9) 6002 yards/***/E

Melrose G.C.
(0189)6822855
Dingleton, Melrose
(9) 5579 yards/**/C

Minto G.C.
(01450) 870220
Minto Village, by Denholme,
Hawick
(18) 5460 yards/**/D

Newcastleton G.C.
(013873) 75257
Holm Hill, Newcastleton
(9) 5748 yards/***/E

Peebles G.C.
(01721) 720197
Kirkland Street, Peebles
(18) 6160 yards/*/C/G/H

The Roxburghe G.C.
(01573) 450333
Kelso, Roxburghshire
(18) 7111 yards/***/F

St Boswells G.C.
(01835) 823527
St Boswells, Roxburghshire
(9) 2625 yards/***/D

Selkirk G.C.
(01750) 20621
The Hill, Selkirk
(9) 5620 yards/***/D

Torwoodlee G.C.
(01896) 752260
Edinburgh Road, Galashiels
(18) 6200 yards/***(Thurs)/D

West Linton G.C.
(01968) 660256
West Linton, Peebleshire
(18) 6132 yards/**/C

Woll G. C.
(01750) 32222
Woll House, Ashkirk, By Selkirk
(9) 6406 yards/***/F

DUMFRIES & GALLOWAY

Castle Douglas G.C.
(01556) 502801
Abercromby Road, Castle Douglas
(9) 5408 yards/***(Thurs pm)/D

Colvend G.C.
(01556) 630398
Sandyhills, by Dalbeattie
(9) 2240 yards/***/D

Crichton Royal G.C.
(01387) 247894
Bankend Road, Dumfries
(9) 6168 yards/***/E

Dalbeattie G.C.
(01556) 611421
Dalbeattie
(9) 4200 yards/***/F

Dumfries & County G.C.
(01387) 253585
Edinburgh Road, Dumfries
(18) 5928 yards/**/B

Dumfries & Galloway G.C.
(01387) 253582
Laurieston Avenue, Dumfries
(18) 5803 yards/**/B

Gatehouse of Fleet G.C.
(01557) 814766
Gatehouse of Fleet
(9) 4796 yards/***/D

Gretna G.C.
(01461) 338464
Gretna
(9) 6430 yards/***/E

Hoddom Castle G.C.
(01576) 300251
Hoddom, Lockerbie
(9) 2274 yards/***/E

Kirkcudbright G.C.
(01557) 330314
Stirling Crescent, Kirkcudbright
(18) 5696 yards/***/D

Langholm G.C.
(013873) 381247
Langholm, Dumfriesshire
(9) 5744 yards/***/E

Lochmaben G.C.
(01387) 810552
Castlehillgate, Lochmaben
(18) 5357 yards/***/C

Lockerbie G.C.
(01576) 203363
Corrie Road, Lockerbie
(18) 5418 yards/***(Sat)/C

Moffat G.C.
(01683) 220020
Coatshill, Moffat
(18) 5218 yards/***(Wed pm)/C

New Galloway G.C.
(01644) 430455
Castle Douglas, Kircudbright
(9) 2503 yards/***/E

Newton Stewart G.C.
(01671) 402172
Kirroughtree Avenue, Minnigaff
(18) 5970 yards/***/C

Portpatrick (Dunskey) G.C.
(01776) 810273
Portpatrick, Stranraer
(18) 5644 yards/***/C/H

Powfoot G.C.
(01461) 700276
Cummertrees, Annan
(18) 6266 yards/**/CF

St Medan G.C.
(01988) 700358
Monreith, Port William
(9) 2277 yards/***/D

Sanquhar G.C.
(01659) 50577
Old Barr Road, Sanquhar
(9) 5594 yards/***/D

Southerness G.C.
(01387) 880677
Southerness, Dumfries
(18) 6566 yards/***/B

Stranraer G.C.
(01776) 703539
Crechmore, Stranraer
(18) 6300 yards/***/C

Thornhill G.C.
(01848) 331779
Blacknest, Thornhill
(18) 6011 yards/***/B

Wigtown and Bladnoch G.C.
(01988) 403354
Lightlands Avenue, Wigtown
(9) 2732 yards/***/E

Wigtownshire County G.C.
(01581) 300420
Mains of Park, Glenluce
(18) 5847 yards/***/C

Artist: **I McPhie THE DRIVE**
Courtesy of: **Burlington Gallery**

211

Artist: **John Lavery NORTH BERWICK** *Courtesy of:* **Sotheby's**

'Hard by in the fields called the links, the citizens of Edinburgh divert themselves at a game called golf, in which they use a curious kind of bat tipt with horn and a small elastic ball of leather stuffed with feathers rather less than tennis balls, but out of a much harder consistency and this they strike with such force and dexterity that it will fly to an incredible distance.'

When Tobias Smollett wrote these words in 1771 golf had already been played in the 'fields' around Edinburgh for at least three hundred years. The seemingly harmless pastime wasn't always popular with the authorities. In 1593 the Town Council of Edinburgh deplored the fact that a great number of its inhabitants chose to spend the Sabbath in the town of Leith where 'in tyme of sermons' many were 'sene in the streets, drynking in taverns, or otherwise at Golf'. Shame on them! Today the east coast of Scotland is famous the world over, not only because it was here that it all began, but also because its many courses remain among the very finest the game has to offer. In a 30 mile coastal stretch between the courses of **Royal Burgess** and **Dunbar** lie the likes of **Muirfield, Gullane, North Berwick, Luffness New** and **Longniddry**—truly a magnificent seven—and there are many others.

Edinburgh

Visitors to the beautiful city of Edinburgh, the so called 'Athens of the North', should have little trouble getting a game. There are numerous first class courses in and around the capital—regrettably we only have space to mention a handful of the best. To the west of the city lie a particularly historic pair, **Bruntsfield Links** and **Royal Burgess**: between them they have witnessed nearly 500 years of golfing history. The latter club in fact claims to be the world's oldest. (A claim hotly disputed I might add by Muirfield's 'Honourable Company'!) These more prestigious courses are of course more difficult to play, but with advance preparation it is possible; restaurants in both clubhouses are of an extremely high standard. Another Edinburgh gem not to be missed is **Braid Hills**; in fact there are two fine public courses here, just south of the city. The **Dalmahoy** Hotel Golf and Country Club situated to the south west of the city nestles at the base of the Pentland Hills and has two excellent 18 hole courses. Dalmahoy, Muirfield, North Berwick and Dunbar, are featured ahead. Towards the east side of Edinburgh is Musselburgh. The old Open championship links is not what it was, alas, although you can still play the nine holes adjacent to Musselburgh racecourse for history's sake. However, perhaps the best place for a game is **Royal Musselburgh,** a beautiful parkland course and a little further out of the city the course at **Newbattle** can also be highly recommended.

Spending a few days in Edinburgh is a real treat whether one is a golfer or not. The city's leading hotels include the magnificent Balmoral Hotel (0131) 556 2414, re-opened in 1991 to great acclaim, and the Caledonian Hotel (0131) 459 9988. The latter's Pompadour Restaurant is quite superb. Among the many other hotels, the Sheraton Grand (0131) 229 9131 is almost on a par with the city's best while the George (0131) 225 1251 is a most impressive edifice and is a great favourite for post-rugby celebrations. Johnstounburn House (01875) 833696 at nearby Humbie offers an out of town alternative as does the Marriott Dalmahoy Hotel (0131) 333 1845 at Kirknewton—golfcourse, restaurants and very much more besides.

Edinburgh is as well blessed with restaurants as it is with hotels. These are some of the many worth considering: The Atrium (0131) 228 8882 and L'Auberge (0131) 556 5888 will delight, whilst the Kalpna (0131) 667 9890 is a first class Indian restaurant. In Leith two noted restaurants are Oysters (0131) 553 6363 and Skippers (0131) 554 1018. Finally, Channings (0131) 315 2226 is a sophisticated and elegant hotel with excellent facilities and a country house feel.

The courses of West Lothian are not as well known as their eastern counterparts. However, two are particularly worth considering, **Bathgate,** a fine moorland course and the **Deer Park** Golf and Country Club at Livingston. Both lie within easy access of Edinburgh and one hotel to consider there is the Chestnut House (0131) 654 1339.

Links Golf

Travellers wishing to explore the delights of the East Coast should aim to pick up the A198 at Prestonpans near Musselburgh. Before it reaches Longniddry the road passes through Seton, where Mary Queen of Scots is known to have sharpened up her golf swing more than 400 years ago. At 13 miles east of Edinburgh, **Longniddry** ought not to be considered as merely a stopping place en route to **Muirfield.** It is a superb course, part links part parkland, with every hole having a view of the sea. **Kilspindie** Golf Club is also worth a little detour while **Luffness New** and the three neighbouring courses of **Gullane** lie only a short distance further along the coast. Each is outstanding in its way, though if you only have time to play two then Luffness New and Gullane Number One are probably the pick—although the former can be difficult to get on! The panoramic view from the top of Gullane Hill on the latter's 7th hole is one of the most famous in golf. The West Links at **North Berwick** has a wealth of charm and tradition; it is one of the most natural courses one is likely to come across and several blind shots must be encountered. Two of its holes, the 14th 'Perfection' and the 15th 'Redan' have been imitated by golf architects all over the world. As at **Dunbar,** there are some splendid views across to Bass Rock.

Time for a 19th hole. Hotels are numerous, as indeed are good restaurants. In Gullane, Greywalls (01620) 842144 has gained an enviable reputation and is literally on the doorstep of Muirfield and the three links of Gullane. La Potiniere (01620) 843214 is a restaurant to savour when in these parts—eating on a par with the outstanding golf. Gullane is also resplendent with guest houses; the Golf Tavern (01620) 843259 is but one recommended illustration. In Aberlady the Kilspindie House Hotel (01875) 870682 and the Wagon (01875) 870319 are both welcoming, as is clearly the Open Arms (01620) 85241 in the pretty village of Dirleton, an excellent restaurant with rooms. The Marine Hotel (01620) 892406 is convenient for North Berwick while other well priced alternatives include the Mallard (01620) 843228, the Royal (01620) 892401, the Point Garry Hotel (01620) 892380 and the Golf Hotel (01620) 892202. Towards Dunbar, in the town itself the Bellevue (01368) 862322 and the Bayswell (01368) 862225 are both comfortable hotels, while the Courtyard (01368) 864169) at Woodush Brae offers award-winning cuisine. South of Dunbar, the Craw Inn (018907) 61253 at Auchencraw is recommended for its fish. Many super establishments are to be found a little inland. Note especially the Harvesters Hotel (01620) 860395 at East Linton and the Tweedale Arms (01620) 810240 at Gifford. Travelling westwards, 15th century Borthwick Castle (01875) 820514 at Gorebridge is another first class establishment. For the touring golfer, a country cottage can serve as an ideal base and both Blakes Country Cottages (01603) 783227 and Mackays (0131) 225 3539 offer a range of self-catering accommodation.

Scotland is the home of golf, and Johnstounburn offers the golfer an opportunity of staying in one of Scotland's original homes. The earliest reference to the estate goes back to 1260, and the house dates to certainly the early 17th century. Since those distant days, Johnstounburn has been cared for and enhanced by influential Scottish families—Borthwick, Broun and Usher—with most of the building on the estate having been effected in the 19th century.

The house sits proudly, surrounded by spacious lawns, gardens and unspoilt countryside overlooking the Lammermuir hills. The eleven bedrooms in the main house are rich in individuality and have been decorated to achieve the standard of comfort required by discerning travellers. Each has a private bathroom, colour television with satellite reception, and direct dial telephone. A further nine bedrooms were added when the coach house (circa 1840), some 300 yards through the gardens, was converted in 1986.

The 'piece de resistance' is the dining room with ornate hand carved wood panelling from floor to ceiling, created in the mid 18th century. After a sumptuous meal from the table d'hote menu featuring the finest fresh local produce, and served by candlelight in traditional style, you can retire to the Cedar lounge and enjoy your coffee in front of an open hearth. Or, if the night is kind, you can stroll in the gardens and experience the tranquillity of the surroundings.

Activities at the hotel include off-road driving, all terrain vehicles and a sporting clay pigeon shoot. You can practise your golf swing on the "fairway course" and participate in "The Johnstounburn Challenge", a match play event invented by the hotel. The famous golf courses of East Lothian—Muirfield, Gullane, North Berwick, Dunbar—are all within thirty minutes drive. There are more than a dozen courses from which to choose. For those not playing (or just taking the day off), Edinburgh city centre is thirty minutes away. To the south lies the beautiful Border region, with many historic castles, houses and gardens scattered about its rolling hills.

Johnstounburn offers comfort and friendly hospitality in a truly outstanding setting, with fine food and wines and a selection of the country's celebrated malt whiskies. Most of all, here you have the opportunity to savour the tradition of Scotland in a house that feels like home.

Johnstounburn House
Humbie
Nr Edinburgh
East Lothian, EH36 5PL
Tel: (01875) 833696
Fax: (01875) 833626

Muirfield

Muirfield is of course much more than one of the world's greatest golf links, it is also the home of the world's oldest golf club. The Honourable Company of Edinburgh Golfers are the direct descendants of the Gentlemen Golfers who played at Leith Links from at least as early as the 15th century. On 7th March 1744 several 'Gentlemen of Honour, skilful in the ancient and healthful exercise of Golf', petitioned the city fathers of Edinburgh to provide a silver club to be played for annually on the links at Leith. The winner of this competition became Captain of Golf and the club was paraded through the city. In 1744 the Edinburgh Golfers formulated the game's first code of rules—The Thirteen Articles—which were adopted almost word for word ten years later by the Royal and Ancient Club at St Andrews.

The company played over the five holes at Leith for almost a hundred years before overcrowding forced the decision to move to the nine hole course at Musselburgh, to the east of the city. Long before they had left Leith the members had begun to dine and play in the famous red uniform; failure to wear this usually resulted in a fine. A minute from the 1830s records how one member was fined two tappit hens for playing golf without his red coat! The Open Championship first came to Musselburgh in 1874 and was held there every third year until 1889. Meanwhile Musselburgh, like Leith, had become terribly crowded and the company decided that the time had come for a second move. Again, they looked to the east and almost twenty miles from Edinburgh, under the lee of Gullane Hill, they discovered Muirfield.

The course was initially designed by 'Old' Tom Morris and opened for play on 3rd May 1891. In its early years the course received much criticism. One professional described it as 'nothing but an auld watter meddie' but it appears that this had more to do with jealousy, because when the Honourable Company left Musselburgh it took the Open Championship with it. It was held at Muirfield in 1892 and never again returned to Musselburgh. Following the success of the 1892 Championship, Muirfield's reputation grew rapidly. In the 1920s Harry Colt and Tom Simpson made substantial revisions to the links and today Muirfield is widely considered to be the fairest, if not the finest test in golf.

Visitors wishing to play at Muirfield must make prior arrangements with the **Secretary, Group Captain J A Prideaux**, who may be contacted by telephone on **(01620) 842123** and by fax on (01620) 842977. For gentlemen golfers there is a requirement that they belong to a recog-

nised golf club and carry a handicap of 18 or less, while for lady golfers (who may only play if accompanied by a gentleman player) the handicap limit is 24. The days on which visitors are welcome are Tuesdays and Thursdays. It should also be noted that by tradition foursome matches are strongly favoured at Muirfield and fourball games will only be permitted in the mornings. All written correspondence should be addressed to **The Secretary, The Honourable Company of Edinburgh Golfers, Muirfield, Gullane, East Lothian, EH31 2EG.** The green fees for 1998 are set at £65 for a single round, with £85 entitling the visitor to a full day's golf.

Travelling to Muirfield (or Gullane) will often be by way of Edinburgh. Gullane is connected to the capital city by the A198. Northbound travellers can avoid Edinburgh by approaching on the A1 which runs to Dunbar to the east of Gullane. From Dunbar the A198 can be picked up. Those coming from the north and west of Scotland will need to travel via Edinburgh. The M8 links Glasgow to Edinburgh, while the M9 should be taken from Stirling and the M90 from Perth.

One of the unique features of Muirfield (or at least unique in terms of a Scottish championship links) is its layout of two separate loops, an outer and an inner. This ensures that the golfer will not have to play several successive holes into or against the same wind direction. Although occasionally quite undulating, the course has only one blind shot (the drive at the 11th) and this contributes much to Muirfield's fairness tag. From the championship tees the links stretch to 6941 yards, and with the often prodigiously thick rough and deep, cavernous bunkers, it can be a very severe test of golf. From the medal tees Muirfield still measures a fairly lengthy 6601 yards, par 70.

Since 1892 the Open Championship has been played at Muirfield on 14 occasions. Before the last war winners included Harry Vardon, James Braid and Walter Hagen. The first Open to be held at Muirfield after the war was in 1948, when Henry Cotton won his third title. Gary Player won in 1959 and Jack Nicklaus in 1966. Perhaps the most dramatic Open in Muirfield's history came in 1972 when Lee Trevino holed his famous chip shot from the edge of the 17th green and in the process stole the title from Tony Jacklin. In recent times British fortunes have revived dramatically, however, with Nick Faldo winning in 1987 and again in 1992, when he so memorably produced 'the best four holes of my life' to deny the unfortunate John Cook. One wonders what the 21st century has in store.

Hole	Yards	Par	Hole	Yards	Par
1	449	4	10	475	5
2	349	4	11	386	4
3	379	4	12	381	4
4	181	3	13	153	3
5	558	5	14	447	4
6	471	4	15	396	4
7	185	3	16	188	3
8	444	4	17	542	5
9	510	5	18	447	4
Out	**3,526**	**36**	**In**	**3,415**	**36**
			Out	**3,526**	**36**
			Totals	**6,941**	**72**

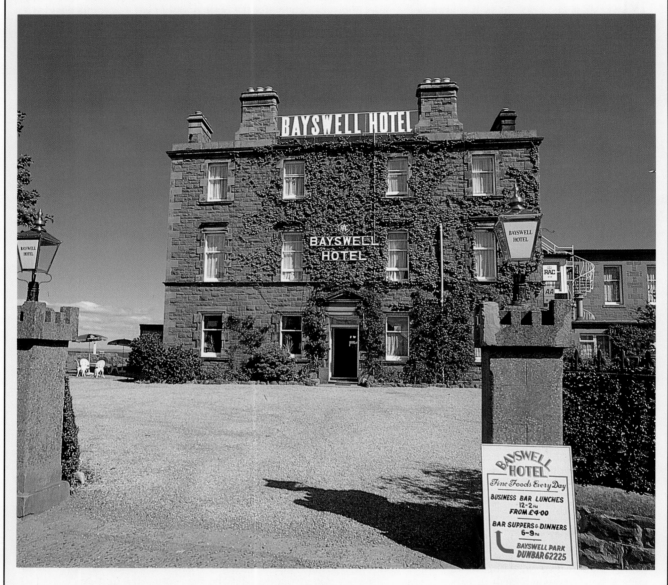

This fine hotel by the sea, elevated on a clifftop, has an idyllic setting and its two restaurants command one of the most spectacular views in East Lothian, overlooking the Firth of Forth, Bass Rock, May Island, the ruins of Dunbar Castle and the Fife coast.

At the Bayswell comfort is a high priority. All fourteen double/twin rooms have en suite facilities, with bath and shower, and have colour television, radio, trouser press, direct-dial telephones and tea/coffee tray. Weekly terms are available and offer excellent value for bed and breakfast. Dinner is served in a restaurant with an adjoining lounge bar—a perfect place to reflect on days past or golf ahead. A fine selection of ales, malt whiskies and liqueurs provides a fine way to start or end the evening.

The hotel is happy to organise golf breaks at a dinner bed and breakfast rate of £42.50 per person per night, based on sharing a twin/double room. Single occupancy is also available. There are 18 golf courses nearby, some of which offer the facility of a golf ticket.

The hotel often has carvery dinners where you can eat as much as you want. Dinner dances take place on most Saturday nights. First class catering and entertainment guarantees great fun for all. Edinburgh, Scotland's historic capital, is only 30 minutes away and the Lammermuir Hills provide a perfect backdrop to the fishing port of Dunbar.

A warm welcome awaits from the resident proprietors who will make your stay as comfortable and relaxing as possible.

The Bayswell Hotel
Bayswell Park
Dunbar, East Lothian
Tel & Fax (01368) 862225
E mail: the bayswellhotel@btinernet.com

Dalmahoy

Dalmahoy, near Edinburgh has a lot in common with Moor Park, near London. Apart from being an easy drive from its country's capital (although it is much easier to escape from central Edinburgh than central London) both have two parkland courses—the one being much more testing than the other; both have staged televised professional tournaments over their championship course and most immediately striking of all is that the courses of Dalmahoy and Moor Park are each overlooked by magnificent mansion houses which act as extraordinarily elegant 19th holes.

Dalmahoy's mansion is a three storey Georgian building, originally designed for the Earl of Morton in 1735. To wander around its interior is an experience itself; many magnificent paintings adorn the walls and a wonderful sense of wellbeing pervades the building. The mansion has in fact been the focal point of a considerable amount of activity in recent times. The Georgian building has been sympathetically restored and is now the centrepiece of a 151 bedroomed luxury hotel and country club. The whole development plan comprised an investment of some £14 million. Lord knows what the Earl of Morton would have thought of it all!

Golf has been played at Dalmahoy since the 1920s, five times Open Champion James Braid designing both courses, the championship **East** and the **West**, in 1927. From the day the very first ball was struck they have been held in extremely high esteem. The courses exemplify all that is best in parkland golf and offer a very real contrast to the nearby challenges of Muirfield, North Berwick and Dunbar. Again, like Moor Park, Dalmahoy's fairways are quite undulating and provide some far-reaching views; Edinburgh Castle sits proudly on the horizon.

Measuring 6677 yards, par 72, the East Course is considerably longer than the West at 5185 yards, par 68. Both however are maintained in the same superb condition all year round. Due to the recent works at Dalmahoy the East Course front and back nines have been reversed, in other words, what was formerly the 10th is now played as the opening hole. This isn't the first time this has happened. The course was played 'this way round' in the 1981 Haig Tournament Players Championship.

That 1981 event witnessed some outstanding golf. On the final day Scotland's Brian Barnes, cheered on by a partisan crowd, stormed around the course in an unbelievable 62 strokes, including an inward nine of just 28. This score enabled him to catch Brian Waites and, inevitably, Barnes went on to win the playoff. As for Dalmahoy, it is now indelibly linked with the Solheim Cup and that memorable week in October 1992 when the world of women's golf was so dramatically turned on its head.

Marriott Dalmahoy Hotel, Golf and Country Club, Kirknewton, Midlothian, EH27 8EB

Director of Golf	Brian Anderson (0131) 333 4105
Green Fees	East WD £50, WE £70/round
	West WD £35, WE £45/round
Restrictions	10 day advance bookings (0131) 333 1845; weekend golf limited.

Directions
The club is 7 miles south west of Edinburgh off the A71 Kilmarnock road. Travelling from Glasgow leave the M8 at junction 3, using the A599 to link with the A71.

Dunbar

In common with much of eastern Scotland it isn't entirely clear when golf was first played at Dunbar. Whilst the Dunbar Golf Club was founded in 1856 following a meeting in the Town Hall, the Dunbar Golfing Society had been instituted in 1794. Furthermore, records suggest that some cruder form of golf had been played in the area at least as early as the beginning of the 17th century. In 1616 two men of the parish of Tyninghame were censured by the Kirk Session for 'playing at ye nyne holis' on the Lord's Day and in 1640 an Assistant Minister of Dunbar was disgraced 'for playing at gouff'. Times, as they say, change and 350 years later 'gouff' is still played at Dunbar, although no one is likely to be censured or disgraced for doing so and there are now 18 splendid holes.

Dunbar is very much a natural links, laid out on a fairly narrow tract of land closely following the contours of the shoreline. It is bounded by a stone wall which runs the full length of the course. While Dunbar is by no means the longest of Scottish links, when the winds blow it can prove to be one of the most difficult—this may have something to do with the fact that there is an 'out of bounds' on the 3rd, 4th, 5th, 6th, 7th, 8th, 9th, 16th, 17th and 18th holes, and the beach can come in to play on the 4th, 5th, 6th, 7th, 12th, 14th, 15th, 16th and 17th—straight hitting would appear to be called for!

Dunbar is without doubt one of the east coast's most attractive links with some splendid views out across the sea towards Bass Rock. The first three holes are played fairly close to the clubhouse, the opening two being relatively tame par fives and the 3rd a spectacular short hole played from an elevated tee. The 4th then takes you alongside the beach as the course begins to move away from the clubhouse. Perhaps the most testing holes occur around the turn, the 9th to the 12th, and there is no let-up either on the closing stretch with the beach readily receiving the mildest of slices. The 18th can also be a card-wrecker with the stone wall out of bounds running the entire length of the fairway to the right.

All the major Scottish Championships have been played at Dunbar, including the Scottish Amateur, Scottish Boys and Scottish Professional Championships. The club has also staged the British Boys Championship

Dunbar's 19th is a comfortable and informal building with views from the lounge of the Firth of Forth and across much of the course. And just one final thought as you relax in the clubhouse—one of the regulations of the Dunbar Golfing Society dated 1794 reads as follows: 'When the expense of each member for dinner amounts to two shillings and sixpence, the club shall be dissolved'. Times, as they say, most certainly change!

The Dunbar Golf Club, East Links, Dunbar, East Lothian, EH42 1LT

Sec/Manager	Liz Thom (01368) 862317
Professional	Derek Small (01368) 862086
Caterer	(01368) 863334
Green Fees	WD £25/round; £35/day
	WE £35/round; £45/day
Restrictions	No visitors on Thursdays

Directions
Dunbar is on the A1 between Berwick-upon-Tweed and Edinburgh. From the Borders take a combination of the A68 and A6137 to Haddington, there picking up the A1.

North Berwick

The golfer who journeys to Ayrshire essentially to inspect the links at Turnberry and Troon, but discovers that he actually prefers Prestwick, is the same player who visits Muirfield (and, yes, enjoys a challenge) but falls in love with North Berwick.

Prestwick charms. North Berwick charms. Both bristle with character. If the Open Championship had begun on the East instead of the West coast of Scotland in the middle of the last century, Musselburgh would doubtless have been the birthplace (it was the then home of the Honourable Company) but the West Links at North Berwick would have made a much better venue.

With the exception of a few staunch traditionalists—Ben Crenshaw immediately springs to mind—today's champion golfers would regard North Berwick as too unpredictable: they abhor any degree of blindness on a golfcourse and expect a good shot always to be rewarded with a perfect level lie. The fact of the matter is that courses like North Berwick and Prestwick are too intricate for their tastes and many top players simply do not possess the varied armoury of shot-making skills necessary to tame a classic 'old fashioned' links. Besides, where is their spirit of adventure?!

North Berwick Golf Club was founded in 1832 although golf had already been played over the site of the present links for centuries. Like the Old Course at St Andrews, the West Links starts and finishes in town—and, like St Andrews, North Berwick is an attractive seaside town that lives and breathes golf. It is claimed that the ghost of Old Tom Morris stalks the fairways of the Old Course. At North Berwick it is the spirit of Ben Sayers, and not even he can master the contours of the legendary 16th green.

North Berwick's setting is one of the most captivating in golf. The first three holes run adjacent to the shore, as, broadly speaking, do the 10th to the 14th on the inward nine—the course being laid out in the shape of a figure of eight. The Forth Estuary is on the golfer's right side as he plays the opening holes. Bass Rock, a miniature Ailsa Craig, and a host of rocky islets command attention, as does a great sweep of sandy beech.

Visitors have always been made extremely welcome at North Berwick. Bookings can be made in advance by phoning the **Golf Office** on **(01620) 892135** (or by fax on 01620 893274). The club's full address is **North Berwick Golf Club, New Clubhouse, Beach Road, North Berwick EH39 4BB**. Green fees in 1998 are £30 per round, £45 per day during the week, £45 per round, £60 per day at weekends. The **Course Manager** is **David Huish**, a former Captain of the British PGA who has been attached to the club since 1967. His son **Martyn Huish** is the resident **Teaching Professional**. Finally, it is worth noting that the Starter may require visitors to produce proof of a current handicap.

The character and eccentricities of North Berwick are apparent from the outset. The opening tee shot is invariably played with a fairway wood or long iron in order to lay up short of a deep gully. This is followed by a short but semi-blind second to a green that occupies a craggy hilltop and slopes sharply towards the sea. The drive at the 2nd must flirt with the shore—a spectacular hole this is—and at the 3rd the approach is hit over an ancient stone wall that traverses the fairway. And so it continues. Along with the 2nd, the finest holes on the outward nine are probably the two par threes, the 4th and 6th, and the par five 9th.

Turning for home, a marvellous vista unfolds from the elevated back tee at the short 10th. Next is a curving par five that hugs the base of some formidable dunes. The 12th is a teasing, bite-off-as-much-as-you-dare dog-leg, and then comes a truly classic sequence of holes. The 13th features another approach over a stone wall but a far more precise second (not to mention an intelligently positioned drive) is required on this occasion to find a green squashed between the wall and the dunes. The 14th is called 'Perfection'—a somewhat controversial name for a blind hole! The real perfection, however, relates to the setting of the green which is perched right on the edge of the links, seemingly on the verge of slipping into the sea. And then you confront the par three 'Redan' and a green complex that is surely the most imitated in golf. Here at North Berwick is the original prototype. If the 'Redan' doesn't defeat you, the incredible slopes of the 16th green probably will. A very difficult 17th and a benign 18th bring you back to reality.

So enjoy North Berwick. Remember to bring that armoury of shot-making skills with you—and leave your lob wedge behind!

Hole	Yards	Par	Hole	Yards	Par
1	314	4	10	154	3
2	417	4	11	489	5
3	448	4	12	369	4
4	166	3	13	339	4
5	361	4	14	359	4
6	140	3	15	180	3
7	334	4	16	364	4
8	462	5	17	381	4
9	490	5	18	266	4
Out	**3132**	**36**	**In**	**2901**	**35**
			Out	**3132**	**36**
			Totals	**6033**	**71**

Key

To avoid disappointment
it is advisable to telephone
in advance

***Visitors welcome at most times
**Visitors usually allowed on
weekdays only
*Visitors not normally permitted
(Mon, Wed) No visitors
on specified days

Approximate Green Fees
A   £40 plus
B   £25 to £40
C   £20 to £30
D   £15 to £25
E   under £15
F   Green fees on application

Restrictions
G Guests only
H—Handicap certificate required
H—(24) Handicap of 24 or less
L —Letter of introduction required
M—Visitor must be a member of
another recognised club

Aberlady G.C.
(01875) 870374
Aberlady, East Lothian
(18) 5410 yards/***/F

Baberton G.C.
(0131) 453 3361
Baberton Avenue, Edinburgh
(18) 6098 yards/***/C/H

Balbardie Park G.C.
(01506) 634561
Balbardie Park, Bathgate
(9) 1237 yards/***/E

Bass Rock G.C.
(01620) 822082
Harperdean, Haddington
(18) 6420 yards/***/B-A

Bathgate G.C.
(01506) 630553
Edinburgh Road, Bathgate
(18) 6362 yards/***/D

Braid Hills G.C.
(0131) 447 6666
Braid Hill Road,Edinburgh
(18) 5239 yards/***/E
(18) 4832 yards/***/E

Braids United G.C.
(0131) 452 9408
Braid Hills Approach, Edinburgh
(18) 5239 yards/***/E
(18) 4832 yards/***/E

Broomieknowe G.C.
(0131) 663 9317
Golf Course Road, Bonnyrigg,
Midlothian
(18) 6046 yards/**/C

Bruntsfield Links G.C.
(0131) 336 1479
Barton Avenue, Davidsons Mains
(18) 6407 yards/**/F/H

Carrick Knowe G.C.
(0131) 337 1096
Glendevon Park, Edinburgh
(18) 6299 yards/***/E

Carrickvale G.C.
(0131) 337 1096
Glendevon Park, Edinburgh
(18) 6299 yards/***/F/H

Castle Park G.C.
(01620) 810733
Gifford, Haddington
(9) 5810 yards/***/D

Craigentinny G.C.
(0131) 554 7501
Craigentinny Avenue, Edinburgh
(18) 5418 yards/***/E

Craigmillar Park G.C.
(0131) 667 0047
Observatory Road, Edinburgh
(18) 5851 yards/**/B/H or L

Dalmahoy Hotel & C.C.
(0131) 333 4105
Dalmahoy, Kirknewton, Midlothian
(18) 6667 yards/**/A/G
(18) 5185 yards/**/A/G

Deer Park G.C.
(01506) 431037
Carmondean, Livingston
(18) 6636 yards/***/D

Dirleton Castle G.C.
(01620) 843496
Gullane, East Lothian
(18) 6466 yards/**/F
(18) 6244 yards/***/F
(18) 5166 yards/***/F

Duddingston G.C.
(0131) 661 1005
Duddingston Road, Edinburgh
(18) 6420 yards/**/B/H

Dunbar G.C.
(01368) 862317
East Links, Dunbar
(18) 6426 yards/***/B-A

Dundas Park G.C.
(0131) 331 1416
Loch Road, South Queensferry
(9) 6800 yards/***/E/M/H

Gifford G.C.
(01620) 810267
Edinburgh Road, Gifford
(9) 6243 yards/**/E

Glen G.C.
(01620) 892726
Tantallon Terrace, North Berwick
(18) 6098 yards/***/D

Glencorse G.C.
(01968) 677177
Milton Bridge, Penicuik, Midlothian
(18) 5217 yards/***/C-B

Greenburn G.C.
(01501) 770292
Fauldhouse, West Lothian
(18) 6210 yards/**/E/H

Gullane G.C.
(01620) 842255
Gullane, East Lothian
(18) 6466 yards/**/F
(18) 6244 yards/***/F
(18) 5166 yards/***/F

Haddington G.C.
(01620) 8233627
Amisfield Park, Haddington,
(18) 6280 yards/**(pm)/D

Harburn G.C.
(01506) 871131
West Calder, West Lothian
(18) 5843 yards/***/D

Honourable Company Of Edinburgh
Golfers
(01620) 842123
Muirfield, Gullane, East Lothian
(18) 6601 yards/(Tues, Thurs
only)/A/H (18)/M/L

Kilspindie G.C.
(018751) 870358
Aberlady, East Lothian
(18) 5410 yards/***/F

Kingsknowe G.C.
(0131) 441 1145
Lanark Road, Edinburgh
(18) 5979 yards/***/C

Liberton G.C.
(0131) 664 3009
Gilmerton Road, Edinburgh
(18) 4882 yards/**/C

Linlithgow G.C.
(01506) 842585
Braehead, Linlithgow, West Lothian
(18) 5858 yards/***(Wed/Sat)/D

Longniddry G.C.
(01875) 852141
Links Road, Longniddry, East Lothian
(18) 6210 yards/**/B-A/H

Lothianburn G.C.
(0131) 445 2288
Biggar Road, Fairmilehead
(18) 5750 yards/**/D

Luffness New G.C.
(01620) 843114
Aberlady, East Lothian
(18) 6122 yards/**/B

Merchants of Edinburgh G.C.
(0131) 447 1219
Craighill Gardens, Edinburgh
(18) 4889 yards/**/C

Mortonhall G.C.
(0131) 447 6974
Braid Road, Edinburgh
(18) 6557 yards/**/B/H

Murrayfield G.C.
(0131) 337 3478
Murrayfield Road, Edinburgh
(18) 5725 yards/**/B/H

Musselburgh G.C.
(0131) 665 2005
Monktonhall, Musselburgh
(18) 6623 yards/***/D

Musselburgh Links G.C.
(0131) 665 5483
Balcarres Road, Musselburgh
(9) 2700 yards/***/E

Musselburgh Old Course G.C.
(0131) 665 6981
Millhill, Musselburgh
(9) 5380 yards/***/F

Newbattle G.C.
(0131) 663 1819
Abbey Road, Dalkeith, Midlothian
(18) 6025 yards/**/D

Niddry Castle & G.C.
(01506) 891097
Castle Road, Winchurch
(9) 5476 yards/***/E

North Berwick G.C.
(01620) 892135
Beach Road, North Berwick
(18) 6033 yards/***/B-A

Polkemmet G.C.
(01501) 743905
Whitburn, Bathgate
(9) 2967 yards/***/E

Portobello G.C.
(0131) 669 4361
Stanley Road, Portobello, Edinburgh
(9) 2419 yards/**/C

Prestonfield G.C.
(0131) 667 1273
6 Prestonfield Road North,
Edinburgh
(18) 6178 yards/**(Sat, Sun pm)/B-A

Pumpherston G.C.
(01506) 432869
Drumshoreland Road, Livingston
(9) 5434 yards/*/E/G

Ratho Park G.C.
(0131) 333 2566
Ratho, Newbridge, Midlothian
(18) 5900 yards/***/B-A

Ravelston G.C.
(0131) 315 2486
24 Ravelston Dykes Road,
Edinburgh
(9) 5200 yards/*/C/G

Royal Burgess G.S.
(0131) 339 2075
Whitehouse Road, Edinburgh
(18) 6494 yards/**/F/L/H

Royal Musselburgh G.C.
(01875) 810276
Prestongrange House, Prestonpans,
(18) 6237 yards/**/B/H

Silverknowes G.C.
(0131) 336 3843
Silverknowes, Parkway, Edinburgh
(18) 6210 yards/***/E

Swanston G.C.
(0131) 445 4002
Swanston Road, Edinburgh
(18) 5024 yards/**/D/H

Tantallom G.C.
(01620) 892114
Westgate, North Berwick
(18) 6420 yards/***/B-A

Torphin Hill G.C.
(0131) 441 4061
Torphin Road, Colinton, Edinburgh
(18) 5024 yards/***/D

Turnhouse G.C.
(0131) 339 1014
Turnhouse Road, Edinburgh
(18) 6171 yards/**/F/G

Uphall G.C.
(01506) 856404
Uphall, West Lothian
(18) 5600 yards/***/D

West Lothian G.C.
(01506) 826030
Airngarth Hill, Linlithgow, West
Lothian
(18) 6578 yards/**/D

Whitekirk G.C.
(01620) 870300
Whitekirk Mains, Dunbar
(18) 6420 yards/***/D

Winterfield G.C.
(01368) 863562
St Margarets,North Road,Dunbar
(18) 5155 yards/***/F

PORT APPIN

OBAN

KILCHRENAN

ARDUAINE   INVERARAY

STRACHUR   TARBET
                  LOCHGOILHEAD

CRINAN   ARGYLL

JURA   Dullatur G.C.
         Blairmore & Strone G.C.   Bishopbriggs G.C.
         Cowal G.C.   Helensburgh G.C.   CUMBERNAULD Westerwood
PORT ASKAIG   Kyles of Bute   DUNOON   GOUROCK   Hotel & G.C.
              G.C.   Innellan G.C.   LANGBANK   Renfrew G.C.
              Port   Bannatyne G.C.   Gleddoch G & C.C.   Haggs Castle G.C.
ISLE OF   KENNACRAIG   WEMYSS BAY   GLASGOW
ISLAY   ISLE OF   Pollok G.C.
   Islay G.C.   BUTE   Rothesay G.C.   BARRHEAD   East Renfrewshire G.C.
   (Machrie)   Kingarth G.C.   Largs G.C.   Torrance House G.C.
PORT ELLEN   FAIRLIE STEWARTON   Lanark G.C.
              ISLE OF   W. Kilbride G.C.   KILWINNING   Strathaven G.C.   LANARK
              ARRAN   ARDROSSAN   Irvine G.C. IRVINE
                        Glasgow Gailes G.C.   KILMARNOCK
         Brodick G.C.   Kilmarnock G.C.   Royal Troon G.C.
         Lamlash G.C.   Western Gailes G.C. TROON   Prestwick St. Nicholas G.C.
                           Whiting Bay   Prestwick G.C. PRESTWICK   Ballochmyle G.C.
   CAMPBELTOWN Blackwaterfoot   ALLOWAY   AYR
   Machrihanish G.C.   G.C.   Belleisle G.C.

         CULZEAN CASTLE
         Turnberry Hotel   AYRSHIRE
         & G.C.

         AILSA CRAIG

                  GIRVAN

Artist: **T. Hodge TOM MORRIS** *Courtesy of:* **Sotheby's**

Ayrshire

An ancient golfing rhyme from the land of Burns runs:
'Troon and Prestwick, old and classy,
Bogside, Dundonald, Glasgow Gailes, Barassie,
Prestwick St Nicholas, Western Gailes,
St Cuthbert, Portland—memory fails,
Troon Municipal (three links there)
Prestwick Municipal, Irvine, Ayr,
They faced the list with delighted smiles -
Sixteen courses within ten miles'.

Even without Turnberry, that 'little corner of heaven on earth', some 15 miles south of Ayr, an extraordinarily impressive list, and little wonder that this small region of Scotland's coast has become nothing short of a Mecca for golfers the world over.

Prestwick, Troon and **Turnberry** have of course each staged the Open Championship. Prestwick was the birth-place of the event back in 1860 and is probably the most classic test of traditional links golf—'penal' the American architects would describe it, on account of the many blind shots. The Open is no longer held at Prestwick but the history of the place is overwhelming and quite mag-netic. Troon and Turnberry are both firmly on the 'Open' rota. It was last played over the latter's Ailsa course in 1994 (Nick Price's great victory) and was last held at Troon in 1997, when it was won by Justin Leonard. Understandably the golfer making a pilgrimage to the Ayrshire coast will be drawn towards this famous trio. However, if time isn't of the essence, it would be bordering on a disgrace not to sample as many of the nearby delights as possible. As the old rhyme relates, within short distance of one another lie a number of outstanding courses, at any of which it may be easier to arrange a game.

While not all roads lead to Ayr, as the largest town on the coast, it's probably as good a starting point as any. Here we find a belle—**Belleisle** to be precise and a most attractive parkland course. Considered by many to be the finest public course outside of St Andrews and Carnoustie and, being somewhat sheltered, it's an admirable retreat from the more windswept links near-by. Furthermore as a municipal course the green fees are relatively cheap.

Just north of Ayr lie a series of outstanding links courses, all within a mile or two of one another. **Western Gailes**, Prestwick and Troon are featured on later pages (as is Turnberry) but also in this area one finds first class courses at **Prestwick St Nicholas, Barassie, Glasgow (Gailes)** and **Irvine** (also known somewhat unfortunately as Bogside). Each warmly welcomes visi-tors and, although they are less busy than the more famous courses, prior telephoning is strongly recom-mended, especially during the peak summer months. Weekdays are inevitably the best times for a visit.

Just as there is a proliferation of golf courses on the Ayrshire coast, so the region is inundated with all man-ner of hotels, guesthouses, pubs and restaurants. A few thoughts follow. To start at a pinnacle, undoubtedly one of the best hotels in Britain is the Turnberry Hotel (01655) 331000, the first ever purpose-built hotel and golf course. Both hotel and restaurant are truly outstanding. For beautiful views over the Isle of Arran, we also rec-ommend nearby Malin Court (01655) 331457. If staying in this area, Culzean Castle (open between April and October) is well worth a visit and in nearby **Girvan** where there is an underrated municipal course, an excel-lent place for liquid refreshment is the King's Arms

(01465) 713322. Golfers may also find the nearby Bardrochat country house hotel (01465) 881232 ideal accommodation—it is particularly good for small groups. If you've food on your mind we suggest you forget about calories and go for a slap-up meal in Splinters! (01465) 713481.

Returning northwards, perhaps the most popular, and certainly the most convenient hotel for Royal Troon is the Marine Highland (01292) 314444. It proudly over-looks the Old Course Championship links and boasts excellent leisure facilities. Two other hotels in Troon are Piersland House (01292) 314747 and the Ardneil (01292) 311611, a less stylish but thoroughly welcoming establish-ment. Highgrove House (01292) 312511 in nearby Loans provides excellent cuisine and agreeable accommoda-tion. A similar commendation is given to Lochgreen House (01292) 313343 in Southwood two miles south of Troon. Two hotels in Ayr to note are Fairfield House (01292) 267461 and the Pickwick (01292) 260111 while close by in Alloway is the excellent Northpark House (01292) 442336 and in Maybole, the Ladyburn Hotel (01655) 740585 is good value. On to Prestwick, which if you've arrived by plane may well be your first port of call. Here, the Carlton Toby (01292) 476811 and the Parkstone (01292) 477286 stand out from the crowd and there are numerous B&Bs and small hotels. The Fairways Hotel (01292) 470396 and North Beach Hotel (01292) 479069 are always popular retreats. Kilmarnock is now a busy industrial centre yet it was here that Robbie Burns' first collection of poems was published. Just to the north of the town at Irvine is the Hospitality Inn (01294) 274272 which, in keeping with its name, is most welcoming. If an escape to the countryside is sought then a trip to Stewarton is highly recommended. Here, set in glorious surroundings, is the redoubtable Chapeltoun House (01560) 482696—quiet and very com-fortable with a first class restaurant. Kilwinning is a final recommendation for this area, the Montgreenan Mansion House (01294) 557733 is superbly situated with excellent facilities including some practice holes to warm up on before sallying forth.

To the north of the famous golfing stretch there is plenty of less testing golf to be found. This may well be necessary in order to restore battered pride! **West Kilbride** (another links type) and **Largs** (a well wooded parkland course) should suit admirably. Both also offer some magnificent views across to Argyll and the Isle of Arran where there are no fewer than seven golf cours-es, and an ideal base to play them from is the Auchrannie Country House Hotel (01770) 302234 and the excellent Kilmichael Country House (01770) 302219. Also roughly due east of Ayr, close to the A76 there is a very good course at **Ballochmyle**.

Glasgow

Glasgow is Britain's third largest city after London and Birmingham and, being Scottish to boot, not surprisingly has a huge number of golf courses. Indeed some wag once said of Glasgow that there was a pub in every street with a golf club around each corner. One interest-ing statistic is that between 1880 and 1910 more than 80 golf courses were built in the Greater Glasgow area—so much for today's golf boom! Unfortunately the problem for the golfing stranger to Glasgow is that many of the city's leading clubs permit visitors to play only if accom-panied by a member. Among the city's more traditional courses—and where arranging a game can be difficult—are **Haggs Castle, Pollok** and **Glasgow Killermont**. Other suggestions include **Renfrew** and **East Renfrewshire**, to the north west and south west respectively, and **Bishopriggs and Cawder** to the north of Glasgow. There are a number of public courses in Glasgow so the visiting golfer confined to Glasgow need not get too depressed. The pick of the municipals are probably **Lethamhill** and **Little Hill**—a game on either is remarkably inexpensive.

Forgetting the golf for a moment, it came as something of a surprise for many south of the border when Glasgow was chosen as European City of Culture for 1990, in succession to Athens and Paris, among others. Of course those familiar with the city will know that it has changed out of all recognition in the past decade or so. Good hotels are not as thick on the ground as golf courses but a list of the best would include the Glynhill Leisure Hotel (0141) 886 9555 which caters equally well for individuals and groups and offers various golfing packages. Others to note are the Glasgow Hilton (0141) 204 5555, the Glasgow Marriott (0141) 226 5577, the Glasgow Thistle (0141) 332 3311 and the less modern (and with a much more attractive exterior) Stakis Grosvenor (0141) 339 8811. One Devonshire Gardens (0141) 339 2001 also combines old-fashioned elegance and service. For more contemporary surroundings Malmasion (0141) 221 6400 is a real gem. As for restaurants, Glasgow is pretty well endowed. Fish lovers will enjoy Rogano (0141) 248 4055 in Exchange Square while those seeking first class French cuisine should head for the Buttery (0141) 221 8188 on Argyle Street. High quality Chinese and Indian restaurants also abound, with the Amber (0141) 339 6121 and Balbir's Ashoka West End (0141) 339 0936 both well worth seeking out. For a sample of Glasgow's culture the Theatre Royal (0141) 332 9000 offers distinguished ballet, opera and drama and the Burrell Collection in Pollok Park is Scotland's leading art gallery.

Time for a spot more golf, and the **Gleddoch House Hotel Golf and Country Club** (01475) 540711 provides the solution. Located at Langbank it is close to the Clyde Estuary and offers views of the Kilpatrick Hills. It is easily accessible from Glasgow by way of the M8 and in a nutshell could be described as a darn good hotel with a darn good restaurant and a darn good golf course! Further north, the course at **Helensburgh** is also worth a visit.

From Glasgow, the great challenges of Troon, Turnberry and Prestwick lie to the south west (the A77 is incidentally the most convenient route), and, of course, to the north west on the shores (or 'bonnie banks') of Loch Lomond is the outstanding **Loch Lomond** Golf Course (featured ahead). Good golf can also be found to the north and east of Glasgow—**Dullatur** is one such place, **Lanark** another. The former is a parkland course whereas Lanark is essentially moorland. For Dullatur a hotel to note is Crow Wood House (0141) 779 3861 and an excellent restaurant, La Campagnola (0141) 779 3405—both are in Muirhead. The Cartland Bridge Hotel (01555) 664426 is recommended for the course at Lanark. Twenty miles or so east of Glasgow near Cumbernauld the **Westerwood Hotel** (01236) 457171 and its golf course offer a fine combination of golf, leisure and accommodation. The golf course is very challenging and calls for many daring shots, which is not altogether surprising since Seve Ballesteros had a hand in its design!

Further Afield

Before heading for the more distant corners of the area, a quick mention for two courses lying due south

of Glasgow: **Torrance House** and **Strathaven** are the pair in question. Both are very easily reached by way of the A726, although Strathaven is quite a bit of a way from the city and by the time you arrive at the course you'll have climbed 700 feet above sea level. But a lovely setting and a most convenient hotel, the Strathaven (01357) 521778 await.

What of the more remote outposts then? There's not a great deal in the way of golfing challenges here—the landscape precludes it—but the countryside is quite glorious and there are some extremely fine hotels and country houses nestling in and around the hills, all making splendid bases for exploring the magnificent scenery of these parts. North of Loch Lomond one finds Stonefield Castle (01880) 820836 at Tarbert alongside Loch Fyne. If inspecting the delights of Oban a detour to Kilchrenan is highly recommended—Ardanaiseig (01866) 833333 is the place—outstandingly relaxing and in a beautiful setting overlooking Loch Awe. Still nearer to Oban at Kilninver, the Knipoch Hotel (01852) 316251 offers great comfort together with all manner of country pursuits.

Two great courses still remain to be charted—those magical 'M's'—**Machrie** and **Machrihanish.** Each enjoys a kind of splendid isolation and is a superb test of traditional links golf. Machrie is to be found on the distant Isle of Islay at Port Ellen. As it can now be reached by plane from Glasgow there can be no excuse for not making the trip—besides, right on the course is the Machrie Hotel (01496) 302310. Many have already made the pilgrimage to Machrihanish and as it too is reachable by air a large number are certain to follow. *Following The Fairways* has also succumbed to its charms and Machrihanish is explored on a later page. There are a number of hotels and guesthouses nearby, both in Machrihanish itself and in Campbeltown, and it's well worth spending a few days here. The Putechan Lodge (01583) 421323 can be highly recommended and, like several local hotels, offers special golfing breaks. Balegreggan Country House (01586) 552062 is renowned for its food, and Ardell House (01586) 810235 offers some good accommodation.

Before you leave the area a mellow tune may come to mind—Mull of Kintyre by one Paul McCartney. The music inspired millions: the golf course and its surrounds will almost certainly give equal satisfaction.

THE TEE SHOT *Courtesy of:* **Burlington Gallery**

The Mansion House at Montgreenan was built by Dr Robert Glasgow in 1817 as a family home and so it remains today, with all the period features including the attractive marble and brass fireplaces, decorative ceiling and plasterwork having been carefully retained. Indeed, the traveller who visits Montgreenan may be forgiven for feeling they have made a journey back in time. Where better to relax and enjoy the peaceful setting and magnificent view of the distant Ailsa Craig and Arran Hills, or to stroll through the 50 acres of beautiful gardens and secluded parklands. Montgreenan prides itself on its high standards of personal service and warm hospitality.

Whatever the occasion, Montgreenan is the ideal venue offering spacious rooms, a secluded setting and quiet, attentive service. The comfortable bedrooms are finished to a deluxe standard with antique and reproduction furniture and offer a choice of luxurious beds including a king size round bed and four posters.

Relax and enjoy the culinary skill of award-winning chef Alan McCall. Seasonal specialities are incorporated into Alan's menus and fresh Scottish fare is always available, making dining at Montgreenan an experience not to be missed. The wine cellar has one of the finest selections of fine wines available in Ayrshire and offers something for every taste, including Montgreenan's own specially selected Bordeaux.

Enjoy the challenge of playing the finest links courses in Ayrshire including Royal Troon, venue for the 1997 British Open Championship, and the magnificent Prestwick Golf Club where the original Open was held in 1860. There are also many interesting courses inland. In fact, there are over 30 courses within 45 minutes of Montgreenan. In addition, Montgreenan has its own 5 hole practice course which allows guests to play at their leisure.

Montgreenan Mansion House Hotel
Montgreenan Estate
Kilwinning
Ayrshire
KA13 7QZ
Tel: (01294) 557733
Fax: (01294) 850397

Royal Troon

O'a the links where I hae golfed
Frae Ayr to Aberdeen,
On Prestwick or Carnoustie and mony mair I ween
What tho' the bents are rough and bunkers yawn aroun'
I dearly lo'e the breezy links, the breezy links o' Troon.
(Gilmour)

When the golfing mind focuses on Troon it invariably thinks of the Postage Stamp, the par three 8th on the Old Course, unquestionably the world's most celebrated short hole. During the 1973 Open Championship, Gene Sarazen, then at the mature age of 71, holed out with his punched five iron shot in front of the watching television cameras. Sarazen declared that he would take with him to heaven a copy of the film to show to Walter Hagen and Co. Legend has it that on hearing of Sarazen's feat an American flew to Britain and travelled to Troon. He strode to the 8th tee and proceeded to strike 500 balls in succession towards the green. Not surprisingly he failed to equal Sarazen's achievement, whereupon he left the course and duly flew home to America. Who said it was only mad dogs and Englishmen?

Anyone contemplating the above ought at least to consult the **Secretary/Manager** first, **Mr J W Chandler** being the gentleman in question. He can be contacted at the **Royal Troon Golf Club, Craigend Road, Troon, Ayrshire KA10 6EP (01292) 311555** or by fax on (01292) 318204.

The Royal Troon Club Golf possesses two 18 hole courses, The **Old** and The **Portland**. Gentleman visitors are welcome to play both courses on Mondays, Tuesdays and Thursdays provided prior arrangement is made with the Secretary. Lady golfers are also welcome, although they are limited to playing on the Portland Course. All visitors must be members of a recognised club and be able to produce a certificate of handicap (maximum 30 for ladies, 20 for men).

In 1998 a green fee of £110 entitles the visitor to a round on each course, while a fee of £70 secures a full day's golf on the Portland Course; both fees are inclusive of lunch. There are no concessionary rates for junior golfers who, in any event, must have attained the age of eighteen before they will be permitted to play over the Old Course. Sets of clubs and trolleys may be hired from the club's **Professional, Brian Anderson (01292 313281)**. A caddy can also usually be organised.

Troon lies just to the north of Prestwick and Ayr. The town can be reached from Glasgow and the north via the A77, which also runs from near Stranraer in the south. The A78 is the coastal road, running from Largs through Irvine to Loans just east of Troon. Travelling from Edinburgh, the A71 should be taken, while from the North of England the best route is probably via the A74 and the A71. Finally, Prestwick Airport is no more than two miles away. Bordering the Firth of Clyde, the wind often blows very fiercely across the links and Troon is hardly a place for the faint-hearted golfer.

The Old Course at Troon has both the longest hole of any Open Championship course—the 6th at 577 yards—and the shortest—the Postage Stamp—which measures a mere 126 yards. In the 11th it also possesses one of the toughest, with its railway out-of-bounds, thick gorse and painfully narrow fairway. Along with the fabled 8th, the best holes at Troon are probably the 7th, which is played from an elevated tee to a stage-like green surrounded by tall dunes and deep pot bunkers, and the 13th, which features a wonderful, naturally undulating fairway.

At 6274 yards the Portland Course represents a more modest test but it is nonetheless a very fine course and although in parts it closely resembles a moorland-type course, it has all the challenges of traditional links golf.

The club is naturally proud of its great history. When it was founded in 1878 by twenty-four local enthusiasts there were originally only five holes. By 1923 it had staged its first Open Championship. Since then the club has held six Opens: in 1950, 1962 (when a rampant Palmer stormed to a six stroke victory) 1973, 1982 (Tom Watson's fourth victory) 1989 (where a dramatic playoff concluded an unforgettable final day's play) and most recently in 1997, when Justin Leonard shot a final round 66 to eclipse the unfortunate Jesper Parnevik..

If you have played all 36 holes at Troon and waged a successful war against the elements you will have earned your drink at the 19th. The clubhouse provides all the usual facilities and the catering has a very good reputation. When you leave you will probably not have a video to take to heaven, but you will at least know that you have visited one of the earth's greatest golfing shrines.

Old Course					
Hole	Yards	Par	Hole	Yards	Par
1	364	4	10	438	4
2	391	4	11	481	4
3	379	4	12	431	4
4	557	5	13	465	4
5	210	3	14	179	3
6	577	5	15	457	4
7	402	4	16	542	5
8	126	3	17	223	3
9	423	4	18	452	4
Out	3,429	36	In	3,668	35
			Out	3,429	36
			Totals	7,097	71

Turnberry

Not so many years ago it was said that the golfing visitor to Scotland journeyed to St Andrews for the history and to Turnberry for the beauty. Incomparable is a word often used to describe Turnberry's setting—magnificent and majestic are two others. Quite what causes Ailsa Craig to be so mesmerising is a mysery, but mesmerising it is and the views towards the distant Isle of Arran and the Mull of Kintyre can be equally captivating and enchanting. Since 1977, Turnberry has possessed history as well as beauty.

The Open Championship of 1977, Turnberry's first, is generally considered to have been the greatest of all championships. Nicklaus and Watson, the two finest golfers of the day, turned the tournament into a titanic, head-to-head confrontation—the 'Duel in the Sun' as it came to be known. On the final day, both having pulled along way clear of the field, Nicklaus held a two stroke advantage as they left the 12th green. "Who in the world can give Jack Nicklaus two shots over six holes and beat him?" asked Peter Alliss—the rest, as they say, is history.

There are two championship courses at Turnberry: the better known **Ailsa** Course, to which the Open returned for a third time in 1994, and the **Arran** Course. *Turnberry Hotel owns and runs both courses and tee times are reserved for hotel residents.* Arrangements can be made prior to arrival at the hotel by contacting the **Golf Operations Manager, Ewen Bowman.** Mr Bowman and his staff can be contacted by telephone on **(01655) 331000** and by fax on (01655) 331706. Letters should be addressed to **The Turnberry Hotel, Turnberry, Ayrshire KA26 9LT.**

In 1998 the summer green fee for hotel residents was £80 for one round over the Ailsa Course. A single round on the Arran Course cost £35.

The hotel and golf courses lie approximately 17 miles south of the town of Ayr off the A77. For those travelling from the Glasgow region, the A77 runs direct from Glasgow to Turnberry and is dual carriageway for much of the journey. Motoring from Edinburgh the A71 is the best route, picking up the A77 at Kilmarnock. Approaching from England, Carlisle is likely to be a starting point (M6 to Carlisle). The distance from Carlisle to Turnberry is one of just under 120 miles, and although there are two choices, the quickest route is to head north on the A74 leaving (in what appears to be no man's land) and joining the A70 towards Ayr. Finally, Prestwick Airport is situated just to the north of Ayr.

From its elevated perch, the red-roofed Turnberry Hotel enjoys a commanding view over both courses. It will have witnessed much of Turnberry's rather turbulent past. During the War the rolling expanse of links had been used as an air base and a vast runway had been constructed. Much levelling of the ground had also taken place and in 1945 the last thing Turnberry must have looked was the setting for two Championship courses. Mackenzie Ross is the architect we all have to thank for the restoration and transformation of the links.

From its medal tees, the Ailsa Course isn't a great deal longer than the Arran, their respective distances being 6440 yards, par 69, and 6014 yards, par 68. The same from the ladies tees are 5757 yards, par 75 and 5501 yards par 72. When Turnberry's second Open was staged in 1986 the Ailsa course weighed in at 6950 yards, par 70 and the fairways had been narrowed to alarming proportions. Greg Norman's second round 63, achieved in far from perfect weather conditions, was a remarkable feat.

After three holes 'inland' as it were, the Ailsa course hugs the shore tightly for a series of dramatic holes between the 4th and the 11th. The 6th, named Tappie Toorie, is possibly the most difficult par three on the course; the lengthy tee shot is to a heavily guarded green across a valley (play it into the wind and you may be short with a driver).

The 9th and the 10th, though, are the holes most likely to be remembered. The 9th 'Bruce's Castle', is played alongside the famous Turnberry lighthouse, built over the remains of Turnberry Castle, birthplace of Robert the Bruce. The championship tee is perched on a pinnacle of rock with the sea crashing below. Play this hole and the wonderfully curving 10th and you can appreciate why parallels have often been drawn between Turnberry and Pebble Beach. Following the par three 11th, the holes turn inland and if the scenery is a little less spectacular the challenge in no way diminishes.

The closing holes in fact produced a marvellous climax to the 1994 Open when Jesper Parnevik birdied five of his final eight holes yet was still overtaken by Nick Price. The popular Zimbabwian birdied the 16th and then eagled the 17th with a putt of fully 60 feet. Watson, Norman and Price—Turnberry's great triumvirate.

				Ailsa Course		
Hole	Yards	Par	Hole	Yards	Par
1	350	4	10	452	4
2	430	4	11	174	3
3	462	4	12	446	4
4	165	3	13	412	4
5	442	4	14	449	4
6	231	3	15	209	3
7	529	5	16	409	4
8	431	4	17	497	5
9	454	4	18	434	4
Out	**3,494**	**35**	**In**	**3,482**	**35**
			Out	**3,494**	**35**
			Totals	**6,976**	**70**

Prestwick

One could be forgiven for thinking that they take their golf a little too seriously at Prestwick—especially when one hears of such stories as the one about the monk from a nearby monastery who played a match against the Lord of Culzean to settle a deadly feud: at stake was the monk's nose!

The truth more likely is that Prestwick folk are a competitive breed. Only nine years after the formation of their club in 1851 the members got together and decided to stage an annual Open competition. The winner of the event was to receive an elegant red belt subscribed for by the members. Whilst there may have been only eight entrants, the 1860 Open marks the birth of the world's most prestigious championship.

Willie Park of Musselburgh (a 'foreigner from the east coast') won the 1860 Open and it was decided that if anyone should win the event three years in succession they would win the belt outright. 'Young' Tom Morris was the greatest player of his day and fittingly enough in 1870 won his third title in as many years. Whereas Tom may have kept the belt, Prestwick didn't keep the Open, or at least not the sole rights, as St Andrews and Musselburgh now joined Prestwick in the dawning of a new era.

In those days the combatants played over a twelve hole course. Today there are eighteen holes, though the distinctive flavour remains (seven of the original greens are in the same place). The modern day golfer must still play over the humps and hillocks, face blind shots and tackle the deep sleeper-faced bunkers and eccentrically contoured greens that are so much the charm of Prestwick.

Visitors wishing to play the historic course are advised to approach **Mr Ian Bunch**, the club's **Secretary**, to book a starting time. Mr Bunch can be contacted at **The Prestwick Golf Club, 2 Links Road, Prestwick, Ayrshire, KA9 1QG,** . **(01292) 477404** or by fax on (01292) 477255. Visitors should note that they are not permitted to play at weekends or after 11am on Thursdays, and that the first tee is reserved for members between the hours of 9am-10am and 12.30pm and 2.45pm. Furthermore, three-ball and four-ball matches are not allowed prior to 9.00am.

In 1998 the green fees are £80 per day. However, on Thursdays and for those arriving after 2.45pm on Mondays, Tuesdays, Wednesdays and Fridays the green fee is £55 for a single round. Sets of golf clubs and caddies can be hired through the **Professional, Frank Rennie, (01292) 479483.**

I suppose, like most things at Prestwick, the clubhouse could be described as having a traditional but friendly atmosphere. Ladies are not permitted in the dining and smoking rooms where jackets and ties must be worn at all times, but all may enter the Cardinal Room where some fine light lunches are offered. Dinners can also be arranged, though some prior warning is necessary.

At one time Prestwick was a fairly remote place. Improved roads and the opening of an international airport has made the area much more accessible from all directions. By road, the A77 runs directly from Glasgow in the north and along the coast from Stranraer in the south. Those travelling from Edinburgh should use the A71, before joining the A77 at Kilmarnock.

From the back markers Prestwick measures 6544 yards and has a par of 71. Perhaps not overly long by modern championship standards, it is nonetheless extremely challenging and local knowledge (not to mention rub of the green) can make a considerable difference. At 346 yards the opening hole is small beer in comparison to the first on the original twelve hole layout—that one measured a lengthy 578 yards and in an age of hickory shafts and gutty balls no doubt proved a stiff bogey six. One can only wonder as to how in the 1870 Open, en route to his aforementioned hat trick, 'Young' Tom Morris managed to hole out in three strokes! Another of Tom's notable achievements at Prestwick occurred in the 1868 Open when he scored the first ever recorded hole in one.

The 3rd hole at Prestwick is probably the most famous. Here the golfer must carry the vast Cardinal bunker which stretches the entire width of the fairway right at the point of the dog-leg. The infamous Pow Burn shapes the difficult 4th and then comes the fabled 'Himalayas'—a blind par three played over a massive dune. Almost every hole at Prestwick bristles with character and curiosity. The 10th 'Arran' and the 13th 'Sea Headrig' are regarded as two of the greatest two-shot holes in golf; the fairway at the 15th is surely one of the narrowest and the bunker at the 17th the most magnetic. As for the 18th, at only 284 yards it must be a straightforward hole? Tell that to the golfer who stands one down to the Lord of Culzean.

Hole	Yards	Par	Hole	Yards	Par
1	346	4	10	454	4
2	167	3	11	195	3
3	482	5	12	513	5
4	382	4	13	460	4
5	206	3	14	362	4
6	362	4	15	347	4
7	430	4	16	288	4
8	431	4	17	391	4
9	444	4	18	284	4
Out	**3,250**	**35**	**In**	**3,294**	**36**
			Out	**3,250**	**35**
			Totals	**6,544**	**71**

Loch Lomond

There maybe a handful of inland courses that are as challenging, as well designed and even one or two that are as perfectly maintained as Loch Lomond, but does any golf course in the world enjoy a more beautiful setting ? Surely not, for the splendour of Loch Lomond is in a class of its own.

The golf course is laid out alongside the legendary "bonnie banks" of Loch Lomond. It is practically encircled by mountains and hills—the start of the Scottish Highlands—and occupies the heart of an historic 800 year old estate, the ancestral home of the Clan Colquhoun who fought with Robert the Bruce. The estate is blessed with an extraordinary wealth of trees including many giant pines and several ancient oaks. Rhododendrons and azaleas provide seasonal splashes of colour while the ruins of a 15th century castle watch over the 18th green. For good measure the clubhouse at Loch Lomond is the palatial Rossdhu House, built in 1773.

Designed by Tom Weiskopf and Jay Morrish, Loch Lomond has already established itself as a favourite among the world's golfing elite. September 1996 saw the inaugural staging of the World Invitation Tournament, won by Denmark's rising star, Thomas Bjorn. During the event Nick Faldo described the course as "absolutely fabulous—as good as any I've seen". Colin Montgomerie called it "faultless". In 1997 the tournament was held the week before the Open Championship at Royal Troon, and it produced another fine champion in Tom Lehman.

The design of the course takes good advantage of the lakeside setting. Either the tee or green is adjacent to the Loch on eight of the holes, and a stream or burn affects another four. In addition to the many varied water hazards, Loch Lomond's defences include some distinctive marshes and an array of dazzling jigsaw shaped bunkers.

Perhaps the most memorable holes on the front nine are the par five 3rd, the extremely photogenic short 5th where the tee shot must be aimed directly at the Loch, and the 6th and 7th—a gorgeous par five and a swinging left to right dog-leg.

On the back nine the par four 15th heralds the start of an extraordinary finish. From an elevated tee the fairway flows down towards a shallow, sloping green beautifully framed by dark woods. The sweeping par five 16th dares you to attempt to carry the burn in front of the green with your second shot. The 17th is a superbly challenging par three with a tee shot across marshes to a tightly bunkered green and the 18th curves spectacularly around Rossdhu Bay to a huge green elegantly perched on the edge of the Loch—a marvellous ending to a marvellous course.

Loch Lomond Golf Club, Rossdhu House, Luss By Alexandria, Dumbartonshire G83 8NT

Sec/Manager	(01436) 655555
Professional	C Campbell
Green Fees	Members and their guests only
Restrictions	As above

Directions
From Glasgow Airport take the M898-A82 North.

Artist: **_Graeme W Baxter 17TH GREEN 'THE BAY'_** _Courtesy of:_ **_Baxter Prints_**

Western Gailes

Sam McKinlay once wrote, 'Western Gailes represents to the true golfer, to the connoisseur of the game, something approaching the ideal in golf.' Squeezed onto a narrow tract of land between the Atlantic Ocean and the Ayrshire coast's ubiquitous railway line, Western Gailes is indeed a marvellous links. It may not have the history of Prestwick (though the club celebrated its centenary in 1987) and the setting may not be as mouth-wateringly beautiful as Turnberry, nor does the links provide quite the stern, uncompromising challenge that is the hallmark of Royal Troon, but if a player wishes to experience a fine blend of all three then Western Gailes is the place to head for.

The 1st hole, with its humpy, hillocky fairway, and its green heavily contoured and partially concealed in a dell could have been plucked from Prestwick. The long par four 2nd is bordered by the railway line—now you could be playing the 11th at Troon. And when you stand on the tee at the par three 7th and gaze out to sea at Ailsa Craig and the Isle of Arran or along the coast which the course hugs for a series of holes you could believe you were at Turnberry. It is classic links golf—deep revetted pot bunkers and meandering burns, thick marram grass topping the dunes, and heather and gorse fringing the fairways.

While Troon and the Ailsa Course are essentially 'out and back' layouts, at Western Gailes the clubhouse sits in the middle of the links. And yet, rather than having two loops of nine—as at Muirfield—the golfer at Western Gailes is lured away from the clubhouse for four holes and invited to play nine close to the sea before being reeled in from the 14th hole onwards. At 6714 yards, par 71, it is long enough and testing enough to have staged many significant championships—it is a regular qualifying venue for the Open Championship and in 1972 hosted the Curtis Cup.

The sequence between the 4th and 7th at Western Gailes is considered one of the finest in golf, and it certainly reveals the course's great variety. The 4th is a medium length two-shotter with a raised and superbly angled Redan style green. The 5th is a big par four that features a minefield of pot bunkers and a fairly narrow entrance to the green—not surprisingly it is the Stroke Index One hole. The 6th is a really characterful par five, its fairway twisting and tumbling towards a green mischievously hidden behind tall dunes. And then comes a famous and much photographed par three. The 7th tee is raised and overlooks the sea From there you play down to a bulb-shaped green backed by dunes and fiercely defended by an assortment of grassy swales and pot bunkers—some revetted and some with wooden sleepered faces. Yes, shades of Turnberry, Troon and Prestwick all in one hole!

Western Gailes Golf Club, Gailes, By Irvine, Ayrshire KA11 5AE	
Secretary	Mr Andrew McBean (01294) 311649 Fax (01294) 312312
Green Fees Restrictions	WD £52/round; £84/day No visitors Thurs, Sat or Sun. Ring to book tee times.
Directions	
The club is on the west coast between Troon and Irvine, two minutes south of Irvine on the A78 Irvine-Greenock road.	

Machrihanish

The chief purpose of *Following the Fairways* is to guide the golfer around the counties of Great Britain and Ireland seeking out the finest golfing challenges (and some of the most welcoming 19th hole establishments). Let us imagine, for once, that we are only allowed to play 18 holes but that we may assemble these 18 from any course in Great Britain and Ireland—a dream round if you like.

If there is any romance in our souls we will conclude this round on the 18th green of the Mahony's Point Course at Killarney, no doubt lining up a twenty footer for a two in the lengthening shadows of the encircling pines, and with the gentle lapping of Lough Leane in the background. And if we are bold we will step on to the 18th tee after tackling the Road Hole 17th at St Andrews. But what do we choose for our opening hole? Well, if we are both romantic and bold we will select the 1st at Machrihanish. Let us hope that we have picked a mild day and that any wind is at our backs.

Machrihanish—the very name borders on the mystical—was founded in 1876 (although it was in fact originally named the Kintyre Golf Club). Situated on the south western tip of the Mull of Kintyre, it is perhaps the most geographically remote of all the great courses in the British Isles.

If the situation is exhilarating and invigorating in itself, the golf course will in no way disappoint—certainly for the lover of traditional links golf, Machrihanish has everything. The layout has altered quite a bit since the late 19th century when it was designed by 'Old' Tom Morris, but the natural character of the course remains. Not only are the fairways among the most naturally undulating in the British Isles, but the greens are some of the most amazingly contoured—awkward stances and blind shots are very much a feature

of Machrihanish.

There is nothing blind about the 1st hole—from the tee the challenge ahead is very visible. It is a long par four of 423 yards and the only way of ensuring that the green can be reached in two shots is by hitting a full-blooded drive across the waters of Machrihanish Bay. From the back tees a 200 yard carry is called for. 'Intimidating' is the description: 'Death or Glory' is the result.

After the 1st the rest must be easy? Not a chance! If the opening hole tests the drive, several of the following holes will test the approach shot, particularly perhaps the 2nd, 7th and 14th. Machrihanish has its own 'Postage Stamp' hole, the 4th—just 123 yards—and there are successive short holes at the 15th and 16th. The course starts to wind down at the 17th and pars here are frequently followed by birdies at the 18th and, of course, considerable celebration at the 19th.

The Machrihanish Golf Club, Machrihanish, by Campbeltown, Argyll PA28 6PT	
Secretary Professional	Mrs Anderson (01586) 810213 Ken Campbell (01586) 810277
Green Fees	WD £23/round; £32/day WE £38
Restrictions	Book starting times with the Professional.
Directions	
The course is on the south-west tip of the Mull of Kintyre. Fly from Glasgow with Loganair, or take a three-hour drive using the A82/A83.	

Key

To avoid disappointment
it is advisable to telephone
in advance

***Visitors welcome at most times
**Visitors usually allowed on
weekdays only
*Visitors not normally permitted
(Mon, Wed) No visitors
on specified days

Approximate Green Fees
A   £40 plus
B   £25 to £40
C   £20 to £30
D   £15 to £25
E   under £15
F   Green fees on application

Restrictions
G Guests only
H—Handicap certificate required
H—(24) Handicap of 24 or less
L —Letter of introduction required
M—Visitor must be a member of
another recognised club

Airdrie G.C.
(01236) 762195
Rochsoles, Airdrie
(18) 6004 yards/**/D/L

Alexandra Park G.C.
(0141) 556 1294
Sannox Gardens, Glasgow
(9) 4016 yards/***/E

Annanhill G.C.
(01563) 521512
Irvine Road, Kilmarnock
(18) 6270 yards/***(Sat)/E

Ardeer G.C.
(01294) 464542
Greenhead, Stevenston
(18) 6630 yards/***(Sat)/D

Auchenharvie G.C.
(01292) 603103
Moor Park Road, Saltcoats
(9) 2456 yards/***/D

Ayr Seafield G.C.
(01292) 441258
Belleisle Park, Doonfoot Road
(18) 5498 yards/***/D/H

Ballochmyle G.C.
(01290) 550469
Ballochmyle, Mauchline
(18) 5952 yards/**/D

Balmore G.C.
(0141) 332 0392
Golf Course Road, Balmore
(18) 5516 yards/***/F

Barshaw G.C.
(0141)889 2908
Glasgow Road, Paisley
(18) 5073 yards/***/E

Bearsden G.C.
(0141) 942 2351
Thorn Road, Bearsden, Glasgow
(9) 6014 yards/***/E

Beith G.C.
(01505) 503166
Threepwood Road, Beith
(18) 5600 yards/***/C

Belleisle G.C.
(01292) 441258
Doonfoot Road, Ayr
(18) 6477 yards/***/C/H

Bellshill G.C.
(01698) 745124
Motherwell Road, Orbiston
(18) 5900 yards/***/C

Biggar G.C.
(01899) 220319
Broughton Road, Biggar
(18) 5229 yards/***/E

Bishopbriggs G.C.
(0141) 762 4883
Brackanbrae Road, Glasgow
(18) 6041 yards/*/F/H/L

Blairbeth G.C.
(0141) 634 3355
Burnside, Rutherglen, Glasgow
(18) 5518 yards/***/C

Blairmore & Strone G.C.
(01369) 840676
High Road, Strone, by Dunoon
(9) 2112 yards/***/E

Bonnyton G.C.
(01355) 302781
Eaglesham, Glasgow
(18) 6255 yards/**/B

Bothwell Castle G.C.
(01698) 852052
Blantyre Road, Bothwell
(18) 6243 yards/**/B/H

Brodick G.C.
(01770) 302349
Brodick, Isle of Arran
(18) 4404 yards/***/D

Brunston Castle G.C.
(01465) 811471
Dailly, Girvan
(18) 6858 yards/***/B

Buchanan Castle G.C.
(01360) 660307
Drymen, Glasgow
(18) 6086 yards/**/B

Bute G.C.
(01700) 83648
Kingarth, Bute
(9) 2497 yards/***(Sat pm)/E

Calderbraes G.C.
(01698) 813425
Roundknowe Road, Uddingston
(9) 5046 yards/*/D

Caldwell G.C.
(01505) 850329
Uplawmoor, Renfrewshire
(18) 6228 yards/**/B

Cambuslang G.C.
(0141) 641 3130
Westburn Drive, Cambuslang
(9) 6072 yards/*/G/F/L

Campsie G.C.
(01360) 310244
Crow Road, Lennoxtown
(18) 5517 yards/***/F

Caprington G.C.
(01563) 521915
Ayr Road, Kilmarnock
(18) 5718 yards/***/E

Cardross G.C.
(01389) 841213
Main Road, Cardross
(18) 6466 yards/**/F

Carluke G.C.
(01555) 771070
Mauldslie Road, Hallcraig
(18) 5805 yards/**/C

Carnwath G.C.
(01555) 840251
Main Street, Carnwath
(18) 5955 yards/**/C

Carradale G.C.
(01583) 431643
Carradale, Campbeltown, Argyll
(9) 2387 yards/***/E

Cathcart Castle G.C.
(0141) 638 9449
Mearns Road, Clarkston
(18) 5832 yards/*/F/H/L

Cathkin Braes G.C.
(0141) 634 4007
Cathkin Road, Rutherglen, Glasgow
(18) 6266 yards/**/C/H/L

Cawder G.C.
(0141) 772 7101
Cadder Road, Bishopbriggs
(18) 6295 yards/**/B/H
(18) 5877 yards/**/B/H

Clober G.C.
(0141) 955 0382
Craigton Road, Milngavie
(18) 4763 yards/*/E

Clydebank Municipal G.C.
(01389) 873289
Glasgow Road, Hardgate
(18) 5612 yards/**/D/H

Clydebank Overtoun G.C.
(0141) 952 8698
Overtoun Road, Dalmur
(18) 5033 yards/***/E

Coatbridge G.C.
(01236) 421492
Townhead Road, Coatbridge
(18) 6026 yards/***/E

Cochrane Castle G.C.
(01505) 320146
Scott Avenue, Craigston
(18) 6226 yards/**/B/H

Colonsay G.C.
(01951) 200316
Scalasaig, Isle of Colonsay
(18) 4775 yards/***/E

Colville Park G.C.
(01698) 265378
Jerviston Estate, Motherwell
(18) 6265 yards/*/G/C

Corrie G.C.
(01770) 810223
Sannox, Isle of Arran
(9) 1948 yards/***/E

Cowal G.C.
(01369) 702216
Ardenslate Road, Kirn, Dunoon
(18) 6251 yards/**/C

Cowglen G.C.
(0141) 632 0556
Barrhead Road, Glasgow
(18) 6098 yards/***/C-D

Craignure G.C.
(01680) 812370
Scallastle, Isle of Mull
(9) 5072 yards/***/E

Crow Wood G.C.
(0141) 779 2011
Garnkirk Estate, Muirhead
(18) 6261 yards/**/C

Cumbernauld G.C.
(01236() 734969
Palacerigg Country Park
(18) 6412 yards/***/E

Dalmally G.C.
(01838) 200370
Orchy Bank, Dalmally
(9) 4514 yards/*/E

Deaconsbank G.C.
(0141) 638 7044
Stewarton Road, Eastwood
(18) 4800 yards/**/F

Dalmilling G.C.
(01292) 263893
Westwood Avenue, Ayr
(18) 5752 yards/*/E

Doon Valley G.C.
(01292) 531607
Hillside, Patna
(9) 5654 yards/***/E

Dougalston G.C.
(0141) 956 5750
Strathblane Road, Milngavie
(18) 5946 yards/**/D

Douglas Park G.C.
(0141) 942 2220
Hillfoot, Bearsden
(18) 5957 yards/*

Douglas Water G.C.
(01555) 880361
Ayr Road, Rigside, Lanark
(9) 2947 yards/**/E

Drumpellier G.C.
(01236) 472 4139
Drumpellier Avenue, Coatbridge
(18) 6227 yards/**/B

Dullatur G.C.
(01236) 723230
Dullatur, Glasgow
(18) 6195 yards/**/F

Dumbarton G.C.
(01389) 732830
Broadmeadows, Dumbarton
(18) 6017 yards/**/D

Dunavert G.C.
(01586) 830677
Southend, Campbeltown, Argyll
(18) 4799 yards/***/E

Easter Moffat G.C.
(01236) 842289
Mansion House, Plains
(18) 6221 yards/**/C

East Kilbride G.C.
(013552) 47728
Chapelside, Nerston
(18) 6419 yards/***/C-B/H

East Renfrewshire G.C.
(01355) 500206
Loganswell, Pilmuir
(18)6100 yards/*/F

Eastwood G.C.
(01355) 500280
Muirshield, Loganswell
(18) 5844 yards/**/B

Elderslie G.C.
(01505) 322835
Main Road, Elderslie
(18) 6175 yards/**/C/H

Erskine G.C.
(01505) 862302
Bishopston, Renfrewshire
(18) 6298 yards/**/B

Ferenze G.C.
(0141) 880 7058
Ferenze Avenue, Barrhead
(18) 5962 yards/**/C/G

Gigha G.C.
(01583) 506287
Isle of Gigha, Kintyre
(9) 5042 yards/***/E

Girvan G.C.
(01465) 714346
Girvan
(18) 5095 yards/***/D

Glasgow (Gailes) G.C.
(01294) 311347
Gailes, by Irvine
(18) 6510 yards/***/A

Glasgow (Killermont) G.C.
(0141) 942 1713
Killermont, Bearsden
(18) 5968 yards/***/A

Gleddoch G.& C.C.
(01475) 540704
Langbank, Renfrewshire
(18) 6375 yards/***/A

Glencruitten G.C.
(01631) 562868
Glencruitten Road, Oban
(18) 4250 yards/***/D

Gourock G.C.
(01475) 631001
Cowal View, Gourock
(18) 6494 yards/**/C/H

Greenock G.C.
(01475) 720793
Forsyth Street, Greenock
(18) 5838 yards/***(Sat)/F/L

Haggs Castle G.C.
(0141) 427 3355
Dumbreck Road, Glasgow
(18) 6464 yards/*/B-A

Hamilton G.C.
(01698) 282324
Riccarton, Firniegair, Hamilton
(18) 6264 yards/*/F/G

Hayston G.C.
(0141) 775 0882
Campsie Road, Kirkintilloch
(18) 6042 yards/**/B

Helensburgh G.C.
(01436) 674173
East Abercromby Street, Helensburgh
(18) 5773 yards/**/C

Hilton Park G.C.
(0141) 956 5125
Auldmarroch Estate, Milngavie
(18) 6707 yards/**/B
(18) 5374 yards/**/B

Hollandbush G.C.
(01555) 893646
Acretophead, Lesmahagow
(18) 5791 yards/***/D

Innellan G.C.
(01369) 830242
Knockmillie Road, Innellan
(9) 2343 yards/***/E

Inveraray G.C.
(01499) 302508
Dalmally Road, Inverary
(9) 5600 yards/***/E

Irvine G.C.
(01294) 275979
Bogside, Irvine
(18) 6408 yards/**/B/H

Irvine Ravenspark G.C.
(01294) 276467
Kidsneuk, Irvine
(18) 6429 yards/***/D

Kilbirnie Place G.C.
(01505) 683398
Largs Road, Kilbirnie
(18) 5517 yards/**A-C

Kilmacolm G.C.
(01505) 872139
Portafield Road, Kilmacolm
(18) 5964 yards/**/B/G/H

Kilmarnock (Barassie) G.C.
(01292) 313920
Hillhouse Road, Barassie,Troon
(18) 6473 yards/*(Wed)/A

Kilsyth Lennox G.C.
(01236) 824115
Tak-Ma-Doon Road, Kilsyth,
Glasgow
(9) 5944 yards/***(W/E am)/E/H

Kingarth G.C.
(01700) 831648
Kilchattan Bay, Isle of Bute
(9) 2497 yards/**/E

Kings Park G.C.
(0141) 630 1597
Carmunock Road, Glasgow
(9) 4142 yards/***/E

Kirkhill G.C.
(0141) 641 7972
Greenless Road, Cambuslang
(18) 5862 yards/***/F

Kirkintilloch G.C.
(0141) 775 2387
Campsie Road, Kirkintilloch
(18) 5269 yards/*/G/D/H/L

Knightswood G.C.
(0141) 959 6358
Lincoln Avenue, Knightswood
(9) 5726 yards/***/E

Kyles of Bute G.C.
(01700) 811601
Tighnabruaich, Argyll
(9) 4778 yards/***(Sun am)/F

Lamlash G.C.
(01770) 600296
Lamlash, Brodick, Isle of Arran
(18) 4640 yards/***/D

Lanark G.C.
(01555) 663219
Whitelees Road, Lanark
(18) 6423 yards/**/B

Langlands G.C.
(013552) 24685
Auldhouse Road, East Kilbride
(18) 6202 yards/***/C

Largs G.C.
(01475) 673594
Irvine Road, Largs
(18) 6220 yards/**/F/H

Larkhall G.C.
(01698) 881113
Burnhead Road, Larkhall
(9) 6700 yards/***/F

Leadhills G.C.
(01659) 74222
Leadhills, Biggar
(9) 4354 yards/***/E

Lenzie G.C.
(0141) 776 1535
Crosshill Road, Lenzie
(18) 5982 yards/**/C/H

Lethamhill G.C.
(0141) 770 6220
Cumbernauld Road, Millerston
(18) 5836 yards/***/E

Linn Park G.C.
(0141) 637 5871
Simshill Road, Glasgow
(18) 5005 yards/***/E

Littlehill G.C.
(0141) 772 1916
Auchinairn Road, Bishopbriggs
(18) 6240 yards/***/E

Lochgilphead G.C.
(01546) 602340
Blarbuie Road, Lochgilphead
(9) 4484 yards/***/E

Loch Lomond G.C.
(01436) 860223
Luss, Alexandria
(18) 7053 yards/*/G

Lochranza G.C.
(01770) 830273
Lochranza, Isle of Arran
(9) 5454 yards/***/E

Lochwinnoch G.C.
(01505) 842153
Burnfoot Road, Lochwinnoch
(18) 6243 yards/**/B/H

Loudoun G.C.
(01563) 820551
Galston, Ayrshire
(18) 5600 yards/**/F

Machrie G.C.
(01496) 302310
Machrie Hotel, Port Ellen, Isle of Islay
(18) 6226 yards/***/B/H

Machrie Bay G.C.
(01770) 850232
Machrie, Isle of Arran
(9) 2143 yards/***/E

Machrihanish G.C.
(01586) 810213
Machrihanish, Campbeltown
(18) 6228 yards/***/C/H

Maybole G.C.
(01292) 612000
Memorial Park, Ayrshire
(9) 2635 yards/***/E

Millport G.C.
(01475) 530306
Millport, Isle of Cumbrae
(18) 5828 yards/***/D

Milngavie G.C.
(0141) 956 1619
Laighpark, Milngavie, Glasgow
(18) 5818 yards/*/G/F

Mount Ellen G.C.
(01236) 872277
Johnston Road, Gartcosh
(18) 5526 yards/**/D/G

Muirkirk G.C.
(01290) 661257
Furnace Road, Muirkirk
(9) 5380 yards/***/E

New Cumnock G.C.
(01290) 423659
Lochmill, New Cumnock
(9) 5176 yards/***/E

Old Ranfurly G.C.
(01505) 613612
Ranfurly Place, Bridge of Weir
(18) 6089 yards/**/F/L/H

Paisley G.C.
(0141) 884 3903
Braehead, Paisley
(18) 6466 yards/*/B/H/L

Palacerigg G.C.
(01236) 734969
Country Park, Cumbernauld
(18) 6444 yards/***/E

Pollok G.C.
(0141) 632 4351
Barrhead Road, Glasgow
(18) 6257 yards/**/B/H/L

Port Bannatyne G.C.
(01700) 502009
Mains Road, Port Bannatyne, Bute
(13) 4730 yards/***/E

Port Glasgow G.C.
(01475) 704181
Devol Road, Port Glasgow
(18) 5592 yards/**/D

Prestwick G.C.
(01292) 477404
Links Road, Prestwick
(18) 6544 yards/**/A/L

Prestwick St Cuthbert G.C.
(01292) 477101
East Road, Prestwick
(18) 6470 yards/**/C

Prestwick St Nicholas G.C.
(01292) 477608
Grangemuir Road, Prestwick
(18) 5952 yards/**/B/H

Ralston G.C.
(0141) 882 1349
Strathmore Avenue, Ralston
(18) 6100 yards/*/G/F

Ranfurly Castle G.C.
(01505) 612609
Golf Road, Bridge of Weir
(18) 6284 yards/**/B/L/H

Renfrew G.C.
(0141) 886 6692
Inchinnan Road, Renfrew
(18) 6818 yards/**/G/F/H/L

Rothesay G.C.
(01700) 502244
Canada Hill, Rothesay, Bute
(18) 5370 yards/***/D/H

Rouken Glen G.C.
(0141) 620 0826
Stewarton Road, Glasgow
(18) 4800 yards/***/E

Routenburn G.C.
(01475) 673230
Greenock Road, Largs, Ayrshire
(18) 5650 yards/**/E/H

Royal Troon G.C.
(01292) 311555
Craigend Road, Troon
(18) 7097 yards/**/A/H/L
(18) 6386 yards/**/B/H/L

Ruchill G.C.
(0141) 946 8793
Brassey Street, Glasgow
(9) 4434 yards/***/E

Sandyhills G.C.
(0141) 778 1179
Sandyhills Road, Glasgow
(18) 6253 yards/***/D/H

Shiskine G.C.
(01770) 860226
Blackwaterfoot, Isle of Arran
(12) 2990 yards/***/D

Shotts G.C.
(01501) 820431
Blairhead, Shotts
(18) 6205 yards/**/C

Skelmorlie G.C.
(01475) 520152
Skelmorlie, Ayrshire
(13) 5056 yards/***(Sat)/C

Strathaven G.C.
(01357) 520421
Overton Avenue, Glasgow Road
(18) 6226 yards/**/B

Strathclyde Park G.C.
(01698) 429350
Motehill, Hamilton
(9) 3147 yards/***/E

Tarbert G.C.
(01880) 820565
Kilberry Road, Tarbert
(9) 4460 yards/***/E

Tobermory G.C.
(01688) 302020
Tobermory, Isle of Mull
(9) 4890 yards/***/E

Torrance House G.C.
(013352) 48638
Strathaven Road, East Kilbride
(18) 6437 yards/***/C

Troon Municipal G.C.
(01292) 312464
Harling Drive, Troon
(18) 6785 yards/***/C
(18) 6501 yards/***/C
(18) 4822 yards/***/C

Turnberry Hotel G.C.
(01655) 331000
Turnberry, Ayrshire
(18) 6976 yards/***/A/H
(18) 6014 yards/***/A/H

Vale of Leven G.C.
(01389) 752351
Northfield Road, Alexandria
(18) 5167 yards/**/D/H

Vaul G.C.
(01879) 2203399
Scarinish, Isle of Tiree
(9) 2911 yards/***/E

Westerwood Hotel & G.C.
(01236) 457171
St Andrews Drive, Cumbernauld
(18) 6601 yards/***/B

Western Gailes G.C.
(01294) 311649
Gailes, by Irvine
(18) 6639 yards/**/A/H

West Kilbride G.C.
(01294) 823911
Fullerton Drive, Seamill
(18) 6542 yards/**/A/L/H

Whinhill G.C.
(01475) 721064
Beith Road, Greenock
(18) 5504 yards/***/E

Whitecraigs G.C.
(0141) 639 4530
Ayr Road, Newton Mearns
(18) 6230 yards/**/B/H

Whiting Bay G.C.
(01770) 700487
Whiting Bay, Arran
(18)4405 yards/***/E/H

Williamwood G.C.
(0141) 637 1783
Clarkston Road, Netherlee
(18) 5878 yards/*/C/G

Windyhill G.C.
(0141) 942 2349
Bal Jaffray Road, Bearsden
(18) 6254 yards/**/B

Wishaw G.C.
(01698) 372869
Cleland Road, Wishaw
(18) 6051 yards/***/C

Old Troon Sporting Antiques

In the field of sporting antiquities, Old Troon Sporting Antiques is one of the best respected and most experienced companies in the world, with a portfolio of regular clients, both private and institutional, in every corner of the globe.

The company has been trading for over ten years and its principal, Bob Pringle, has been involved in collecting golf memorabilia for a number of decades. Throughout his career Bob has followed a philosphy of buying—and dealing in—quality rather than quantity. Today he is known as a leading authority in the sale of golf's most important artifacts.

All areas of golf collectables are covered, and these include golf clubs, golf balls, original paintings—both in oil and watercolour—original prints, mezzotints and lithographs, porcelain, silver and gold objects, early golf games, books, ephemera and everything else connected with golf. Everone has favourites and Bob is no exception, specialising in original paintings, golf clubs and balls. There is no one place in the world today that has a larger stock of original golf art, clubs and balls for sale than Old Troon Sporting Antiques.

As an adjunct to the Art side, Bob Pringle handles the work of internationally renowned watercolour artist, Kenneth Reed FRSA, world-wide. Commissions are sought for his work from private individuals and private golf clubs to the highest governing bodies of the game, The Royal and Ancient Golf Club of St. Andrews and the United States Golf Association of America.

The company has exhibited at the Asia Golf International in Singapore, at the Japan Golf Exhibition in Tokyo and each year at The Open in Great Britain, the premier tournament in golf.

Golf antiques appear in the most unlikely places and Old Troon Sporting Antiques is forever on the lookout for quality items. If you have any quality items relating to golf in any way then you are invited to get in touch with Bob Pringle by writing to the address below.

Old Troon Sporting Antiques
49 Ayr Street, Troon, Ayrshire
Scotland KA10 6EB
Tel. (01292) 311822
Fax. (01292) 313111

Artist: **Linda Hartough** **ROYAL TROON** *Courtesy of:* **Old Troon Sporting Antiques**

Artist: **Cecil Aldin THE 5TH & 13TH GREENS** *Courtesy of:* **Burlington Gallery**

Fife Choice Golf

Many years ago, watching an England versus Scotland soccer game at Wembley, I remember being amused by one of the banners carried by a group of Scottish supporters which boldly declared, 'Remember Bannockburn'. Being a pigheaded Englishman I thought to myself, they ought to remember it—it was just about the only battle they won in centuries. Of course, all is now abundantly clear—the Scots were far too busy priming their golfing skills to bother themselves fighting the Sassenachs.

As long ago as 1457 the Scottish Parliament, unimpressed by the performance of its sharpshooters, felt that too much golf and football were to blame for the lack-lustre performances on the battlefields. An act was passed stating that because of their interference with the practice of archery, the 'fute-ball and golf be utterly cryit down and nocht usit'. History would seem to suggest that the Scots didn't take a blind bit of notice, and golf steadily grew in popularity. Juggle the figures that make up 1457 and we have 1754, perhaps the most significant date in golf's history—the year the Society of St Andrews golfers drew up its written rules of golf.

Today **St Andrews**, deep in the Kingdom of Fife, is the place every golfer in the world wants to visit. Even if you have only swung a club at the local municipal you'll be itching to do the same at St Andrews. However, for those contemplating a pilgrimage to the centre of the golfing world it should be said that St Andrews has several near neighbours that warrant the most discerning attention. Between Dunfermline, to the west of Fife, and St Andrews lie what are undoubtedly some of the finest courses in Scotland.

Travelling Around the Coast

For six hundred years Dunfermline was the country's capital and the body of its most famous king, Robert the Bruce, lies buried in Dunfermline Abbey (minus his heart, apparently, which is in Melrose Abbey). The town has two courses, **Dunfermline** and **Pitreavie**. Both are parkland courses at which visitors are welcome provided some prior arrangement is made. Neither is unduly hard on the pocket. For those wishing to spend a day or two in the old royal town, the appropriately named King Malcolm Thistle Hotel (01383) 722611 provides convenient comfort. Alternatively, the Keavil House (01383) 736258 at Crossford has excellent accommodation and good food.

East of Dunfermline there is a testing links at **Burntisland** with fine views over the Firth of Forth and there are again two courses in Kirkcaldy, the **Dunnikier Park** and **Kirkcaldy** golf clubs, (and make sure you pronounce it Ker-coddy!) Dunnikier Park is a public course. One other good golf club to note in the area is **Aberdour**. A peaceful night's sleep can be found at the Long Boat Inn (01592) 890625 in Kinghorn and good fare is abundantly available at the Old Rectory Inn (01592) 651211 in Dysart. In Burntisland, Kingswood (01592) 872329 is most convenient. Beyond Kirkcaldy, out along a glorious stretch of spectacular coast are Fife's famous five—**Leven Links, Lundin Links, Elie, Balcomie** and of course **St Andrews**. The first two are often considered as a pair, probably on account of there being very little land in between (an old stone wall serves as the boundary). Two proud clubs share the 6433 yards links at Leven, the Leven Golfing Society and Leven Thistle, however, the visitor is always made to feel welcome—as indeed he or she is at the more hilly Lundin—an excellent course, which although very much a links has an abundance of trees on the back nine.

Elie, or the Golf House Club, lies a short distance from the two across Largo Bay, the A917 linking the town with Leven. Elie is famed for its unique periscope by the first tee and for the fact that it was here that James Braid fashioned many of the skills that won him five Open Championships. A charming and very natural links—you won't see trees anywhere here—and not too demanding in length, several of the holes are laid out right alongside a rocky shoreline. A ballot system operates at Elie during the summer but otherwise there are no general restrictions on times visitors can play.

Following the aforementioned A917 eastwards from Elie, the town of Crail is soon reached. Just beyond the town at Fifeness is the magnificent Balcomie links, home of the two hundred year old **Crail Golfing Society**. Together with St Andrews it is featured a few pages on. Incidentally, when visiting St Andrews, or if just passing by, try to visit the **British Golf Museum** (01334) 478880—right next to the 1st tee on the **Old Course** it provides a memorable insight into the glorious game.

The Old Manor Country House Hotel
Lundin Links, Near St Andrews,
Fife KY8 6AJ
Tel: (01333) 320368 Fax: (01333) 320911
Freephone: (0800) 9802420

Play St Andrews and the Championship courses of Fife.

Free golf booking service for guests and special rates for individuals and societies.

The Old Manor overlooks Largo Bay and Lundin Golf Course in the picturesque seaside village of Lundin Links, near St Andrews.

Delightful accommodation in 24 superior rooms, fine dining in the Aithernie restaurant or interesting food and real ale in the unique Coachman's Bistro can all be found at The Old Manor.

In addition to the numerous hotels in St Andrews, there is plenty of accommodation near to the other great links courses of Fife and it is generally inexpensive. A great number are geared almost solely towards the interests of the golfing community and are situated within pitching distance of the nearest fairway. Here are a few thoughts. In Lundin Links, the Old Manor Hotel (01333) 320368 is highly thought of with a particularly good restaurant while less grand accommodation can be enjoyed at the Lundin Links Hotel (01333) 320207, an especially popular retreat for golfers. The Golf Hotel (01333) 330209 in Elie is self explanatory and extremely popular. On a fine day, before the season reaches its height, Elie is a particularly charming place to be. Just a short distance away in Anstruther, is the popular Craws Nest Hotel (01333) 310691—located midway between Elie and Crail it's an excellent base. In Anstruther one might also visit the Smugglers Inn (01333) 310506, a cosy 300 year old tavern. The Cellar (01333) 310378 is a really pleasant restaurant specialising in seafood. Crail is a delightful fishing village and here the Golf Hotel (01333) 450206 is another obvious choice. It's a place of great character and is one of Scotland's oldest licensed inns. Still in Crail, the Caiplie Guest House (01333) 450564 is good value and the Balcomie Links Hotel (01333) 450237 is very convenient as its name suggests. Two other restaurants that can be strongly recommended for the area are found a little inland, namely, Ostlers Close (01334) 655574 at Cupar and the exceptional Peat Inn (01334) 840206 on the road to Cupar. For people who consider themselves golfing gourmets, this establishment should be very high on their list. A number of pleasant bedrooms complete the picture. Further north, at the interestingly named Wormit, you will find Sandford House (01382) 541802, a country house hotel which comes highly recommended.

It isn't an overstatement to say that **St Andrews** is the centre of the golfing world. As early as 1691 it was described as the 'Metropolis of Golfing'. With pilgrims today making the trip from all corners of the globe the number of hotels and guesthouses is understandably considerable. The St Andrews Old Course Hotel (01334) 474371, sumptuously refurbished, is unquestionably one of Scotland's leading hotels and, overlooking the most famous hole in golf, the Road Hole 17th on the Old Course, couldn't be better positioned. More aesthetically pleasing than prior to its restoration, it now oozes class both within and without. The hotel's own golf course, the highly acclaimed Peter Thomson-designed **Duke's Course** is featured on a later page. Rufflets Hotel (01334) 472594 just outside the town is also an excellent base with award-winning gardens while another room with a view can be booked at the Rusacks Hotel (01334) 474321, formerly the Golf Inn, which oozes golfing history (the restaurant is also good and rather appropriately named the Niblick). The other hotels which might just hint at a round of the good old game include the St Andrews Golf Hotel (01334) 472611 and the Scores Hotel (01334) 472451—both are good value and pleasant.

There is also any number of comfortable guesthouses and B&Bs in town; noteworthy examples include the Albany (01334) 477737, Arran House (01334) 474724 and the Amberside (01334) 474644. One final thought for hungry souls is the popular Grange Inn (01334) 472670 in nearby Grange Village—an excellent eating place. While golf clearly takes centre stage one should not forget the pleasant coastline nearby (scenes from Chariots of Fire were filmed on St Andrews' vast sands), nor the 12th century cathedral and Scotland's oldest university.

Inland Golf

Just as the leading courses of Surrey aren't all heathland and gorse, neither are those of Fife all seaviews and sandhills. **Ladybank** is actually only a few miles north of Leven but is completely different in character with heathland fairways and much pine and heather—a very beautiful course and well worth a visit. North of Ladybank lies **Cupar,** one of the oldest 9 hole golf courses in Scotland and a clubhouse that has to be approached through a cemetery (slightly older even

than the golf course!)

In an area steeped in history, **Glenrothes** is a relative newcomer to the scene. Young, perhaps, but an excellent course nonetheless. Situated to the west of the town it is a fairly hilly parkland type, offering many superb views. A friendly welcome awaits but the names of two of the holes worry me a little—the 11th, titled 'Satan's Gateway' and the 18th 'Hells End'!

A restful 19th is clearly in order and fortunately in Glenrothes quality places abound. The Balgeddie House (01592) 742511 is secluded and most relaxing, while the charming Rescobie Hotel (01592) 742143 at Leslie and the Rothes Arms (01592) 753701 should also placate the soul. Letham is only a short distance from Ladybank and here Fernie Castle (01337) 810381 is recommended. Equally convenient and comfortable is the Lomond Hills Hotel at Freuchie (01337) 857329. Not to be forgotten either is the classical mansion Balbirnie House (01592) 610066 at Markinch, a luxury hotel set in over 400 acres of landscaped woodland and situated adjacent to **Balbirnie Park** Golf Club. The restaurant here is also first class.

Two other courses that are well worth visiting if journeying inland in Fife are at **Thornton,** where the River Ore makes for some challenging holes, and at **Lochgelly**—convenient if travelling between Dunfermline and Kirkcaldy. The final mention though goes to **Scotscraig,** an Open Championship qualifying course at Tayport. Although close to the sea it is actually a downland type course rather than a true links, but is an admirable test of golf. Following that testing game at Scotscraig one is likely to be left with a difficult decision: to the north, Carnoustie and many other great challenges await—but then no golfer who has experienced the pleasures of the Kingdom of Fife ever left easily.

"Tee it high and let it fly"
at the 'Golf International' 1998 Hotel of the Year

Balbirnie House is a privately owned country house hotel situated by Markinch, equidistant from Edinburgh and St Andrews in the heart of the ancient kingdom of Fife. Under the personal supervision of the Russell family, this wonderful Georgian mansion, recognised as one of Scotland's finest Grade 'A' listed houses, maintains the warmth and friendliness of its old days combined with the needs of today's house guests. The emphasis is on personal service. Once a home to few Balbirnie is now a home from home to many. Awards include the coveted 4AA Red Star rating and top Scottish Tourist Board rating of 5 Crowns Deluxe as well as the Macallan Taste of Scotland Hotel of the Year. Balbirnie offers a quite outstanding dining experience with dishes which are sometimes classical and at other inventive with a light modern Scottish approach. The house itself is the centrepiece of a 416 acre park which is landscaped in the style of Capability Brown. The estate includes specimen trees and one of the most important rhododendron collections in Scotland.

Views from the house extend over fine lawns, trimmed yew hedges and interesting flowering borders to the golf course beyond. For the golf enthusiast the hotel is ideally situated just a short chip from the first tee of Balbirnie Park

golf course, a challenging and beautifully landscaped 18 hole 6210 yard par 71 parkland course. Locally, the championship courses of Leven Links, Lundin Links and Ladybank offer the opportunity to sample Scottish golf at its very best. The Mecca of St Andrews (5 courses) is only half an hour by car and possibly the hardest test of all, Carnoustie, is 45 minutes away. All-in-all there are over a hundred golf courses within one hour of Balbirnie, many being well renowned, and justly so.

Within the perimeter of the park itself extensive recreational and leisure pursuits are available. Doorstep golf, horse riding (horses can be brought to the front door ready to ride around the three mile bridle path within the park), jogging and woodland walking. The park is home to an abundance of wildlife. A charming craft centre is located close to the hotel and incorporates a leather workshop, a goldsmith and jewellers and a pottery.

Balbirnie has many special arrangements for sporting pursuits with local operators near the park, all with high quality facilities, and the hotel is happy to tailor a package to the individual's requirements and budget.

Balbirnie House
Balbirnie Park, Markinch
Fife KY7 6NE
Tel: (01592) 610066 Fax: (01592) 610529
E mail: balbirnie@btinternet.com
Web site: http://www.balbirnie.co.uk

St Andrews

If there is such a thing as a truly global sport then it has to be golf. From parochial beginnings on the east coast of Scotland it is now played on every continent, in every conceivable corner. Not only are there golf courses on the exotic islands of Tahiti and Bali but there is one in the Himalayas and there is one in the Arctic. Golf has even been played on the Moon. For all this there remains but one home—St Andrews.

Whilst we will never be able to put an exact date on the time golf was first played on the famous links, several documents refer to a crude form of the game being played as early as the mid 1400s. As for the right to play at St Andrews, which, of course, the whole world enjoys, the origins are confirmed in a licence dated 1552 drawn up by the Archbishop of St Andrews. It permitted the Archbishop to breed rabbits on the links and confirmed the right of the citizens of St Andrews to 'play at golf, futeball, schueting, at all gamis with all uther, as ever they pleis and in ony time'. Furthermore the proprietor was bound 'not to plough up any part of the said golf links in all time coming.' Organised golf came to St Andrews in 1754 when twenty two Noblemen and Gentlemen formed the St Andrews Society of Golfers. In 1834 the Society became the Royal and Ancient Golf Club.

Not only can all the world play at St Andrews, but all the world wants to and arranging a game on the **Old Course** can be a little difficult. The St Andrews Links Trust handles all matters relating to times of play and they should be contacted well in advance. The summer months are naturally the busiest period and it is best to write to the Trust twelve months prior to intended play, offering if possible a number of alternative dates. The address to write to is **The St Andrews Links Trust, Pilmour Cottage, St Andrews, Fife, KY16 9SF.** The **General Manager, Mr Alan McGregor** and his staff can be contacted by telephone on **(01334) 466666**, by fax on (01334) 477036 and via the Internet. The handicap limits to play on the Old Course are 28 for men and 36 for ladies, and a handicap certificate or letter of introduction is required. It should also be noted that there is no Sunday golf on the Old Course. In 1998 the green fee for a round in summer is priced at £72.

In addition to the Old Course there are four other eighteen hole links at St Andrews: the **New Course**, which dates from 1895, the **Jubilee** (1897)—recently lengthened and improved by Donald Steel—the **Eden** (1914) and the new **Strathtyrum Course.** No handicap certificate is required to play over any of the above four courses and the green fees for 1998 on each are £31 £29, £21 and £16 respectively. A nine hole course, the Balgove, is also available (at a modest green fee of £7 for 18 holes), together with a driving range and extensive practice facilities.

St Andrews is situated 57 miles north east of Edinburgh. For northbound travellers the most direct route to take is the M90 after crossing the Forth Road Bridge. The A91 should be joined at junction 8. This road can be followed to St Andrews. Southbound travellers should head for Perth which is linked in turn to Dundee by the A85 and to the north of Scotland by the A9. From Perth a combination of the A90 and the A913 takes one to Cupar where the A91 can be picked up.

It was nature that fashioned St Andrews and over the centuries the Old Course has seen little change. Its myriad tiny pot bunkers remain both a fascination and a frustration—providing just enough room, as Bernard Darwin put it, 'for an angry man and his niblick'. Laid out on a narrow strip of land ranging from 50 to 100 yards in width, St Andrews is famed for its enormous double greens. There are seven in all and some are more than an acre in size. With little definition between the fairways there tends to be no standard way of playing a particular hole and as a rule the wind direction will determine the preferred line. Individual holes are not likely to be easily remembered the first time of playing, especially as one will probably be walking the course in a semi-trance. History is everywhere, and on the first hole as you cross the bridge over the Swilcan Burn a voice from somewhere says, 'they've all walked this bridge'—and of course they have, just as they've all passed through the Elysian Fields, tackled Hell Bunker, the Beardies and the Principal's Nose. And then of course they've all faced the Road Hole with its desperate drive and even more desperate approach and then finally strolled over the great expanse of the 18th fairway towards the Valley of Sin with the famous R & A clubhouse beyond.

Hole	Yards	Par	Hole	Yards	Par
1	370	4	10	380	4
2	411	4	11	172	3
3	399	4	12	316	4
4	463	4	13	429	4
5	564	5	14	567	5
6	416	4	15	459	4
7	372	4	16	426	4
8	178	3	17	461	4
9	356	4	18	354	4
Out	**3,529**	**36**	**In**	**3,547**	**36**
			Out	**3,529**	**36**
			Totals	**7,076**	**72**

The Duke's Course (St Andrews)

No hotel in the world enjoys a better golfing situation than the five star Old Course Hotel at St Andrews. With views over much of the historic links, it literally overlooks the 17th fairway of the Old Course, the most famous—and most infamous—hole in golf.

Guests of the sumptuous hotel have no special playing privileges on the Old Course—a round cannot be guaranteed. This fact was the major spur behind the hotel owner's decision to construct a new 18 hole championship course within St Andrews. Good links land simply wasn't available so the new course had to be built on an inland site. A few traditionalists were aghast at the notion, although the quality of the end-product has converted all but the diehards. Moreover, perhaps two things should be immediately emphasised. Firstly, the Duke's Course, as it is called, is not the exclusive preserve of hotel residents—it is open to the golfing public—and secondly, sound choices were made with regard to selection of both site and architect.

The Duke's Course was built over a 330 acre site at Craigtoun, just two miles (or a five minute drive) from the Old Course Hotel. It occupies high ground with commanding views over the town of St Andrews, the Eden Estuary and north along the coast to Arbroath and Carnoustie. A mixture of undulating farmland and parkland prior to construction, it included many mature trees, notably silver birch and larch, plus a fair smattering of sentinel pines.

Most traditionalists were persuaded of the wisdom of creating the new course as soon as it was announced that Peter Thomson had been appointed as course architect. A five-time winner of the Open, including the 1955 Championship at St Andrews, the Australian's reputation as a leading course designer has been built around his appreciation of traditional—even classical—principles of golf architecture. To these values he adds a very distinctive personal style and plenty of imagination. Work on the new course began in 1993 and the Duke's was officially opened during the 1995 St Andrews Open.

The design of the Duke's Course encapsulates its architect's philosophies. According to Thomson, 'golf is a game of strategy. It should be played on the ground not in the air. . . the challenge is getting the ball to the green not merely landing on it'. Notwithstanding the nature of the terrain, there is a genuine links feel to many of the holes. Subtle contours have been incorporated into the fairway landing areas and around many of the greens, several of which are plateaued. Pitch and run shots are also encouraged.

The bunkering is particularly impressive. Many are of a links pot-bunker style, not just around the greens but also on the edges, and occasionally in the centre of the fairway! In this respect, and with its isolated stands of trees and burns affecting four of the holes, the Duke's Course resembles Carnoustie. For strategic as well as visual enhancement, gorse, broom and heather have been introduced to the site with the result that on the higher parts of the course there is a distinct heathland-cum-moorland flavour to the holes—a hint of Ganton perhaps?

The round commences with two strong holes. The 1st is a meandering par five and at the 2nd you drive over a marshy area then play an approach to a narrow bunkerless green. Next comes a scenic short hole—the 3rd—enclosed by birch woods with a plateaued green defended by a burn and a deep central bunker. The 4th and 5th are two of the best par fours on the Duke's Course. The wide fairway of the 6th is a welcoming sight whilst a cluster of traps await you to the right of the 7th fairway and two very large bunkers protect the entrance to the green on the formidable par three 8th. You return to the clubhouse by way of a curving fairway and a demanding second to a cleverly angled green.

The second nine also begins with a strong hole. The 10th sweeps dramatically downhill from the tee; then dog-legs to the left and is crossed by a burn as it climbs towards the green. The 11th is a huge par five and is followed by a tough par three where the green is perched on a plateau. The 13th charges downhill and features some impressive fairway bunkering. Now comes one of the best and most strategic two-shotters of the round. The drive on the 14th is to a fairway bisected (vertically and diagonally) by a burn. The brave drive is to the right half of the fairway and it sets up a much easier second.. The par five 15th looks a birdie opportunity on the card but the approach is severely uphill and the green is guarded by no fewer than eight bunkers. The 16th green is also fiercely defended and the round concludes with an attractive par three and a testing uphill par four with a big, two-tiered stage-like green.

Green fees to play the Duke's in 1998 were £40 per round for hotel residents. Non residents pay £50 per round Mondays to Fridays and £55 per round at weekends. The **Golf Professional** is **John Kelly**. He and his staff can be contacted on **(01334) 474371** and by fax on (01334) 477668.

Hole	Yards	Par	Hole	Yards	Par
1	517	5	10	429	4
2	488	4	11	610	5
3	156	3	12	212	3
4	439	4	13	397	4
5	375	4	14	472	4
6	565	5	15	533	5
7	467	4	16	429	4
8	212	3	17	191	3
9	415	4	18	404	4
Out	**3594**	**36**	**In**	**3677**	**36**
			Out	**3594**	**36**
			Totals	**7271**	**72**

Crail Golfing Society

On 23rd February 1986 the seventh oldest golf club in the world celebrated its bicentenary. Some three years before the Bastille was stormed a group of eleven gentlemen met at the Golf Inn in Crail and together formed the Crail Golfing Society. The records of that historic day are still preserved; indeed remarkably the Society possesses a complete set of minutes from the date of its inception. In those early days the Society members wore scarlet jackets with yellow buttons and dined at the Golf Inn after a day on the links. The local punch flowed and a good time was doubtless had by all—now those were the days!

Since 1895 the club has played over the Balcomie Links which is located approximately two miles north east of Crail at Fifeness. Earlier the Society had used a narrow strip of land at Sauchope, slightly closer to Crail (and of course to the Golf Inn).

The atmosphere is still jovial and visitors are made most welcome. With the exception of a few competition days there are no general restrictions on times of play. However, individual visitors are advised to telephone the **Professional, Graeme Lennie** the day before playing. He can be contacted on **(01333) 450278** or **(01333) 450960**. Societies, or golfing parties, are equally welcome and advance bookings can be made at all times apart from during the peak summer period. Written enquiries should be addressed to **The Manager, Crail Golfing Society, Balcomie Clubhouse, Crail, Fife KY10 3XN**. The Manager, **Jim Horsfield**, can be reached by telephone on **(01333) 450686** and by fax on (01333) 450416.

The green fees for 1998 are pitched at £20 per round, £30 per day during weekdays or £25 per round and £38 per day at weekends. Juniors can play for £9.50 during the week and £12 at weekends but only if accompanied by a full fee paying adult—otherwise the adult fee is applicable.

The Balcomie Links is ideal for 'holiday golf'. Without being overly long (5922 yards, par 69)—though the wind can affect distances greatly—it offers some exceptionally spectacular scenery and, similar to Cruden Bay further north, a nearby castle casts a watchful eye. Balcomie Castle, where Mary of Guise, mother-to-be of Mary Queen of Scots, spent her first few days in Scotland, comes complete with ghost.

The course is always well maintained and the greens especially have acquired an enviable reputation. The holes have been laid out so that each provides a view of the sea. There is an unusual balance to the round with the front nine containing six par fours and the back nine only three; as for the par threes, the second nine boasts four short holes including the 18th. There are some rather interesting names too: 'Fluke Dub' (4th) 'Hell's Hole' (5th) and 'Lang Whang' (11th). The aforementioned 'Hell's Hole' really lives up to its name. You stand on the tee of the fearsome 5th at Crail and decide whether to 'go for it' or not—ie whether to go for a brave carry over rocks, sea and sand or to play safe.

The temptation for many on crossing the Forth Road Bridge is of course to head straight for the Royal and Ancient. Although St Andrews may be the undisputed sovereign in the so-called Kingdom of Fife, there are also a number of handsome princes. Balcomie stands comparison with the best and is a course of which the two hundred year old society can justifiably be proud.

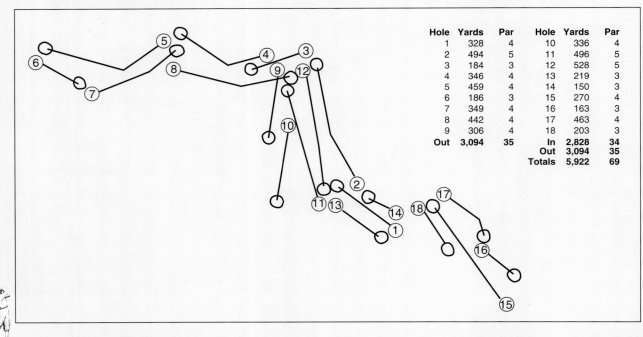

Hole	Yards	Par	Hole	Yards	Par
1	328	4	10	336	4
2	494	5	11	496	5
3	184	3	12	528	5
4	346	4	13	219	3
5	459	4	14	150	3
6	186	3	15	270	4
7	349	4	16	163	3
8	442	4	17	463	4
9	306	4	18	203	3
Out	**3,094**	**35**	**In**	**2,828**	**34**
			Out	**3,094**	**35**
			Totals	**5,922**	**69**

Aberdour G.C.
(01383) 860080
Seaside Place, Aberdour
(18) 5460 yards/***(Sat)/C

Anstruther G.C.
(01333) 310956
Shore Road, Anstruther
(9) 4537 yards/***/D

Auchterderran G.C.
(01592) 721579
Woodend Road, Cardenden
(9) 2525 yards/***/D

Balbirnie Park G.C.
(01592) 752006
Markinch, Glenrothes
(18) 6210 yards/***/B-A

Ballingry G.C.
(01592) 860086
Crosshill, Lochgelly
(9) 6482 yards/***/E

Burntisland Golf House Club
(01592) 873247
Dodhead, Burntisland
(18) 5908 yards/***/C-B

Canmore G.C.
(01383) 724969
Venturefair Avenue, Dunfermline
(18) 5474 yards/***/C

Cowdenbeath G.C.
(01383) 511918
Cowdenbeath
(9) 6552 yards/***/E

Crail G.S.
(01333) 450686
Fifeness, Crail
(18) 5720 yards/***/C-B

Cupar G.C.
(01334) 653549
Hilltarvit, Cupar
(9) 5300 yards/***/D

Dunfermline G.C.
(01383) 723534
Pitfirrane, Crossford, Dunfermline
(18) 6244 yards/**/B

Dunnikier Park G.C.
(01592) 261599
Dunnikier Way, Kirkcaldy
(18) 6601 yards/***/D

Earlsferry Thistle G.C.
(01333) 330301
Golf Club House, Elie, Leven
(18) 6261 yards/**/B-A
(9) 2277 yards/**/B-A

Elie Golf House Club
(01333) 330301
Elie, Leven
(18) 6261 yards/**/B-A
(9) 2277 yards/**/B-A

Falkland G.C.
(01337) 857404
The Myre, Falkland
(9) 2622 yards/***/F

Glenrothes G.C.
(01592) 758686
Golf Course Road, Glenrothes
(18) 6444 yards/***/D

Kinghorn G.C.
(01592) 890345
McDuff Crescent, Kinghorn
(18) 5629 yards/***/E

Kirkcaldy G.C.
(01592) 260370
Balwearie Road, Kirkcaldy
(18) 6004 yards/***(Sat)/C

Ladybank G.C.
(01337) 830814
Annesmuir, Ladybank
(18) 6641 yards/***/B

Leslie G.C.
(01592) 620040
Balsillie, Leslie
(9) 4940 yards/***/E

Leven Links G.C.
(01333) 421390
The Promenade, Leven
(18) 6434 yards/***/B

Lochgelly G.C.
(01592) 780174
Cartmore Road, Lochgelly
(18) 5491 yards/***/D

Lundin Links
(01333) 320202
Golf Road, Lundin Links
(18) 6377 yards/**(Sun)/C/H

Lundin Ladies
(01333) 320832
Woodie Lea Road, Lundin Links
(9) 4730 yards/***/F

Methil G.C.
(01333) 425535
Links Road, Leven
(18) 6434 yards/***/C

Pitreavie (Dunfermline) G.C.
(01383) 722591
Queensferry Road, Dunfermline
(18) 6032 yards/***/C

St Andrews (01334) 475757
(18) 7076 yards/**(Sun)/A/H/L(Old)
(18) 6604 yards/***/F(New)
(18) 5094 yards/***/F(Strathtyrum)
(18) 6805 yards/***/F(Jubilee)
(18) 6112 yards/***/F(Eden)
(9) 1520 yards/***/F(Balgove)
(18) 7271 yards/***/A(Dukes)

St Michaels G.C.
(01334) 839365
Leuchars, St Andrews
(9) 5510 yards/***(Sun am)/D

Saline G.C.
(01383) 852591
Kinneddar Hill, Saline
(9) 5302 yards/***(Sat)/E

Scoonie G.C.
(01333) 427057
North Links, Leven
(18) 5500 yards/***/F

Scotscraig G.C.
(01382) 552515
Golf Road, Tayport
(18) 6496 yards/**/B/M

Thornton G.C.
(01592) 771111
Station Road, Thornton Village
(18) 6177 yards/***/C-B

Tulliallan G.C.
(01259) 730396
Alloa Road, Tullliallan, Kincardine
(18) 5982 yards/**/F

Artist: **Paul Gribble** **THE DRIVE OFF** *Courtesy of:* **Rosenstiels**

Artist: **Arthur Weaver GLENEAGLES** *Courtesy of:* **Burlington Gallery**

Inland Gems

If, as the song says, the streams of the mountains please you more than the sea then it is to the likes of **Gleneagles**, **Pitlochry** and **Murrayshall** you will head. If you are one of the diehards who think there is but one form of golf then you will probably set course for **Carnoustie**, **Monifieth** and **Montrose**. Then again, if it is felt that variety is the spice of golf a choice combination of the two can be devised. The heart of Scotland has much to offer of everything.

While there is an inevitable temptation to head for the 'bigger clubs', the Gleneagles and the Carnousties, the region boasts a staggering number of smaller clubs where golf can be equally enjoyable. **Taymouth Castle** and **Callander** are perhaps two of Scotland's lesser known courses, at least to many south of the border, yet they are two of the most scenic courses one is likely to find anywhere. At Callander in early spring the deer come down from the Perthshire hills to forage, a glorious sight, while the course at Taymouth Castle is situated in a conservation area surrounded by beautiful woods.

For golfers travelling northwards, before Gleneagles is reached some excellent golf is to be found at **Falkirk Tryst**, **Glenbervie** (Larbert), **Braehead** and **Alloa**, while over to the west of the Central region and somewhat isolated is picturesque **Buchanan Castle**. The town of **Stirling** is known as the 'Gateway to the Highlands' and Stirling's golf course has a beautiful setting beneath the Ochil Hills and in the shadow of Stirling Castle.

The world renowned **Gleneagles Hotel** (01764) 662231 near Auchterarder is a superb base, not only to secure a game on one or more of its own magnificent courses (see feature) but also for exploring the many fine golf courses nearby. However, there is certainly no shortage of very good alternatives for a night's stay. Three miles away the Auchterarder House Hotel (01764) 663646 is excellent and is set amid beautiful gardens. Duchally House (01764) 663071 also has great charm. In Cleish, Nivingston House (01577) 850216 is a small, very pleasant family-run hotel—ideal for the M90 (exit 5), while at Dunblane set in its own 3000 acre estate is the celebrated Cromlix House

(01786) 822125 (note especially the marvellous restaurant). Stirling, with its splendid castle offers the Park Lodge (01786) 474862, Fintry the outstanding Culcreuch Castle (01360) 860228, Callander the Roman Camp Hotel (01877) 330003 with its first rate accommodation and restaurant, and Drymen the Buchanan Arms (01360) 860588 a former coaching inn, now modernised with a leisure centre.

After Gleneagles, **Blairgowrie** is probably the best known inland course and it too is featured on a later page. However, the golfer should undoubtedly pay a visit to the 'fair city of Perth'. The **King James VI** Golf Club on Moncrieffe Island is steeped in history while nearby at Scone—former crowning place of kings—is the **Murrayshall** Country House Hotel and its attractive golf course (see ahead). A round here is strongly recommended and the hotel (01738) 551171 offers some of Scotland's best accommodation and cuisine. To the south of Perth at Glenfarg lies the welcoming Glenfarg Hotel and Restaurant (01577) 830241, a true golfing haven set in beautiful surroundings and ideal for St Andrews, Gleneagles and Carnoustie. Visitors tackling Blairgowrie have a choice of two excellent hotels. Dupplin Castle (01738) 623224 is a magnificent country house well situated for all the area's attractions and Altamount House Hotel (01250) 873512 provides stunning Scottish cuisine in a delightful atmosphere.

Those wishing to stay in Blairgowrie itself should consider the **Rosemount** Golf Hotel (01250) 872604 or the Moorfield House Hotel (01828) 627303. Another really first class hotel is Kinloch House (01250) 884237, a delightful example of a Scottish country house.

A little distance to the west of Perth there is more fine golf at **Crieff** where there are 27 holes (note the Crieff Hydro (01764) 655555 and a very pretty 9 hole course even further west at **St Fillans** where the Four Seasons (0176485) 333 is a charming place to stay. To the north of our region and tucked away amid some breathtaking scenery **Dalmunzie House** (01250) 885224 should not be forgotten; situated at Spittal O'Glenshee, the hotel has its own spectacular 9 hole golf course where drives are said to travel further in the rarified atmosphere! The

Artist: **Graeme W Baxter** **THE GLENEAGLES HOTEL, MONARCH'S COURSE** *Courtesy of:* **Baxter Prints**

Ardeonaig Hotel (01567) 820400 near Killin combines splendid views with comfortable accommodation, and in this respect Kinnaird (01796) 482440 can also never be too highly praised. This is a superb hotel where fishermen as well as golfers will be content.

Returning to Blairgowrie, if a game cannot be arranged on either of the club's outstanding courses, then the heathland course at **Alyth** is very close and certainly won't disappoint. The Lands Of Loyal (01828) 633151 is a comfortable hotel close to the course and the nearby Losset Inn (01828) 632393 is more modest but equally accommodating. Drumnacree House (01828) 632194 is another winner—excellent food and good value accommodation. Perth's delights as mentioned are at hand to the south, while to the west is **Taymouth Castle** and to the north along the A9 stands **Pitlochry**. The latter is another course many will choose to play, for this is one of the most attractive in Britain—a veritable 'theatre in the hills'. Green fees at all these courses are relatively inexpensive and certainly very good value. Still further north the scenic 9 holer at **Blair Atholl** is also worth a visit. In Strathtay, near Pitlochry a recommended 19th hole is the Grantully Hotel (01887) 840207, while Westlands of Pitlochry (01796) 472266 is another to offer good quality and value.

More ideas for a relaxing stay include the Kenmore Hotel (01887) 830205 in Kenmore, ideal for Taymouth Castle. Scotland's oldest inn is the Killiecrankie Hotel (01796) 473220 in Killiecrankie (north of Pitlochry). Other ideas include the sporty Ballathie House (01250) 883268 at Kinclaven by Stanley, and the Log Cabin (01250) 881288 at Kirkmichael. Indeed, the list is almost endless, such is the popularity of this magnificent area.

Closer to the Coast

Some of Scotland's greatest links courses are to be found between Dundee and Montrose on the Tayside coast. However, just to the north west of Dundee lies **Downfield** one of the country's finest inland courses. Indeed, five times Open Champion Peter Thomson rates this heavily wooded parkland course as one of the best inland courses in the world. It is said that Downfield is very popular with American visitors because it reminds them of some of their better courses 'back home'.

East of Dundee, the Medal Course at **Monifieth** has staged the Scottish Amateur Championship, while **Panmure** at Barry has in the past hosted the Seniors' Championship. Both are classic links courses and fairly inexpensive to play over. **Carnoustie** is, of course, one of Scotland's greatest golfing shrines and along with Montrose, Gleneagles, Letham Grange, Murrayshall and Blairgowrie is featured ahead. **Montrose,** like Monifieth, is a public links (two courses at each in fact) and when the winds blow can be extremely difficult. As earlier noted, green fees along this great coastal stretch are relatively cheap and provided some forward planning is done a game is possible at most times.

A brief word on staying in the area. In Carnoustie, the Glencoe Hotel (01241) 853273 is very convenient, as are the Park Hotel (01674) 763415 and Links Hotel (01674) 671000 in Montrose which both offer golfing packages. Perhaps the pick of the many hotels in Dundee is the Angus Thistle Hotel (01382) 226874. The Castleton House (01307) 840340 by Glamis is another establishment few will find fault with, and for those seeking excellent value, the Kingsley Guesthouse (01241) 873933 in Arbroath provides exactly that. Moorfield House (01828) 627303 in Cupar Angus is also well worth trying. Back in Carnoustie, one restaurant worth trying is 11 Park Avenue (01241) 853336.

Finally, two inland courses to the north east of Tayside which strongly merit attention are **Edzell** and **Letham Grange**. The former, just north of Brechin, and in a charming village is a beautiful heathland course where some marvellous mountain views can be enjoyed. The Glenesk Hotel (01356) 648319 is but a par four away. Letham Grange is a hotel and country club (01241) 890373 and is situated at Colliston near Arbroath. The hotel is a splendidly restored Victorian mansion with 36 holes of golf now on offer, is well worth a visit.

Artist: **Graeme W Baxter THE GLENEAGLES HOTEL, KINGS COURSE** *Courtesy of:* **Baxter Prints**

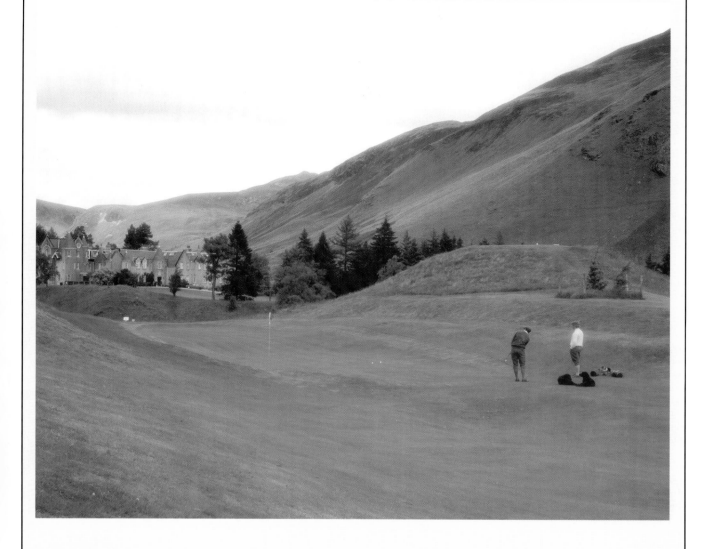

Dalmunzie House enjoys a glorious position in the mountains of the Scottish Highlands. The hotel stands in its own 6000 acre mountain estate. It is owned and run by the Winton family who have been in the glen for a number of decades and have many years of experience looking after guests. Taste of Scotland cooking with one AA rosette, attention to detail and unobtrusive service ensure a comfortable stay at all times.

The house itself is cosy, the atmosphere is homely and the welcome both genuine and warm, the emphasis being on friendliness rather than pomp and splendour.

All of the bedrooms have en suite facilities, are of individual character and all are centrally heated.

Their charming decor and restful tranquillity reflect the ambience found elsewhere at Dalmunzie.

Many activities can be pursued here. The hotel has its own private golf course, and in addition there is a tennis court and games room for the family complete with bar billiard table. River and loch fishing as well as shooting and stalking can all be easily arranged. Some of Scotland's finest mountains surround the hotel and for cross country and alpine skiers the Glenshee Ski Centre is only a few minutes drive away.

Dalmunzie House Hotel
Spittal O' Glenshee
Blairgowrie
Perthshire
Scotland PH10 7QG
Tel : (01250) 885224
Fax: (01250) 885225

The Roman Camp Hotel sits on the north bank of the River Tieth amongst 20 acres of mature and secluded gardens which nestle by the picturesque village of Callander, the gateway to the Trossachs and the Highlands of Scotland.

The house was originally built as a hunting lodge for the Dukes of Perth in 1625 and was given its name from the conspicuous earth mounds, believed to be the site of a Roman fort, which are visible across the meadow to the east of the walled garden.

The building has grown over many years as each consecutive family has added their own embellishments to this lovely home. The most obvious of these are the towers, one of which contains a tiny chapel.

Today, under the guidance of Eric and Marion Brown, the traditional country house atmosphere still evokes its alluring charm. As you enter, you will notice the abundance of freshly cut flowers, their scent lingering in the air, and be greeted by great log fires.

The library and drawing room are of grand proportions with an atmosphere of warmth and relaxation and are places to enjoy and reflect on the day's sport, especially after dinner in the company of friends and a fine malt. The tapestry-hung dining room is crowned by a richly painted 16th century style ceiling. Here, dinner is served at candlelit tables, laid with fine silver and crystal, while you choose from menus of local game and fish, prepared by the chef and accompanied by vegetables and herbs from the hotel's gardens.

Each of the bedrooms has its own distinctive style and character and is equipped with all the little thoughtful extras to make your stay as comfortable as possible.

At the Roman Camp country house you are within easy reach of many championship and picturesque golf courses and the hotel can arrange tee times at the local course, just two minutes walk from the hotel.

A stretch of river three quarters of a mile long runs through the gardens, enabling guests to fish for wild brown trout and salmon on the private beat at no extra charge. There is also the opportunity for the hotel to arrange fishing on the many lochs and other private beats surrounding Callander.

The Roman Camp is the perfect country house hotel to make your favourite country retreat.

The Roman Camp
Callander
FK17 8BG
Tel: (01877) 330003
Fax: (01877) 331533

Gleneagles

There is a vast oil painting that hangs in the Tate Gallery in London; the artist is John Martin and the painting is titled 'The Plains Of Heaven'. Some may know it well, others will wonder what on earth I'm gibbering on about—suffice to say that it depicts in the most vivid colours imaginable the artist's impression of Paradise. I suspect that John Martin wasn't a golfer. Blasphemy isn't intended but for many of us who stalk the fairways of the world, Gleneagles is just about our best idea of how heaven might look—give or take a couple of angels.

The Gleneagles Hotel and its golf courses are set in the heart of some of the most glorious Perthshire countryside. Surrounded by the foothills of the Grampian Mountain range, everywhere one turns there is a shock of colour. The mountains themselves often appear wrapped in purples and blues. Heather, silver birch and rowan cover the crisp moorland turf. With so much around one could be forgiven for losing a little concentration, yet the golf too is glorious and for those wishing to enjoy their golf in leisurely five star surroundings there really is nothing quite like Gleneagles.

The land was first surveyed with a view to designing one or more golf courses before the first World War and James Braid was called in to direct affairs. By 1919 the **King's** and **Queen's** courses were both open for play. Braid's work met with instant acclaim and in 1921 the forerunner of the Ryder Cup was staged at Gleneagles, when a team of British professionals played a team from America.

Until quite recently The Gleneagles Hotel maintained four 18 hole golf courses, the Prince's and Glendevon courses being opened in 1974 and 1980 respectively. Subject to making a booking through the Golf Office all were open to the general public. Golf became so popular at Gleneagles that at times it came close to resembling a fairways version of Piccadilly Circus and since 1st January 1990 golf at Gleneagles has been restricted to hotel residents, Gleneagles members and their guests.

The Prince's and Glendevon courses no longer exist either—but for a very good reason: in May 1993 a Jack Nicklaus-designed championship course opened for play. It is Nicklaus' first course in Scotland and, like his first ventures in England (St Mellion) and Ireland (Mount Juliet), it has generated an enormous amount of interest. Laid out on land previously utilised by the Prince's and

Glendevon courses, plus adjacent acquired land, the **Monarch's** Course measures in excess of 7000 yards from the championship tees.

Things are certainly happening apace at Gleneagles and a sparkling new clubhouse has also been constructed. Its architectural style is in keeping with the Edwardian hotel. In 1998 the green fee for hotel residents is £80 per round (on any of the three courses). **Greg Schofield,** the Gleneagles' golf **Professional** can be reached on **(01764) 662231.** or by fax on (01764) 694383.

Located approximately midway between Perth and Stirling and half a mile west of Auchterarder, Gleneagles is easily reached by road. The A9, which in fact links Perth to Stirling is likely to prove of most assistance. Travelling from the Glasgow region a combination of the A80 and the M80 should be taken to Stirling. Those approaching from further south can avoid Glasgow by following the A74 and the M74/M73 joining the A80 below Stirling. Motoring from Edinburgh the best route is to cross the Forth Road Bridge via the A90 heading for Dunfermline and thereafter taking the A823 road to Auchterarder. Southbound travellers will find the A9 helpful if coming from the Highlands via Blair Atholl and Pitlochry, while from the north east of Scotland, the A92 links Aberdeen to Dundee and Dundee is in turn linked to Perth by the A85. The Gleneagles Hotel can also be reached by rail, with a bus meeting trains from Gleneagles station.

Measuring 6471 yards, par 70, the King's course is some 500 yards longer that the Queen's at 5965 yards, par 68. Perhaps the best known hole at Gleneagles is Braid's Brawest, the 13th on the King's Course—a tough par four requiring a long straight drive to carry a ridge and a second to a raised and heavily guarded sloping green. Other fine holes include the highly characterful 3rd, the par three 5th, the cavalier 9th and the extremely picturesque 14th.

Many will have first viewed the glories of Gleneagles through the medium of television. The BBC Pro-Celebrity series was staged on several occasions during the 1970s and in the mid 1980s the European Tour brought the Scottish Open to Gleneagles. It was played over the King's Course for 6 years, before 'moving east' to Carnoustie-and then disappearing altogether . . . Paradise Lost?!

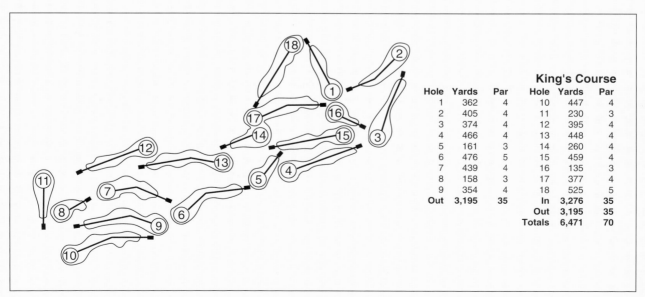

King's Course					
Hole	Yards	Par	Hole	Yards	Par
1	362	4	10	447	4
2	405	4	11	230	3
3	374	4	12	395	4
4	466	4	13	448	4
5	161	3	14	260	4
6	476	5	15	459	4
7	439	4	16	135	3
8	158	3	17	377	4
9	354	4	18	525	5
Out	3,195	35	In	3,276	35
			Out	3,195	35
			Totals	6,471	70

Ideally situated in the heart of Scotland's golfing country and only half an hour's drive from St Andrews—the home of golf—the Glenfarg hotel is the perfect base for a golfing break. An abundance of superb and varied courses lie close at hand—parkland, woodland, heath, links and highland—each offering a different and exciting challenge.

The hotel has a well earned reputation amongst players throughout the UK and further afield, and many return annually to enjoy the comfort, good food and friendly service that is the hallmark of the Glenfarg.

This welcoming hotel is managed by a keen and active golfer and offers a comprehensive golf booking service at nearby courses—apart from St Andrews these include Gleneagles, Carnoustie, Rosemount and Dalmahoy as well as 70 others within 40 minutes drive!

The hotel provides an array of golfing packages ranging from 'Hackers Heaven' breaks to 'Champagne Specials'. Bargain breaks are available from as little as £69 for two nights, including golf.

After a day on the fairways the period candlelit restaurant offers an exciting menu which changes daily. The hotel's award-winning chef uses only the very best of local produce sizzling Scotch steaks, Tay salmon, venison or pheasant or maybe haggis in Drambuie cream . . . delicious!

If you prefer a more informal atmosphere, you can enjoy a glass of real ale and a delicious range of home-cooked bar meals either in the lounge bar or on the picturesque riverside terrace surrounded by the beautiful Perthshire scenery.

The Glenfarg has seventeen bedrooms, all en suite with direct dial telephone and colour TV including satellite channels. In addition to the lounge bar areas, a public bar offers pool, darts and that all-important opportunity to talk to the locals—about the day's game or whatever takes your fancy.

Whether you're a single handicapper or a weekend hacker the Glenfarg Hotel will suit you to a tee . . . For a brochure on tailormade golfing breaks to suit all budgets, telephone, fax or write to Steve Whiting.

The Glenfarg Hotel & Restaurant
Glenfarg Nr Kinross
Perthshire
PH12 9NU
Tel: (01577) 830241
Fax: (01577) 830665

Carnoustie

Walter Hagen—a shrewd judge you might think—once described Carnoustie as the greatest course in the British Isles. There are many who would agree with the great man, though doubtless the disciples of St Andrews and several honourable gentlemen at Muirfield would beg to differ. Greatest or not, very few would dispute that when the winds blow—as they invariably do in these parts—Carnoustie is the toughest of all our championship links.

In the days when the Campbells and the MacDonalds were busy slaughtering each other up in the Highlands, down at Carnoustie more civilised pursuits were taking place. Records suggest that golf was being played on the adjoining Barry Links as early as the 16th century. The first official club at Carnoustie—today there are six—was founded in 1842 and golf was played over a ten hole course laid out by Allan Robertson. Later, 'Old' Tom Morris came on the scene and extended the links to a full 18 holes, but the present championship course didn't really take shape until James Braid made several alterations in 1926. By 1931 Carnoustie was ready to stage its first Open Championship.

As previously mentioned there are presently six clubs at Carnoustie and play is now over three 18 hole courses: the **Championship**, the **Burnside** and the **Buddon**. Administrative matters are in the hands of the Carnoustie Golf Links Management Committee and those wishing to visit Carnoustie should direct correspondence to the committee's **Secretary, Mr E J C Smith**. Their full address is **The Carnoustie Golf Links Management Committee, Links Parade, Carnoustie, Tayside, DD7 7JE**. Contact by telephone can be made on **(01241) 853789** and by fax on (01241) 852720. Handicap certificates are required for the Championship course and starting times must be booked in advance.

In 1998, the green fees to play at Carnoustie are £52 for a single round on the Championship course with £62 securing a round over both the Championship and Burnside courses and £60 for a round over the Championship course and Buddon Links.. Fees to play just the Burnside course (£19 per round or £28.50 per day) or Buddon Links(£15 per round or £22.50 per day) are good value. It is also possible to obtain a three day pass for £156 which allows one round a day over the Championship course and unlimited play on the Burnside or Buddon. Details of these day tickets can be obtained by phoning the above number. Caddies can also be arranged.

The cluster of clubs that go to make up Carnoustie's permanent golfing village provide all the usual amenities for the visiting golfer—golf shops for clothing, equipment and club hire and of course a more than adequate 19th hole. Travelling to Carnoustie shouldn't present too many problems. The Forth Road Bridge and the M90 link the Edinburgh region with Perth. Perth in turn is linked to Dundee by the A85 (dual carriageway all the way) and Dundee to Carnoustie by the A390. Those on golfing tours will quite likely be coming via St Andrews. The A91 (A919) runs from St Andrews towards Dundee. It picks up the A92 just before the Tay Road Bridge and on crossing the bridge the A930 should immediately be joined. Approaching from northerly directions, the A92 runs from Aberdeen (and beyond) to within a couple of miles of Carnoustie at Muirdrum, while the A958 links the town with Forfar. Carnoustie can also be reached by train with connections from Perth, Dundee and Aberdeen.

It isn't only the wind that makes Carnoustie such a difficult test. When the championship tees are in use the course stretches close to 7000 yards. From the club medal tees, 6941 yards is still a formidable proposition. The bunkering at Carnoustie is extremely impressive. A few courses may have more bunkers but nowhere are they quite so cavernous or as consistently well positioned.

Scotland is the land of Burns. It is also the land of burns—streams or creeks anywhere else in the English-speaking world—and Carnoustie is famous for them. The ubiquitous Barry Burn and its wee brother Jockie's Burn traverse the fairways in the most unfriendly of places, often in front of greens and across the spot you'd ideally like to drive to. More than anything else though, Carnoustie is renowned for its incredibly tough finishing stretch. The 16th is an exceptionally long short hole, the 17th has the Barry Burn meandering across its fairway, making it a particularly difficult driving hole and at the 18th the Burn crosses in front of the green, necessitating one of the most exciting (or nerve-racking) closing shots in golf.

Each of the five Opens held at Carnoustie has produced a great champion: Tommy Armour (1931), Henry Cotton (1937), Ben Hogan (1953), Gary Player (1968) and Tom Watson (1975). Many consider Hogan's victory in 1953—he won by four strokes with ever decreasing rounds of 73-71-70-68—to be the greatest ever performance in a major championship. The Open is scheduled to return to Carnoustie in 1999.

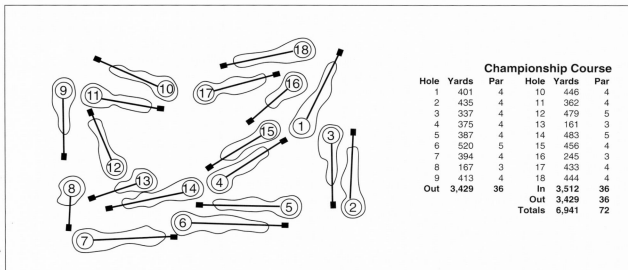

Championship Course

Hole	Yards	Par	Hole	Yards	Par
1	401	4	10	446	4
2	435	4	11	362	4
3	337	4	12	479	5
4	375	4	13	161	3
5	387	4	14	483	5
6	520	5	15	456	4
7	394	4	16	245	3
8	167	3	17	433	4
9	413	4	18	444	4
Out	**3,429**	**36**	**In**	**3,512**	**36**
			Out	**3,429**	**36**
			Totals	**6,941**	**72**

Blairgowrie

With so many outstanding courses to choose from, all within fairly close proximity of one another, even the most blinkered of diehard Englishmen would be forced to concede that Scotland is just about the finest place on earth for a week's golfing holiday. Given seven precious days a large number of would-be travellers on opening their maps of Scotland are likely to plan a trip thus: three days on the west coast playing Prestwick, Turnberry and Troon; a day in the middle visiting Gleneagles, finishing with three on the east coast taking in Carnoustie, St Andrews and Muirfield. Marvellous stuff of course, but many of the golfing sages hold the opinion that such an itinerary misses out the finest gem of all—the Rosemount Course at Blairgowrie.

There are in fact two 18 hole courses at Blairgowrie, the older and more celebrated **Rosemount,** designed by James Braid and the **Lansdowne** Course, a fairly recent addition, the work of Peter Alliss and Dave Thomas. On each, golf is played over beautiful moorland fairways, lined by great forests of pine, larch and silver birch. A liberal sprinkling of purple heather and gorse add considerable colour to an already majestic setting—as one obviously bewitched observer put it, 'somebody seems to have gone mad with a paintbrush!'

Measuring 6588 yards, par 72 from the medal tees (6239 yards, par 70 from the forward tees) the Rosemount Course may not be the toughest challenge one is likely to face but it must rank among the most enchanting. The course and surrounding landscape abound with wildlife, from pheasants and partridge to deer and winter geese, but the golfer who lifts his head too much is likely to suffer over the closing stretch—the 16th, 17th and 18th are all difficult holes, especially the 16th where the golfer must twice confront the infamous Black Loch.

The official course record at Rosemount stands at 64, though in 1973, during a practice round for the Sumrie Better-Ball tournament, professional Lionel Platts achieved an amazing ten consecutive birdies between the 8th and 17th—quite obscene don't you think?! The Lansdowne course is slightly longer than its older brother, and many would say a much sterner test—either way a game on each is strongly recommended.

It need hardly be added that Blairgowrie with its two courses—three if one includes the aptly named Wee Course, a short nine-holer—has a more than adequate 19th. Lunches, high teas, dinners and light snacks are all offered. There are also two bars—comfortable places where many will choose to go and celebrate a magnificent day's golfing in one of the most glorious settings the game has to offer. Planning a week's golf?

Blairgowrie Golf Club, Golf Course Road, Blairgowrie, Perthshire, PH10 6LG

The Starter	(01250) 872594 (tee reservations)
Sec/Manager	J N Simpson (01250) 872622
Professional	Charles Dernie (01250) 873116
Green Fees	WD £50 (£60 per day)
	WE £50 (£75 per day)
Restrictions	Handicaps required

Directions
Two miles south of Blairgowrie off the A93

Letham Grange

There are 'dreamers' and there are 'doers'. Once in every blue moon—thank heavens—the two combine.

Soon after the late Sir Henry Cotton officially opened Letham Grange in 1987, Malcolm Campbell, the then editor of *Golf Monthly* bravely announced, 'We now have the "Augusta of Scotland" '. In a generally critical article a second leading UK golf magazine later lambasted this judgement saying it was, 'a bit like trying to sell blended whisky as a twelve year old malt.' But then we are a nation of 'knockers' aren't we? Of course Letham Grange isn't the equal of Augusta, where the azaleas and dogwoods run riot, but it is a wonderfully enjoyable place to play golf nonetheless and there is at least one parallel in the manner of its creation. Like Augusta, Letham Grange is the result of one man's dream. Down in Georgia the guiding force was a man named Jones; up in Angus it was a man called Smith. Letham Grange was Ken Smith's dream and aside from the quality of the end product I wouldn't be quick to criticise Letham Grange for the very fact that Ken Smith had the guts, vision and determination to do something about his dream.

It is an extraordinary place. Letham Grange is where a typical and, until recently, 'oh so timeless' Scottish country estate confronts a 20th century 'hotel and country club golf' head on. In fact, the Victorian mansion which presides over the heavily wooded and rolling estate had become derelict by the mid 1970s, before the golfing dream was conceived. This same mansion is now one of Scotland's most luxurious 19th hole retreats. Moreover, time no longer stands still at Letham Grange for since 1991 the estate has boasted two 18 hole courses—the slightly revised 1987 layout now being called the **Old Course**(!)

At 5528 yards, par 68, the **New Course** is more than 1000 yards shorter than its older sister (6614 yards, par 73) and there are none of the water hazards that make the Old Course at once potentially treacherous and positively spectacular.

The finest run of holes at Letham Grange occurs between the 2nd and 4th on the Old Course—a stunning sequence and one which has been compared with the celebrated 10th, 11th and 12th at St Mellion. The pick of these is probably the two-shot 4th where the player drives from an elevated tee (usually with an iron), threading it along an ever-narrowing fairway and then fires an approach across the corner of an encroaching lake to a stage-like green. Another superb hole is the par three 9th: here the green is once again the 'wrong side' of water and is set at such an angle that only the very bold, precisely struck tee shot will be rewarded. Not a hole for the nit-picking 'knockers'.

Letham Grange Hotel and Golf Courses, Colliston, by Arbroath, Angus, DD11 4RL

Golf Administrator	David Speed(01241) 890373
	Fax (01241) 890725
Green Fees	Old WD £24; WE £33
	New WD £15; WE £24
	Above prices per round
Restricted	Tuesday, Friday and weekend mornings

Directions
The club is 4 miles north of Arbroath off the A933.

In the heartland of golf lies the superb new Letham Grange Hotel and Golf Courses. The magnificent Victorian mansion nestles within the panoramic Letham Grange Estate.

The mansion has been restored to its former glory as a top quality, four star hotel with 20 bedrooms, offering a style and standard of living which is both traditional and sumptuous. In addition 22 modern bedrooms are available in the Letham Grange Golf Estate accommodation.

36 holes of magnificent golf! Widely acclaimed as one of the premier courses in Scotland, the Old Course provides a blend of tree-lined parkland and open rolling fairways. With water playing a major role, the course is both scenic and dramatic.

The New Course, although slightly shorter—and without the water hazards—offers golfers a more relaxed and less arduous round. However, it can be deceptive!

Letham Grange Hotel
Colliston
by Arbroath
DD11 4RL
Tel: (01241) 890373
Fax: (01241) 890725

Set on a hillside overlooking the Vale of Strathmore to the Sidlaw Hills beyond, lies the Lands of Loyal. This impressive Victorian mansion was built in the 1830s, commissioned by Sir William Ogilvy, who on his return from Waterloo chose Loyal Hill as the site for this magnificent home. The Lands of Loyal was subsequently owned by a succession of families until it was converted into an hotel in 1945.

Since then it has been very prominent in the area, holding fond memories for the oldest generations. It is also highly regarded as a second home to country sportsmen who have remained loyal for many years. More recently extensive refurbishment of the public rooms has further enhanced the unique atmosphere of this much respected country house hotel.

The restaurant is highly acclaimed in its own right, with a style of cuisine that is both traditional and imaginative, making full use of local fish and game. An extensive wine list, is available to complement your meal.

The Lands of Loyal makes an ideal base for the ambitious golfer. Perthshire has 30 golf courses in total with remarkable variety. All courses are within an hour's drive of the hotel with some of the most famous and desirable spots only a few minutes away.

As fundamentally a sportsman's hotel, The Lands of Loyal appreciates the needs of the golfer. Very early breakfasts and unusually flexible dining arrangements, quality packed lunches etc, are offered courteously. Private rooms for parties can be requested in advance.

The hotel management are delighted to arrange a complete itinerary for the golfer, whether an individual or a group. Tee times can be arranged and any correspondence with golf clubs will gladly be undertaken..

The Lands of Loyal provides a complete and competitive golfing package. A full colour brochure and tariff is available on request.

Karl-Peter & Patricia Howell
The Lands of Loyal Hotel
Alyth
Perthshire
Scotland PH11 8JQ
Tel: (01828) 633151
Fax: (01828) 633313

Montrose

Perhaps there are two things that strike you most when you arrive at one of the famous golfing links on the east coast of Scotland:. The first will almost certainly be the thought, 'So this is where it all started'—which can often leave one slightly numb. The second, and equally numbing, is likely to be the thought, 'Will this wretched wind ever die down?' The famous links at Montrose is just such a place.

Golf has been played on Montrose links since the 16th century and according to the best records it is the fifth oldest course in the world. By course is meant the **Medal Course**, for there are two 18 hole links at Montrose, the Medal and the shorter **Broomfield Course**, the former having altered surprisingly little through the ages. One interesting fact is that in the 1800s, at a time when one or two more famous clubs had only 5 holes, the Medal Course at Montrose boasted 25! All of which were played in a unique tournament in 1866 won by a Mr T Doleman from Glasgow who played the 25 holes in 112 strokes. Willie Park, winner of the first Open Championship in 1860, finished second scoring a 115.

In common with St Andrews and Carnoustie, Montrose is a public links and although three golf clubs play over the two courses—the Royal Montrose, Caledonia and Mercantile Clubs—both courses are managed by the Montrose Links Trust who handle all administrative matters.

Apart from their length—the Medal Course measures 6470 yards (par 71) and the Broomfield 4865 yards (par 66)—the two courses differ in other respects. The Broomfield is laid out on the landward side of the Medal and is considerably flatter. With its many subtle—and many not-so-subtle—undulations the Medal is by far the more testing so it is not surprising that major championships are held here. These have included the Scottish Professional Championship, the Scottish Amateur Championship, and the British Boys

Championship and Internationals. This year the course has been selected as a Final Qualifying venue for the 1999 Open.

For twelve of its eighteen holes, the Medal Course follows the line of the dunes, with the 4th and 6th being especially memorable. However, some of the best holes appear at the end of the round—the 16th (Gully) being a particularly long par three and the 17th (Rashes) with its raised green, one of those par fours requiring, as a caddy once put it, three damned good shots to get up in two! For a 19th hole, visitors are more than adequately catered for by the golf clubs, each of which has a clubhouse adjacent to the links.

There are no airs and graces about Montrose—it is what might be described as a good honest links. But if you've come to Scotland to admire the golf, then Montrose is clearly one that shouldn't be missed.

Montrose Links Trust, Traill Drive, Montrose Angus, DD10 8SW	
Sec/Manager	Mrs Margaret Stewart (01674) 672932
Professional	Kevin Stables (01674) 672634
Green Fees	Medal WD £22, WE £30
	Broomfield WD £10 WE £14
	Above prices per round
Restrictions	Medal: No visitors Saturdays before 230 pm or Sundays before 10 am. Handicap certificates required.
	Broomfield: No restrictions.
Directions	
North of Montrose, signposted off the A92.	

Murrayshall

Perth is a legendary place, a city steeped in history and one surrounded by stunning natural beauty. Perthshire the county evokes thoughts of everything Scottish. To North Americans, mention of the very word 'Perthshire' is enough to send them drooling. It is arguably one of the most romantic places in the world and for golfers, whether from the New World or the Old, the contemplation of a game of golf in the heart of Scotland is enough to make us forget a tweaked three footer (well almost).

It is often said that a person's golfing education is incomplete until he or she has swung a club in Scotland. And how can you visit Scotland without visiting Perth, the ancient crowning place of kings? To the south west of Perth, and half an hour's drive away is Gleneagles which, along with St Andrews and Augusta, is surely one of the three best known golfing centres in the world. Almost due north of Perth and again about 30 minutes by road is Blairgowrie and the delights of the Rosemount and Lansdowne courses. A little further, but still no more than an hour, are St Andrews and Carnoustie. Perth cannot be a bad place sitting amidst all this finery! But there is more. Right on the city's doorstep, not four miles from the town centre, is a comparatively modern golfing jewel—the Murrayshall Country House Hotel and Golf Course.

Murrayshall is where the peacocks strut, the pheasants call and the deer run freely in the woods. Designed by J Hamilton Stutt and opened in 1981, the golf course is set in 300 acres of truly rolling parkland The holes weave their way in and out of the copses and alongside ponds. In fact, there is quite a lot of water at Murrayshall—little lakes, ponds and streams—but the golfer is guided over and around them via quaint stone bridges. Some 200,000 tulips adorn the hotel grounds and golf course. Yes, Murrayshall

makes folks drool and perhaps at least smile after that missed three foot putt.

From the back markers, Murrayshall measures 6446 yards, par 73. The forward tees reduce the course to around the 6000 yards mark. It isn't a long course by any means but is both attractive and challenging and certainly full of interest. Many of the fairways are bordered by magnificent oaks, copper beeches and chestnuts—not to mention those marvellous tulips. There are also some wonderful views from the higher parts of the course.

Notable holes include the 3rd, one of those par four and a half holes; the short 4th, where if you mishit you will land in the pond; the severely dog-legged 7th—so severe that it is known as the 'dog's grave'—and most people's favourite, the short par four 10th where the approach is played over water to a raised green.

Murrayshall Country House Hotel and Golf Course, Murrayshall, Scone, Perthshire, PH2 7PH	
Golf Manager/	Alan Reid (01738) 552784
	Fax (01738) 552595
Professional	Book through the Golf Manager
Green Fees	WD £22/round, £30/day
	WE £27/round, £45/day
	Reduced rates for hotel residents.
Directions	
Perth is easily reached from all directions, being linked to Edinburgh by the M90, the Highlands by the A9 and Dundee by the A35. Murrayshall is 2 miles out of Perth on the A94 heading towards New Scone.	

The Altamount House Hotel, a Georgian built residence, was built as a private house in 1806. It is beautifully situated in over six acres of grounds with extensive gardens and mature woodlands, yet it is only minutes away from the centre of the delightful Perthshire town of Blairgowrie. Inside, the house is tastefully furnished with elegant panelling, pinewood doors and many original features.

There are several golf courses nearby. The famous Rosemount course is a must for all discerning golfers. But there are many more wonderful courses in the surrounding area, including the new Strathmore Golf Centre at Alyth, which consists of two brand new uncrowded and undiscovered courses.

There are only seven en suite bedrooms, complete with all the facilities normally found in top class hotels. The small number of bedrooms ensures that full attention is paid to the welfare of all guests.

While the golf and the accommodation are unlikely to disappoint even the most discerning and demanding of sportsmen, the cuisine cannot fail to satisfy in the charming refined ambience of the dining room. Great pride is taken in the superb Scottish cuisine with top quality dishes being freshly prepared from the finest local ingredients. Silver cutlery and fine china complement cooking of the highest standard which has earned the hotel many awards and an enviable reputation.

Add to the above a welcoming relaxed atmosphere generated by your hosts Robert and Sally Glashan and you have a recipe for an ideal break. Whatever you desire, this is Scotland at its best.

Altamount House Hotel
Blairgowrie
Perthshire
PH10 6JN
Tel: (01250) 873512
Fax: (01250) 876200

Key

To avoid disappointment
it is advisable to telephone
in advance

***Visitors welcome at most times
**Visitors usually allowed on
weekdays only
*Visitors not normally permitted
(Mon, Wed) No visitors
on specified days

Approximate Green Fees
A   £40 plus
B   £25 to £40
C   £20 to £30
D   £15 to £25
E   under £15
F   Green fees on application

Restrictions
G Guests only
H—Handicap certificate required
H—(24) Handicap of 24 or less
L —Letter of introduction required
M—Visitor must be a member of
another recognised club

Aberfeldy G.C.
(01887) 820535
Taybridge Road, Aberfeldy
(18) 5972 yards/**/D

Aberfoyle G.C.
(01877) 382493
Braeval, Aberfoyle
(18) 5218 yards/***/C

Alloa G.C.
(01259) 722745
Schawpark, Sauchie
(18) 6240 yards/**/D

Alva G.C.
(01259) 760431
Beauclerc Street, Alva
(9) 2423 yards/**/D/H

Alyth G.C.
(01828) 632268
Pitcrocknie, Alyth
(18) 6226 yards/***/F

Arbroath G.C.
(01241) 875837
Elliot, Arbroath, Angus
(18) 6090 yards/**/C

Arbroath Artisans G.C.
(01241) 875872
Elliot. Arbroath
(18) 6185 yards/*/F

Auchterarder G.C.
(01764) 662804
Ochil Road, Auchterarder
(18) 5778 yards/***/C/H

Bishopshire G.C.
(01592) 780203
Kinneswood, Kinross
(10) 4700 metres/***/E

Blair Atholl G.C.
(01796) 481274
Blair Atholl, Perthshire
(9) 5620 yards/***/D

Blairgowrie G.C.
(01250) 872622
Rosemount, Blairgowrie
(18) 6588 yards/***(Wed)/B-A/H
(18) 6895 yards/***(Wed)/B-A/H
(9) 4654 yards/***(Wed)/F/H

Bonnybridge G.C.
(01324) 812822
Larbert Road, Bonnybridge
(9) 6060 yards/***/F

Braehead G.C.
(01259) 725766
Cambus, by Alloa
(18) 6041 yards/***/D/H

Brechin G.C.
(01356) 622383
Trinity, by Brechin, Angus
(18) 6200 yards/***/C-B/H

Bridge of Allan G.C.
(01786) 832332
Sunlaw, Bridge of Allan, Stirling
(9) 4932 yards/***(Sat)/E

Buchanan Castle G.C.
(01360) 660307
Drymen
(18) 6015 yards/***/F

Caird Park G.C.
(01382) 434706
Mains Loan, Dundee
(18) 6303 yards/***/C

Callander G.C.
(01877) 330090
Aveland Road, Callander
(18) 5125 yards/***/C/H

Camperdown G.C.
(01382) 434706
Camperdown Park, Dundee
(18) 6561 yards/***/E

Campsie G.C.
(01360) 310920
Crow Road, Lennoxtown
(18) 5517 yards/**/D

Carnoustie
(01241) 853789
Links Parade, Carnoustie, Angus
(18) 6941 yards/***/A/H
(Championship)
(18) 6020 yards/***/B/H (Burnside)
(18) 5420 yards/***/C/H (Buddon)

Comrie G.C.
(01764) 670055
Cowden Way, Comrie
(9) 4040 yards/***/D

Craigie Hill G.C.
(01738) 622644
Cherrybank, Perth
(18) 5386 yards/**/D

Crieff G.C.
(01764) 652909
Perth Road, Crieff
(18) 6402 yards/***/C
(9) 4772 yards/***/D

Crieff Hydro G.C.
Crieff, Perth
(01764) 651615
(9) 2137 yards/***/D

Dalmunzie Hotel & G.C.
(01250) 885224
Spittal of Glenshee, Blairgowrie
(9) 2035/***/E

Dollar G.C.
(01259) 742400
Brewlands House, Dollar
(18) 5242 yards/***/D

Downfield G.C.
(01382) 825595
Turnberry Avenue, Dundee
(18) 6822 yards/***/C-B/H

Dunblane New G.C.
(01786) 823771
Perth Road, Dunblane
(18) 5957 yards/**/C

Dunkeld and Birnam G.C.
(01350) 727524
Fungarth, Dunkeld
(9) 5240 yards/***/D

Dunning G.C.
(01764) 684747
Rollo Park, Dunning, Perth
(9) 4836 yards/***/D/G

Edzell G.C.
(01356) 647283
High Street, Edzell, by Brechin
(18) 6348 yards/***/F/H

Falkirk G.C.
(01324) 611061
Stirling Road, Cumlins, Falkirk
(18) 6230 yards/***/D

Falkirk Tryst G.C.
(01324) 562415
Burnhead Road, Larbert
(18) 6053 yards/**/C/H

Forfar G.C.
(01307) 462120
Arbroath Road, Forfar, Angus
(18) 6052 yards/***/B-A/H

Foulford G.C.
(01764) 652407
Sma'Glen, Nr Crieff
(9) 916 yards/***/E

Glenalmond G.C.
(01738) 880275
Trinity College, Glenalmond
(9) 5812 yards/*/G

Glenbervie G.C.
(01324) 562605
Stirling Road, Larbert
(18) 6469 yards/**/B-A/L

Gleneagles Hotel & G.C.
(01764) 663543
Auchterarder
(18) 7081 yards/*/A/G
(18) 6471 yards/*/A/G
(18) 5965 yards/*/A/G

Grangemouth Municipal G.C
(01324) 711500
Polmont Hill, Polmont, Falkirk
(18) 6314 yards/***/E

Green Hotel G.C.
(01577) 863407
Beeches Park, Kinross
(18) 6257 yards/***/D
(18) 6456 yards/***/D

Kenmore G.C.
(01887) 830226
Kenmore, Aberfeldy
(9) 6052 yards/***(Thurs pm)/D

Killin G.C.
(01567) 820312
Killin
(9) 5200 yards/***/D

King James VI G.C.
(01738) 445132
Moncreiffe Island, Perth
(18) 5664 yards/**/D

Kirriemuir Players G.C.
(01575) 573317
Kirriemuir, Angus
(18) 5510 yards/**/C/H

Leitie Links G.C.
(01828) 633322
Alyth, Blairgowrie
(9) 1719 yards/***/E

Letham Grange G.C.
(01241) 890373
Letham Grange, Colliston
(18) 6614 yards/**/B
(18) 5528 yards/**/C

Milnathort G.C.
(01577) 864069
South Street, Milnathort
(9) 5969 yards/***/D

Monifieth Links G.C.
(01382) 532767
Dundee, Angus
(18) 6657 yards/***(Sat)/B/H
(18) 5123 yards/***(Sat)/B

Montrose Links Trust
(01674) 672932
Traill Drive, Montrose, Angus
(18) 6470 yards/**/C
(18) 4865 yards/**/E

Muckhart G.C.
(01259) 781423
Drumburn Road, Muckhart, Dollar
(18) 6034 yards/***/C/H

Murrayshall Hotel & G.C.
(01738) 552784
Murrayshall, Scone, Perth
(18) 6446 yards/***/B

Muthill G.C.
(01764) 681523
Peat Road, Muthill, Crieff
(9) 4700 yards/***/D

North Inch G.C.
(01738) 636481
Hay Street, Perth
(18) 5178 yards/***/E

Panmure G.C.
(01241) 855120
Barry, Angus
(18) 6317 yards/***(Sat)/B-A

Pitlochry G.C.
(01796) 472792
Golf Course Road, Pitlochry
(18) 5811 yards/***/C/H

Polmont G.C.
(01324) 711277
Maddiston, by Falkirk
(9) 3033 yards/**/E/H

St Fillans G.C.
(01764) 685312
St Fillans, Perthshire
(9) 5268 yards/***/D

Stirling G.C.
(01786) 473801
Queens Road, Stirling
(18) 6438 yards/**/C/H

Strathtay G.C.
(01350) 727797
Dalguise, Dunkeld
(9)4980 yards/**/E

Taymouth Castle G.C.
(01887) 830228
Kenmore, by Aberfeldy
(18) 6066 yards/***/C/H

Tillicoultry G.C.
(01259) 750124
Alva Road, Tillicoultry
(9) 2528 yards/***/E

Whitemoss G.C.
(01738) 730300
Dunning, Perthshire
(18) 6000/**/D

Artist: **Bill Waugh ROYAL DORNOCH** *Courtesy of:* **Burlington Gallery**

Mist-covered mountains and bottomless lochs, bagpipes, whisky and haggis. I doubt whether there is a more romantic place in the world than the Highlands of Scotland. I doubt also that there is a place quite so shatteringly beautiful. The area extends from the Cairngorms northwards, encompassing the Great Glen and the Western Isles, across the entire north east corner of Scotland. This part of the country was at one time covered by a dense forest of pine broken only by the soaring granite peaks of the Grampian mountain range. This was the home of the savage Caledonian tribe, a land where wolves hunted in packs. Nowadays very little of the forest remains. As for the wolves, most of them were killed by the Caledonians, but then unfortunately most of the Caledonians were killed by the Romans. No wonder they called life 'nasty, brutish and short'!

Aberdeen and Moray

Let us make a start in the north east. Forgetting the wolves, the savages and the Romans, what we need is a good 18 holes—and, of course, a suitable 19th. Aberdeen is a fine place to begin. Balgownie and Murcar lie right on the town's doorstep and are unquestionably two of the finest courses in Scotland. Balgownie links is the home of the **Royal Aberdeen** Golf Club and is featured ahead but **Murcar** is certainly not overshadowed and is a true championship test. It is a classic Scottish links with plenty of sandhills and a meandering burn and is quite a bit more undulating than Balgownie.

If the above are the best two courses around Aberdeen, (there are dozens in the area) and they are to the north of the city then perhaps the most spectacular is to the south at **Stonehaven**, laid out right alongside the lashing North Sea. And in total contrast to Stonehaven—and indeed to Aberdeen's great links layouts is the new 'American-style' course at **Newmachar**, north west of the city.

There are even more hotels in Aberdeen than golf courses but a large number are modern and somewhat unattractive and many may prefer to stay outside the town where establishments such as the excellent Ardoe House (01224) 867355 can be found. One other hotel strongly recommended by the golfing fraternity is the Atholl (01224) 323505 in Kings Gate. Many of the city's innumerable guesthouses provide a friendly ambience with Cedars Private Hotel (01224) 583225 a prominent example. An excellent seafood restaurant to visit is Atlantis (01224) 591403 while Gerard's (01224) 639500 and the Silver Darling (01224) 576229 are highly thought of. Our final thought is the excellent Marcliffe at Pitfodels (01224) 861000 on the western outskirts of the city.

North of Aberdeen, the popular Udny Arms (01358) 789444 at Newburgh enjoys a peaceful situation overlooking the Ythan Estuary and is a total contrast to the modern hotels of Aberdeen. Due west of the city another striking location is found at Kildrummy by Alford. Here the Kildrummy Castle (019755) 71288 is a first class establishment. To the north west, the Pittodrie House Hotel (01467) 681444 at Pitcaple enjoys glorious surroundings and in Old Meldrum one finds the similarly splendid Meldrum House Hotel (01651) 872294, which is convenient for the **Old Meldrum** course, and the many championship courses in the area.

Looking to play outside Aberdeen, the golfer is faced with two equally appealing choices—one can either head north along the coast towards Cruden Bay, or alternatively head inland along the A93. The latter choice broadly involves following the path of the River Dee and will take the traveller through some truly magnificent scenery. The 18 hole courses at **Banchory**, **Aboyne**, **Ballater** and **Braemar** all lie along this road and not surprisingly boast spectacular settings. There are several superb places in which to stay as you golf your way along the Dee. Near Banchory, Raemoir House (01330) 8024884 is outstanding and the Tor-na-Coille (01330) 822242 has excellent facilities, as does the Banchory Lodge Hotel (01330) 822625. Aboyne offers the Birse Lodge Hotel (01339) 886253 while the especially attractive town of Ballater boasts a number of fine establishments. Tullich Lodge (013397) 55406 is one of the leading mansion houses in Scotland with delightful bedrooms and excellent food, but also note the Craigendarroch Hotel (013397) 55858 with its fine restaurant and first class leisure facilities. Darroch Learg (013397) 55443 and Balgonie Country House (013397) 55482 are also of a very good standard. Should you time it right then Braemar boasts that magnificent spectacle, the Highland Games.

Banchory Lodge Hotel
Banchory, Banchory on Royal Deeside,
Aberdeen AB31 5HS
Tel: (01330) 822625 Fax: (01330) 825019

The Banchory Lodge Hotel combines Georgian charm with the distinctive leisured atmosphere of a country house.

The public rooms, including the dining room, where cuisine of a very high standard is served, offer superb views of the River Dee. All 24 bedrooms are individually furnished and have private bathrooms, colour television and tea-making facilities.

There is ample opportunity for sport and relaxation, with local golf courses, tennis courts, putting and bowling, forest walks and nature trails nearby. Salmon fishing on the River Dee can also be arranged.

Journeying due northwards from Aberdeen, **Cruden Bay** is clearly the first stopping point. A truly splendid golf links this, situated some 23 miles north of Aberdeen on Scotland's Buchan Coast. It is detailed on a later page. The old fishing and whaling town of **Peterhead** has an interesting seaside course where fierce sea winds can make scoring tricky. The Red House Hotel (01779) 812215 in Cruden Bay is recommended as a good place to take shelter.

From fishing port to Georgian elegance—the **Duff**

House Royal Golf Club at Banff is overlooked by an impressive baroque-style mansion. The course too has a touch of class having been designed by Alister Mackenzie immediately prior to his constructing the legendary Augusta National course in America—note the many two-tiered greens. Although not far from the sea, Duff House is very much a parkland type challenge. Nearby **Royal Tarlair** at Macduff is well worth a visit and like Duff House is always beautifully maintained. To the south of Banff along the A947 **Turriff** can also be recommended, while even further inland (but a marvellous drive anyway) from the Banff/ Macduff area on the A97, is the charming course at **Huntly** and the very relaxing Castle Hotel (01466) 792696. West of Huntly lies the well run and excellent Craigellachie Hotel (01340) 881204. Returning to Macduff, the Fire Arms Hotel (01261) 32408 is convenient and in Banff's High Street, the Country Hotel (01261) 815353 is another to note. Also to be found in Banff is the charming Carmelite House Hotel (01261) 812152. Just to the south is Eden House (01261) 821282, a former fishing lodge and very agreeable too. Nearby, Cullen Bay has the welcoming Cullen Bay Hotel (01542) 840432.

Crossing the salmon-filled River Spey at Fochabers the City of **Elgin** is soon reached. Of the few cathedrals in this part of the world Elgin, the capital of Morayshire, has a beautiful one that dates from the 13th century. It also has one of the finest inland golf courses in the north of Scotland. A mile or so south of the city and some distance away from the often fierce coastal winds, the course is sheltered by many pines and silver birch. Inevitably, it occupies a glorious setting with distant purple hills forming a spectacular horizon.

Inland from Elgin, a drive through the Glen of Rothes will lead the golfer to **Dufftown** where there is a pleasant and not too difficult course, but if a coastal challenge is sought then Lossiemouth is the place to head for. Here, the **Moray** Golf Club has two links courses, the championship 'Old Course', which is more than a hundred years old and the 'New Course', a little over ten years old. Whilst the fighter aircraft from nearby RAF Lossiemouth may occasionally irritate, it would be difficult to find a finer combination of superb natural golf and scenic splendour.

In Elgin, two hotels; the Mansion House (01343) 548811 and Mansefield House (01343) 540883 are recommended and in Rothes, the Rothes Glen (01340) 831254 is superbly relaxing. In Forres, the Knockomie Hotel (01309) 673146 is very accommodating. Finally in Lossiemouth, ideal for golf at Moray, is the adjacent Stotfield Hotel (01343) 812011.

The Highlands

In Scotland, where there is land there is golf and although the Highland region may be a wild and somewhat remote part of the country it nonetheless has its share of golfing gems—and more than that, in the minds of many, it has in **Royal Dornoch** the finest of them all.

As well as its gems, the region has a number of golf's genuine outposts, none more so than the **Gairloch** Golf Club situated in the far west of Scotland with views across to the Isle of Skye. There are 9 holes at Gairloch, each wonderfully named. The 6th, however, baffles me—'Westward Ho!' is its title?! The 9th has more of a Celtic ring to it—'Mo Dhachaidh'. There is no Sunday golf at Gairloch, though visitors can play at all other times. Others in the 'lonely' category include **Fort Augustus** on the edge of Loch Ness and **Fort William**, a moorland course laid out in the shadows of Ben Nevis. In addition, the intrepid golfer will find a number of courses to play in the Western Isles and the Hebrides, although the scenery may cause many to lift their heads too quickly.

Further south, the area around Aviemore has become an increasingly popular holiday retreat, particularly for winter sports enthusiasts. However, whilst the skis must go on the roof, the golf clubs can fit in the boot, and there are five or six courses at hand each of which possesses a truly glorious setting. Picking two of the best, the **Kingussie** and **Boat of Garten** golf clubs lie either side of Aviemore close to the A9. Both have spectacular courses at which visitors are always made welcome. Neither is particularly long, though the hills at Kingussie and the narrow fairways and small greens at Boat of Garten can make scoring extremely difficult and you are more likely to see eagles than score one! At Boat of Garten you may also catch a glimpse of one of the famous ospreys which nest in the area. Boat of Garten is featured ahead.

Some thoughts for the 19th include in the Newtonmore-Kingussie area, the Highlander (01540) 673341 and the Osprey (01540) 661510, both pleasant hotels, and the Cross (01540) 661166 is an outstanding restaurant in Kingussie with charming rooms. Near Fort William one finds Inverlochy Castle (01397) 702177, one of the country's finest hotels and restaurants, while two other gems are the remote Arisaig House (01687) 650622 on the western coast and in Ballachulish, the Ballachulish Hotel (01855) 811606. In Boat of Garten, the Boat (01479) 831258 is convenient overlooking the golf course (note the special 'golf weeks'). The Dalrachney Lodge (01479) 841252 at Carrbridge caters exceptionally well for golfing and fishing guests. Both Seafield Lodge (01479) 872152 and the Grant Arms Hotel (01479) 872526 in Grantown-on-Spey are comfortable and good value, whilst nearer the coast at Advie is the gracious Tulchan Lodge (01807) 510200. We also recommend Muckrach Lodge (01479) 851257 and Auchendean Lodge (01479) 851347 at Dulnain Bridge. Both make a fine base for touring the region.

Inverness, as the so-called 'Capital of the Highlands', is where many may choose to spend a day or two—the Loch Ness monster lives nearby and the famous fields of destruction at Culloden Moor are only a few miles to the east. Golfers may wish to note the **Inverness** 18 hole course just south of the town centre. However, many are drawn towards **Nairn** (16 miles away) where in addition to the magnificent championship links—see feature—there is an excellent second course, **Nairn Dunbar**.

Both Inverness and Nairn have a number of good hotels. Near the former, Dunain Park (01463) 230512 is outstanding and the 18th century Kingsmills (01463) 237166 is also ideal. Near to the famous battlefield is the impressive Culloden House Hotel (01463) 790461 where a portrait of the Bonnie Prince will welcome you. Relaxation and comfort can also be found at Glenruidh House (01463) 226499 and Ballifeary House Hotel (01463) 235572. In Nairn, the Golf View Hotel (01667) 452301 is situated right alongside the famous championship course but there are strong recommendations also for the Claymore House Hotel (01667) 453731, the Newton Hotel (01667) 453144, the charming Lochloy House (01667) 455355 and the Clifton Hotel (01667) 453119 (good restaurant here), all in Nairn.

On the Chanonry Peninsula, linked to Inverness by way of the Kessock Bridge, the A9 and the A832, is the flattish links course of **Fortrose and Rosemarkie**—surrounded by sea and well worth a visit. **Strathpeffer Spa**, a moorland course, is one of the prettiest stepping stones for those heading north of Inverness along the A9, and Craigdarroch Lodge Hotel (01997) 421265 will provide comfort. Alternatively, the Royal Hotel (01381) 600217, Cromarty, is pleasant. This road passes through **Tain**, home of the famous Glenmorangie whisky, and where there is another outstanding 18 holes—but by now most will be itching to reach Dornoch. If you do decide to sample the whisky, the appropriately named Morangie House (01862) 892281 should oblige.

Royal Dornoch is regularly ranked among the top ten golf courses in Britain. For those wishing to reflect on their day's golf, the Dornoch Castle (01862) 810216 the Royal Golf Hotel (01862) 810283, Burghfield House (01862) 810212 and the Mallin House Hotel (01862) 810335 can all be recommended. Having played Royal Dornoch, many will surely wish to inspect the nearby golf course at **Skibo Castle**. Both are explored separately ahead.

There are two fine courses a short distance to the north at Dornoch—**Golspie** and **Brora**. Both are testing links courses set in the most majestic surroundings with views to distant hills and along what is a truly spectacular coast. Brora (where the greens are reputed to be the equal of those at Royal Dornoch and are ringed by electric fences to keep the sheep out!) stretches out right alongside three miles of deserted sandy beach. Being so far north golf can be played at absurdly late hours during the summer months and at both the green fees are very inexpensive. In Brora, the Royal Marine (01408) 621252 and the Links (01408) 621225 hotels are both strategically placed on the aptly named Golf Road, while another well titled hotel can be found at Golspie, the Golf Links Hotel (01408) 633408.

Beyond Brora we really are getting remote! However, the A9 makes it all the way to John O'Groats. There are 18 hole courses at **Wick** and **Reay**, but the furthest north is **Thurso**, not too far from the Dounreay Power Station, and if you do make it there accommodation in true country house style is available at the Melvich Hotel (01641) 531206. I should imagine it gets pretty cold in these parts but if you are still looking for fresh challenges then there is always the golf club in the Arctic—fittingly called the 'Polar Bear Club'—and which, I suppose it goes without saying, was founded by Scotsmen!

Artist: **Graeme W Baxter** **ROYAL DORNOCH** _Courtesy of:_ **Baxter Prints**

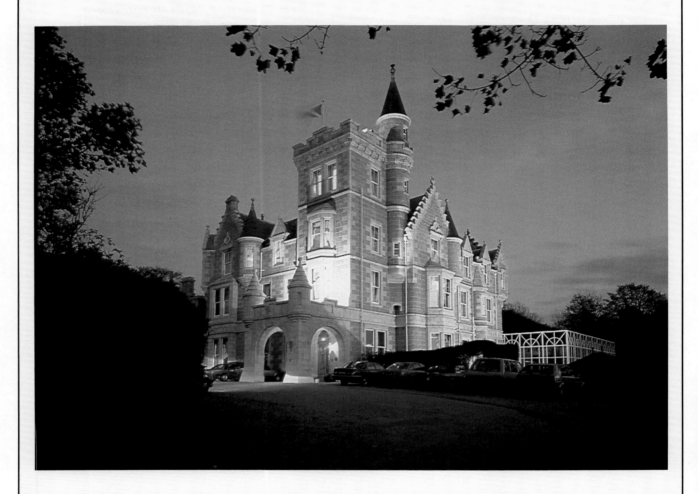

Ardoe House Hotel is a Scottish baronial style mansion with commanding views over beautiful Royal Deeside. Within easy reach of many of the North East Scotland's golf courses, the hotel is also conveniently situated close to Aberdeen, only a few minutes drive from the city centre. Set in thirty acres of its own grounds, the stunning exterior of the hotel is matched by an equally impressive interior. Features include ornate mouldings, wood panelling and log fires with delightful public rooms providing areas for rest and relaxation.

A complete refurbishment of this Victorian house took place in the late 1980s with additions in the early 90s sympathetic to the original building. The result is a superb venue for business or pleasure with seventy-one bedrooms displaying a high level of excellence, both for their generous proportions and luxuriousness. Bedrooms have all the facilities necessary to ensure a most comfortable stay, including a hospitality tray and fresh fruit. The hallmarks of Ardoe House are the commitment to maintaining high standards of comfort, fine cuisine and service which is attentive yet unobtrusive and a warmth of hospitality unrivalled anywhere.

The hotel is presently a popular base for golf parties playing the many challenging courses of the North East, in particular, Deeside and the coast, both of which are readily accessible from the hotel.

The restaurant at Ardoe House is very popular with both guests and the local community. An excellent reputation is enjoyed due, in the main, to the consistently high standards of cuisine achieved by using the best and freshest of ingredients combined into mouth-watering dishes by a team of dedicated award-winning chefs eager to maintain and enhance this reputation.

Golf packages, which include accommodation in a deluxe room with a full Scottish breakfast, four course dinner and packed lunch are available all year round. Details are available on request from the manager.

Ardoe House Hotel
Blairs
South Deeside Road
Aberdeen
AB12 5YP
Tel: (01224) 867355
Fax: (01224) 861283

Royal Aberdeen

Founded in 1780, Royal Aberdeen is the sixth oldest golf club in the world. For the first thirty five years of its existence the club was known as The Society of Golfers at Aberdeen, with membership of the society being determined by ballot. They were clearly a meticulous group of gentlemen for in 1783 they became the first to introduce the five minute limit on searching for golf balls. A sensible idea, you may think, but one that has caused the modern day Aberdeen golfer much distress—a subject to which I shall return in due course.

In 1815, on the eve of the Battle of Waterloo, the Society changed its name to the Aberdeen Golf Club and in 1903 the Royal prefix was bestowed on the club.. Originally the members played over a strip of common land between the Rivers Don and Dee but in the second half of the 19th century the club acquired its own course at Balgownie on the northern side of the River Don. Today Balgownie Links is regarded as one of Scotland's greatest championship courses.

Ron MacAskill is the **Director of Golf** and **Head Professional** at Royal Aberdeen Golf Club and **Sandra Nicholson** is the **Administration Secretary**. They may be contacted for tee reservations Monday to Friday on **(01224) 702571** while the pro shop can be contacted all week on **(01224) 702221**. All correspondence should be addressed to: **The Royal Aberdeen Golf Club, Links Road, Bridge of Don, Aberdeen, AB23 8AT.**

Visitors are made extremely welcome at Royal Aberdeen and they may play at Balgownie on any day subject to making a tee reservation. The green fees for 1998 are set at £45 per round or £60 per day during the week (the tee being available between 10.00–11.30 and 2.00-4.00) with a £50 fee for a single round at the weekend (available after 3.30pm).

Travelling to Aberdeen is made fairly straightforward by the A92. From the south this road passes along the coast from Dundee via Arbroath, Montrose and Stonehaven to Aberdeen. It also connects the town to Fraserburgh in the north. Those approaching from the north west should find the A96 helpful (it in fact runs directly from Inverness.) Other roads which may prove of assistance are the A947 from Oldmeldrum and the A93 which links Aberdeen to Perth and passes through Blairgowrie. The links itself is situated two miles north of Aberdeen and can be sighted immediately to the right after crossing the River Don.

From its medal tees, Balgownie measures 6372 yards, par 70 (SSS 71) with the forward tees reducing the length to 6104 yards, par 69. Although perhaps not overly long, the course is very exposed to the elements and the wind can often make a mockery of some of the distances. There is also a considerable spread of gorse and the rough can be very punishing. It should be added that there are no fewer than ninety-two bunkers—ten of which appear on the short par three 8th! Balgownie has the traditional 'out and back' links layout, the front nine hugging the shore and the back nine returning on the landward side towards the clubhouse.

The outward nine is definitely the more interesting of the two halves—the eminent golf writer Sam McKinlay was moved to say: 'There are few courses in these islands with a better, more testing, more picturesque outward nine than Balgownie'. However, the most difficult hole on the course is possibly the last hole—a lengthy par four, well bunkered and usually played into the teeth of the prevailing wind.

Golfers may also wish to investigate the club's second course, the shorter Silverburn Course which measures 4066 yards, par 60.

Royal Aberdeen has played host to a number of major events including the British Youth's Championship, the Scottish Amateur Championship and the Northern Open Championship. In 1993, the British Seniors Championship was played over the Balgownie links. Numerous exhibition matches have also taken place; participants have included Tom Morris Junior, Harry Vardon, James Braid, John H Taylor, Walter Hagen and Henry Cotton.

I now return to the matter of the five minute rule. In the opening paragraph, I mentioned how in 1783 the Aberdeen Golfers had introduced the five minute limit on searching for lost balls. Well, somebody somewhere, it seems, didn't approve and 200 years later a plague of crows was sent to deliver retribution. Throughout the long summers of 1983 and 1984 the crows determined that no one should search for his ball. They descended on the links stealing Titleists and Top-Flites, Pinnacles and Penfolds. Several members had more than one ball stolen in a round. Numerous suggestions were put forward as to how to rid the links of this turbulent pest but alas to no avail. Even a crow trap was built but still they plundered. Then, just as suddenly as they came, they left, never it is presumed to return. Sanity restored, Balgownie became once more one of Britain's friendliest links.

Hole	Yards	Par	Hole	Yards	Par
1	409	4	10	342	4
2	530	5	11	166	3
3	223	3	12	383	4
4	423	4	13	375	4
5	326	4	14	390	4
6	486	5	15	341	4
7	375	4	16	389	4
8	147	3	17	180	3
9	453	4	18	434	4
Out	**3,372**	**36**	**In**	**3,000**	**34**
			Out	**3,372**	**36**
			Totals	**6,372**	**70**

Royal Dornoch

Usually when a person describes his first visit to a golf course as 'the most fun I've had playing golf in my whole life,' very little is thought of it. However, when that person happens to be Tom Watson, five times Open Champion, one tends to sit up and take notice. Like Ben Crenshaw, Nick Faldo and Greg Norman who have also made the pilgrimage, Watson was enchanted by the 'Star of the North'.

There are two words that are normally associated with Royal Dornoch; one is 'greatness' and the other is 'remoteness'. Situated fifty miles north of Inverness, Dornoch enjoys a kind of splendid isolation. It is often described as the course every golfer wants to play but the one that very few actually do.

So what is the charm of Dornoch? Firstly, there's the setting (this is when people forgive its remoteness!) Bordered by the Dornoch Firth and a glorious stretch of sand, distant hills with their ever-changing moods fill the horizon creating a feeling that one is playing on a stage. And then of course, there's the history: Royal Dornoch Golf Club dates from 1877 but mention is made of golf being played on the links at least as early as 1616. Writing in the 17th century Sir Robert Gordon wrote of Dornoch: 'About this town are the fairest and largest links on any part of Scotland, fit for Archery, Golfing, Ryding and all other exercises; they doe surpasse the fields of Montrose and St Andrews.' Finally, and most importantly, there's the very links itself—described on more than one occasion as the most natural golf course in the world; to quote Tom Watson again, 'One of the great courses of the five continents.'

Mr John Duncan is the **Secretary/Manager** and he may be contacted on **(01862) 811220**. All written correspondence should be addressed to the **Secretary/Manager, Royal Dornoch Golf Club, Golf Road, Dornoch, IV25 3LW**. Reservations and enquiries may be made on **(01862) 810219.,** by fax on (01862) 810792 or on the Internet at http://www.cali.co.uk/RDGC **Andrew Skinner** is the club's **Professional**; he may be reached on **(01862) 810902**.

Visitors are welcome at Royal Dornoch seven days a week. However, it is wise to telephone the club prior to setting off to make a tee reservation as an ever-growing number of people are now making the trip and during the months of June to August the links can get busy. The cost of a single round on the **Championship Course** in 1998 is set at £45 between Monday and Friday and £55 at the weekend. A three day ticket is available for consecutive weekdays priced at £110 in 1998. There is a second eigh-

teen hole course at Dornoch, the **Struie Course** measuring 5438 yards, par 69. A day ticket, enabling a round over both courses is available (between Monday and Friday only) at a cost of £50. A day ticket for the Struie Course alone can be purchased for £19 (£13 per round) with £80 securing a full week's golf.

Travelling to Dornoch gets ever easier. The A9 runs from Perth to John O'Groats, Perth being linked to Edinburgh by the M90. There are regular flights from London and other parts of the country to Inverness Airport and the links itself has an adjacent landing strip for light aircraft; moreover, there is now a road bridge over the Dornoch Firth and this reduces the motoring time from Inverness to 50 minutes.

By today's standards Dornoch could probably be described as being of only medium length, the links measuring 6514 yards, par 70 (SSS 73). However, the last thing in the world that Dornoch is, is an easy course. It has been said that the prevailing wind at Dornoch comes from every direction but even when the winds don't thunder in from across the Firth or down from the hills, the links can be the proverbial 'smiler with the knife'.

Although the club was founded in 1877, ten years later when 'Old' Tom Morris was brought from St Andrews to survey the links there was still only a rather crude nine hole layout. The master craftsman set to work and not only completely redesigned the nine but extended the course to a full eighteen holes. By using the natural contours of the terrain many magnificent plateau greens were created and despite major alterations made to the links by John Sutherland and John H Taylor thirty years later, it is the plateau greens that remain the hallmark of Dornoch. Among the most classic holes are the 4th, 5th (Watson's favourite), 10th, 14th and 17th.

Donald Ross, considered by many to be the greatest of all golf architects was born in Dornoch and between 1895 and 1899 was the professional and head green keeper at Dornoch. Several of the great American courses he later designed incorporate many of Dornoch's features.

Today there are signs that Dornoch is at last shedding its remoteness tag. In 1985 the club staged the Amateur Championship for the first time in its history—this being in the minds of many alarmingly overdue—and in 1999 Dornoch will host the Ladies' Home Internationals. It may be to indulge in pure fantasy but one cannot help wondering what it would be like if the hallowed links were ever visited by the greatest of all compliments.

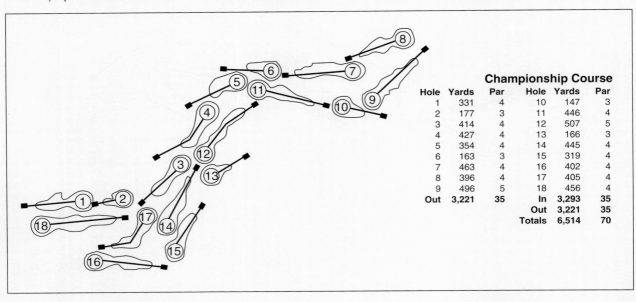

Championship Course

Hole	Yards	Par	Hole	Yards	Par
1	331	4	10	147	3
2	177	3	11	446	4
3	414	4	12	507	5
4	427	4	13	166	3
5	354	4	14	445	4
6	163	3	15	319	4
7	463	4	16	402	4
8	396	4	17	405	4
9	496	5	18	456	4
Out	**3,221**	**35**	**In**	**3,293**	**35**
			Out	**3,221**	**35**
			Totals	**6,514**	**70**

Cruden Bay

One often reads of famous golf clubs having been founded in local hotels and hostelries: Deal (The Black Horse), Crail (The Golf Inn) and Hoylake (The Royal) to name but three. Well, the birth of Cruden Bay apparently took place during a meeting in the North of Scotland Bank—one presumes a much more sober affair! The precise date of the meeting was 16th June 1898 and in March the following year the Cruden Bay Hotel and Golf Course was opened.

The hotel (long since demolished) and the 18 hole golf course were originally both owned by the Great North of Scotland Railway Company. Within a month of their opening the company staged a professional tournament which attracted many of the day's leading players, including Harry Vardon (then Open Champion), James Braid and Ben Sayers. The event proved an outstanding success with Vardon taking the first prize of £30.

Today the club's full address is the **Cruden Bay Golf Club, Aulton Road, Cruden Bay, Peterhead, Aberdeenshire AB42 0NN**. In addition to the 18 hole **Championship Course** there is also a well-kept 9 hole short course, the **St Olaf**.

The present **Secretary** is **Mrs Rosemary Pittendrigh**. She may be contacted via the above address and by telephone on **(01779) 812285**, and fax: **(01779) 812945**. The club's **Professional, Robbie Stewart**, can be reached on **(01779) 812414**. Casual visitors are welcome at Cruden Bay, although not surprisingly certain restrictions apply during Saturdays and Sundays. It is generally advisable to telephone the club to make an advance reservation, particularly as a starting sheet is in operation daily from April to September. Visitors should also note that they are not permitted to play the 18 hole course between 4.30 pm and 6.30 pm on Wednesdays and that at weekends, unless accompanied by a member, handicap certificates must be provided. No specific restrictions relate to the St Olaf course.

In 1998 the green fee to play on the Championship course is priced at £35 for a weekday ticket, with £45 payable at weekends (reduced to £30 after 3.30 pm). Under 18s pay £20 and £25 respectively. A day's golf on the St Olaf course can be obtained for £10 during the week and £15 at weekends. (Half price for juniors)

Cruden Bay is situated on Scotland's Buchan Coast, some 23 miles north of Aberdeen and seven miles south of the old whaling port of Peterhead. The course itself has a dramatic setting with Slains Castle providing a rather eerie backdrop. Bram Stoker, who spent several summers in Cruden Bay is reputed to have been inspired by the castle when writing his Dracula stories. Fortunately the surrounding countryside bears little resemblance to Transylvania and strangers should find travelling in the area a pleasant experience. The best route from the south is probably the A92 coastal road which runs from Dundee via Montrose and through Aberdeen. Leave the A92 near Newburgh and follow the A975 direct to Cruden Bay. The A92 approaches from the north via Fraserburgh and Peterhead.

Originally laid out by Old Tom Morris but substantially revised by Tom Simpson, Cruden Bay is very much a traditional links and there are a number of blind and semi-blind shots. Measuring 6395 yards from the back tees, par is a fairly tight 70 (SSS 71). From the ladies' tees the course measures 5761 yards (par 74). A good old Scottish burn is a prominent feature of the course affecting several of the holes. There are a number of vast sand dunes and hills to be negotiated while the beach too (if one is a little wayward) can come into play around the 14th and 15th. The finest sequence of holes, however, comes between the 4th, one of the finest par threes in golf, and the 7th. The views over the Bay of Cruden naturally add to the pleasure of the round, and it isn't difficult to comprehend why *Golf World* magazine ranks Cruden Bay amongst its top 50 courses in the British Isles—and why in November 1995 *Golf Magazine* (an American publication) rated it 98th best course in the world.

The magnificently appointed clubhouse has the kind of atmosphere one comes to expect in this part of the world—very friendly—and casual dress may be worn at all times. Meals are served throughout the day with lunches, high teas, dinners and some delightful steak suppers being offered in addition to bar snacks.

South of Hadrian's Wall, Cruden Bay is probably not as well known as it ought to be. The legions who arrange their golfing trips around the more traditional favourites often miss out on some of Scotland's finest courses. Cruden Bay should be included in anyone's itinerary—it is a genuinely spectacular course and perhaps of equal importance, a place where the warmest of welcomes can be guaranteed.

Hole	Yards	Par	Hole	Yards	Par
1	416	4	10	385	4
2	339	4	11	149	3
3	286	4	12	320	4
4	193	3	13	550	5
5	454	4	14	397	4
6	529	5	15	239	3
7	392	4	16	182	3
8	258	4	17	428	4
9	462	4	18	416	4
Out	**3,329**	**36**	**In**	**3,066**	**34**
			Out	**3,329**	**36**
			Totals	**6,395**	**70**

Nairn

A glorious setting, a superb championship course and a warm welcome to visiting golfers—that, in the proverbial nutshell, is Nairn. In 1987 the club celebrated its centenary and played host to both men's and ladies' Scottish Amateur Championships. In 1994 the club staged the British Amateur Championship and in September 1999 Nairn is due to host the 37th Walker Cup.

Designed by Archie Simpson and modified two years later by 'Old' Tom Morris, the present layout owes much to the work of James Braid, arguably the greatest of all Scottish golf architects. Nairn is very much a traditional links with the opening holes stretching out along the shoreline. At the 10th comes the inevitable about-turn, and the head for home. It is a fine test of golf and with the abundant heather, the great sea of gorse and the distant mountains providing a spectacular backdrop, this is a veritable heaven.

Being so far north Nairn has probably not received the recognition it must surely deserve—at least in terms of attracting professional tournaments. Yet with an airport (Inverness) a mere 8 miles away and an adequate road and rail network, Nairn ought not to be considered too remote in the way that Royal Dornoch traditionally is.

From the medal tees the course measures 6452 yards, par 71. Nairn is certainly no monster and accuracy rather than length should determine the quality of scoring. The front nine is the shorter of the two although the prevailing south-westerly may well cause this to be the tougher half. Anyone suffering a bout of the dreaded sliced tee-shot is likely to find himself doing battle with the Moray Firth—the early holes really do run very close to the sea.

Perhaps the best series of holes, however, are found on the back nine, namely holes 12, 13 and 14. Anyone who can manage three pars here can call himself a golfer. Staying out of the gorse and avoiding the numerous well-positioned bunkers is undoubtedly the key to a good round, for with the magnificent, and not overly large greens, there is no excuse for poor putting at Nairn.

And so, as they say, to the 19th and at Nairn that means entering one of the most relaxing clubhouses in Britain. Built in 1990, it was extended in 1997 with the addition of the Gordon Bulmer Wing and a newly fitted pro shop. During summer the club hosts a number of open competitions and these are invariably well supported. It isn't difficult to imagine why. For those of us who enjoy our golf in pleasant and dramatic surroundings and who occasionally feel the urge to get away from it all, there can surely be no finer place to visit than Nairn.

Nairn Golf Club, Seabank Road Nairn, Highland IV12 4HB	
Secretary	Jim Somerville (01667) 453208
	Fax (01667) 456328
Professional	Robin Fyfe (01667) 452787
Green Fees	WD £40
	WE £45
Restrictions	No fourballs before 9.30 am
Directions	

Directions
Eight miles from Inverness airport, situated on the town's western shore.

Boat of Garten

Ask a golfer who has never been to the Highlands of Scotland which are the country's three most scenic inland courses and he'll probably say Loch Lomond, Gleneagles Kings and Gleneagles Queens. Ask the same question of a golfer who has savoured the delights of Boat of Garten and he'll probably give you a different answer. Boat of Garten's scenery is nothing short of awesome.

At Loch Lomond you play much of the round alongside the 'Bonnie Banks', at or near water level. At Gleneagles you climb the foothills and gaze at the distant peaks. When you play golf at Boat of Garten there is a sense of being right in amongst the mountains. Nowhere else does the air seem as crisp or as invigorating. The accompanying views are utterly enchanting as the golf course wanders—and frequently plunges—through avenues of birch and rowan liberally sprinkled with heather and broom.

Like the Kings and Queens at Gleneagles, Boat of Garten was designed by James Braid. Measuring a shade under 6000 yards from the back tees it is not the longest of challenges, yet it is anything but easy! The fairways are generally quite narrow and they really do undulate significantly. Moreover, several of them ripple in a links-like manner thus awkward stances are not uncommon. There are occasional blind shots too, making Boat of Garten something of an inland Cruden Bay—an old fashioned, thoroughly bewitching test of golf.

The only plain hole at Boat of Garten is the 1st, a modest par three played over flat terrain. But then the excitement begins. At the 2nd you drive downhill to one of those rippling fairways that changes gear midway, climbing to a green sitting roughly at eye level. The 3rd is another short hole, this time played over a valley of heather, while the 4th is a dramatic par five where the fairway cascades in tiers before once again rising in front of the green. The 5th hole is more 'up' than 'down' but is equally spectacular. And so it continues. The 6th and 8th are both very strong two-shotters and the front nine concludes with a par three at which sand, heather and broom all conspire to ensure that the only place to be is on the green.

The highlights of the back nine are the views from the 12th tee—a glorious panorama—the complexities of the 13th (an unusual green site here), the eccentricities of the 15th (where both the drive and approach are blind!) and the all-round star quality of the 18th, a wonderful finishing hole that features an exciting downhill tee shot, a gently curving fairway and a green perched precariously on a hilltop. A thrilling conclusion to an exhilarating round.

Boat of Garten Golf Club PH24 3BQ		
Gen Manager	Paddy Smyth (01479) 831282	
Professional	J R Ingram (01479) 831282	
Green Fees	WD £21/round; £26/day	
	WE £26/round; £31/day	
Restrictions	Handicap certificates required	
Directions		

Directions
Situated east of the A9, 5 miles north of Aviemore.

Culloden House

Culloden House is a handsome Georgian mansion with a tradition of lavish hospitality stretching back hundreds of years. Among its famous visitors was Bonnie Prince Charlie who fought his last battle by the park walls. The house stands in 40 acres of elegant lawns and parkland, enhanced by stately oaks and beech trees.

The long term Scottish resident staff, dedicated to your comfort and service, are on-hand at all times to extend a warm welcome to all visitors to their hotel. Culloden House is decorated to the highest standard, particularly the comfortable drawing room which is decorated with magnificent Adam-style plasterwork.

Dining is a memorable experience at Culloden House. The emphasis in the Adam style dining room is on friendly and unobtrusive service matched by the highest standards of cuisine. The wine cellars hold a superb range of wines from the great vineyards of the world and there is a wide selection of aged malt whiskies.

Every bedroom is individually decorated and has direct dial telephone, television, trouser press, bath and shower. Guests can choose from four poster rooms, standard rooms or a room with a jacuzzi. The Garden Pavilion, situated by the ancient listed walled garden, and the newly refurbished west wing Pavilion on the main house, offer the discerning non-smoking guest luxurious suite and junior suite accommodation.

Leisure facilities include a hard tennis court, sauna, free weights and exercise bicycle with future plans for spa development. There is so much to visit in the area—golf, fishing and shooting can be arranged and the Highlands, Loch Ness and Inverness are just waiting to be explored. Also nearby are Cawdor Castle, the Clava Cairns and Culloden Battlefield.

Situated three miles from the centre of Inverness, off the A96 Inverness-Nairn Road, Culloden House extends the best of Scottish hospitality to all its guests.

Culloden House
Inverness IV1 2NZ
Tel: (01463) 790461
Fax: (01463) 792181
Toll Free Fax: (USA) 1800 3737987

Cruden Bay

Ⓞne often reads of famous golf clubs having been founded in local hotels and hostelries: Deal (The Black Horse), Crail (The Golf Inn) and Hoylake (The Royal) to name but three. Well, the birth of Cruden Bay apparently took place during a meeting in the North of Scotland Bank—one presumes a much more sober affair! The precise date of the meeting was 16th June 1898 and in March the following year the Cruden Bay Hotel and Golf Course was opened.

The hotel (long since demolished) and the 18 hole golf course were originally both owned by the Great North of Scotland Railway Company. Within a month of their opening the company staged a professional tournament which attracted many of the day's leading players, including Harry Vardon (then Open Champion), James Braid and Ben Sayers. The event proved an outstanding success with Vardon taking the first prize of £30.

Today the club's full address is the **Cruden Bay Golf Club, Aulton Road, Cruden Bay, Peterhead, Aberdeenshire AB42 0NN**. In addition to the 18 hole **Championship Course** there is also a well-kept 9 hole short course, the **St Olaf**.

The present **Secretary** is **Mrs Rosemary Pittendrigh**. She may be contacted via the above address and by telephone on **(01779) 812285**, and fax: **(01779) 812945**. The club's **Professional, Robbie Stewart**, can be reached on **(01779) 812414**. Casual visitors are welcome at Cruden Bay, although not surprisingly certain restrictions apply during Saturdays and Sundays. It is generally advisable to telephone the club to make an advance reservation, particularly as a starting sheet is in operation daily from April to September. Visitors should also note that they are not permitted to play the 18 hole course between 4.30 pm and 6.30 pm on Wednesdays and that at weekends, unless accompanied by a member, handicap certificates must be provided. No specific restrictions relate to the St Olaf course.

In 1998 the green fee to play on the Championship course is priced at £35 for a weekday ticket, with £45 payable at weekends (reduced to £30 after 3.30 pm). Under 18s pay £20 and £25 respectively. A day's golf on the St Olaf course can be obtained for £10 during the week and £15 at weekends. (Half price for juniors.)

Cruden Bay is situated on Scotland's Buchan Coast, some 23 miles north of Aberdeen and seven miles south of the old whaling port of Peterhead. The course itself has a dramatic setting with Slains Castle providing a rather eerie backdrop. Bram Stoker, who spent several summers in Cruden Bay is reputed to have been inspired by the castle when writing his Dracula stories. Fortunately the surrounding countryside bears little resemblance to Transylvania and strangers should find travelling in the area a pleasant experience. The best route from the south is probably the A92 coastal road which runs from Dundee via Montrose and through Aberdeen. Leave the A92 near Newburgh and follow the A975 direct to Cruden Bay. The A92 approaches from the north via Fraserburgh and Peterhead.

Originally laid out by Old Tom Morris but substantially revised by Tom Simpson, Cruden Bay is very much a traditional links and there are a number of blind and semi-blind shots. Measuring 6395 yards from the back tees, par is a fairly tight 70 (SSS 71). From the ladies' tees the course measures 5761 yards (par 74). A good old Scottish burn is a prominent feature of the course affecting several of the holes. There are a number of vast sand dunes and hills to be negotiated while the beach too (if one is a little wayward) can come into play around the 14th and 15th. The finest sequence of holes, however, comes between the 4th, one of the finest par threes in golf, and the 7th. The views over the Bay of Cruden naturally add to the pleasure of the round, and it isn't difficult to comprehend why *Golf World* magazine ranks Cruden Bay amongst its top 50 courses in the British Isles—and why in November 1995 *Golf Magazine* (an American publication) rated it 98th best course in the world.

The magnificently appointed clubhouse has the kind of atmosphere one comes to expect in this part of the world—very friendly—and casual dress may be worn at all times. Meals are served throughout the day with lunches, high teas, dinners and some delightful steak suppers being offered in addition to bar snacks.

South of Hadrian's Wall, Cruden Bay is probably not as well known as it ought to be. The legions who arrange their golfing trips around the more traditional favourites often miss out on some of Scotland's finest courses. Cruden Bay should be included in anyone's itinerary—it is a genuinely spectacular course and perhaps of equal importance, a place where the warmest of welcomes can be guaranteed.

Hole	Yards	Par	Hole	Yards	Par
1	416	4	10	385	4
2	339	4	11	149	3
3	286	4	12	320	4
4	193	3	13	550	5
5	454	4	14	397	4
6	529	5	15	239	3
7	392	4	16	182	3
8	258	4	17	428	4
9	462	4	18	416	4
Out	**3,329**	**36**	**In**	**3,066**	**34**
			Out	**3,329**	**36**
			Totals	**6,395**	**70**

Key

ABERDEEN & MORAY

Aboyne G.C.
(01339) 886328
Formaston Park, Aboyne
(18) 5975 yards/***/C

Alford G.C.
(01975) 562178
Montgarry Road, Alford
(18) 5290 yards/***/D

Auchenblae G.C.
(01561) 320308
Auchenblae, Laurencekirk
(9) 2174 yards/***/E

Auchmill G.C.
(01224) 715214
Auchmill, Aberdeen
(18) 5439 metres/***/F

Ballater G.C.
(01339) 755567
Ballater, Aberdeenshire
(18) 6127 yards/***/C/H

Banchory G.C.
(01330) 822365
Kinneskie, Banchory
(18) 5245 yards/***/C/H

Balnagask G.C.
(01224) 871286
St Fitticks Road, Aberdeen
(18) 5468 yards/***/F

Bon Accord G.C.
(01224) 633464
Golf Road, Aberdeen
(18) 6384 yards/***/F

Braemar G.C.
(01339) 741618
Cluniebank, Braemar
(18) 4916 yards/***/C

Buckpool G.C.
(01542) 832236
Barhill Road, Buckie
(18) 6259 yards/***/C

Caledonian G.C.
(01224) 632443
Golf Road, Aberdeen
(18) 6384 yards/**/F

Cheyne G.C.
(01569) 762702
Fetteressoe, Stanehaven
(18) 6685 yards/***/E

Cruden Bay G.C.
(01779) 812285
Aulton Road, Cruden Bay
(9) 4710 yards/**/B-A/H
(18) 6395 yards/**/B-A/H

Cullen G.C.
(01542) 840685
The Links, Cullen, Buckie
(18) 4610 yards/***/D

Deeside G.C.
(01224) 867697
Bieldside, Aberdeen
(18) 5972 yards/**/B/H
(9) 6632 yards/**/B/H

Duff House Royal G.C.
(01261) 812062
Barnyards, Banff
(18) 6161 yards/***/C/H

Dufftown G.C.
(01340) 820325
Tomintoul Road, Dufftown
(18) 5308 yards/***/D

Dunecht House G.C.
(01330) 860404
Dunecht, Skene
(9) 3135 yards/***/F/G

Elgin G.C.
(01343) 542338
Hardhillock, Elgin
(18) 6401 yards/***/D-C

Forres G.C.
(01309) 672250
Muiryshade, Forres
(18) 6236 yards/***/D

Fraserburgh G.C.
(01346) 516616
Philorth, Fraserburgh
(18) 6278 yards/***/C

Garmouth and Kingston G.C.
(01343) 870388
Garmouth, Fochabers, Moray
(18) 5616 yards/***/D/H

Grantown-on-Spey G.C.
(01479) 872079
Grantown-on-Spey, Moray
(18) 5672 yards/***/D

Hazlehead G.C.
(01224) 315747
Hazlehead Park, Aberdeen
(18) 5303 metres/***/F
(18) 5673 metres/***/F
(9) 2531 metres/***/F

Hopeman G.C.
(01343) 830687
Hopeman, Moray
(18) 5531 yards/***/C

Huntly G.C.
(01466) 792643
Cooper Park, Huntly
(18) 5399 yards/***/F

Insch G.C.
(01464) 820363
Golf Terrace, Insch
(9) 5488 yards/***/D

Inverallochy G.C.
(01346) 582000
Inverallochy, Nr Fraserburgh
(18) 5137 yards/***/E

Inverurie G.C.
(01467) 624080
Blackhall Road, Inverurie
(18) 5711 yards/***/D

Keith G.C.
(01542) 882469
Fife Park, Keith
(18) 5791 yards/***/C

Kemnay G.C.
(01467) 642225
Monymusk Road, Kemnay
(9) 5502 yards/***(Mon/Tues/Thurs pm)/E

Kings Links G.C.
(01224) 641577
Golf Road, Kings Links, Aberdeen
(18) 5838 metres/***/D

Kintore G.C.
(01467) 632631
Balbithan Road, Kintore, Inverurie
(18) 5997 yards/***/D

Longside G.C.
(01779) 821558
Longside, Peterhead
(18) 5201 yards/***/D/H

Macdonald G.C.
(01358) 720576
Hospital Road, Ellon
(18) 5986 yards/***/F

Moray G.C.
(01434) 812018
Stotfield Road, Lossiemouth
(18) 6667 yards/***/B/H
(18) 6005 yards/***/C/H

Murcar G.C.
(01224) 704370
Bridge of Don, Aberdeen
(18) 6241 yards/***/F/H

Newburgh-on-Ythan G.C.
(01358) 789058
Newburgh, Aberdeenshire
(18) 6162 yards/***/D
(9) 6438 yards/***/D

Newmachar G.C.
(01651) 863002
Swailend, Newmachar
(18) 6605 yards/**/B/H

Nigg Bay G.C.
(01224) 871286
Balnagask, Aberdeen
(18) 5984 yards/***/F/G

Old Meldrum G.C.
(01651) 872648
Kirkbrae, Old Meldrum
(18) 5442 yards/***/C

Peterculter G.C.
(01244) 734994
Burnside Road, Aberdeen
(18) 5947 yards/***/D

Peterhead G.C.
(01779) 472149
Craigewan Links, Peterhead
(18) 6173 yards/***/F/H
(9) 4322 yards/***/F/H

Portlethen G.C.
(01224) 781090
Badentoy Road, Portlethen
(18) 6707 yards/***(Sat am)/C/H

Rosehearty G.C.
(01346) 571645
Rosehearty, Fraserburgh
(9) 1684 yards/***/E

Rothes G.C.
(01340) 831277
Blackhall, Rothes
(9) 4956 yards/***/E

Royal Aberdeen G.C.
(01224) 702571
Balgownie, Bridge of Don
(18) 6372 yards/**/A/H
(18) 4033 yards/**/B/H

Royal Tarlair G.C.
(01261) 832897
Buchan Street, Macduff
(18) 5866 yards/***/D

Spey Bay G.C.
(01343) 820424
Spey Bay, Fochabers, Moray
(18) 6092 yards/***/D

Stonehaven G.C.
(01569) 762124
Cowie, Stonehaven
(18) 5103 yards/**/C

Strathlene G.C.
(01542) 831798
Portessie, Buckie
(18) 5957 yards/***/D

Tarland G.C.
(01339) 881413
Tarland, Aboyne
(9) 5812 yards/***/D

Torphins G.C.
(01339) 882115
Golf Road, Torphins, Banchory
(9) 2342 yards/***/D

Turriff G.C.
(01888) 562982
Rosehall, Turriff
(18) 6105 yards/***/C/H

Westhill G.C.
(01224) 742567
Westhill Heights, Westhill, Skene
(18) 5291 yards/*/C/G

THE HIGHLANDS

Abernethy G.C.
(01479) 821305
Nethybridge
(9) 4986 yards/***/E

Aigas G.C.
(01463) 782942
By Beauly, Invernesshire
(9) 2439 yards/***/D

Alness G.C.
(01349) 883877
Ardross Road, Alness
(9) 5160 yards/***/E

Askernish G.C.
(01878) 700541
Askernish, Lochboisdale, South Uist
(9) 5042 yards/***/E

Boat of Garten G.C.
(01479) 831282
Boat of Garten
(18) 5837 yards/***/C/H

Bonar Bridge G.C.
(01549) 421248
Bonar Bridge, Ardgay
(9) 2313 yards/***/E

Brora G.C.
(01408) 621417
Golf Road, Brora, Sutherland
(18) 6110 yards/***/C

Carnegie Club
(01862) 894600
Skibo Castle, Dornoch
(18) 6671 yards/***/A/H

Carrbridge G.C.
(01479) 841623
Carrbridge
(9) 2623 yards/***/C

Cawdor Castle G.C.
(01667) 404615
Nairn, Invernesshire
(9) 1161 yards/***/E

Colonsay G.C.
The Hotel, Colonsay, Argyll
(01951) 200316
(18) 4774 yards/***/E

Craignure G.C.
(01680) 812370
Craignure, Isle of Mull
(9) 5072 yards/***/E

Durness G.C.
(01971) 511364
Balnakeil, Durness
(9) 5545 yards/***(Sun am)/E

Fort Augustus G.C.
(01320) 366660
Markethill, Fort Augustus
(9) 5454 yards/***(Sat pm)/E

Fortrose and Rosemarkie G.C.
(01381) 620529
Ness Road East, Fortrose
(18) 5858 yards/***/C

Fort William G.C.
(01397) 704464
Turlundy, Fort William
(18) 6217 yards/***/F

Gairloch G.C.
(01445) 712407
Gairloch
(9) 2046 yards/***(Sun)/D

Golspie G.C.
(01408) 633266
Ferry Road, Golspie, Sutherland
(18) 5836 yards/***/E

Helmsdale G.C.
(01431) 821240
Helmsdale, Sutherland
(9) 1860 yards/***/E

Invergordon G.C.
(01349) 852715
Cromlet Drive, Invergordon
(9) 6028 yards/***/E

Isle of Coll G.C.
(01879) 230334
Isle of Coll, Argyll
(9) 2053 yards/***/E

Inverness G.C.
(01463) 239882
Culcabock Road, Inverness
(18) 6226 yards/**/F

Kingussie G.C.
(01540) 661600
Gynack Road, Kingussie
(18) 5504 yards/***/C

Lochcarron G.C.
(01520) 722252
Lochcarron, Strathcarron
(9) 3578 yards/***/E

Lybster G.C.
(01593) 721215
Main Street, Lybster, Caithness
(9) 1898 yards/***/E

Muir of Ord G.C.
(01463) 870825
Great Northern Road, Muir of Ord
(18) 5202 yards/***/C/H

Nairn G.C.
(01667) 453208
Seabank Road, Nairn
(18) 6745 yards/***/A/H

Nairn Dunbar G.C.
(01667) 452741
Lochloy Road, Nairn
(18) 6712 yards/***/A/H

Newtonmore G.C.
(015403) 673328
Golf Course Road, Newtonmore
(18) 6029 yards/***/D

Reay G.C.
(01847) 811288
By Thurso, Caithness
(18) 5884 yards/***/D

Royal Dornoch G.C.
(01862) 810219
Golf Road, Dornoch, Sutherland
(18) 6514 yards/***/A/H
(18) 5438 yards/***/D/

Sconser G.C.
(01478) 613059
Sconser, Isle of Skye
(9) 4798 yards/***/E

Skeabost G.C.
(01470) 532202
Skeabost Bridge, Isle of Skye
(9) 1528 yards/***/E

Spean Bridge G.C.
(01397) 704954
Spean Bridge, Fort William
(9) 2203 yards/***/E

Stornoway G.C.
(01851) 702240
Stornoway, Isle of Lewis
(18) 5178 yards/***(Sun)/D

Strathpeffer Spa G.C.
(01997) 421219
Strathpeffer
(18) 4792 yards/***/D

Tain G.C.
(01862) 892314
Tain, Ross-shire
(18) 5082 yards/***/E

Tarbat G.C.
(01862) 871236
Portmahomack
(9) 2368 yards***(Sun)/E/H

Thurso G.C.
(01847) 893807
Newlands of Geise, Thurso
(18) 5818 yards/***/E

Tobermory G.C.
(01688) 302020
Erray Road, Tobermary
(9) 4890 yards/***/E

Torvean G.C.
(01463) 711434
Glenurquhart Road, Inverness
(18) 5784 yards/***/D

Traigh G.C.
(01687) 450377
Back of Kewppoch, Arisaig
(9) 2405 yards/***/E

Wick G.C.
(01955) 602726
Wick, Caithness
(18) 5976 yards/***/C

ORKNEY AND SHETLAND ISLES

Asta G.C.
(01598) 880231
Scalloway, Shetland
(9) 2023 yards/***/E

Orkney G.C.
(01856) 872457
St Ola, by Kirkwall, Orkney
(18) 5411 yards/***/E

Shetland G.C.
(01595) 840369
PO Box 18, Lerwick
(18) 5776 yards/***/E/H

Stromness G.C.
(01856) 850772
Ness, Stromness, Orkney
(18) 4762 yards/***/D

Whalsay G.C.
(01806) 566481
Skantaig, Shetland
(18) 6009 yards/***/E

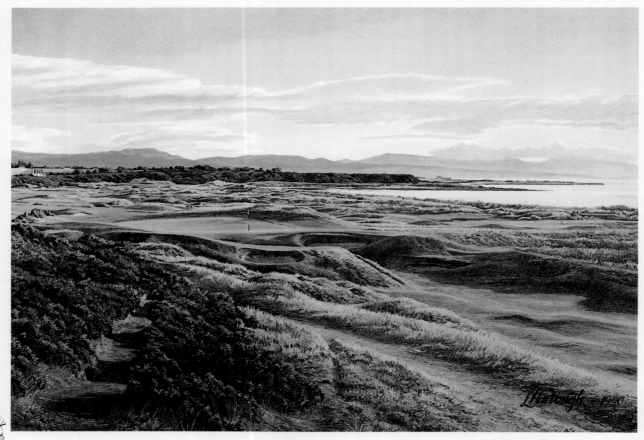

Artist: **Linda Hartough ROYAL DORNOCH** *Courtesy of:* **Old Troon Sporting Antiques**

'Heaven on Earth' was how Andrew Carnegie described Skibo—his glorious castle which is now home to the Carnegie Club. Looking at the property today and particularly if you're a golfer, few could disagree.

The Scottish-born American steel tycoon and philanthropist left his home at the age of 13 for America where he made his fortune. Returning home he searched the county for a Highland home—he settled at Skibo. Celtic inhabitants titled it "Schythertolle" or fairyland of peace. Carnegie acquired the property 100 years ago and set about making it into one of the world's great residences. Guests, a veritable who's who of the day, were regaled in style, enjoying traditional Highland and other pursuits including golf, fishing, shooting, riding and tennis. Today, the Carnegie Club recreates the aura of Carnegies time, providing members with a delightful retreat from a busy world.

Food, accommodation and service are of the highest standard and today some classic sporting opportunities are available. Carnegie's original golf course has been reconstructed to provide an outstanding eighteen hole championship links and there are several other courses nearby including the renowned Royal Dornoch. Members enjoy the friendship that befits being part of a small international clan, who appreciate traditional values, good sportsmanship and the beauty of the Highlands.

The enchantingly beautiful estate, which covers over 7000 remote acres, is particularly private. That said, nearby Inverness enjoys good rail, air and road links, so there is no problem in reaching the estate. It also benefits from a mild and comparatively dry climate due mainly to the Gulf Stream and the 'Fohn'. The castle is particularly well sheltered by its topography and is sited on an elevated south-facing terrace offering spectacular views over the estate.

The castle also offers magnificent reception and bedrooms with a nostalgic atmosphere of the grand Edwardian era. In addition to the castle there are secluded lodges close by, so members can live in the castle but enjoy the privacy of their own lodges.

A delightful turn of the century swimming pavilion houses an original heated marble pool, a Clarins Spa, as well as health and gymnasium facilities in an elegant environment.

There are many celebrities who have spoken of the delights of Skibo Castle, but of all today's lucky guests it would be more appropriate to reflect on Andrew Carnegie's words 'Heaven on Earth'. His house, his dream, his heaven still lives on in the Carnegie Club at Skibo Castle. For more information please contact the numbers below.

The Carnegie Club at Skibo Castle
Dornoch, Sutherland
IV25 3RQ
Tel: (01862) 894600
Fax: (01862) 894601

Carnoustie, Scotland

Royal Dornoch, Scotland

Turnberry, 10th Hole, Scotland

Turnberry, 18th Hole, Scotland

Muirfield, 4th Hole, Scotland

Royal Troon, Scotland

Ailsa Course, Turnberry, Scotland

Prestwick, Scotland

Pictures by Graeme W Baxter courtesy of Baxter Prints, see page 352 for order details

Portmarnock, Ireland

Lahinch, Ireland

Killarney Killean Course, Ireland

Ballybunion, Ireland

Royal County Down, Ireland

Pictures by Graeme W Baxter courtesy of Baxter Prints, see page 352 for order details

Artist: **Douglas Adams** *THE LINKS* Courtesy of: **Burlington Gallery**

It is no secret that Northern Ireland has experienced a turbulent history—what is less widely known, however, is that it is a stunningly beautiful place. It is a land of forests and lakes, of mountains and glens. It boasts some of the most spectacular coastal scenery in the British Isles and where else can you view the handiwork of a giant? So much in a country no larger than Yorkshire.

The quality of golf is equally outstanding. There are approximately seventy courses in all, a large number of which are to be found close to the coast enjoying some quite splendid isolation. Belfast, which is about the size of Bristol, has no shortage of good courses, and not just parkland types either, and then, of course, there are the two jewels in the crown—Portrush and Newcastle, or if you prefer, **Royal Portrush** and **Royal County Down**.

Belfast and County Down

Belfast is a likely starting point and getting there should be fairly straightforward. Approaching from Dublin it is a case of following the N1 and the A1, while from Britain car ferries run regularly from Stranraer. And travelling by air is even simpler should you be thinking of hiring a car when you arrive.

Having declared nothing but your urge to break 80, resist at all costs the temptation to zoom off northwards to Portrush or southwards to Newcastle—Belfast offers much more than you probably imagine. The best known golf course immediately at hand is the appropriately named **Royal Belfast**. It is situated just outside the city on the north coast alongside Belfast Lough and is a classic example of well manicured parkland golf. A number of holes here are very scenic, particularly around the turn and there is considerable challenge to combine with the charm. Royal Belfast, together with **Ardglass**, **Portstewart**, **Portrush** and **County Down**, is featured on a later page.

Remaining in Belfast, **Malone** Golf Club at Dunmurry is one of the leading inland courses in all Ireland—a visit is therefore strongly recommended—and two 'Parks' are also decidedly worth inspecting. The first is Belvoir (pronounce it, 'Beever') and the second is Shandon. **Belvoir Park** lies five miles south of the city centre, **Shandon Park** just to the north: both are championship courses. The former is definitely the pick of the two with its magnificent tree-lined fairways, however Shandon has the advantage of offering some interesting views over historical Stormont.

Clandeboye Golf Club, situated not too far from Royal Belfast along the Bangor Road offers a different challenge. Clandeboye is more wooded and 'heathy' with a considerable splash of gorse. There are two courses, the more difficult Dufferin and the Ava. Very close by golfers should also note the **Blackwood** Golf Centre.

To the south of Newtownards, **Scrabo** Golf Club is worth an inspection—its opening hole is reckoned to be the toughest in Ireland—and circling back towards Belfast, **Lisburn** is almost in the same league as Malone and Belvoir Park.

A good base is required from which to visit these courses. In Belfast itself, the Wellington Park Hotel (01232) 381111 offers comfortable rooms and a thriving nightlife, particularly at weekends. Alternatively, the Europa Hotel (01232) 327000 is both modern and very comfortable but the most popular choice for golfers will probably be the Culloden Hotel (01232) 425223 at Holywood (very convenient for Royal Belfast). The Culloden is an impressive building, a baronial styled Victorian mansion. Its restaurant is particularly recommended. Another good eating place in Holywood is

Sullivans (01232) 421000 and on the subject of sumptuous fare, Belfast offers Speranza (01232) 230213 and Nick's Warehouse (01232) 439690. Belfast in fact is becoming renowned for its eating places and Roscoff (01232) 331532 and Manor House (01232) 238755 are two further places that offer particularly appealing fare. The former is particularly excellent. Whatever you do though don't forget to sample one or two of the local pubs—in most the atmosphere is tremendous. The Marine Court Hotel (01247) 451100 is recommended for those wishing to stay in Bangor, but for a cosy inn the best bet is to head towards Crawfordsburn where the Old Inn (01247) 853255 is a superb hostelry—full of character, its food is first class and there are some delightful bedrooms. Finally, adjacent to the new Blackwood Golf Centre (and obviously convenient for Clandeboye Golf Club as well) is the elegant Clandeboye Lodge Hotel (01247) 852500. Incidentally, the restaurant at Blackwood, the intriguingly named Shanks (01247) 853313 is very well thought of.

Relaxed, well fed, well lubricated and swing nicely grooved, the next golf course to play is **Kirkistown Castle**. It lies near the foot of the Ards Peninsula (once described somewhat alarmingly as the proboscis of Ulster!) Kirkistown is a real old-fashioned gem. James Braid assisted in the design of the course and is reputed to have commented wistfully 'If only I had this within 50 miles of London'. The town of Portaferry is no great distance away and the Portaferry Hotel (012477) 28231 is a marvellous place to spend the night. It is another of those cosy inns (note the splendid seafood here).

If you're not in a rush it is worth spending some time on the Ards Peninsula. It is a remote and beautiful corner of Ireland and Lough Strangford is one giant bird sanctuary and wildlife reserve. From Portaferry, take a ferry to Strangford and from here a short drive will take you to Ardglass on the coast. Perched on craggy rocks, the layout is reminiscent of some of the better seaside courses in Cornwall. A true 'hidden gem', Ardglass may be Northern Ireland's best kept golfing secret.

Beyond St John's Point and around Dundrum Bay, a journey of approximately twelve miles, lies Newcastle, an attractive seaside town and where, as the famous song tells you, 'the mountains of Mourne sweep down to the sea'. For golfers it is a paradise. Royal County Down Golf Club is quite simply one of the greatest courses in the world. For those lucky people who can enjoy a few days here, the Burrendale Hotel (013967) 22599 on Castlewellan Road is very popular with golfers (and only about a five minute drive from the course). Equally recommended is the Slieve Donard Hotel (013967) 23681 which practically adjoins the famous links—in fact you'll be aiming a couple of drives at its spires. There are, alas, fewer and fewer hotels nowadays able to combine old-fashioned elegance with modern comforts but the Slieve Donard is a memorable example. Newcastle is a holiday town and good quality guesthouses and bed and breakfasts abound. If one is staying in the area some sightseeing is strongly advised. To the south and west the mountain scenery is quite magnificent while the southern coastal road takes in some very different but beautiful views. Smuggling was once notorious here and, before reaching the border, we recommend that you smuggle in a quick 18 holes at **Warrenpoint**, where Ronan Rafferty learnt to play. Also try to make an excuse to visit Annalong and more specifically Glassdrumman Lodge (01396) 768451. This is a really delightful place to stay and dine—just ask Nick Faldo!

The Causeway Coast

Our journey now takes us back northwards, past Belfast to the Antrim coast. Here there is perhaps the most spectacular scenery of all and, equally important, yet more glorious golf.

Now, what kind of being can pick thorns out of his heels whilst running and can rip up a vast chunk of rock and hurl it fifty miles into the sea? Who on earth could perform such staggering feats? The answer is Finn McCool (who, alas, is not eligible for Ryder Cup selection). Finn was the great warrior giant who commanded the armies of the King of all Ireland. He inhabited an Antrim headland, probably not far from Portrush in fact. Having fallen madly in love with a lady giant who lived on the Hebridian Island of Staffa, Finn began building a giant bridge to bring her across the water. Either Finn grew fickle or the lady blew him out but the bridge was never completed Still, the Giants Causeway remains a great monument to one Finn McCool.

Royal Portrush is a monument to the Royal and Ancient game. However, don't limit your golf to Portrush—there are three other superb 18 hole courses nearby. To the east of Portrush, **Ballycastle** has an attractive situation overlooking an inviting stretch of sand and, if it didn't look so cold, the sea would be equally inviting. It is nothing like as tough as Portrush, more of a holiday course really, but tremendously enjoyable all the same.

Midway between Ballycastle and Portrush there is a pleasant nine holes at **Bushfoot** in Portballintrae and where the Bayview Hotel (012657) 31453 is a comfortable base. One should visit the famous Bushmills Distillery nearby—the oldest distillery in the world where whiskey has been produced since 1608. Just think what Finn might have done after a magnum of Black Bush. Equally popular with golfers it would appear is the Hillcrest Country House (01261) 731577 which offers exceptional value golf packages out of Bushmills. Another popular place to stay is the excellent Bushmills Inn (012657) 32339—ideal for those who wish to avoid both kinds of drinking and driving! Portrush's most celebrated eating place is Ramore on the quay, where there is a top class restaurant (01265) 824313 and a casual wine bar (01265) 823444. Those who have overindulged in Portrush and are seeking a comforting bed for the night should look (or stumble) no further than the excellent Magherabuoy House (01265) 823507. Alternatively we can recommend the Royal Court Hotel (01265) 822236, whose location high above the famous links is the envy of every hotel in Ireland and the Causeway Coast Hotel (01265) 822435.

Four miles west of Portrush and further along the coast is the fishing town of Portstewart. The Edgewater Hotel (01265) 833314 in town is near the golf club and there are numerous small hotels and B&Bs. Also convenient for both Portrush and Portstewart is Maddybenny Farm (01265) 823394, one of the finest guesthouses in the country. Further west again lies the course at **Roe Park** set in the grounds of the Radisson Roe Park Hotel (015047) 22222, a fine hotel with course to match.

One final course remains to be played on the splendid Causeway coast. **Castlerock** lies a few miles across the River Bann from Portstewart. Again a classic links set amid towering sand dunes, a game here will test every aspect of your game! There are many golfing delights in Northern Ireland that we have not explored, however, should Castlerock be your last port of call you'll have no excuse for not leaving Ireland a contented soul.

Further inland close to Ballymena you will find Galmgom Manor (01266) 881001 which is situated close to the golf course at the nearby castle. Another fine stopover is the Adair Arms Hotel (01266) 653674 set in the centre of Ballymena, but a good base for the local courses.

Artist: **N. Arthur Lorraine A MIXED FOURSOME** _Courtesy of:_ **Burlington Gallery**

Culloden Hotel

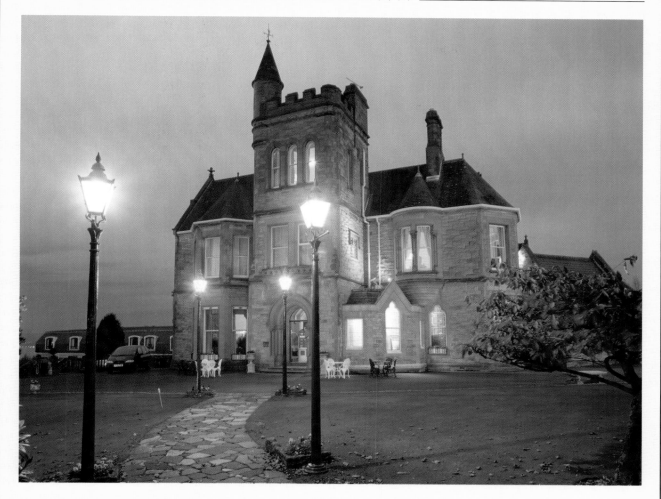

Northern Ireland's Five Star Hotel

Standing on the wooded slopes of the Holywood Hills, overlooking Belfast Lough and the County Antrim coastline, is the magnificent Culloden Hotel. Northern Ireland's only 5 star hotel and a member of the exclusive *Small Luxury Hotels of the World*, the Culloden offers guests the highest level of personalised friendly service combined with discreet efficiency. Originally built as a Bishop's Palace, the hotel is set in 12 acres of secluded gardens and yet is only six miles from Belfast city centre.

This fine hotel offers 90 bedrooms and some of the most magnificent suites in Ireland. As you would expect from a hotel of perfection and prestige, each guest room is exquisitely decorated and tastefully furnished to provide a true feeling of calm and relaxation.

Residents have full use of the exclusive Elysium Health Spa, which offers facilities such as a swimming pool, sauna, needle shower, and fitness suite, as well as a health and beauty salon. Guests may also make use of the excellent facilities in the Cultra Inn located in the hotel grounds.

The hotel's Mitre Restaurant can seat 150 diners, serving both table d'hôte and à la carte menus. Its small marble dance floor, baby grand piano and beautiful view over the gardens and the County Antrim coast make it a most luxurious restaurant. The superb cuisine and friendly service have won the Mitre Restaurant many top awards.

The Culloden is perfectly situated for the sailing and golfing visitor. Golfing enthusiasts have the added advantage of privileged tee-off times at the Royal Belfast Golf Club, which is within easy walking distance of the hotel.

The hotel provides residents with a hospitality car for travelling to and from Belfast City Airport, Belfast city centre and the Royal Belfast golf course.

Northern Ireland's only 5 Star Hotel

Culloden Hotel
Bangor Road Holywood
Co Down BT18 0EX
Tel: (01232) 425223
Fax: (01232) 426777
E mail: res.cull@hastingshotels.com
Internet: http:\\www.hastingshotels.com

The magnificent Slieve Donard Hotel is located in Newcastle, County Down, just 45 minutes south of Belfast.

Situated "where the Mountains of Mourne sweep down to the sea", the Slieve Donard Hotel stands in six acres of private grounds which extend to an extensive golden strand. Originally a luxurious railway hotel, the Slieve Donard offers 4 star accommodation and excellent facilities. It is the most popular hotel in the Province for a conference, holiday or golf break. All of its 134 luxury bedrooms are beautifully appointed with all the modern facilities you would expect from a top international hotel.

The Slieve Donard Hotel is the first choice for golfers who play at the world famous Royal County Down Golf Club. It is only two minutes through a beautiful hedged, arched walk to the course. Other courses close at hand are Kilkeel, Ardglass and Warrenpoint.

The hotel warmly welcomes all golfers and can arrange starting times with local courses, including Royal County

Down. A hospitality car can be provided by the hotel for residents.

Within the hotel, the Elysium Leisure Spa is a must for all visitors, with tennis, swimming in the luxurious indoor pool, putting on the lawn, or a relaxing sauna or jacuzzi. Other popular venues are Chaplin's Bar and the Percy French, an informal pub/restaurant in the grounds of the hotel, named after the writer of "The Mountains of Mourne".

The Slieve Donard is truly one of Ireland's great holiday hotels - renowned for its warm welcome, the efficiency and courtesy of its service, and, of course, for the gourmet food and fine wines served in the Oak Restaurant. Newcastle town is the gateway to the magnificent Mourne Mountains and Tollymore Forest Park where guests can enjoy excellent fishing, hiking on clearly marked trails, and pony-trekking.

The Slieve Donard is a member of Hastings Hotels, the leading group of hotels in Northern Ireland—a further guarantee of its excellence.

Slieve Donard Hotel
Downs Road, Newcastle
Co Down
Tel: (013967) 23681
Fax: (013967) 24830
E mail: res.sdh@hastingshotels.com
Internet: http:\\www.hastingshotels.com

Royal County Down

Approximately thirty miles to the south of Belfast and beneath the spectacular gaze of the Mountains of Mourne there lies the most beautiful golf course in the world. A daring statement perhaps, but will anyone who has visited disagree?

Royal County Down is situated in Newcastle and the course stretches out along the shores of Dundrum Bay. It was originally laid out in 1889 by 'Old' Tom Morris from St Andrews, who for his labours, we are told, was paid the princely sum of four guineas. In a way though, there was little that Old Tom had to do, for Royal County Down is also one of the world's most natural golfing links.

Within four years of the first ball being struck the course was considered good enough to stage the Irish Open Amateur Championship which was duly won by the greatest amateur of the day, John Ball. Before the 20th century had dawned, County Down was already being considered the finest course in all Ireland and some were even extending the accolade further.

Beautiful and natural, what next? Degree of difficulty. 'It was, in fact, the sternest examination in golf I had ever taken', the words of the very knowledgeable and well travelled golf writer Herbert Warren Wind. From its championship tees, Royal County Down measures 7037 yards, par 71. The fairways are often desperately narrow, the greens small, slick and not at all easy to hold; there are a number of blind tee shots amid the dunes and the rough comprises heather and thick gorse. Imagine what it's like in a fierce wind! Royal County Down is one of the toughest courses in the world.

Those wishing to pay homage should telephone the club well in advance of intended play. Visitors are certainly welcome, but the course can naturally only accommodate so many. Weekends are best avoided as indeed are Wednesdays, but Mondays, Tuesdays, Thursdays and Fridays are relatively easy for visitors; a letter of introduction from the golfer's home club is helpful. The **Secretary, Mr Peter Rolph** can be approached by telephone on **(013967) 23314** and by fax on (013967) 26281. The address to write to is **Royal County Down Golf Club, Golf Links Road, Newcastle, Co. Down. BT33 0AN**. The club's **Professional, Kevan Whitson,** can be contacted on **(013967) 22419**. In summer 1998 the green fees are £60 per round during the week with £70 payable at the weekend.

Visitors looking for a more sedate (but equally beautiful) challenge should take note of the **Annesley Links** at Royal County Down. Recently upgraded under the direction of Donald Steel, this course now measures 4681 yards,

par 66 (par 68 for ladies). It is open to visiting golfers all week, with green fees currently set at £15 during the week and £20 at weekends.

The thirty mile journey from Belfast is via Ballynahinch along the A24 and the A2. The road is a good one and it should take less than an hour. From Dublin to the south the distance is about ninety miles and here the route to follow is the N1 to Newry and then again the A24, this time approaching Newcastle from the west.

Unlike many of the great natural links courses, Royal County Down doesn't have the traditional 'out and back' type of layout; rather there are two distinct loops of nine. The outward loop, or half, is closer to the sea and hence is more sandy in nature and the dunes are consistently larger. You can hear the breaking of the waves as you play down the 1st fairway and your first blind tee shot comes as early as the par four 2nd. It is said that you can always spot the first time visitor to Newcastle for he walks up the 1st fairway backwards, so enchanting is the view behind!

Among the finest holes on the front nine are the 3rd with its extraordinary split-level fairway, the par three 4th, the dog-legged 5th, the 8th and the 9th, where an uphill drive must be targeted at the red spire of the Slieve Donard Hotel and followed (assuming the drive has successfully flown the hill and descended into the valley below) by a long second shot to a well guarded plateau green—a particularly memorable hole to conclude what many people consider to be the finest nine holes in golf.

The back nine may not have so many great sandhills, but there is still a plentiful supply of heather and gorse. Of the better holes perhaps the 13th, where the fairway curves its way through a beautiful heather-lined valley and the very difficult 15th stand out.

Given its rather remote situation and the lack of facilities or space to cope with a vast crowd of spectators the Open could sadly never be staged at Royal County Down. The Amateur Championship has been played here though, Michael Bonallack completing a hat trick of victories in 1970. The Irish Amateur Championship visits Newcastle regularly and there have been some truly memorable finals. In 1933, Eric Fiddian playing against Jack McLean, holed in one at the 7th in the morning round and then again at the 14th in the afternoon. A magical moment in a magical setting—and I don't suppose Fiddian felt too sore when McLean eventually won the match.

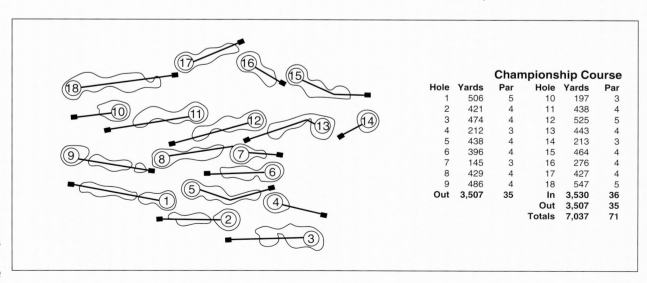

Championship Course					
Hole	Yards	Par	Hole	Yards	Par
1	506	5	10	197	3
2	421	4	11	438	4
3	474	4	12	525	5
4	212	3	13	443	4
5	438	4	14	213	3
6	396	4	15	464	4
7	145	3	16	276	4
8	429	4	17	427	4
9	486	4	18	547	5
Out	**3,507**	**35**	**In**	**3,530**	**36**
			Out	**3,507**	**35**
			Totals	**7,037**	**71**

Royal Portrush

In May 1988, Royal Portrush celebrated its one hundredth birthday. One could say that this famous club was born with a golfing silver spoon in its mouth. Within four years of its foundation patronage was bestowed, and there could never be a finer natural setting for a championship links. The course is laid out amid huge sand dunes which occupy slightly elevated ground providing commanding views over the Atlantic. And what views! The Antrim coast is at its most spectacular between the Giant's Causeway and Portrush and overlooking the links are the proud ruins of a magnificent castle, Dunluce, from which the championship course takes its name. The first professional the club employed was Sandy Herd, who went on to win the Open Championship in 1902, and as if by way of a final blessing, in 1951 Portrush became the first (and to this day the only) club in Ireland to stage the Open Championship

There are in fact two championship courses at Portrush. When people talk of 'the championship links' they are invariably referring to the **Dunluce** Course—this is where the Open and the 1993 Amateur Championship were staged—but there is also the **Valley** Course which can stretch to 6278 yards and is used for many important events. Somewhat surprisingly it has only twenty bunkers.

Visitors are made very welcome at Portrush and can play either course on any day of the week except Wednesday and Friday afternoons. The Valley course is also closed to visitors on Sunday mornings. It is always wise to telephone the club in advance as the tees may have been reserved and Portrush is popular in the summer.

In 1998 the green fees to play over the Dunluce Course are set at £55 per round between Monday and Friday and £65 for a single round at weekends and bank holidays (when available). Visitors may play a second round for an additional charge of £25. Fees for the Valley Course are £22 per round during the week and £30 at weekends, with an extra round costing a further £10. Golfing societies are equally welcome, subject of course to prior arrangement with the **Secretary, Wilma Erskine.** She may be contacted by writing to the **Royal Portrush Golf Club, Portrush, Co. Antrim. BT56 8JQ Tel: (01265) 822311** or fax: (01265) 823139; the club's

Professional, Dai Stevenson, can be reached on **(01265) 823335.**

The golf club lies about half a mile from Portrush town. Portrush itself is easily accessible as it is linked by coastal road to Portstewart and Ballycastle, and to Belfast by major road—a distance of approximately sixty miles. Londonderry is about thirty five miles to the west. The club is located immediately off Bushmills Road and don't forget to visit the famous distillery when you're in the area—it's less than 10 minutes from the links and is guaranteed to do wonders for your golf!

Although golf has been played at Portrush for more than a hundred years, the Dunluce Course bears little resemblance to the original championship course. Harry Colt is responsible for the present layout and we all owe him a great debt. Work was carried out between 1929 and 1932 and he is said to have considered it his masterpiece—and Harry Colt built many a great course. Bernard Darwin wrote in *The Times* after viewing the links during the 1951 Open: 'It is truly magnificent and Mr H S Colt, who designed it in its present form, has thereby built himself a monument more enduring than brass'.

Portrush's most celebrated holes are the 5th and the 14th. The 5th, 'White Rocks', is one of the most exhilarating two-shot holes in golf. From the tee, there is a splendid view of the Antrim Coast towards the White Rocks and the Giant's Causeway beyond. However spellbound you may be, considerable care is required with both the drive and the approach. The hole is properly a dog-leg and although a brave drive can cut the angle, failure will result in a trip into the deep, deep rough—over-hit your second and you're in the Atlantic! The green here nearly fell into the sea some years ago but a retaining wall was built and it has been saved. The 14th is titled 'Calamity', and not without good reason—a par three of over 200 yards in length, the direct line to the pin requires a very precise shot to carry an enormous ravine—mishit this one and you can be playing your next shot from at least fifty feet below the hole.

The course poses a considerable challenge but it's a fair one nonetheless. In the 1951 Open only twice during the entire tournament did a player break 70. Silver spoon or not, you can be sure my good friend Finn McCool would have been mightily impressed.

Dunluce Course					
Hole	Yards	Par	Hole	Yards	Par
1	392	4	10	478	5
2	505	5	11	170	3
3	155	3	12	392	4
4	457	4	13	386	4
5	384	4	14	210	3
6	189	3	15	365	4
7	431	4	16	428	4
8	384	4	17	548	5
9	475	5	18	469	4
Out	3,372	36	In	3,446	36
			Out	3,372	36
			Totals	6,818	72

Portstewart

The Causeway Coast of Northern Ireland—essentially the coast of Antrim with a bit of County Londonderry stuck on—has long been regarded as a fine place for a golfing break with three very good courses and one outstanding championship links to play. The last-mentioned is, of course, Royal Portrush, the only golf links in Ireland to have staged the Open Championship, the three supporting courses being Ballycastle, Portstewart and Castlerock. In the last few years all this has changed. It is not the opening of a new course (although some might describe it as such) but rather the extraordinary transformation of one of the supporting cast. Portstewart now ranks among the greatest courses in Ireland. How come? Two words will suffice, Thistly Hollow.

Visitors to Portstewart have always marvelled at the magnificent 425 yard, par four 1st hole. 'The best opening hole in Ireland' is the proud boast, and only the members at Portrush seem to grumble loudly. Of course the difficulty of having such a spectacular starter is that the main course has got a lot to live up to. Although the following seventeen holes at Portstewart were considered well above average, they were not able to sustain the sensation of wonder—that is until now. After playing the glorious 1st, golfers used to gaze up into the nearby range of sandhills, known as Thistly Hollow, and ruminate on how fantastic it would be if only they could build some golf holes amidst those towering dunes. Well now they have—and that is why Portstewart is such a fantastic golf course.

One of the people best able to tell you how this came about—for he presided over much of it—is the club's enthusiastic **Secretary, Michael Moss**. Visitors wishing to explore the awesome sandhills and the rest of the links are advised to contact the club a little in advance. The full address is **Portstewart Golf Club, 117 Strand Road, Portstewart, Co Londonderry, BT55 7PG**. Mr Moss can also be contacted by telephone on **(01265) 832015** and by fax on **(01265) 834097**, while Portstewart's **Professional, Alan Hunter** can be reached on **(01265) 832601**.

Although it is easy to get carried away with the major reshaping of the **Championship** Course it should be pointed out that there are now 45 holes of golf to enjoy at Portstewart. The short 18 hole **Old** Course has been around for a little while but a new nine hole course, the **Riverside 9** has evolved following the aforementioned

reshaping of the championship links. Broadly speaking, what has happened is that much of the former back nine at Portstewart has become the Riverside 9 and the new holes have been 'inserted' to immediately follow the famous 1st. This is only roughly what has happened for the 'new' 18th is still more or less the 'old' 18th—confused? The best bet is to pay a visit!

Portstewart welcomes visitors, although a round on the championship course is not normally possible on Saturdays and only limited times are available on Sundays. The summer green fee in 1998 for the championship course is £40 during the week and £60 at the weekend. A full eighteen holes on the Riverside 9 is priced at £10 midweek and £15 at weekends, while at similar times the green fee for the Old Course is £8 and £12 respectively.

Portstewart is situated right on the coast, some 4 miles from Coleraine and no greater a distance from Portrush which is to the east of Portstewart. The road that links each to the other is the A2. Belfast is approximately 65 miles away, though its airport is a little nearer. From there one doesn't have to journey through the capital to get to the Causeway Coast—the A26 is a very direct route. Londonderry is about 30 miles to the west and there is a second airport there.

So having played the splendid dog-leg 1st with its superbly elevated tee (every bit as exhilarating as the 5th at Portrush) and amphitheatre-like green, instead of gazing up into the sandhills the golfer playing the championship links must now get in amongst them. The 'new' front nine holes at Portstewart are being compared favourably with the back nine holes at Tralee Golf Club in County Kerry—and anyone who has played that exceptional links, designed by Arnold Palmer, will know that this is a mighty compliment. The views that these holes afford are also quite breathtaking and at times quite terrifying! The sight from the back tee at the 2nd, a stunning par four, provides an early example of both sensations. There are two tremendous short holes, the 3rd and the 6th, but perhaps even better are the long dune-fringed, sweeping par five 4th, and the classic stroke index one 5th.

The golfer may feel in a world of his own as he plays these holes but then that's Portstewart—a quite extraordinary golf course.

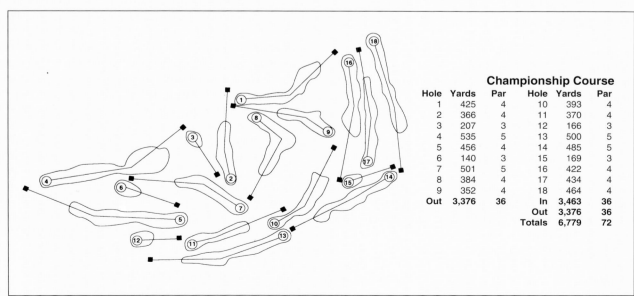

Championship Course					
Hole	Yards	Par	Hole	Yards	Par
1	425	4	10	393	4
2	366	4	11	370	4
3	207	3	12	166	3
4	535	5	13	500	5
5	456	4	14	485	5
6	140	3	15	169	3
7	501	5	16	422	4
8	384	4	17	434	4
9	352	4	18	464	4
Out	**3,376**	**36**	**In**	**3,463**	**36**
			Out	**3,376**	**36**
			Totals	**6,779**	**72**

The Causeway Coast in the North of Ireland is highly famed for its spectacular scenery, Bushmill's whiskey and the Giant's Causeway—and of course its long established reputation for fine links courses. Royal Portrush, Portstewart and Castlerock have all been established for over one hundred years and retain all the excellent qualities of ocean-side golf at its very best. Just along the coastline, Roe Park golf course is set in the historic Roe Valley, by the market town of Limavady on the lower reaches of the fine salmon fishing River Roe.

Roe Park course opened in 1992, followed in 1995 by the opening of the four star Radisson Roe Park Hotel, all set in a country Georgian estate. With its natural boundaries provided by the River Roe and with only minimal ground-shaping work required, this fine 18 hole parkland course already enjoys the historic ambience of its distinguished neighbours. Radisson Roe Park is Northern Ireland's only hotel with its own 18 hole golf course and the character of this Georgian estate is carried right through the impressive facilities—even the driving range is situated within an old walled garden.

The layout of the course, designed by the renowned local architect, Frank Ainsworth, makes full use of the local natural features. Water comes into play on at least six of the holes, and the entire layout is dominated by the central mound locally known as Drumceatt, with its historic links back to St Columba and the Convention of Drumceatt held in 575AD.

Rapidly gaining a deserved reputation for its excellent fairways, tricky greens and memorable holes, the course provides a most enjoyable test for golfers of all abilities.

In competition with seven strong par fours of around 400 yards, the holes causing most comment are the 15th, a short par four of only 272 yards, tempting the longer hitters to play direct to the green over a small lake (reminiscent of the 10th at the Belfry), the 12th, a beautifully sculptured par three over an attractive little pond, well stocked with water lilies and under hit golfballs! and the now mandatory 'signature hole', the 6th—again a par three surrounded by the Coach House, the walled garden, the castle and a tricky uphill approach over a deep and receptive chasm.

The course opens with a 400 yard par four and finishes with a 420 yard tester, so a combination of power and finesse are definite requirements—together with a second visit to work out the intricacies of the greens.

For golf-related enquiries, there is a direct line to golf reception on **(015047) 60105**. This gives you access to a computer-based advance booking system, ensuring a fuss free and friendly welcome on arrival. Advance bookings for both individuals and groups are essential, particularly at weekends. The standard green fee for 1998 is £20, certainly attractive for such comprehensive surroundings. Golf buggies, clubs and general golf equipment are all available for hire, while the resident PGA professional, **Seamus Duffy**, provides lessons and tips both on course and on the driving range (featuring 10 floodlit bays). Golf academies and clinics are also available for groups and/or corporate golf days. The Coach House Brasserie, just above the pro-shop, is ideal for individuals or groups to enjoy the rewards of well earned refreshments after their exertions on the golf course.

As many of the distinguished 'seniors' playing in the Annual British Seniors event at Royal Portrush have found, staying at Radisson Roe Park provides everything the discerning golfer requires—right on the doorstep.

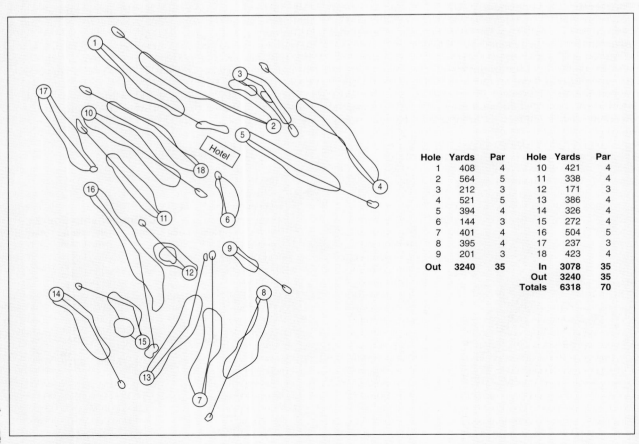

Hole	Yards	Par	Hole	Yards	Par
1	408	4	10	421	4
2	564	5	11	338	4
3	212	3	12	171	3
4	521	5	13	386	4
5	394	4	14	326	4
6	144	3	15	272	4
7	401	4	16	504	5
8	395	4	17	237	3
9	201	3	18	423	4
Out	**3240**	**35**	**In**	**3078**	**35**
			Out	**3240**	**35**
			Totals	**6318**	**70**

Radisson Roe Park Hotel and Golf Resort

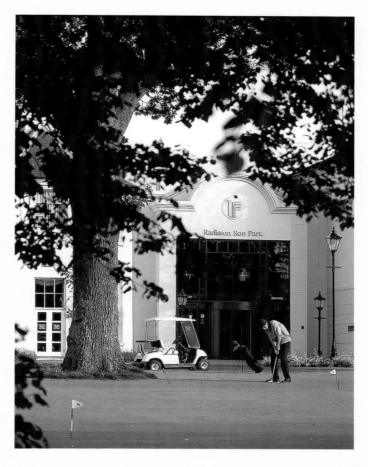

Situated in the picturesque Roe Valley countryside, Radisson Roe Park is Northern Ireland's only hotel and golf resort. This four star hotel is centred around the original building of Mullagh House, dating from the mid 18th century, and combines the elegance and charm of a country parkland estate with Radisson's renowned standards of service and hospitality. Radisson Roe Park is located outside the market town of Limavady in the north west of Ireland, 20 miles due west of Portrush.

The hotel is set in the heart of its own 18 hole parkland course, a challenging 6318 yards with a par of 70. The 10 bay floodlit driving range, pro-shop and resident PGA combine to offer the golfer a leisure break made to measure.

Sixty-four spacious bedrooms, including five suites and a large selection of rooms to sleep up to five adults, are all fully equipped with today's essentials. Residential leisure packages are available for both individuals and groups.

During their stay, residents enjoy complimentary membership of The Fairways Leisure Club, the hotel's superb fitness centre, featuring its own indoor heated pool, sauna, steam room, jacuzzi and full gymnasium. Also located in the Leisure Club is Eden Health and Beauty Salon, providing a range of luxurious treatments for both men and women, including a golfer's tonic to relieve aching muscles after a game of golf!

After working out in the gym or the challenge of the course, treat yourself in the 19th hole, The Coach House Brasserie, which serves a range of international cuisine from snacks to something more substantial. Alternatively, the award-winning elegant Courtyard Restaurant serves fine dining table d'hôte and à la carte menus, featuring the best of local produce. Relax for a quieter moment after your meal in the resident's lounge, O'Cahan's Bar, named after an old local legend.

Whether your pleasure is sporting, touring or pure relaxation, Radisson Roe Park welcomes you. A holiday can be based entirely on-site at Radisson Roe Park or you could use the hotel from which to visit the breathtaking surrounding countryside—east to the Causeway Coast, including the Giant's Causeway, Bushmill's distillery and Dunluce Castle or west to the coastline of Donegal's Inishowen Peninsula or Atlantic Drive. Other golf courses within a 30 mile radius include Royal Portrush, Portstewart, Castlerock, Ballyliffin and Rosapenna.

Radisson Roe Park Hotel and Golf Resort
Roe Park
Limavady
BT49 9LB
Tel: (015047) 22222
Fax: (015047) 22313
E mail: reservation@radisson.nireland.com.

Royal Belfast

Just as London is famed for the quality of its heathland courses, so Belfast is renowned for the quality of its parkland challenges. Within a short distance of the city centre are the likes of Belvoir Park, Shandon Park, Malone, Lisburn and, perhaps most famous of all, Royal Belfast.

Founded in 1881, Royal Belfast is the oldest golf club in Ireland. It's golf course is situated at Craigavad to the east of the city on the southern shores of Belfast Lough. The club's home has not always been here—there were two previous sites—but since 1925 it has enjoyed this genuinely spectacular location. The course was designed by Harry Colt, the same architect who transformed the links courses at Royal Portrush and Royal Dublin and who created a splendid layout at nearby Belvoir Park.

The land at Craigavad tilts consistently towards the Lough (something to remember when lining up putts!). This slope was used to dramatic effect in Colt's routing which includes no fewer than 13 distinct changes of direction. There is a good mix of uphill and downhill holes as well as left and right angled dog-legs. On the higher parts of the course golf is played along mature tree-lined avenues with occasional glimpses of the Lough. Down on the waterfront there is a very open, almost links feel to some of the holes. Colt's talent for cunning placement and elegant shaping of bunkers is also very evident, although in recent years Donald Steel has added and removed a few hazards to compensate for the effects of modern equipment.

The round begins with a strong two-shotter, a slightly uphill, curving dog-leg to the left, and is immediately followed by the first of several exhilarating downhill tee shots. After touring the fringes of the property, the course turns towards the Lough at the 5th and 6th. The 7th, an outstanding par three, swings back uphill but the 8th charges back down again to a green situated close to the shore. A few loughside joggers may pass comment on your drive at the 9th, and then come two of the best and most characterful holes on the course.

The 10th is a short par four that dog-legs to the left. The tee shot must be precisely placed for the green nestles in a tight, pocket-like corner, its entrance protected by an assortment of over-hanging trees and a bunker that eats into the front right side. The 11th is an intimidating par three played slightly uphill over rocky terrain that is covered in gorse bushes and scrub. The tempo momentarily relaxes at the next hole then builds to a strong finish with the 18th, a beautifully landscaped par five, providing a fitting finale to a most pleasurable round.

Royal Belfast Golf Club, Station Road Craigavad, Co Down BT18 0BP	
Sec/Manager	Susanna Morrison (01232) 428165 Fax (01232) 421404
Professional	Chris Spence (01232) 428586
Green Fees	WD £30/round WE £40/round
Restrictions	Proof of handicap required. Ring beforehand for bookings.
Directions	

The club is 7 miles north east of Belfast on the A2 Bangor road, about a mile outside Holywood.

Ardglass

The golfer in a hurry—or the golfer without a soul—will travel to Portrush from Belfast by journeying inland, by driving through the heart of Northern Ireland after picking up the A26 at Ballymena, bypassing the Causeway coast. That same person will head speedily for Newcastle, travelling due south via Ballynahinch. A bally idiot you might think.

The route to Newcastle we recommend is a very leisurely trip round the Ards Peninsula. Such a route will please the birdwatcher, for the road runs alongside Strangford Lough—one of the finest bird sanctuaries in Europe—fascinate the country house enthusiast and historian, as the road passes several magnificent houses as well as numerous castles, abbeys and monuments, and delight the golfer, for a game could be sneaked in at Kirkistown Castle. On reaching Portaferry the traveller takes a quick ferry ride and then heads for Ardglass, just seven scenic miles away along the coast of Co Down. The Mountains of Mourne loom on the horizon and Newcastle is just 12 miles beyond Ardglass. Now we suggest that all and sundry make a decent length pit stop.

Ardglass is an historic little town. It has a great seafaring tradition and was once, though it's hard to believe now, the busiest port in Ulster. It is particularly famous for its collection of 14th to 16th century castles (there are about half a dozen of them in various states of ruin) and is apparently celebrated for its herrings, though I cannot recall ever having sampled any. Perhaps they are a speciality at the 19th hole of Ardglass Golf Club? 18 holes of golf here will certainly create an appetite, though my guess is that the first-time visitor will be even more keen on getting back out and playing a second round on what is unquestionably one of the most spectacular and sporting courses in Ireland.

What makes Ardglass so enjoyable is its dramatic layout with several tees and greens overlooking the ocean. Measuring little more than 6000 yards it is not particularly long, although it has a really rugged feel and is part links, part clifftop in nature. Much of the course is overrun with vast swathes of purple heather.

The front nine holes are the more memorable, especially the first five which all run right alongside the sea. The par three second is many people's favourite—and many people's undoing—with its tee shot needing to be fired across a rocky inlet. A real death-or-glory hole and somewhat reminiscent of the 3rd at Tralee. By contrast the 18th offers a good chance of a closing birdie. Then, of course, it is off to the 19th, which being Ardglass is a converted ancient castle, and time to relax with a drink or two—unless, that is, you are a golfer in a hurry, or a golfer without a soul.

Ardglass Golf Club, Castle Place Ardglass, Co Down BT30 7TP	
Club Manager	Debbie Polly (01396) 841219 Fax (01396) 841841
Professional	Philip Farrell (01396) 841022
Green Fees	WD £14 WE £20
Directions	

The club is seven miles south of Downpatrick on the B1 and about 12 miles from Newcastle.

Key

To avoid disappointment it is advisable to telephone in advance

***Visitors welcome at most times
**Visitors usually allowed on weekdays only
*Visitors not normally permitted (Mon, Wed) No visitors on specified days

Approximate Green Fees
A   £40 plus
B   £25 to £40
C   £20 to £30
D   £15 to £25
E   under £15
F   Green fees on application

Restrictions
G   Guests only
H—Handicap certificate required
H—(24) Handicap of 24 or less
L —Letter of introduction required
M—Visitor must be a member of another recognised club

CO ANTRIM

Ballycastle G.C.
(012657) 63319
Cushendall Road, Ballycastle
(18) 5882 yards/***/D-C

Ballyclare G.C.
(01960) 322696
Springvale Road, Ballyclare
(18) 6282 yards/**/D/H

Ballymena G.C.
(01266) 861487
Raceview Road, Broughshane
(18) 5245 metres/***(Sat)/D/H

Bushfoot G.C.
(012657) 31317
Portballintrae, Bushmills
(9) 5572 yards/***/D/H

Cairndhu G.C.
(01574) 583324
Coast Road, Ballygally, Larne
(18) 6112 yards/***(Sat)/D

Carrickfergus G.C.
(01960) 363713
North Road, Carrickfergus
(18) 5765 yards/**/D

Cushendall G.C.
(01266) 771318
Shore Road, Cushendall, Ballymena
(9) 2193 metres/***/E

Gracehill G.C.
(01266) 51209
141 Ballinlea Road, Stranocum
(9) 5377 metres/***/E

Greenacres G.C.
(01960) 354111
153 Ballyrobert Road, Ballyclare
(18) 5820 yards/***/E

Greenisland G.C.
(01232) 862236
Upper Road, Greenisland
(9) 5887 yards/***(Sat)/D

Lambeg G.C.
(01846) 662738
Bells Lane, Lambeg, Lisburn
(9) 4583 yards/***/E

Larne G.C.
(01960) 382228
Ferris Bay Road, Islandmagee, Larne
(9) 6082 yards/***/E

Lisburn G.C.
(01846) 677216
Eglantine Road, Lisburn
(18) 6647 yards/**(am)/B

Massereene G.C.
(01849) 428096
Lough Road, Antrim
(18) 6559 yards/***(Fri)/C/H

Royal Portrush G.C.
(01265) 822311
Bushmills Road, Portrush
(18) 6818 yards/**(am)/A/H(24)
(18) 6278 yards/**(am)/C/H(24)

Whitehead G.C.
(01960) 353631
McCraes Brae, Whitehead
(18) 6362 yards/**(Sat)/D/G

CO ARMAGH

Ashfield G.C.
(01693) 868180
Freeduff, Cullyhana
(18) 5616 yards/***/E

County Armagh G.C.
(01861) 525861
Newry Road, Armagh
(18) 5649 metres/**/D

Craigavon Golf & Ski Centre
(01762) 326606
Silverwood, Lurgan
(18) 6496 yards/***/E

Edenmore G.C.
(01846) 611310
Drumnabreeze Road, Craigavan
(9) 6152 yards/***/E

Lurgan G.C.
(01762) 322087
The Demesne, Lurgan
(18) 5836 metres/***(Sat)/C

Mallusk G.C.
(01232) 843799
Newtonabbey
(9) 4444 metres/***/F

Portadown G.C.
(01762) 355356
Gilford Road, Portadown
(18) 5649 metres/**/C

Silverwood G.C.
(01762) 326606
Turmoyra Lane, Lurgan
(18) 6459 yards/**(am)/E/M

Trandragee G.C.
(01762) 841272
Trandragee, Craigavon
(18) 5446 metres/***(Thurs/Sat)/D

BELFAST

Ballyearl G.C.
(01232) 848287
Doagh Road, Newtonabbey
(9) 2362 yards/***/E

Balmoral G.C.
(01232) 381514
Lisburn Road, Belfast
(18) 5488 metres/**/C

Belvoir Park G.C.
(01232) 491693
Newtownbreda, Belfast
(18) 6516 yards/***(Wed)/B/H

Cliftonville G.C.
(01232) 746595
Westland Road, Belfast
(9) 2853 yards/**/D

Dunmurry G.C.
(01232) 610834
Dunmurry Lane, Belfast
(18) 5348 metres/**(Fri/Sat)/C/H

Fortwilliam G.C.
(01232) 370770
Downview Avenue, Belfast
(18) 5642 yards/***(Sat)/C

Gilnahirk G.C.
(01232) 448477
Manns Corner, Upper Brawiel Road
(9) 5398 yards/***/F

Knock G.C.
(01232) 483251
Summerfield, Dundonald
(18) 6435 yards/**/B/H

Malone G.C.
(01232) 612758
Upper Malone Road, Dunmurry
(18) 6476 yards/***(Sat/Wed)/A

Mount Ober G.& C.C.
(01232) 401811
Ballymaconaghy Road, Knockbracken
(18) 5391 yards/**/E

Ormeau G.C.
(01232) 640700
Park Road, Belfast
(9) 5306 yards/***/D

Shandon Park G.C.
(01232) 401856
Shandon Park, Belfast
(18) 6252 yards/***/C

CO DOWN

Ardglass G.C.
(01396) 841219
Castle Place, Ardglass
(18) 6048 yards/**/C

Ardminnan G.C.
((012477) 71321
15 Ardminnan Road, Portaferry
(9) 2766 metres/***/E

Banbridge G.C.
(018206) 62211
Huntly Road, Banbridge
(18) 5000 metres/**/D

Bangor G.C.
(01247) 270922
Broadway, Bangor
(18) 6424 yards/**/C

Blackwood G.C.
(01247) 852706
Clandeboye
(36)/***/F

Bright Castle G.C.
(01396) 841319
Bright, Downpatrick
(18) 7143 yards/***/D/H

Carnalea G.C.
(01247) 270368
Station Road, Bangor
(18) 5584 yards/***/D

Clandeboye G.C.
(01247) 271767
Conlig, Newtownards
(18) 6648 yards/**/C/G
(18) 5755 yards/**/C/G

Crossgar G.C.
(01396) 831523
Derryboye Road, Crossgan
(9) 4139 metres/***/E

Donaghadee G.C.
(01247) 883624
Warren Road, Donaghadee
(18) 5760 yards/***(Sat)/D

Downpatrick G.C.
(01396) 615947
Saul Road, Downpatrick
(18) 5615 metres/***/D

Helens Bay G.C.
(01247) 852815
Helens Bay, Bangor
(9) 5176 metres/***(Sat)/F

Holywood G.C.
(01232) 423135
Nuns Walk, Demesne Road
(18) 5153 metres/***/C

Kilkeel G.C.
(01693) 765095
Mourne Park, Ballyardle
(9) 6625 yards/***(Sat)/C

Kirkistown Castle G.C.
(012477) 71233
Cloughey, Newtownards
(18) 5596 metres/**/D-C

Mahee Island G.C.
(01247) 541234
Comber, Mahee Island
(9) 5580 yards/***/D

Ringdufferin G.C.
(01396) 828812
Toye, Killyleagh
(18) 4698 metres/***/E

Royal Belfast G.C.
(01232) 428165
Holywood, Craigavad
(18) 5963 yards/***/B/H/M

Royal County Down G.C.
(013967) 23314
Newcastle
(18) 7037 yards/**/A/H
(18) 4681 yards/**/D/H

Scrabo G.C.
(01247) 812355
Scrabo Road, Newtownards
(18) 5699 metres/***/D/H

Spa G.C.
(01238) 562365
Grove Road, Ballynahinch
(18) 6003 metres/**/D

Temple G.C
(01846) 639213
60 Church Road, Boardmills.
(9) 5451 yards/***/E

Warrenpoint G.C.
(016937) 53695
Lower Dromore Road, Warrenpoint
(18) 6215 yards/***(Wed)/D/H

CO FERMANAGH

Castlehume G.C.
(01365) 327077
Castle Hume, Eniskillen
(18) 6139 metres/***/D

Enniskillen G.C.
(01365) 325250
Enniskillen
(18) 5588 metres/***/D/H

CO LONDONDERRY

Brown Trout G.& C.C.
(01265) 868209
Agivey Road, Aghadovey, Coleraine
(9) 2800 yards/***/E

Castlerock G.C.
(01265) 848314
Circular Road, Castlerock
(18) 6687 yards/***/C/M
(9) 2457 metres/***/C/M

City of Derry G.C.
(01504) 46369
Prehan, Londonderry
(18) 6487 yards/***/D/H
(9) 2354 yards/***/D/H

Foyle G.C
(01504) 352222
Alder Road, Londonderry
(18) 6678 metres/***/D

Kilrea G.C.
(01266) 821048
Drumagarner Road, Kilrea
(9) 4326 yards/*(Tues/Wed/Sat)/E

Moyola Park G.C.
(01648) 468468
Shanemullagh, Castledawson
(18) 6522 yards/**/D

Portstewart G.C.
(01265) 832015
Strand Road, Portstewart
(18) 6779 yards/**/A/H
(18) 4733 yards/***/E
(9) 2662 yards/***/E

Roe Park G.C.
(015047) 60105
Limavaddy
(18) 6318 yards/***/C

CO TYRONE

Aughnacloy G.C.
(016625) 57050
99 Tullyvar Road, Aughnacloy
(9) 3017 metres/***/E

Dungannon G.C.
(018687) 727338
Mullaghmore, Dungannon
(18) 5433 metres/***/D

Fintona G.C.
(01662) 841480
Fintona
(9) 6250 yards/***/F

Killymoon G.C.
(016487) 63762
Killymoon, Cookstown
(18) 6013 yards/***/D/H

Newtownstewart G.C.
(016626) 61466
Golf Course Road,
Newtownstewart
(18) 6100 yards/***/E

Omagh G.C.
(01662) 241442
Dublin Road, Omagh
(18) 5633 metres/***/D
(18) 5429 metres/***/D

Strabane G.C.
(01504) 382007
Ballycolman, Strabane
(18) 5552 metres/***/D/H/M

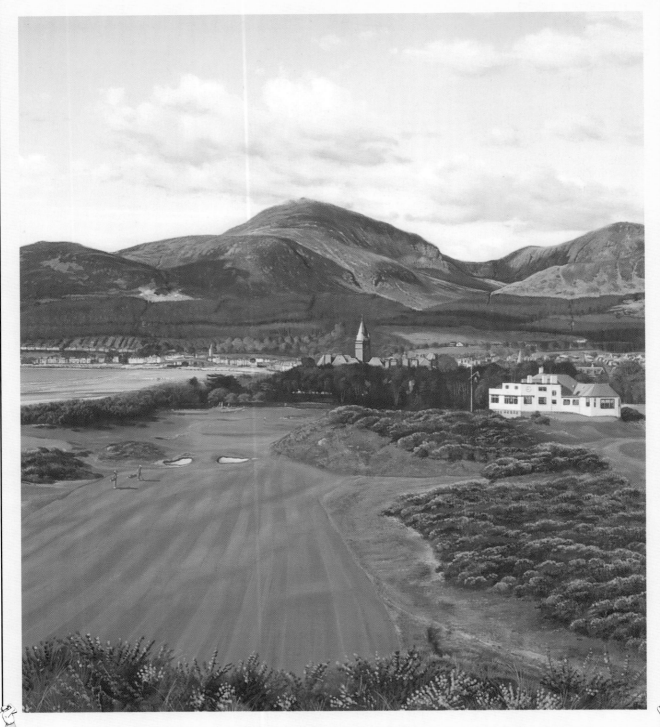

Artist: **Graeme W Baxter ROYAL COUNTY DOWN, IRELAND** *Courtesy of:* **Baxter Prints**

Artist: **Graeme W Baxter 15TH, PORTMARNOCK, IRELAND** Courtesy of: **Baxter Prints**

The Unicorn Restaurant & Apartments

It would plainly be wrong to describe Ireland as the gourmet capital of the world. Paris, New York, London and other notables would surely cry Non! No Way! No! But that isn't to say there are not a number of Irish culinary gems in the world's friendliest capital. One such jewel is The Unicorn.

In the heart of Dublin but off the main drag and a five iron shot from St Stephen's Green you will find this small but enchanting haven. The Unicorn is in the charge of the engaging Jeff Stokes and Giorgio Casari (formerly of La Caprice). Today the Unicorn goes from strength to strength and is a legendary meeting place for Dubliners and visitors alike. For the traveller, it is a joy to settle in with such a lively, jovial crowd. As Hugh Leonard wrote in the *Sunday Independent*; "If there is a friendlier restaurant in town, or one with better service, lead me to it."

The menu offers Italian fare of excellent quality accompanied by a good wine list. So if you are planning a day on one of the fairways or racecourses in the environs of Dublin, then win, lose or draw, book a table here. If you are unable to make dinner then the lunchtime 'long buffet' is excellent with antipasto, grilled aubergine and courgettes, seafood salad, red beans with tuna, salami and a plethora of vegetable salads.

Conde Naste in its new *Traveller* magazine recommends the Unicorn as the place to be on a Saturday night in Dublin. Keith Floyd who spent three months in Italy filming proclaimed that he has seldom enjoyed such a refreshingly homely and simple but delicious lunch as that offered at The Unicorn.

In addition to the excellent restaurant, The Unicorn offers smart, serviced apartments. One apartment has a double bedroom, another two, and there are three other studios available. Jeff and his design partner, for the project Deidre Whelan have created most attractive and comfortable interiors. One of the most appealing aspects is the excellent use of space within the apartments. Not a single foot is wasted. The small kitchenette in the two bedroomed apartment is an excellent example of this.

Stay at the Unicorn and take advantage of its central location to enjoy all Dublin has to offer. The apartments are reasonably priced and make a perfect base for a short trip to the capital. Perhaps the appeal of The Unicorn is best summed up by Trevor White in his review in *Food & Wine* magazine; "What is the secret of a successful restaurant? Unusually good food? Excellent service? A sense of theatre?

The answer of course, is a subtle blend of the three and nowhere in Ireland is the mixture employed to greater effect than at The Unicorn." Visitors from Paris, New York and London, to name but three cities, will surely be equally impressed.

The Unicorn Restaurant & Apartments
12B Merrion Court
Merrion Row
Dublin 2
Tel: (00 353) 1 676 2182
Fax (00 353) 1 662 4757

From the time you arrive in Ireland and crack your first drive straight down the middle, to the time you leave, having holed that tricky putt on the final green (and then drained your last drop of Guinness at the 19th), you cannot fail to be impressed by the natural charm and helpfulness of the Irish people. Nowhere is it more immediately apparent than in Dublin—what a contrast to many of the world's capital cities! Nothing seems rushed and nothing seems too much trouble. You see, the Irish welcome is quite simply second to none. As the century comes to a close we would recommend as warmly as ever a visit to this delightful island.

Dublin

Within ten miles of the city centre there are four great links and at least twenty other courses, most of which are of a very high standard. Two of the links are at Portmarnock—world-famous **Portmarnock** Golf Club and the impressive **Portmarnock Hotel and Golf Links.** The other two—and what a contrasting pair they make—are **Royal Dublin** to the south of Portmarnock, and **The Island** to the north near Malahide. All four links courses are explored later in this chapter. Not too far from Malahide (and close to Dublin Airport) is the championship parkland layout of the **St Margaret's Golf & Country Club.** Again, we investigate the course later in this chapter.

In Malahide the Grand Hotel (00 353) 1 845 0000 provides a perfect place to base oneself when playing the North Dublin courses. It is particularly handy for The Island and is less expensive (and certainly more attractive) than the majority of the capital's more centrally located hotels. The Portmarnock Hotel and Golf Links (00 353) 1 846 0611 has 108 luxury bedrooms and is the first choice of many golfers visiting Portmarnock. However, if one does wish to be more in the middle of things then among the better hotels in Dublin are the Shelbourne (00 353) 1 676 6471, the Berkeley Court (00 353) 1 660 1711 (which is possibly the best), the Burlington (00 353) 1 660 5222, Mont Clare (00 353) 1 661 6799 and Jury's (00 353) 1 660 5000. A recommended hotel for St Margaret's is the Forte Posthouse (00 353) 1 844 4211. Also well worth noting is the Royal Marine in Dun Laoghaire (00 353) 1 280 1911. In Howth, the King Sitric (00 353) 1 832 5235 is a well known seafood restaurant, and again particularly convenient for the courses to the north of Dublin. Good restaurants abound in the centre of Dublin and suggestions could include La Stampa (00 353) 1 677 8611, Patrick Guilbaud (00 353) 1 676 4192, Dobbins (00 353) 1 676 4679, Le Coq Hardi (00 353) 1 668 9070 and Locks (00 353) 1 454 3391. Visiting a Dublin bar is an experience in itself and ought not to be missed. One final thought for those of you visiting Dublin, try the Unicorn (00 353) 1 676 2182 - some good value but beautifully furnished apartments here and a restaurant to make you smile whatever the standard of your golf!

If most of the celebrated links golf courses are found to the north of Dublin, there are many more parkland challenges to the south and west of the capital, indeed, the city is practically encircled by golf courses. Without question the most talked about inland course in the south Dublin area is the Tom Craddock/Pat Ruddy designed **Druids Glen** golf course at Kilcoole in Co Wicklow, just south of Bray. Druids Glen, the Arnold Palmer designed course at the Kildare Country Club, **The K Club** (00 353) 1 627 3333 and **Luttrellstown Castle** (00 353) 1 808 9900 at Clonsilla are

all explored ahead. The hotels at these establishments are also outstanding.

In pre-Druids Glen days the leading club to the south of Dublin was **Woodbrook**. It too has played host to the Irish Open, in addition to many other important tournaments. Woodbrook offers a mixture of semi-links and parkland golf and has recently been extensively renovated.

A few miles further down the coast is the pleasant course at **Greystones**, from the back nine of which there are some marvellous views of the Wicklow Mountains, and a nearby 18 hole golf and hotel complex, the attractively priced **Charlesland** Golf and Country Club Hotel (00 353) 1 287 6764—more great views. Near the town of Wicklow, **Blainroe** Golf Club has a much improved—and pretty demanding—championship length layout, and there is a very scenic course at **Woodenbridge**. It's a bit of a drive from Dublin, but well worth it. Just south of Wicklow at Brittas Bay is **The European Club**, which is explored in our South East Ireland section.

Following a round in South Dublin, Roly's restaurant (00 353) 1 668 2611 in Ballsbridge is recommended. The Stillorgin Park Hotel (00 353) 1 288 1681 is very lively, while in Bray, not far from Greystones an evening spent at the Tree of Idleness (00 353) 1 286 3498 should be extremely relaxing. The Wicklow area is well served by Fitzpatricks Castle Hotel (00 353) 1 284 0700 and the Glenview Hotel (00 353) 1 287 3399, which is close to Druids Glen. Finally, a really attractive pair of Co Wicklow courses are **Powerscourt** and **Rathsallagh**. Both are featured ahead. For truly superb accommodation there is Rathsallagh House (00 353) 4 540 3112 and in Rathnew, the outstanding Tinakilly House (00 353) 404 69274 and Hunter's Hotel (00 353) 404 40106. It is well worth emphasising that the above are just a rich part of Irelands many golf courses - there are many more who welcome visitors and offer good value green fees with clubhouses of excellence. A final thought is to consider The City West Hotel and Golf Course, a well turned out establishment.

North of Dublin

Thirty miles north of Dublin in the charming village of Baltray near Drogheda is the **County Louth** Golf Club. Baltray, as the course is known, enjoys a wonderfully remote setting, but while it may be a peaceful place the course will test your game to the full. Baltray is featured ahead. Also make a note of the **Seapoint Golf Club** another handsome spot. One needn't look far for a bed as the club offers its own accommodation and meals are available. (Telephone (00 353) 41 22329 for details.) However, if there's no room at the 19th the best bet is either the Boyne Valley Hotel (00 353) 41 37737 in Drogheda, or the Neptune (00 353) 41 27107 in nearby Bettystown.

This latter hotel is very close to the **Laytown and Bettystown** links which, while not in the same class as Baltray, certainly poses enough problems. It is the home club of the former Ryder Cup player Des Smyth. Just north of Baltray (in fact visible just beyond the 14th tee at Co Louth) is the newly opened **Seapoint** Golf Club at Termonfeckin.

Further north the course at **Dundalk** deserves inspection. Again it's not in the same league as Baltray, but then very few are. Still, it's definitely worth visiting if only for the tremendous scenery it offers. Although very much a parkland type challenge, the course is set out alongside the shores of Dundalk Bay with the Mountains of Mourne and the Cooley Mountains providing a spectacular backdrop. The Ballymascanlon House (00 353) 42 71124 in Dundalk is very good value if a night's stopover is required, while for an outstanding restaurant try Quaglinos (00 353) 42 38567.

Dundalk provides a fine base for playing our final recommendation in the north east, the course at **Greenore** where a more dramatic location couldn't be wished for. Alongside Carlingford Lough, Greenore have recently built three new holes which are destined to be the envy of every golf course in Ireland. You don't believe it? Then go and visit—you'll be made most welcome!

Travelling Inland

For those who enjoy horseracing as well as golf (this must include near enough every Irishman), a good route to take out of Dublin is the N7. Given a clear road the Curragh is little more than half an hour's drive away. This is the Newmarket of Ireland. Golf has been played on the great stretch of heathland since the 1850s and the **Curragh** Golf Club was founded in 1883 making it the oldest golf club in the Republic. Rather like England's senior links, Westward Ho!, the fairways are shared with the local farmer's sheep. There's also a nearby army range—one presumes golf is rarely uneventful at the Curragh! It's actually a very

good course and the green fees are typically modest. Barberstown Castle (00 353) 62 88157 at Celbridge is an excellent place to head for after a day on the heath, especially if a game of golf has been combined with a day at the races. Others to note include Moyglare Manor (00 353) 16 286351 at Maynooth, a delightful Georgian country house and the Hotel Keadeen (00 353) 45 31666 in Ballymany.

Venturing further inland, **Mullingar** in County Westmeath, **Headfort** near Kells and **Royal Tara** at Navan (both in County Meath) and **Tullamore** in County Offaly are four of Ireland's best 'established' parkland layouts. Mullingar is probably the pick of the bunch, but all enjoy delightful locations and welcome visitors at most times. Those planning to stay in the area might consider the Hodson Bay Hotel (00 353) 902 92444 in Athlone or the Greville Arms (00 353) 44 48563 in Mullingar. Alternatively, Dunderry Lodge (00 353) 46 31671 is a restaurant to delight.

Finally, two hotel golf courses that are not exactly close to Dublin, but decidedly worth inspecting, are at the **Nuremore** Hotel (00 353) 42 61438, near Carrickmacross in Co Monaghan and the spectacular **Slieve Russell** Hotel course (00 353) 49 264444 at Ballyconnell in Co Cavan (featured in our North West section). Both offer comfortable accommodation and a myriad other facilities.

Artist: **Brid Clarke PORTMARNOCK** *Courtesy of:* **Portmarnock Golf Club**

Portmarnock

One day in 1893, a Scot named W L Pickeman domiciled in Dublin was riding his bicycle along the road from Baldoyle to Portmarnock when, so the story goes, looking across the estuary it occurred to him that he was looking at magnificent golfing terrain. . . .

Portmarnock is located to the North of Dublin and lying on a peninsula is surrounded by water on three sides. It can be as tough a challenge as any in the world—more than 7000 yards from the back tees with the rough often mercilessly punishing (knee-high in parts!) But Portmarnock, rather like Muirfield, offers a genuinely fair challenge. There is only one blind shot, there are no hidden traps and the greens are among the finest in the world. As for that rough, well, as an obviously straight-hitter once remarked, you've no business being there in the first place and you cannot really argue with that! Portmarnock has its beauty too. . . to the south, the Hill of Howth and the great sweep of Dublin Bay and to the north west, Drogheda and the distant Mountains of Mourne. On a fine day the links provides the player with a spectacular 360 degree vista; all in all it is a truly wonderful place to pursue the Royal and Ancient game.

The **Secretary** at Portmarnock is the very helpful **Mr John J Quigley**. He may be contacted by writing to **Portmarnock Golf Club, Portmarnock, Co Dublin,** by telephone on **(01) 846 2968** and by fax on (01) 846 2601 (the code is (00 353) 1 from the UK) The club's **Professional** is **Joey Purcell**, who can be reached on **(01) 846 2634**.

Providing visitors possess a handicap of 24 or less they are very welcome to play the famous links, although ladies cannot play at weekends or on bank holidays. It seems that half of Dublin wants to play Portmarnock (not to mention you and me) and the course can be extremely popular. The wisest move is to telephone the club before you set off. The green fees as set in 1998 are £65 from Monday to Friday (although there are no visitors on Wednesdays) and £80 at the weekend (subject to availability). Golfing societies are equally welcome subject to prior arrangement with the Secretary.

It is far easier to travel to Portmarnock than to many of the country's other great golfing attractions. The capital is very well served by international flights and Dublin's airport is only six miles from the links. From Britain, it is also worth noting that both B&I and Sealink sail regularly to Dublin. As mentioned, Portmarnock lies to the north of the capital, a distance of about eight miles. By road it's essentially a case of heading for Portmarnock village and then looking out for signs—

from Dublin the course should be signposted off to the right, and from Malahide, look to your left.

The casual visitor will not have to attempt the full 7000 yards plus, but he's still likely to be facing a good 6800 yards so he'd better have his game in fine fettle! Happily there is a relatively gentle break-in with three holes measuring less than 400 yards. The course then changes direction and the 4th, the stroke one hole confronts you. Normally, the wind will be with you, but don't bank on it! A number of second shots will be played to plateau greens which can be very difficult to hold and a good Irish pitch-and-run may be needed frequently. Two outstanding holes to note on the front nine are the par five 6th and the 8th. The most celebrated holes on the back nine are undoubtedly the 14th and the 15th. The former has been described by Henry Cotton as one of the greatest par fours in golf and it's easy to see why. The hole is played towards the sea along a gently curving, tumbling fairway; the narrow green sits on a plateau and is protected by two bunkers set into a natural rise just short of the green, with many humps and hillocks surrounding the putting surface—nothing but a precise second shot will do. As for the 15th, Ben Crenshaw has called it, 'one of the greatest short holes on earth'. Out of bounds in the form of the beach lurks the length of the hole to the right. Even then there is no let up and the five-four-four finish is one of the toughest around.

The gentle wind down of course begins at the 19th. Portmarnock has a splendid clubhouse, though not the original, which unfortunately burned down. The atmosphere is tremendous and some very good value snacks are offered daily with dinner also possible during the week.

The club has staged many great championships in the past including, somewhat surprisingly, the (British) Amateur Championship which was won—it goes without saying—by an Irishman. The World Cup was played at Portmarnock in 1960, Palmer and Snead winning for the United States, while winners of the Irish Open on this links have included Americans Crenshaw and Hubert Green and an illustrious quartet of European stars: Ballesteros, Langer, Woosnam and Olazabal—proving the old adage that a great course will always produce a great champion.

In 1991 Portmarnock successfully hosted the Walker Cup and there are many who consider it a travesty that the Ryder Cup matches did not come here in 1993.

Venue for the Jameson International Golf Challenge Finals (1997/8)

Hole	Metres	Par	Hole	Metres	Par
1	360	4	10	338	4
2	376	4	11	391	4
3	364	4	12	142	3
4	433	4	13	517	5
5	363	4	14	376	4
6	551	5	15	174	3
7	168	3	16	528	5
8	367	4	17	432	4
9	400	4	18	376	4
Out	**3,382**	**36**	**In**	**3274**	**36**
			Out	**3,382**	**36**
			Totals	**6,656**	**72**

The K Club (Straffan)

In timeless fashion, and without a care in the world the River Liffey meanders its way through the ancient Straffan Estate in Co Kildare en route to Dublin and the Irish Sea. In 1988 the estate was acquired by Ireland's largest, and possibly most ambitious company, Jefferson Smurfit—undoubtedly the great attraction being the vast 19th century Straffan House, one of the most striking country houses in Ireland. Such a company, such an estate—a heady mix if ever there was one. For some time it had been the dream of company chairman Dr Michael Smurfit to develop a 'world class country club'. At Straffan he saw the potential for an extremely grand, even palatial 5 star hotel (the restored and extended Straffan House) and sufficient land to build a challenging championship length golf course, one good enough to host national and international tournaments. Thus the Kildare Country Club, or The K Club as everyone calls it, was born.

When it came to the design of the golf course the word 'challenging' was clearly given special emphasis, for though four leading golf architects submitted proposals for the 18 hole layout, it seems there was not much of a contest once Arnold Palmer and his team had presented their ideas. Palmer had already created one course in Ireland, the ultra-spectacular links at Tralee on the west coast. Now was the opportunity to demonstrate his swashbuckling design theories on an inland site, just 25 miles south west of Dublin.

The golf course (which measures 7178 yards from its championship tees) was officially opened in 1991. To suggest that Palmer has succeeded in creating a challenging layout would be a gross understatement. With holes weaving their way through an extraordinary landscape, the unsuspecting golfer is likely to be awestruck and amazed by some of the shots he is asked to take on. . . Straffan is no ordinary golf course.

Notwithstanding its youth, The K Club has become the home of the European Open, one of the most prestigious events on the PGA European Tour. In its inaugural staging of the championship in 1995, Bernhard Langer holed a putt of at least 80 feet for an eagle three on the final green, before going on to win a sudden death play-off.

The **Director of Golf** at The K Club is **Paul Crowe** and the **Professional** is **Ernie Jones.** Visitors can make tee reservations by telephoning **(01) 601 7300,** by faxing on (01) 601 7399 or via e mail at golf@kclub.ie. All players must be golf club members and have a handicap. The green fee in 1998 is £120 with a reduced rate of £80 per person for groups of 16 and more.

Time then for us to 'attack' Arnie's golf course. A long straight drive at the 1st, carrying the large fairway bunker should set up a relatively easy opening par five. The same, however, cannot be said of the 2nd where two very precise shots are essential. The drive must be perfectly positioned, for the approach is downhill to a smallish green guarded by trees on one side and water on the other. And so the gauntlet is laid down. There are two par threes in the first five holes, the 5th being the more demanding, but for most people the round really comes alive at the par five 7th.

From tee to green this is one long, dramatic, 'S shaped' voyage of discovery as the hole double dog-legs its way over sand, rough and water and in between a plethora of colourful trees and shrubs. The green occupies its own pretty little island and is sandwiched between two arms of the River Liffey. A quaint old iron bridge transports players to and from the island. Our friend the River Liffey is an inseparable companion for the entire length of the 8th (a hooker's nightmare) and then comes the 9th, an intimidating par four with a giant tree standing defiantly in the centre of the fairway.

There is absolutely no let up on the back nine, indeed the drama most definitely increases. The 12th is probably the best par three on the course. The tee shot here must be struck over a small lake to a superbly angled green—between the lake and green is a deep beach-like bunker where the sand literally runs into the water's edge. The downhill par five 13th rivals the 18th as the most exhilarating hole: like the 7th, it is a double dog-leg with a highly elusive and heavily contoured green. From the 15th to the end of the round a series of heroic shots alongside or across water are called for. Two daring water carries in fact confront us at the 16th and a good drive at the last begs one final question: shall we risk a watery grave and go for the 18th green in two—a real grandstand finish in front of the magnificent clubhouse? Well, what would Arnie do?

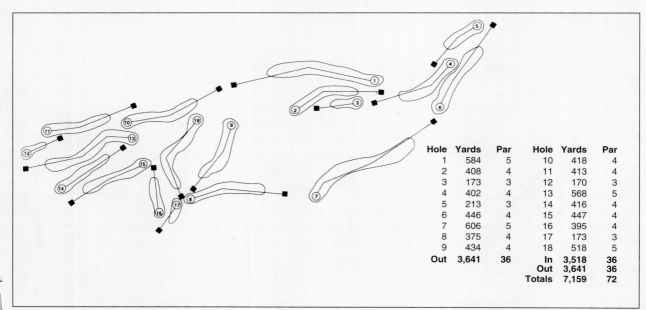

Hole	Yards	Par	Hole	Yards	Par
1	584	5	10	418	4
2	408	4	11	413	4
3	173	3	12	170	3
4	402	4	13	568	5
5	213	3	14	416	4
6	446	4	15	447	4
7	606	5	16	395	4
8	375	4	17	173	3
9	434	4	18	518	5
Out	**3,641**	**36**	**In**	**3,518**	**36**
			Out	**3,641**	**36**
			Totals	**7,159**	**72**

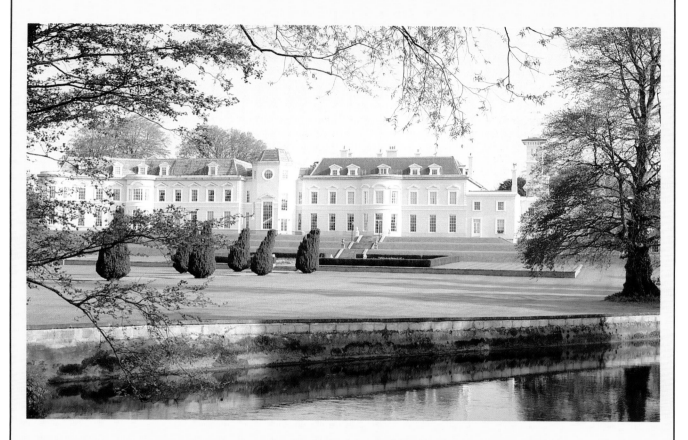

The 15th of July 1991 saw the official opening of the Kildare Hotel and Country Club, widely acclaimed as Ireland's premier resort development and a five star complex to rival the very best that Europe can offer.

The Kildare Hotel and Country Club has been developed at a cost of £27.5 million by Jefferson Smurfit Group plc. Ireland's world class hotel and sporting facility encompasses an 18 hole golf course designed by the legendary Arnold Palmer, salmon and trout fishing, indoor and outdoor tennis, exercise, swimming and croquet.

The entire project was created in less than three years and involved the complete renovation of the existing Straffan House. A new wing was added in the style of the existing house, establishing in the process a 45 bedroom hotel, whose exacting standards have few equals.

The bedrooms and suites are complemented by exquisitely appointed self-contained apartments and a magnificent three bedroom lodge in the grounds. Meetings and private dining take place in the Tower and River rooms, where work can happily be combined with play by taking advantage of the wide range of leisure and recreational activities.

The Kildare Country Club, now known simply as The 'K' Club, is a multi-facility sporting paradise. Members, hotel guests and visitors alike can enjoy the championship golf course, river and lake fishing, indoor and outdoor tennis, squash, gym, swimming pool, beauty treatment rooms, sauna and solarium.

The golf course has received many excellent reviews and has already hosted many national and international tournaments. Covering 177 acres of prime Co Kildare woodland, the course has a championship length of 7178 yards and a testing par of 72 (four par fives, four par threes and ten par fours).

Among eighteen exquisitely and imaginatively sculpted holes, particularly outstanding memories could stem from the huge par five 7th, the water-clad 8th or the spectacular par three 17th. Every hole, however, has its own challenge and beauty.

In the words of Arnold Palmer himself, reflecting proudly on his creation whilst standing on the terrace of the elevated clubhouse sited behind the eighteenth green; "We could draw for 100 years and not come up with as good a vision as we have here."

The Kildare Hotel and Country Club
Straffan
Co Kildare
Ireland
Tel: (00 353 1) 601 7200 (Hotel) 601 7300 (Clubhouse)
Fax: (00 353 1) 601 7299 (Hotel) 601 7399 (Clubhouse)
e mail: golf@kclub.ie

Portmarnock Hotel & Golf Links

From Co Kerry to Co Wicklow and from Co Donegal to Co Dublin, more links courses have been built in Ireland since the mid 1970s than have appeared in Britain this century.

It was Eddie Hackett who first set the ball rolling. The genial Irishman roamed the western shores of Ireland and left his mark at such wonderful places as Connemara, Enniscrone, Murvagh and, most famously, Waterville.

Then in the 1980s two of the greatest names in golf, Robert Trent Jones and Arnold Palmer, crossed the Atlantic and headed for the dunes at Ballybunion and Tralee. By the time they departed, Co Kerry had two more precious gems and the south west of Ireland was fast establishing itself as the greatest golfing region in the world.

Now enter Pat Ruddy. Never one to miss out on things, he summoned a helicopter and proceeded to scour the entire coast of Ireland before concluding that Brittas Bay in Co Wicklow was the perfect place to put down some roots. The dunes, the marram grass—everything else was in place. He created the European Club there, and then teamed up with Tom Craddock to build a second links course for Ballyliffin Golf Club in Co Donegal.

The Glashedy Links at Ballyliffin opened in August 1995. It is the country's most northerly situated course and is destined to become one of its greatest. But it wasn't the only outstanding links that was preparing to take its bow that summer. For the majority of the Irish—particularly those living in Dublin—there was one much closer to home.

The Portmarnock Hotel & Golf Links lies adjacent to Portmarnock Golf Club. The hotel, once the home of the Jameson (whiskey) family, became fully operational in June 1996. The new links was designed by Bernhard Langer, a three-time winner of the Irish Open, and the architect was Stan Eby. Together they have produced a masterpiece.

Perhaps the most immediately striking aspect of the links is how natural it appears. There is nothing flamboyant about the design and it is refreshing to see that no fewer than five of the par fours measure less than 380 yards. The course flows, almost gracefully, from green to tee to green. As at St Andrews and Ballybunion Old Course there are no lengthy walks in between holes.

The other very obvious feature is the quality and extent of the bunkering. There are almost 100 bunkers in total and each has been painstakingly and skilfully constructed with steep revetted faces, similar to Carnoustie and Muirfield. In fact, the Portmarnock Hotel links bears more of a resemblance generally to those two great Scottish courses than to neighbouring Portmarnock. More specifically, the front nine is reminiscent of Carnoustie and the back nine of Muirfield, although it could be argued that the final four holes are more thrilling than those at either of the Scottish links.

In true Carnoustie style then, the opening few holes demand a 'keep your head down' approach. The views are hardly distracting but the challenge is very evident. The landscape becomes more appealing from the 8th hole onwards. Aside from the climactic finish, the 8th is possibly the finest hole on the course. The fairway dog-legs sharply to the left before tumbling in classic links fashion towards a severely sloping green perched amid some very wild-looking dunes.

The par three 9th calls for an extremely precise shot to a table-shaped green, the 12th surely rivals the 14th at Baltray as the best short par four in Ireland and the 13th is an all-or-nothing par three.

The great finish begins at the 15th, where the approach must somehow be threaded past (or over) a sea of deep traps. The 16th is played from a superbly elevated tee. The 17th is yet another formidable short hole—beware the very cavernous greenside bunker—and the 18th descends from a lofty tee to an amphitheatre green surrounded by towering sand dunes and devilish pot bunkers. The perfect stage for a winning birdie!

Visitors are able to play the course on any day of the week but should make advance arrangements. The **Golf Director, Moira Cassidy**, can be reached by telephone on **(01) 846 1800** and by fax on (01) 846 2442. For hotel residents the green fees in 1998 are £30 per round midweek and £50 at weekends. For non residents, they are £50 per round throughout the week.

Venue for the Jameson International Golf Challenge Finals (1997/8)

Hole	Metres	Par	Hole	Metres	Par
1	320	4	10	467	5
2	350	4	11	406	4
3	172	3	12	316	4
4	512	5	13	135	3
5	409	4	14	312	4
6	462	5	15	352	4
7	405	4	16	354	4
8	323	4	17	171	3
9	139	3	18	365	4
Out	**3,092**	**36**	**In**	**2,878**	**35**
			Out	**3,092**	**36**
			Totals	**5,970**	**71**

The Portmarnock Hotel and Golf Links is Irelands newest and most talked about hotel and PGA championship links course. It is also the first golf course that the International Management Group (IMG) has developed in Ireland. It is therefore fitting that The Masters champion Bernhard Langer chose this magnificent setting to design his first links course and it has been an instant success staging the Irish Open, the World Cup and the Walker Cup.

Portmarnock is located on the east coast of Ireland and can be found just 30 minutes drive north of the capital Dublin one of Europes liveliest cities, and 15 minutes from Dublin International Airport, the hotel is on the north side of the peninsula so this golfing haven is within easy reach of all travellers.

Overlooking the links is the former Jameson (of whiskey fame) family home, which has been carefully redeveloped into a 103 luxury bedroomed hotel. It boasts a superbly appointed first class restaurant, where fresh local produce is served all year round. Bars, conference and function facilities are also available so whether on business or holiday all your needs will be taken care of.

As the house was owned by the Jameson's there have been some notable guests including all manner of royalty. The surrounding area is also steeped in history, so strolling through the 180 acres you will find the 12th century church of St Marnock and The Ogham Stone which has the earliest written characters known to have been used in Ireland.

As well as the course at Portmarnock there are many other championship standard golf courses within easy reach of the hotel so as a base you will be pushed to find any finer. For the non-golfer there is an abundance of activities to keep you occupied, fishing, walking, sailing or just driving through the beautiful dcountrysie there will be something here for everyone.

The course designer, Bernhard Langer has described it like this "There are very few locations in Europe that could have allowed me the opportunity and landscape to design such a classic championship links.I hope all those who play it discover its magic and its challenging beauty", and once youv'e played it I'm sure you will.

Portmarnock Hotel & Golf Links
Portmarnock
Co Dublin
Ireland
Tel: (00 353 1) 846 1800
Fax: (00 353 1) 846 2442

St Margaret's

I wonder what Old Tom Morris would have made of the recently opened St Margaret's Golf and Country Club. Not a lot probably. I'm not suggesting that he would necessarily disapprove of it but he probably wouldn't understand it. In fact, it would probably be as much a mystery to him as the jumbo jet aircraft at nearby Dublin Airport. Old Tom inhabited a very different world. It was Old Tom who designed the original golf links at Lahinch in Co Clare and Lahinch is about as different from St Margaret's as it is possible for a golf course to be. In many ways (historically, geographically and technically for a start) Dublin's lavish new parkland layout is the antithesis of the famous west coast links, the so called 'St Andrews of Ireland'. One of the advantages of being a present day golfer, however, is that it is possible to play both courses and discover that such contrasting challenges can be equally enjoyable.

There is a favourite saying among purveyors of real estate that the two most important aspects of a property are its location. . . . and its location! Situated close to the international airport and not far from the centre of Dublin, no club in Ireland is better placed to capture the attention of an ever increasing golf hungry public. Aesthetically speaking, the St Margaret's site was a fairly unremarkable piece of farmland before the bulldozers and the architects appeared on the scene. Now no one could ever describe St Margaret's as unremarkable—unrecognisable, yes. It is undoubtedly a very fine golf course and one without any obvious weaknesses.

Responsible for a very welcoming atmosphere is **Chief Executive, Tony Judge** who can be contacted by telephone on **(01) 864 0400.** There are no specific restrictions as to the time when visitors can play although advance booking is recommended. The green fees in 1998 are £40 per round—both during the week and at weekends.

From its championship tees, St Margaret's measures a shade under 7000 yards, or in other words, when the elements are stirred it can be a brute! Most players of course will not have to confront the many challenges from the back markers but playing from the forward tees in no way diminishes the character of the holes. This is because the real strength and flavour of St Margaret's lies in the great range of approach shots that the player is invited to take on. Perhaps the best example of this is provided by the 7th,

where following a downhill drive the approach shot to the green invokes memories of the celebrated par three 12th at Augusta—with water and a bunker in front of what is a raised and narrow putting surface and twin bunkers posing menacingly behind the flag at the back of the green.

As one might expect on a modern championship styled course, water not only features prominently, but shapes a number of fairways and greens at St Margaret's. The hole immediately following the 'slice of Augusta,' the dramatic par five 8th, illustrates the point perfectly. Here the golfer must avoid a lake to the left of the tee, another to the right of the fairway and a third which bisects the fairway immediately in front of the green—it all adds up to one of the most perilous journeys in Ireland!

On the back nine, the 12th is an absolute beauty but the 'piece de resistance' has to be the glorious finishing hole. The long, twisting par four 18th at St Margaret's features a dramatically positioned green which nervously overlooks a lake and which is in turn imperiously overlooked by the large clubhouse. It makes for a spectacular climax to the round, although golfers might feel more comfortable playing this hole wearing a blindfold. Blind shots at St Margaret's? Come back Old Tom.

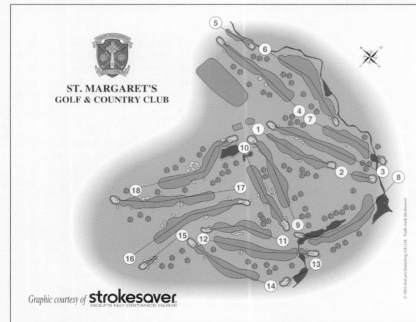

ST. MARGARET'S
GOLF & COUNTRY CLUB

Hole	Yards	Par		Hole	Yards	Par
1	358	4		10	395	4
2	149	3		11	366	4
3	509	5		12	474	5
4	456	4		13	194	3
5	174	3		14	402	4
6	458	4		15	180	3
7	374	4		16	535	5
8	525	5		17	512	5
9	398	4		18	458	4
Out	**3,401**	**36**		**In**	**3,516**	**37**
				Out	**3,401**	**36**
				Totals	**6,917**	**73**

Graphic courtesy of **strokesaver**
GOLF'S No1 DISTANCE GUIDE

With its location just ten minutes from Dublin airport and only 20 minutes from the city centre, for any golfer visiting Dublin a round of golf at St Margaret's is a must. The course designers, Tom Craddock and Pat Ruddy, have created at St Margaret's Golf and Country Club a course which, within two years of opening, has been accolated as one of Ireland's premier golfing venues.

The designers have turned a couple of hundred acres of flat farmland into a magnificent expanse of sculpted parkland. The modern design approach makes use of water hazards and each of the 18 holes is framed by manmade hills and huge undulating greens.

Challenging in terms of length the course has five par fives and four par threes—the rest being par fours. Flexible teeing allows the middle and high handicap golfer a fairer challenge on this course.

The par five 8th measures 525 yards and is set to become one of the most notorious holes in Europe. It features a lake to the left of the tee, a second lake to the right on the second shot and a third lake in front of the green. The 12th is perhaps the most picturesque of all the holes and features a generous rollercoaster fairway that dips between lakes and across a brook below the majestic elevated green.

The 18th hole is one of the finest in golf today and not for the faint hearted. The overall design of the course, the obvious attention to every small detail and the sheer beauty of the features all combine to inspire an excellent round of golf.

The clubhouse is designed with luxury in mind. It has a spacious bar ideal for relaxing after a challenging round of golf. The clubhouse also boasts a spike grill, luxury golf shop, an elegant restaurant and purpose-built conference suite. The overall effect is a welcoming building suitable for relaxing or conducting business. Corporate days and society outings are welcomed and expertly catered for under the guidance of Denis Kane and his experienced and friendly staff.

St Margaret's is designed as a place where golf is to be played recreationally and competitively. The club played host to the 1994/95 Ladies Irish Open. Over the last two years it has also played host to the Golf Writers Home Internationals, the Cork Dry Gin Foursomes and hosted the 1997 Irish Seniors Open.

For intending visitors bookings are simple—phone Gillian Harris, Reservations Manager, to reserve a tee time (pre booking is recommended).

St Margaret's Golf & Country Club
St Margaret's
County Dublin Ireland
Tel: (00 353 1) 8640400
Fax: (00 353 1) 8640289
E mail: stmarggc@indigo.ie
Website: http://www.fusio.ie/web1/stmargarets

Luttrellstown Castle

'I love it over here', said the great Seve Ballesteros to his Irish host. 'You have a wonderfully relaxed way of doing things. Surely there's an Irish word for our "Mañana"?' 'Good heavens, no', replied the stunned host, nothing quite so urgent!.'

An apocryphal story perhaps, but you understand the point. Go to Luttrellstown Castle and you'll experience the feeling. Luttrellstown is situated at Castleknock near Phoenix Park, just seven miles from the centre of Dublin yet it seems a world apart. It is not as if the spectacular castle and its splendid grounds are caught in a time warp—a great deal has happened here of late—but there is an air of timelessness about the place and, yes, it is wonderfully relaxing. Moreover, for golfers it has a special appeal since the opening in July 1993 of the Luttrellstown Castle Golf and Country Club.

As far as I am aware, 'the great Seve' (a three time winner of the Irish Open) has never been to Luttrellstown but an equally legendary figure has, namely the American, Gene Sarazen. At a sprightly 91 years of age, golf's 'Oldest Member' visited Luttrellstown Castle and took a buggy ride out to view the pristinely new golf course. He didn't play, but as he journeyed around the layout he was heard to declare, "This is one of the finest parkland courses I have ever seen." A spellbound Sarazen had no doubt been charmed by the majesty of the surroundings but as one who has played golf all over the world for some 80 odd years, he must know a really good course when he sees one. Despite his Italian ancestry, Sarazen is an American through-and-through and he lives in Florida where fine golf courses are two a penny. What I suspect he liked about Luttrellstown is that it is a thoroughly Irish parkland course in a thoroughly Irish setting. Had he been given a guided tour around the nearby K Club he might have imagined he was back in Florida, with all its vast manmade mounds, its beach like bunkers and plethora of do-or-die shots across water.

Luttrellstown is very different. There is no shortage of water. Mind you, indeed there are several dramatic water carries to be confronted during the 18 holes, but this is what the purists would describe as a very natural parkland course. The beautifully landscaped ponds and lakes exist primarily for the benefit of wildlife not golfers. There is no overt mounding but with gently undulating terrain and a glorious assortment of trees (ancient oaks, limes, beeches and a sprinkling of cedar and pine) there is plenty of definition to the holes and no need to frame the fairways with huge hills. And who in any event would wish to hide away the many delightful vistas—the serenity of the Dublin Mountains, the glimpses of an adjoining wooded glen with its waterfalls and cascades, an ancient bridge, a Doric Temple and an ivy-clad castle?

Under the skilful direction of architect Dr Nicholas Bielenberg, the golf course accommodates and takes advantage of its natural inheritance. From the championship markers it measures over 7000 yards (par 72) although from the forward and ladies' tees the challenge is less daunting. There are several highly memorable holes, with a particularly strong sequence between the 7th and 12th (the par three 10th was Sarazen's favourite) and none that could be described as dull. The putting surfaces are among the best conditioned in Ireland and the clubhouse—built in Finnish pine—is one of the country's most stylish   yes, Luttrellstown has charmed this writer as well! But I am sure no visitor will be disappointed by a trip to Luttrellstown Castle. With 1998 green fees set at £40 per round, £60 per day during the week and £45 per round, £65 per day at weekends (with group discounts available on request) there can be few more enjoyable places to while away the hours.

Tee reservations can be made by telephoning the club's **Professional, Graham Campbell** and his staff on **(01) 808 9988**, on fax no (01) 808 9989, or by e mail at golf@luttrellstown.ie.

Hole	Metres	Par		Hole	Metres	Par
1	384	4		10	171	3
2	472	5		11	325	4
3	386	4		12	526	5
4	352	4		13	403	4
5	338	4		14	396	4
6	202	3		15	415	4
7	358	4		16	153	3
8	127	3		17	493	5
9	508	5		18	375	4
Out	**3,127**	**36**		**In**	**3,257**	**36**
				Out	**3,127**	**36**
				Totals	**6,384**	**72**

Set in the grounds of the magnificent 560 acre Lutrellstown Castle estate, the course is being hailed as one of Ireland's finest, having hosted the Guardian Irish Open in 1997.

Dublin City, although a mere 15 minutes away, never intrudes as you savour the peace and beauty of the estate. Though cleverly exploiting the natural contours, the course has retained the integrity of a mature and ancient parkland. This championship facility offers many excellent features and is particularly renowned for the quality if its greens.

The clubhouse, which is of log construction and unique in Ireland, provides superb facilities for individuals and groups alike. A first class bar and restaurant, private meeting rooms and conference facilities and a well stocked pro shop all contribute to making this the ultimate destination for the discerning visitor.

The castle is internationally renowned as a venue for exclusive private and corporate entertaining. The 14 bedrooms and reception rooms have been restored and modernised to provide every possible comfort. Accommodation is also available on the estate in the self catering Courtyard Apartments.

Enquiries for additional information and bookings should be addressed to Adrienne Clarke at Luttrellstown Castle.

Luttrellstown Castle Golf & Country Club
Castleknock Dublin 15
Republic of Ireland
Tel: (00 353 1) 8089900 (Castle) 8089988 (Golf)
Fax: (00 353 1) 8089901 (Castle) 8089989 (Golf)
E mail Castle: enquiries@luttrellstown.ie
E mail: Golf: golf@luttrellstown.ie

Druids Glen

The brief was straightforward enough: 'Go and build the best inland course in Ireland . . . and then send us the bill.' Straightforward (and generous) but not simple. Better than Killarney? Better than The K Club and Mount Juliet? Before it was finished the hype began. There was no point in being modest: 'Druids Glen, Co Wicklow The Garden of Eden in the Garden of Ireland'. The burning question then, does it live up to its billing?

Druids Glen opened in 1995 and was immediately selected to host the 1996 Irish Open. This was such a success that the course was chosen as the Open venue for 1997 and 1998. Colin Montgomerie won in 1996 and 1997 and returns to aim for the hat trick in 1998. Druids Glen is indeed a special and stunning place. The chosen site near Newtownmountkennedy, the Woodstock estate at Kilcoole , was beautiful to begin with—not to mention historic. It was also perfect for building a golf course—undulating, well wooded and well watered. Today, the landscape is not so much beautiful, as shatteringly beautiful. And yes, the golf course is quite possibly the finest inland course in Ireland. It is certainly the most imaginatively conceived and the most visually striking.

Tom Craddock and Pat Ruddy are the architects of Druids Glen. It was they who relished and boldy rose to the challenge. Their design is an inspirational one—in both senses of the word. It is impossible to visit Druids Glen and not be reminded of Augusta. It was by no means the only influence but Druids Glen resembles Augusta National more than any other course on this side of the Atlantic—Jack O'Connor has seen to that.

Landscape gardener and nurseryman extraordinaire, O'Connor was commissioned to 'add background colour'. In fact, he went brilliantly berserk. At any time of the year, even in midwinter, Druids Glen is a riot of colour. When I asked the club if he might be able to provide me with the names of a few of the more unusual flowers and shrubs that had been planted, together with a list of some of the amazing trees that adorn the course, I was promptly sent a seven page fax! It makes incredible reading. The variety and the commitment (again in more senses than one) is staggering. Moreover, I have now become an authority on gold lonicera baggesoros or, if you prefer, hebe buxafolia. I also know that the large Celtic cross that has so magically sprouted on the face of the 12th tee was planted with dark green dwarf hebes and yellow spirea. The fax concluded with the words, 'Planting and landscaping continues'!

The famous American course architect, Charles Blair Macdonald once suggested, 'Putting greens are to golf courses what faces are to portraits'. The greens at Druids Glen are remarkable in terms of both contouring and condition. One could even go so far as to describe them as pioneering. In this regard, the designers were able to call upon the expert services of the renowned agronomist, James Lynch. He advised on the introduction of a new strain of creeping bent grass. The result is that Druids Glen can boast some of the best putting surfaces in Ireland.

Some golf courses begin benignly (in relative terms) then build to a dramatic climax; the new course at Adare is a good example, as is The K Club. The design of Druids Glen adopts a different approach. It starts strongly—the beautifully sweeping par four 1st where the green, according to the fertile imagination of Pat Ruddy 'lurks like a dangerous woman in the sunlit trees' (!) and the short 2nd (which was inspired, believe it or not, by the 17th at St Andrews) are two of the best holes on the course—and it finishes in a blaze of glory. In between, there are two purple patches. One on the front nine from the 7th to the 9th and another on the back nine, from the cathedral-like 12th (it is here that the druids built their altar) to the 14th—the Amen Corner of Ireland. As for the finishing blaze of glory, the 17th at Druids Glen is a potentially terrifying par three played across water to an island green—the first of its kind in Ireland. Water again threatens at the 18th, this time in the form of three lakes close to the green which, according to my friend Jack O'Connor, have been planted with 600 water lilies, and cascade over weirs one into the other.

Visitors are very welcome at Druids Glen. Subject to making a tee reservation they can play on any day of the week for a green fee (in 1998) of £75 (£65 for groups of 16 or more) with slightly lower rates between mid-October and mid-April. The **Golf Director, Aidan Murphy**, can be contacted by telephone on **(01) 287 3600** and by fax on (01) 287 3699. The 19th hole facilities at Druids Glen are as impressive as one might expect, the clubhouse being the restored and extended 18th century Woodstock House.

So then, 'Druids Glen, Co Wicklow—the Garden of Eden in the Garden of Ireland'? Why not. But then again, would the druids have sanctioned such biblical links? We'll compromise and declare that for golfers it is Shangri-la.

Venue for the Jameson International Golf Challenge Finals (1997)

Hole	Yards	Par	Hole	Yards	Par
1	445	4	10	440	4
2	190	3	11	522	5
3	339	4	12	174	3
4	446	4	13	471	4
5	517	5	14	399	4
6	476	4	15	456	4
7	405	4	16	538	5
8	166	3	17	203	3
9	389	4	18	450	4
Out	**3,373**	**35**	**In**	**3,653**	**36**
			Out	**3,373**	**35**
			Totals	**7,026**	**71**

Royal Dublin

The links at Royal Dublin may be the closest thing in Ireland to the Old Course at St Andrews. Laid out over a narrow track of land, it is the only one of Ireland's great links that stretches out and back in traditional 'Scottish' style. Harry Colt is credited as the architect rather than Mother Nature but it is a very minimalist design. Like St Andrews the land is essentially flat with subtle undulations (although Royal Dublin's fairways do not possess the Old Course's myriad little humps and hillocks). Wind and pin position dictate a player's strategy, the greens are kept firm and fast, and bump and run is king.

The golf club dates from 1885. Initially 'home' was a confined area in Phoenix Park, but in 1889 the club moved to its present site at Bull Island, still within the city limits. Bull Island is accessed by a wooden bridge and the duneland terrain is shared by golfers, bird watchers and botanists. It is an extraordinary domain—the backdrop is industrial and not particularly pretty but the island itself is a haven, a true sanctuary.

A combination of greater length and the prevailing wind ensures that the inward nine is invariably the tougher half. However, the outward nine includes arguably the two best holes, namely the par four 5th and the par five 8th. The former is called 'Valley', an apt description since the hole funnels along a narrow corridor of dunes; and the fairway has more undulations than any other. There is an out of bounds to the right of the hole and the left side of the green is guarded by a very deep pot bunker. The 8th curves from left to right, its green sitting on a plateau with a sharp fall-away to the left and a truly cavernous trap eating into the front right.

The inward nine starts to bare its teeth at the 11th, a tough par five that features another out of bounds all along the right edge of the fairway and a severely contoured two-tier green. The 12th is a long par three to a bowl-shaped green and the 13th is a formidable two-shotter where the entrance to the green is cambered and very narrow—again rather appropriately, the hole is called 'Dardanelles'.

The most famous hole at Royal Dublin is the 18th, 'Garden', a right-angled par four. The approach must be fired directly over an out of bounds field (the eponymous garden) to reach the green in two. Royal Dublin has staged many important championships over the years and the closing hole has provided many dramatic finishes. Christy O'Connor once finished 2-3-3 to win a tournament. Between 1983 and 1985 the club hosted the Irish Open Championship and the winners were Ballesteros, Langer and, in centenary year, Ballesteros again—the Spaniard defeating the German in a thrilling sudden death play-off.

Royal Dublin Golf Club,
Bull Island, Dollymount, Dublin 3

Manager	John Lambe (01) 833 6346
	Fax (01) 833 6504
Professional	Leonard Owens (01) 833 6477
Green Fees	WD £50; WE £60
Restrictions	No visitors Weds or any day between
	12.30 and 2.00.

Directions
The club is 15-20 minutes out of Dublin city centre on the road to Clontarf through Fairview.

Venue for the Jameson International Golf
Challenge Finals (1998)

The Island

When an American golfer travels to Scotland he feels compelled to visit the great Open Championship links—St Andrews, Muirfield, Carnoustie, Turnberry and Troon. That same person visiting Ireland will want to play at one or more of its famous five—Portmarnock, Ballybunion, Lahinch, Portrush and County Down. But what if he is an informed adventurer—a devotee of classic links golf who has already paid homage to those hallowed shrines? Well, when in Scotland he must decide whether to travel north to Dornoch and Cruden Bay or south to Machrihanish. And when he visits the Emerald Isle? Of course there is an array of glittering links courses to explore, but if he is 'in the know' and is a genuine connoisseur of traditional, old-fashioned links golf, he will not wish to roam far from Dublin. He will head straight for The Island Golf Club near Malahide.

Although founded over a century ago, The Island is Ireland's greatest golfing secret. There are several reasons for this, chief of which is the links' close proximity to Royal Dublin and Portmarnock, two very well established championship venues. Another is that until quite recently the principal mode of transport to The Island was by ferry. In fact it isn't literally an island—the course occupies a peninsula and the club's founders chose to build their clubhouse on the tip of that peninsula, directly across the estuary from Malahide. The rather eccentric voyage discouraged many but for those with a spirit of adventure it merely added to the allure and charm of the links.

The Island enjoys some of the most naturally rugged terrain on the east coast. It has been called 'the Lahinch of the east', and the sandhills dwarf those at Portmarnock. When the course was originally laid out (it is not clear by whom), little attempt was made to tame the landscape and the links was built right in amongst the dunes. Although changes have occurred over the years (the ferry was discontinued in 1973 when a newly sited clubhouse opened) the course has kept its essential character. In 1990, the club's centenary year, a revised layout was unveiled. It included several new holes but also retained the best of the old layout, including the wonderful sequence between the 12th and the 15th, which tour the tip of the peninsula.

American writer Jim Finegan eloquently summarised the attractions of The Island in his book *Emerald Fairways and Foam Flecked Seas:* "The Island is a great course, compelling our respect for the testing quality of its holes, winning our admiration for its naturalness, endowing us from start to finish with the unique joy of seaside golf at its best. The world should be beating a path to its door".

The Island Golf Club,
Corballis, Donabate, Co Dublin

Sec/Manager	John Finn (01) 843 6104
	Fax (01) 843 6860
Professional	Kevin Kelliher (01) 843 5002
Green Fees	WD £40/round; £50/day; WE £50
Restrictions	Booking essential. Very limited
	availability Wed, Thur, Sat, Sun.

Directions
From the airport, take the Dublin-Belfast road (N1). Two miles past Swords make a right turn towards Donabate then follow the signs to The Island.

Powerscourt

There was a time when golfing visitors to Ireland took a quick look around Dublin—sneaking in a round, perhaps, at Portmarnock—then raced off to the magical west. Now there has been some serious reappraisal. During the 1990s three outstanding courses (plus a handful of above average layouts) have opened in County Wicklow, directly south of Dublin. The first was Rathsallagh, the second Druids Glen and the most recent is Powerscourt—the closest to Dublin, situated just 12 miles south of the city at Enniskerry.

All three courses provide classic parkland golf, which is not surprising since each was laid out in the grounds of a well wooded estate. Indeed, Powerscourt is probably the most famous estate in all Ireland. Its name dates back to 1300 when the land was acquired by the Norman Le Poer family. In the 17th, 18th and 19th centuries the estate was owned by the Wingfields, who built Powerscourt House and gradually developed the gardens. Today those gardens cover 45 acres and are stunningly beautiful—a dash of Italy and a hint of Japan in the heart of Ireland.

The course is approached via an avenue of towering beech trees. You then turn into the golf club and are confronted by a handsome Georgian style clubhouse. Powerscourt House is close to the 1st tee and you are surrounded by rolling countryside. But there is still one more striking feature—Sugarloaf Mountain. Along with Croagh Patrick in Co Mayo this is Ireland's most famous peak and it dominates the horizon at Powerscourt.

The design is refreshing. The architect, Peter McEvoy, has placed an emphasis on subtlety and harmony and has not attempted to force or manufacture the spectacular. The course flows with the land and there are only two water hazards in the entire layout. And yet there is enormous variety. The first five holes, for instance, comprise a medium par four dog-legging mildly to the right, a par five that swings to the left, a short hole, a teasingly short par four where the tee shot must flirt with an out of bounds, and a big par three that plunges dramatically downhill. As for the quality of the greens, *Golf Monthly* described them in March 1996 as "18 of the best shaped putting surfaces since God had a hand in shaping Prestwick".

The variety continues. At the 8th McEvoy has employed old-fashioned crossbunkers while at the 11th, a tough two-shotter, there are no bunkers. The par three 16th occupies a 'secret corner' of the course and here is where you confront water—but you must also avoid three pot bunkers. Finally a huge par five and a sweeping par four guide you back to that most elegant of 19th holes.

Powerscourt Golf Club, Powerscourt Estate, Enniskerry, Co Wicklow	
Golf Manager	Bernard Gibbons (01) 204 6033
Professional	Paul Thompson (01) 204 6033
Green Fees	WD £50
	WE £60
Restrictions	Bookings preferred.
Directions	
12 miles south of Dublin off the N11, just south of Bray and adjacent to the village of Enniskerry.	

Rathsallagh

It must be wonderful to own a property right on the edge of a golf course; to be able to rise early and sneak out for a few holes before breakfast. A less expensive alternative is to spend a few days at Rathsallagh House in CoWicklow. It is a luxurious home-from-home and, importantly, it has a splendid 18 hole championship golf course at the bottom of its garden.

Nestling beneath the Wicklow Mountains near Dunlavin, Rathsallagh is a large estate with centuries of history. The golf course is a mere youngster, although you would never know. It was designed by Peter McEvoy and Christy O'Connor Jr (the architects of Fota Island) and opened for play in 1994. Gently rising and falling, the course meanders its way through more than 250 acres of mature parkland and woodland. Giant beech trees, oaks and limes adorn the grounds and some of the holes are played amid great avenues of trees, while others are attractively routed alongside winding streams and ponds.

The Irish press have been quick to lavish praise on the course. John Redmond described it as, 'Augusta without the azalea' and added, 'I would have no hesitation in declaring that it is as good a layout and challenge as you will find anywhere in Irish golf'. Comparisons with Augusta may be stretching the imagination a little but Rathsallagh is undoubtedly a fine course and on a glorious spring or summer's day there can be few more pleasant places to play golf. And imagine how colourful it becomes in autumn when those giant trees turn crimson and gold.

The most distinguishing feature of Rathsallagh is the quality of the putting surfaces—their design, construction and condition. Each of the greens is beautifully shaped and as they were built to USGA specification, they are extremely quick.

Among many strong holes on the front nine one might single out the par four 2nd, a beautifully conceived hole with a broad, sweeping fairway bordered by towering trees and a heavily guarded green. But the most celebrated sequence begins at the 6th, a zig-zagging minefield of a par five. The 7th is a very picturesque short hole and the 8th, an almost L-shaped par four where the approach must be fired across sand and water.

The finest holes on the back nine are possibly the 10th, which sweeps dramatically downhill, the par three 13th and the 15th which features a vast greenside bunker. As for the most difficult hole at Rathsallagh, how about the 18th—from the back tee it measures 450 yards and runs uphill towards a huge and severely contoured green. Anyone achieving a birdie at this hole deserves to be granted the freedom of Rathsallagh.

Rathsallagh Golf Club, Dunlavin, Co Wicklow, Ireland	
Director of Golf	Michael Birmingham (00 353) 45 403316
Green Fees	£25 (Mon), £30 (Tues-Thurs), £40 (Fri-Sun)
Restrictions	Telephone in advance to reserve tee times. Members only weekends before 11.00 am.
Directions	
Rathsallagh lies 1 mile south of Dunlavin and 30 miles from the centre of Dublin. From south Dublin travel via Tallacht and Blessington and from north Dublin via the Nass-Kilcullan bypass.	

Converted from Queen Anne stables when the main house was burnt to the ground in 1798 this large, comfortable farmhouse is situated in 500 acres of peaceful parkland surrounded by some of the most beautiful countryside of Eastern Ireland.

The addition of full modern amenities has done nothing to spoil the traditional splendour of the house where welcoming log fires combine with full central heating to ensure your comfort. The delightful bedrooms are individually decorated with care and attention; all are large and luxurious and offer en suite bathrooms with enormous bath towels.

The atmosphere is happy and relaxed in this hotel with its huge variety of diversions. The 18 hole championship golf course, set in 252 acres of mature parkland, was designed by Irish golfing legend Christy O'Connor Jr and Peter McEvoy, former world amateur champion and English captain. The course is not restricted to residents and members, although residents enjoy a reduced green fee. Rathsallagh also has a hard tennis court, near the indoor heated swimming pool alongside the sauna which is upstairs from the full size billiard table. Croquet and

archery are practised on the lawn. Alternatively, you could stroll around the award–winning two acre walled garden, or relax with a whiskey in the fully licensed bar. For the racing enthusiast the hotel is ideally situated for the Irish National Stud, along with Curragh, Punchestown, and Goff's sales paddock.

For a change, deer-stalking can be arranged, while your host, Joe O'Flynn, a former master of the local hunt can arrange fox-hunting in season. Besides the outstanding natural beauty of the surrounding areas there is also a variety of historic sites well worth a visit, not least of these being Glendalough and Russborough House.

At the end of such a day, the real log fire of the restaurant provides a pleasing welcome. The cooking is superb with the emphasis on fresh, local produce, while the too-tempting sweet trolley fairly groans with luscious offerings.

Naturally, Rathsallagh is fully able to cater for business meetings and offers, amongst other things, a fully equipped purpose-built conference room and helipad.

Rathsallagh Country House and Restaurant
Dunlavin
Co Wicklow
Ireland
Tel: (00 353 45) 403112
Fax: (00 353 45) 403343

County Louth (Baltray)

Golfing visitors to the east coast of Ireland can almost be forgiven if having arrived in Dublin they fail to travel any real distance beyond the fair city. Dotted around the fringes of Ireland's capital are numerous first rate challenges, something like 20 courses within 10 miles (or half an hour's drive) of O'Connell Street. (How many within thirty minutes of Piccadilly Circus?)

There is great variety too with classic links courses to the north, including world famous Portmarnock and Royal Dublin and some very pleasant, well manicured parkland courses to the south and west of the city. The quality of golf isn't the only reason why so many decide not to venture away from Dublin—the city and its people have much to offer. But I did say at the beginning, 'can *almost* be forgiven', because one of the greatest courses in Ireland lies no more than 40 miles north of Dublin (and about an hour's drive) just beyond Drogheda in the small fishing village of Baltray. This is where County Louth Golf Club is situated, and a truly magnificent and totally natural golf links.

Baltray, as everyone calls it, is one of the least widely known of Ireland's great championship links. Give the Club a major professional tournament and all this would probably change, but for the moment Baltray retains a fairly low profile, which doubtless suits many of the members! Not that they won't welcome you, mind you, for this must be one of the most friendly and informal clubs around. A genuinely relaxed Saturday afternoon atmosphere prevails throughout the week.

One gentleman who helps maintain the marvellous mood is the **Secretary, Michael Delany**. Visitors wishing to arrange a game at Baltray should contact him in advance of intended play either by writing to him at **County Louth Golf Club, Baltray, Co Louth, (041) 22329** fax (041) 22969, (00 353) 41 from Great Britain. The green fees in 1998 are £40 during the week and £50 at the weekend with reduced rates for juniors. Club competitions may make it difficult to arrange a game for the weekend but usually the only other day to try to avoid is Tuesday. Golf societies normally visit Baltray on Mondays and Thursdays. One other person you may wish to consult before striding out on to the links is the club's affable **Professional, Paddy McGuirk, (041) 22444**.

As already mentioned, Baltray is about an hour's drive from Dublin—less from the city's airport which is located 8 miles north of the capital. The road to pick up, both from Dublin and the airport is the N1. It links the city with Drogheda (and indeed carries on towards Belfast)

and is well signposted—if you follow the course of the River Boyne towards the sea you cannot go far wrong, but make sure you journey north of the river.

We were about to stride out onto the links, and tackle all 6567 yards, par 73 from the medal tees (6783 yards, par 73 from the back markers). The first two holes tempt us to open the shoulders (after all, the rough doesn't look too menacing) but on both holes a wayward drive can easily find a bunker, and this is the story all the way around. Architect Tom Simpson may have been presented with a wonderful piece of golfing terrain to work with when he designed the course in the 1930s, but he clearly put an enormous amount of thought into the positioning of bunkers and other hazards. The good shot at Baltray, however, is always rewarded, no more so than at the par five 3rd where the second must be played blind over a rise in the fairway to a narrow green. The 4th is only a drive and a pitch but it is a classic links hole with a tumbling, folding, dune-lined fairway. The 5th green is actually perched high in these dunes. It is a splendid short hole and one of Baltray's 'four little gems'.

For many the most exciting holes appear between the 12th and 16th at the far end of the links, the part closest to the sea and where nature presents the dunes at their wildest. The entire 12th fairway appears to have been carved out of the surrounding towering sandhills. The shot to the green has to be targeted through a gap in the dunes and only a perfect long iron will suffice—spray it to the left or right and disaster awaits. The 13th is almost as difficult but the far reaching views from the elevated 14th tee will placate the most wounded souls. This is a beautiful and historic part of the world and as you drive at the 14th (a hole which is arguably the finest short par four in Ireland) the broad estuary of the River Boyne, famed for its 17th century battle, stretches out ahead. Over your shoulder are the far off romantic Mountains of Mourne. Another fine par four comes at the 16th where the angled approach is played into an amphitheatre green. It is a superb dog-leg hole, and again one of several at Baltray. A new championship tee has added considerable teeth to the par five 18th, however from the forward tees it still offers a real chance of a finishing birdie.

The way to celebrate such a feat at Baltray is with a drop of the famous black and white stuff—almost, but not quite obligatory. Good food and overnight accommodation in the clubhouse can also be arranged. Like every good Irish golf club, Baltray has 19 splendid holes.

Hole	Yards	Par	Hole	Yards	Par
1	433	4	10	398	4
2	482	5	11	481	5
3	544	5	12	410	4
4	344	4	13	421	4
5	158	3	14	332	4
6	531	5	15	152	3
7	163	3	16	388	4
8	407	4	17	179	3
9	419	4	18	541	5
Out	**3,481**	**37**	**In**	**3,302**	**36**
			Out	**3,481**	**37**
			Totals	**6,783**	**73**

Artist: **Bill Waugh** **THE BEST VIEW IN GOLF** *Courtesy of:* **Burlington Gallery**

Continuing to wander down through the counties of Ireland, County Laois is the next we come across. There's only one 18 hole course, the **Heath** and no guesses as to the type of golf offered. The course is laid out on common land and rather like the Curragh, there's a fair chance that you'll spot more sheep than golfers. Also like the Curragh it is a most historic course and has special apeal to those interested in the game's heritage.

Stumbling into County Carlow we find probably the best inland course (aside from Mount Juliet) in south east Ireland. **Carlow** is a superb course: well bunkered and well wooded, it presents a considerable test of golf but a very fair one nonetheless. Carlow is highlighted later in this chapter. There are a number of convenient hotels in Carlow itself but for a real treat stay in Castledermot at **Kilkea Castle** (00 353) 503 45156, a splendidly converted 12th century castle. Kilkea has its own turf nursery and has opened an 18 hole golf course in the grounds. The Seven Oak Hotel (00 353) 503 31308 in Carlow also offers good food; plain by comparison with the stately hotels of the area, but excellent value. A very popular restaurant is also found in Castledermot, the Doyles School House (00 353) 503 44282.

Kilkenny is one of those places that has to be visited. It's a town steeped in Irish history. In medieval times it housed the Irish Parliament, then there's the famous Kilkenny Castle, an impressive collection of churches and Kytelers Inn. The city's golf course is a bit of a youngster in comparison, but it's a fine parkland course, very typical of Ireland's better inland courses. The Newpark Hotel (00 353) 562 2122 is just one of several comfortable establishments in the town.

Nearby, Thomastown is the setting for the magnificent **Mount Juliet** complex (00 353) 562 4455, featuring 18 spectacular holes designed by Jack Nicklaus (see ahead) and a luxurious country house hotel and excellent restaurant. Less formal but thoroughly gracious accommodation can be found at Hunters Yard at Mount Juliet (00 353) 56 24725. It is an 18th century converted stable block packed with character. For non residents, the Loft Restaurant is good value with a good atmosphere and excellent food. One mile from Thomastown and adjacent to Jerpoint Abbey is the Abbey House (00 353) 562 4192—a highly recommended guesthouse.

From Kilkenny it's a pleasant drive to **Borris** where there is an excellent 9 holer and it's certainly not a long way to Tipperary either. Visitors to the county with the famous name should slip a game in at **Clonmel**. This is a fairly isolated part of Ireland and you may just have the course to yourself on a quiet weekday.

A good place to put the feet up after a game is the Hotel Minella (00 353) 52 22388, considered by many the best in this area, or alternatively, the Clonmel Arms Hotel (00 353) 522 1233. Not too far away in Cashel, (and be sure to visit the magnificent Rock) the Cashel Palace Hotel (00 353) 626 1411 and its restaurant, the Four Seasons are quite outstanding. The former Archbishop's Palace also has some magnificent gardens in which to reflect on one's swing. Before heading down to Waterford a quick recommendation for the 18 hole course at **Courtown**, close to the north Wexford coast which boasts some fabulous beaches—in fact the golden sands stretch practically all the way south to Wexford town. A charming place to stay when playing Courtown is Marlfield House (00 353) 55 21124 at Gorey, one of the finest country houses in Ireland.

The world famous Waterford crystal factory is reason enough for stopping a while in the Waterford area, but there are other sound reasons too. The first is **Waterford Castle**, the kind of place you dream about: an ivy-clad 12th century castle dominating a small island which can only be reached by ferry. Today, the castle is one of Ireland's finest hotels (00 353) 51 78203. Moreover, the island isn't quite so small that space could not be found for an 18 hole golf and country club! The course, designed by Ryder Cup golfer Des Smyth, opened in the summer of 1992.

The other good reasons for visiting Waterford are **Tramore** Golf Club and **Waterford** Golf Club—both offer very good parkland golf. The former, just 15 minutes from Waterford, is a real test and is good enough to have staged the Irish Amateur Championship in 1987. The latter, however, is possibly more enjoyable having greater variety, especially on the back nine which features a magnificent downhill finishing hole. The course is described in greater detail on a later page.

Either side of Waterford there has been much golf course building activity and both **West Waterford** Golf Club at Dungarvon and **St Helen's Bay** are well worth inspecting from a base such as the Ferrycarrig Hotel (00 353) 53 22999 in Wexford. Alternatively try the cosy cottages beside St Helens Bay (00 353) 53 33234. The restaurant here is held in particularly high regard. Additional places to stay include Jurys (00 353) 51 32111, a focal point for the town. Those visiting the Dungarvon area should certainly try to visit Lawlors Hotel (00 353) 58 41122, another hotel with a reputation for entertaining.

But we end our journey in **Rosslare**. Having started our tour of south east Ireland on a heath, we end on a links. Rosslare may not have the glamour of a Portmarnock or a Royal Dublin but for lovers of the traditional game—rolling sand dunes and a hammering wind—it will do perfectly.

Those of you seeking immediate sustenance, or possibly a place to shelter after your ferry crossing should certainly consider Kelly's Strand Hotel (00 353) 32114. There are good facilities here, making it a fine base from which to commence or conclude a journey in this truly delightful land. One final thought before we move on, golfers might care to visit the splendidly named Ballyhack. A restaurant to mention here is the Neptune (00 353) 51 389284 on the harbour—excellent seafood and an ideal place in which to reflect upon your day's golf.

*Artist: **A B Frost** FORE Courtesy of: **Rosenstiel's***

Carlow

While it may be little known internationally, Carlow Golf Club has a proud reputation in Ireland. In 1978 it hosted the Irish Close Championship—normally the preserve of links courses—and in its annual poll of Ireland's 'Top 30 Golf Courses', the Irish Golf Institute rate Carlow among the country's top three inland courses built before 1990.

Strictly speaking, Carlow is a parkland type course and it certainly boasts a wealth of wonderfully mature trees., However, in places it has much more of a moorland, even heathland feel and the subsoil is quite sandy. In fact Carlow is something of a cross between Yorkshire's Moortown and Fulford—and it's just as good.

The course was designed by Cecil Barcroft, a native of Portrush. It opened in 1922 and was remodelled in 1937 by Thomas Simpson, assisted by Molly Gourlay. Visitors have always been made very welcome. The current **Secretary** at Carlow is **Margaret Meaney** and she can be contacted by telephone on **(0503) 31695** or fax **(0503) 40065**. Advance bookings are recommended and although it is naturally much easier to arrange a game during the week, weekend golf is always a possibility. The 1998 green fees are set at £22 on weekdays and £27 at weekends. Weekly and fortnightly tickets can also be purchased and reduced rates are available for parties of 12 and over. Carlow's **Professional** is **Andrew Gilbert** and he can be reached on **(0503) 41745**.

The county town of Carlow is located approximately 50 miles south of Dublin and the road linking each to the other is the N9. The same road joins Carlow with Thomastown (Mount Juliet), Kilkenny and Waterford to the south. The golf club is situated just to the north of the town, immediately off the Dublin Road.

From the championship tees Carlow is certainly no monster, measuring just over 6500 yards, (5974 metres) but it has a fairly tight par of 70 and is never 'torn apart'. The round begins with a pair of very contrasting par fours. The 1st is one of Carlow's toughest, a lengthy dog-leg left to a heavily guarded green: only a long straight drive up the right hand side of the fairway will suffice. At the 2nd, though, the sensible shot is to lay up with an iron off the tee, still leaving only a pitch to the green: a big smash with a driver might get you close to the green but it might also cause you to take a drop out of the water hazard. Probably the best two holes on the front nine are the stroke one 7th where the fairway meanders around to the left yet tries to throw your ball off to the right—a marvel-

lously sited green here—and the spectacular downhill 8th where if you were prudent and held back on the 2nd tee no one could begrudge you now winding up and letting fly from this superbly elevated tee.

The real fun, however, is still to come. Carlow's back nine is exceptionally good and precision becomes the name of the game. A deft pitch is required over an attractive pond at the 10th and disaster can befall the shot that misses the green at the 12th: Carlow's rough is nothing if not punishing! A trio of par fours, the 14th, 15th and 16th guide you into deepest Co Carlow—each is a really fine hole. The 16th, which is played through a tunnel-like valley, is perhaps the most demanding two-shotter of the entire round, and is followed immediately by the most celebrated par three hole. I mentioned 'precision' earlier, well, tackling the 17th at Carlow has been likened to threading a needle. How's your eyesight! The par five 18th offers the chance of a closing birdie and a grandstand finish as it tumbles downhill all the way back to the clubhouse. A good ending to a memorable round.

Carlow is less than 25 miles from Mount Juliet. It offers a very different type of challenge from the new Nicklaus designed course, but if you happen to be in this delightful part of 'Middle Ireland' why not play the pair? You won't regret it, that's for certain.

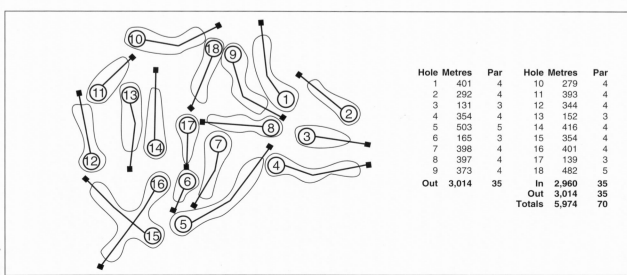

Hole	Metres	Par		Hole	Metres	Par
1	401	4		10	279	4
2	292	4		11	393	4
3	131	3		12	344	4
4	354	4		13	152	3
5	503	5		14	416	4
6	165	3		15	354	4
7	398	4		16	401	4
8	397	4		17	139	3
9	373	4		18	482	5
Out	**3,014**	**35**		**In**	**2,960**	**35**
				Out	**3,014**	**35**
				Totals	**5,974**	**70**

Mount Juliet

Joseph II of Austria (1741-1790) was an enlightened despot and a thoroughly miserable soul to boot. He wrote his own epitaph: 'Here lies a man who never succeeded in anything he attempted.' When, and let's hope it's a long, long way off, people begin to consider a fitting epitaph for Jack William Nicklaus someone should suggest, 'Here lies a man who succeeded in almost everything he attempted'.

Not content to go down in history as merely the greatest golfer who ever lived, the 'Golden Bear' is determined to establish himself as one of the finest golf architects the world has known. Jack's original career goal was to better Bobby Jones' record of 13 major championship victories: by 1986 he had totalled 20. Many believe that he would have won even more major titles had he not devoted so much of his energy to designing championship golf courses. But then again, had he not done so there would of course be no Muirfield Village, no St Mellion, no Glen Abbey—and no Mount Juliet.

Nicklaus once said, 'Building a golf course is my total expression. My golf game can only go on so long. But what I have learned can be put into a piece of ground to last beyond me'. Mount Juliet estate is a heavenly piece of ground, in fact 1500 acres of sublimely beautiful Irish countryside through which the River Nore flows and on which Jack Nicklaus has built a masterly 18 hole golf course.

Situated approximately 75 miles south of Dublin (via the N7/N9) on the outskirts of Thomastown in Co Kilkenny, Mount Juliet may just be the ultimate golfing oasis. The Mount Juliet Hotel, a splendidly refurbished 18th century mansion house, and the golf course have only recently opened yet the reputation of both is already immense. Some people are predicting that Mount Juliet will become the Turnberry or Gleneagles of Ireland, yet there appears to be none of their overt 'flashiness' or commercial brashness. Everything about Mount Juliet seems very understated and the ambience is at once graceful and peaceful. In front of the great house, somewhere between the hotel reception and the 11th tee, is a veritable Garden of Eden. Amid the ancient oaks, beeches and lime trees a hundred colours dazzle the eye and Mount Juliet's famous parading pheasants can simply vanish into the floral background. It is the perfect place for an early morning 'get your mind

together' stroll before going out and tackling Jack's formidable but spectacular parkland layout.

Unlike Gleneagles, golf at Mount Juliet is not restricted to residents and golf club members, although hotel guests do pay reduced green fees. Advance bookings can be made for any day of the week by telephoning the club on **(056) 73064.** The **Director of Golf, Kate MacCann,** can be contacted On (056) 73082 and the **Professional, Mark Reid,** is available on (056) 73063. Handicap certificates are required and the non-resident green fees for 18 holes in summer 1998 are £70 midweek and £75 at weekends. Special group rates are available and there are reductions for those teeing off after 4.30pm. Visitors may also wish to inspect Mount Juliet's impressive new David Leadbetter Golf Academy.

The course officially opened on 14th July 1991 and a vast crowd was present to watch Nicklaus play a friendly match against Christy O'Connor Sr. Even bigger crowds assembled in June 1993 to watch Mount Juliet's first Irish Open, won by Nick Faldo—his third successive victory in the event—and again in 1994 and 1995 as Bernhard Langer and Sam Torrance also claimed Irish Open titles.

Although it is certainly a mighty challenge from the back markers (all 7101 yards of it) each hole has four sets of tees so one needn't get too despondent! From the medal tees the course measures 6641 yards and from the ladies' tees, 5472 yards, par 73.

When writing the piece on East Sussex National I fantasised about a 'dream nine holes' made up entirely from some of the finest holes on East Sussex National's West Course. To that nine I'm now going to add the 2nd, 3rd, 5th, 8th, 10th, 11th, 13th, 14th and 18th from the Mount Juliet course. This collection will provide three exceptional short holes: the 3rd (which has a serious water carry), the 11th (over a plunging valley occupied by a cascading stream and rockery) and the 14th (with its marvellous backdrop of trees); three par fours: the 2nd (a beautifully shaped dog-leg), the 13th (a hint of Augusta's back nine) and the 18th (a classic Nicklaus closing hole) as well as three outstanding par fives, namely the double dog-legging 5th, the 8th (a fabulous elevated tee here) and the 10th (where, like the 5th, a real sea of traps must be negotiated en route to a superbly angled green). A dream round for sure, but sweet dreams? Potential nightmares, I reckon!

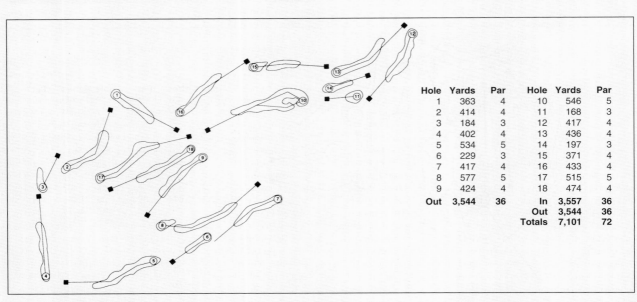

Hole	Yards	Par	Hole	Yards	Par
1	363	4	10	546	5
2	414	4	11	168	3
3	184	3	12	417	4
4	402	4	13	436	4
5	534	5	14	197	3
6	229	3	15	371	4
7	417	4	16	433	4
8	577	5	17	515	5
9	424	4	18	474	4
Out	**3,544**	**36**	**In**	**3,557**	**36**
			Out	**3,544**	**36**
			Totals	**7,101**	**72**

The European Club

'Rugged dunes, deep bunkers and sea breezes; fast running fairways, large undulating greens that invite the pitch-and-run approach and acres of tall waving marram grass. This is the very essence of golf—as it was at the beginning and was always meant to be'.
(Pat Ruddy)

Legend has it that when W L Pickeman pedalled along the estuary from Baldoyle and saw the great stretch of linksland at Portmarnock he almost fell off his bicycle. Almost a century later, Robert Trent Jones was led deep into the sandhills at Ballybunion and has never been the same man since. Imagine then how Pat Ruddy must have felt when he first saw the vast expanse of 'rugged dunes' and 'tall waving marram grass' just south of Brittas Bay in Co Wicklow. What effect on a man with golf in his soul?

Another legend is developing, for it is being claimed that Ruddy drove a JCB on to the same stretch of land in 1987 and didn't venture out the other side until 1993, and they believe it everywhere in Ireland, except at St Margaret's.

It is the proud boast of golfers at Mount Juliet that they play 'the course that Jack built'. In Co Wicklow we can now experience the links that Pat built, and whatever else Pat Ruddy achieves in his life the European Club will stand as his monument to golf.

Let us straight away say that it has enormous potential. The word 'great' should be used very sparingly in relation to golf courses but the links at Brittas Bay is undoubtedly a great links. It has many great qualities. The sandhills are not quite of Ballybunion-like proportion but they dwarf those at Portmarnock and Baltray. Better still, the golf course never leaves the dunes. There is balance and consistency and no feeling of mild disappointment, as is sometimes expressed in relation to the final few holes at Lahinch and Newcastle—and indeed with regard to the first few at Portmarnock and Ballybunion. The Irish Sea is the golfer's constant companion. You see it as you leave the 1st green, you hear it as you approach the 3rd and smell it as you stroll down the 7th—and you can almost touch it as you play along the 12th and 13th.

There are at least six genuinely great holes: the beautifully flowing downhill 3rd, the 7th with its fairway bordered by haunting marshland, the 8th, the 11th, the 12th and the fabulous 17th which plunges through a secluded dune-lined valley. These could all be described as great holes, and one final treat—or is it shock—awaits at the 18th, but who are we to spoil the surprise?

Ruddy's dream is that the European Club will one day be spoken of in the same breath as Ireland's 'Big Four' of Portmarnock, Portrush, Ballybunion and Newcastle. Most who have seen the course believe he has an evens chance of succeeding, and people who know Pat Ruddy will tell you that he eats such odds for breakfast.

We will probably have to wait a little while, however, before the European Club can be properly or fairly compared with the aforementioned 'Big Four'—it is still a trifle raw for one thing, but then the course was only fully opened for play in May 1993. What is certain is that you are made to feel very relaxed at Brittas Bay. A unique 'welcome to the family' atmosphere is developing. Ruddy says he wants to encourage a 'spirit of simplicity' and to recreate the mood of a time when golf was enjoyed in less hurried, less crowded and less pretentious circumstances. 'I've been to clubs where you see guys dressed like undertakers. Golf is meant to be fun', he says.

The course and club facilities are open to visitors seven days a week. The only restriction as such is that the number of players is carefully controlled. Priority is naturally given to those who have made advance arrangements, so booking a tee time is recommended. The club's telephone number is **(0404) 47415** Fax (0404) 47449. The green fees in 1998 are set at £35 per round weekdays and weekends.

Brittas Bay is approximately 40 minutes south of Dublin and the European Club is slightly closer to the capital than Baltray (Co Louth) is to the north. It is often claimed that a golfer hasn't experienced the full flavour of Irish links golf until he or she has made a pilgrimage to Ballybunion. One day the same might be said about Brittas Bay. The golf course is genuinely amazing and when a club is very personally run by a man whose motto in life is 'Grab some sticks and let's go golfing', how can you possibly resist?

Hole	Yards	Par	Hole	Yards	Par
1	390	4	10	415	4
2	160	3	11	385	4
3	505	5	12	470	4
4	455	4	13	600	5
5	395	4	14	165	3
6	185	3	15	410	4
7	470	4	16	415	4
8	410	4	17	395	4
9	420	4	18	445	4
Out	**3,390**	**35**	**In**	**3,700**	**36**
			Out	**3,390**	**35**
			Totals	**7,090**	**71**

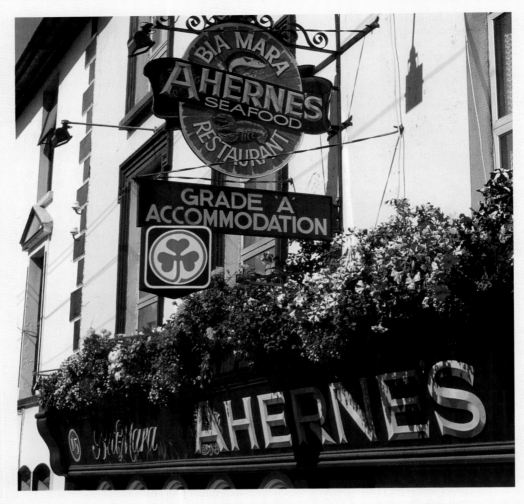

Welcome to Aherne's. Nestling in the heart of picturesque Youghal, halfway between Cork and Waterford, you will find an internationally renowned landmark specialising in the freshest of locally caught seafood. The bountiful fishing grounds provide a wide and varied supply—lobster, prawns, turbot, sole, salmon, monkfish, crab, mussels and clams—and the care and flair with which they are prepared has earned Aherne's a well-deserved place in all the leading travel and good food guides.

The Fitzgibbon family (third generation) offer a unique destination for the tourist and business traveller alike. Enjoy the personal and friendly welcome, whether you prefer a light meal in one of the bars or lingering over your meal in the comfortable surroundings of the award-winning restaurant.

And after your meal settle into the comfort of one of the twelve luxurious bedrooms. All are generous in size, tastefully decorated and furnished with carefully chosen antique pieces of furniture that blend perfectly together. Despite this traditional ambience, all rooms are fully supplied with modern amenities such as large en suite

bathrooms, direct dial telephone, hairdryer, trouser press and colour TV.

For those who enjoy a stroll there are all the delights of East Cork to discover—one of the prime tourist areas on the splendid south coast of Ireland. Youghal itself is home to Ireland's first post-Norman university, founded in 1462, the still used 12th century Collegiate church and the unique clock tower. And there is always the surrounding spectacular scenery to enjoy.

For sportsmen the opportunities are endless—deep sea and river angling, equestrian facilities and two Blue Flag beaches. And, of course, the golf. Youghal has an 18 hole golf course and there are sixteen other courses within an hours drive, including the championship courses of Fota Island, Lee Valley, Monkstown and Waterford.

So for the committed touring golfer what better base could there be in South West Ireland than Aherne's, where a gruelling day on the course can be comforted, or an ecstatic round celebrated with a truly superb seafood meal.

Aherne's
163 North Main Street
Youghal
Co Cork
Tel: 00 353 24 92424
Fax: 00 353 24 93633
E mail: ahernes@tinet.ie

CLIFFS OF MOHER
N67
M18
LAHINCH
Lahinch GC
CLARECASTLE
Dromoland Castle GC
N7
Shannon GC
LIMERICK
TARBERT
Adare GC
Castleroy GC
Ballybunion GC
Limerick GC
CASHEL
BALLYBUNION
TIPPERARY
Co Tipperary G&CC
N21
N24
N20
Tralee GC
TRALEE
Dingle G.C.
Dooks GC
Killarney
MALLOW GC
GLENBEIGH
KILLARNEY
Harbour Point GC
CORK
Cork GC
N70
N22
Waterville GC
Muskerry GC
Douglas GC
Fota Island GC
WATERVILLE
KENMARE
Lee Valley G&C
Monkstown GC
BANTRY
N71
SKIBBEREEN

Artist: **Graeme W Baxter** **KILLARNEY, IRELAND** *Courtesy of:* **Baxter Prints**

On entering the warmth and elegance of Midleton Park Hotel, you will receive the luxury and personal service you deserve. The hotel is situated only ten miles from Cork Airport and car ferry terminal and the business capital of the south, yet in a location very removed from city living and the interruptions of everyday life. Of all the counties in Ireland, Cork is the largest. In the path of the Mid Gulf Stream the climate is temperate, the scenery intoxicating and the choice of pursuits almost endless.

Golf is, of course, one of the specialities of the hotel and there is a selection of packages tailored to suit your requirements for that well deserved getaway.

For the golf fanatic, the hotel is situated only four miles from the picturesque but challenging par 72 championship, Fota Island Golf Course which would satisfy the most discerning of golfers.

For non golfers, it is just seven miles to the seaside village of Ballycotton with its unspoilt sandy beaches and relaxing mountain walks and at Fota Island Wildlife Park you can see the rarest species of wildlife from all five continents. No other county in Ireland offers such a fine tapestry of beauty, historical riches and sporting and leisure possibilities.

To round off the perfect day, Midleton Park offers you the ideal place to relax with its luxurious guest rooms and award-winning restaurant where you can sample local cuisine and catches from the local waters. For a less formal atmosphere, there is the option of the comprehensive lounge menu which is available throughout the day. In the hotel bar you can indulge and sample the 'spirit of Ireland' the local distilled and world famous Irish whiskeys. . . Jameson and Midleton Rare to name just two. You can also visit the 18th century distillery which has been restored.

The hotel also offers excellent business and conference facilities with three superior conference suites and four syndicate rooms catering for anything from 2 to 400 delegates. Daily delegate and 24 hour delegate rates are available on request.

The Midleton Park Hotel is a hotel where you can combine business and pleasure and discover a welcome as warm as the memories you will take back.

Midleton Park Hotel
Midleton
Co Cork Ireland
Tel: (00 353 21) 631767
Fax: (00 353 21) 631605

County Clare and County Limerick

We begin our brief tour of south west Ireland in County Clare where **Lahinch** is found. The famous links is featured ahead but ideas for staying in the area must include the excellent Aberdeen Arms Hotel (00 353) 65 81100—good food here. In Ennis, Mungovans (00 353) 65 24608 offers first rate accommodation as does Auburn Lodge (00 353) 65 21247. Slightly nearer Limerick in Newmarket-on-Fergus, Hunter's Lodge (00 353) 61 368577 is inexpensive and very welcoming while **Dromoland Castle** (00 353) 61 368144 is for the true connoisseur—the person who stayed at Ashford Castle will probably be staying here. Again the hotel has a golf course, although Dromoland's course has 18 holes and has recently been upgraded. The Clare Inn Hotel (00 353) 61 368161 is very convenient for Dromoland golfers who wish to save some punts. Not far from Dromoland, **Shannon** Golf Club is also well worth a visit—friendly and a very good parkland golf course. It is handy for the airport, as is the Great Southern Hotel (00 353) 61 471122.

Around Limerick, the most exciting development is the new Robert Trent Jones designed course at Adare Manor (00 353) 61 396566, one of the finest hotels in Ireland. **Adare** Golf Club is featured ahead. Close by, the Dunraven Arms (00 353) 61 396633 offers pleasant accommodation and the Mustard Seed (00 353) 61 396451 is a restaurant of excellence. Another course with accommodation (in the shape of twelve holiday cottages) and worth a visit is the **Limerick Country Club** (00 353) 61 351881, while golf is just one of a number of sporting pursuits to be enjoyed from the Clonlara Hotel (00 353) 61 354141.

Kerry's Gold

If we have crossed the Shannon via the Tarbert Ferry, **Ballybunion** is the first great club we come across in County Kerry. Like **Killarney**, **Waterville** and **Tralee** it is explored later in this chapter. Killarney provides the most central base and as an enormously popular tourist destination has numerous hotels and guesthouses. Undoubtedly one of the best places to base oneself is the Killarney Country Club (00 353) 64 44655, four miles from Killarney Golf Club at Faha—superb accommodation and a friendly welcome await. Among other fine establishments in Killarney are the Aghadoe Heights (00 353) 64 31766 (stunning views and an outstanding restaurant here), the Muckross Park Hotel (00 353) 64 31938, the Great Southern (00 353) 64 31262, the very attractive Cahernane (00 353) 64 31895, the International (00 353) 64 31816 and the Castlerosse (00 353) 64 31144. Eating establishments are equally plentiful. The panoramic restaurants of the Hotel Europe (00 353) 6431900 provide a feast for the eyes as well as the palate while Gabys (00 353) 64 32519 comes highly recommended. To the south of Killarney, the Park Hotel Kenmare (00 353) 64 41200 is where our friends from Dromoland Castle will now be heading. Also in Kenmare, Sheen Falls Lodge (00 353) 64 41600 is extremely welcoming and rapidly establishing itself as one of the finest hotels in the country. It is set within woodland on the banks of the River Sheen—delightful. For an intimate and inexpensive stopover in Killarney, Kathleen's Country House Hotel is highly recommended (00 353) 64 32810, as is the 19th Green guesthouse (00 353) 64 32868, almost adjacent to the famous golf club.

Tralee is about 20 miles north west of Killarney. The links is actually some eight miles from the town itself; the journey takes a little longer than you expect but no golfer in the world should be disappointed when he reaches this course. Perhaps the best hotel for golfers in Tralee itself is the Mount Brandon Hotel (00 353) 66 23333 but more adjacent in Barrow is the popular Barrow House (00 353) 66 36437 guesthouse. One hotel to match the quality of the golf at Ballybunion is undoubtedly Glin Castle (00 353) 68 34173 at Glin, near Limerick while two hotels to note in Ballybunion are the Marine (00 353) 68 27522—a good seafood restaurant here—and the Ballybunion Golf Hotel (00 353) 68 27111.

There are very reasonable 18 hole courses at **Dingle** (Ballyferiter) and **Dooks** but **Waterville** is the other great course in County Kerry. Waterville is one of the longest courses in Europe when played from the back tees. It has its charm as well though and has been described as 'the beautiful monster'. Suggestions for a 19th hole in Waterville include the elegant Waterville House (00 353) 66 74244, recently upgraded and extended, and the Butler Arms Hotel (00 353) 66 74144. Two restaurants to savour here are the Huntsman and the Smugglers Inn (00 353) 66 74330.

Cork and Tipperary

Coming down from rather dizzy heights, County Cork deserves an inspection. In the city itself, **Cork** Golf Club at Little Island is decidedly worth a visit. About five miles east of the town centre the course overlooks Cork Harbour and is one of the top ten inland courses in Ireland. It was at Little Island that one of Ireland's legendary golfers Jimmy Bruen learnt to play. Other golfing challenges near to Ireland's second city include **Muskerry** (a spectacular challenge) **Monkstown, Harbour Point** and **Douglas,** plus two very fine new 18 hole courses, the much acclaimed **Fota Island** (see feature page) and **Lee Valley**.

A delightful place to stay in Cork—and particularly convenient for Fota Island is Midleton Park (00 353) 21 631767. Other options include the Arbutus Lodge (00 353) 21 501237 while less expensive, but equally welcoming, is the popular Rochestown Hotel (00 353) 21 892233. Just outside Cork in Shanagarry is Ballymaloe House (00 353) 21 652531, where the restaurant is particularly outstanding. Cork also boasts the Silver Springs Hotel (00 353) 21 507533, which has numerous leisure facilities including its own 9 hole golf course.

Down on the coast at the Old Head of Kinsale there is a spectacular new course, the **Old Head**, which is featured ahead. Kinsale itself is packed with superb restaurants, while further east, but still on the coast lies the historic town of **Youghal** with a very pleasant 18 holes. Here the Walter Raleigh Hotel (00 353) 24 92011 and Ahernes (00 353) 24 92424 offer pleasant and friendly accommodation. Further inland at **Mallow** the order of the day is an enjoyable round of golf followed by a relaxing stay at Longueville House (00 353) 22 47156—sheer bliss!

We complete this all too brief introduction to golf in the south west of Ireland in Co Tipperary—not strictly 'south west', but then not a great distance from the delights of County Kerry either. Between Tipperary and Cashel stands Dundrum House (00 353) 62 71116: a splendid hotel and an 18 hole golf course, **County Tipperary** Golf & Country Club designed by Philip Walton await.

Once the seat of the O'Brien clan, Dromoland Castle has all the imposing stature you'd expect of the Kings of Munster. It stands proud on its own lakeside setting - a location that instantly highlights it as a very exceptional hotel indeed.

The warm red carpet in the expansive reception hall reflects the warmth of the Dromoland welcome - a genuine attitude further supported by a subtle combination of informality and efficiency.

The numerous lounges are of truly regal proportions, extremely comfortable with exquisite decor. A cosy bar and a relaxing snooker room are two additional options to help pass the evening hours.

The magnificence of the hotel is more than equalled by the quality of the French and indigenous cuisine, the Earl of Thomond Room restaurant having won an Egon Ronay star as Best Hotel Restaurant in Ireland. With its expansive views, it's an ideal setting to while away some delightful hours accompanied by the finest of wines from one of the most extensive cellars in the country.

Golfing guests can enjoy the challenge of the hotel's own 18 hole golf course, the new clubhouse with facilities which include a restaurant, bar, pro shop, health and leisure centre, and for an even greater challenge the championship courses of Lahinch and Ballybunion are nearby.

Anglers are catered for with trout in the hotel's own lake and salmon and trout in the nearby Shannon. An hour away, the more adventurous can tackle some deep sea angling on the west coast. Hunting of a different kind starts on November 1st for snipe, pheasant and duck.

With Shannon International Airport only 8 miles away, it's not surprising that Dromoland has proved a very popular location for international conferences and seminars. Its prestigious reputation adds a unique status to any such event or management think tank.

If the O'Briens of old returned to day, they could only but be impressed. The manicured lawns, calm elegance, finest in food and facilities, it's true what they say - there is only one Dromoland.

Dromoland Castle
Newmarket-on-Fergus
Co Clare
Ireland
Tel: (00 353 61) 368144
Fax: (00 353 61) 363355

Ballybunion

Ballybunion is a place of true pilgrimage. To golfers this is where gold has been struck, not once, but twice with two of the greatest golf courses in the world lying side by side. The Old Course at Ballybunion has long been regarded as the ultimate test in links golf. It lies in a remote corner of County Kerry close to the Shannon estuary amid the largest sandhills in the British Isles. It has a very wild beauty—no course could be closer to the sea and a number of the holes run right along the cliff edges. It's incredibly spectacular stuff and when the wind lashes in from the Atlantic, it is not a place for faint hearts.

The **Old** Course was begun in 1896, although a full eighteen holes were not completed until thirty years later. The renowned American writer Herbert Warren Wind said of the creation: 'It is the finest seaside course I have ever seen'. When Tom Watson first visited in 1981 (and he has returned many times since), he instantly supported Wind's contention and went on to tell the members as much in a personal letter of thanks to the club. What then of the New Course (now known as the **Cashen** Course) constructed in the mid 1980s? Architect Robert Trent Jones had this to say: 'When I first saw the piece of land chosen for the new course at Ballybunion, I was thrilled beyond words. I said it was the finest piece of links land I had ever seen. I feel totally confident that everyone who comes to play at Ballybunion will be as thrilled as I was by the unique majesty of this truly unforgettable course'.

Happily, Ballybunion isn't jealous of its treasures and visitors are always made to feel welcome. The **Golf Manager** at Ballybunion is **Jim McKenna.** He can be contacted by telephone on **(068) 27146** or by fax on (068) 27387. The code from the UK is (00 353 68). The professional at Ballybunion, **Brian Callaghan,** can also be reached on the above number. A full day's green fee in 1998 is priced at £72. This entitles the visitor to a round over both the Old and the Cashen—not of course compulsory, but if the body can take it (and it's likely to receive a fair battering en route) it would be a tragedy not to play the pair. A single round over the Old Course is priced at £55 in 1998 with £30 payable for 18 holes on the Cashen.

Helped by the lavish praise of Messrs Watson and Co, Ballybunion has become a lot busier in recent years and visitors should book some time in advance of intended play. Weekdays are naturally the easiest times for a visit and Sundays should be avoided if a game on the Old Course is sought.

The nearest airports to Ballybunion are at Shannon, a distance of approximately sixty miles to the north east, and the new Kerry Airport at Farranfore, some thirty miles due south. Cork's airport is about eighty miles to the south east. From either Cork or Shannon the journey can take about an hour and a half but there cannot be a soul on earth who wouldn't enjoy a trek through the south west of Ireland. From Shannon, travel via Limerick and from Cork via Mallow and Listowel. From Ballybunion town the course is about a mile's drive along the coast.

There is certainly no shortage of land at Ballybunion and, if necessary, both courses could be stretched to 7000 yards—an alarming prospect! From the medal tees the two are of fairly similar length, the Old measuring 6503 yards, par 71, the Cashen 6477 yards, par 72. But don't be fooled by the scorecard—each is a monster when the mood takes it.

The truly great holes on the Old Course begin at the 6th which has a frighteningly narrow entrance to a plateau green. The 7th fairway runs its entire length along the shore—one of the most spectacular par fours one is likely to play. The 8th is a shortish downhill par three, but if you miss the green you can be in serious trouble. And so it continues with the 11th being perhaps the most famous hole on the course. The sight from the tee is intimidating to put it mildly—the Atlantic waves are beneath you to the right, with some enormous sand dunes to the left. The fairway drops in tiers until it finally culminates on a windswept plateau green overlooking the ocean. It is unquestionably one of the greatest two-shot holes anywhere in the world.

The Cashen Course is arguably more dramatic! The sand hills are even more massive, and some of the carries required from the tee are prodigious. Some people rate the course on a par with the Old. Most critics don't agree, although it certainly includes some magnificent holes.

The 19th at Ballybunion, a brand new clubhouse opened by Tom Watson in 1993, is a grand place for recuperation. It is conveniently situated midway between nature's two masterpieces. Nowhere are stories swapped so enthusiastically and perhaps nowhere will you hear so often the phrase, 'Just wait until next time!' Gold diggers them all.

Venue for the Jameson International Golf Challenge Finals (1993 - 96)

Old Course

Hole	Yards	Par	Hole	Yards	Par
1	377	4	10	356	4
2	434	4	11	443	4
3	217	3	12	185	3
4	504	5	13	485	5
5	508	5	14	136	3
6	364	4	15	228	3
7	417	4	16	483	5
8	151	3	17	379	4
9	455	4	18	381	4
Out	**3,427**	**36**	**In**	**3,076**	**35**
			Out	3,427	36
			Totals	6,503	71

Waterville

How often have you read, or heard it said that 'Waterville is for the Big Man?' Given that Waterville is very much in the land of the Little People this sounds terribly exclusive. Wot, no Irishmen? Unlike Ballybunion, the name of the place sounds rather Anglo-French but the major influence has undoubtedly been American. In fact, modern Waterville is very much the result of an American dream.

Oddly it was an Anglo-American fisherman who first 'discovered' Waterville. Not your average fisherman, but one Charles Chaplin who regularly came here after the war to escape the clutches of stardom. In Waterville he found total peace (as well as some marvellous fishing).

The man we have to thank for creating the golfing majesty that is Waterville Links is an Irish-American, John A Mulcahy. Like all the others who had explored this part of the world he fell in love with the area, and like Castlerosse of Killarney fame he was both extremely wealthy and extremely crazy about golf. In the early seventies Mulcahy talked to leading Irish course designer Eddie Hackett—and the rest is history.

Immediately Mulcahy's Waterville opened for play, it was showered with the highest praise. Of course, it helped that Mulcahy was able to bring his buddies over from America, and that they happened to include people like Sam Snead, Art Wall and Julius Boros, but their enthusiasm for Waterville and the beauty of its situation was genuine. In any event, people like Henry Cotton, Tom Watson and Ray Floyd have since been and marvelled at the creation, the last named in particular who thought it, 'the finest links I have ever played'.

Today, more and more people are 'discovering' Waterville, although at most times the links is still relatively and wonderfully uncrowded. The reason for this is its remoteness. Waterville is 50 miles from Killarney and the nearest airport is at Farranfore—by car a journey time of approximately one and a half hours. The international airports at Cork and Shannon are 100 and 110 miles away respectively. But what a journey it is! The direct route from all points is via Killarney, and Killarney is the starting point for the Ring of Kerry, one of the most scenic roads in the world. Whether the approach to Waterville is 'along the top' via Killorglin and Cahiraveen (this is the quicker but less dramatic route) or 'along the bottom' via Kenmare and Parknasilla, much of the Ring of Kerry will be taken in. Nobody in their right minds could arrive at Waterville uninspired and surely nobody will leave on anything less than a high.

In 1998 the green fee at Waterville is set at £50 per round, seven days per week, but with a special rate of £30 for those teeing off before 8.00 am from Monday to Thursday. Second rounds are available on request. Tee times can be guaranteed by making an advance booking with the office. In this instance a 25 per cent deposit is payable one month in advance of the date of playing. The **Secretary/Manager** at Waterville is **Noel Cronin.** He can be contacted by telephone on either **(066) 74545 or (066) 74102** and by fax on (066) 74482. From the UK the code is (00 353) 66. The club's **Professional, Liam Higgins** can be reached on **(066) 74102.**

The danger of encouraging the description of a golf course as being 'for the big man' is that it risks putting off anyone who cannot thump a ball 300 yards. Naturally it is an advantage to be able to hit the ball like Liam Higgins, who once holed in one at the 16th—all 350 yards of it—but if you've got a twitchy short game, you are still going to be struggling, and besides, how often are you going to be asked to play Waterville from the championship tees? From the forward tees Waterville is no more or less frightening than the other great links courses of Ireland, and it is certainly as enjoyable.

Although there are some good holes on the front nine, notably the 3rd and 4th, it is the back nine at Waterville that everyone raves about. In golfing terms, this is life in the fast lane. The dunes are high and the fairways tumble. There are some spectacular carries and magnificent vantage points and three holes that are widely regarded as being world class—I refer to the 11th, 12th and 17th.

The 12th and 17th are both longish, short holes. On both the tee shot must be carried over a sea of dunes and at the 12th, the 'Mass Hole', over a gaping gully as well. If the 12th tee is elevated then the 17th must be on a mini-mountain. In fact it is on 'Mulcahy's Peak', a purpose-built tower of a tee from which there is a superb view, not just down to the elusive green but across the entire links.

The 11th, 'Tranquillity' is rated by many to be the greatest par five in Ireland. The fairway winds its entire length beneath sand dunes that are reminiscent of Ballybunion or Birkdale. It is possible to reach the green in two, for much of the last eighty yards or so is downhill, but only if the drive has been perfectly positioned.

It's funny how the world not only turns but sometimes turns on its head. In the 19th century just about every self-respecting Irishman living in Co Kerry wanted to explore America. Now every self-respecting American wants to explore Co Kerry—to see the lovely Ring of Kerry and to play the glorious links of Kerry. But remember, Waterville isn't just for the Big Man, Waterville is for Everyman.

Venue for the Jameson International Golf Challenge Finals (1993 - 96)

Hole	Yards	Par	Hole	Yards	Par
1	430	4	10	475	4
2	469	4	11	496	5
3	417	4	12	200	3
4	179	3	13	518	5
5	595	5	14	456	4
6	371	4	15	392	4
7	178	3	16	350	4
8	435	4	17	196	3
9	445	4	18	582	5
Out	**3,519**	**35**	**In**	**3,665**	**37**
			Out	**3,519**	**35**
			Totals	**7,184**	**72**

Geographically speaking, Waterville is something of an Irish Dornoch. No-one could pretend that it is anything but remote, but then who would really want it to be anything else? With remoteness comes the peace of a lost world; with remoteness comes charm.

Waterville sits at the far end of the Ring of Kerry. West of Waterville there is nothing for 2000 miles, save the Atlantic Ocean, while completing the circle to the North, South and East are brooding mountains, majestic lakes, soft hills and babbling streams.

It may surprise some to learn that golf has been played at Waterville from at least the early 1880s. Initially it was by those gallant and indomitable men who laid the trans-Atlantic cable, so bringing the New World close to the old. The land that these pioneering golfers played over was classic, sandy links terrain—greatly exposed to the elements, but neatly maintained by the local sheep.

Until the late 1960s Waterville was largely its own best-kept secret. About this time a second team of golfing pioneers led by the visionary Irish-American Jack Mulcahy determined that Waterville links should realise its full potential. 'Determined' is the word for in a few short years they, to adopt the words of leading Irish golf writer Pat Ruddy, 'transformed Waterville from a cosy localised scale to the pinnacles of world class'.

In the 20 years since 'modern' Waterville Links opened for play it has been showered with praise—but there is more to Waterville than spectacular golf. For one thing the 19th hole is one of the most comfortable clubhouses in Ireland and for lovers of golfing art and memorabilia it is a genuine treasure trove. And then there is Waterville House, the Irish residence of the owners of Waterville links and a temporary home to guests who enjoy an intimate and timeless country house ambience.

Built in the late 18th century and recently refurbished, Waterville House presides serenely on the shores of Ballinskelligs Bay. It has ten bedrooms all overlooking the pure waters of Butler's Pool (a favourite old fishing haunt of Charlie Chaplin) the wider seascapes and landscapes of the Atlantic and the magnificent, untouched countryside. In addition to the warm hospitality and fine cuisine (note the hearty Irish breakfast!) Waterville House offers its guests a heated pool, sauna, steam room, snooker and billiard room and golf practice facilities including a putting green.

Finally though, let us return to the nearby links and close with a few more choice words from Pat Ruddy. 'Waterville offers a person a splendid golfing challenge and a delicious taste of life as it must have been for primeval man—earth and clear sky, mountain and ocean and the ever present and teasing winds'.

Waterville House & Golf Links
Waterville
Co. Kerry Ireland
Tel: (00 353 66) 74102
Fax: (00 353 66) 74482
E mail: wvgolf@iol.ie
Website: http//www.watervillegolf.com/golf.html

Adare

If you are the world's most famous golf course architect you can afford to be choosy. If there is one place in Ireland (perhaps on earth) where you would seek to build a links course, it is amidst the sandhills of Ballybunion. And if there is one place in Ireland (above all others) where you might wish to design a parkland course, where else than in the grounds of Adare Manor? The incomparable Robert Trent Jones and the incomparable Adare Manor—a golf match made in heaven.

Just as the great man was mesmerised when he first saw the linksland at Ballybunion, so he couldn't help but be charmed when he first set eyes on Adare Manor. Only Ashford Castle has an equal capacity to bewitch the first time visitor. Adare Manor has both beauty and history. For a century and a half it was the ancestral home of the Earls of Dunraven, one of the great families of Ireland. In recent times it has established a reputation as one of the world's finest hotels. Today it has a Robert Trent Jones designed championship golf course.

Actually, it didn't need a genius to spot the golfing potential of Adare Manor. (Merely one to bring it to fruition!) The site has many natural advantages. The River Maigue flows, and occasionally meanders, through the heart of the estate. From giant oaks, beech trees and ash to glorious cedars and towering pines, few estates in Ireland have such a wealth and mix of splendid mature trees. Then there are the romantic ruins of an Augustinian abbey (built in 1313) and a Franciscan friary (1464). The Earls of Dunraven left a wonderful legacy—and it is one that all golfers (hotel residents and non-residents alike) can now experience.

The course opened for play in August 1995. The 1998 green fees are £36 per round, £60 per day for residents and £45 per round, £60 per day for non-residents. All golf enquiries should be directed to the **Golf Administrator, Barry Deane** by telephone on **(061) 395044** and by fax on (061) 396987. From outside Ireland the code is (00 353) 61.

A theme that distinguishes many of the best golf courses in the world is the way the level of drama increases as the round progresses. The challenge doesn't necessarily become any greater but subtlety gradually surrenders to drama. When you walk from the 10th green on the Old Links at Ballybunion your heart begins to pound—especially when you peer down the 11th fairway!

The inland equivalent to this sensation occurs when you stand on the tee of the par three 11th at Adare. Already several very good holes have been played. The par five 7th, where the fairway curves tantalisingly around the edge of a lake, couldn't be described as anything less than spectacular, but equally strong are some of the more subtle par four holes, notably the 2nd, 5th, 8th and 10th. Also by this time the famous Trent Jones jigsaw-shaped bunkers and the magnificently contoured greens may have exacted their toll.

. . . So you are standing on the 11th tee at Adare—heart pounding. Only a perfectly struck iron will find the putting surface, which is surrounded by traps and set at an angle on the 'wrong side' of the River Maigue. Assuming you survive this watery duel, the fairway at the 12th charges uphill then sweeps down to the left towards a sea of sand and a green backed by beautiful trees. The 13th carves a path through an extraordinary avenue of woodland, the 14th heads out towards the ruined abbey and the 15th turns back in the direction of the manor. Accompanying the 15th for its entire length is the River Maigue—a slicer's nightmare. The 16th is a stunning par three played directly beside the manor across a lake. It is modelled on the famous 4th at Baltusrol and in terms of fear-inducement is somewhat reminiscent of the 17th at Kiawah Island. Adare's 17th journeys back through the woods and then comes the classic and yes, dramatic, par five 18th. Trent Jones regards it as possibly the greatest finishing hole in golf. Perhaps he is a little biased, but for sheer panache it is hard to beat.

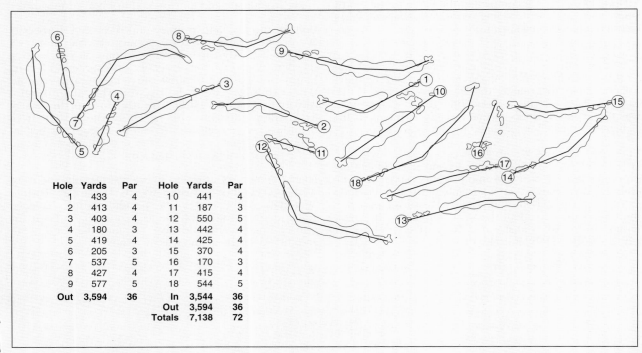

Hole	Yards	Par	Hole	Yards	Par
1	433	4	10	441	4
2	413	4	11	187	3
3	403	4	12	550	5
4	180	3	13	442	4
5	419	4	14	425	4
6	205	3	15	370	4
7	537	5	16	170	3
8	427	4	17	415	4
9	577	5	18	544	5
Out	**3,594**	**36**	**In**	**3,544**	**36**
			Out	**3,594**	**36**
			Totals	**7,138**	**72**

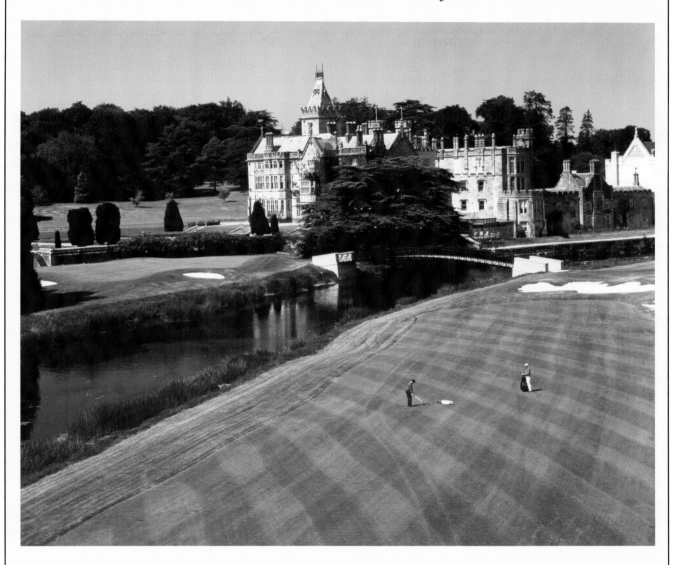

Adare Manor, an RAC five star hotel, is located 22 miles from Shannon airport in the picturesque village of Adare, Co. Limerick. Home for the past two centuries to the Earls of Dunraven, Adare Manor has been lovingly transformed into a world class hotel with 63 luxury bedrooms.

Adare Manor Hotel is an architectural masterpiece of towers, turrets and stonework, with full leisure facilities including an indoor heated swimming pool, fitness centre, sauna, horse riding, fishing and clay pigeon shooting.

The restaurant is famed for its wonderful European food with an Irish influence. From its windows one can view the parterre gardens and the golf course. The famous long gallery is modelled on the Hall of Versailles and will seat over 200 for gala dinners.

The 18 hole championship course was designed by one of the most respected and best known golf course architects in the world, Robert Trent Jones, Sr.

The course, constructed to world class standards, stretches over 230 acres of the 840 acre estate. A 14 acre lake, one of three on the course, dominates the front nine. The River Maigue meandering through the back nine creates a sense of beauty and challenge, particularly on the 18th hole, which Mr Jones foresees as one of the finest finishing par 5 holes in the world.

Each hole has four tees, built to greens specification, with a championship yardage of 7138. The Adare Golf Club has an exquisite parkland atmosphere with a magnificent variety of trees.

Adare Manor Hotel & Golf Club
Adare
Co Limerick
Ireland
Tel: (00 353 61) 396566 Golf 395044
Fax: (00 353 61) 396124 Golf 396987
USA toll free reservations: 800 462 3273 (800-Go Adare)

Killarney

Killarney is often described as 'paradise on earth', and not merely by we blasphemous golfers. This is Ireland's most famous beauty spot; somehow the lakes here seem a deeper and clearer blue and the mountains a more delicate shade of purple. It is a place where even the most miserable of wretches would be forced to smile.

The two golf courses of the Killarney Golf and Fishing Club take full advantage of the majestic surroundings. A Gleneagles afloat perhaps? Not really. The golf at Killarney is parkland rather than heathland or moorland, but it can generate a similar degree of pleasure and, like Gleneagles, can be a welcome retreat from the tremendously testing links courses nearby. A place to soothe one's damaged pride.

Killarney has lived through a somewhat chequered history. Golf has been played here since the late 19th century. The first course was nothing grand, laid out in an old deer park owned by the Earl of Kenmare. However, in 1936 the Earl's very keen golfing heir, and a great character of his time, Lord Castlerosse, decided that Killarney deserved a course that would reflect the glorious setting. Eighteen holes were laid out by Sir Guy Campbell and the new course opened in 1939. Castlerosse, who had played a very active role in the design, was pleased with the creation but continued to suggest imaginative improvements, unfortunately, not all of which were carried through following his untimely death in 1943. In the 1970s a second eighteen holes were built and the two present courses, **Mahony's Point** and **Killeen** are each a combination of the old holes and the new. Basking beside the shores of Lough Leane and encircled by the splendour of the Macgillicuddy Reeks and the Carrauntoohill Mountains, Killarney really is a golfer's dream.

This dream will be further enhanced in 1999 when the club opens its third championship course. Designed by Donald Steel, the new Lackabane Course will measure 6450 metres from the championship tees.

The present **Secretary** at Killarney is the affable **Tom Prendergast**, who may be contacted by telephone on **(064) 31034** (from the UK **(00 353 64) 31034**). Any written correspondence should be addressed to The Secretary, **Killarney Golf and Fishing Club, O'Mahony's Point, Killarney, Co. Kerry, Ireland.** The club's **professional, Tony Coveney** can be reached on **(064) 31615.** As seems to be the case with all of Ireland's great courses, visitors are warmly greeted—and they come from every foreseeable golfing country! There are no specific restrictions on playing during the week,

although some do exist at the weekend, so it's always a good idea to telephone the club before making any firm arrangements. The green fee in 1998 for either course at Killarney is £35 per round, seven days per week. Handicap certificates are required for both courses.

Killarney is the most accessible of Kerry's golfing delights, the town being linked to both Limerick (70 miles) and Cork (60 miles) by major road. The nearest airport is at Farranfore (Kerry Airport). The golf club lies about three miles west of the town off the N72 Killorglin Road and is well signposted. Those staying in the area might note that Killarney is the starting point of the famous one hundred mile Ring of Kerry road, which takes in surely some of the most marvellous scenery to be enjoyed anywhere in the world.

In such a setting, inspired golf is clearly on the cards (or so one hopes!) **Mahony's Point** is still probably the better known of the two courses, largely on account of its spectacular finishing holes, although in 1991 and 1992 it was the **Killeen** Course that hosted the Carrolls Irish Open, and on both occasions victory went to Nick Faldo. The Killeen also staged the 1996 Curtis Cup match, won by Great Britain and Ireland. It is in fact the longer of the two courses, measuring 6474 metres, par 72, compared with Mahony's Point, which measures 6164 metres, par 72.

Among the better holes on the Killeen Course are the dog-legged 1st, which follows the curve of Lough Leane's shore, the stunning par three 3rd, also alongside the water's edge and the exacting 13th—one of Castlerosse's favourites from the Campbell layout—a long par four which has a stream crossing the fairway to catch the mishit second.

On the Mahony's Point Course the celebrated finish begins at the par five 16th where the course returns toward Lough Leane. The 18th is the hole everyone remembers. It's a par three, which is fairly unusual at the end of a round, and the tee shot is played directly across the edge of the lake, practically all carry. Rhododendron bushes and pine trees frame the green: very beautiful, yet potentially very treacherous. 'The best short hole in the world', enthused Henry Longhurst. He also suggested that it might be a fitting place to end one's days. I can think of many worse places than the 18th green on Mahony's Point, but to pass over the club's magnificently appointed 19th hole would be at best anti-social.

Venue for the Jameson International Golf Challenge Finals (1993 - 96)

Mahony's Point Course

Hole	Metres	Par	Hole	Metres	Par
1	341	4	10	344	4
2	404	4	11	426	4
3	431	4	12	215	3
4	141	3	13	435	5
5	448	5	14	344	4
6	360	4	15	268	4
7	169	3	16	458	5
8	532	5	17	373	4
9	296	4	18	179	3
Out	**3,122**	**36**	**In**	**3,042**	**36**
			Out	**3,122**	**36**
			Totals	**6,164**	**72**

Tralee

Like the Beatles, there will never be another Arnold Palmer. In his prime he attacked golf courses the way Errol Flynn attacked pirates. He led golf away from its stuffy, gin and tonic, plus fours image and took a vast army of hero-worshipping fans with him. When he stopped winning golf tournaments around the world, Palmer became involved in golf course design. Now let's face it, a man whose middle name is 'Charge' is unlikely to construct humdrum golf courses. Hardly! He designs courses that any golfer with high blood pressure ought to steer well clear of. Tralee's golf course, perched on the edge of the incomparably dramatic coast of County Kerry, is one that should carry such a health warning.

Tralee (the golf course is actually eight miles north west of the town at Barrow) understandably prides itself on being the first golf course that Arnold Palmer designed in Europe. Apparently, he had been looking to build across the water for some time but until the mid 1980s when he was approached by some remarkably astute Irish gentlemen he hadn't found a venue that suited. Doubtless the Irish chatted him up good and proper as only they can, but Palmer didn't need the Ancient Mariner's treatment. One look at the proposed site convinced him. 'I have never come across a piece of land so ideally suited for the building of a golf course', he declared.

For decades Tralee golfers had played on a rather ordinary 'town course.' When they discovered the tract of links land at Barrow they sensed they had discovered something very special—hence the bold approach to Palmer and the decision to 'quit town' and head for the coast.

The drive from Tralee to Barrow doesn't remotely hint at the pot of gold that awaits at the end of the long, winding road. The situation is sensational in the extreme and Palmer was the perfect choice to lay out a daring and heroic course alongside such a beautifully rugged coastal stretch: a seascape described by Peter Dobereiner as being 'in a different class even to California's Monterey Peninsula.'

The **Club Supervisor** at Tralee is **Mr Michael O'Brien** who can be contacted by telephone on **(066) 36379** or by fax: (066) 36008 (00 353 66 from the UK). The club's full address is, **Tralee Golf Club, West Barrow, Ardfert, County Kerry.** Visitors wishing to test their skills at Tralee must be in possession of a current handicap and advance booking with the club is required. The best days to arrange a game at Tralee are Mondays, Tuesdays, Thursdays and Fridays when there are no general restrictions. No visitors are allowed on Sundays and there are no Wednesday green fees during June, July and August but in

other months the tee is available from 7.30-10.30. Visitors can also book to play on Saturdays from 11.00-1.20. The green fees in 1998 are set at £45 per round but there is an Early Bird Special of £35 for those wanting to tee off between 7.30 and 9.00 am and on Fridays in June, July and August between 7.30 and 3.30.

Measuring 6252 metres (about 6900 yards) from the championship tees, Tralee has the appearance of being two courses rather than one. The gentler outward half opens with an exacting par four where the second shot immediately guides you to the edge of the precipice—one of several greens overlooking the ocean and in this case, down over a vast, desolate beach that featured prominently in the film Ryan's Daughter. The 2nd is a banana-shaped par five that follows the cliff edges—invigorating stuff! Then comes the classic short 3rd across the rocks, a hole that often reminds American visitors of Pebble Beach. The view of the hole from the championship tee is enough to make a brave man tremble. The 6th, 7th and 8th ('Palmer's Loop') offer more exhilarating golf and provide views of a ruined 12th century castle and an old smugglers' haunt, but it is the back nine holes that leave most first-timers gasping.

After passing in front of the clubhouse and playing the 10th the golfer then disappears into another world, a world of extraordinarily wild and massive dunes. This is where Palmer (and Mother Nature) really went to town. In true Arnie fashion, desperately daring carries are the order of the day. The par four 12th is surely one of the most examining two-shot holes in golf. Although slightly downhill it is invariably played into the teeth of the wind—and my, how it can blow in these parts! The second must be fired over a huge ravine which continues around the left side of what is a painfully narrow table green. Barely do you have time to regain your breath when you must confront the par three 13th—there the tee shot must carry an even deeper chasm! As you play these holes, all around are magnificent vistas of the Atlantic Ocean, the Dingle Peninsula and the great sweep of Kerryhead. The drama doesn't let up and the downhill, par three 16th (reminiscent of the 15th at Ballybunion Old), and the dog-legged 17th (which is called 'Ryan's Daughter') are two more outstanding holes. On reaching the magnificently appointed clubhouse you will probably feel that you've tackled more than just an extraordinary golf course—you may even feel you have challenged Palmer head to head. But then that's Tralee—a unique golfing experience.

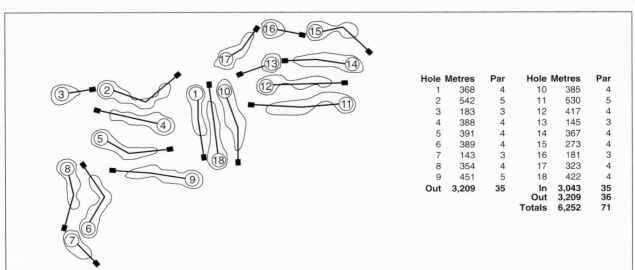

Hole	Metres	Par	Hole	Metres	Par
1	368	4	10	385	4
2	542	5	11	530	5
3	183	3	12	417	4
4	388	4	13	145	3
5	391	4	14	367	4
6	389	4	15	273	4
7	143	3	16	181	3
8	354	4	17	323	4
9	451	5	18	422	4
Out	**3,209**	**35**	**In**	**3,043**	**35**
			Out	**3,209**	**36**
			Totals	**6,252**	**71**

Fota Island

For many years overseas golfers have tended to view Co Cork as a mere gateway to the delights of Co Kerry. Arriving by boat or plane, most have simply passed through Ireland's second city before descending upon Killarney, then on to Ballybunion, Waterville and Tralee. But things are beginning to change. Cork Golf Club with its fine layout at Little Island (designed in the 1920s by master architect Alister MacKenzie) has at last been discovered, while no great distance away on historic Fota Island Christy O'Connor Jr and Peter McEvoy have fashioned a course of sufficient quality that it has hosted the 1995 and 1996 Irish Amateur Open.

Fota Island lies to the east of the city in Cork Harbour—it is only in recent times that it has been connected by causeway to the mainland. Despite its rather mystical, Norse sounding name, it was a Norman family who first developed the island and it remained in family ownership until 1975. Today the 780 acre estate is listed among the Inventory of Outstanding Landscapes of Ireland. It is beautifully wooded, has a handsome Regency house, wildlife park, striking arboretum and gardens, and since 1993, one of the country's finest parkland golf courses.

In an article assessing new developments in Ireland *Golf World* magazine described Fota Island as the 'pick of the bunch'. *Golf Monthly* has also been very generous in its praise: 'It's a mark of imaginative design when a new course appears old before the paint has dried . . . some of the innovations evoke other times and other values'. The latter coment is a reference to the course's very natural, almost old fashioned look.

Although water hazards feature quite prominently in the design, the inspiration is more St Andrews than Sawgrass. The greens at Fota are generally large and undulating and are defended by grassy swailes and deep pot bunkers—there is even a shared double green.

Measuring 6886 yards, par 72, the course is suffciently long to test the top professionals (in 1995 the club staged the Irish Club Professionals Championship as well as the Irish Amateur Open) but invariably rewards 'brain rather than brawn'. The par five 18th is widely acknowledged as the finest and most dramatic hole at Fota Island. The green here is guarded by a nest of pot bunkers at the front and a small lake at the back; sixes and sevens are common, but so too are birdies and even eagles.

The clubhouse is the perfect place to relax. Being built from medieval stone it rivals Luttrellstown and with the Niblick restaurant overlooking the 18th you will be well catered for in all departments.

Fota Island Golf Club, Fota Island, Carrigtwohill, Co Cork, Ireland	
General Manager	Kevin Mulcahey (00 353) 21 883700
Professional/ Reservations	Kevin Morris (00 353) 21 883710
Green Fees	WD £28/round, £40/day WE £33/round, £45/day
Restrictions	None
Directions	7 miles from Cork City on Fota Island.

Old Head

You look at the brochure, you read the reviews and still you wonder whether it's half as good as they say. The Old Head Golf Links near Kinsale—what was Joe Carr calling it "the eighth wonder of the golfing world"? Well, as co-designer he would say that, wouldn't he! But why should Christy O'Connor Sr be telling everyone he meets that he has just seen "six of the best holes in all of golf" ? And then there was the article by leading Irish golf writer Charlie Mulqueen declaring Old Head to be "a golfing location that will never be rivalled in terms of drama and beauty". Strong stuff.

One evening in March 1997 this editor found himself in Kinsale exploring 'the nicest small town in Ireland' (not to mention the nation's culinary capital) and eagerly looking forward to a morning visit to Old Head. Since the course was not due to be opened until the summer this was something of a sneak preview.

Anticipation turned to frustration when the curtains were drawn back to reveal a foggy, chilly day. It was no less fogbound as I reached the narrow neck of land that joins Old Head to the rest of Co Cork. Driving past the ghostly castle ruins I could just make out the ocean, crashing against the rocks some 200 feet below. Fortunately the fog lifted a little as I approached the 2nd tee and I knew this was the first of the acclaimed clifftop holes. . . . The moment of truth. Was this really the Cypress Point or Pebble Beach of Ireland? In a word, yes! It was—it is—an astonishing sight. The entire fairway runs along the edge of the cliffs while the green appears all set to fall into the sea. The 3rd is a par three, again its green overlooks the abyss, while the 4th is a longer and if anything more spectacular version of the 2nd.

While Old Head seems destined to be compared with the celebrated courses of the Monterey Peninsula, a flavour of two other great courses is experienced on the back nine. The fairway on the par four 15th is not only bordered to the right by the ocean but it cascades in terrace-like fashion from a high tee. In this respect it is very reminiscent of the fabled 11th on the Old Course at Ballybunion. A magnificent par three and a huge par five lead you to the 18th tee which is overlooked by the 19th century Old Head lighthouse. The drive that follows is pure Turnberry.

Old Head is undoubtedly a great golf course. Exactly how great it is too early to say. At the time of my visit many of the bunkers were still being shaped and the fairways seemed a trifle raw—the subtleties have still to be developed. But I'll say this—Charlie Mulqueen did not exaggerate. Even on a foggy day in March the Old Head Golf Links appeared visually incomparable, stunning, magical. . . .

Old Head Golf Links, Kinsale, Co Cork, Ireland	
Golf Office	(00 353) 21 778444
Green Fees	WD £50; WE £60
Restrictions	None
Directions	20 miles south of Cork City via Kinsale; follow signs to the 'Old Head.'

The Old Head of Kinsale is one of the most remarkable developments ever conceived in the history of golf—one of the most spectacular and scenic golf courses you are likely to find anywhere in the world. Set on an Atlantic promontory that will never be rivalled in terms of drama and beauty, nine holes run along the coastline, unique amongst the world's great links courses.

The Old Head is ideally located on the South Coast of Ireland, 30 minutes drive from Cork International Airport. It is easily accessible from the other great links courses of south west Ireland such as Ballybunion, Waterville and Lahinch.

The course is set on a rugged, roughly heart shaped and historic peninsula rising hundreds of feet above dramatic cliffs, surrounded by ocean on all sides and commanding spectacular views. The Old Head peninsula comprises around 220 acres, with the golf course situated on the flat area of the headland, allowing composition of a 7100 yard, par 72 golf course, configured as two returning loops of nine holes plus a practice ground facility.

A number of the most famous names in Irish golf are associated with the project; the course was designed by a combination of Ireland's greatest past golfing heroes and recognised contemporary design experts led by Joe Carr, Ron Kirby, Paddy Merrigan and Eddie Hackett. Carr said of the course "The Old Head of Kinsale as a golf links, will in my estimation rate with the great courses in the world.

Its location, scenic reality and spectacular terrain remind me of Cypress Point and Pebble Beach, two of America's most famous courses. To be associated with the design of this course is to me the thrill of a lifetime. I see Old Head as a golfers' paradise with the potential of being the eighth wonder of the world in golfing terms."

The Old Head of Kinsale is a national monument and an ancient Roman site, fortified by a castle at the narrowest part of the headland. Other landmarks include the lighthouse which was built in 1853 and the small stone circles which are thought to be the remains of Iron Age dwellings.

The ancient harbour town of Kinsale is about seven miles north of Old Head—one of the most attractive towns in Ireland, it is today considered the gourmet capital of the country. A cosmopolitan seaside town, it boasts three busy yacht marinas and many excellent restaurants and bars. The golfer is assured of being very well catered for here.

The course has taken over ten years to develop, mainly due to environmental objections, but now the clubhouse and course are completed and the result is beyond any expectations—a unique golfing experience. The magnificent location and the quality of the course will make this a truly memorable experience for golfers of all standards, with the vagaries of the Atlantic winds providing a fresh challenge each day.

Old Head Golf Links
Kinsale
Co Cork Ireland
Tel: (00 353) 21 778444
Fax : (00 353) 21 778022
E mail: info@oldheadgolf.ie
Website: www.globalgolf.com

Lahinch

On the rugged coast of County Clare, two miles from the spectacular Cliffs of Moher lies the 'St Andrews of Ireland'.

In 1892, officers of the famous Black Watch Regiment stationed in Limerick discovered a vast wilderness of duneland. Being good Scotsmen, they knew at once that this was the perfect terrain for a golf links. On Good Friday 1893, Lahinch was duly founded. The obvious choice of person to design the course was 'Old' Tom Morris of St Andrews. Tom accepted but then other than laying out the tees and greens, he felt there was little he could do. He said: 'I consider the links is as fine a natural course as it has ever been my good fortune to play over'. More praise was to follow. In 1928, Dr. Alister Mackenzie was invited to make a number of adjustments to the links. On completion he suggested that 'Lahinch will make the finest and most popular course that I, or I believe anyone else, ever constructed'. Not perhaps the most modest statement ever made but coming from a man who would very shortly design Cypress Point and later help to to create the legendary Augusta, it can hardly be taken lightly.

Visitors wishing to play at Lahinch will find the Club extremely welcoming. The only restrictions are as follows: Monday to Friday between 9am and 10am and 12.00 to 1.30pm and at weekends between 8am and 11am and 12.30pm to 2pm. The present **Secretary** is **Mr Alan Reardon**, who can be contacted by telephone on **(065) 81003** or by fax on (065) 81187. The **Professional, Robert McCavery,** can be reached on **(065) 81408.**

Since Dr Mackenzie's alterations, there have been two 18 hole courses: the championship Old Course and the shorter Castle Course, the latter having been extended from nine holes to eighteen in 1975. Green fees in 1998 to play on the Old Course were set at £45 per round, £55 per day between April and September, with a reduced rate of £40 per round for midweek golf between January and March and in November and December.

Green fees on the Castle Course were £25 per round, £35 per day during summer and £20 per round in winter. Certain discounts are available to those staying in local hotels. Golfing societies are equally welcome and bookings can be made for any day other than Sunday.

Travellers coming from Britain (or indeed Europe and America) should find Lahinch more accessible than any of the great links of Co Kerry. International flights to Shannon are frequent and Lahinch is located approximately thirty miles to the north west of the airport. On leaving Shannon, Ennis is the town to head for, and thereafter, Ennistimon, just two miles from Lahinch. The road passes through some marvellous countryside, and incidentally, do try to visit the Cliffs of Moher—in places they rise to a sheer drop of over six hundred feet, the highest in Europe. Golfers on a west of Ireland pilgrimage approaching from Ballybunion should cross the Shannon via the Tarbert Ferry. It leaves every 30 minutes—on the hour and at half past.

The **Old Course** at Lahinch is not as tough as a Portmarnock or a Waterville. It doesn't have the length for a start, but then it's anything but straightforward. The golfer who enjoys the challenge of Ballybunion will fall in love with Lahinch. The seascapes are just as dramatic and the fairways twist and tumble in a similar fashion. A premium is placed on accurate tee shots and the slightest straying will put you amongst the dunes. Many greens sit on natural plateaux and can be tricky to hold. It isn't easy to select the best holes, for so many are memorable, but perhaps the finest sequence is found between the 7th and 10th—four really tremendous par fours.

The most famous holes, however, are undoubtedly the 5th and 6th, both of which Mackenzie was forbidden to touch. Having won four Open Championships at Prestwick, 'Old Tom' clearly relished the blind shot and this is what is called for at both the 5th (Klondyke) and the 6th (Dell). Not too many quibble with the 5th—it is a par five, although the blind second shot is over a prodigious sandhill and the green is a further two hundred yards on. The 6th however, is a par three! The green nestles between two steep sand dunes and all the player sees from the tee is a white marker-stone placed on the fronting hill to indicate the current pin position—'hit and hope' perhaps, but charming all the same.

The par 70 **Castle Course** is literally over the road from the Old and occupies much more level ground. The fairways wind their way around the remains of O'Brien's Castle. It presents an attractive, if slightly less demanding challenge, and some £300,000 has recently been spent on upgrading the course.

The clubhouse at Lahinch is marvellously intimate and certainly an excellent place to adjourn to should the heavens open. And you'll have ample warning of the impending doom for legend has it that the goats that graze on the dunes will always make an early retreat towards the shelter of the 19th. A bit of Irish mist? Try telling that to the members!

Old Course					
Hole	Metres	Par	Hole	Metres	Par
1	352	4	10	412	4
2	468	5	11	126	3
3	138	3	12	434	4
4	391	4	13	250	4
5	441	5	14	446	5
6	142	3	15	422	4
7	365	4	16	178	3
8	320	4	17	400	4
9	351	4	18	487	5
Out	**2,968**	**36**	**In**	**3,155**	**36**
			Out	**2,968**	**36**
			Totals	**6,123**	**72**

RULE XXXII
A player may stand out of bounds to play a ball lying within bounds.

Artist: **Charles Crombie** **RULE XXXII** *Courtesy of:* **Rosenstiel's**

Resting in its own 100 acre estate is the historic mansion of Mount Falcon. Originally built in 1876 by John Fredrick Knox, it overlooks the Moy Valley towards the changing hues of the heathery slopes of the Ox mountains in the distance.

The owner, Constance Aldridge, plays the part of hostess to her visitors who quickly realise that, in keeping with the tradition of the house, they will experience the friendliness and attention given to a personal guest rather than simply another booking. Here, you can relax beside a log fire in the tranquillity of gracious rooms filled with antique furniture and fresh flowers picked from the garden.

Frequently acclaimed in international good food guides, the hotel was awarded the 'Host of the Year' award by Egon Ronay in 1997, the superb menu is traditional country house cuisine. It includes local ingredients, fresh produce from the estate as well as well as fresh rod-caught salmon from the Mount Falcon Fishery on the River Moy. The delicious food is accompanied by a comprehensive selection of fine wines and after dinner coffee and drinks are served in the drawing room.

There are ten bedrooms all enjoying views of the estate. All the bedrooms have private bathrooms as well as all the amenities you would expect of a good hotel.

Mount Falcon is the ideal base from which to explore the magnificent countryside of County Mayo. Beautiful beaches, rugged coastline, lakes and mountains are all on the doorstep as are the fascinating sites of ancient Celtic history.

For the golfer, the first class 18 hole course of Enniscrone is only ten miles away and Ballina also has a good 18 hole course. Horse riding is available in the area and the lively old fashioned town of Ballina is worth a visit.

For the serious fisherman, Mount Falcon has excellent facilities having catered for generations of country sportsmen. The River Moy is Ireland's most prolific salmon river and three miles away the large limestone loughs, Conn and Cullen, provide some of the finest fishing for brown trout in Europe.

In the winter months, the castle can arrange excellent rough shooting for woodcock and snipe.

Mount Falcon Castle
Ballina, Co Mayo
Ireland
Tel: (00 353 96) 70811
Fax: (00 353 96) 71517
E mail: mfsalmon@iol.ie

Without any shadow of doubt some of the greatest golf courses in the world are to be found in the south west of Ireland. But as any Irishman worth his Guinness will tell you, great golf in the west of Ireland certainly isn't confined to the south western corner—it starts from County Donegal downwards. Apart from its magnificent golf, the south west is renowned for its beautiful scenery: majestic Killarney, the glorious Ring of Kerry and the Dingle Peninsula—stunning for sure but further north can be equally spectacular. This is what W M Thackeray had to say of the area around Westport: 'It forms an event in one's life to have seen the place, so beautiful is it, and so unlike all other beauties that I know of'. Clearly inspired, he continued: 'But the Bay—and the Reek which sweeps down to the sea—and a hundred islands in it, were dressed up in gold and purple and crimson, with the whole cloudy West in a flame'. Marvellous! And have you ever been to Connemara?

Donegal

And have you ever been to Donegal! I don't suppose many golfers are likely to begin a tour in the very far north and head all the way downwards but we shall have a go all the same. (It is possible I suppose if one were approaching from the Causeway Coast?) Let us start at **Ballyliffin** on the very northern tip of Donegal, not far from Malin Head. Now Ballyliffin is a club we overlooked in the early editions of _Following The Fairways_. This has now been rectified (see feature ahead). Suffice to say at this juncture that we believe it has the potential to become the 'Dornoch of Ireland'—or even, perhaps, the 'Ballybunion of the North'. Two recommended hotels in Ballyliffin are the Strand Hotel (00 353) 77 76107 and the Ballyliffin Hotel (00 353) 77 76118, while Rossaor House (00 353) 77 76498—with its amazing views—is one of several fine guesthouses.

Rosapenna is our next port of call. Like Ballyliffin it is somewhat isolated, but a fine 18 hole course nonetheless. It was laid out in 1893 by Old Tom Morris and is part links, part inland in nature. The place has a bleak beauty and the coast is very dramatic—note the spectacular nearby Atlantic Drive. Rosapenna is explored further ahead. The Rosapenna Golf Hotel (00 353) 74 55301 provides a very comfortable and convenient base while those looking for really deluxe accommodation might consider Rathmullan House (00 353) 74 58188 in Rathmullan, a Georgian building with splendid gardens. Not far from Rosapenna there is a magnificently situated course at **Portsalon** and three other Donegal links courses to recommend are **Dunfanaghy, North West (Buncrana)** and **Narin and Portnoo**. Further inland, 18 holes can be played at **Letterkenny** and again at **Ballybofey & Stranorlar** where the Kee's Hotel (00 353) 74 31018 provides a perfect base for exploring the mountains and hills of Donegal.

Donegal town, famed for its tweeds and woollens, has one of the longest courses in Ireland measuring 7200 yards (try playing it in a fierce wind!) The course is actually outside of the county town at **Murvagh**. A truly great course this and again we explore it on a later page. There are a number of hotels and guesthouses in Donegal and for golfers looking for a lively night there is the Schooner Inn (00 353) 73 21671 on Upper Main Street. More sedate accommodation is to be found at Rossnowlagh, here the splendid Sand House Hotel (00 353) 72 51777 enjoys superb views over Donegal Bay and there is a short 9 hole golf course within the hotel grounds. Other possibilities in Donegal town include the Abbey Hotel (00 353) 73 21014 and the Hyland Central

(00 353) 73 2107 while outside the town one finds two really pleasing establishments, St Ernan's House (00 353) 73 21065, which enjoys a delightful wooded setting with views of Donegal Bay or alternatively, Harvey's Point (00 353) 73 22208 with its loughside setting and excellent restaurant. A little south of Rossnowlagh is **Bundoran**, another tough, though fairly open links. Right in the middle of the course is the Great Northern Hotel (00 353) 72 41304 which has 150 rooms.

The West

Our next visit is a more established favourite. **County Sligo**, or **Rosses Point** as it is commonly known, is rated among the top ten courses in Ireland and is the home of the prestigious West of Ireland Amateur Championship. Laid out right alongside the Atlantic coast, it is a true links and can be greatly affected by the elements. This great course is tackled ahead. County Sligo and surrounds is another charming area of Ireland. It is the country of W B Yeats and the landscape is dominated by the formidable Ben Bulben mountain. An outstanding seafood restaurant is located in Rosses Point—the Moorings (00 353) 98 25874. The Sligo Park Hotel (00 353) 71 60291, Ballincar House Hotel (00 353) 71 45361 and the Yeats Country Ryan Hotel (00 353) 71 77211 are all very convenient for the course. To the south of Sligo at Riverstown, Coopershill (00 353) 71 65108 is another fine and extremely welcoming hotel and at Colloney, Markree Castle (00 353) 71 67800 is superb. Rosses Point is marketed alongside **Enniscrone, Donegal, Connemara** and **Carne** Golf Club at belmullet as one of the 'West Coast Links' but there are many other fine golfing challenges in this part of Ireland and a neighbour of Rosses Point is the links at **Strandhill**, adjacent to Sligo airport.

Perhaps the most underrated of the West Coast links is Enniscrone. Laid out on the shores of Killala Bay it is, to quote Peter Dobereiner, 'an undiscovered gem of a links.' The best places to stay nearby are the Downhill Hotel (00 353) 96 21033 in Ballina and the Mount Falcon Castle (00 353) 96 70811 just south of the town. Both hotels are really welcoming and they are also convenient for the links at Belmullet. The latter has a delightfully laid-back country house atmosphere. Note also a superb inn on the quay at Ballina, the lively River Boat (00 353) 96 22183.

A short drive from Ballina and we reach **Westport**, Thackeray's paradise. The town nestles in the shadows of the massive Croagh Patrick mountain. It was on its peak that St Patrick is said to have fasted and prayed for 40 days. The golf course (from which there are many marvellous views of Croagh Patrick) is another on the grand scale—7000 yards when fully stretched. It's a relatively new course having been designed by Fred Hawtree in 1973. Although some holes run spectacularly along the shoreline (note particularly the superb par five 15th which curves around Clew Bay) Westport is most definitely a parkland type course and is a very friendly club. The Irish Amateur Championship has been played here twice in recent years. There is no shortage of good accommodation in Westport and many hotels offer golfing packages. One of the most comfortable hotels in town is the Hotel Westport (00 353) 98 25122 near Westport House, although the Castlecourt Hotel (00 353) 98 25444 is also popular with travel-weary golfers and in nearby Newport, Newport House (00 353) 984 1222 is first class. Also highly commended for those seeking a homely atmosphere in one of Ireland's top inns, Healy's Hotel (00 353) 94 56443. Approximately twenty miles away at Cong stands the redoubtable

Ashford Castle (00 353) 92 46003 a place fit for a king and possibly the finest hotel in Ireland. Its setting on the edge of Lough Corrib is quite breathtaking; it also boasts a 9 hole golf course within the grounds of the hotel .

Connemara Golf Club (see feature page) is located about 30 miles south of Westport amid very rugged country. It is a wild, remote and incredibly beautiful part of the world. The links course at Ballyconneely must be one of the toughest one is ever likely to meet. Despite the remoteness there are several first class establishments at hand. The best places for a night's stay are the Rock Glen Country House Hotel (00 353) 95 21035, the Ardagh Hotel and Restaurant (00 353) 95 21384 and the Abbeyglen Castle Hotel (00 353) 95 21201. All three are in Clifden and all are good. They need to be—you'll need a medicinal whiskey or two and a good night's sleep before (or after) tackling Connemara. Another superb establishment is found close by in Cashel Bay, the Cashel House Hotel (00 353) 95 31001—a delightful country house with marvellous gardens.

On to Galway—a fascinating and lively city. Golfwise, there is the established **Galway** Golf Club at Salthill, and the new **Galway Bay** Golf and Country Club near Oranmore, the creation of Christy O'Connor Jr. This is an idyllic location for a good break - some excellent holiday homes here as well (00 353) 91 790500. Galway has a number of centrally located hotels including the Great Southern Hotel (00 353) 91 64041 and Ardilaun House (00 353) 91 21433. In Spiddal, the Bridge House (00 353) 918 3118 is a cosy inn, and at Oranmore, very convenient for Galway Bay, is the Oranmore Lodge Hotel (00 353) 91 94400. Also convenient is the Glenlo Abbey (00 353) 91 26666, a restored 18th century house and church .

Finally to a part of Ireland perhaps more renowned for its fishing than golf. The Roscommon-Athlone area doesn't have many courses but both **Athlone** Golf Club and **Roscommon** Golf Club are worth exploring and there is also the outstanding **Glasson** Golf & Country Club which is featured ahead, along with Slieve Russell. Among a number of pleasant places to stay we can recommend the Hodson Bay Hotel (00 353) 902 92444 which is surrounded by Athlone golf course itself, the Prince of Wales Hotel (00353) 902 72626, also in Athlone, and the Abbey Hotel (00 353) 903 26240 in Roscommon.

Artist: **Roy Perry SEVEN IRON** *Courtesy of* **Rosenstiel's**

An historic Irish castle, dating back to the 13th century, Ashford is now one of the finest hotels in the world. Enter the main reception hall and the feeling of genuine history is matched only by the warmth of the welcome. Solid oak beams and wood panelling reflect a more formal age, but the most modern facilities and comforts are reassuring signs that Ashford is very much a hotel of today, and it's that same sense of elegant luxury which has entitled Ashford to host former US Presidents, European royalty and international celebrities.

For the past seven years, Ashford Castle has been nominated 'Best Hotel in Ireland' by Egon Ronay. Experience the finest food and wine in the George V dining room or in the Connaught Room gourmet restaurant where the most fastidious palate is treated to the exquisite delights of French cuisine.

Standing on the shore of Lough Corrib, Ireland's second largest lake, it's no surprise that Ashford offers its guests some of the most sporting salmon, trout, pike and perch fishing in the West of Ireland. But if golfing is more your bag, the hotel grounds comfortably accommodate Ashford's own 9-hole golf course and golf clubs are available. For variety and an even stiffer challenge two additional courses are less than fifty miles away. Ashford also boasts an indoor equestrian centre and health centre comprising a gymnasium, sauna, steam room and conservatory. Golf and the health centre are free to residents of the castle.

With its spacious grounds offering their own calming air of quiet it's no surprise that Ashford is consistently chosen by national and international corporations and organisations for conferences and management get togethers.

Seven centuries since the first brick was laid, the setting, atmosphere and discreet luxury have made Ashford Castle more than a unique hotel—it's an experience.

Ashford Castle
Cong
Co. Mayo
Ireland
Tel: (00 353 92) 46003
Fax: (00 353 92) 46260

Ballyliffin

Picture this—365 acres of spectacular duneland surrounded by curvaceous hills and soaring mountains. The only other boundary is the sometimes stormy, sometimes sparkling Atlantic Ocean.

Ballyliffin enjoys such a setting. Ireland's most northerly golf club is situated close to Malin Head on Donegal's Inishowen Peninsula. The links hugs the shore beside Pollan Bay and overlooks a vast stretch of sand. The massive bulk of Binion Hill slips into the sea at one end of the bay and at the other are the ancient ruins of Carrickabraghy Castle. Just off the coast, surveying everything, is Glashedy Rock, Ballyliffin's own Ailsa Craig.

But it isn't just the hidden beauty of the location that captivates and casts a spell over all who travel to Ballyliffin. Nick Faldo made a surprise visit in June 1993 and went away describing **The Old Links** as the most natural golf course he had ever played.

Stories began to circulate of an undiscovered links that possessed the most amazing rippling fairways. Overseas commentators started to call Ballyliffin 'the Dornoch of Ireland.' Then, in the summer of 1995, the club unveiled a second 18 hole course, the appropriately named **Glashedy Links**, designed by Pat Ruddy and Tom Craddock.

The new course is, quite simply, a diamond of a links. Laid out on predominantly higher ground above and beyond The Old Links, it revels in the majesty of the setting. The sandhills are generally larger and the terrain more sweepingly undulating. If The Old Links is guaranteed to charm, so Glashedy Links is certain to thrill.

Visitors who wish to be charmed or thrilled, can make tee reservations by telephoning the **Secretary/Manager, Karl O'Doherty** on **(077) 76119** or by fax on (077) 76672. Green fees in 1998 for The Old Links are £17 per round midweek, £20 at weekends and for the Glashedy Links, £25 per round midweek and £30 at weekends.

Glashedy Links has been designed in heroic fashion with vast greens and deep revetted bunkers. With its championship tees stretching the course to 7102 yards (par 72) it is much longer than The Old Links (6612 yards, par 71) but there are fewer awkward stances to contend with—provided, that is, you keep to the fairways.

There is no gentle break-in on the Glashedy Links. It opens with three formidable par fours, each measuring over 420 yards from the back tees. The green at the 1st is perched, rather enticingly, between two large sandhills; the threat of hitting out of bounds looms at the 2nd—as

does an alarmingly cavernous bunker in front of the green—and the landing area appears painfully narrow from the elevated tee at the 3rd. The dunes increase in size as you approach the dog-leg at the 4th and just as the fairway swings to the right and a cross bunker reveals itself, so Glashedy Rock comes fully into view directly behind the green. It is a magical moment.

Glashedy becomes an almost constant companion for the remainder of the round. It dominates the backdrop to the par three 5th, the first of the short holes. Stand on the tee of this hole on a lovely summer's evening with the sun reflecting off the sea and you may think Ballyliffin the most heavenly place on earth. At least, until your ball plummets into one of a series of gaping pot bunkers which practically encircle the green. The 6th is perhaps the most gentle of the par fours and after a vertigo-inducing tee shot at the 7th, where you play from the top of an enormous sandhill down to a green sited almost 100 feet below, the course flows gracefully back to the clubhouse.

The second nine is longer and tougher! Holes 10-12 weave a path through The Old Links and lead the golfer back out towards the higher, wilder duneland behind the great sandhill. Then begins a superb sequence of holes. The 13th is a massive par five—uphill and breathtaking in both senses of the word. Its rollercoasting fairway shadowed by towering sandhills is reminiscent of Ballybunion. The view over the shoulder, however, (back to Glashedy) is pure Turnberry. The 14th is arguably the best and most seductive of the short holes, and the 15th with its exhilarating downhill drive and fairway, which this time dog-legs to the left, is another excellent two-shotter.

From the 16th tee the course returns towards the clubhouse. It is a testing and potentially perilous journey home—an arrow-straight par four into the prevailing wind, a second par five that seems to stretch forever and a day, and finally, a classic finishing hole. The 18th is a sweeping dog-leg where the approach has to be targeted between tall dunes to find a heavily guarded green.

While some may think it a little premature to judge the quality of the new course no one could deny that it is both beautiful and dramatic. There seems every possibility that it will one day take its place alongside Portrush and Newcastle as one of the three great courses in the north of Ireland. Add the unique character of The Old Links to the equation and you have an extraordinary golfing destination. The Ballybunion of the North, perhaps?

Glashedy Links

Hole	Yards	Par	Hole	Yards	Par
1	426	4	10	397	4
2	432	4	11	419	4
3	428	4	12	448	4
4	479	5	13	572	5
5	177	3	14	159	3
6	361	4	15	440	4
7	174	3	16	426	4
8	422	4	17	549	5
9	382	4	18	411	4
Out	**3,281**	**35**	**In**	**3,821**	**37**
			Out	**3,281**	**35**
			Totals	**7,102**	**72**

County Sligo (Rosses Point)

Which is the best golf course in Ireland? Is it the Old Course at Ballybunion? Or perhaps Portmarnock near Dublin? Or what about the two 'Royal' courses north of the border, Portrush and County Down? These four courses invariably receive the most nominations in the age-old favourite 19th hole debate. But there is another golf course that many people believe deserves to be spoken of in the same breath and that is County Sligo, more commonly known as Rosses Point.

Of this magnificent five, Royal County Down at Newcastle has perhaps the strongest claim to possessing the finest front nine holes and Ballybunion the greatest back nine. But taking each of the eighteens as a balanced whole, Rosses Point must have a creditable claim—indeed Peter Alliss has been quoted as saying 'Rosses Point stands right at the very top of the list of Irish golf courses.' Another famous supporter is the great Tom Watson. If he were asked to name his three favourite links courses in Great Britain and Ireland (excluding those at which he won an Open Championship!) he would probably rattle off the names Ballybunion, Royal Dornoch and Rosses Point.

As well as having a glorious golf course, County Sligo Golf Club enjoys a glorious situation. The golf links (and the surrounding countryside) is dominated by the extraordinary mountain, Benbulben, which is a dead ringer for Cape Town's Table Mountain. Immediately adjacent to the links is a wonderfully sweeping bay with three beautiful beaches: little wonder that the scenery so intoxicated Ireland's greatest poet, W B Yeats.

Visiting golfers who wish to become similarly intoxicated by the golfing challenge are advised to contact the club in advance. The **Golf Secretary** at Rosses Point can be contacted by telephone on **(071) 77134** (from the UK the code is 00 353 71) and by fax on (071) 77460. There is no firm requirement that visitors produce handicap certificates but they must, however, be players of a 'reasonable standard'. The club's **Professional, Leslie Robinson** can be reached by telephone on **(071) 77171**. Finally, the green fees for summer 1998 are £27 per round, £40 per day during the week and, subject to availability, £35 per round, £50 per day at weekends.

Rosses Point is often tagged 'remote', not as remote as Waterville but more so than most of Ireland's finest golfing attractions. Naturally, it depends where one is coming from but there is an airport (County Sligo) just 20 minutes drive away at Strandhill. The town of Sligo is no more than 10 minutes away from the links (via the R291 road); Donegal is about one hour's drive north (N15) and Westport approximately an hour and a half to the south west (N17/N5/N60).

The 1st at Rosses Point is a medium length par four, fairly straight and gently uphill all the way to a well protected green. The 2nd is much more severely uphill and the approach shot, although likely to be no more than a short iron, can be very difficult to judge. On reaching the green at the 2nd one can feel on top of the world, almost literally, for the panoramic view from here is as vast as it is sensational. Benbulben is genuinely awe-inspiring, a geological freak which, if located in a more widely known part of the world, would be universally acclaimed. From such dizzy heights the Atlantic looks positively inviting—so does the downhill drive at the 3rd! This hole can be reached with two well struck shots but a series of fiendishly positioned bunkers await to punish the less accurate.

The 4th is a fine par three where the green sits on a natural plateau and this is followed by another vertigo-inducing tee shot at the 5th. The 6th is perhaps the weakest hole on the course and the 7th looks fairly straightforward for a stroke index one hole—that is until your second shot plummets into the brook in front of the green. The brook reappears on the 8th, which is a magnificent and much photographed dog-leg. The front nine concludes with the excellent par three 9th where the green is surrounded by bunkers.

The 10th and 11th offer the closest views of Benbulben and they are a very good pair of par fours. A fairly blind par five is followed by the difficult one-shot 13th, where the tee looks down over the sea and sands. Then comes Tom Watson's favourite. The 14th is a superb and extremely testing par four and when the wind is blowing can make even the 8th seem tame. If the wind is against on the 14th then it will be so again on the 15th, which is bad news because the drive needs to be carried far over some very wild dunes close to the shore. The 16th is the longest par three at Rosses Point and the 17th calls for a long uphill second to an amphitheatre green. Then at long last, comes a fairly gentle hole! It is the last and if you play it on a fine summer's evening you may be lucky enough to see the sun setting behind the 18th green: now wouldn't that be the perfect end to a perfect round!

Hole	Metres	Par	Hole	Metres	Par
1	347	4	10	351	4
2	278	4	11	368	4
3	457	5	12	486	5
4	150	3	13	162	3
5	438	5	14	394	4
6	379	4	15	367	4
7	393	4	16	196	3
8	374	4	17	414	4
9	153	3	18	336	4
Out	**2,969**	**36**	**In**	**3,074**	**35**
			Out	**2,969**	**36**
			Totals	**6,043**	**71**

The Sand House, a 4 star hotel, is an oasis of comfort, luxury and tranquillity. Standing on the edge of the Atlantic Ocean overlooking Donegal Bay its unique rear garden is the vast ocean which laps onto miles of golden sands including the EC Blue Flag beach at Rossnowlagh. Over 40 years experience has fashioned the style with which you are greeted by the Britton family and their friendly staff at this delightful hotel.

The hotel's 40 en suite bedrooms are individually and tastefully decorated and furnished to a high standard of comfort with antiques gathered over the years in keeping with its country house style. Many overlook the sea and a limited number have four poster beds. In the elegant dining room guests can sample such house specialities as Donegal Bay salmon, sea trout, scallops, crab and lobster as well as prime beef, lamb, veal and game in season. Locally smoked salmon, fresh bay oysters and mussels are

served throughout the day in the cosy lounge bar. Guests can relax after dinner in the cocktail lounge or in one of the other two comfortable bars, or appreciate the calm and beauty of the sea from the comfort of the delightful conservatory.

The Sand House Hotel is the ideal touring base for the Donegal Highlands, Fermanagh Lakelands and Sligo, Yeats County. For the energetic the hotel has an all-weather tennis court, croquet and miniature golf. Swimming, board sailing, surfing, canoeing and water skiing can also be enjoyed right outside the hotel.

South Donegal is a golfer's paradise with a choice of three superb championship links within a 40 minute drive—Donegal Murvagh (15 minutes), Bundoran (20 minutes) and Rosses Point (40 minutes). Enniscrone and Strandhill are two other excellent links within easy reach.

The Sand House Hotel
Rossnowlagh
Donegal Bay
Ireland
Tel: (00 353 72) 51777
Fax: (00 353 72) 52100

Donegal

The Irish have an inborn wanderlust that is perhaps rivalled only by Australians and New Zealanders. This partly explains how, wherever you go in the world, you bump into an Irishman, sooner rather than later. And why sooner rather than later, you'll hear the phrase 'to be sure' or 'tis grand'. It also partly explains why the names of numerous relatively small towns in Ireland are famous the world over—places like Limerick, Blarney and Tipperary for example. Another place that just about everybody has heard of is Donegal—not for its rhymes, kisses or songs of course but for its tweed. Yet like Limerick, Blarney and Tipperary not all that many people born outside Ireland have visited Donegal. Every golfer however, given the chance, should visit the country's most north westerly county. There are many wonderful courses here and they are all wonderfully uncrowded. And every brave golfer should visit Donegal, the county town itself, and play its majestic links at nearby Murvagh.

Why only every brave golfer? This is because to get the most out of Murvagh you must enjoy a mighty challenge. It is the longest golf course in Ireland. A local joke is that if you are a short hitter you can spend a full day at Murvagh and not complete 18 holes. Donegal really is a tiger of a links: from the Championship tees it measures over 7100 yards (or 6547 metres as the card will tell you.) In reality, most of us are never going to tackle the links from the tiger tees and while it is still a very long course from the tees of the day, real challenge becomes entwined with real pleasure.

Murvagh enjoys considerable seclusion. It is not exactly off the beaten track—Donegal is only six miles away—but quite a bit of the course is bordered by some fairly thick woodland, and being situated on a peninsula, there is an added feeling of isolation. The other border, of course, is the great Atlantic Ocean.

Few golf clubs are as keen for visitors to come and experience the charms of their course as Donegal (the club is understandably proud of the fact that Nick Faldo visited the course in 1993). The green fees in 1998 are a modest £18 per day during the week with £25 payable at weekends and on bank holidays. The club operates a timesheet system from May 1st to September 30th. Also restrictions apply on Mondays, which is ladies' day. . Donegal's **Secretary, John McBride** can be contacted by telephone on **(073) 34054** (00 353 73) from the UK, and by fax on (073) 34377. There is no professional at the club but the **Steward**, **Eugene McLoughlin** is very helpful. Meals and snacks are available in the clubhouse throughout the day although players are requested to place an order for meals before teeing off.

As already mentioned, Murvagh is approximately six miles from the centre of Donegal. The linking road is the N15 and the route off to the golf course is signposted. The town itself is about an hour's drive from the nearest airport which is at Sligo and again the route is the N15. Knock Airport is 80 miles away and Belfast 110 miles. Sligo Airport is obviously the most convenient and anyone playing golf at Donegal should try to include a game at County Sligo (or vice versa). Rosses Point and Murvagh—what a double for links enthusiasts!

Rather like at Rosses Point, the course opens with a fairly gentle hole. This time it is a par five and like every par five at Murvagh (there are four others) it is a dog-leg, but the approach to the green is not too demanding and the putting surface is fairly large. Things start to hot up at the 2nd. This is a very tough par four that plays every bit of its 416 yards. Thick, tangling rough lines the left hand side of the fairway on this hole and there is an out of bounds on the right. As for the green, it sits on a natural shelf.

Neither the 3rd or 4th is an easy hole and the 5th can be a horror. This is one of two really tremendous par threes at Donegal; the tee shot must be struck perfectly to carry a ravine—mishit it slightly and you can be playing your second from sand 30 feet below the green. Beyond the green is the beach. A brilliant sequence of holes comes after the 5th. This is where the course runs close to Donegal Bay and the views (if you care to clamber up the sandhills) are tremendous.

Perhaps the most memorable holes on the back nine at Murvagh are the 10th, 11th and 15th, while the most demanding are the 12th and 16th. The former is once again a huge par five; from the back tees it is (as some wag once suggested) a reasonable train journey and, as on most three-shot holes, the key is the second. If we are talking train distances then as par threes go the 16th must be the equivalent of the Trans-Siberian Express! One could sit behind this green all day and not see anyone reach the green with their tee shot. When the elements are stirred this is the kind of hole where, in days gone by, Jack Nicklaus would have peeled off his sweater and teed up with his driver. But then, Donegal is a place where another of those lovely Irish expressions 'good crack' takes on a new meaning.

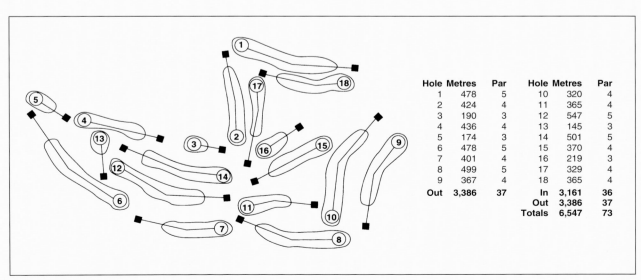

Hole	Metres	Par	Hole	Metres	Par
1	478	5	10	320	4
2	424	4	11	365	4
3	190	3	12	547	5
4	436	4	13	145	3
5	174	3	14	501	5
6	478	5	15	370	4
7	401	4	16	219	3
8	499	5	17	329	4
9	367	4	18	365	4
Out	**3,386**	**37**	**In**	**3,161**	**36**
			Out	**3,386**	**37**
			Totals	**6,547**	**73**

Slieve Russell

The unsuspecting traveller's first impression of the Slieve Russell Hotel is that it must be an incredible mirage. The knowledgeable golfer's lasting impression of Slieve Russell is that it is an extraordinary oasis.

Deep in the countryside of Co Cavan a remarkable new hotel and championship golf course has seemingly 'sprung from nowhere' and now demands to be discovered. Ballyconnell is the place—a small town in a quiet, sleepy part of the world, one much more renowned as a fisherman's paradise than a golfer's—although this would appear set to change. The landscape of this part of Ireland is dominated by numerous lakes, hence all the fishing, and one other rather more unusual feature, drumlins. (Remember them from your geography studies of glacial drift?) These are curvaceous little hills or mounds and they are dotted all over the valleys of west Cavan. So a land of lakes and curvaceous mounds? Clearly Mother Nature intended...

Mother Nature aside, the founder and guiding force behind the development of Slieve Russell has been successful local entrepreneur, Sean Quinn. His original concept was for the 18 hole golf course to complement the extensive leisure facilities of a luxury 150 bedroomed hotel. The Slieve Russell Hotel opened its doors in 1990 but sometime before the projected opening date for the golf course (summer 1992) it became apparent that this was to be no typical hotel resort type course. It would not have been hyperbole to suggest that the Slieve Russell construction team, lead by architect Paddy Merrigan, were busy creating a masterpiece.

Slieve Russell is most definitely a parkland golf course although occasionally the extreme contouring—both natural and strategically introduced—produces an almost links type feel. Two large lakes, connected by a wandering stream are the dominant features of the design and are responsible for creating several outstanding and dramatic holes. Water in fact must be confronted as early as the 2nd, a truly marvellous swinging dog-leg hole where, after trying to avoid the lake to the left of the fairway with the drive, the approach must then be played over the stream to a raised and two tiered green. The severity of the undulations (including some of the putting surfaces!) will be understood by the time the rollercoasting 3rd has been played. Both the 2nd and 3rd are superb par four holes but the quartet of par threes will probably create an even greater impression on the mind of the first time visitor—especially perhaps the 16th, an absolute gem of a short hole, and the amazing par five 13th, where for its entire length the fairway follows the curving edge of the second lake. You stand on the tee at the 13th and the green is straight ahead—the direct route to the flag however requires a water carry of some 400 yards!

Slieve Russell Hotel Golf & Country Club, Ballyconnell, Co Cavan, Ireland	
Director of Golf	P J Creamer (00 353 49) 26444 Fax (00 353 49) 26474
Green Fees	Resident Sun-Fri £20; Sat £26 Non resident Sun-Fri £28; Sat £36 Above prices per round.
Restrictions	Bookings preferred.
Directions	
Take the N3 from Dublin, leaving on the R200 for Ballyconnell at Belturbet.	

Glasson

It is becoming known as the 'Glasson experience': you don't just go and play Glasson you experience it. Clever marketing? Maybe. But it is true. Glasson has the capacity to overwhelm in at least four different ways. Firstly, there is the setting—it is simply sublime. Secondly, the welcome is one of the warmest you are ever likely to receive. Thirdly, there is the course itself—one of the most interesting you are ever likely to play. And finally, perhaps no golf club in the world offers the opportunity to roll up at its gates in quite so stylish a manner.

The setting: Glasson is the Killarney of the Irish Midlands. There is not much in the way of mountain scenery but Lough Ree is every bit as enchanting as Lough Leane. Moreover, the golf course at Glasson makes better use of its lakeside setting than either of the courses at Killarney. The site is quite elevated in places, allowing Lough Ree to be seen from almost every hole. From the highest parts of the course there are breathtaking 360 degree views.

The welcome: Glasson Golf and Country Club is the realisation of a dream—Tom and Breda Reid's dream. A charming and modest couple, together with their daughter Fidelma who is the Club Operations Manager, they provide a very personal, 'family' welcome. Considerable care and attention to detail has gone into the design of their course as well as the accompanying off-course facilities. In fact, the 19th is one of the best of many great holes at Glasson.

The golf course: Christy O'Connor Jr has designed several courses in Ireland but probably none is destined to be as famous (or as photographed) as his work at Glasson. And Christy knows it: "it is one of the most scenic pieces of land I have ever seen". There are tantalising glimpses of Lough Ree as you play down the fairways of the 1st and 2nd and you confront it head on at the par three 3rd. The 6th hole sweeps down to the most attractive area on the front nine, a point where the 6th and 8th greens and 7th tee converge, and where each is separated from the other by an attractive water hazard. The dramatic approach to the 8th is one no golfer will quickly forget. Nor could anyone tire of playing the skilfully designed par four 13th, the stunning par five 14th and the extraordinary par three 15th where both the tee and green protrude into the waters of Lough Ree.

The stylish arrival: Glasson has its own lakeside jetty, enabling golfers to arrive by cruiser after journeying from the west of Ireland along the River Shannon. Did you ever hear of a better way of getting one up on your opponent even before you hit a ball?

Glasson Golf & Country Club, Glasson, Athlone, Co Westmeath, Ireland	
Golf Manager	Fidelma Reid (00 353 902) 85120
Green Fees	Mon-Thur £25; Fri/Sun £28; Sat £30
Restrictions	Best to book with Golf Office
Directions	
Glasson is 75 miles from Dublin via the N6 and 6 miles north east of Athlone on the N55 Cavan/Longford road.	

Rosapenna

There is perhaps no more romantic adventure in all the golf world than a journey to Rosapenna and Portsalon, the obscure, almost forgotten links on the rugged Donegal coast'—*Links of Heaven*, Richard Phinney and Scott Whitley.

Imagine the scene about a hundred years ago: Old Tom Morris, his legendary beard now a whiter shade of grey, surveys his work. Rosapenna he concludes, must be the most natural links he was ever invited to lay out. "I'll accept a few guineas for my efforts but perhaps Mother Nature should take most of the credit." He retires to the elegant hotel, fraternises with the holidaying English gentry over dinner then takes an evening stroll along one of the most beautiful stretches of coast he has ever seen.

After Tom Morris came Harry Vardon and James Braid—not only in respect of their impact on the world of golf, but both made the trip to Rosapenna. And, being celebrated course architects as well as players, neither could resist tinkering with Old Tom's design.

Then times became hard. Long before the outbreak of World War Two the numbers of holidaying English gentry began to dwindle. The hotel lost its way and as a consequence, Rosapenna became almost forgotten—that is, until Frank Casey came along. Here isn't the place to discuss the life and times of Frank Casey—besides he is a modest man—suffice to say he presides over a marvellous 'new' Rosapenna Golf Hotel. The condition of the links (which is managed by the hotel) would bring a twinkle to Old Tom's eye and it is rapidly shedding its 'forgotten' tag. Furthermore, 18 additional holes, designed by Pat Ruddy in a vast stretch of adjoining duneland, should be open by the millennium. Rosapenna is going places.

The present links appears very much as Vardon and Braid left it. True, it now measures 6374 yards (par 70) but there is an unmistakably old-fashioned flavour about Rosapenna. It is also a course of two halves, or rather two distinct loops. The first 10 holes occupy fairly level ground beside Sheephaven Bay while the remaining eight holes wind their way around—and eventually career over the top of a vast hill that overlooks Mulroy Bay on one side and Sheephaven Bay on the other. Throughout the round there are glimpses of the Donegal Hills and the imperious (and splendidly named) Muckish Mountain.

Among the most memorable holes within the first loop are the 4th, with its incredibly contoured green, and the par three 6th, where the tee shot must be fired across a chasm of dunes to find an elusive table shaped green. On the back nine a cattle grid and country road have to be negotiated at the quaint old 12th, but the outstanding hole is undoubtedly the 13th, a brilliantly designed dog-leg that charges downhill towards Mulroy Bay.

Rosapenna Hotel & Golf Course, Downings, Co Donegal, Ireland	
Manager	Frank Casey (00 353) 74 55301 Fax (00 353) 74 55128
Green Fees Restrictions	WD £20, WE £25 Visitors welcome; bookings preferred.
Directions	25 miles north west of Letterkenny via the R245 from Milford.

Portsalon

Where in the world can you play golf alongside a beach as pure and as perfect as the one at Portsalon? The official answer is nowhere. A few years ago an international panel of travel writers adjudged Portsalon Strand 'The Second Most Beautiful Beach in the World'. Apparently there is a more beautiful one in the Philippines but it has no golf course. And the beach really does come into play at Portsalon!

The 'romantic journey' referred to above in *Links of Heaven* can never adequately prepare first time visitors for the drama of Portsalon's setting. Tucked away on the tip of the Fanad Peninsula on the northern shores of Lough Swilley, the Knockalla Mountains provide a stunning backdrop. Linking with heather-clad hills, they shield and semi-circle the links, creating a stage-like effect. Add the glistening waters of Lough Swilley, those glorious golden sands and 18 spectacular holes to the equation and for we blasphemous golfers, *this* is the links of heaven.

Local enthusiasts have played golf amid such natural splendour for more than a century. The club was established in 1891 and became one of the founding members of the Golfing Union of Ireland. Again, like Rosapenna, the links benefitted in its early years from the close proximity of a stylish hotel and when the hotel faded, so did the fame of Portsalon—although not before it twice hosted the Irish Ladies Championship. The great May Hezlet triumphed at Portsalon in 1905 and Mabel Harrison won when the event returned in 1912.

By modern standards the course is quite short, weighing in at 5880 yards, par 69. In terms of character and charm, however, it has very few peers. A journalist from *Fore* magazine inspected the links in 1995 and it seems was no less captivated than Phinney and Whitley. When he put pen to paper he declared, 'If I could play only one golf course for the rest of my life I would choose Portsalon. No contest'. Presumably he avoided hooking his opening drive into the sea, remained similarly dry at the par three 2nd ('the best short hole in the British Isles') and survived the vertigo-inducing tee shot at the 3rd, before successfully threading his approach between the twin rocky outcrops that guard the entrance to that green.

Portsalon is an extraordinary golf course. At the 6th players must occasionally wade across water to drive from an island tee, and on the 13th, they have to climb (or scale) a tee known as 'The Matterhorn'. There are blind holes, fairways that rollercoast and greens so heavily contoured that they resemble crumpled duvets. Extraordinary? Better make that eccentric. Yes, Portsalon is an eccentric, turn of the century masterpiece. Long may it remain so.

Portsalon Golf Club, Portsalon Fanad, Co Donegal, Ireland	
Secretary	Peter Doherty (00 353) 74 59459 (Tel and fax)
Green Fees Restrictions	WD £14 WE £17 None, but it is best to ring ahead for bookings
Directions	20 miles north of Letterkenny via Ramelton, Milford. and Kerrykeel.

Connemara

Not many people reading this book will have visited the moon and, unless NASA is keeping an extraordinary secret under wraps, only one man has ever played golf there—our friend from La Moye and Fulford, Admiral Alan Sheppard. I suspect the closest most of us are ever likely to get to experiencing golf in a lunar-like landscape is if we visit Connemara on the west coast of Ireland.

While much of County Kerry basks in picture-post-card prettiness, the countryside of Connemara boasts a truly rugged kind of splendour. Some of Connemara appears almost prehistoric. Great grey rocks are strewn all over a hilly, green landscape. Connemara National Park is surely where Finn McCool and his giant buddies staged an all-night rock throwing party but forgot to clear up afterwards. The village of Ballyconneely is about as far west as you can go in Connemara without slipping into the Atlantic and Ballyconneely is where Connemara Golf Club is found.

Before 1973 it used to be reckoned that the only people who ventured this far west were lost. This of course was in the days before golf came to Ballyconneely. Connemara's championship golf links is worth discovering. It may not be in quite the same league as Rosses Point to the north or Ballybunion to the south but it is a wonderful golfing experience.

Connemara hosted its first professional tournament, the Carroll's Irish Matchplay Championship, in 1980, and the AIB Connemara pro-am, held in September, is now recognised as one of the major fixtures on the Irish PGA calendar.

Ballyconneely is 9 miles south of Clifden (where transatlantic aviators Alcock and Brown fell to earth) some 15 to 20 minutes along a fairly deserted road. Clifden is joined to Galway by the N59, a distance of approximately 50 miles and a journey that no one should rush. According to Thackeray this is 'one of the most beautiful districts that is ever the fortune of the traveller to examine.' Thackeray was biased, but a thousand watercolours cannot lie. The N59 also links Clifden with Westport to the north east and the route via Leenane (where 'The Field', which starred Richard Harris was filmed) is at least as dramatic.

Golfing visitors to Connemara are always made extremely welcome. Greatly responsible for the hospitable atmosphere at the club is the **Secretary/ Manager John McLoughlin**. It is advisable to contact Mr McLoughlin in advance for tee reservations. The club's address is **Connemara Golf Club, Ballyconneely, Clifden, Co Galway.** Telephone on **(095) 23502** or fax on (095) 23662 (from the UK the code is 00 353 95). During the summer months and at holiday weekends a starting sheet system is operated. Subject to the above, and being able to provide proof of handicap, there are no general restrictions on the times when visitors may play. Green fees for 1998 are £25 in summer—between April and October—and £16 for the rest of the year. The club's new **Professional** is **Hugh O'Neill**, who has recently moved from Galway GC.

Few clubhouses enjoy a better vantage point than the one at Connemara. Perched on high ground, there are not only some magnificent views over the ocean (particularly splendid when the western sun dips into the sea on a summer's evening) but also across much of the course. It is a wonderful place in which to relax. But first we must tackle the course.

The first seven holes at Connemara occupy the flattest part of the links. They are by no means easy holes—very testing ones, in fact—but in the opinion of many they serve as mere appetisers for the feast that follows. Some of the holes between the 8th and 18th are as good as any one is likely to play: 'So good they are nearly ridiculous' reckoned Irish golf writer Pat Ruddy. The 8th is the stroke index one hole and the approach is a very testing one to a broad but plateau green. As for the 9th, it is a real gem of a hole. Again a two-shotter, the player drives downhill from a magnificently placed high tee. Over the player's shoulder as he drives is a mountainous backdrop, the famous Twelve Bens, and stretching out ahead is the sea, the Atlantic Ocean—the next terra firma being Long Island.

If the 9th is a memorable hole, the par three 13th is out of this world. This is where landscape is replaced by moonscape. As at the 9th, an exhilarating downhill tee shot is called for. From the back tees a long-iron shot will be needed as the carry is all of 200 yards. The 14th, a par five where you can really open the shoulders, and the 15th, which is a little reminiscent of the 14th at Portmarnock with its uphill second to a shelf-like green, are two more marvellous holes. Water can play the devil at the 16th while the 17th and 18th are a pair of par fives that seem to stretch for ever and a day.

If you've played Connemara from the back tees (well over 7000 yards) the chances are you'll be breathless by the finish. Breathless at Connemara—like being on the moon.

Hole	Metres	Par		Hole	Metres	Par
1	331	4		10	383	4
2	366	4		11	151	3
3	145	3		12	399	4
4	335	4		13	180	3
5	342	4		14	460	5
6	175	3		15	349	4
7	482	5		16	370	4
8	418	4		17	468	5
9	344	4		18	475	5
Out	**2,938**	**35**		**In**	**3,235**	**37**
				Out	**2,938**	**35**
				Totals	**6,173**	**72**

A delightful converted shooting lodge built in 1815, the Rock Glen is now a 29 bedroomed cosy first class country house hotel nestling in the heart of Connemara.

Lush pasture rolls from the door down to the shore of the narrow bay where Connemara's mountain range, the Twelve Bens, drift in and out of the clouds.

Family run, the restaurant is renowned locally for its excellent cuisine which has earned it two AA Rosettes.

The cosy bar, where plump armchairs out-number bar stools, has a turf fire which glows all year round. Guests can enjoy a pleasant evening of musical entertainment with the resident pianist. Spontaneous sing-songs occur regularly, and you are invited to join in. Coffee is served in the drawing room where you can relax and enjoy the conversation. There is also a cosy sun lounge which can be a delight to all even on the dullest day.

The all-weather floodlit tennis course is in excellent condition and is free to residents and there is also a superb full size snooker table. The bedrooms, 15 of which are on the ground floor, are all individually and comfortably decorated with private bathroom, radio and television, trouser press, hairdryer, and direct dial telephone.

The hotel is ideally situated for the golf enthusiast. Connemara's 18 hole championship course is in a spectacular setting on the coast, with the Twelve Bens in the background. It is just a 15 minute drive from the hotel. Lessons are also available on request, golf clubs and caddy cars can also be hired at the club.

For the non-golfer the area is perfect for walking, hill climbing, river, lake and deep-sea fishing. Miles of sandy beaches for the swimmer and pony trekking (Clifden is famous for its Connemara ponies) can all be arranged at the reception desk.

John and Evangeline Roche, their family and staff look forward to welcoming you to the Rock Glen where you may recall the pleasures of leisurely and more sedate way of life, then return home refreshed, rested and fit.

Rock Glen Country House Hotel
Clifden
Connemara
County Galway Ireland
Tel: 00 353 95 21035
Fax: 00 353 95 21737
E mail: rockglen@iol.ie

Key

To avoid disappointment
it is advisable to telephone
in advance

***Visitors welcome at most times
**Visitors usually allowed on
weekdays only
*Visitors not normally permitted
(Mon, Wed) No visitors
on specified days

Approximate Green Fees
A   £40 plus
B   £25 to £40
C   £20 to £30
D   £15 to £25
E   under £15
F   Green fees on application

Restrictions
G   Guests only
H—Handicap certificate required
H—(24) Handicap of 24 or less
L —Letter of introduction required
M—Visitor must be a member of
another recognised club

CO CARLOW

Borris G.C.
(0503) 73143
Deerpark, Borris
(9) 6026 yards/***/D

Carlow G.C.
(0503) 31695
Deerpark, Dublin Road, Carlow
(18) 6532 yards/***/D

CO CAVAN

Belturbet G.C.
(049) 22287
Erne Hill, Belturbet
(9) 5347 metres/***/E

Blacklion G.C.
(072) 53024
Toam, Blacklion
(9) 6098 yards/***/E

Cabra Castle G.C.
(042) 67904
Kingscourt
(9) 5839 yards/***/F

County Cavan G.C.
(049) 31514
Arnmore House, Drumellis, Cavan
(18) 5519 metres/***/D

Slieve Russell G.C.
(049) 26444
Slieve Russell Hotel, Ballyconnell
(18) 6580 yards/***/B/H/M

Virginia G.C.
(049) 48066
Virginia
(9) 4900 metres/***/E

COUNTY CLARE

Clonlara G.C.
(061) 354141
Clonlara
(9) 5289 metres/***/E

Dromoland Castle G.C.
(061) 368144
Newmarket on Fergus
(18) 6098 metres//***/B/H

East Clare G.C.
(061) 921322
Bodyke
(9) 5675 metres/***/E

Ennis G.C.
(065) 24074
Drumbiggle, Ennis
(18) 5316 metres/**(Sun)/C/M

Kilkee G.C.
(065) 56048
East End, Kilkee
(9) 5900 metres/***/D

Kilrush G.C.
(065) 51138
Parknamoney, Kilrush
(9) 2739 yards/***/F

Lahinch G.C.
(065) 81003
Lahinch
(18) 6123 metres/***/A/H/M
(18) 5138 metres/***/B/H/M

Shannon G.C.
(061) 471849
Shannon Airport, Shannon
(18) 6874 yards/**/B/H/M

Spanish Point G.C.
(065) 84198
Spanish Point, Miltown Malbay
(9) 1787 yards/***/D

Woodstock G.C.
(065) 29463
Shanaway Road, Ennis
(18) 5879 metres/***/C

CO CORK

Bandon G.C.
(023) 41111
Castlebernard, Bandon
(18)5879 metres/***/C

Bantry Park G.C.
(027) 50579
Donemark, Bantry
(9) 2973 yards/***/D

Berehaven Park G.C.
(027) 70700
Millcove, Castletownbere
(9) 4763 metres/***/E/H/M

Charleville G.C.
(063) 81257
Ardmore, Charleville
(18) 6430 yards/**/D

Cobh G.C.
(021) 812399
Ballywilliam, Cobh
(9) 2518 yards/**(W/E am)/E

Coosheen G.C.
(028) 28182
Schull
(9) 3362 metres/***/E

Cork G.C.
(021) 353451
Little Island, Cork
(18) 6115 metres/**(Thurs)/B/H

Doneraile G.C.
(022) 24137
Doneraile, Cork
(9) 5528 yards/**(W/E am)/F

Douglas G.C.
(021) 895297
Douglas, Cork
(18) 5644 metres/**(Tues)/C

Dunmore G.C.
(023) 33352
Muckross, Clonakilty
(9) 4464 yards/***(Sun)/D

East Cork G.C.
(021) 631687
Gortacrue, Midleton
(18) 5207 metres/**/D/H

Fermoy G.C.
(025) 31472
Carrin Cross, Fermoy
(18) 5550 metres/***(Mon/Wed)/F

Fota Island G.C.
(021) 883710
Carrigtwohill, Cork
(18) 6891 yards/***/B

Frankfield G.C.
(021) 361199
Douglas, Cork
(9) 5191 yards/***/E

Glengarriff G.C.
(027) 63150
Glengarriff
(9) 2047 metres/***/E

Harbour Point G.C.
(021) 353094
Clash Road, Little Island, Cork
(18) 5773 metres/***/B

Kanturk G.C.
(029) 50534
Fairy Hill, Kanturk
(9) 5527 metres/***/E

Kinsale G.C.
(021) 773258
Ringenane, Belgooly
(9) 2666 metres/**/D/M
(18) 6500 yards/**/D/M

Lee Valley G.& C.C.
(021) 331721
Clashanure, Ovens
(18) 6705 yards/**/B/H

Macroom G.C.
(026) 41072
Lackaduve, Macroom
(9) 5439 metres/***/D/H

Mahon G.C.
(021) 362480
Cloverhill, Blackrock
(18) 4818 metres/***/E

Mallow G.C.
(022) 21145
Ballyellis, Mallow
(18) 6559 yards/**(Tues)/D

Mitchelstown G.C.
(025) 24072
Mitchelstown
(15) 5057 metres/***/D

Monkstown G.C.
(021) 841376
Parkgarriffe, Monkstown
(18) 5669 metres***/B/H(20)/M

Muskerry G.C.
(021) 385297
Carrigrohane, Blarney
(18) 5426 metres/**(Mon/Tues)/D

Raffeen Creek G.C.
(021) 378430
Ringaskiddy
(9) 5800 yards/***/D

Skibbereen G.C.
(028) 21227
Licknavar, Skibbereen
(18) 5774 yards/***/D

Youghal G.C.
(024) 92787
Knockaverry, Youghal
(18) 5664 metres/***(Wed)/D/H/M

CO DONEGAL

Ballybofey & Stranorlar G.C.
(074) 31093
Stranorlar, Ballybofey
(18) 5913 yards/*(not am)/D/H

Ballyliffin G.C.
(077) 76119
Ballyliffin, Cardonagh
(18) 6612 yards/***/C/M
(18) 7102 yards/***/B/M

Buncrana G.C.
(077) 62279
Buncrana
(9) 2020 yards/***/F

Bundoran G.C.
(072) 41302
Great Northern Hotel, Bundoran
(18) 6159 yards/***/D/H

Chloic Cheann Fhaola G.C.
(074) 65416
Cloughaneely, Falcarragh
(9)/***/F

Cruit Island G.C.
(075) 43296
Kincasslagh, Dungloe
(9) 5297 yards/***/E

Donegal G.C.
(073) 34054
Murvagh, Donegal
(18) 6249 yards/**(Mon)/C/H/M

Dunfanaghy G.C.
(074) 36335
Dunfanaghy, Letterkenny
(18) 5006 metres/***/D

Greencastle G.C.
(077) 81013
Moville, Greencastle
(18) 5386 metres/**/D

Gweedore G.C.
(075) 31140
Derrybeg, Gweedore
(18) 6201 yards/***/E

Letterkenny G.C.
(074) 21150
Barnhill, Letterkenny
(18) 6239 yards/***/D

Narin and Portnoo G.C.
(073) 21722
Narin, Portnoo
(18) 5322 metres/**(Sun)/F/H

North West G.C.
(077) 61027
Lisfannon, Fahon, Lifford
(18) 5968 yards/***/D/H/M

Otway G.C.
(074) 58319
Saltpans, Rathmullen
(9) 4134 yards/***/E

Portsalon G.C.
(074) 59459
Portsalon, Letterkenny
(18) 5878 yards/***/D

Redcastle G.C.
(077) 82073
Redcastle, Moville
(9) 5528 yards/***/D

Rosapenna G.C.
(074) 55301
Downings, Rosapenna
(18) 6374 yards/***/C

CO DUBLIN

Balbriggan G.C.
(01) 841 2229
Blackhall, Balbriggan
(18) 5881 metres/***/D

Balcarrick G.C.
(01) 843 6957
Corballis, Donabate
(18)6912 yards/***/D

334

Ballinascorney G.C.
(01) 451 2082
Ballinascorney
(18) 5464 yards/***/D

Beaverstown G.C.
(01) 843 6439
Beaverstown, Donabate
(18) 5551 metres/**/D/H

Beech Park G.C.
(01) 458 0100
Johnstown, Rathcoole
(18)5730 metres/**/C

Carrickmines G.C.
(01) 295 5972
Carrickmines, Dublin
(9) 6103 yards/***/C/G

Castle G.C.
(01) 490 4207
Woodside Drive, Rathfarnham
(18)5653 metres/**/B

Clontarf G.C.
(01) 833 1892
Malahide Road
(18) 5459 metres/**/B

Coldwinters G.C.
(01) 864 0324
Newton House, St Margarets
(18) 5973/***/E

Corballis G.C.
(01) 8436583
Donabate
(18) 4971 metres/***/F

Corrstown G.C.
(01) 864 0553
Corrstown, Killsallaghan
(18) 5584 yards/*/G

Deer Park Hotel & G.C.
(01) 832 6039
Howth Castle, Howth
(18) 6503 yards/***/D
(18) 6778 yards/***/D

Donabate G.C.
(01) 843 6346
Donabate
(18) 6187 yards/**/F

Dublin Mountain G.C.
(01) 458 2570
Gortlum, Brittas
(18) 5433 metres/***/A/H

Dun Laoghaire G.C.
(01) 280 3916
Eglinton Park, Dun Laoghaire
(18) 5712 yards/**/B

Edmondstown G.C.
(01) 493 1082
Edmondstown, Rathfarnham
(18) 5663 metres/***/B/H

Elm Green G.C.
(01) 269 3438
Nutley House, Donnybrook
(18) 5422 metres/***/A/H/M

Finnstown Fairways G.C.
(01) 628 0644
Newcastle Road, Lucan
(9) 2695 yards/***/D

Forrest Little G.C.
(01) 840 1763
Forrest Little, Cloghran
(18) 6451 yards/**/F/H/M

Foxrock G.C.
(01) 289 3414
Torquay Rd, Foxrock
(9) 6234 yards/**/C

Grange G.C.
(01) 493 2299
Grange Road, Rathfarnham
(18) 5517 metres/***/A/M

Hazel Grove G.C.
(01) 452 0911
Mount Seskin Road, Jobstown,
Tallaght
(9) 5225 yards/**/D

Hermitage G.C.
(01) 626 8072
Lucan
(18) 5814 metres/***/B/H(24)/M

Hibernian G.C.
(01) 851 0565
Citywest G.C., Saggart
(18) 6441 yards/***/B

Hollywood G.C.
(01) 843 3007
Hollywood, Ballyboughal
(18) 5674 yards/***/D

Howth G.C.
(01) 832 3055
Carriackbrack Road, Sutton
(18) 5618 metres/***/C/H/

Island G.C.
(01) 84366104
Corballis, Donabate
(18) 6658 yards/***/A

Killiney G.C.
(01) 285 2823
Ballinclea Road, Killiney
(9) 5626 metres/***/C/M

Kilmashogue G.C.
(088) 682360
College Road, Whitechurch
(18) 5320 metres/***/E

Kilternan Hotel G.C.
(01) 295 5559
Enniskerry Road, Kilternan
(18) 4952 metres/***/C/H(24)

Lucan G.C.
(01) 628 2106
Celbridge Road, Lucan
(18) 5650 metres /***/C

Luttrellstown Castle G.C.
(01) 808 9988
Castleknock, Dublin 15
(18) 6384 metres/**/A/M

Malahide G.C.
(01) 846 1611
Beechwood, The Grange, Malahide
(18) 6619 yards/**/B-A/H/M
(9) 6257 yards/**/B-A/H/M

Milltown G.C.
(01) 497 6090
Lower Churchtown Road
(18) 5638 metres/***/A/H/M

Newlands G.C.
(01) 459 3157
Clondalkin
(18) 5714 metres/**/B

Portmarnock G.C.
(01) 846 2968
Portmarnock
(18) 6497 metres/**/A/L/M
(9) 3478 yards/**/A/L/M

Portmarnock Hotel G.C.
(01) 846 1800
Strand Road, Portmarnock
(18) 5970 metres/***/A/H

Rathfarnham G.C.
(01) 493 1201
Newtown, Rathfarnham, Dublin 16
(9) 5787 yards/**(Tues)/C

Royal Dublin G.C.
(01) 833 6346
Bull Island, Dollymount, Dublin 3
(18) 6076 metres/**/A

Rush G.C.
(01) 843 8177
Rush
(9) 6850 yards/**/D/H

St Annes G.C.
(01) 833 6471
Bull Island, Dollymount, Dublin 5
(18) 5797 metres/***/C

St Margaret's G.& C.C.
(01) 864 0400
St Margaret's, Dublin
(18) 6900 yards/***/B-A

Skerries G.C.
(01) 849 1567
Hackestown, Skerries
(18) 6113 metres/**/C/H(20)

Slade Valley G.C.
(01) 458 2739
Lynch Park, Brittas
(18) 5337 metres/**/C/H

Stackstown G.C.
(01) 494 4561
Kellystown Road, Rathfarnham
(18) 5952 metres/***/D-C

Sutton G.C.
(01) 832 2965
Cush Point, Barrow Road, Sutton
(9) 2859 yards/***(Tues/Sat)/C

Swords G.C.
(01) 840 9819
Balheary Avnue,. Swords
(18) 5677 metres/***/E

Turvey G.C.
(01) 843 5169
Turvey Avenue, Donabate
(9)/***/E

Westmanstown G.C.
(01) 820 5817
Clonsilla, Dublin
(18) 6400 yards/***/C

CO GALWAY

Athenry G.C.
(091) 794466
Palmerstown, Oranmore
(18) 5552 metres/***(Sun)/D

Ballinasloe G.C.
(0905) 42126
Ballinasloe, Rosgloss
(18) 5868 metres/***/D/M

Bearna G.C.
(091) 592677
Corboley, Bearna
(18) 6164 metres/***/F

Connemara G.C.
(095) 23502
Ballyconneelly, Clifden
(18) 6173 metres/***/C/H

Connemara Isles G.C.
(091) 572498
Lettermore, Connemara
(9) 5720 yards/***/E

Galway G.C.
(091) 522033
Blackrock, Salthill, Galway
(18) 6376 yards/**(Tues)/C

Galway Bay G.& C.C.
(091) 790500
Renville Oranmore
(18) 6453 metres/***/E

Gort G.C.
(091) 632244
Laughtyshaughnessy, Gort
(9) 4976 metres/***(Sun am)/E

Loughrea G.C.
(091) 841049
Bullaun Road, Loughrea
(18) 5613 yards/***/D

Mountbellew G.C.
(0905) 79259
Shankhill, Mountbellew
(9) 5564 yards/***/F

Oughterard G.C.
(091) 552131
Gortreevagh, Oughterard
(18) 6141 yards/***/D/H

Portumna G.C.
(0509) 41059
Ennis Road,Portumna
(18) 5776 yards/***/D

Tuam G.C.
(093) 28993
Barnacurragh, Tuam
(18) 6321 yards/**/D

CO KERRY

Ardfert G.C.
(066) 34744
Sackville, Ardfert
(9) 4754 yards/***/E

Ballybunion G.C.
(068) 27146
Sandhill Road, Ballybunion
(18) 6503 yards/***/A/H(24)/L
(18) 6477 yards/***/A/H(24)/L

Ballyheigue Castle G.C.
((066) 33555
Ballyheigue, Tralee
(9) 6292 metres/***/D

Beaufort G.C.
(064) 44440
Churchtown, Beaufort
(18) 6792 yards/***/B

Castlegregory G.C.
(066) 39179
Stradbally, Castlegregory
(9) 5488 yards/***/D

Ceann Sibeal G.C.
(066) 56255
Ballyferriter, Tralee
(18) 6650 yards/***/C

Dooks G.C.
(066) 68205
Dooks, Killorglin
(18) 6010 yards/**/C/H/M

Kenmare G.C.
(064) 41291
Kenmare, Killarney
(9) 5950 yards/***/D

Kerries G.C.
(066) 22112
Tralee
(9) 2718 metres/***/E

Killarney G.& C.C.
(064) 31034
O'Mahony's Point, Killarney
(18) 6743 yards/***/B/H
(18) 7083 yards/***/B/H

Killorglin G.C.
(066) 61979
Steelroe, Killorglin
(18) 6464 yards/***/B

Parknasilla G.C.
(064) 45122
Parknasilla, Sneem
(9) 4834 yards/***/D

Ross G.C.
(064) 31125
Ross Road, Killarney
(9) 5898 metres/***/E

Tralee G.C.
(066) 36379
West Barrow, Ardfert
(18) 6252 metres/**(Weds)/A/H/M

Waterville G.C.
(066) 74102
Ring of Kerry, Waterville
(18) 7184 yards/***/A/H/M

CO KILDARE

Athy G.C.
(0507) 31729
Geraldine, Athy
(18) 6308 yards/**/D

Bodenstown G.C.
(045) 87096
Bodenstown, Sallins
(18) 5788 metres/**/D
(18) 5428 metres/**/D

Castlewarden G.& C.C.
(01) 458 9254
Castlewarden, Straffan
(18) 6008 metres/**/D

Cill Dara G.C.
(045) 521433
Kildare Town
(9) 6426 yards/***/D

Clongowes G.C.
(045) 868202
Clongowes Wood, Clane
(9) 4674 metres/***/F

Craddockstown G.C.
(045) 897610
Naas
(18) 6134 metres/***/D

Curragh G.C.
(045) 441714
Curragh
(18) 6603 yards/***/D

Highfield G.C.
(0405) 31021
Highfield House, Carbury
(18) 6278 yards/***/E

Kilcock G.C.
(01) 6284074
Kilcock
(9)/***/E

Kildare Country Club 'K' Club
(01) 6273111
Straffan
(18) 6368 metres/**/A/H

Kilkea Castle
(0503) 45156
Castledermot
(18) 6200 metres/***/B

Killeen G.C.
(045) 866003
Killenbeg, Kill
(18) 5452 yards/***/D

Knockanally G.& C.C.
(045) 869322
Donadea, N. Kildare
(18) 6424 yards/***/B

Leixlip G.C.
(01) 624 4978
Leixlip
(18) 5550 metres/***/D

Naas G.C.
(045) 874644
Kerdiffstown, Salins, Naas
(18) 5660 metres/***/D

Woodlands G.C.
(045) 860777
Coill Dubh, Naas
(9) 4839 metres/***/F

CO KILKENNY

Callan G.C.
(052) 25136
Geraldine, Callan
(9) 5844 metres/***/E

Castlecomer G.C.
(056) 41139
Dromgoole, Castlecomer
(9) 6515 yards/***/C

Kilkenny G.C.
(056) 65400
Glendine, Kilkenny
(18) 6450 yards/***/C/M

Mount Juliet G.C.
(056) 73064
Thomastown
(18) 7101 yards/***/A/H

CO LAOIS

Abbey Leix G.C.
(0502) 31450
Abbey Leix, Portlaoise
(9) 5680 yards/***/E

Heath G.C.
(0502) 46622
The Heath, Portlaoise
(18) 5736 metres/***/D/H/M

Mountrath G.C.
(0502) 32558
Knockanina, Mountrath
(9) 5300 yards/***/E

Portarlington G.C.
(0502) 23115
Garryhinch, Portarlington
(18) 6206 yards/***/D/L

Rathdowney G.C.
(0505) 46170
Coulnaboul West, Rathdowney
(9) 6086 yards/***/F

CO LEITRIM

Ballinamore G.C.
(078) 44346
Crevy, Ballinamore
(9) 5680 yards/***/F

Carrick on Shannon G.C.
(079) 67015
Woodbrook, Carrick on Shannon
(9) 5584 metres/***/D

CO LIMERICK

Abbeyfeale G.C.
(063) 32033
Dromtrasna Collins
(9) 4004 yards/***/E

Adare G.C.
(061) 396566
Adare
(18) 7138 yards/***/A

Adare Manor G.C.
(061) 395044
Adare
(18) 5800 yards/***/D/H

Castletroy G.C.
(061) 335753
Castletroy, Limerick
(18) 6335 yards/**/B

Killeline G.C.
(069) 61600
Newcastle West
(18) 5924metres/***/D

Limerick G.C.
(061) 412492
Ballyclough, Limerick
(18) 5938 metres/**(Tues)/B/H/M

Limerick County G.& C.C.
(061) 351881
Ballyneery
(18) 6137 metres/***/C

Newcastle West G.C.
(069) 76500
Ardagh, Newcastle West
(18) 5482 yards/***(Sun)/D

CO LONGFORD

County Longford G.C.
(043) 46310
Dublin Road, Longford
(18) 6008 yards/***/D/H(24)

CO LOUTH

Ardee G.C.
(041) 53227
Townparks, Ardee
(18) 6200 yards/***/D/H

County Louth G.C.
(041) 22329
Baltray, Drogheda
(18) 6783 yards/**/B/H/M

Dundalk G.C.
(042) 21731
Blackrock, Dundalk
(18) 6776 yards/***(Tues/Sun)/C

Greenore G.C.
(042) 73678
Greenore, Dundalk
(18) 6506 yards/***/D/H(20)

Killinbeg G.C.
(042) 39303
Killin Park, Dundalk
(12) 3322 yards/***/E

Seapoint G.C.
(041) 22333
Termonfeckin
(18) 6339 metres/***/

Townley Hall G.C.
(041) 42229
Tullyallen, Drogheda
(9) 5221 metres/***/EC

CO MAYO

Achill Island G.C.
(098) 43456
Keel, Achill
(9) 2723 yards/***/E

Ashford Castle G.C.
(092) 46003
Cong
(9) 2896 yards/***/D

Ballina G.C.
(096) 21050
Mossgrove, Shanaghy, Ballina
(9) 5702 yards/***/D

Ballinrobe G.C.
(092) 41118
Claremorris Road, Ballinrobe
(18) 6234 metres/***/D

Ballyhaunis G.C.
(0907) 30014
Coolnaha, Ballyhaunis
(9) 5393 yards/***/E

Carne G.C.
(097) 82292
Carne, Belmullet
(18) 6058 metres/***/D

Castlebar G.C.
(094) 21649
Rocklands, Castlebar
(18) 5698 metres/***(Sun)/D

Claremorris G.C.
(094) 71527
Rushbrook, Castlemaggaret
(9) 6454 yards/***/F

Mulrany G.C.
(098) 36262
Mulrany, Westport
(9) 6380 yards/***/E/M

Swinford G.C.
(094) 51378
Brabazon Park, Swinford
(9) 5230 yards/***/E

Westport G.C.
(098) 28262
Carrowholly, Westport
(18) 6950 yards/***(Sun)/C

CO MEATH

Ashbourne G.C.
(01) 835 2005
Anderstown, Ashbourne
(18) 5778 metres/***/C

Black Bush G.C.
(01) 825 0021
Thomastown, Dunshaughlin
(18) 6930 yards /***/D
(9) 2800 yards/***/E

Gormanston G.C.
(01) 841 2203
Franciscan College, Gormanston
(9) 2170 yards/*/F

Headfort G.C.
(046) 40857
Kells
(18) 6480 yards/***(am)/D/H

Laytown and Bettystown G.C.
(041) 27170
Bettystown, Drogheda
(18) 5668 metres/***/C/H

Moor Park G.C.
(046) 27661
Mooretown, Navan
(18) 5600 metres/***/F

Royal Tara G.C.
(046) 25508
Bellinter, Navan
(18) 5757 metres/***(Tues)/D
(9) 3184 metres/***/D

Trim G.C.
(046) 31463
Newtownmoynagh, Trim
(18) 6870 yards/***/D

CO MONAGHAN

Castleblayney G.C.
(042) 41139
Muckno Park, Castleblayney
(9) 2678 yards/***/E

Clones G.C.
(047) 56017
Hilton Park, Scotshouse, Clones
(9) 5790 yards/***/E

Mannan Castle G.C.
(042) 61714
Donaghmoyne, Carrickmacross
(9) 5804 metres/***/E

Nuremore G.C
(042) 64016
Carrickmacross
(9) 5906 metres/***/C

Rossmore G.C.
(047) 81316
Rossmore Park, Monaghan
(18) 6082 yards/***/E-D

CO OFFALY

Birr G.C.
(0509) 20082
The Glenns, Birr
(18) 5748 metres/***/D/H(26)

Castle Barna G.C.
(0506) 53384
Daingean
(18) 5595 metres/***/E

Edenderry G.C.
(0405) 31072
Boherberry, Edenderry
(9) 5791 yards/**/E

Tullamore G.C.
(0506) 21439
Brookfield, Tullamore
(18) 6314 yards/***/D/H/M

CO ROSCOMMON

Athlone G.C.
(0902) 92073
Hodson Bay, Athlone
(18) 5922 metres/***/D/H(22)

Ballaghadereen
(0907) 60295
Ballaghadereen, Roscommon
(9) 5663 yards/**/E

Boyle G.C.
(079) 62192
Roscommon Road, Boyle
(9) 4957 metres/***/E

Castlerea G.C.
(0907) 20068
Clonalis, Castlerea
(9) 5466 yards/***(Sun)/E

Roscommon G.C.
(0903) 26382
Moate Park, Roscommon
(18) 6162 metres/**/D

Strokestown G.C.
(078) 33303
Cloonfinlough, Strokestown
(9)5230 metres/***/E

CO SLIGO

Ballymote G.C.
(071) 83089
Carrigans, Ballymote
(9) 5152 yards/***/E

County Sligo G.C.
(071) 77186
Rosses Point
(18) 6043 yards/**/C-B/M

Enniscrone G.C.
(096) 36297
Ballina Road, Enniscrone
(18) 6720 yards/**/D

Strandhill G.C.
(071) 68188
Strandhill
(18) 6032 yards/***/D/M

Tubbercurry G.C.
(071) 85849
Ballymote Road, Tubbercurry
(9) 5490 metres/***/E

CO TIPPERARY

Ballykisteen G.&C.C.
(062) 33333
Ballykisteen, Monard
(18) 6765 yards/***/C/M

Cahir Park G.C.
(052) 41474
Kilcommon, Cahir
(9) 5690 yards/***/E

Carrick on Suir G.C.
(051) 640047
Garravoone, Carrick on Suir
(9) 5948 yards/***(Sun)/E

Clonmel G.C.
(052) 24050
Mountain Road, Clonmel
(18) 5768 metres/***/D

County Tipperary G.& C.C.
(062) 71116
Dundrum House,Dundrum, Cashel
(18) 6709 yards/***/C

Nenagh G.C.
(067) 31476
Beechwood, Nenagh
(18) 5491 metres/***/D/H/M

Rockwell College G.C.
(062) 61444
Rockwell College, Cashel
(9) 4136 yards/*/F

Roscrea G.C.
(0505) 21130
Derryvale, Dublin Road, Roscrea
(18) 5750 metres/***/D

Templemore G.C.
(0504) 31522
Manna South, Templemore
(9) 5442 yards/***/E

Thurles G.C.
(0504) 21983
Turtulla, Thurles
(18) 6494 yards/**(Tues)/C

Tipperary G.C.
(062) 51119
Rathanny, Tipperary
(18) 6385 yards/***/D

CO WATERFORD

Dungarvan G.C.
(058) 44707
Knocknagranagh, Dungarvan
(18) 6134 yards/***/D

Dunmore East G.C.
(051) 383151
Dunmore East
(9) 2408 yards /***/E

Faithlegg G.C.
(051) 82241
Faithlegg House, Faithlegg
(18) 6057 metres/***/C/H

Goldcoast G.C.
(058) 42249
Ballinacourty, Dungarven
(9) 5786 metres/***/D

Lismore G.C.
(058) 54026
Ballyin, Lismore
(9) 5715 yards/***/D/H

Tramore G.C.
(051) 386170
Newtown Hill, Tramore
(18) 6622 yards/***/C/H/M

Waterford G.C.
(051) 76748
Newrath, Waterford
(18) 6237 yards/***/C/M

Waterford Castle G.C.
(051) 71633
The Island, Waterford
(18) 6209 metres/***/B

West Waterford G.C.
(058) 43216
Coolcormack, Dungarvan
(18) 6771 yards/***/D

CO WESTMEATH

Delvin Castle G.C.
(044) 64315
Delvin
(18) 6300 yards/***/D/H

Glasson G.C.
(0902) 85120
Athlone
(18) 7083 yards/***/B

Moate G.C.
(0902) 81271
Ballinagarby, Moate
(9) 5348 yards/***/E

Mount Temple G.C.
(0902) 81545
Mount Temple, Moate
(18) 6500 yards/***/D/H

Mullingar G.C.
(044) 48366
Belvedere, Mullingar
(18) 6200 yards/**/C

CO WEXFORD

Courtown G.C.
(055) 25166
Kiltennel, Gorey
(18) 5898 metres/***/C

Enniscorthy G.C.
(054) 33191
Knockmarshal, Enniscorthy
(18) 6266 yards/***/D/H/M

New Ross G.C.
(051) 21433
Tinneranny, New Ross
(9) 6133 yards/***(Tues/Sun)/D

Rosslare G.C.
(053) 32203
Rosslare Strand, Rosslare
(18) 6554 yards/***/C/H/M
(9) 3153 yards/***/D/H/M

St Helens Bay G.& C.C.
(053) 33234
St Helens, Kilrane
(18) 6163 yards/***/C

Tara Glen G.C.
(055) 25413
Ballymoney, Courtown
(9)/***/F

Wexford G.C.
(053) 42238
Mulgannon, Wexford
(18)6120 yards/***/D/H/M

CO WICKLOW

Arklow G.C.
(0402) 32492
Abbeylands, Arklow
(18) 404 metres/***/D/H/M

Baltinglass G.C.
(0508) 81350
Baltinglass
(9) 5554 yards/***/E

Blainroe G.C.
(0404) 68168
Blainroe
(18) 6788 yards/***/C/H

Bray G.C.
(01) 286 2484
Ravenswell Road, Bray
(9) 5761 metres/**/C

Charlesland G.& C.C.
(01) 287 6764
Greystones
(18) 6739 yards/***/B

Coollattin G.C.
(055) 26302
Coollattin, Shillelagh
(9)6203 yards/***/D

Delgany G.C.
(01) 287 4536
Delgany
(18) 5290 metres/***/C/M

Djouce Mountain G.C.
(01) 281 8585
Roundwood
(9) 5762 metres/***/E

Druids Glen
(01) 287 3600
Kilcoole, Co Wicklow
(18) 7026 yards/***/A

The European Club
(0404) 47415
Brittas Bay
(18) 7090 yards/***/B

Glenmalure G.C.
(0404) 46679
Greenane, Rathdrum
(18) 5237 metres/***/C

Greystones G.C.
(01) 287 4136
Greystones
(18) 5401 metres/***/B

Kilcoole G.C.
(01) 287 2066
Kilcoole
(9) 5506 metres/**/D

Old Conna G.C.
(01) 282 6055
Ferndale Road, Bray
(18) 6551 yards/**/B/H

Powerscourt G.C.
(01) 276 0503
Enniskerry
(18) 6410 metres/***/A

Rathsallagh G.C.
(045) 403316
Nr Dunlavin
(18) 6956 yards.***/B

Roundwood G.C.
(01) 281 8488
Newtownmountkennedy
(18) 6685 yards/***/F

Tulfarris Hotel & C.C.
(045) 864574
Blessington
(9)2806 yards/***/F

Wicklow G.C.
(0404) 67379
Dunbar Road, Wicklow
(9) 6260 yards/**/D

Woodbrook G.C.
(01) 2824799
Dublin Road, Bray
(18) 5966 metres/***(Tues)/B-A

Woodenbridge G.C.
(0402) 35202
Woodenbridge, Arklow
(18) 6318 yards/***(Sat)/B

Top: **Golf Hotel Blue Green, Seignosse**
Middle: **Blue Green Pleneuf-Val Andre**
Bottom: **Golf Hotel Blue Green, Grenoble Charmeil**

While Scotland is home to golf and England the village cricket pitch and pub, France plays host to dining beyond comparison. The French love to eat, they love to drink and from time to time they enjoy the odd round of golf. Several of the courses are fairly private but many also welcome visitors, and the 19th hole, needless to say, is often excellent. Tour operators have been quick to pick up on this and provide some really excellent packages, which are available for small or large parties alike.

While it is not my job to push business their way it is fair to say that they know the courses and nearby hotels and can more often than not provide tailor-made packages at great value.

I would always save some time to go off the beaten track and investigate new courses or restaurants and certainly with Sterling in such great shape as I write (June 1998) then a trip is very much on the cards and so without further ado let's go.

Pas de Calais

It is perhaps no coincidence that this, the most accessible region of France for the British golfer, is also considered by many to hold some of the finest French courses.

The two at **Le Touquet (21 05 68 47)** namely La Mer and La Forêt, certainly do rank with the best, with La Mer a links course of championship standard, and La Forêt a slightly less demanding and shorter course which meanders through picturesque woodland.

The accommodation at this resort is, like the golf, of a very high standard. Le Manoir (21 06 28 28) is one hotel which has for many years catered exceptionally well for both the sporting and gastronomic tastes of its guests. Equally as popular is the Hôtel Westminster (21 05 48 48) a four star hotel with excellent facilities, as is the new Grand Park Plaza Hotel. The Hôtel Le Bristol is recommended for its comfort, charm and friendly staff. A smaller family run hotel, The Red Fox (21 05 27 58) is one to consider. A restaurant to note amongst many is Flavio (21 05 10 22).

Slightly north of Le Touquet, lies **Hardelot (21 83 73 10)** with its Les Pins and Les Dunes courses, each with their own clubhouse, and each worthy of comparison with the challenges at Le Touquet. Les Pins has noticeable similarities to The Berkshire, sharing as it does the same designer in Tom Simpson. Les Dunes, despite the name is also a parkland course, albeit a very hilly one, and in the opinion of some will one day surpass its elder brother in reputation.

While many will be tempted to make base camp for the whole area at Le Touquet, there is an excellent alternative on the courses at Hardelot in the Hôtel du Parc (21 33 22 11).

Further north still is the typically testing links course at **Wimereux (21 32 43 20)** where the prevailing wind dictates playing conditions. For those inclined to take cover at the first hint of a channel breeze, a trip inland to **St Omer (21 38 59 90)** may be the answer. This is, however, no easy option covering undulating terrain with a challenge worthy of any great golf course in its last four holes.

As for accommodation in these parts, there is a wide variety from which to choose. In Wimereux itself, the two star Hotel Paul et Virginie is of note, while further inland there are some fine chateaux. The Chateau Tilques (21 88 99 99) is a classic of its kind, and the Hôtel-Château Clery (21 83 19 83) at Hesdin L'Abbé is another not to miss. St Hubert (21 39 77 77) is a restaurant with rooms of real character and also worthy of consideration.

A word, finally, on two other courses to consider if planning a prolonged stay in the region, or fresh fields for the seasoned campaigner. The **Belle Dune (22 23 45 50)** course south of Le Touquet is particularly recommended while nearby **Golf Nampont-St-Martin (22 29 92 90)** is an enjoyable test in very pleasant surroundings with a 15th century clubhouse.

Chantilly, Versailles, Paris

There are some quite exceptional courses and magnificent châteaux-hotels to be found in this area. In the heartland of French racing, set in the ancient Forest of Chantilly, lies the four star **Golf Hôtel Blue Green Chantilly** (44 58 47 77). Here you can step straight out of a luxurious hotel on to the golf course dotted with gardens in the French style. The layout is traditional and undemanding but well placed bunkers invite risk-laden approaches. Also in Chantilly, **Golf de Chantilly** (44 57 04 03) is a perfect parkland course rated as one of the best in Europe. The sister course, **Chantilly Longeres** (44 57 04 43) also boasts some fine holes. Recommended accommodation includes the three star **Golf Hôtel Blue Green Mont Griffon** (34 68 10 10) which has its own 18 hole links course with magnificent views over the Ysieux Valley. There are also excellent chateaux-hotels at Gouvieux (44 62 38 38) and Bazincourt-Sur-Epte (32 55 11 61). Other recommended courses include the two at **Le Prieure**, the recently designed John Jacobs course at **Apremont** (44 25 61 11) and the manicured splendour of **Rebetz** (44 49 15 54).

Golf Hotel Blue Green Mont Griffon

No visitor to Paris should overlook the **Golf National** (30 43 36 00) west of the city. The L'Albatros course at just over 7000 yards is the venue for the French Open, and the many water hazards make for a round which demands consistently good shot making. The second course, L'Aigle, is shorter and certainly more 'fun'. All tour operators also extol the attractions of **Yvelines** (34 86 48 89) and the two courses at **La Vaucouleurs** (34 87 62 29) with their tree-lined fairways.

The modern three star Novotel San Quentin is ideally situated fot Golf Nationale. However, for those enamoured of the more classical tradition of French accommodation, Hôtel Abbaye des Vaux de Cernay (34 85 23 00) is four star refinement, as is the prestigious Trianon Palace, (30 84 38 00) ideally situated for golf, Versailles and Paris itself.

In and around Paris itself there are a host of golf courses, all with something special to offer. **Golf Blue Green Guerville** (30 92 45 45), near Nantes la Jolie is a pretty course with gently sloping fairways. **Golf Regional d'Ile de France** offers 45 holes in a recreation centre south west of Paris. To the south east, bordering on the forest of Sénart, **Golf Blue Green Villeray** has 18 holes in very pretty surroundings. **Golf Blue Green Marolles-en-Brie** has nine holes on a wooded and undulating course, while **Golf Blue Green Chevry** offers a 9 hole green oasis in the urban surrounds. A similar distance to the north of the city is **Golf Blue Green Saint Aubin**, which has varied

fairways with bunkers and water hazards that make for an interesting round. To the north, **Golf Blue Green Villennes-sur-Seine** (39 08 18 18) is a family club with excellent practice facilities, but if you don't want to travel far there is a nine hole par 3 course on the banks of the Seine at **Golf de L'Ile Fleurie** which is only 10 minutes from the centre of the city.

Normandy

There are many who consider that Normandy has, in Deauville and Omaha Beach, courses to match the standards set up the coast at Le Touquet and Hardelot. **Golf Champ de la Bataille** (32 35 03 72) set in the grounds of a magnificent Louis XIV château south of Rouen, is well off the beaten golfing track but found in most tour operators' programmes. A slightly mundane opening hole leads to some of the most spectacular golf holes to be found in France, and unquestionably the most beautiful natural surroundings. Another superb course in the area is **Golf Blue Green Beuzeval-Houlgate** (31 24 80 49) and only ten minutes from Deauville. Designed by Peter Alliss and Dave Thomas in 1980, this is a truly picturesque course.

Rouen makes as good a base as any for those golfers keen to play Champ de Bataille and then head off towards Chantilly and Paris. One local hotel for golfers to consider is the Hôtel Mercure Champs de Mars (35 52 42 32) in Rouen. Just north of the city at the **Rouen-Mont-St-Aignan Club** (35 76 38 65) there are some difficult holes to be negotiated on this well established hilly course. Rouen itself is a gorgeous city stuffed full of excellent restaurants. You'll be waddling round the golf course if you stay here long. One restaurant to note near Rouen is Butte at Bonsecours (35 80 43 11) a real treat.

The attractions of Normandy for most golfers though are to be found on or near the coast, where **Deauville** (31 14 48 48) is the pick of the resorts. The original 18 holes here are another Tom Simpson parkland creation from 1929, while a further nine were added in the 1960s courtesy of Henry Cotton. Although Deauville is not memorable for its length, tight fairways and well bunkered greens call for accurate shot making on the exceptionally well maintained course. The views from the course out over Deauville and Trouville are magnificent, and these two resorts are popular destinations in their own right.

Justifiably popular with golfers is the four star Hôtel du Golf Deauville (31 14 24 00), which elegantly complements its golfing surroundings and is matched in quality only by the Hôtel Royal (31 98 66 33) and Hôtel Normandy (31 98 66 22). For those seeking slightly less refinement there is still excellent value to be had in the area, at the Orion Apartments and good three star accommodation can be found at, Trouvilles Hôtel Mercure (31 87 38 38).

The other course on the coast where golfers and critics are united in their approbation is the **Omaha Beach** (31 21 72 94). The course comprises three loops of nine holes, each of individual character. La Mer is considered the most spectacular, offering the best views out over the D Day beaches, La Bocage runs through the valley and groves of apple trees, while L'Etag is renowned for its water hazards.

Omaha Beach is about an hours drive from Deauville and accommodation is not as plentiful, although there is an excellent three star golf hotel at the centre of the complex, The Chenevière (31 51 25 25). This is a 19th century château with excellent cuisine.

There are certainly many other courses well worth playing. **Étretat** (35 27 04 89) a links course perched on a clifftop is one of the more spectacular and the Golf Hôtel Dormy House (35 27 07 88) there is recommended. Around Caen, where the three star Hotel Friendly lives up to its name, there are two inland courses to note, **Golf de Clécy** (31 69 72 72) and **Golf de Caen** (31 94 72 09) as well as the links course **Cabourg-Le Home** (31 91 25 56).

Closer to Deauville are the recently developed courses at **St Gatien** (31 65 19 99) (the Hôtel Le Chos is well thought of) and **St Julien** (31 64 30 30) which come into the "well worth a visit" especially for the clubhouse at the latter and three distinctly different sets of nine holes at the former. **Golf L'Amirauté** (31 14 42 00) designed by a Scotsman in American style, is often compared favourably to the Golf Nationale and has a modern three star hotel close by also known as L'Amirauté.

Brittany

Brittany is well served by British tour operators, which makes its undoubted attractions all the more accessible. In many respects the inland course and club at **La Freslonnière** (99 14 84 09), near Rennes typifies the high standard of golf, excellent facilities and fine cuisine awaiting the golfer visiting Brittany, yet like Champ de la Bataille it is set inland and away from the more obvious seaside resorts. This excellent course is carved from woodland and has more than its fair share of water hazards.

Other courses of merit in this area include the **Golf de Rennes St Jacques** (99 30 18 18) and the **Golf des Rochers**. **Golf Blue Green Cicé Blossac** (99 52 79 79) which with its wide fairways and large greens is reminiscent of an American country club. A little further north **Golf Blue Green Pléneuf-Val André** (96 63 01 12) has a magical coastal setting with cliffs, beaches and amazing seascapes.

Further along the Brittany coast, twenty minutes from Brest, the **Golf-Hôtel Blue Green Brest-Iroise** (98 85 16 17) offers an 18 hole course designed along British lines with a hilly layout giving splendid views over the Monts d'Arrée and Iroise sea. The converted water mill, Ar Milin (99 00 33 91) at Chateaubourg is another ideal base for golfers visiting this region, although in Rennes itself there is plenty of excellent accommodation.

For most golfers, though, these courses will be played as an excursion south from the delights of St Malo, Dinard and Dinan. Of the many courses in this region, the **Golf Club des Ormes** (99 73 49 60) has over the years become the most popular. A classic parklands course in the grounds of a 16th century chateau, it wends its way through woods and lakes and is a most attractive challenge. The Golf Hôtel des Ormes is popular, and an alternative to this modern, well appointed creation is the Hôstellerie Abbatiale, Le Tronchet, an abbey dating back to the 16th century which stands on the banks of Lake Mirloup.

The abbey stands on **St Malo-Le Tronchet** (99 58 96 69)

course, one of the better new courses—almost as popular as Des Ormes itself.

For a testing piece of links golf, the course at **Dinard (99 88 32 07)** is the one to try, with views as breathtaking as the prevailing wind which gives this rather short course its bite. An elegant place to recuperate from the experience is the four star Grand Hôtel (99 88 26 26) in Dinard which needs no further recommendation.

West of Dinard there is some enjoyable but less demanding golf along the coast that will suit players of all abilities, especially those reduced to enjoying the views. The journey from the **Club des Sables-d'Or-les-Pins, (96 41 42 57)** along to **St Samson (96 23 87 34)** is well worth the effort.

Golf de L'Odet, (98 54 87 88) is arguably the prettiest course in South Brittany (it is also near several good restaurants The Ferme du Letry in Bénodet (98 57 01 27) and L'Agape (98 56 32 70) at Ste-Marie are two of note). Considerable amounts of money have been spent improving the course and it is now a fair test for high and low handicappers alike, not forgetting the resident British professional. There is a good quality hotel Bains de Mer (98 57 03 41) nearby at Bénodet, but golfers wanting a more central base in this region may prefer to stay further south closer to the three most highly rated courses, **Golf de St Laurent (97 56 85 18)**, **Golf Le Val Queven (97 05 17 96)** and **Golf de Baden (97 57 18 96)**. A hotel to consider is Le Manoir de Ménec (98 39 47 47).

Golf de St Laurent has played host to numerous French amateur and professional championships and the long tree-lined fairways with water hazards and strategically placed bunkers do not disappoint. There are those who would claim, however, that the number one course is now Val Queven, which despite its relative youth, has the best greens in the region and requires accurate, and often courageous, shot making. While Golf de Baden has its fair share of taxing holes, the picturesque setting and relative ease of this course by comparison has ensured its popularity with visiting golfers.

A firm favourite in the hotel stakes here is the Hotel Fairway, a three star hotel right on the St Laurent course which arguably merits four star status if only for the excellent cuisine. Just a few hundred yards away from the hotel can be found the excellent Maeva Cottages, a collection of one and two room studio apartments.

By way of contrast, mention must be made of the Château de Locguenole, a four star hotel with a Michelin rosette, close to Val Queven, St Laurent and one of France's shorter championship courses, **Golf Ploemeur Océan (97 32 81 82)**.

Also of note are the Hostellerie Abbatiale, Le Bono, an old Breton priory now a three star hotel overlooking the Baden course and well situated for **Golf de Rhuys Kerver (97 45 30 09)** which is renowned for its impenetrable gorse thickets but is nevertheless an enjoyable collection of 18 holes.

Western Loire

Leaving Brittany for what passes as Western Loire the first course encountered is possibly France's most famous golfing landmark and certainly the course most British golfers would instantly recognise as French. **Golf de la Bretesche (40 88 30 03)** is built around the imposing lines of a 14th century chateau. As a test of golf the course does not disappoint. Accuracy is called for from tee to tree-lined fairways, culminating in an unforgettable tour de force around the chateau and lake. The Bretesche (51 76 86 96) is a hotel to savour.

As the perfect partner for this golfing experience, try the four star Manoir du Rodoir (99 90 82 68) at La Roche Bernard, a newly renovated mill. Or experience the cottages in the grounds of the 250 acre La Bretesche estate, where peace and quiet reign supreme. Also make a note of Auberge Bretonne (99 90 60 28) an outstanding restaurant.

Just south of La Bretesche lie two more popular French courses in **Golf de la Baule (40 60 46 18)** and **Golf de la Savenay (40 56 88 05)**. La Baule is rated as one of the best courses designed by Peter Alliss and Dave Thomas. The first nine holes are set amongst chestnut and oak trees, while the second nine follow the valley's undulations around the almost obligatory lake. With nine holes added in 1994 and a Jack Nicklaus Academy with excellent facilities, the La Baule complex is now one of the largest in France. There are apartments and villas here which are first class.

The four star Hôtel Royal-Thalasso (40 11 48 48) in La Baule has traditional elegance and beautiful furnishings, but alternatives equally hard to fault are the four star Hermitage (40 11 46 46) and Castel Marie Louise (40 11 48 38) both situated on the sea front at La Baule.

Golf de Savenay is a more recent development and typically spectacular, wandering over parkland through chestnut woods and presenting a series of interesting and varied challenges, so much so that it has risen rapidly in the estimation of many golfers.

Ranked alongside this and a touch further down the coast is the outstanding **Golf Club St Jean-de-Monts (51 58 82 73)** occupying an impressive piece of headland with an opening hole which is definitely not for the faint-hearted. The quality of the links challenge here is matched by the testing parkland course inland at **Golf de la Domangère (51 07 60 15)**. The related Hôtel du Golf La Domangère a converted 15th century manor house is also an exceptional three star hotel.

The Hôtel Altea Le Sloi, also comes highly recommended, a modern three star hotel close to the St Jean de Monts course and well placed too for **Golf Des Fontenelles (51 54 13 94)** set in scenic green countryside with a plethora of water hazards.

Those golfers tempted by the well maintained American style golf available at **Port Bourgenay (51 23 35 45)** may prefer to select the hotel there and there are also P&V Club Apartments in Bourgenay.

The Loire

Moving back towards Paris, near Orléans, we have **Golf Blue Green Limére Orléans (38 59 25 15)**, an 18 hole course that winds its way through the ancient Sologne forest. Host to the French professional championships in 1992 and 1993 and the French Amateur in 1995 this is a challenging layout that will give pleasure to both high and low handicappers. The adjoining hotel, Domaine des Portes de Solonge (38 49 99 99) comes highly recommended.

Golf Blue Green Limére Orléans

Further south, and home to one of France's best and most exclusive clubs, **Les Bordes** (54 87 72 13) owned by the Baron Bic, is immaculately maintained and has all the features expected of a true championship course.

The fairytale Château Golf Hôtel Des Sept Tours and the course itself are in many ways reminiscent of La Bretesche, although the golf is not quite as demanding. The chateau is also ideally situated for the golf at Touraine and Ardrée.

The **Touraine** (47 53 20 28) course has a picturesque setting and a number of challenging holes, but **Golf Blue Green Ardrée-Tours** (47 56 77 38) is more popular. Perhaps deservedly so as it retains interest throughout the length of its 18 holes which are set in the wooded park of a Loire chateau with a river and lake enhancing the design and making for a memorable test of golf.

Golf Blue Green Ardée Tours

To match the châteaux and the excellent Jean Bardet (47 41 41 11) at Tours, **Les Haukes Roches** (47 52 88 88) is undoubtedly one of the finest properties in the area and well placed for Ardrée and Sept Tours. Also commended in this area around Tours is the Château de Beaulieu (47 53 20 28).

Two courses which feature as prominently as Ardrée are **Golf Blue Green Avrillé** (41 69 22 50) and **Anjou Golf and Country Club** (41 42 01 01). While d'Avrillé has taken time to mature into an interesting test of golf with scenic surrounds, the Anjou course, designed by the British architect Fred Hawtree, has remained something of a well kept secret until now and this is a course to be enjoyed by all standards of golfer.

As for accommodation in the area to the west of Tours, there are two fine chateaux-hotels, Du Plessis and De Noirieux, as well as the three star Grand Hôtel de Solesmes (43 95 45 10). Golfers favouring the Grand Hotel may also care to try out the beautifully maintained course **Golf de Sable-Solesmes** (43 95 28 78) which has three 9 hole layouts set between the Forest of Pince and the River Sarke.

One final thought in this area. It is worth a detour to the western coast to try out the **Golf Blue Green la Prée de la Rochelle**. Links courses are rare in France and this sheltered site overlooking the bay of Aguillon offers a taste of Scotland.

Bordeaux and Biarritz

Trekking south through Cognac country where, by the way, there is a course surrounding the home of the Martell family which actually has a par 3 for a nineteenth hole, the visiting golfer with a taste for wine may be forgiven for leaving his clubs in the car. Bordeaux is the world's finest wine producing region and, while **Les Golfes du Médoc** (05 56 70 11 90), may be considered one of the premier clubs, it is the premier crus of Mouton-Rothschild and Lafite that have placed Médoc firmly on the world map.

The two courses at Médoc, Les Chateaux and Les Vignes, are nevertheless worthy of their reputation, with the more established Chateau Course to be found in most 'top ranking' compilations. The long, well bunkered fairways in the style of a Scottish links course are well maintained and the greens are superb.

In Médoc itself, Le Pont Bernet is a three star hotel with excellent facilities. Le Relais de Margaux, a chateau of impeccable quality is also ideally situated for the golf at Médoc, Pessac and Lacanau.

In the Dordogne, the **Golf-Hôtel Blue Green Castlenaud** (05 53 01 60 19) just north of Agen has 18 holes that run uphill and downdale, with some water hazards to test your shot making abilities. The hotel's restaurant La Menuisière is also highly praised.

Golf-Hôtel Blue Green Castlenaud

In Lacanau the Golf Hôtel Latitudes (56 03 92 92) on the actual **Lacanau** course is an excellent base for touring the area. The course itself is very picturesque and hosted the French professional championships back in 1983, so it will come as no surprise to learn that accurate shot making is required around the tree-lined fairways and over the numerous water hazards.

As an alternative to overnighting in Lacanau there is offer the four star La Reserve in Pessac, and the Hotel Mercure, five minutes from the course. Further north on the Médoc peninsula itself try the Château Cordeillan Bages, a four star hotel with great character.

Just a little south of Lacanau, there are two courses worthy of note. **Golf Blue Green Bordeaux-Pessac** (57 26 03 33) just out of Bordeaux offers 27 holes while **Golf Blue Green Gujan** (56 66 86 36) close to Arcachon's seawater

Golf Blue Green la Prée de la Rochelle

Golf Blue Green Bordeaux-Pessac

Golf du Haut-Poitou

POITIERS

LA ROCHELLE

LIMOGES

N141

N141

D728

SAINTES

N150

Cognac

Cognac

ANGOULÊME

Golf de la
Cote de Beauté

ROYAN

COGNAC

N141

Hirondelle

N10

N10

N21

SOULAC

N215

A10

N10

PERIGUEUX

Sporting Club
de Cameyrac

N89

N21

Lacanau

Bordeaux Lac

BERGERAC

D936

BORDEAUX

ARCACHON

N250

A63

N113

MARMANDE

Castelnaud
VILLENEUVE-
sur-LOT

Arcachon

A62

MIMIZAN

D46

N10

AGEN

N124

MOLIETS

Moliets

MONT-de
MARSAN

N21

VIEUX-BOUCAU

Seignosse

Hossegor

A63

HOSSEGOR

BAYONNE

AUCH

BIARRITZ

Golf de Chiberta

A64

ST-JEAN-
de-LUZ

Golf de Chantaco

LESCAR
PAU

La Nivelle

Artiguelouve
Pau

TARBES

N117

N734

D834

N21

N113

LOURDES

N125

SPAIN

Luchon

BAGNERES-
de-LUCHON

Golf Blue Green Gujan

lake also has 27 holes. The trees here make for some tight approaches but the lakes, rough heather, trees and natural terrain combine to form arguably one of the best tests of golf in the region.

Golfers looking to combine Gujan with the courses to the north would be well advised to consider the accommodation available in Bordeaux itself. The four star Hôtel Burdigala (56 90 16 16) with its 18th century facade is very highly recommended. The two star Hôtel Continental (56 52 66 00) is delightful, as are the many restaurants to be found in Bordeaux.

A golfing holiday in this area would not be complete nowadays without a visit to **Château Des Vigiers (53 61 50 00)** which lies inland from Bordeaux surrounded by vineyards. This is an impressive Donald Steel designed course with a magnificent 16th century chateau-hotel at the heart of the complex.

Bordeaux may have its wine but Biarritz is a celebrated resort with golf to match. To the north, the first course encountered on the journey down from Bordeaux is the Robert Trent Jones creation **Golf de la Côte d'Argent (58 48 54 65)** (Moliets) which overlooks the Atlantic. Despite its location the Moliets course is another combination of water, trees and dense rough relieved by some generous fairways. A course not to be missed. Some good accommodation exists here as well. Equally highly rated and the creation of another American architect, Robert van Hagge, is the course at **Blue Green Golf-Hôtel Seignosse (58 43 17 32)** which has been compared in design to the Augusta National and is a favourite of José-Maria Olazabal. This is our International Golf Venue of the Year and is featured separately at the beginning of *Following the Fairways*.

Flying the flag for Britain is the Tom Morrison-designed course at **Hossegor (58 43 56 99)** which we shall liken to Sunningdale, courtesy of the huge pine trees which shelter the course from the sea. Hossegor can offer the modern Lacotel (58 43 93 50) which does overlook the lake and has one of the best restaurants in town, and there are also P&V apartments at Moliets-Plage.

In Biarritz itself we have a former residence of Napoleon III, the Hôtel du Palais (59 41 64 00) as well as the magnificent Regina et du Golf which overlooks the bay to one side and the golf course to the other. In many respects the Biarritz course does not match the hotels for quality, however when the wind blows it develops a challenging character compounded by slick greens.

A more recognised test of golf and the slightly less glamorous Hôtel de la Résidence can be found on another Tom Simpson designed course at **Chiberta (59 63 83 20)** just to the north of Biarritz. This combination of links and parkland golf, offers a well maintained variety. A slightly more demanding challenge awaits at **Arlanques** with its undulating terrain, though the marvellous views do compensate for what can be a somewhat ardous trek.

A final recommendation in this area is **Golf Blue Green Pau-Artiguelouve (05 59 83 09 29)** in the shadow of the Pyrenees. Designed by French champion, Jean Garailde, this is a tight and testing course and a good examination

of technical ability. Trees, lakes and well placed bunkers leave little room for a stray shot. For those who fall in love with the area, Pau Artiguelouve has special arrangements with local hotels and can also arrange games at Chiberta, **Pau Golf Club (59 32 02 33)**—the oldest course in continental Europe.

Golf Blue Green Pau-Artiguelouve

The Riviera

Before concentrating on the golf to the east of Marseilles and the choice along the coast, brief mention must be made of Montpellier and Nîmes in Languedoc-Roussillon.

The course **Nîmes Campagne (66 70 17 37)** has attracted more than its fair share of accolades and is probably the course not to be missed when on holiday in the region. The **Golf Club de Montpellier Massane (67 87 87 87)** will be well known to those who have followed the fortunes of PGA tour qualifiers and is acknowledged as typically American in design. The same if not more could be said of Robert Trent Jones' **La Grande Motte (67 56 05 00)** which as one would expect offers a superb test of golf.

Accommodation in the Montpellier and La Motte region is purpose built and modern, although there is a fair selection of hotels around Arles, Avignon and Nîmes. However, here is a good hotel with its own golf course at **Golf-Hôtel Blue Green Fontcaude (67 03 34 30)** Chris Pittman has created a championship course here out of the garrigue—the wild scrubland peculiar to the region—which offers 18 holes over a gently undulating landscape with a further 9 hole course. For those who like a different challenge the hotel offers special arrangements with the **Cap d'Agde (67 26 54 40)** a Ronald Fream championship course overlooking the sea.

Golf-Hôtel Blue Green Fontcaude

There are those who would head straight for **Golf de Barbaroux (94 69 63 63)** en route to the courses concentrated above St Tropez, but the discerning golfer might opt to make first for **Domaine de Frégate (94 32 50 50)**. This is an excellent course offering the kind of challenge expected of a Ronald Fream design.

Frégate, though, is no alternative to Barbaroux, which should be experienced at all costs. This is an exceptional course both in terms of beauty and the standard of golf demanded, carrying the hallmark of the Dye Brothers. The Hostellerie du Golf de Barbaroux is a four star hotel at the heart of the course.

Clustered to the west of Fréjus are three courses which command spectacular views of the Provence countryside and the Mediterranean. Of the three, it is the most recently completed **St Endreol (94 99 22 99)**, development which attracts most attention. Its signature hole is the 13th, a par 3 played to an island green. The testing course runs through some magnificent countryside which may be some consolation to those driven to despair by their mounting score.

Golf Blue Green Sainte Maxime (94 49 26 60) and **Golf de Roquebrune (94 82 92 91)** offer limited but perhaps more manageable challenges by comparison. As beautifully situated as the course at St Maxime is the four star Hotel Playa Maxime, while the Golf Plaza impresses and is similarly rated. In St Raphael, we have the Excelsior (94 95 02 42)

which is adjacent to the Casino on the sea front or self catering apartments along the coast at Cap Esterel (94 95 02 42).

Either way, access to **Golf d'Esterel (94 82 47 88)** is a prerequisite when preparing your itinerary around St Raphael. Another Robert Trent Jones creation which has played host to PGA tour events, Esterel has rapidly become popular with golfers of all abilities and has a reputation for being challenging but fair.

The Latitudes Hotel at Esterel serves the visiting golfer well. This is a modern three star hotel overlooking the course and only five minutes from St Raphael.

Around Cannes there is definitely no shortage of quality golf. The **Riviera Golf (92 97 67 67)** clubhouse is one of the most impressive in France while the course, again designed by Robert Trent Jones, boasts a typical combination of forest and water hazards which render it something of a picturesque challenge.

Another Van Hagge creation at **Royal Mougins (92 92 49 69)** will not disappoint those golfers who enjoy Seignosse and Les Bordes, while the hands of Alliss and Thomas are again evident in the redesigned layout of **Cannes-Mougins (93 75 79 13)** host to the Volvo Cannes Open. Nearby **Mandelieu** has also played host recently to a Tour event, this time on the ladies circuit, and proved very popular with the players. After Pau and Biarritz this is the third oldest course in France.

One final recommendation in the vicinity of Cannes goes to **St Donat**, which can prove a rewarding experience for high and low handicappers alike in typically picturesque surroundings.

As for accommodation in the resort, quality is the key. Four highly recommended luxury hotels are The Royal Hôtel Casino (92 97 70 00) near Mandelieu, Hôtel de Mougins (92 92 17 07) one kilometre from Cannes-Mougins, the four star Martinez (92 98 73 00) on the Croisette and the equally highly rated Hôtel Majestic (92 98 77 00). Self catering in Cannes is raised to luxurious levels at the Royal Mougins complex with its exceptional facilities. Restaurants also abound, try the Moulin de Mougins (93 75 78 24) its incredible, some pleasant rooms here as well.

Golf Blue Green Sainte Maxime

There are of course those who like their golf packaged slightly differently and two Club Med villages at Dieulefit and Opio Valbonne cater for golfers.

Golf d'Opio Valbonne (93 12 00 08) itself enjoys an excellent reputation with two distinctly different sets of nine holes, and an excellent on-course golf hotel, originally a 17th century manor house, while the **Grasse Country Club** (93 60 55 44) course offers fantastic views and an enjoyable round for any golfer with some notion of accuracy and placement. There are some incredible hotels and restaurants in the area, Bastide St-Antoine (a restaurant with rooms) (93 09 16 48) is outstanding.

Moving back up towards central France, we come to **Golf de Toulane** (93 60 31 30). The first course in Europe to be designed by Gary Player it may enjoy a remote location on the edge of Alpes-Maritime, but this is golf at its most invigorating.

Further north in the foothills of the Alps, there are three sister courses in the Lyon/Grenoble area that could gently grow a star from a beginner. **Golf Blue Green Lyon Chassieu** (78 90 84 77) close to Lyon city centre is a typical meadowland 18 hole course which is ideal for learning golf. Close by in Grenoble, **Golf de Grenoble-Uriage** (76 89 03 47) is a 9 hole course with excellent practice facilities. The **Golf-Hôtel Blue Green Grenoble Charmeil** (76 93 67 28) offers 18 holes and practice facilities together with a comfortable hotel with a really fine restaurant. It's an interesting course. Is the influence Scottish or American? If you're not aware of the differences in approach to golf design, this course may help you decide which you like best, as you change from one style to the other almost every hole.

Golf-Hôtel Blue Green Grenoble Charmeil

The Alps

Further up into the Alps themselves, dominated by the snow-capped peak of Mont Blanc, **Chamonix** (50 53 06 28) a couple of miles south of the town on the road to Les Houches, is unquestionably the region's leading golf course. Robert Trent Jones designed this smallish but delightfully scenic course, open throughout the summer and autumn from May to November. It is small, but there is really not much space in which these fellows can carve out their designs. Still, as you would expect from the master, the ubiquitous water hazards and some tricky par 3's combine to make Chamonix a true test.

As with all the courses in the Alps, golf is only half the story. Skiing, I hear you say, is the other half. Chances are however you're not really going to come across many skiers in the summer—well at least you hope you won't at Megève **Golf du D'Arbois** (50 21 29 79) where some of the fairways actually transform into ski slopes during the winter months. At over 4000 feet up in the mountains it is daunting enough as it is without having to worry about skiers crossing your path. Indeed of all the courses, Megéve is the most ski-orientated—even the clubhouse is set amidst a ski-lift station, sharing its facilities with the

various ski-shops and cafés way up near the top of Mount D'Arbois. The course is open between June and early November, depending on when the snow arrives. But it is a popular course, so beware the months of July and August when the fairways are practically full.

Abour 25 miles west of Megéve sits the 5216 yard, par 69 **Golf du Lac D'Annecy** (50 60 12 89) at Talloires, commanding the most superb views over the lake. The spectacle perhaps compensates for the lack of yardage, which even by Alpine standards is low. One interesting feature of the course is the insurance fee, charged before players are let loose on the criss-cross fairways. Fore! **Les Arcs,** (79 07 43 95) **Tignes** (79 06 37 42) and **Meribel** (79 00 52 67) also boast their own golf courses in the area. If your driving leaves something to be desired, look no further than **Royal Club d'Evian** (50 26 85 00), where there is a fine teaching school. In the area the Royal Hôtel at Evian (50 26 85 00) has its own course and offers free golf to its residents. More important perhaps is the free entry to the Casino in Evian—also owned by the hotel.

One of the delights about a holiday in the mountains is that you can make the most of a whole variety of other leisure activities. Walks, mountain biking, tennis, white water rafting, skiing and swimming are just some of the options available. If you are a lover of good wine, good living and the great outdoors this is a holiday location for the summer as well as the winter.

France is a large and dramatically beautiful country which offers much. Its easy to access and can provide a really good holiday attraction. Its golf courses are well maintained and the authorities encourage fast play - (although this is not always the case). In France good living is life and good golfing a satisfactory but far from essential bonus. From glorious Seignosse to the style of Paris or Chantilly, France has great appeal. We wish you well on your travels and your golf and hope that you find that little restaurant off the beaten track that hopefully makes life so worthwhile.

Further Information

Telephoning - prefix number with 0033 +

    1, Paris and surrounding area
    2, North West
    3, North East
    4, South East
    5, South West

French Tourist Board -   0891 244123
                   00 33 149 52 53 54

Blue Green UK Ltd -   0121 212 0066

A selection of tour operators to contact -

3D Golf	0800 333 323
A Golfing Experience	0181 - 205 7138
Cresta Golf	0161 - 929 1311
Fields Fairway	00 33 321 33 85 23
French Golfing Holidays	01277 374374
Relaix & Chateaux	0171 287 0987
BDH	0181 644 7881

How to get there -

Eurostar	0345 303030
Air France	0181 742 6600
British Airways	0345 222111
Brittany Ferries	01752 221321
Stenna Ferries	0990 707070
P&O Ferries	0181 575 8555

St Andrews, Swilcan Bridge, Scotland

St Andrews, Swilcan Burn, Scotland

St Andrews, Snow Scene, Scotland

St Andrews, R & A, Scotland

*St Andrews, 17th Hole, Scotland

*St Andrews, Old Course, Scotland

Pictures by Graeme W Baxter courtesy of Baxter Prints, see page 352 for order details

Limited & Open Edition Prints by Denis Pannett

Turnberry, 27 x 20 ins

Gleneagles, 27 x 20 ins

Wentworth, 20 x 16 ins

Sunningdale, 20 x 16 ins

Belfry, 17 x 10 1/2 ins

St Andrews - Sea Shore, 17 x 10 1/2 ins

Royal Dornoch, 17 x 10 1/2 ins

Moor Park, 17 x 10 1/2 ins

St Pierre, 17 x 10 1/2 ins

Walton Heath, 17 x 10 1/2 ins

All Denis Pannett prints limited and open editions are signed, supplied mounted (not framed)
with polythene covering.

Open Edition Prints by Denis Pannett & Order Form

North Berwick, 17 x 10 ½ ins

Royal Liverpool, 17 x 10 ½ ins

The Berkshire, 17 x 10 ½ ins

Gleneagles (Hotel), 17 x 10 ½ ins

All Denis Pannett prints limited and open editions are signed, supplied mounted (not framed)
with polythene covering.

Golf at Gleneagles

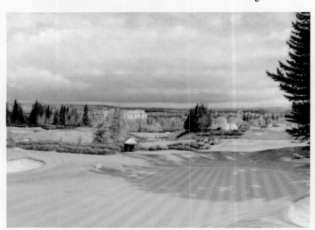

The Gleneagles Hotel, Kings Course, Scotland

The Gleneagles Hotel, Queens Course, Scotland

The Gleneagles Hotel, Monarchs Course, Scotland

*The Gleneagles Hotel, Queens Course, Scotland

Following the Fairways Competition

We are constantly looking for up to date information to improve Following the Fairways. Please could you therefore help us with our research by filling in the following information. All entrants will be placed in a draw and the winner will receive a complimentary weekend for two at one of our hotels and golf courses. Two runners up will receive a case of Jameson Irish Whiskey each.

Best New Course Played - - - - - - - - - - - - - - - *Best Course Played* - - - - - - - - - - - - - - -
How many years has the Jameson International Golf Challenge been in existence ? - - - - - - - -
Best Par 3 - *Best Par 4* - - - - - - - - - - - - - - - -
Best Par 5 - - - - - - - - - - - - - - - - - - - *Best Clubhouse (19th hole)* - - - - - - - - - - - - - -
At what Golf Course is the Jameson Ancestral Home located ? - - - - - - - - - - - - - - - - - - -
Best Pub/Hotel Stayed At -
Name seven golf courses that have staged the Jameson International Golf Challenge ? - - - - - -
- -

Order Form

The following prints can be found on pages 135 & 187	Edition	Price (£)	Qty.	Cost
What shall I take for this?	N/A	31.50		
The Only Way	N/A	31.50		
The First, Kings Course	600	85.00		
The Caddie	600	85.00		
The Lucky Dog	N/A	31.50		
Addressing the Ball	N/A	31.50		
Seven Iron	N/A	35.00		
To Halve the Match	N/A	35.00		
Ballesteros Hole, The Belfry	N/A	on application		
Augusta National, 16th Hole	850	150.00		
The following prints can be found on pages 349 & 350	Edition	Price (£)	Qty.	Cost
Turnberry	850	75.00		
Gleneagles	850	75.00		
Wentworth	850	52.00		
Sunningdale	850	52.00		
Belfry	N/A	23.50		
St Andrews - Sea Shore	N/A	23.50		
Royal Dornoch	N/A	23.50		
Moor Park	N/A	23.50		
St Pierre	N/A	23.50		
Walton Heath	N/A	23.50		
North Berwick	N/A	23.50		
Royal Liverpool	N/A	23.50		
The Berkshire	N/A	23.50		
Gleneagles (Hotel)	N/A	23.50		
Postage and Packing				£5.00
All prices include VAT			**Total**	

Order Form

Edition	Edition	Price (£)	Qty.	Cost
Golf in England - Page 186				
Royal Lytham & St Annes, England	N/A	29.50		
The Belfry, 10th Hole, England	N/A	29.50		
The Belfry, 18th Hole England	N/A	29.50		
Royal St George's, England	N/A	29.50		
Wentworth England	N/A	29.50		
Sunningdale England	N/A	29.50		
*Royal St Geroge's, England	850	110.00		
*Royal Birkdale, England	850	110.00		
Golf in Scotland - Page 268				
Carnoustie, Scotland	N/A	29.50		
Royal Dornoch, Scotland	N/A	29.50		
*Turnberry, 10th Hole, Scotland	850	110.00		
*Turnberry, 18th Hole, Scotland	850	110.00		
*Muirfield, 4th Hole, Scotland	850	110.00		
Royal Troon, Scotland	N/A	29.50		
Ailsa Course, Turnberry, Scotland	N/A	29.50		
Prestwick, Scotland	N/A	29.50		
The Home of Golf - Page 348				
St Andrews, Swilcan Bridge, Scotland	N/A	29.50		
St Andrews, Swilcan Burn, Scotland	N/A	29.50		
St Andrews, Snow Scene, Scotland	N/A	29.50		
St Andrews, R&A, Scotland	N/A	29.50		
*St Andrews, 17th Hole, Scotland	850	110.00		
*St Andrews, Old Course, Scotland	850	110.00		
Golf at Gleneagles - Page 350				
The Gleneagles Hotel, Kings Course, Scotland	N/A	29.50		
The Gleneagles Hotel, Queens Course, Scotland	N/A	29.50		
The Gleneagles Hotel, Monarchs Course, Scotland	N/A	29.50		
*The Gleneagles Hotel, Queens Course, Scotland	850	110.00		
Golf in Ireland - Page 269				
Portmarnock, Ireland	N/A	29.50		
Lahinch, Ireland	N/A	29.50		
Killarney, Killean Course, Ireland	N/A	29.50		
Ballybunion, Ireland	N/A	29.50		
Royal County Down, Ireland	N/A	29.50		
Postage and Packing			£5.00	
All prices include VAT			Total	

* These prints are numbered, individually signed and embossed.
I enclose a cheque for the sum of £_____ payable to Kensington West Productions Ltd
Please debit my: Access/Visa/Amex/Diners card by the sum of £_____

No_____   Expiry Date _____

Name_____   Address _____

_____   Tel. No. _____

All orders should be sent to: Kensington West Productions Ltd.
5 Cattle Market, Hexham, Northumberland NE46 INJ Tel: 01434 609933 Fax: 01434 600066